The Historiography of Genocide

Edited by

Dan Stone
Professor of Modern History, Royal Holloway, University of London

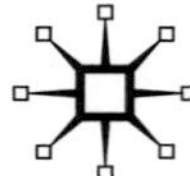

First published 2008 by
PALGRAVE MACMILLAN
Houndmills, Basingstoke, Hampshire RG21 6XS and
175 Fifth Avenue, New York, N.Y. 10010
Companies and representatives throughout the world

PALGRAVE MACMILLAN is the global academic imprint of the Palgrave Macmillan division of St. Martin's Press, LLC and of Palgrave Macmillan Ltd. Macmillan® is a registered trademark in the United States, United Kingdom and other countries. Palgrave is a registered trademark in the European Union and other countries.

ISBN-13: 978-1-4039-9219-2 hardback
ISBN-10: 1-4039-9219-3 hardback

This book is printed on paper suitable for recycling and made from fully managed and sustained forest sources. Logging, pulping and manufacturing processes are expected to conform to the environmental regulations of the country of origin.

A catalogue record for this book is available from the British Library.

Library of Congress Cataloging-in-Publication Data

The historiography of genocide / edited by Dan Stone.
p. cm.
Includes bibliographical references and index.
ISBN 1–4039–9219–3 (alk. paper)
1. Genocide—History. 2. Crimes against humanity—History.
I. Stone, Dan, 1971–

HV6322.7.H57 2008

304.6'630722—dc22 2007048561

10 9 8 7 6 5 4 3
17 16 15 14 13 12 11 10 09

Printed and bound in Great Britain by
CPI Antony Rowe, Chippenham and Eastbourne

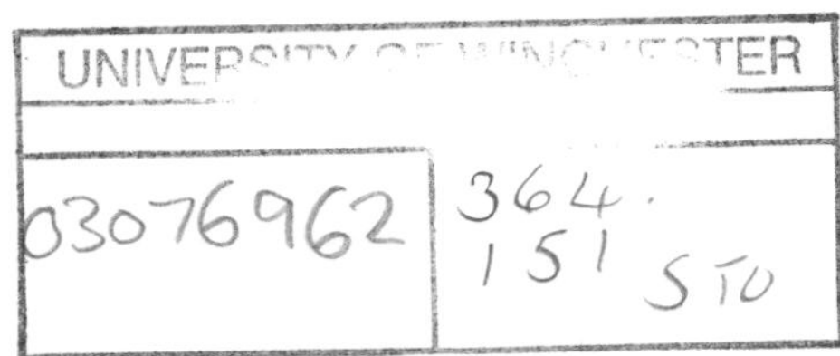

The Historiography of Genocide

Also by Dan Stone:

BREEDING SUPERMAN: Nietzsche, Race and Eugenics in Edwardian and Interwar Britain

COLONIALISM AND GENOCIDE (*co-editor with A. Dirk Moses*)

CONSTRUCTING THE HOLOCAUST: A Study in Historiography

HANNAH ARENDT AND THE USES OF HISTORY: Imperialism, Nation, Race and Genocide (*co-editor with Richard H. King*)

HISTORY, MEMORY AND MASS ATROCITY: Essays on the Holocaust and Genocide

RESPONSES TO NAZISM IN BRITAIN 1933–1939: Before War and Holocaust

THE HISTORIOGRAPHY OF THE HOLOCAUST (*editor*)

THEORETICAL INTERPRETATIONS OF THE HOLOCAUST (*editor*)

Contents

Charts

Tables

Notes on the Contributors

Tony Barta is a Research Associate at La Trobe University, where he taught European and Australian history and founded the History and Film programme in 1985. In addition to his work on genocide in Australia, he has written on twentieth-century Germany, and on historiography, media and historical understanding. He is the editor of *Screening the Past: Film and the Representation of History* (1998).

Doris L. Bergen is the Chancellor Rose and Ray Wolfe Professor of Holocaust Studies at the University of Toronto. She is the author of *Twisted Cross: The German Christians in the Third Reich* (1996) and *War and Genocide: A Concise History of the Holocaust* (2003) and the editor of *The Sword of the Lord: Military Chaplains from the First to the Twenty-First Centuries* (2004). Her research focuses on issues of religion, gender, ethnicity and violence, particularly in the context of Nazi Germany, the Holocaust and World War II.

Donald Bloxham is Reader in History at the University of Edinburgh. He is author of *The Great Game of Genocide: Imperialism, Nationalism, and the Destruction of the Ottoman Armenians* (2005), *The Holocaust: Critical Historical Approaches* (2005, with Tony Kushner) and *Genocide on Trial: War Crimes Trials and the Formation of Holocaust History and Memory* (2001). He is editor, with Mark Levene, of the Oxford University Press monograph series *Zones of Violence*.

Alfred A. Cave is Professor of History at the University of Toledo. He is the author of *Jacksonian Democracy and the Historians* (1964), *An American Conservative in the Age of Jackson* (1969), *The Pequot War* (1996), *The French and Indian War* (2004), *Prophets of the Great Spirit* (2006) and numerous articles primarily on the ethnohistory of Early America.

Ann Curthoys is Manning Clark Professor of History, Australian National University. Following research into the unpublished manuscripts of Raphael Lemkin in New York in December 2003, she has prepared for publication with the journal *Patterns of Prejudice* a draft chapter Lemkin wrote on Tasmania as genocide; she has also written a chapter for Dirk Moses, ed., *Genocide and Colonialism* (2005). With John Docker, Ann co-edited *Aboriginal History* (vol. 25, 2001), a special section entitled '"Genocide"? Aboriginal History in International Perspective', for which they wrote the introduction 'Genocide: Definitions, Questions, Settler-Colonies'.

Veena Das is Kriger-Eisenhower Professor at the Department of Anthropology, Johns Hopkins University. Her most recent book is *Life and Words: Violence and the Descent into the Ordinary* (2006). She is an honorary fellow of the American Academy of Art and Sciences and elected Member of the Third World Academy of Sciences. She holds an honorary doctorate from the University of Chicago.

John Docker is a Visiting Fellow at the Humanities Research Centre, Australian National University. On 26 February 2004, he gave a paper entitled 'Raphael Lemkin's History of Genocide and Colonialism' at the United States Holocaust Memorial Museum, Center for Advanced Holocaust Studies, Washington D.C., which has been put on the Museum's website. He is the author of *1492: The Poetics of Diaspora* (2001), and a chapter for Dirk Moses, ed., *Empire, Colony, Genocide* (forthcoming 2008).

Fatma Müge Göçek is Associate Professor of Sociology and Women's Studies at the University of Michigan, Ann Arbor. She is author of *Rise of the Bourgeoisie, Demise of Empire: Ottoman Westernization and Social Change* (1995) and *East Encounters West: France and the Ottoman Empire in the Eighteenth Century* (1999) and editor of *Social Constructions of Nationalism in the Middle East* (2002). She is co-organiser of the Workshop on Armenian/Turkish Scholarship (WATS).

Robert M. Hayden is Professor of Anthropology, Law and Public & International Affairs and Director of the Center for Russian & East European Studies at the University of Pittsburgh.

Robert K. Hitchcock is Professor and Chair of the Department of Anthropology at Michigan State University in East Lansing, Michigan, USA. His work focuses on human rights, development, refugees and resettlement, especially in southern Africa and North America. He has published several papers on genocides of indigenous peoples. He is the author of *Kalahari Communities: Bushmen and the Politics of the Environment in Southern Africa* (1996), and a co-editor of *Hunters and Gatherers in the Modern World: Conflict, Resistance, and Self-Determination, Endangered Peoples of Africa and the Middle East: Struggles to Survive and Thrive* (2000), *Indigenous Peoples' Rights in Southern Africa* (2004) and *Updating the San: Myth and Reality of an African People in the 21st Century* (2006). Currently, he is working on a book on the Ju/'hoansi San of Namibia since independence and doing research on dam-related resettlement in Africa.

Adam Jones is currently Visiting Fellow at the Yale Genocide Studies Program. He holds a PhD in Political Science from the University of British Columbia. He has published two books on the mass media and political transition, and two edited volumes on genocide: *Gendercide and Genocide* (2004) and *Genocide, War*

Crimes & the West: History and Complicity (2004). His scholarly articles on gender and conflict have appeared in *Review of International Studies, Ethnic & Racial Studies, Journal of Genocide Research, Journal of Humanitarian Assistance,* and other publications. He serves as executive director of Gendercide Watch (www.gendercide.org), a Web-based educational initiative that confronts gender-selective atrocities against men and women worldwide.

Ben Kiernan is the A. Whitney Griswold Professor of History and Professor of International and Area Studies at Yale University. He is founding Director of Yale's Cambodian Genocide Program and its Genocide Studies Program (www.yale.edu/gsp). In 2000–3, he also served as Convenor of the Yale East Timor Project. Kiernan is the author of *How Pol Pot Came to Power: Colonialism, Nationalism and Communism in Cambodia, 1930–1975* (2nd edn, 2004) and *The Pol Pot Regime: Race, Power and Genocide in Cambodia under the Khmer Rouge, 1975–1979* (1996). He is a member of the Editorial Boards of *Critical Asian Studies, Human Rights Review,* the *Journal of Human Rights,* the *Journal of Genocide Research* and *Zeitschrift für Genozidforschung.* His 2002 anthology *Conflict and Change in Cambodia* won the *Critical Asian Studies* Prize for that year. He is also editor of *Burchett: Reporting the Other Side of the World, 1939–1983* (1986) and *Genocide and Democracy in Cambodia: The Khmer Rouge, the United Nations, and the International Community* (1993), and co-editor with Robert Gellately of *The Specter of Genocide: Mass Murder in Historical Perspective* (2003).

Thomas E. Koperski is a humanities area researcher specializing in interdisciplinary approaches to the social sciences. Currently he is in the graduate program in Political Science at the University of Nebraska-Lincoln. His interests range from globalization and its impacts and management, development of governmental systems, human rights of indigenous peoples worldwide and the emerging field of bio-politics. He has done research on genocides of indigenous peoples and on the rights of indigenous peoples in southern Africa, and has published articles in *The Indigenous World.*

Jean-Louis Margolin is senior lecturer in history at the University of Provence in Aix-en-Provence, and Deputy Director of the Research Institute on South-East Asia (IRSEA/CNRS) in Marseille. He is the author of *Singapour 1959–1987: Genèse d'un nouveau pays industriel* (1989) and a number of articles on Singaporian economic and political history during the twentieth century. He is currently engaged in a comparative historical analysis of the political background of development strategies followed in South Korea, Taiwan and Singapore. He has also worked on political mass crime in East Asia, and more specifically on repression under Asian communist regimes, using a comparative approach that led to his contribution to the *Black Book of Communism* (1997), as well as to specific studies on the Cambodian genocide. He is a member of the editorial boards of *Espaces-Temps*, a social sciences journal, and of *Moussons*, dedicated to Southeast Asia.

A. Dirk Moses teaches history at the University of Sydney, Australia. He is the author of *German Intellectuals and the Nazi Past* (2007), and editor of *Empire, Colony, Genocide* (forthcoming 2008), *Colonialism and Genocide* (2007, with Dan Stone), and *Genocide and Settler Society: Frontier Violence and Stolen Indigenous Children in Australian History* (2004).

David Moshman is a professor of educational psychology at the University of Nebraska, where he teaches adolescent development, cognitive development and related courses. He is the author of *Adolescent Psychological Development: Rationality, Morality, and Identity* (2nd edn, 2005). He also teaches and writes about the psychology of genocide, including issues of conceptualization and denial. His chapter 'Genocidal Hatred: Now You See It, Now You Don't' appeared in R. J. Sternberg, ed., *The Psychology of Hate* (2005).

Victoria Sanford is Associate Professor of Anthropology at Lehman College, City University of New York. She is the author of *Buried Secrets: Truth and Human Rights in Guatemala* (2003), *Violencia y Genocidio en Guatemala* (2003) and (co-editor with Asale Angel Ajani) of *Engaged Observer: Anthropology, Advocacy and Activism* (2006). She is completing a book entitled *Morality and Survival* about child soldiers in Guatemala and Colombia. Her current research is on feminicide and impunity in contemporary Guatemala.

William A. Schabas is Director of the Irish Centre for Human Rights at the National University of Ireland, Galway, where he also holds the chair in human rights law. He is the author of 12 books dealing in whole or in part with international human rights law, including *Introduction to the International Criminal Court* (2nd edn, 2004), *Genocide in International Law* (2000), *The Abolition of the Death Penalty in International Law* (3rd edn, 2003), *International Human Rights Law and the Canadian Charter* (1996), *The Death Penalty as Cruel Treatment and Torture* (1996) and *Précis du droit international des droits de la personne* (1997). He has also published more than 150 articles in academic journals, principally in the field of international human rights law. Professor Schabas is editor-in-chief of *Criminal Law Forum*, the quarterly journal of the International Society for the Reform of Criminal Law.

In May 2002, the President of Sierra Leone appointed Professor Schabas to the country's Truth and Reconciliation Commission, upon the recommendation of Mary Robinson, the United Nations High Commission for Human Rights.

Professor Schabas has often been invited to participate in international human rights missions on behalf of non-governmental organizations such as Amnesty International (International Secretariat), the International Federation of Human Rights, and the International Centre for Human Rights and Democratic Development to Rwanda, Burundi, South Africa, Kenya, Uganda, Sudan, Cambodia and Guyana. He has worked as a consultant to the Ministry of Justice of Rwanda, the United States Agency for International Development and the Organization for Security and Cooperation in Europe. He was a delegate of the International Centre for Criminal Law Reform and Criminal Justice Policy to the United Nations Diplomatic Conference of Plenipotentiaries on the Establishment of an International Criminal Court, Rome, 15 June–17 July 1998. He is a member of the board of several international human rights organizations and institutions, including the International Institute for Criminal Investigation, of which he is chair, and the International Institute for Human Rights (Strasbourg), of which he is treasurer.

From 1991 to 2000, William Schabas was professor of human rights law and criminal law at the Département des sciences juridiques of the Université du Québec à Montréal, a Department he chaired from 1994 to 1998; he now holds the honorary position of *professeur associé* at that institution. He has also taught as a visiting or adjunct professor at McGill University, Université de Montréal, Université de Montpellier, Université de Paris X-Nanterre, Université de Paris XI, Université de Paris II Pantheon-Assas, Dalhousie University and University of Rwanda, and he has lectured at the International Institute for Human Rights (Strasbourg), the Canadian Foreign Service Institute, the United Nations Institute for Training and Research and the Pearson Peacekeeping Centre. He is a member of the Quebec Bar, and was a member of the Quebec Human Rights Tribunal from 1996 to 2000. Professor Schabas was a senior fellow at the United States Institute of Peace in Washington during the academic year 1998–9. In 1998, Professor Schabas was awarded the Bora Laskin Research Fellowship in Human Rights by the Social Sciences and Humanities Research Council of Canada.

Dan Stone is Professor of Modern History at Royal Holloway, University of London. He is the author of *Breeding Superman: Nietzsche, Race and Eugenics in Edwardian and Interwar Britain* (2002), *Constructing the Holocaust: A Study in Historiography* (2003), *Responses to Nazism in Britain, 1933–1939: Before War and Holocaust* (2003) and *History, Memory and Mass Atrocity: Essays on the Holocaust and Genocide* (2006); editor of *Theoretical Interpretations of the Holocaust* (2001) and *The Historiography of the Holocaust* (2004); and co-editor of *Colonialism and Genocide* (2007, with A. Dirk Moses) and *Hannah Arendt and the Uses of History: Imperialism, Nationalism, Race and Genocide* (2007, with Richard H. King). He is a member of the editorial boards of the *Journal of Genocide Research* and *Patterns of Prejudice*.

Scott Straus is Assistant Professor of Political Science at the University of Wisconsin, Madison. Straus is the author of two books on Rwanda: *The Order of Genocide: Race, Power, and War in Rwanda* (2006), and, with Robert Lyons, *Intimate Enemy: Images and Voices of the Rwandan Genocide* (2006). *The Order of Genocide* received the 2006 Award for Excellence in Political Science and Government from the Association of American Publishers. Straus also co-authored, with David Leonard, *Africa's Stalled Development: International Causes and Cures* (2003), and he translated Jean-Pierre Chrétien's *The Great Lakes of Africa: Two Thousand Years of History* (2003). Straus has additionally published articles in *Foreign Affairs, Genocide Studies and Prevention*, the *Journal of Genocide Research* and the *Wisconsin International Law Journal*.

Ian Talbot is Director of the Centre for Imperial and Post-Colonial Studies at the University of Southampton. He has published extensively on the Partition of India and on Pakistan history. His most recent works include, *Divided Cities: Partition and Its Aftermath in Lahore, Amritsar* (2007) and *Pakistan: A Modern History* (2005).

Robert van Krieken teaches and researches in sociology and socio-legal studies in the Department of Sociology and Social Policy at the University of Sydney. His books include *Children and the State, Norbert Elias* and *Sociology: Themes and Perspectives*, and his journal publications include studies of the historical sociology of child welfare, violence and civilization, state-formation and changing forms of subjectivity. His current research addresses a number of questions in the history and sociology of law, including transformations in family law and legal reasoning as a mode of knowledge-production.

Anton Weiss-Wendt received his PhD in modern Jewish history from Brandeis University. Before joining the Norwegian Holocaust Centre in Olso he taught Soviet history at Keele University in the UK. His intellectual interests include, but are not limited to, comparative genocide and prosecution of war crimes, East European and Soviet history. He has published in *Journal of Genocide Research, Holocaust and Genocide Studies, Nationalities Papers* and *Journal of Baltic Studies*. His book, *Murder Without Hatred: Estonians, the Holocaust, and the Problem of Collaboration*, is forthcoming. In his current research project he examines the connection between war crimes trials and the Cold War.

Nicolas Werth is Director of Research at CNRS (Centre National de la Recherche Scientifique) in Paris. After studying at the Ecole Normale Supérieure, he taught for eight years in Minsk and Moscow, and was cultural attaché at the French Embassy in Moscow during the period of perestroika. He came to CNRS in 1989, where he specializes in the social and political history of the USSR, in particular the Stalinist period and the question of state violence. He is the author of many works, including *Etre communiste en URSS sous Staline* (1981), *La vie quotidienne des paysans soviétiques de la Révolution à la Collectivisation, 1917–1939* (1984), *Les procès de Moscou* (1987), *Histoire de l'Union soviétique, de l'Empire russe à la CEI, 1900–1991* (1991, 5th edn, 2001), *Rapports secrets soviétiques. La société russe dans les rapports confidentiels, 1921–1991* (1995), *L'Ile aux cannibales* (2006), *La Terreur et le désarroi. Staline en son système* (2007) and *Les Années Staline* (2007). He has also co-edited *Histoire du Goulag Stalinien* (2004, 7 volumes) and contributed to *The Black Book of Communism* (French edn, 1997, English edn, 1999).

Jürgen Zimmerer is Lecturer in International History at the University of Sheffield, UK. His areas of research include comparative genocide, African history, the transnational history of European colonialism and representations of the imperial world in various European countries (Germany, Great Britain and Portugal). He is co-editor of the *Journal of Genocide Research* and president of the International Network of Genocide Scholars. Recent publications include *Deutsche Herrschaft über Afrikaner. Staatlicher Machtanspruch und Wirklichkeit im kolonialen Namibia* (2001), *Genocide in German South-West Africa: The Colonial War of 1904–1908 and Its aftermath* (co-edited, 2003; English translation 2006), *Verschweigen-Erinnern-Bewältigen. Vergangenheitspolitik in globaler Perspektive* (edited, 2004), *Raphael Lemkin 'On Genocides': The 'Founder of the Genocide Convention' as a Historian of Mass Violence*, (co-edited, 2005) and *Von Windhuk nach Auschwitz. Beiträge zum Verhältnis von Kolonialismus und Holocaust* (forthcoming).

Introduction

Dan Stone

In the introduction to *The Historiography of the Holocaust*, which appeared in 2004, I noted that in due course it would be necessary to produce a similar book for the historiography of genocide. The rapidity with which this turned out to be the case was surprising, and reflects the fact that genocide studies is one of the fastest-growing disciplines in the humanities and social sciences. Of course, this growth in the literature does not apply equally to all cases of genocide, and that on genocide in Bangladesh, Iraq, Burundi, Ethiopia or East Timor remains relatively limited, which is why they are regretfully omitted from this book. But it is also not the case that the historiography of genocide has grown only with respect to the 'canon' of genocides: the Armenian genocide, the Holocaust, Cambodia and Rwanda. Rather, there has been a steady growth of literature on colonial genocides, especially in North America, Australia and German South West Africa (though nothing like the same extent on, for example, the Belgian Congo, the Caribbean, Peru or Argentina); as well as an attempt to understand communist regimes (the USSR and China, Cambodia is a special case here) and other forms of mass atrocity such as the Partition of India, or the violence of twentieth-century South American regimes through the lenses of genocide studies. Such an approach does not please everyone; indeed, arguments about whether or not genocide took place in India or Australia can often obscure as much about a particular history as they can reveal (if it is genocide, what more needs to be said, why should we try and understand the patterns of interaction, violent or otherwise, that lie behind the events?). Yet, it is also the case that these debates can bring and have brought considerable energy and vigour to historiographical and broader cultural debates.

That said, it remains to be seen whether or not such a thing as a recognizable discipline of genocide studies really exists. One critic argues that 'genocide studies is not a discipline but a field dealing with a certain phenomenon and therefore is not theoretically bound to a specific set of methods.'[1] Certainly, there are journals, notably the *Journal of Genocide Research*, scholarly bodies, and no shortage of international conferences. But what is discussed at these forums has the tendency to become, beyond the addition of more detail to particular case studies, a merry-go-round of definitional debates. In other words, the 'discipline' cannot even agree on the meaning of its basic terms. Some scholars feel that this is a problem peculiar to genocide studies, but it can also be regarded, if not as a sign of strength, at least as a sign of fluidity, genuine intellectual engagement with a profoundly moving and difficult topic, and critical debate. The lack of clarity in the field can also therefore be an indication of great potential, and not just a reflection of the conceptual confusion built into the concept from its invention by Raphael Lemkin.[2]

If that potential is to be released, then, as Mark Levene points out, scholars need to do more than just engage in 'comparative genocide studies'.[3] That is not to make the unrealistic demand that scholars must learn many languages and conduct research in many countries before they can pronounce on the meaning of genocide. It means, rather, that instead of contenting themselves with drawing similarities and dissimilarities between cases of genocide, they must attempt to develop general, empirically informed, theoretical statements about genocide as such – what it is, when it happens, who supports it, and so on.

The problem is that, even where some sort of consensus to be arrived at as to the meaning of genocide – say, by agreeing to stick with Lemkin's definition or the United Nations' version of it – there is no guarantee that this would facilitate agreement as to any other question pertaining to genocide. We might end by showing only that a certain number of genocides have taken place throughout human history, and that in each case circumstances differ so widely that it is impossible to make general statements about, for example, what kind of person takes part in genocide or what political or economic circumstances are most conducive to its occurrence. Or we might wish to collapse all '–cide' terms (politicide, ethnocide, democide, indigenocide and so on) so that there is no distinction between, say, ethnic cleansing and genocide, and all cases of mass atrocity are termed genocide.[4] As Anton Weiss-Wendt reminds us with salutary sobriety in his challenging chapter, there is much basic work yet to do before genocide studies can rightfully take its place among the other interdisciplinary specialisms.

Readers of this volume can make up their own minds as to how far the volume succeeds in bringing coherence to the field. But what it does do is offer up to date and comprehensive assessments of the large literature relating to theories of genocide and to many cases of genocide from the colonial period onwards.

The historiography of genocide is a classic case of 'uneven development'. The literature on the Holocaust – which, for good or ill, has provided many of the theoretical frameworks and research strategies for analyzing other genocides – is unmanageably large. My chapter on this subject omits as much as it mentions.

By contrast, Victoria Sanford's chapter on Guatemala refers to relatively few authorities for the simple reason that they do not exist in anything like the same numbers. In that case, and in the case of events that are less obviously examples of genocide, such as the Partition of India, that shortage of historical literature (not *per se*, but from a genocide studies perspective) is perhaps unsurprising. But in the cases of Australia and North America it is remarkable that, given the enormous historiography on the colonial period and frontier conflict in both places, there is not more that directly addresses the question of genocide. Mark Levene is right when he notes the 'dearth of really good overviews of settler-native conflict in the New World.'[5] Alfred A. Cave's chapter goes a long way to correcting this situation, but obviously there is scope for more, especially since it is clear that so many historians who write on American Indians and Australian Aborigines shy away from confronting the question of genocide.

What has happened here is that the study of genocide has been dominated since the 1980s – when Leo Kuper's pioneering work appeared – by political scientists in the North American liberal tradition.[6] Their aim (obviously laudable in itself) was to prevent genocide, and to this end they sought to analyze past occurrences of the phenomenon in order to draw up typologies and thus to provide 'early-warning' signals of likely genocidal situations in the world.[7] This process is critically analyzed by Ann Curthoys and John Docker and by David Moshman in their treatments, which look at the development of the idea of genocide since Lemkin and the trend to typologization, respectively. Historians, who traditionally focus on the particular and not the general, did not play an active role in the development of this work; indeed they were somewhat suspicious of it. In recent years, though, a new generation of historians, anthropologists and, most impressively, political scientists such as Scott Straus, has turned to a more strictly historical approach to genocide. Thus, many scholars are likely to locate the origin of genocide less in a single moment, decision or blueprint (which is, problematically for history-writing, demanded by the UN Convention's legal interpreters, who need to demonstrate 'intent') than in a radicalizing dynamic, a process in which even perpetrators themselves may be unclear about how and when they have passed over into the moral abyss and moved from discrimination to violence to genocide. Tony Barta's idea of 'construing intent through action', which he put forward over 20 years ago, seems to bear more relation to reality than the search for incriminating documents that reveal an 'intent to destroy', finding which is, of course, an exceptionally rare occurrence.

What this new cohort who pay more attention to historical detail have also shown, if often only implicitly, is that genocide – in contrast to what was suggested by the earlier political science paradigm – is not committed by aberrant lunatics in faraway places about which we know little and desire to know even less. Rather, genocide has historically been committed by 'us' in the West, in settler colonial situations, as Jürgen Zimmerer shows, and continues to be committed across the world in the name of development, as Robert K. Hitchcock and Thomas E. Koperski show in their study of indigenous peoples. Furthermore, where it was once simple to assume that genocide was committed in backward countries ruled by savage despots, A. Dirk Moses shows that the number of social theorists and philosophers who have seen a meaningful relation between modernity and genocide – even if not in the direct sense popularized by Zygmunt Bauman in his simplistic reading of Weber – means that we can no longer glibly take it for granted that genocide is only ever part of someone else's history. This is the uncomfortable conclusion also reached by Doris Bergen and Adam Jones, whose analyses of the roles played in genocide by religion and gender respectively should give us pause for thought about our own traditions – in this case, whoever 'we' are – as much as others'.

But genocide, as everyone who picks up this book will know, is not a stable concept; indeed it epitomizes what is meant by the phrase 'essentially contested concept'. One man's genocide is another man's unfortunate bout of disease-drive 'population readjustment', as Robert van Krieken and Veena Das demonstrate in their conceptual chapters. In the case of the Armenian genocide, the Turkish government continues to exploit uncertainties and lack of knowledge to propound its negationism. And even in the cases of Cambodia and Rwanda there is a good deal of debate about the basic characteristics of the events, as Ben Kiernan and Scott Straus show. In the cases of Yugoslavia, India, China and the Soviet Union, there is little consensus as to the applicability of the term 'genocide', nor is there agreement that even if the events could be so described, that doing so would necessarily be the most cogent or informative way of approaching them. Ian Talbot argues for the usefulness of the term when discussing Partition, but his is a minority voice, though one that is definitely getting louder. That mass death has occurred in modern China no historian would seek to deny, but Jean-Louis Margolin provides an instructive demonstration that mass murder and genocide are conceptually distinct, even if the moral or criminal difference in this instance may be negligible. And while many have sought to make the genocide label stick to the Soviet Union, especially in their treatment of the Ukrainians in the 'terror famine', Nicolas Werth shows that it is perhaps only with great caution that one can find a convincing case of genocide in the course of Stalin's reign. Robert M. Hayden's analysis of Yugoslavia is, however, the most contentious here, since, while he is disputing neither that terrible things occurred in Bosnia in the early 1990s nor that the Serbs were the main guilty party – it is important to state this clearly, since his work has often been misinterpreted by propagandists – he is taking on the decision of the International Criminal Tribunal for the Former Yugoslavia that 'genocide' is the correct way of interpreting those events. To some this conclusion is an affront to common sense, or politicized hair-splitting; but it reveals that the concept of genocide, however clear it might seem in one's preferred definition (most scholars believe that the UN Convention has problems) does not always correspond clearly to the demands of writing history.

It is because writing about the past, when done well, is complex and messy, that those who seek to produce typologies of genocide as a guide to future political action, are often sceptical of the work of historians. Scholars of genocide sometimes have the tendency to be rather self-congratulatory, as if those who do not spend their lives researching, writing about or actively trying to prevent genocide are any less concerned about its occurrence. Within the still fairly small community of genocide studies, this self-congratulatory tone sometimes spills over into unattractive internecine debates about the 'correct' relationship between academic research and political activism. One activist has written in a public, online forum that 'lawyers and activists make history. Most historians just write about it.'[8] It is not my intention here to overturn this division between 'activists' and 'historians'; rather, I wish to suggest that the dichotomy is a false one, drawn for rhetorical effect. The inclusion here of an important essay by the leading scholar of law and genocide, William Schabas, should make it clear that a concern with prosecuting perpetrators has historically been at the heart of genocide studies, as it continues to be. The 'pioneers of genocide studies' may have believed that they were changing the world by writing about genocide. Perhaps it is even the case that those who devote themselves to genocide prevention have prevented a genocide from taking place. But the new cohort of genocide scholars – which is not necessarily the same thing as a generational shift – that has been responsible for the rapid growth of the field over the last decade, perhaps has a more cautious approach. Those who undertake historical, anthropological, legal, sociological or philosophical research into genocide are, one ventures to suggest, at least as alarmed by the thing that they study as those who pioneered the field in the 1980s. It is precisely because they are careful scholars that they do not make grand claims for the significance of their work in terms of preventing genocide. Those who have little patience for scholarship do not need to engage with it; but there are many ways to engage with (and change) the world and, if this collection of essays succeeds in demonstrating that the scholarly engagement with genocide is not the least meaningful of them it will have justified its existence.

Notes

1. C. Gerlach, 'Extremely Violent Societies: An Alternative to the Concept of Genocide', *Journal of Genocide Studies*, 8, 4 (2006), 463.
2. See A. D. Moses, 'The Holocaust and Genocide', in *The Historiography of the Holocaust*, ed. D. Stone (Basingstoke: Palgrave Macmillan, 2004), pp. 533–55; A. Rabinbach,

'The Challenge of the Unprecedented: Raphael Lemkin and the Concept of Genocide', *Simon Dubnow Institute Yearbook*, 4 (2005), pp. 397–420.

3. See M. Levene, *Genocide in the Age of the Nation State. Vol. 1: The Meaning of Genocide* (London: I. B. Tauris, 2005).
4. See M. Shaw, *What is Genocide?* (Cambridge: Polity Press, 2007), pp. 48–62 for the argument that there is no real distinction between ethnic cleansing and genocide. See also B. Lieberman, *Terrible Fate: Ethnic Cleansing in the Making of Modern Europe* (Chicago, IL: Ivan R. Dee, 2006).
5. M. Levene, 'Nation-States, Empires, and the Problems of Historicizing Genocide: A Response to Wolfgang Reinhard and Anthony Pagden', *Journal of Genocide Research*, 9, 1 (2007), 131.
6. See Moses, 'The Holocaust and Genocide'; idem., 'Conceptual Blockages and Definitional Dilemmas in the "Racial Century": Genocides of Indigenous Peoples and the Holocaust', *Patterns of Prejudice*, 36, 4 (2002), 7–36.
7. H. Fein, 'Genocide: A Sociological Perspective', *Current Sociology*, 38, 1 (1990), pp. 1–126.
8. G. Stanton, communication to H-Genocide, 29 November 2002 (www.h-net.org/~genocide).

I. Concepts

1
Defining Genocide[1]

Ann Curthoys and John Docker

Genocide is one of those rare concepts whose author and inception can be precisely specified and dated. The term was created by the brilliant Polish-Jewish jurist Raphael Lemkin (1900–59), in his book *Axis Rule in Occupied Europe: Laws of Occupation, Analysis of Government, Proposals for Redress*, published in the USA in 1944. Lemkin was also the prime mover in the discussions that led to the 1948 United Nations (UN) Convention on the Prevention and Punishment of the Crime of Genocide. The concept was immediately recognized worldwide to be of contemporary significance and future importance, for it calls attention to humanity at its limits. It is a major concept in international law, for its framework of group experience and rights challenges both a stress on the individual as the subject of law and the exclusive jurisdiction of modern nation states. It has led to the reconceptualization of the whole of human history as involving a history of genocide, for it amply fulfills Croce's dictum, so important for twentieth- and twenty-first-century historical writing, that history is written out of the urgent concerns and dangers of the present.[2] Since the beginning, it has been embroiled in argument and controversy, which show no sign of abating as the pressing contexts of world history continuously change. Questions that have arisen over the past 60 years include: Are there forms of genocide which do not involve mass killing? What are the criteria for assessing intention in genocidal events and processes? Do genocides necessarily involve state action or leadership? Should mass killing based on political categories be called genocide? What is meant by cultural genocide? And finally, to what extent must our definition of genocide for the purposes of historical scholarship conform to the definition used in international law? Despite the different answers scholars have given to these questions, the usage of 'genocide' as a meaningful and suggestive term in international law, history, and social science continues to grow, as this present volume attests.

Raphael Lemkin defines 'genocide'

We necessarily begin with a portrait of Raphael Lemkin and his originating definition.[3] Lemkin was born on 24 June 1900 in Bezwodne, a village near the small city of Wolkowysk (now Vaulkovisk). When Lemkin was growing up, Wolkowysk was part of Tsarist Russia; between the World Wars it was located in Poland, and is now in Belarus. In his unfinished autobiography, 'Totally Unofficial Man', written in 1958 not long before he died, Lemkin recalls that from childhood he was stirred by historical accounts of extermination. He read about the destruction of the Christians by Nero; the Mongols overrunning Russia, Poland, Silesia, and Hungary in 1241; the persecution of Jews in Russia by Tsar Nicholas I; the destruction of the Moors in Spain; and the devastation of the Huguenots. He confides that from an early age he took a special delight in being alone, so that he could feel and think without outer disturbances, and that loneliness became the essential condition of his life.[4]

Lemkin gained his doctor of laws at the University of Lvov in 1926; after a year of study in Heidelberg, Rome, and Paris, he became a public prosecutor in Warsaw.[5] In 1933, the year of Hitler's election to government in Germany, Lemkin sent a paper to a League of Nations conference in Madrid on the Unification of Penal Law.[6] He proposed that the crimes of barbarity and vandalism be considered as new offences against the law of nations. Acts of barbarity, ranging from massacres and pogroms to the ruining of a group's economic existence, undermine the fundamental basis of an ethnic, religious, or social collectivity. Acts of vandalism concern the destruction of the cultural heritage of a collectivity as revealed in the fields of science, arts, and literature. Lemkin argued that the destruction of any work of art of any nation must be regarded as an act of vandalism directed against 'world culture'.[7] Lemkin always regretted that the 1933 conference did not enact his proposals in international law. He felt that if they had been ratified by the 37 countries represented at Madrid, the new laws could have inhibited the rise of Nazism by declaring that attacks upon national, religious, and ethnic groups were international crimes and that the perpetrators of such crimes could be indicted whenever they appeared on the territory of one of the signatory countries.[8]

In 1939, Lemkin fled Poland and reached Stockholm in Sweden, where he did extensive research on Nazi occupation laws throughout Europe. On 18 April 1941, he arrived in the United States via Japan. He thought help for European Jewry, including his own family, could only come from the United States, which he saw as a nation born out of moral indignation against oppression, and a beacon of freedom and human rights for the rest of the world. Yet he also records that as he travelled by train to take up an appointment teaching law at Duke University, he saw at the chillingly named Lynchburg station, Virginia, toilet signs saying 'For Whites' and 'For Colored'. He recalls that in Warsaw 'there was one single Negro in the entire city', employed as a dancer in a popular nightclub. Lemkin contrasts the 'feeling of curiosity and friendliness' that prevailed 'towards this lonely black man in Poland' with attitudes in Poland towards its 'three million' Jews. Lemkin says that he asked the 'Negro porter if there were indeed special toilets for Negroes', but was met with a puzzled look mixed with hostility; he observes that after 17 years in the United States he now understood that the porter must have thought he was making fun of him.[9] This enigmatic anecdote indicates at the very least that an ambivalence about the moral history of the United States remained to his last days, especially revealed in his unpublished papers and the controversy, discussed in detail later in this chapter, in which he was involved in the early 1950s over whether or not African-American history and experience constituted genocide.[10]

What was notable about Lemkin's 1933 proposals concerning barbarity and vandalism was the width of his formulations. In a similar spirit, 11 years later, chapter nine of *Axis Rule* proposed his new concept of 'genocide', deriving the term from the Greek word *genos* (tribe, race) and Latin *cide* (as in tyrannicide, homicide, fratricide). Genocide is composite and manifold; it signifies a coordinated plan of different actions aiming at the destruction of the essential foundations of life of a group. Such actions can, but do not necessarily, involve mass killing. They involve considerations that are cultural, political, social, legal, intellectual, spiritual, economic, biological, physiological, religious, and moral. Such actions involve considerations of health, food, and nourishment; of family life and care of children; and of birth as well as death. Such actions involve consideration of the honour and dignity of peoples, and the future of humanity as a world community.[11]

In 1933, Lemkin had focused on what he would later call genocide as an episode or act or event. In 1944, he saw genocide as also a process, a process that may include destructive episodes or acts or events. A key passage on the opening page of chapter nine states:

> Genocide has two phases: one, destruction of the national pattern of the oppressed group; the other, the imposition of the national pattern of the oppressor. This imposition, in turn, may be made upon the oppressed population which is allowed to remain, or upon the territory alone, after removal of the population and the colonization of the area by the oppressor's own nationals.[12]

Lemkin here defines genocide as a twofold process of destruction and replacement, a process that entwines genocide and colonization.

In the post-war years Lemkin worked tirelessly in the fledgling UN circles to persuade relevant committees to pass a convention banning genocide.[13] At the same time, in 1947 he began writing a history describing many examples of genocide in the past, which he could submit as memoranda to influential delegates.[14] For this research, Lemkin gained financial assistance from various sources, such as the Viking Fund and the Lucius N. Littauer Foundation in New York, as well as from the Yale Law School, which provided him with an office and research support.[15] When he left his position teaching international law at Yale in 1951, he was supported by organizations of East European ethnic communities in the US, such as the Lithuanian American National Council and the Ukrainian Congress Committee of America, with whom he had developed close political ties.[16]

Lemkin's book on the history of genocide remained unfinished and unpublished when he died in 1959. Yet the various manuscript chapters and research notes and cards are now being explored.[17] They make fascinating reading. The book kept expanding, taking in examples from antiquity to modernity. In particular, he pursued the linking of colonization with genocide made in chapter nine of *Axis Rule* to include European colonizing around the world, including that of the Americas, by the Spanish from 1492 and later in North America by the English, French, and post-independence Americans. He is highly critical of Columbus as an egregious genocidist (Lemkin's own term) who set the historical example for the future of Spanish colonization in the Americas, instituting slavery and catastrophic loss of life. He develops a sophisticated methodology that permits the possibility of multifaceted analyses of settler-colonial histories in relation to genocide. He carefully distinguishes between cultural change and cultural genocide. He points out that the relationship between oppressor and victim in history is always unstable, and that in world history there are many examples of genocidal victims transforming into genocidists, the formerly persecuted into the persecutors of others. He points to recurring features in historical genocides: mass mutilations; deportations under harsh conditions often involving forced marches; attacks on family life, with separation of men and women and taking away of the opportunity of procreation; removal and transfer of children; destruction of political leadership; and death from illness, hunger, and disease through overcrowding on reserves and in concentration camps.[18]

Lemkin's views on humanity and violence were double-edged, both optimistic and pessimistic. He fervently hoped and believed that international law could restrain or prevent genocide. Yet he also argued that genocide has followed humanity through history, that it occurs between groups with a certain regularity just as homicide takes place between individuals. In retrospect, we can see Lemkin's historical conceptions and legal thinking emerging from a 1930s and 1940s context where émigré intellectuals were attempting to reprise and develop traditions of cosmopolitanism and internationalism which they saw being engulfed by Nazism, itself a culmination of nineteenth-century nationalism and colonialism. Figures like Walter Benjamin, Freud, Lemkin, Hannah Arendt, Erich Auerbach, Albert Einstein, and Leo Spitzer were concerned that humanity should establish a duty of care to all the world's peoples and cultures.[19] Central to Lemkin's thought were notions of world culture and the oneness of the world, valuing the variety and diversity of human cultures.[20] Yet as we shall see, in the post-war world, riven as it was by the racial divide and the Cold War (with its sense, shared by Lemkin himself, of an absolute gulf between two monolithic opposed blocs, the Communist and the 'Free World'), the notion of a common humanity was pushed ever further to the margins.

When Lemkin died in New York on 28 August 1959, seven people attended his funeral. Most of his family had perished in the Holocaust.[21] Yet he left a rich legacy, for genocide quickly proved to be a protean and productive, if contested, concept.

The United Nations Convention on Genocide, 1948

One immediate source of complication is that Lemkin in effect produced, or influenced into being, two definitions, the discursive definition in chapter nine of *Axis Rule* and the codified definition of the 1948 UN Genocide Convention. Although the latter was based on the former, a tortuous political process in a divided Cold War atmosphere meant that what emerged was a narrower definition than the one Lemkin originally proposed. In the deliberations of the various committees, there were, Leo Kuper records, major controversies regarding the groups to be protected, the question of intent, the inclusion of cultural genocide, the problem of enforcement and punishment, the extent of destruction which would constitute genocide, and the essential nature of the crime.[22] The Soviet representatives, for example, led the attack to exclude political groups. Kuper feels that one 'must acknowledge that there was cause for anxiety that the inclusion of political groups in the Convention would expose nations to external interference in their internal affairs'. In the controversy over cultural genocide, Kuper observes that the roles of the national delegations were somewhat reversed, with the Soviet Bloc pressing for its inclusion, while the Western European democracies were opposed. Presumably, Kuper notes, the 'representatives of the colonial powers would have been somewhat on the defensive, sensitive to criticism of their policies in non-self-governing territories'.[23] Lemkin especially regretted the exclusion of cultural genocide ('very dear to me').[24]

The Articles of the UN Convention on the Prevention and Punishment of the Crime of Genocide, United Nations General Assembly 9 December 1948, became widely known and quoted.[25] Article II sets out the key clauses of the definition:

> In the present Convention, genocide means any of the following acts committed with intent to destroy, in whole or in part, a national, ethnical, racial or religious group, as such:
>
> 1. Killing members of the group;
> 2. Causing serious bodily or mental harm to members of the group;
> 3. Deliberately inflicting on the group conditions of life calculated to bring about its physical destruction in whole or in part;
> 4. Imposing measures intended to prevent births within the group;
> 5. Forcibly transferring children of the group to another group.

The omission of political and cultural genocide was cause for regret in some quarters, and both have remained issues in scholarly and legal debate ever since. The case of cultural genocide is especially complex. Leo Kuper reflects that while cultural genocide was dropped from the Convention it survived in vestigial form in the prohibition on the forcible transfer of children from one group to another, and in the term 'ethnical' group, suggesting protection of groups with distinctive culture or language.[26] We would also argue that the notion of 'mental harm' was and is open to being interpreted as implying cultural as well as psychological genocide.

While cultural genocide was muted in the 1948 Convention and political genocide was omitted, in Lemkin's 1944 definition in *Axis Rule* the cultural and political were both strongly present as part of the manifold ways the essential foundations of life of a group were being destroyed.[27] We might say that Lemkin's 1944 definition, and the Lemkin-influenced definition enshrined in the 1948 Convention, acted in subsequent thinking about genocide like a double helix, neither reducible one to the other nor wholly separable.

An early sociology of genocide: Jessie Bernard, 1949

The extreme violence and extent of slaughter and mass death of World War II left many intellectual fields epistemologically shaken and uncertain: how did their discipline now look in the light of such catastrophe?[28] Sociology became one of the fields most affected. Indeed, the crisis posed to sociology, with its functionalist inheritance and normative assumptions, is a recurring theme in the history of attempts to define genocide. A very early sociological engagement came from Jessie Bernard in 1949. Bernard, who would later become well known for her arguments concerning gender, sex, marriage, motherhood, and family life, as well as for *Marriage and Family among Negroes* (1966), which examined the effects of racism on Black culture, discussed genocide in her book *American Community Behavior*. In the preface to the 1962 edition, Bernard says that in the 1940s most sociology curricula gave little recognition to problems engendered by competition and conflict, in a world in which war, strikes, revolutions, rebellions, and riots were endemic. Her aim was to rectify this omission by studying 'community disorganization', not least violence, for the 'extraordinary importance of this phenomenon has seemed to demand sociological consideration'.[29] The final section of the book, 'The World Community', drew directly on Lemkin's essay 'Genocide – A Modern Crime' (*Free World*, April 1945) to argue that race and ethnic conflict on the world stage had experienced an 'unexpectedly brutal turn', in Germany taking the form of 'genocide, so-called, that is, of exterminating whole peoples', for example, 'that an estimated 6 million Jews were systematically destroyed in gas chambers'. The weapons in the arsenal of genocide, she adds, could also include, in relation to occupied peoples, 'reducing the birth rate by keeping the sexes separated, chronic undernourishment, specific vitamin deficiencies'. Sometimes the 'objective is not to destroy the people as physical beings but to destroy them as bearers of culture'. In such situations, liberal arts training is forbidden because it might stimulate national thinking; religious sanctions must be thoroughly wrecked. Nevertheless, Bernard noted, referring to post-war desires for decolonization, increasingly 'the darker races are rebelling against their status as exploited peoples', accompanied by support from world opinion; the Apartheid mode of race relations in South Africa, for example, was on the defensive.[30]

It would soon be the turn of the United States to be on the defensive in the court of world opinion, somewhat to the dismay of Lemkin himself.

We Charge Genocide: condemning the treatment of African Americans, 1951

Genocide as a legal convention proved almost immediately to be troubling and problematic in the context of the Cold War. Both sides recognized that the charge of 'genocide' might be made against the other, and each wished to avoid being charged. This struggle was the strongest within the US in the early 1950s, where two groups, in particular, competed to have the UN consider accusations of genocide: Eastern European émigrés wanted charges of Soviet genocide while radical African Americans sought charges of American genocide. It is to the latter we now turn.

In *The Archaeology of Knowledge* Michel Foucault advised that in the history of ideas we should never forget the importance of notions and phenomena like 'threshold, rupture, break, mutation, transformation'.[31] Such could well be said of a momentous event in American and African American history.

In December 1951, only 11 months after the Genocide Convention went into effect, having at last attracted the necessary 20 signatures, a petition entitled *We Charge Genocide* was presented by Paul Robeson and others to the UN Secretariat in New York. At the same time, William L. Patterson, the petition's main author, presented it to the UN General Assembly in Paris.[32] This was not the first African American attempt to seek redress through the UN; W. E. B. Du Bois for the National Association for the Advancement of Colored People (NAACP) had petitioned it in 1947. The Civil Rights Congress (CRC) petition, however, was the first attempt to charge the US with genocide under the UN Convention.[33] In brief, it argued that the lynching and other forms of assault on the lives and livelihood of African Americans from 1945 to 1951, especially the frenzied attacks on returning Black American veterans, amounted to genocide.[34] While well remembered in African American historiography and historical consciousness,[35] this petition had until very recently been largely forgotten by genocide studies, though this situation, in a fast-moving field, is rapidly changing.[36] We believe that, as an early indicator of the impact of the Convention and the issues involved in applying its ideas in practice, *We Charge Genocide* needs to be featured in the conceptual history of genocide.[37]

The originator of the petition was the CRC, a vigorous, fearless, and always controversial Communist-led organization that fought for African American rights at a time when, historian Gerald Horne argues, a 'reign of terror' was being conducted against Blacks.[38] Patterson was national secretary of the CRC from 1946 to 1956; he was also a lawyer and a member of the Communist Party.[39] The CRC focused its campaigns on cases of racist repression, and attracted the support of well known people like Jessica Mitford (her married name Decca Treuhaft), who became its East Bay leader in California, and Dashiell Hammett, who went to jail as a result of being a trustee of CRC's Bail Fund, as well as African American entertainers like Paul Robeson, Josephine Baker, and Lena Horne. In addition to skilled legal challenges, it engaged in picketing, demonstrations, and petitioning, for example, in the cases of Willie McGee, Rosa Lee Ingram, the Trenton Six, and the Martinsville Seven.[40] The CRC strongly believed that a focus on Jim Crow laws and deprivation of Blacks' rights would be an embarrassment for the US abroad and might hasten overdue reform. (In this it was prophetic; such tactics were successfully adopted by the American Civil Rights movement a decade later.[41])

We Charge Genocide is a remarkable document. On the inside cover was a black-and-white full-page photo of two young Black men hanging from a tree, the next page having the caption: 'THE FACE OF GENOCIDE. The two young Negro men, Dooley Morton and Bert Moore, were murdered in a brutal double lynching at Columbus, Mississippi. Such horrifying violence is only one of the many crimes against the Negro people of the United States which together form the major crime of genocide.' The opening title pages reprinted Articles II and

III of the 1948 Genocide Convention. They also list the writers, alongside William L. Patterson, of *We Charge Genocide*: Richard O. Boyer, Howard Fast, Yvonne Gregory, Dr Oakley Johnson, John Hudson Jones, Leon Josephson, Stetson Kennedy, and Elizabeth Lawson.[42] There was also another list of names, of the petitioners, who included Du Bois, Paul Robeson, Jessica Mitford, and Ben Davis.[43] Then followed a powerfully worded 'Introduction' by Patterson: 'Out of the inhuman black ghettos of American cities; out of the cotton plantations of the South, comes this record of mass slayings on the basis of race, of lives deliberately warped and distorted by the willful creation of conditions making for premature death, poverty and disease.' Such a record called aloud for condemnation of injustices that constituted a 'daily and ever-increasing violation' of the UN Convention. Patterson reminded readers that it was 'sometimes incorrectly thought that genocide means the complete and definitive destruction of a race or people'. He pointed out that the Genocide Convention defined genocide as 'killing members of the group', and that genocide is any intent to destroy, *in whole or in part* – this phrase Patterson italicized – a national, racial, ethnic, or religious group. Thus, as well as 'killing members of the group', genocide is constituted in 'causing serious bodily or mental harm'. The petition would maintain, Patterson said, that the 'oppressed Negro citizens of the United States' suffer from genocide as the result of the 'consistent, conscious, unified policies of every branch of government'.[44]

The petition called upon the United Nations to 'act and to call the Government of the United States to account'.[45] It directly addressed the question of UN responsibility and powers concerning US race relations. Genocide, it contended, could not be sequestered as an internal affair of the US, but was a problem for the world. To destroy the 'racist theory of government of the U.S.A.' would sound the 'death knell of all racist theories'.[46] The world had fought the crimes of Nazism 'against the heroic Jewish people'; every word voiced by US Supreme Court Judge Robert H. Jackson in his opening address to the Nuremberg trial of the Nazi leaders 'applies with equal weight' to racist perpetrators in the US.[47] It urged the world to consider the urgency of its request in terms of the US threat to world peace, because Hitler has already demonstrated that 'domestic genocide develops into the larger genocide that is predatory war'.[48] Already, it observed with 'peculiar horror', the 'genocidal doctrines and actions of the American white supremacists' against the African American people – looting and burning of homes, killing of children, raping of women – are being exported to the 'colored people of Asia'.[49]

> White supremacy at home makes for colored massacres abroad. Both reveal contempt for human life in a colored skin ... It was not without significance that it was President Truman who spoke of the possibility of using the atom bomb on the colored peoples of Asia ...[50]

Not only is the treatment of African Americans a world issue, but also the General Assembly is invested, the petition urged, with the power to receive the indictment and act on it. Furthermore, it claimed (erroneously) that by avowedly accepting the Covenant of the United Nations, the United States had made the Genocide Convention an inseparable part of US law: 'the Genocide Convention ... supersedes, negates and displaces all discriminatory racist law on the books of the United States and the several states.'[51]

The petition refers to the 'institutionalized oppression and persistent slaughter' of the African American people on the basis of 'race' in recognizable Lemkinian language. It will, it says in the Opening Statement, present 'tragically voluminous' evidence of 'acts committed with intent to destroy, in whole or in part, a national, ethnical, racial or religious group as such', that is, the 15 million Black people of the United States. And indeed the petition as a whole *does* powerfully present its case, indicting the US state at every level, arguing, for example, that 'more than 10,000 Negroes' have been killed. They are killed by the Ku Klux Klan, 'that organization which is chartered by the several states as a semi-official arm of government and even granted the tax exemptions of a benevolent society'. Frequently they have been framed and murdered by sham legal processes and a supportive legal bureaucracy. They are killed by police not only in the South but in every city in the US: 'in the back rooms of sheriff's offices, in the cells of county jails, in precinct police stations and on city streets'. When the bodies of murdered African Americans are found, they have often been 'horribly mutilated'. African Americans live in a state of terror of being lynched or shot, which contravenes that part of the Genocide Convention forbidding the causing of serious mental harm to members of a group.[52]

The petition quotes the Convention on genocide as 'deliberately inflicting on the group conditions of life calculated to bring about its destruction in whole or in part', and draws attention to the existence and effects of such conditions in the US.[53] 'From birth to death', it says, 'Negro Americans are humiliated and persecuted, in violation of the Charter and the Convention. They are forced by threat of violence and imprisonment into inferior, segregated accommodations, into jim crow busses, jim crow trains, jim crow hospitals, jim crow schools, jim crow theaters, jim crow restaurants, jim crow housing, and finally into jim crow cemeteries.'[54] In violation of the Convention, there is a mass of segregationist American law, 'written as was Hitler's law', solely on the basis of 'race'. In many American states it was a crime for a 'white person to marry a Negro'. There was no true democracy in the US, because in 'huge and decisive areas' where African Americans were the preponderant population, they were prevented from voting by 'terror' supported not only by Governors, Senators, Judges, and peace officers, but also by the Government of the United States, its Congress, and its Executive branch. The Supreme Court refused to intervene in blatantly framed cases leading to electrocution, and in general the Supreme Court has 'delivered a people – Americans it was supposed to protect – to degradation and violence'. The government, neither by executive nor judicial action, has done nothing to void the many 'racist anti-Negro laws of the several states', though it clearly had the power to do so.[55] Although the petitioners, recalling Shylock's anguished cry in *The Merchant of Venice*, protested 'this genocide as human beings whose very humanity is denied and mocked', they also spoke as 'patriotic Americans' who acknowledged that the 'American Dream was for justice, justice for all men, regardless of race, creed, or color'. 'We cannot believe', they concluded, 'that the General Assembly will not condemn the crimes complained of in this petition.'[56]

The General Assembly did not adopt the petition. Given both the limitations of UN power and responsibility at this time, and the Cold War context, there was no way it could succeed in producing a UN indictment of the United States. Nevertheless, Patterson thought that the action itself of presenting the petition to the United Nations was a signal symbolic success in drawing attention to the situation of African Americans in the post-war world: 'An ideological and moral victory had already been won, the moral bankruptcy of U.S. leaders even in the UN had been exposed'; he also reported that his visit to Paris had 'received a good European press', and that a total of 45,000 copies of the petition were sold in the United States.[57]

Within the United States, as Anson Rabinbach has also pointed out, the reception of the petition was marked by two main features – race and the Cold War.[58] The racial divide was generally clear: while many African Americans supported it, most American whites did not. The Cold War divide was even clearer: pro-Soviet commentators were in favour, and anti-Soviet opinion against. Without exception, law academics were adamantly opposed because any attempt to apply the Genocide Convention to the US situation would affect the integrity of 'our nation'.[59] One of these law academics was Lemkin himself, who, Patterson later wrote, 'argued vehemently that the provisions of the Genocide Convention bore no relation to the U.S. Government or its position vis-à-vis Black citizens'. When the *New York Times* on 18 December 1951 asked Lemkin what he thought, he replied that the accusations were a manoeuvre to 'divert attention from the crimes of genocide committed against Estonians, Latvians, Lithuanians, Poles and other Soviet-subjugated peoples'. Patterson and Paul Robeson, he thought, were 'un-American' elements, serving a foreign power.[60] Later, on 14 June 1953, Lemkin wrote an op-ed piece for the *New York Times* in which he argued that African Americans had conditions of increasing prosperity and progress in the US; though they might experience discrimination, they had not suffered 'destruction, death, annihilation', the essence of genocide. (This seems to us a narrowing of both his own original definition and that of the UN Convention.) In response to the *New York Times* op-ed, Oakley Johnson, one of those who helped write *We Charge Genocide*, wrote to Lemkin protesting that scare tactics and discrimination were not the case of White Americans frightening individual Black Americans but of creating anguish in a racial group as a group; it concerned the terrorizing of a whole race of people who were coloured.[61]

Why was Lemkin so hostile to the *We Charge Genocide* petition? Samantha Power observes that Lemkin intensely felt that concerns about discrimination and prejudice were the province of the United Nations Universal Declaration of Human Rights (which was passed by the General Assembly on 10 December 1948, a day after the Genocide Convention). In Lemkin's irritated view, the Universal Declaration of Human Rights, dealing with individual problems, not with the group rights of peoples as demanded by the concept of genocide, represented a diversion from the Genocide Convention; the danger was that the two conventions would be confused in the public mind.[62] Rabinbach argues that Lemkin, dismissing *We Charge Genocide* as concerned with discrimination, not destruction, was also anxious that charges of racial genocide within the US might mean the final blow to American ratification of the Genocide Convention.[63] In our view, *We Charge Genocide* had made it very clear, by addressing in careful and detailed ways the specific terms of Article II of the Convention, that it was throughout speaking to African American group experience.

Disturbing questions, we believe, remain concerning Lemkin and his attitudes to African American history and people: perhaps there was a fundamental lack of sympathy. It might be fruitful to compare Lemkin in this regard to Einstein, who actively supported the struggle for African American human rights and enjoyed long-standing friendships with African American intellectuals and cultural figures such as Paul Robeson, Du Bois, and Marian Anderson.[64] There are also questions to be pursued concerning Lemkin's attitudes towards Africa and Africans. Dominik J. Schaller, analyzing Lemkin's unpublished manuscripts, expresses dismay at Lemkin's views on European colonial rule in Africa, commenting that Lemkin swayed between condemnation and admiration. In terms of the German colonial war against the Herero in Namibia, Schaller feels that there can be no doubt that Lemkin 'regarded his concept of genocide' as 'perfectly applicable to the events of 1904–1908'. Yet Lemkin also, he points out, fell in with a myth that the Herero, unable to reconcile themselves to subjection and loss of independence, chose to kill themselves in a kind of national suicide, with particular blame being attached to the Herero women. Lemkin considered that the imposition of Belgian colonial rule in the Congo, and the forced labor of the indigenous population that accompanied it, was genocide. Lemkin, however, described the 'native militia' in the pay of the Belgians as 'savages' and 'cannibals'. Schaller says that Lemkin has to be recognized as an 'enthusiastic advocate of colonialism' by European powers in Africa, seeing it as a necessary task that Europeans bring 'civilisation' to the continent. Schaller concludes that the ways Lemkin perceived Africans 'can only be described as racist': 'Africans are portrayed as either weak-willed and helpless victims or as bloodthirsty cannibals.'[65]

Perhaps Lemkin can be compared here with Hannah Arendt. Anne Norton points out that Arendt trivialized and infantilized African American demands for civil rights, and in general constituted Africa and African Americans as outside world history.[66] Ned Curthoys contends that Arendt 'adjudges the real tragedy of colonialism as its abrogation of European humanism and republican values, rather than its invasion and displacement of existing indigenous cultures', and that, unlike Sartre, Arendt refused to acknowledge 'those dimensions of colonialism and imperialism that constituted physical and cultural genocide'.[67] In relation to other exiled European intellectuals in the US, we might also think of Adorno and Horkheimer's notorious judgement in *Dialectic of Enlightenment* that jazz was a mere manifestation of nature, nature interacting with the demands of the American mass entertainment industries; borrowing harsh terms from Nietzsche, Adorno and Horkheimer refer to jazz as stylized barbarity and a system of non-culture. In these terms, Adorno and Horkheimer – and, it would very much appear, their contemporaries and fellow exiles Arendt and Lemkin – were conforming to a long tradition of European superiority and contempt towards Africa. Cosmopolitanism was defeated by profound persisting Eurocentrism.[68]

There was also the ever-pressing Cold War context. Anton Weiss-Wendt suggests that from about 1949, Lemkin, in a desperate and futile attempt to get the United States to ratify the Convention, increasingly aligned himself with the US side in the Cold War, and accordingly adopted a strongly anti-Communist stance. Furthermore, he became closely allied with (and financially supported by) particular organizations of East European ethnic communities in the US, who had enthusiastically adopted the new term 'genocide' in their denunciations of Soviet power, and whom he advised for an exhibit on 'Communism Exterminates Nations: Exhibit of Genocide in Lithuania' in 1951.[69]

It was not only Lemkin for whom Cold War considerations – which were persistently and perhaps inseparably entwined with American race politics – are relevant in terms of rejection of the petition. Such considerations, which were to inflect most discussions of genocide from the 1950s to the 1980s, were, in fact, so strong in relation to the petition that they fuelled intra-racial divisions in the Black anti-racist struggle. When he presented *We Charge Genocide* to the UN in Paris, Patterson encountered opposition on Cold War grounds from the three African American members of the American delegation to the UN Human Rights Commission, namely Channing Tobias, chairman of the board of the NAACP; Edith Sampson, a lawyer from Chicago; and Ralph Bunche.[70]

The effect of Cold War politics was to produce a stalemate, with neither side successfully bringing genocide charges against the other. As each side recognized this, discussions of genocide and the Convention subsided during the 1950s.[71]

Tightening the definition: Pieter Drost, 1959

In the years following *We Charge Genocide*, concern began to develop in genocide scholarship that the 1948 Convention was not leading to any legal action. The Convention seemed to be quiescent in the context of the Cold War, for the USSR ratified it in May 1954, while the US steadfastly refused to do so. In 1959, Pieter N. Drost, a Dutch legal academic, in *Genocide: United Nations Legislation on International Criminal Law*, raised what he saw as important difficulties inhibiting the Convention's operation as international law. It is limited, for example, to national application and interpretation: 'It orders state officials to combat crimes by state officials. Obviously, when the state itself by its own officers commits genocide against its own citizens, the Convention as it stands today, will remain a dead letter.' Drost also felt that the decision to exclude political groups was most regrettable, 'but hardly surprising in view of political conditions both within and between states'. He was pleased, however, that cultural genocide did not survive committee discussions to become part of the 1948 Convention. In Drost's view, genocide is 'collective homicide and not official vandalism or violation of civil liberties': 'It is directed against the life of man and not against his material or mental goods.' Protection of culture is an 'international concern of the highest order', but it belongs primarily to international law concerned with human rights and perhaps to the field of minority rights; it is 'foreign to the field of criminal law' concerned with 'group murder'. Drost argues that in terms of international criminal law the complicity of a government is not required for genocide to be a crime: 'Genocide may occur against the sincere and strenuous efforts of a government in power.' Genocide becomes international criminal law when it denotes two conceptions, 'group' and 'kill': 'If both elements were present, the crime appears.' Drost believed that Article II of the Convention was defined by two elements, intent and destruction.[72]

Drost's view that genocide should be defined as 'group murder' for the concept to become effective in international criminal law represented a substantial narrowing of the concept from Lemkin and the UN Convention. It would also become an influential and continuing position in genocide studies, and foreshadows the late twentieth-century development of bodies like the International Criminal Court. Drost's conception, however, while it recognizes the importance of intent in Article II, also seems to put aside intent as a key element in defining genocide. If, in Drost's formula, genocide simply combines group and kill, where is intent? Who or what has intent to commit genocide?

Genocide in Hannah Arendt's *Eichmann in Jerusalem*, 1963–1964

In a still-controversial and much-discussed book, Hannah Arendt pondered the relationship between the new concept and the events which had given rise to it. Her series of articles written in *The New Yorker*, based on her observation of the

1961 Eichmann trial in Israel, was published in book form in 1963 with the famous and arresting title *Eichmann in Jerusalem: A Report on the Banality of Evil*. In the body of the book, she used the term 'genocide' rarely and incidentally (and did not use the term 'Holocaust' at all). In one of her occasional mentions, she points out that until the 1940s Jewish historical consciousness had emphasized a long history of suffering but not the notion that the Jewish people would not survive, and remarks: 'They had never been confronted with genocide.'[73] In the book's postscript, written in 1964, she considers more closely the question of whether 'genocide' is the best term to use for the Nazi atrocities against the Jewish people. In addressing the question of 'what kind of crime is actually involved here – a crime, moreover, which all agree is unprecedented', she suggests that the problem with the term 'genocide' is that even though it was introduced explicitly to describe this new crime, it is inadequate 'for the simple reason that massacres of whole peoples are not unprecedented'. 'They were', she goes on, 'the order of the day in antiquity, and the centuries of colonization and imperialism provide plenty of examples of more or less successful attempts of that sort.'

So Arendt looks for a description that is more precise, and comes up with 'administrative massacres'; this is a term, she says, that 'arose in connection with British imperialism' in the sense that 'the English deliberately rejected such procedures as a means of maintaining their rule over India'. She likes it not only because it captures the distinctness of the Nazi atrocities, their bureaucratic character, but also because it dispels the prejudice that 'such monstrous acts can be committed only against a foreign nation or a different race.' The term makes it clear that 'this sort of killing can be directed against any given group.'[74] While her nomenclature did not catch on, her emphasis on the unprecedented character of what had happened was to prove highly influential. The term 'Holocaust', a translation into English from *shoah*, the Hebrew word for catastrophe, came, in the wake of the Eichmann trial, to be used instead. As Peter Novick comments, 'what had formerly been one of a variety of terms came, in the early sixties, to be (still usually uncapitalized) the most common one; by the late sixties (usually capitalized), it had become clearly dominant.'[75] The particular association of 'genocide' and 'Holocaust' that is now so common was not to emerge for some considerable time.

Jean-Paul Sartre's 'On Genocide', 1967: the US in Vietnam

In 1967, the Cold War context was still in evidence in the writing and reception of Jean-Paul Sartre's famous essay, 'On Genocide', written on behalf of Bertrand Russell's International War Crimes Tribunal, of which Sartre was executive president. The Tribunal had been created on 13 November 1966 to investigate whether the American war in Vietnam was violating international law. Particular aspects for investigation included the 'crimes against peace' postulated by the Nuremberg trials, the rules of war fixed by international conventions, and the question whether there were acts by American forces 'which can legally be called acts of genocide'. Sartre's 'On Genocide' was adopted at the end of the Tribunal's second session, held in Denmark in late 1967, the Tribunal then unanimously declaring 'the United States guilty of the crime of genocide'.[76] While Western governments ignored it, the Tribunal made a significant and eventually influential contribution to debates over the morality and conduct of the war in Vietnam.

Although Sartre's knowledge of Lemkin was rather vague, his linking in the essay of colonization with genocide would uncannily reprise Lemkin's own approach. Taking French colonization in Algeria as his primary example of settler colonialism, Sartre argues that colonization is 'by its very nature an act of cultural genocide', always involving the systematic liquidation of all the 'characteristics of the native society'. 'For the subject peoples', Sartre writes, 'this inevitably means the extinction of their national character, culture, customs, sometimes even language'. In Algeria, he argues, the colonial troops maintained their authority by 'terror', by 'perpetual massacre', which Sartre saw as 'genocidal in character' since it aimed at the destruction (and here he quotes from Article II of the Convention) of a part of an ethnic, national, or religious group, in order to terrorize the remainder and to 'wrench apart the indigenous society'.[77]

In the Algerian case, the desire to destroy and replace indigenous society was inhibited by the desire to use Algerian labour. There was, however, no such inhibition in Vietnam. In Sartre's view, the American interest in Vietnam issued primarily from its imperial desire for world control. With no direct *economic* interests in Vietnam, there was nothing to prevent the US from envisaging genocide. Against what he called the 'people's war' of the Vietnamese, the Americans pursued an anti-guerilla strategy of 'total genocide' in the spirit of neo-colonialism, installing by *coup d'état* a head of state who would serve their interests and the interests of local privileged strata, while engaging in a war whose intent was to destroy 'the masses' who supported the resistance to American aims and actions. The methods used by the Americans included in the South massive bombing, ruining of crops, murder, rape, looting, and 'concentration camps'; and in the North systematic destruction of the economic base, deliberate attacks against civilians, and destruction of hospitals, schools, and places of worship, leading to serious psycho-social 'mental harm' among children. All these actions, Sartre sought to demonstrate, were directly culpable in terms of Article II of the Convention. The Vietnamese as a national group would be destroyed, Sartre wrote, economically, politically, and culturally and to a certain extent physically.[78]

We can, says Sartre, read American 'genocidal intent' as implicit in 'the facts'. Such intent is not necessarily 'premeditated', and it is impossible to decide if it is conscious or not, though, Sartre adds, 'the Puritan bad faith of Americans works wonders.' The American soldiers may at first have conceived of themselves as 'liberators', not as 'occupation troops'. But when they realized that the Vietnamese did not want them there, Sartre contends, their frustration turned to racism. Such racism, 'anti-black, anti-Asiatic, anti-Mexican' (and here he is particularly close to arguments in *We Charge Genocide*), has 'deep historical roots' in the United States. Proof of this is that 'the United States government refused to ratify the Genocide Convention' because it would have conflicted with the laws of several states.[79] Sartre suggests that the American policymakers permitted racism, torture, shooting of unarmed women, kicking wounded Vietnamese in the genitals, cutting the ears off dead men to take home for trophies, and so on because similar practices were legally tolerated and allowed to flourish in the 'anti-black racism of Southern whites'. The spirit of genocide entered the minds of the soldiers, who saw all Vietnamese as enemies (and in a 'people's war' only civilians are visible) and then tortured and killed men, women, and children in Vietnam merely because they were Vietnamese, just as 'Hitler killed the Jews because they were Jews.'[80] Deploying genocide to defeat the Vietnamese guerillas and their supportive masses, 'at least in part', would have an 'admonitory value', as a warning to those everywhere in the Third World not to engage in anti-American guerilla struggles, and indeed as a warning to humanity as a whole, to be submissive. 'The group', he concludes, 'which the United States wants to intimidate and terrorize by way of the Vietnamese nation is the human group in its entirety'.[81]

Sartre does make a striking case for regarding the American war in Vietnam as genocide legally and conceptually. In 1974, the American philosopher of law Hugo Adam Bedau in an essay 'Genocide in Vietnam?' sympathetically examined Sartre's application of the Genocide Convention and its notions of specific genocidal intent, concluding that Sartre had almost proved his case, but not quite, and that further 'conceptual argument' and 'evidential researches' were required.[82] We agree, and suggest that Sartre's wrestling with the notion of intent provides an early example of just how vexed the question of 'intent' can become.

Although Sartre's essay was received initially within a Cold War context, over time it came to be read as a serious contribution to genocide studies, in particular, to the analysis of the relationship between genocide, colonization, and decolonization. In 1981 Leo Kuper, a scholar of African colonialism, gave it a critically sympathetic reading in his book *Genocide*. He agreed that it was possible to make the argument that the 'level and nature of the destruction rained on Vietnam by the U.S.A. was suggestive of genocide', though he also thought that Sartre's attempt to establish intent was weakened by 'extravagant generalization'. Yet, he mused, this was a problem not only for Sartre; there was a serious difficulty for anyone wishing to establish genocidal intent in a court of law: 'governments hardly declare and document genocidal plans in the manner of the Nazis.' As for public opinion and accountability, the requirement of intent 'provides an easy means for evading responsibility'.[83]

Kuper was cautiously supportive of Sartre's linking of colonization and genocide: '[an] affinity between colonialism and genocide can be accepted, though with much qualification, and we can extract from Sartre's argument some of the significant elements in this relationship.' Kuper considered that Sartre extravagantly claimed that colonization as such involved genocide, whereas Sartre should have distinguished between settler and other kinds of colonialism. Nevertheless, the 'course of colonization' of North and South America, the West Indies, and 'Australia and Tasmania', Kuper observes, has certainly been 'marked all too often by genocide'. (Kuper's lack of clarity on the fact that Tasmania is part of Australia has been unfortunately shared by many international genocide scholars, and brings the whole field into some disrepute, especially among Australian historians.)

Kuper also agrees with Sartre's view that genocide is less restrained when the labour of subject peoples is not required; this consideration, Kuper feels, would be applicable to understanding genocides of hunting and gathering peoples.[84] He supports Sartre's notion of 'genocidal massacre' in relations between colonizer and colonized, especially when there was an 'extremely brutal conquest, as in the French conquest of Algeria'. Unlike Sartre, however, Kuper also wishes to stress genocide as potentially an aspect of decolonization. Colonizers, he argues, create dangerously 'plural' or divided societies, arbitrarily yoking together in the same political unit peoples of different race or ethnicity or religion, with the result that there have been many genocides during decolonization by and among and within ex-colonized groups.[85]

Are genocides necessarily state-directed and controlled?

The 1980s saw a major attempt to redefine the meaning of 'genocide' to refer only to instances of mass killing under the direction of the state. This drive came from two sources. On the one hand, there was a growing attention to the Holocaust (especially, as Peter Novick has shown, in the United States), which profoundly influenced both scholarly and popular thinking about genocide; this influence was so great that in many quarters the Holocaust became synonymous with genocide in a way that had not been the case earlier.[86] In some quarters, the whole project of comparative genocide studies was unacceptable, for it was seen to deny the 'uniqueness' of the Holocaust.[87] On the other hand, there was within the growing field of comparative genocide scholarship continuing dissatisfaction with the exclusion of political groups. Though he shared this dissatisfaction, Leo Kuper thought it unhelpful to create new definitions of genocide 'when there is an internationally recognized definition' and the Genocide Convention could become the basis for effective action.[88] Some key scholars, however, did not agree, and set about devising new definitions and typologies.

In 1982, the American sociologist Irving Louis Horowitz, in the augmented third edition of his book *Taking Lives: Genocide and State Power*, takes as his subject the 'essential nexus between genocide and statecraft': 'most acts of genocide are highly organized activities of the state.' In this view, genocide is 'collective murder', a 'singular type of mass murder, a historically distinct event that had its ultimate expression in the Holocaust'. Like Marx, Horowitz sees the state as an evil in history that should wither away in order that the 'dignity of humanity' can be restored. Much like Jessie Bernard in 1949, he also felt that sociology, in its concern for derivative issues such as social structure and function, was in danger of settling into being a second order, not fundamental, discipline. To redeem itself from a dominant structural functional approach, sociology should study basic issues of life and death, and the most extreme form of such is genocide, which now must become social science's directing framework.[89]

Horowitz's primary argument is that genocide is to be distinguished from other kinds of destructive violence. In addition to its 'systematic character', genocide is conducted with the 'approval of, if not direct intervention by, the state apparatus'; it 'reflects some sort of political support base within a given ruling class or national group'. Genocide is 'always a conscious choice and policy'. In these terms, Horowitz feels, the 'fate of the Armenians is the essential prototype of genocide in the twentieth century.' Sometimes, Horowitz notes, genocide can be an 'episodic and even sporadic event', as in the Jim Jones mass suicide in Guyana in 1978. The conduct of 'classic colonialism', however, Horowitz asserts, was invariably linked with genocide as 'systematic mass extermination' by a state power against a 'relatively powerless group or sector'. Here he refers to the actions of nineteenth-century imperialist nations (decimation of Zulu tribesmen by British troops, the Dutch-run slave trade, the virtual depopulation of the Congo by Belgians) and the liquidation in the Americas of 'ancient Indian civilizations'. Horowitz observes that it is the 'hypocritical heritage' of European and American nations and cultures to proclaim concepts of democracy and liberty for their own populations while 'systematically destroying others'.[90]

Yet certain cases worry Horowitz, not least those concerning African Americans and Vietnam. He wishes to distinguish genocide, for instance, from vigilantism, which represents the 'maintenance of order without law, or some kind of mass participation without corresponding state support', though he is also uneasy about this example, agreeing that categories such as genocide and vigilantism are not absolute and there is a 'slim line between systematic and sporadic destruction'. After all, he notes, in the period between 1865 and 1920 the vigilante practices of the Ku Klux Klan had the 'assistance of legislative assemblies and court houses in Southern states'. Sporadic destruction may also, he reflects, take more lives than systematic annihilation; and he does not wish to offer apologetics for the 'brutality of hostile White power structures toward their Black communities'. Nevertheless, he wishes to hold on to the distinction between genocide and vigilantism because while genocide refers to political structure, vigilantism refers only to events of a 'social' character. In these terms, what happened to American Black communities must be 'distinguished from the sort of systematic extermination associated with the concept of genocide'. It is clear from his endnote references that Horowitz is referring to, but rejecting, the claim of the 1951 *We Charge Genocide* petition that post–World War II African Americans, as a group, were victims of genocide.[91]

Horowitz is also conceptually troubled by the undeclared American war in Vietnam, referring here to critics of the war like Bedau who have seriously considered the case that American destruction is an instance of genocide. Horowitz agrees that the line between war and genocide 'becomes profoundly blurred'. Horowitz himself gives no clear verdict, but when he writes that the 'widespread use of mass violence by state authorities against one portion of a population clearly has spillover potentials for another part of humanity, sometimes thousands of miles away',[92] he is very much in sympathy with a key position of both *We Charge Genocide* and Sartre's essay 'On Genocide' in relation to American wars in South-East Asia. In our reading, Horowitz's desire to define genocide with certainty as systematic state-directed mass death is unsettled by the examples of African American history and the violence perpetrated by the USA in Vietnam.

In the mid-1980s two striking essays by the historian Tony Barta sharply questioned the now-dominant view that genocide is to be defined as systematic and state-directed, an always consciously chosen policy. Barta, an expert in German history with a good general knowledge of Australian history, felt that such definitions were inadequate in relation to European settler colonialism, his example Australian colonial history since 1788. In a 1984 essay, 'After the Holocaust: Consciousness of Genocide in Australia', Barta called for renewed attention to the important passage in chapter nine of *Axis Rule* that links genocide with colonization, Lemkin contending here that genocide proceeds in two phases: 'destruction of the national pattern of the oppressed group' followed by the 'imposition of the national pattern of the oppressor'. Barta movingly evokes how such a two-phase pattern of destruction and imposition quite clearly occurred in relation to the Aboriginal peoples and their societies and cultures on the Australian continent. Barta also comments that because in Australia genocide had come to be understood as synonymous with the Holocaust, Australian colonial history was not recognized as genocide and Australians were failing to take responsibility for a dreadful history.[93]

In a subsequent essay, 'Relations of Genocide: Land and Lives in the Colonization of Australia' (1987) Barta again drew attention to that crucial passage in Lemkin linking genocide with colonization. Barta contended that genocide studies had come to focus too much on those parts of Lemkin's 1944 book and the 1948 Genocide Convention that insisted on conscious policy and intention as proof of genocide. 'I will not, I hope', Barta says, 'beg the question of how relationships might be expressive of intentions; I expect to construe intentions from action (and inaction) and from words as well.' But, he adds, he will 'assume of actions that they imply relationships, and entail consequences, which people do not always envisage clearly'.[94]

Barta engages directly with Horowitz's characterization of a 'genocidal society' founded on the example of Germany in its Nazi period, a society where genocide is constituted in a state bureaucratic apparatus pursuing a systematic destruction of an innocent people. Barta argues that in settler-colonial societies the reverse might be true: while the whole bureaucratic apparatus might officially be directed to protect the indigenous people of a land or continent, 'a whole race is nevertheless subject to remorseless pressures of destruction inherent in the very nature of the society.' In this sense Australia, in the whole 200 years of its existence, is, Barta contends, a genocidal society. Marxism, Barta proposes, can make a valuable contribution to the understanding of genocide. He interprets in Marxist terms that part of Lemkin's 1944 definition linking genocide with colonization as a two-phase process of destruction and imposition. He refers here to Marx in 1843 remarking that 'one is too easily tempted to overlook the *objective nature of the relationships* and to explain everything from the *will* of the persons acting', and alludes as well to Marxist aspects of Sartre's analyses in 'On Genocide'. For Barta, what Lemkin recognizes as a two-phase process of destruction and imposition establishes between colonizer and colonized relations of genocide, relations which do not necessarily correspond to the intentions of individuals or state authorities. In these processes and relationships, intentions could be – and here Barta is supporting Sartre's view of American motives in their war in Vietnam as possibly unconscious – muddled and obscure. Nor do actors in a historical situation necessarily know what the consequences of their actions might be. What is clear, however, Barta suggests, is that the colonizers of the Australian continent, whether or not they desired to protect the Aboriginal inhabitants, insisted on the taking of the land. Such taking possession of the land proceeded by notions of individual ownership and private property, notions alien to the history and society of the colonized; colonization established on the continent two 'totally incompatible forms of economy and society', and neither government authorities nor settlers would countenance the defeat of their overall aim, the incorporation of the continent into 'the capitalist economy'. Dispossession of the land for the colonized had disastrous – genocidal – consequences for the Aboriginal peoples who had lived with the land for many thousands of years.[95]

We can, then, Barta says, now construe intention in a more complex way in relation to genocide, colonization, and the 'relations of destruction' settler colonialism historically establishes. Genocidal intent inhered in the fatal and absolute policy of the colonizers, from metropolitan authorities to local government officials to settlers, to take the land, and even when the terrible human effects of taking the land became clear, at no stage did government authorities or the settlers ever consider withdrawing from the continent, a continent which they had invaded and which was not theirs. Such a conception of intention also has consequences, Barta suggests, for the assigning of responsibility for genocide in settler-colonial situations. Barta recognizes that a focus on relations of genocide could imply that no specific individual or authority is to blame. What, however, we should do, Barta says, is 'critically' explore a settler-colonial society as a 'whole system'.[96]

In effect, what we should be doing is not so much assigning blame as creating a historical consciousness that would be highly critical of British and Australian colonization in Australia since 1788. In these terms, Barta's essays of the mid-1980s can be seen as responding to and developing, within the framework of genocide studies, the historiography that, from the 1970s, had grown in Australia questioning comforting national myths. At the same time, his essays prefigured a major interest in the late 1990s and early 2000s in investigating genocide in relation to European settler colonialism worldwide and the relation of such settler colonialism to Nazism and World War II.

Genocide, mass killing, and intent

Barta's was a minority voice, however, for the rest of the twentieth century. Genocide scholarship continued to be dominated by social scientists seeking to emphasize state action and mass killing rather than the nature and consequences of colonization. An influential example was Frank Chalk and Kurt Jonassohn's edited collection *The History and Sociology of Genocide* (1990). They sought to exclude from 'genocide' much of what Lemkin and even the 1948 UN Convention had included. Most of the wide-ranging aspects and processes Lemkin had regarded as genocide, in terms of undermining the essential foundations of life of a group, should instead, they argued, be construed as acts of 'ethnocide'. Genocide proper they saw as concerned with the 'physical extermination of a group'. They also thought that the Convention was disablingly deficient in its narrow definition of groups; it is 'of little use to scholars'. They wonder if they should make up a new term altogether, but think no, because they couldn't think of an alternative and also the term genocide is now so widely accepted. They decide to offer 'our own definition', with a focus on genocide as mass killings and the annihilation of groups:[97] '*Genocide* is a form of one-sided mass killing in which a state or other authority intends to destroy a group, as that group and membership in it are defined by the perpetrator.'[98] Chalk and Jonassohn are pleased that this definition leaves open the nature of the victim group, and so can include groups excluded by the UN Convention. They also insist that genocides are 'always performed by a *state or other authority*'. Their definition is followed by a fourfold typology, based on the motives of the perpetrator, which will cover (while allowing for further research) all genocides.[99]

In social-scientific fashion, Chalk and Jonassohn believe that the focus in their work, as in the work of other North American scholars such as Roger W. Smith and Helen Fein, on genocide as mass killing is a sign that 'in spite of their occasional differences students of genocide are close to a consensus about the essential components of the core cases in the field.'[100] Their pithy definition, then, is proffered in a normative spirit: this is what genocide studies should do from now on.

In the same year, 1990, Helen Fein, in her long essay 'Genocide: A Sociological Perspective', also sought a compact definition that could be universally applied. She finds Chalk and Jonassohn's definition, however, to be too narrow. Like Bernard and Horowitz before her, Fein protests at the proscriptions of modern sociology that work to exclude consideration of violence, war, and disaster as basic to the discipline. She argues that Chalk and Jonassohn's definition has certain problems, for example, in limiting the perpetrator to a state or other authority; their emphasis on mass killing omits other forms of intentional biological destruction that Lemkin identified; and their notion of one-sided killing seems too restrictive or absolute. Fein also wishes to reconcile her 'sociological definition' with the 'legal definition' of the UN Convention.[101]

> Genocide is sustained purposeful action by a perpetrator to physically destroy a collectivity directly or indirectly, through interdiction of the biological and social reproduction of group members, sustained regardless of the surrender or lack of threat offered by the victim.[102]

While Fein does not identify the perpetrator with the state and includes interdiction of biological and social reproduction as forms of destruction, she nevertheless remains close to a particular strand of genocide studies that we can see working its way from Drost through Horowitz to Chalk and Jonassohn, of reducing genocide to physical destruction of a group.[103] Early in her essay Fein considers the question of intent 'when killings occur during war and colonization', and is particularly critical of Barta's 1987 essay, arguing – wrongly – that Barta 'simply' proposes to 'eliminate intent' as a criterion of genocide.[104] She returns to this 'problematic' issue in a later section, part five, concerning the mass death of indigenous peoples. Here Fein contends that 'Barta's approach, redefining genocide as a product of social relations without intent', may lead to a 'paradoxical disdain or disinterest in assessing the responsibility for the death of indigenous people'; it leads the observer, Fein continues, to 'overlook state and collectively planned mass murders and acts of omission leading to death'.[105] This seems to us a serious misreading of Barta's 1987 essay, where, as we have seen, Barta explicitly says that he is not denying intent, rather, he is redefining it in colonizing situations of contradictory desires and unforeseen consequences. In the confusion and messiness of colonization, with metropolitan authorities, local governments and settlers often pulling in different ways in relation to care of the indigenous people, there was, nevertheless, unanimity of intent to take the land, so leading inevitably to the destruction of the foundations of life of Aboriginal groups across the continent, that is, to genocidal relations. He then calls for settler-colonial societies like Australia – and, by implication, Britain, the invading imperial society at the time – to take responsibility in heightened and critical consciousness of the genocidal disasters they historically created in massive destruction of indigenous societies across the world.

The critiques of Barta's 1987 essay by sociologists like Fein indicate a tension between history and sociology within genocide studies. Where the sociological approach reveals a hubris to create a definition that will be universally applicable and assumes that intent and purpose in society are always clearly known or ascertainable, the historical approach – from Lemkin in his manuscript essays and notes through Sartre and Kuper and Barta to more recent comparative scholarship concerned with genocide and colonization – acknowledges the messiness of history, the frequent obscurity of motives, the salience of unintended consequences.[106]

Recent debates

With the demise of the Soviet Union and the end of the Cold War, the international law of genocide had a new opportunity to operate. The 1990s witnessed genocides in Rwanda and Bosnia and renewed attempts to establish instruments of international law under which charges of genocide could be laid. The Genocide Convention had already been given a new lease of life when the US finally ratified it on 19 February 1986. After his disastrous visit on 5 May 1985 to West Germany's Bitburg Cemetery to commemorate the 40th anniversary of World War II, President Reagan decided to appease the many critics of his appearance at Bitburg by bullying US ratification of the Genocide Convention through Congress, albeit along with interpretations and disclaimers about the Convention that had the effect of immunizing the US from being charged with genocide.[107] After much discussion and consultation, the International Criminal Court was established in 2002, its jurisdiction limited to the 'most serious crimes of concern to the international community as a whole', namely genocide, crimes against humanity, war crimes, and the crime of aggression.[108]

These legal changes did a great deal to stimulate new scholarly interest in genocide. During the 1990s, genocide scholarship emerged as a distinct field with its own international association (the International Association of Genocide Scholars, founded in 1994), conferences, and journals (*Journal of Genocide Research* and *Zeitschrift für Genozidforschung*). In January 2005, the International Network of Genocide Scholars had its foundational meeting in Berlin. The field has expanded beyond the small group of social scientists and legal theorists who had mainly championed it during the 1980s to include a much wider range of disciplines, fields of study, and approaches.

Historians, in particular, have taken a new interest in genocide, deploying divergent approaches. One group was historians of the Holocaust, a vast and diverse field of scholarship. Steven Katz provided in 1994 a systematic exposition of the view that the Holocaust was the only genocide, exacerbating an already large academic debate on the Holocaust's uniqueness or otherwise.[109] The journal *Holocaust and Genocide Studies*, founded in 1986, implied in its title a distinction between the Holocaust and other genocides and, as Dirk Moses points out, gave nearly all its attention to the Holocaust. In this scholarship, as Moses says, 'the original master category, genocide, was replaced by a new one, Holocaust.'[110]

Many other historians, however, saw the idea of genocide in terms closer to Lemkin's own. Lemkin's insight, for example, that genocide has always existed in human history was taken up in the field of world history, with Jared Diamond in *The Rise and Fall of the Third Chimpanzee* (1991) arguing that humanity has always practised genocide against other humans.[111] In *The Other Side of Eden* (2000), Hugh Brody suggests that genocide intensified with the appearance of agricultural societies, an argument he eloquently develops by focusing on the relentless ways that the ever-restless, indeed nomadic, agricultural peoples have spread over the globe, destroying the foundations of life of hunter-gatherer peoples like the Inuit of Canada, the San of southern Africa, and the Aborigines of Australia.[112]

The idea of genocide as wide-ranging and linked to colonialism, articulated by Lemkin, Sartre, and Barta among others, has become an increasingly influential position. It can be seen in Sven Lindqvist's *Exterminate all the Brutes* (1996), Ward Churchill's denunciation of the colonization of the Americas post-1492 in *A Little Matter of Genocide* (1997), and the Australian Human Rights Commission's *Bringing Them Home* (1997), a report on Aboriginal child removal.[113] It continues in the work of historians investigating Lemkin's unpublished manuscripts where he studies colonial genocides;[114] and in historians like Jürgen Zimmerer, Dirk Moses, and Wendy Lower who are exploring how much previous European colonizing inspired Nazi genocidal practices including colonizing projects in the land mass east of Germany. In her *Nazi Empire-Building and the Holocaust in Ukraine* (2005), Lower, referring to Lemkin's manuscript arguments linking genocide to centuries of imperialistic warfare, forced migrations, frontier violence, and the displacement of non-Europeans in the Americas, Australia, and Africa, writes of the Nazi plans, visions, and practices in the territories they conquered and occupied in Eastern Europe:

> one finds in Hitler's, Himmler's, and Rosenberg's imaginings of the new Aryan paradise references to the North American frontier, the British Empire in India, and the European exploitation of Africans in the late nineteenth century. In Heinrich Himmler's SS propaganda publication, *Der Untermensch*, one reads about the life-and-death struggle between Germans and Jews alongside Nazi claims to Eastern European territory depicted as 'black earth that could be a paradise, a California of Europe.'[115]

Paul Celan's poem 'Breathturn' suggests that in history we can listen to the roar as Truth steps among humanity, right into the metaphor flurry.[116] So we can say that as a concept, genocide, born in the turmoil of a world war in one of humanity's most dreadful centuries, continuously interacting with always-disputed historical situations, will continue to be passionately argued and fought over, for it brings to the fore the most fundamental of questions: the character of humanity as a species, history as progress, the ethical bases of societies, and the honour of civilizations and nations.

Notes

1. We would like to thank Ned Curthoys and Dirk Moses for suggestions and references; we owe a huge debt to Rhonda Y. Williams for invaluable assistance in African American historiography and careful reading of the essay.
2. See A. Curthoys and J. Docker, *Is History Fiction?* (Sydney: UNSW Press, 2006), pp. 111–14.
3. There is growing biographical and public interest in Lemkin, including the staging of a play early in 2006 in New York, *Lemkin's House*, by Catherine Filloux, at the 78th Street Theater Lab. See N. Genzlinger, 'Looking Back With Despair at a Life of Fighting Genocide', *New York Times* Theater Review, 13 February 2006. (Our thanks to Nick Mirzoeff for this reference.)
4. R. Lemkin, 'Totally Unofficial Man', in *Pioneers of Genocide Studies*, eds, S. Totten and S. L. Jacobs (New Brunswick, NJ: Transaction Publishers, 2002), pp. 366–9, 370, 379–80, 387–92.
5. Our thanks to James Fussell, who conducts the invaluable website preventgenocide.org and is writing an eagerly awaited biography of Lemkin.
6. Lemkin, 'Totally Unofficial Man', p. 373.
7. Lemkin's 1933 proposals can be accessed at http://www.preventgenocide.org/lemkin/madrid 1933-english.htm. See also S. Power, *"A Problem from Hell": America and the Age of Genocide* (New York: HarperCollins Perennial, 2002), pp. 21–3, and A. D. Moses, 'Genocide and Settler Society', in *Genocide and Settler Society: Frontier Violence and Stolen Indigenous Children in Australian History*, ed. A. D. Moses (New York: Berghahn, 2004), p. 21.
8. R. Lemkin, *Axis Rule in Occupied Europe: Laws of Occupation, Analysis of Government, Proposals for Redress* (New York: Columbia University Press, 1944), pp. xiii, 92–3;

also 'Genocide as a Crime under International Law', *American Journal of International Law*, 41, 1 (1947), 147.

9. Lemkin, 'Totally Unofficial Man', pp. 378–81, 385.
10. Concerning enigmatic anecdotes involving a traveller, cf. Michael Rothberg, 'W.E.B. Du Bois in Warsaw: Holocaust Memory and the Color Line, 1949–1952', *The Yale Journal of Criticism*, 14, 1 (2001), 175–6, discussing a story Du Bois tells in an essay 'The Negro and the Warsaw Ghetto', published in the Communist Party journal *Jewish Life* in 1952.
11. Lemkin, *Axis Rule in Occupied Europe*, ch. IX, 'Genocide', pp. 79–95; for an extended evocation of chapter nine, see A. Curthoys and J. Docker, 'Introduction – Genocide: definitions, questions, settler-colonies', *Aboriginal History*, 25 (2001), 5–11.
12. Lemkin, *Axis Rule in Occupied Europe*, pp. xi, 79–80.
13. The story is told in some detail in Power's *"A Problem from Hell"* and in A. Weiss-Wendt, 'Hostage of Politics: Raphael Lemkin on "Soviet Genocide"', *Journal of Genocide Research*, 7, 4 (2005), 551–9.
14. Power, *"A Problem from Hell"*, p. 54f.
15. See J. Docker, 'Are Settler-Colonies Inherently Genocidal? Re-reading Lemkin', in *Empire, Colony, Genocide*, ed. A. D. Moses (New York: Berghahn, 2008).
16. T. Elder, 'What you see before your eyes: documenting Raphael Lemkin's life by exploring his archival papers, 1900–1959', *Journal of Genocide Research*, 7, 4 (2005), 472; Weiss-Wendt, 'Hostage of Politics', 556.
17. See J. Docker, 'Raphael Lemkin's History of Genocide and Colonialism', paper for United States Holocaust Memorial Museum, February 2004; A. Curthoys, 'Raphael Lemkin's "Tasmania": An Introduction' and R. Lemkin, 'Tasmania', ed. A. Curthoys, *Patterns of Prejudice*, 39, 2 (2005), 162–96, reprinted in *Colonialism and Genocide*, eds, A. D. Moses and D. Stone (London: Routledge, 2007), pp. 66–100; A. Rabinbach, 'The Challenge of the Unprecedented – Raphael Lemkin and the Concept of Genocide', *Simon Dubnow Institute Yearbook*, 4 (2005), 397–420; M. A. McDonnell and A. D. Moses, 'Raphael Lemkin as Historian of Genocide in the Americas', *Journal of Genocide Research*, 7, 4 (2005), 501–29.
18. Docker, 'Are Settler-Colonies Inherently Genocidal? Re-reading Lemkin'.
19. Cf. K. Clark, 'M. M. Bakhtin and "World Literature"', *JNT: Journal of Narrative Theory*, 32, 3 (2002), 266–92; and N. Curthoys, 'The Émigré Sensibility of World Literature: Historicizing Hannah Arendt and Karl Jaspers' Cosmopolitan Intent', *Theory and Event*, 8, 3 (2005). Apropos Einstein see F. Jerome, *The Einstein File: J. Edgar Hoover's Secret War against the World's Most Famous Scientist* (New York: St. Martin's Press, 2002).
20. Lemkin, *Axis Rule in Occupied Europe*, pp. 91 and 91 n51; 'Totally Unofficial Man', p. 377; 'Genocide – A Modern Crime', *Free World* (April 1945), 39–43, accessed at http://www.preventgenocide.org/lemkin/freeworld1945.htm.
21. Power, *"A Problem from Hell"*, pp. 78 and 535 n48.
22. L. Kuper, *Genocide: Its Political Use in the Twentieth Century* (New Haven: Yale University Press, 1981), chapter 2, 'The Genocide Convention', pp. 19–39.
23. Kuper, *Genocide*, pp. 24–5, 29, 31. See also W. A. Schabas, *Genocide in International Law: The Crime of Crimes* (Cambridge: Cambridge University Press, 2000). Our thanks to Dirk Moses for this reference.
24. Lemkin, 'Totally Unofficial Man', p. 393.
25. See, for example, Power, *"A Problem from Hell"*, pp. 62–3; also http://www.preventgenocide.org/law/convention/text.htm.
26. Kuper, *Genocide*, p. 31. Cf. A. D. Moses, 'Genocide and Settler Society in Australian History', pp. 22–3, and his chapter 'The Holocaust and Genocide', in *The*

Historiography of the Holocaust, ed. D. Stone (Basingstoke: Palgrave Macmillan, 2004), p. 542.

27. Cf. Kuper, *Genocide*, p. 30; Curthoys and Docker, 'Introduction – Genocide: Definitions, Questions, Settler-Colonies', 10.
28. Cf. Curthoys and Docker, *Is History Fiction?*, pp. 116–17.
29. J. Bernard, *American Community Behavior*, rev. ed. (New York: Holt, Reinhart and Winston, 1962 [1949]), pp. v–vii.
30. Ibid., pp. 438–9.
31. M. Foucault, *The Archaeology of Knowledge*, trans. A. M. Sheridan Smith (New York: Harper Colophon, 1972), pp. 3–6; Curthoys and Docker, *Is History Fiction?*, p. 182.
32. W. L. Patterson, *The Man Who Cried Genocide: An Autobiography* (New York: International Publishers, 1971), p. 184. G. Horne, *Black and Red: W.E.B. Du Bois and the Afro-American Response to the Cold War 1944–1963* (Albany, NY: State University of New York Press, 1986), p. 181, says Patterson would have liked Du Bois to fly to Paris to present the petition, but Du Bois's doctors advised against it. On 19 February 1951 Du Bois had been indicted as an 'unregistered foreign agent' and was handcuffed before appearing in court; he would be subsequently acquitted (pp. 151, 178).
33. Patterson, *The Man Who Cried Genocide*, pp. 10–11, 171–7, 180, 183–4, 185f. The *We Charge Genocide* petition, p. 143, refers to *Appeal to the World*, prepared by Du Bois for the NAACP, 1947.
34. *We Charge Genocide: The Historic Petition to the United Nations for Relief from a Crime of the United States Government Against the Negro People* (New York: Civil Rights Congress, 1951), p. 8.
35. See, for example, M. Biondi, *To Stand and Fight: The Struggle for Civil Rights in Postwar New York City* (Cambridge, MA: Harvard University Press, 2003), pp. 200–1; also R. D. G. Kelley, *Freedom Dreams: The Black Radical Imagination* (Boston: Beacon Press, 2002), pp. 58–9. Our thanks to Rhonda Y. Williams for these as for other helpful references.
36. See Rabinbach, 'The Challenge of the Unprecedented', 412–15; Elder, 'What you see before your eyes', 486–7; Weiss-Wendt, 'Hostage of Politics', 551–9.
37. Cf. Rothberg, 'W.E.B. Du Bois in Warsaw', 174.
38. G. Horne, *Communist Front? The Civil Rights Congress, 1946–1956* (Toronto: Associated University Presses, 1988), pp. 13–21, 48, 69. In her scintillating *A Fine Old Conflict* (New York: Alfred A. Knopf, 1977), Jessica Mitford writes that when she moved to Oakland in 1947, she became assistant to 'Hursel Alexander, a black organizer who was executive director of the East Bay Civil Rights Congress', then a 'dynamic, predominantly black organization with some five hundred active dues-paying members'; she later became its executive secretary (pp. 104–7, 118). Patterson often came from New York to meet with CRC chapters around the country and she describes him as a 'formidable figure' (p. 127). In chapter 8 she evokes her visit to Mississippi prompted by the Willie McGee case, also protested by Albert Einstein and Josephine Baker (p. 162).
39. See Patterson, *The Man Who Cried Genocide*, pp. 9–10.
40. Horne, *Communist Front?*, pp. 13–21, 48, 69.
41. Cf. M. L. Dudziak, *Cold War Civil Rights: Race and the Image of American Democracy* (Princeton, NJ: Princeton University Press, 2000), and P. M. Von Eschen, *Race Against Empire: Black Americans and Anticolonialism 1937–1957* (Ithaca, NY: Cornell University Press, 1997).
42. In *The Man Who Cried Genocide*, p. 179, Patterson provides brief biographical information for some of these co-authors: 'Richard Boyer, historian and author;

Elizabeth Lawson, biographer and pamphleteer; Yvonne Gregory, writer and poet; and Dr Oakley Johnson, scholar in British and American literature.'

43. Cf. Patterson, *The Man Who Cried Genocide*, p. 180. Apropos Davis, see G. Horne, *Black Liberation/Red Scare: Ben Davis and the Communist Party* (Newark, DE: University of Delaware Press, 1994), pp. 9, 13.
44. *We Charge Genocide*, pp. xi–xiii; also 32.
45. Ibid., pp. xii–xiii; also 31, 35–6.
46. Ibid., p. xii.
47. Concerning the postwar use of the term 'holocaust' by the Communist Party and those close to it in referring to the Nazi genocide of the Jews, cf. P. Novick, *The Holocaust in American Life* (New York: Houghton Mifflin, 2000), pp. 93–4, and Rothberg, 'W.E.B. Du Bois in Warsaw', 174: 'During this era .... Communism provided a discursive space in the United States in which the articulation of genocide and colonialism could first be attempted – and this long before the intellectual vogue for either Holocaust or postcolonial studies.'
48. *We Charge Genocide*, p. 31.
49. Ibid., pp. 3, 7; also p. 57.
50. Ibid., p. 7.
51. Ibid., p. xii. In his autobiography *The Man Who Cried Genocide*, p. 175, Patterson reflected that he knew that the UN 'could not pass laws binding upon the United States or any other government. But the UN rostrum was in the center of the world stage'.
52. *We Charge Genocide*, pp. 3–4, 6, 8–9, 19, 144.
53. Ibid., p. 5.
54. Ibid.
55. Ibid., pp. 6–9, 36, 57, 178–9, 182–3. Cf. Jerome, *The Einstein File*, pp. 72, 74.
56. Ibid., pp. 7–8, 195–6.
57. Patterson, *The Man Who Cried Genocide*, pp. 197, 199, 207, 212; Horne, *Communist Front?*, p. 169.
58. Rabinbach, 'The Challenge of the Unprecedented', pp. 401, 411–16.
59. Cf. Elder, 'What you see before your eyes', 470, concerning the strong opposition by the American Bar Association to treaties including the UN Convention.
60. Patterson, *The Man Who Cried Genocide*, pp. 179, 191.
61. Elder, 'What you see before your eyes', 486–7.
62. Power, *"A Problem from Hell"*, pp. 74–5.
63. Rabinbach, 'The Challenge of the Unprecedented', 413–14.
64. In *The Einstein File* Jerome writes that, on Robeson's invitation, Einstein in September 1946 became co-chairman of a group that Robeson was establishing, the American Crusade to End Lynching. Jerome draws attention to an incident of 16 April 1937 involving Marian Anderson; after the great diva had given a concert to a standing-room only audience at Princeton's McCarter Theatre, she was, nonetheless, refused a room in Princeton's Nassau Inn; Einstein immediately invited her to stay at his home and their ensuing friendship would last for the rest of his life (pp. 76–8, 82, 85, 126, 132–3).
65. D. J. Schaller, 'Raphael Lemkin's view of European colonial rule in Africa: between condemnation and admiration', *Journal of Genocide Research*, 7, 4 (2005), 531–8.
66. See A. Norton, 'Heart of Darkness: Africa and African Americans in the Writings of Hannah Arendt', in *Feminist Interpretations of Hannah Arendt*, ed. B. Honig (University Park, PA: Pennsylvania State University Press, 1995).

67. N. Curthoys, 'The Refractory Legacy of Algerian Decolonisation: Revisiting Arendt on Violence', in *Hannah Arendt and the Uses of History: Imperialism, Nationalism, Race, and Genocide*, eds, R. H. King and D. Stone (New York: Berghahn, 2007).
68. See T. W. Adorno and M. Horkheimer, *Dialectic of Enlightenment* (London: Verso, 1979), pp. 127–8, and J. Docker, *Postmodernism and Popular Culture: A Cultural History* (Melbourne: Cambridge University Press, 1994), p. 38; also Rabinbach, 'The Challenge of the Unprecedented', 409.
69. Weiss-Wendt, 'Hostage of Politics', 555; Elder, 'What you see before your eyes', 488.
70. Patterson, *The Man Who Cried Genocide*, pp. 189–9; Horne, *Communist Front?*, pp. 172–3. (Eleanor Roosevelt headed the American delegation, and she also was chair of the UN Human Rights Commission.) Horne, *Black and Red*, refers to Du Bois's dislike of 'certain Blacks' like Tobias and Sampson who travelled to third world countries on behalf of the State Department in order to rebut charges that the United States was racist towards people of colour. J. D'Emilio, *Lost Prophet: The Life and Times of Bayard Rustin* (New York: Free Press, 2003), pp. 178–9, says that Rustin, a major African American advocate of Gandhian non-violence, while he condemned in the postwar years the assault on civil liberties that right-wing anti-communism inspired, stayed away from any involvement with the CRC 'because its policies mimicked the line of the Communist Party'; Rustin also advised a North Carolina pacifist not to invite Paul Robeson to give a concert in Chapel Hill because Robeson was very closed identified with the Communist Party. See also C. Anderson, *Eyes Off the Prize: The United Nations and the African American Struggle for Human Rights, 1944–1955* (Cambridge: Cambridge University Press, 2003), chapter 4, 'Bleached Souls and Red Negroes', pp. 166–209. A different version of this essay, which is extremely hostile to Patterson, is a chapter, 'Bleached Souls and Red Negroes: The NAACP and Black Communists in the Early Cold War, 1948–1952', in *Window on Freedom: Race, Civil Rights, and Foreign Affairs, 1945–1988*, ed. B. G. Plummer (Chapel Hill, NC: University of North Carolina Press, 2003), pp. 93–113; see especially pp. 96–7 for its dismissive portrait of Patterson and the CRC and their motives in writing and presenting the *We Charge Genocide* petition.
71. When they did happen within the US, Peter Novick comments, 'they focused almost exclusively on the crimes – often real, sometimes imagined – of the Soviet bloc': *The Holocaust in American Life*, p. 101. See also Rabinbach, 'The Challenge of the Unprecedented', 415–16, 419.
72. P. N. Drost, *Genocide: United Nations Legislation on International Criminal Law* (Leyden: A. W. Sythoff, 1959), Introduction and pp. 10–11, 30, 32, 40, 44. Cf. Moses, 'The Holocaust and Genocide', p. 544.
73. H. Arendt, *Eichmann in Jerusalem: A Report on the Banality of Evil*, rev. ed. (New York: Penguin Books, 1994) (first published 1963), p. 153. On another occasion, she describes the concept of 'crimes against humanity' as used in Israeli law as 'strange', in including 'both genocide if practiced against non-Jewish peoples (such as the Gypsies or the Poles) and all other crimes, including murder, committed against either Jews or non-Jews, provided that these crimes were not committed with intent to destroy the people as a whole', pp. 244–5.
74. Arendt, *Eichmann in Jerusalem*, p. 288.
75. P. Novick, *The Holocaust and Collective Memory: The American Experience* (London: Bloomsbury, 2000), pp. 133–4.
76. J.-P. Sartre, *On Genocide, and a Summary of the Evidence and the Judgments of the International War Crimes Tribunal*, ed. A. El Kaïm-Sartre (Boston: Beacon Press, 1968), pp. 3–6, 23, 53.

77. Sartre, *On Genocide*, pp. 62–3.
78. Ibid., pp. 67–9, 74–6.
79. Kuper, *Genocide*, p. 29, writes in general terms that one reason that, by the end of 1978, 30 years after its adoption by the UN, the United States was not among the 84 nations which had ratified the Convention is concern that it would expose nations to external interference in their internal affairs. On the more specific claim concerning state laws, Power, *"A Problem from Hell"*, p. 67, remarks that only a wildly exaggerated reading of the Genocide Convention could have left southern lawmakers vulnerable to genocide charges. Carol Anderson, *Eyes Off the Prize*, p. 180, argues, nonetheless, that the State Department was very aware of the *fear* of southern senators that the Genocide Convention was a back-door method of enacting federal anti-lynching legislation, or might allow the UN to prosecute lynchers who had been acquitted in US courts.
80. Sartre, *On Genocide*, pp. 78–82.
81. Ibid., pp. 69–76, 85.
82. H. A. Bedau, 'Genocide in Vietnam?', in *Philosophy, Morality, and International Affairs*, eds, V. Held, S. Morgenbesser and T. Nagel (New York: Oxford University Press, 1974), pp. 15, 22–46. The volume was a production of the Society for Philosophy and Public Affairs founded in 1969, formed, said the editors in their Introduction, 'due to the concern, outrage, and sense of helplessness aroused in varying degrees among philosophers by the Vietnam War' (p. vii).
83. Kuper, *Genocide*, pp. 33–5.
84. Here both Kuper and Sartre before him prefigure Patrick Wolfe's more recent exploration of the difference between societies requiring the labour of the colonized and those requiring primarily their land; only the latter witness what Wolfe calls 'the logic of elimination'. See P. Wolfe, 'Land, Labor, and Difference: Elementary Structures of Race', *American Historical Review*, 106, 3 (2001), 866–905.
85. Kuper, *Genocide*, pp. 14–17, 45–6, 54, 57–61, 207. Concerning Sartre and Algeria, see Curthoys, 'The Refractory Legacy of Algerian Decolonisation'.
86. Novick, *The Holocaust in American Life*.
87. See D. Stone, 'The Historiography of Genocide: Beyond "Uniqueness" and Ethnic Competition', *Rethinking History*, 8, 1 (2004), 127–42, for a detailed discussion of the uniqueness debates.
88. Kuper, *Genocide*, p. 39.
89. I. L. Horowitz, *Taking Lives: Genocide and State Power, augmented third edition* (New Brunswick: Transaction Books, 1982), pp. xi–xiv, 3–4, 10; see also pp. 44–6 concerning different societal types: genocidal societies; deportation or incarceration societies; torture societies; harassment societies; traditional shame societies; guilt societies; tolerant societies; permissive societies. Such types form a continuum and may be found in any one nation or system, whether capitalist, socialist, or other. What distinguishes genocidal from other types of domination and authority is 'state-perpetuated violence'. On p. 62 Horowitz observes that the United States 'illustrates all eight elements in this typology'.
90. Horowitz, *Taking Lives: Genocide and State Power*, pp. 10, 17–19, 23, 57, 59.
91. Ibid., pp. 10–11, 21 n7, 38, 47, 54–6, 67 n24.
92. Ibid., pp. 56 and 67 n25.
93. T. Barta, 'After the Holocaust: Consciousness of Genocide in Australia', *Australian Journal of Politics and History*, 31, 1 (1984); cf. A. Curthoys, 'Genocide in Tasmania: The History of an Idea', in *Empire, Colony, Genocide*, ed. Moses.
94. T. Barta, 'Relations of Genocide: Land and Lives in the Colonization of Australia', in *Genocide and the Modern Age: Etiology and Case Studies of Mass Death*, eds,

I. Wallimann and M. N. Dobkowski (New York: Greenwood Press, 1987), pp. 238–9. Note that Lemkin also saw intent as important, yet also often difficult to establish. In his unpublished book manuscript on the history of genocide he suggested that in colonizing situations intent was difficult to specify, for example, in his analysis of Tasmania. Cf. Curthoys, 'Raphael Lemkin's "Tasmania": An Introduction' and Lemkin, 'Tasmania'. In his manuscript writings on Spanish colonization from 1492, Lemkin noted that the metropolitan Spanish government never authorized slavery in New Spain and that in 1500 Queen Isabella ordered Governor Bobadilla to respect the liberty and safety of the Indians, but Bobadilla, who had many Indian slaves, paid no attention to the royal order; when Queen Isabella instituted a new system to replace slavery with *encomienda* in order to protect the Indians and assist in their peaceful conversion to Christianity, the colonists quickly took advantage of the new situation, using *encomienda* as a cloak for renewed slavery, now rendered more odious, Lemkin comments, by the hypocrisy involved. See Docker, 'Are Settler-Colonies Inherently Genocidal? Re-reading Lemkin'.

95. Barta, 'Relations of Genocide', pp. 237–41, 246–7. Barta refers to Marx, 'The Defence of the Moselle Correspondent: Economic Distress and Freedom of the Press', 1843, in *Writings of the Young Marx on Philosophy and Society*, eds, L. D. Easton and K. H. Guddat (New York: Doubleday Anchor, 1967), pp. 144–5.
96. Barta, 'Relations of Genocide', pp. 242–3, 246–9.
97. F. Chalk and K. Jonassohn, *The History and Sociology of Genocide: Analyses and Case Studies* (New Haven, CT: Yale University Press, 1990), pp. 4, 8–11, 15–16, 18, 23.
98. Ibid., p. 23.
99. Ibid., pp. 25–6, 29.
100. Ibid., p. 22; cf. R. W. Smith, 'Human Destructiveness and Politics: The Twentieth Century as an Age of Genocide', in *Genocide and the Modern Age*, eds, Wallimann and Dobkowski, pp. 21–39.
101. H. Fein, 'Genocide: A Sociological Perspective', *Current Sociology/La sociologie contemporaine*, 38, 1 (1990), pp. v, 5–6, 13, 23–4, 37.
102. Ibid., p. 24.
103. Cf. discussion in Moses, 'The Holocaust and Genocide', pp. 544–5.
104. Fein, 'Genocide: A Sociological Perspective', p. 15.
105. Ibid., pp. 15, 79–83.
106. Cf. Moses, 'The Holocaust and Genocide', p. 534, for a discussion of sociologists and their generic concepts and typologies. Cf. also J. Docker, review of A. Dirk Moses, ed., *Genocide and Settler Society: Frontier Violence and Stolen Indigenous Children in Australian History*, in *Australian Historical Studies* (April 2006).
107. Power, *"A Problem from Hell"*, pp. 160–6. See also G. M. Hartman, ed., *Bitburg in Moral and Political Perspective* (Bloomington, IN: Indiana University Press, 1986); I. Levkov, ed., *Bitburg and Beyond: Encounters in American, German, and Jewish History* (New York: Shapolsky Publishers, 1987). Thanks to Dirk Moses for these references.
108. Rome Statute Of The International Criminal Court; http://www.Preventgenocide.org/law/icc/statute/part-a.htm#2
109. Novick, *The Holocaust in American Life*, pp. 196–203. See also A. Rosenberg and E. Silverman, 'The Issue of the Holocaust as a Unique Event', in *Genocide in Our Time*, eds, M. N. Dobkowski and I. Wallimann (Ann Arbor, MI: University of Michigan Press, 1992); A. S. Rosenbaum, ed., *Is the Holocaust Unique? Perspectives on Comparative Genocide* (Boulder, CO: Westview Press, 1996).
110. Moses, 'The Holocaust and Genocide', pp. 535, 551.

111. J. Diamond, *The Rise and Fall of the Third Chimpanzee* (London: Vintage, 1992), pp. 250–78. See also T. Barta, 'Mr Darwin's shooters: on natural selection and the naturalizing of genocide', *Patterns of Prejudice*, 39, 2 (2005), 116–37, reprinted in *Colonialism and Genocide*, eds, Moses and Stone, pp. 20–41.
112. H. Brody, *The Other Side of Eden: Hunter-Gatherers, Farmers, and the Shaping of the World* (London: Faber and Faber, 2002), pp. 144, 189; cf. Curthoys and Docker, *Is History Fiction?*, pp. 27–8.
113. S. Lindqvist, *"Exterminate all the Brutes": One Man's Odyssey into the Heart of Darkness and the Origins of European Genocide* (New York: The New Press, 1996); W. Churchill, *A Little Matter of Genocide: Holocaust and denial in the Americas 1492 to the Present* (San Francisco: City Lights Books, 1997); The Australian Human Rights Commission, *Bringing Them Home: A National Inquiry into the Separation of Aboriginal and Torres Strait Islander Children from their Families* (Sydney: HREOC, 1997).
114. See *Journal of Genocide Research*, 7, 4 (2005), passim.
115. W. Lower, *Nazi Empire Building and the Holocaust* (Chapel Hill, NC: University of North Carolina Press, 2005), p. 19.
116. P. Celan, *Breathturn* (1967), trans. Pierre Joris (Los Angeles: Sun and Moon Press, 1995), pp. 214–15.

2
Problems in Comparative Genocide Scholarship

Anton Weiss-Wendt

Introduction

The field of comparative genocide studies has grown beyond recognition over the past two decades, though more quantitatively than qualitatively. On the surface, everything looks good: the number of books on genocide has tripled within less than a decade; the field of comparative genocide studies has its own professional association and journals; more and more colleges and universities offer courses on genocide; several research institutions dedicated to the study of genocide have been established. If we are talking numbers, comparative genocide studies are indeed a great success. Upon close examination, however, genocide scholarship is ridden with contradictions. There is barely any other field of study that enjoys so little consensus on defining principles such as definition of genocide, typology, application of a comparative method, and timeframe. Considering that scholars have always put stress on prevention of genocide, comparative genocide studies have been a failure. Paradoxically, nobody has attempted so far to assess the field of comparative genocide studies as a whole. This is one of the reasons why those who define themselves as genocide scholars have not been able to detect the situation of crisis. This article looks at the conceptual and institutional development of comparative genocide scholarship and outlines major problems that its practitioners face.

Comparative genocide scholarship is still in its infancy. With the exception of two studies that appeared in 1959 and 1972,[1] the scholarly community came to appreciate the work of Raphael Lemkin only in the late 1970s. Another 15–20 years passed before the name of Lemkin acquired its rightful place among the leading humanists of the twentieth century.[2] Until well into the mid 1990s, the discourse on comparative genocide was largely limited geographically to North America. In Europe, in Germany in particular, 'genocide' has long been used as a synonym for the word 'Holocaust'.

Holocaust versus genocide studies

The field of comparative genocide studies was born into the opposition to the dominant Holocaust discourse.[3] What may be seen as an act of revolt has largely informed the subsequent development of the field and its unduly militant character. Some scholars, who tend to pose as unofficial spokesmen for genocide studies, have been attacking the Holocaust establishment ever since. The harshest critic proved to be Henry Huttenbach, who has taken on the U.S. Holocaust Memorial Museum (USHMM) and the historians associated with it in the newsletter that he established in 1994. Thus, he called USHMM 'the Great House of Nazi criminality on the Potomac River'.[4] Any shortcoming of genocide studies, including the delayed introduction of comparative methodology, Huttenbach blamed on Holocaust studies.[5] The fact that the USHMM, in an unprecedented move, on 24 June 2004, shut down normal operations for 30 minutes to draw attention to the situation in Darfur earned no mention from Huttenbach.

Despite claims to the opposite, there is no antagonism between the fields of Holocaust and genocide studies. With the exception of a few senior scholars who support the 'uniqueness' thesis,[6] most Holocaust historians stay away from this debate altogether. Historians feel comfortable within the well-established field of Holocaust studies and are disinclined to venture outside its narrow confines. Most often, though, scholars dealing with the Nazi mass murder of the Jews are simply uninformed about developments in comparative genocide scholarship. Holocaust studies have traditionally been a conservative field with a moralistic overtone. Consider that the first comprehensive studies of the Nazi persecution of Sinti and Roma (Gypsies) came out only in the mid and late 1990s, and that the major study of the Nazi policy towards the Soviet Prisoners of war, which was published in 1978 in German, has never been translated into English.[7] Those among the Holocaust historians who see benefits of merging the two fields, however, may be discouraged from fully committing themselves to comparative genocide studies due to the criticism to which they are sometimes subjected by certain genocide scholars. Each Holocaust historian who has not used a comparative method in his or her study runs a danger of being accused of promoting the 'uniqueness' thesis. Stuart Stein in a recent article in *Journal of Genocide Research (JGR),* for example, spoke disparagingly of Christopher Browning's book *The Path to Genocide.* Stein said nothing about Browning's arguments or the evidence that he used to substantiate them, while blasting the latter for not defining the term genocide.[8] Unsurprisingly then, of the best-known experts on the Holocaust perhaps only Omer Bartov and, to a lesser degree, Christopher Browning have responded to the call by becoming part of a broader discussion on genocide. It is not even clear what hampers the integration of Holocaust studies into the larger field of genocide studies more – the inability of Holocaust scholars to expand into new terrain, the rigidity of historical establishment, or the cold welcome that historians, in general, often receive from their colleagues working on genocide. In any event, the conspiracy theory is unlikely to provide a satisfactory explanation.

Critics who view the field of Holocaust studies as too narrow tend to overlook the advanced methodology that the Holocaust historians have developed over the decades. For example, the concept of collaboration – thoroughly researched and extensively applied in Holocaust studies – is non-existent in genocide studies. Genocide scholars operate with larger categories such as victims and perpetrators, ignoring the marginal ethnic groups who can at different times be both (Mahmood Mamdani has pointedly described this situation as 'when victims become killers'). Consider how little we know about the Kurds who were encouraged by the Special Organization to take advantage of the helpless Armenians and who were later subjected to mass deportation, or the Twa, a tiny minority in Rwanda who were suppressed by the Hutu and the Tutsi throughout history and who in 1994 were incited to take part in genocide. To my knowledge, only a few authors, including anthropologist Christopher Taylor, sociologist Christian Scherrer, and historians Mark Levene and Donald Bloxham have addressed this issue consistently.[9]

Debate on the definition of genocide

Scott Straus has counted 21 different definitions of genocide. Genocide has been a legal, political, moral, and empirical concept that means different things to different people.[10] There are several scholars, including Helen Fein, Leo Kuper, Herbert Hirsch, and Kurt Jonassohn, who question the very rationale for the debate on definition. In view of the 'bewildering array of definitions', as Kuper put it, the UN Genocide Convention is indeed the only reasonable option.[11] Usually, the dissenters express their disagreement by refusing to participate in the argument. Nobody has dared to put it plainly: the debate on definition of genocide is futile! Scholars may continue arguing about the term 'genocide' for decades, without reaching any conclusions, or even a working definition more functional than that agreed upon in 1948. It is practically impossible, considering all the different professional backgrounds of the participants in the discourse (put it to vote?). Some commentators have objected to the UN Genocide Convention as a political compromise between major international players. However, international law is made up of political agreements. Were the discussion on the definition of genocide to be reopened today at the UN – which is rather unlikely – politics would come to dominate the debate much the same as they did 60 years earlier.

A non-specialist looking at the bulk of scholarship on genocide would inevitably come to the conclusion that the focus of comparative genocide studies has been legal definition and conceptual classification. In other words, scholars come together to argue whether this or that case of mass murder constitutes genocide. The International Association of Genocide Scholars (IAGS), for example, asks its new members, as part of a questionnaire, to give their definition of genocide. *JGR*, in the seventh year of its existence, proclaimed as one of its goals to continue the debate on terminology, beginning with the term 'genocide'.[12] There exist entire institutions, for example the Australian Institute for Holocaust & Genocide Studies, that make discourse about the use and meaning of the term genocide their prime objective.[13] Imagine if every book and conference on the Bolshevik Revolution were to open with a lengthy discussion about the use and meaning of the term revolution!

The debate over the definition of genocide has reached such a level of abstraction that sometimes it is not even clear whether it has anything to do with humanity at all. As an illustration, I am reproducing a paragraph from one of the articles recently published in *JGR*:

> The basic problem stems from training the analytical lens on genocide, which is essentially a meta-concept designating a variable mixture of policies, processes, and behaviors, which can be traced to numerous influences (variables), involving diverse combinations of role type participants significant to the development of these clusters of mass killings and related policies. This anchors the study of comparative mass made killings at the wrong end of the continuum. These complex clusters are composed of numerous lower order policies, processes, and behaviors that need to be analyzed first so as to enable the development of useful typologies that can be employed in higher order analyses. Whilst this may smack of abstracted empiricism, meta-deductive analyses have failed to produce tangible results.[14]

One can ask whether the author, Stuart Stein, is actually talking about one group of humans killing another group of humans, or is engaged in hollow theorizing. Unfortunately, this kind of detached discourse neither informs nor helps to prevent genocide. As Hirsch has recently noted, the study of genocide must focus on humanity, using methodology as a tool rather than a goal.[15]

Sometimes one cannot avoid the impression that the intellectual heap surrounding the word genocide has been largely generated by genocide scholars themselves. 'Why is the twentieth century the century of genocide?' Mark Levene entitled one of his articles; Eric Weitz put 'a century of genocide' on the cover of his book; 'the crime of crimes' is the subtitle of William Schabas's study. When somebody like William Rubenstein, then, argues, that 'contrary to popular belief, recent genocides have not been common and have occurred only rarely and unpredictably,' it begins to sound almost like a blasphemy.[16] Whether we want to acknowledge it or not, genocide sells, as does the

Holocaust.[17] One time when it was pointed out to Huttenbach, who does not always operate with accurate facts,[18] that of the several hundreds of thousands of Hutu who had fled Rwanda in the wake of the genocide about 10 percent perished, and not 90 percent as he had argued, Huttenbach made a fascinating statement. The unaccounted for Hutu refugees were most likely slaughtered in a genocidal attack, according to Huttenbach, because 'the subject of concern in these pages is genocide.'[19] In other words, we should attach the word genocide to just any event because genocide is what we study.

Israel Charny, who tends to speak on behalf of the whole of humanity, urges scholars to consider every case involving a massive loss of human life as genocide. All those who refuse to include all instances of mass killing in the category of genocide, according to Charny, do not have genuine concern for the victims, whom they prefer to forget.[20] Evoking the issue of denial, Charny calls all the scholars who disagree with his view 'a prominent pest', 'argumentative hair-splitting "definitionalists"' who lack 'a common-sense appreciation of the tragic fate of any given people'.[21] Unwittingly, Charny makes into 'the enemies of the people' also such well-respected historians as David Chandler, Norman Naimark, Barbara Green, and Isabel Hull, who all have reservations about using the term genocide in their respective studies of Cambodia, ex-Yugoslavia, Ukraine, and German South West Africa.[22] Some scholars object to using the word 'genocide' altogether, proposing an alternative terminology.

Dissatisfied with the legal definition of genocide, Rudolf Rummel coined another term, *democide*. According to Rummel, democide denotes not only premeditated killing but also unintentional death by government, for example, excessive mortality among prisoners in camps and during deportations. To justify the need for the new term, Rummel refers to the staggering number of civilians killed in violent conflicts other than wars. Indeed, it was Rummel who in 1985 pioneered the statistical study of mass killing. The figures that Rummel cites in his studies, however, come entirely from secondary sources, many of them dated. As Tomislav Dulić has recently demonstrated, Rummel's method of estimation is fundamentally flawed.[23] Altogether, figures and graphs, or 'the statistics of democide' as Rummel calls it, have little practical value, telling us nothing about the phenomenon of genocide. Although Rummel points out that democide is different from genocide, he insists that the later is a constituent of the former. By arguing that genocide simultaneously is and is not democide, Rummel in effect sows even more confusion. The use of the terms like 'kilomurders', 'hell-state', and 'mortacracy'[24] further undermines the argumentative prowess of Rummel's scholarship.

The prominence of the term *gendercide* has been associated with the name of Adam Jones. Jones emphasizes the factor of gender in general and the victimization of men in particular in genocide. Drawing on the concept originally proposed by Mary Warren, he defines gendercide as 'gender-selective mass killing'.[25]

Jones cites numerous examples from history that are supposed to demonstrate that the gender identity of the victims was more important than their racial, ethnic, or socioeconomic identity. In effect, he engages in decontextualization. As Maureen Hiebert has noted in her review of Jones's edited collection of essays, the latter fails to provide empirical evidence that the perpetrators targeted a specific group for destruction because of its gender.[26] Even more problematic is how some scholars, including Jones, approach the testimonies of women who fell victim of rape during military conflict. The human rights movement scored a big victory when mass rape committed during the Yugoslavian wars of succession was recognized as a war crime. Rose Lindsey, who has studied war-related violence against women, observes a pattern of using rape victims' testimonies to validate one's theoretical model. The voice of the survivor gets muffled, as the testimony is cut out of context and edited. The conclusion that survivors perceive rape as part of a genocidal assault on their identity, according to Lindsey, is questionable; most survivors have multiple readings of why they were raped. Lindsey has strong words for scholars like Jones:

> Is theory developed for theory's sake? Or do academics developing theory on rape have the objective of future prevention within the aims of their theoretical discourse? The separation of praxis and academia arguably makes it more difficult to prevent these events from recurring. It also gives little back to the survivors, without whom there would be no theory.[27]

Essentially, Lindsey's account raises the issue of professional ethics.

From the standpoint of analysis or empirical observation, the terms democide, gendercide, and ethnocide (Fein, Charny), are of as little use as the terms gynocide (Mary Daly), geracide, elitocide (all Jones), linguicide, planetocide, omnicide (all Charny), etc. Such constructs as *genocidal killing* (Markusen), *genocidal massacre* (Chalk and Jonassohn), or *genocidal pogrom* (Scherrer)[28] pose the same logical problem as Rummel's democide: an act of mass murder can be defined either as genocide or as something else. By the same token, it is unreasonable to describe an event as partial genocide (can we speak, for example, of 'partial war crime' or 'half revolution'?).

Of twenty or so different terms that incorporate the Latin derivative *cide* only one has been warranted. I am referring to the concept of *politicide* introduced in the late 1980s by Barbara Harff. Herself a political scientist, Harff sought to fill the void left by the UN Genocide Convention, which fails to mention political groups. She has emphasized that in contrast to genocide, in politicide the victimized groups are defined primarily in terms of their political opposition to the regime.[29] Despite the narrow definition of politicide, some scholars have compromised this term by using it indiscriminately to cover borderline cases that fall outside the scope of the UN Genocide Convention.

Comparative method

The field of studies that prides itself on comparative analysis, genocide studies lack a clearly defined methodology. The question is whether subject-specific methodology could be devised at all, taking into account the interdisciplinary character of the field. Lawyers, historians, sociologists, psychologists, political scientists, and most recently anthropologists – the scholars who contribute to the study of genocide bring with them methods of inquiry that they have learned in their profession. Social scientists and historians disagree on the very principle of comparison. To define genocide, as Chalk explains, sociologists select a number of cases that they study for the purpose of outlining their common elements.[30] Historians, however, consider any comparison that accentuates only similarity dubious.[31] In spite of the benefits of cross-fertilization, it is essentially impossible to create a universally accepted methodology. Huttenbach, as a historian, has proposed a simple solution – to train specialists who would be well versed in two or more genocides.[32] Logical as it may sound, this proposition can hardly be implemented in practice if we were to apply rigidly the standards adopted in the historical profession.

A historian is somebody who is expected to do archival research in original languages (and sometimes oral interviews). Consider an example: Charles Mironko, a highly qualified scholar fluent in Kinyarwanda and Swahili who has conducted original research in Rwanda.[33] According to Huttenbach, it would be preferable if Mironko mastered, say, the Khmer and Serbo-Croatian languages, did some work in the archives, and ideally conducted interviews with survivors and perpetrators living in Cambodia, ex-Yugoslavia, and in numerous other countries. Not only would that be difficult to accomplish in practice but also potentially damaging to this particular scholar's research on the Rwanda genocide, which requires concentration. Without negating the advantages of multi-genocide expertise, the only tangible outcome in this case appears to be the achievement of the necessary qualifications to become a certified genocide scholar.

Assume for a second that Mironko, after years of hard work, had learned the required languages, which enabled him to examine original documents and to interview the survivors. Next he would have to decide on the principles of comparison: what exactly he should be comparing and what is it that he wants to demonstrate through this comparison. Even some sociologists concede that each case should be examined in terms of its social, economic, and cultural setting so as to elucidate its particularities. A comparative study is first of all an interdisciplinary and cooperative project[34] and not an amalgamation of different methodologies or a thrust to gain expertise in as many cases as possible.

Comparative genocide scholarship comprises purely theoretical works, collections of essays, and monographs that compare two or more cases bound by a certain argument. No discussion is possible without mentioning the names of

Fein and Kuper, who stood at the beginning of comparative genocide studies. In her book, *Accounting for Genocide* (1979), Fein introduced the concept of 'universe of obligation'. She found a common trait in all genocides, namely the stigmatization of victims by the dominant group – something now commonly referred to as dehumanization – as a prerequisite for their physical destruction. She used the quantitative method to explain why the level of persecution of the Jews in Nazi-occupied Europe varied from country to country. Fein was the first sociologist to attempt such an all-encompassing approach. In spite of her innovative approach, Fein failed to demonstrate effectively that the extent of Jewish victimization corresponded with the degree of German control and the level of interwar antisemitism in each European country.[35] Cases like Estonia or the Netherlands simply do not fit into the theoretical model that Fein proposed. Fein's pioneering study demonstrates both the advantages and limitations of a sociological comparison.

Kuper, a South African-born lawyer, was probably the first scholar to present an array of case studies (Ottoman Turkey, Nazi Germany, Stalinist Russia, Indonesia, Bangladesh, Cambodia, Burundi) bound up in a theoretical model. His book, *Genocide: Its Political Use in the Twentieth Century* (1981), broke new theoretical ground by proposing a typology of genocide. Kuper emphasized the dangers inherent in pluralist societies, particularly if combined with a utopian project. Four years later, Kuper, who once said that 'I am not pursuing analysis simply in its own right', published a book dealing specifically with the prevention of genocide. *The Prevention of Genocide* criticized the United Nations' inaction in the face of genocide and proposed to extend the protection of the UN Genocide Convention to political groups.[36]

The first and most cited compilation was published in 1990 by Frank Chalk and Kurt Jonassohn. *The History and Sociology of Genocide*, which is effectively a summary of the genocide course that Chalk and Jonassohn have taught at Concordia University since 1981, has a theoretical part followed by the analysis of 21 different cases, from antiquity until today. For almost a decade, scholars and instructors have used this compilation as a reference book. *Century of Genocide*, edited by Charny, Samuel Totten, and William Parsons, has a similar outline. The editors apparently had a preference for a more conventional interpretation of the 14 cases from the twentieth century that they had selected for this collection, thus overlooking the most recent scholarship. This omission, however, has been compensated for by the decision to include survivors' testimonies for each case. The two-volume *Encyclopedia of Genocide* (1999) was a valuable addition to genocide scholarship, even though the selection of entries and the style of writing reflected the idiosyncrasy of its editor, Charny. The three-volume *Encyclopedia of Genocide and Crimes Against Humanity* (2005), edited by Dinah Shelton, is more professionally done: the entries are comprehensive and easy to use; photographs and maps are carefully selected and executed.

The most recent, scholarly rigorous, and comprehensive collection of essays came out of an international conference organized by Robert Gellately and Ben Kiernan in 2000. The book is divided into four parts, looking at genocide from the perspectives of colonialism and modernity and covering the entire twentieth century.[37] Generally, the overall quality of compilations is difficult to assess as they consist of individual contributions that present unique perspectives on certain topics. Monographs enable a more objective look into the state of the field of comparative genocide studies. With so much emphasis put on the element of comparison, there are surprisingly few studies that take on that approach – perhaps no more than a few dozen articles and books.

One of the first and truly comparative studies was published in 1992 by Robert Melson, a political scientist and Africanist by training. Melson compared the Holocaust and the Aghet (mass murder of Armenians in the Ottoman Turkey), underlining the common elements of ideology, revolution, and war. The differences between the two cases, however, were as important. Melson referred, in particular, to minority status, violent ideology, and the means of genocide.[38] The connection between genocide and total war, first proposed by Kuper and then validated by Melson, has received additional emphasis in Jay Winter's works.[39] Another successful attempt at comparison was undertaken by Edward Kissi. In his study of political violence in Ethiopia and Cambodia in the late 1970s, Kissi deals with two radical Marxist regimes that strove to eliminate their real or perceived opponents and which were later charged with genocide. As Kissi demonstrates in the case of revolutionary Ethiopia, the Mengistu government did not specifically target ethnic groups and at times responded to the killings carried out by the armed opposition, which made it markedly different from Democratic Kampuchea.[40] By effectively linking empirical research and theory, Kissi's study furthers our understanding of genocide in general and these two regimes in particular. Fein, who used the same template of revolutionary/counterrevolutionary violence, fared worse in her comparison of Cambodia and Indonesia. In spite of her painstaking analysis that accounted for both differences and similarities in the uses of terror by Pol Pot and Suharto, Fein failed to overcome a major contradiction: even though Indonesia experienced a revolutionary situation in 1965, the actual revolution did not happen.[41]

Some comparisons tend to be rather mechanical. Scholars who specialize in one particular genocide have a tendency to look for a similar set of factors also in other genocides. That is what Ben Kiernan, an expert on Cambodia, effectively does in his comparison of Pol Pot and Enver Pasha. The imbalance becomes apparent from the outset, as Kiernan focuses on Pol Pot's earlier years but mainly discusses Enver Pasha's post-genocide career. Despite his emphasis on similarities, Kiernan concedes that 'what is missing from the Young Turk precedent, of course, is communism. We still need to determine whether that was a crucial distinguishing factor between the two cases of genocide.'[42] To find the answer to this question one did not need to engage in a comparative exercise, as Kiernan did. Kiernan took it even further in his article, 'Twentieth-Century Genocides: Underlying Ideological Themes From Armenia to East Timor'.[43] This particular piece of scholarship looks more like a list of most common causes of genocide exhibited across the globe in the past century, as if the author was checking the respective fields of a giant table. The purpose of a comparative study that nullifies the very principle of contextualization remains unclear.

Eric Weitz's book, *A Century of Genocide*, testifies to the lack of contextualization as a persistent problem in comparative genocide scholarship. Weitz thinks that he found the common denomination that brings his four selected cases – Nazi Germany, Stalinist Russia, Cambodia, and ex-Yugoslavia – together. Racial theory is the most problematic of the three criteria that Weitz uses in his analysis. In the case of Soviet nationality policy, racial categorization was conspicuously missing. Indeed, as Francine Hirsch points out in her rebuttal of Weitz, the Soviet concept of race was strikingly different from that of the Nazis.[44] Neither did the Serbs, of all ethnic groups in the rump Yugoslavia, have a penchant for racial thinking. Unable to corroborate his argument with solid empirical evidence, the author is forced to rely on quotations taken out of context. Thus, in order to fit the selected cases into his theoretical construct Weitz deliberately overlooks the difference between 'racializing' individuals according to their ethnicity, that is, discrimination, and the Nazi racial policy that spelled death to millions.[45]

At first glance, Norman Naimark does not do anything different from Weitz, by placing the selected five cases from the twentieth century, including the Holocaust and the Armenian genocide, into the category of ethnic cleansing. What distinguishes Naimark's book is its broad scope. For example, Naimark examines the situation of the ethnic Greeks and the Armenians in the Ottoman Empire all the way to the Treaty of Lausanne of 1923, which he considers a watershed event in modern European history. Without diminishing the factor of integral nationalism, Naimark contends that ethnic cleansing is a modern phenomenon implemented by nation states. At the same time he notes that 'comparative reflection on the problems of ethnic cleansing also leads to the conclusion that each case must be understood in its full complexity, in its own immediate context, rather than merely as part of a long-term historical conflict between nations.'[46] The right balance between micro and macro history, convincing arguments, and the fine style of writing – all these have made Naimark's *Fires of Hatred* one of the most frequently assigned texts for university courses on genocide and ethnic cleansing.

The more cases scholars incorporate into their analyses, the more problems it may create. Benjamin Valentino's *Final Solutions* is a case in point. The book offers no new historical interpretation of the eight different cases the author

has selected, but rather a confusing mixture of generalizations. Valentino prefers using the category of mass killing, without reaching a definite conclusion whether it is complementary to or distinct from genocide. He overemphasizes the role of political and military leaders in genocide at the expense of a structural explanation. In his opinion, leaders are likely to consider mass killing under one of the following circumstances: building a communist utopia; carrying out ethnic cleansing; and extinguishing a guerilla movement. In the cases of Soviet Russia, China, and Cambodia he suggests a monocausal explanation, according to which the communist regimes targeted the political opposition that had opposed the policy of mass collectivization of agriculture. The fall of communism, according to Valentino, had automatically reduced the probability of genocide in the world. Equally simplistic are Valentino's attempts to explain why some communist regimes did not tread the path of genocide – because of a relatively small (peasant) population.[47]

William Rubenstein was the first who sought to write a complete history of genocide. Rubenstein avoided the debate on modernity by approaching the problem of genocide chronologically. Rubenstein may not be incorrect in his argument that 'genocide in the age of totalitarianism, 1914–79' was conditioned by ideology, the collapse of the elite structure in Europe, and total war.[48] Well-written, the book may appeal to the general reader but not necessarily to specialists. At times Rubenstein appears to gloss over particular historical events, spending as much time discussing, for example, Rwanda as he does the Israeli–Palestinian conflict. Rubenstein has a tendency to accept the lower estimate for victims of genocide, and he uses sources selectively. Mark Levene was careful to avoid these pitfalls in his landmark study, *Genocide in the Age of the Nation State*. The first two volumes (out of the four planned), dealing with the methodological issues and the earlier cases of genocide, respectively, were published in 2005. As the title of the book suggests, Levene refers the phenomenon of genocide to the emergence of Europe as a dominant power. While working with broad categories, Levene emphasizes the importance of historical interpretation. The only problem that Levene may stumble against in the course of his historical investigation is his attempt to come up with an 'ideal type of genocide' (à la Roger Griffin's generic concept of fascism).[49] Considering the scope and thoroughness of Levene's research, his study may become what Raul Hilberg's *Destruction of the European Jews* is for students of the Holocaust.

In some cases, authors seem to utilize a comparative method to stress the importance of a particular genocide they have been working on. That is the impression one gets after reading Vahakn Dadrian's article in *JGR* that compares the genocides of the Armenians, Jews, and Tutsis. While denigrating the Rwandan genocide to the status of a civil war and emphasizing the lack of a preconceived Nazi plan to murder the European Jews, Dadrian accentuates the history of anti-Armenian violence in the Ottoman Empire, advancing an intentionalist interpretation of the Armenian genocide. Dadrian disputes a widespread view that some Armenians managed to escape deportations and eventually survived. He notes that in the case of Smyrna, for example, a German general blocked the deportation against the wishes of the Ottoman regime, threatening a military intervention. Dadrian contends that the German Foreign Office in Berlin supported the stance of the general, even though elsewhere he has argued for the complicity of Germany in the genocide.[50]

In the final analysis, none of the studies mentioned above – probably with the exception of Melson's and Kissi's books – can be recommended as a model, mainly because the theoretical template offered by the author fails to account for the particularities of each of the cases under consideration. This raises the question of whether the comparative method is ever effective. Stein joins Huttenbach in his condemnation of case studies, which according to the former fail to produce usable typologies or theoretical models.[51] To follow this line of argumentation, any case study of the Bolshevik Revolution missing a comparative element must be faulty. To take this example one step further, consider what other instances of revolutionary upheaval could be compared to the Bolshevik takeover of October 1917. The French, English, and Russian Revolutions, as well as the Paris Commune, would all make a good comparison. It may get more complicated, however, if we decide to add to this list the Industrial Revolution and Stalin's 'Revolution from above'. Indeed, someone may want to make a comparative analysis of the Industrial Revolution and Stalin's Revolution. This is certainly possible, but utterly pointless! This kind of comparison, unfortunately, happens all too often in genocide studies. Huttenbach, for example, urges scholars to pursue a comparison of the witch-hunt and the persecution of Jews, as both of these groups have been attacked as scapegoats throughout history. According to Huttenbach, the comparative approach enables scholars to 'experiment' with various definitions of genocide.[52]

It is not coincidental that two of the best-selling books on genocide have been written by individuals who do not necessarily associate themselves with comparative genocide studies. Peter Balakian is a literary scholar and poet while Samantha Power, who at one time worked as a Balkan war correspondent, has been involved with human rights. These two authors write with passion and are not afraid to appear controversial or politically incorrect (Power in particular). Balakian grabbed the attention of critics and readers alike with his memoir, *Black Dog of Fate*, which described an Armenian American boy becoming aware of the Armenian genocide. Power grabbed headlines with her damning condemnation of American foreign policy in the face of genocide.[53] Both authors have a firm grip on primary sources, weaving them masterfully into powerful prose. Power and Balakian have the skill that many other scholars working on genocide lack – they write well. In terms of mobilizing public opinion behind the campaign to prevent genocide and to recognize past injustices,

Power's and Balakian's books did more than most others. This has been indirectly acknowledged by the Institute for the Study of Genocide, which awarded Power's *"A Problem From Hell"* and Balakian's *The Burning Tigris: The Armenian Genocide and America's Response* the Raphael Lemkin Prize for best scholarly book on genocide for 2003 and 2005, respectively.

Failures and successes

Students of genocide have encountered more problems than they are able to resolve. One of many issues on which scholars disagree is that of chronological limits. Is genocide essentially a modern phenomenon that occurred for the first time in German South West Africa in 1904–5 and persisted throughout the twentieth century, or has genocide always plagued humanity? In a memorable sentence some 25 years ago, Kuper declared that, 'the word is new, the crime ancient.'[54] Jonassohn has modified this statement, by arguing that successful analyses of recent cases of genocide require much greater attention to the historical antecedents of the genocidal events.[55] The question is, however, how far back in time we should go in order to comprehend the phenomenon of genocide. Kate Cushing at Keele University, for example, teaches a seminar on genocide and tolerance in Europe with a heavy focus on the Middle Ages and the period of the Enlightenment.

Several scholars have attempted to devise a typology of genocide that is supposed, among other things, to help to delineate the difference between premodern and modern genocides. Roger Smith, for example, identifies five forms of genocide – retributive, institutional, utilitarian, monopolistic, and ideological – referring to revenge, conquest, gain, power, and purification as the main motivations to carry out mass murder. Chalk and Jonassohn have developed a similar typology, based on the motive of a perpetrator. Dadrian, who is best known for his work on the Armenian genocide, has come out with five different types of genocide: cultural, latent, retributive, utilitarian, and optimal. Fein distinguishes between ideological, retributive, developmental, and despotic genocides.[56] The problem with all these typologies is that the proposed categories often overlap. Let us try to fit, for example, the Rwandan genocide into one of the above typologies. According to Chalk and Jonassohn, the crime of genocide is usually committed as an attempt to eliminate a threat, spread terror, acquire wealth, or implement an ideology. The 1994 genocide, as well as the earlier massacres of the Tutsis in Rwanda – as René Lemarchand has emphasized – were carried out in response to the massacres of the Hutu in neighbouring Burundi and the incursions of the Rwandan Patriotic Front. By committing genocide, the Hutu extremists sought to beat their Tutsi countrymen into submission once and for all. To justify their abominable goals, Hutu Power made use of the Hamitic theory that described the Tutsi minority as alien invaders. At the same time, many ordinary Hutu partook in the crime in order to acquire the murdered Tutsis' property and personal effects. This one example further demonstrates that – as Dulić has remarked – 'human behavior patterns regularly fail to conform to theoretical models.'[57]

Fein thinks of the spread of genocide in the twentieth century and the simultaneous growth of international humanitarian law as a paradox.[58] Unintentionally, Fein has answered the question as to what makes genocide a modern phenomenon – a combination of popular and political will to stamp it out of human existence. Since genocide is a legal concept, it will not be incorrect to apply the formula *nulla poena sine lege* to the public discourse on the meaning of genocide. Before the critical mass of concerned citizens and governments had recognized a purposeful physical destruction of certain groups of people a crime, it could not be called one. The word genocide could not have entered into our modern vocabulary if it had not been for the crusading work of such individuals as Edmund Morel, who launched a public campaign to stop atrocities in Congo Free State, or Johannes Lepsius, who dedicated his life to the defence of the Armenian minority in Ottoman Turkey. ICTY and ICTR own as much to Nuremberg as they do to the failed attempt to prosecute the architects of the Armenian genocide. This qualitative leap in perceptions signals the emergence of civic society. That is what makes the Armenian, Jewish, and Rwandan genocides distinct from the Albigensian crusades, the witch-hunt, and the European conquest of Americas.

I agree with scholars like Valentino and Stein who propose to use mass killing as a unit of analysis along with genocide. Although mass killing is not a legal concept, using this term would allow us to reintegrate both the pre-twentieth-century cases – particularly those committed by colonial powers – and the cases from the past century which involved massive victimization but did not amount to actual genocide – for example, Stalinist Russia or ex-Yugoslavia – into the analytical framework without violating the integrity of comparative genocide studies.

In spite of numerous problems, it would be wrong to say that comparative genocide scholarship has not seen any progress at all. Within the field of comparative genocide studies, I would argue, lawyers and historians have established the most successful symbiosis. The cooperation between the two professions began in the aftermath of the Second World War when historians were called upon to work through millions of pages of documents in preparation for the International Military Tribunal at Nuremberg. The legal investigation into Nazi crimes conducted first in post-war Germany, and later in Israel, the United States, Canada, Australia, and the United Kingdom, benefited both justice and history. As Erich Haberer has contended, 'the creative tension between the requirements of law and those of history generated invaluable evidence and documentary resources.'[59] Scores of Holocaust historians, including Hilberg (†) and Browning, participated in war crimes trials, either as researchers or expert witnesses. For over a decade now, historians have been utilizing police and court records in reconstructing the history of past genocides. Hopefully, the upcoming generation of genocide scholars will find the records of the International Criminal Tribunals for the former Yugoslavia and Rwanda (and now Cambodia) as useful as Holocaust historians have found the documentation presented at the Military Tribunals in Nuremberg and Tokyo and the numerous smaller trials throughout Europe.

Unsurprisingly, probably the best works in comparative genocide studies are those examining the development of international justice. What makes the books by Yves Beigbeder, Howard Ball, and Gary Bass high-quality scholarship is their preference for a balanced empirical analysis over a heated theoretical discourse. The same applies to a comparative study of the court cases involving Holocaust denial by Robert Kahn.[60] In chronological order, the above authors follow the creation and maturity of the international justice system, from Leipzig and Constantinople all the way to The Hague and Arusha. What some among the most radical adherents of the comparative method may dismiss as 'linear', in my opinion is the strength of these studies.

Anthropologists have made probably the most valuable contribution to genocide studies in the recent years. I deliberately omitted the word 'comparative', because the major problem that the anthropologists have yet to address is how to incorporate a comparative analysis into the case studies. Anthropologists work with the category of culture, basing their analyses of human behaviour on the interviews they conduct. Alexander Laban Hinton is one of the pioneers who started applying the methodology used in cultural anthropology to the study of genocide. Although Hinton was not the first to conduct interviews with the survivors and perpetrators of the Cambodian genocide, he asked different kind of questions from his predecessors. In his research Hinton has demonstrated that the Khmer Rouge utilized cultural models of revenge, patronage, and obedience to force the rank-and-file to murder and torture. Hinton argues that by replacing the traditional hierarchy with a new class structure, the Pol Pot regime had effectively assumed the role of the head of the family, to obey which was the norm. He further contends that cultural norms preexisting in Khmer society had informed the forms of violence and the willingness of ordinary Cambodians to commit it in the name of the Angkar.[61] Christopher Taylor put forward a similar argument in his book, *Sacrifice as Terror*. Taylor argues that the highly ritualized forms of torture applied to the Tutsi victims during the genocide reflected the common perceptions of physical health and illness in Rwanda.[62]

What is missing in these and other anthropological studies is a comparative element, by introducing which scholars would have inevitably had to de-emphasize the aspect of uniqueness of each particular culture. Although Hinton mentioned the Moscow show trials of the 1930s in his book, he did not go any further with the comparison of Pol Pot's Cambodia and Stalin's Russia. Otherwise, he would have probably attached more attention to such collective and personal traits as circumstantial pressure, enmity, and last but not least ideology. Taking into consideration that the anthropologists have entered the field only recently, however, it would be fair to mention that the number of anthropological studies dealing specifically with genocide is very limited. In the case of Soviet Russia, for example, Catherine Merridale was the first to address the issue of death systematically.[63] A welcome attempt to look at the phenomenon of genocide from the anthropological perspective was recently undertaken by historian Dan Stone. Taking a pessimistic view that humankind is prone to violence, Stone argues that partaking in genocide generates the atmosphere of a festival – similar to ancient blood offerings – that leads to further brutalization.[64]

Institutional development

The foundation for comparative genocide studies, as we know them today, was laid in the early 1980s. In 1982, after three years in the making, Charny organized a landmark International Conference on the Holocaust and Genocide in Tel Aviv. The conference was marred by controversy, as the Israeli government backed the Turkish demand to drop from the programme speakers on the Armenian genocide. The conference organizers persevered, however. In the United States, one of the first panels on genocide was organized by Hirsch at the annual meeting of the American Political Science Association convention in Chicago in 1983. As Hirsch recalled, the conference organizers had difficulties deciding where to place the panel, whose subject did not fit conventional categories.[65]

The first research institutions dedicated to the study of genocide came into existence in 1982. Established with the assistance of Simon Wiesenthal, the Institute for the Study of Genocide found home at the John Jay College for Criminal Justice in New York City. Unfortunately, as the Institute's executive director Fein had remarked, it had failed to secure funding as well as to devise an agenda.[66] Around the same time, Charny founded a research institute in Jerusalem. Unwittingly, Charny had cemented the notion of the Holocaust and genocide as two separate phenomena, when he incorporated the verbal construct 'Holocaust and genocide' into the name of the institute. The next attempt, at Montreal in 1986, was more successful. The Montreal Institute for Genocide Studies was a natural outgrowth of the course started by Chalk and Jonassohn at Concordia University. The first enterprise of the Institute was to start publishing a series of Occasional Papers, which continues until today. Based in the Departments of History and Sociology/Anthropology, the Institute has attracted MA and PhD students who work on comparative aspects of genocide and gross human rights violations.

One of the most important initiatives ever launched materialized in 1981 under the name the Cambodian Genocide Project. Based at Yale University, the new research centre was connected with the name of Gregory Stanton. Stanton and Kiernan, both PhD students at the time, were among the first Westerners to visit post-Khmer Rouge Cambodia. While Stanton arrived in Phnom Penh as the director of a consortium of American relief groups, Kiernan's path to genocide studies was less direct; as an undergraduate student Kiernan sympathized with the Pol Pot regime only to denounce it publicly several years later. A major breakthrough in the operations of the Cambodian Genocide Program occurred in 1994 when it won $800,000 contract from the US Government to conduct research in Cambodia. For over two decades, Stanton lobbied with various national governments to bring the Khmer Rouge to justice.[67] The long-awaited agreement, signed between the Cambodian government and the UN in 2004 to start prosecuting the crimes committed in Democratic Kampuchea between 1975 and 1979, would have been virtually impossible without Stanton's resolve.[68]

The next wave of institutional expansion occurred in North America and Australia in the 1990s, and in Europe mainly within the last five years. In Australia, the Center for Comparative Genocide Studies was established at Macquarie University in Sydney in 1993. Seven years later the Center reconstituted as an independent educational entity under the name the Australian Institute for Holocaust and Genocide Studies. Considering the history of the settlement of the continent, the Institute has paid particular attention to the study of the decimation of the Aborigines. The Institute is currently based at the University of New South Wales and provides for students from the four Sydney universities. The first, similar institution in Europe was founded at the Ruhr University in Bochum in 1994. The particularity of the Institute for Diaspora and Genocide Studies is its double focus on genocide and forced migration. Post-traumatic stress disorder is another issue of interest for German researchers. Since 1999 the Institute has published a biannual journal, *Zeitschrift für Genozidforschung*, which unfortunately failed to register with the larger community of genocide scholars outside of Germany. The Raphael Lemkin Institute for the Study of Xenophobia and Genocide at the University of Bremen focuses on Nazi Germany within the broader context of genocide. Between 1997 and 2001 the Institute published a series, *Schriftenreihe des Raphael-Lemkin Instituts*.

At present there exist three different models of research institutions with a focus on genocide. The first and most common model is a research institute attached to a university such as Concordia in Montreal (1986), New South Wales in Sydney (1993), Yale (1994), Minnesota (1997), Uppsala (1998), and Amsterdam (2002). Senior scholars and research fellows associated with these centres and study programmes usually teach or pursue a graduate degree at the respective university. The second group of research centres is only nominally affiliated with a university, concentrating on research and conferences, for example, the Institute for the Study of Genocide at the City University of New York (1982), the Institute for Diaspora and Genocide Studies at Ruhr University in Bochum (1994), and the Raphael Lemkin Institute for the Study of Xenophobia and Genocide in Bremen (1994). Finally, there are institutions situated within a larger research unit such as the Department of Holocaust and Genocide Studies at the Danish Institute for International Studies in Copenhagen (1999) and the Committee on Conscience (COC) at USHMM (1995). One of their objectives is to contribute to policymaking. In addition to research and teaching, all of the above institutions are heavily involved with the general public, organizing public lectures and commemorative events, and in some cases engaging in school outreach.

The two most successful institutions, representing two different models, are, in my opinion, the Genocide Studies Program at Yale University and the COC at USHMM. The Yale Genocide Studies Program is built around the Cambodian Genocide Program, which boasts the best archival collection outside of Cambodia documenting the crimes perpetrated by the Khmer Rouge. Thanks to the continual effort of their colleagues at Yale, scholars now have access to the records of Pol Pot's secret police, 22,000 biographical and bibliographical references, 6,000 photographs, as well as data on prisons, execution sites, and so on. Taking one particular case of genocide as a point of departure, the Yale Genocide Studies Program has become a model centre for scholarship that brings together researchers from different disciplines working on various aspects of genocide.

The COC has chosen a different path. Making full use of the resources of the USHMM with which it is affiliated, COC disseminates knowledge about current instances of genocide and gross human rights violations. Consisting essentially of a single staff member, Law Professor Jerry Fowler, COC has been doing very important work by organizing public events and monitoring violent conflicts worldwide. The COC website is probably the best of all the organizations dedicated to the prevention of genocide. In 2003 COC produced a DVD, a conversation with General Roméo Dallaire, commander of the UN Mission in Rwanda.[69] The important ethical questions regarding UN decision-making that Dallaire has raised in his interview make it an excellent educational tool. Following Fowler's visit to the Sudan–Chad border where he collected testimonies from refugees who had fled Darfur, in July 2004 COC issued a 'genocide emergency warning' for Darfur. Alongside Sudan, COC currently has Chechnya, the Balkans, and Central Africa on its watch list. The criticism waged against the COC as makeweight of the USHMM is completely unfounded.[70] It should be admitted, though, that the activities organized by COC and USHMM rarely overlap, attracting different audiences.

The decision to create a professional association of genocide scholars grew out of the second 'Remembering for the Future' conference in Berlin in 1994. As a result of the discussion between Fein, Melson, Charny, and Smith, a new organization was born. Fein agreed to serve as the first president of the newly established Association of Genocide Scholars, affiliated with the Institute for the Study of Genocide in New York. The Association's first meeting took place a year later at William and Mary College and attracted about 40 participants. The continual growth of the field was formally recognized when in 1999 the Association of Genocide Scholars added the word 'International' to its name.

In January 2005 a new academic association came into existence, the European Network of Genocide Scholars (ENOGS). The creation of ENOGS was timely considering the growing interest in the study of genocide in Europe in general, and in Germany in particular. Symbolically, the inaugural conference in Berlin focused on the Namibian War of 1904–8. A year later, ENOGS boasted 93 members, representing 22 different countries. Remarkably, one-third of the members come from outside of Europe, mainly from the US. This is both an encouraging and troubling trend, as the ENOGS appears to have taken over some of the functions of the International Association of Genocide Scholars (IAGS). Indeed, in early 2006 ENOGS changed its name to the International Network of Genocide Scholars.

It is difficult to tell now who among the scholars was the first to start teaching genocide at university level, or at any level at all. Apparently, several scholars had conceived of the idea of a new field of studies simultaneously around 1980–1. Next they attempted to summarize the existing knowledge on genocide in course syllabi. Some of the instructors were historians such as Huttenbach at City University of New York and Joyce Apsel at State University of New York, or sociologists such as Jonassohn and Chalk at Concordia University. Jonassohn and Chalk have been teaching genocide as a two-semester course since 1980. They argue that the study of the pre-modern cases of genocide encourages a more rigorous analysis, as students are forced to take temporal and cultural distance. In 1998, Fein and Apsel published a selection of course syllabi entitled *Teaching About Genocide: A Guidebook for College and University Teachers*.

The first Master's programme in Holocaust and genocide studies in the United States was established at Richard Stockton College in New Jersey in 1999. In Europe, the most extensive study programme is currently offered at Royal Holloway, University of London. With the recent new hire, five members of staff at Royal Holloway provide a broad expertise on genocide. Nevertheless, these and similar programmes continue teaching genocide in conjunction with the Holocaust, which effectively dominates the curriculum. Statistics regarding courses on genocide are unavailable. The number of university-level genocide courses has grown exponentially, though it is rather unlikely that they will ever become as prevalent as Holocaust-focused modules. In Europe, for example, the predominance of the Holocaust over all other cases of genocide has been bolstered through the establishment of the Task Force for International Cooperation on Holocaust Education in 2000 and the subsequent introduction of Holocaust Remembrance Day. This decision has effectively removed the Holocaust from history, placing it into realm of current politics.[71]

In 1985, the Institute on the Holocaust and Genocide in Israel launched a newsletter called *Internet on the Holocaust and Genocide*, which was the first such publication to appear. Ten years and 56 issues later the newsletter was transferred to the newly founded Center for Comparative Genocide Studies at Macquarie University in Australia. Under its director, Colin Tatz, the newsletter continues to be published under the name *International Network on Holocaust and Genocide*. The Institute for the Study of Genocide in New York has been publishing its newsletter since 1988.

A similar publication started by Huttenbach in 1994, *The Genocide Forum* (*GF*), promoted a comparative approach to the study of genocide. Although the objective of the *GF* was to stimulate a dialogue among students of genocide, it by and large remained a mouthpiece of the editor. The provocative, confrontational tone taken on by Huttenbach alienated potential contributors. When a scholarly exchange did take place in the *GF*, it assumed a grotesque form. For example, Huttenbach pointed out numerous fallacies in Steven Katz's analysis, without giving any page references. In his reply, Katz suggested that Huttenbach – whom he compared to the editor of *Der Stürmer* – had not actually read the book. Huttenbach then called Katz 'a bruised author whose book has been subjected to serious criticism'.[72] Ironically, Huttenbach has been continually violating his own dictum, which goes as follows: 'all too often personality clashes and emotional ties stand in the way of a balanced handling of the very sensitive issues inherent in the study of genocide.'[73]

Huttenbach perceived *GF* as an alternative to *Holocaust and Genocide Studies* (*HGS*), a journal published by Oxford University Press in association with the USHMM, which he had heavily criticized. It is true that *HGS* has published only a handful of articles on cases of genocide other than the Holocaust (with the Armenian genocide featuring most prominently). The Assistant Editor of *HGS* has explained that the journal rarely receives quality submissions unrelated to the Holocaust. Potential contributors prefer submitting their articles elsewhere, because they think that the journal affiliated with the USHMM is only pursuing a Holocaust agenda. This is ironic as it is incorrect. One-third of all books in the journal's review section, for example, deal with cases of genocide unrelated to the Nazi mass murder of Jews.

In 1999, *GF* was upgraded to the *JGR*, published by Routledge. For the first six years of its existence the *JGR* had lacked a proper peer-reviewing system, which resulted in the uneven scholarly quality of the articles. Nevertheless, *JGR* has played an important role in shaping the academic discourse on genocide.

Since January 2005 *JGS* has been published as the official journal of the newly founded ENGS. Dominik Schaller and Jürgen Zimmerer stepped in as co-editors and the editorial board was expanded. The decision of the Editor-in-Chief of *JGS* to move its operations to Europe was perceived by many in the field as odd. It would have been only natural if *JGS* had formally become the official publication of the much larger and better-established IAGS. In response, in 2006 IAGS launched its own journal, *Genocide Studies and Prevention*, with Hirsch, Totten, Eric Markusen, and Alex Alvarez, as co-editors. As a result, comparative genocide studies – already deeply divided – now have two rival associations represented by two different journals.

The problem of representation of genocide remains as topical as ever. Beside exhibits devoted to one or another case of genocide, such as Tuol Sleng in Phnom Penh, USHMM in Washington, D.C., or the Armenian Genocide Institute and Museum in Yerevan, to name just a few, genocide as a phenomenon has not yet made it into permanent exhibitions worldwide. Just how contentious the subject of genocide is, can be seen in the example of the National Museum of the American Indian, which opened on the Washington Mall in autumn 2004. To avoid controversy, the museum curators not only shunned away from using the word genocide anywhere in the exhibit but also omitted direct references to the destruction of the indigenous population on the American continent. Regretfully, as far as the universal issue of genocide is concerned, the new Yad Vashem Museum in Jerusalem failed to depart from its mandate as 'the Holocaust Martyrs' and Heroes' Remembrance Authority.' Rather unexpectedly, the first permanent exhibition with the focus on genocide was set up in a country normally not associated with genocide research: Norway. The Norwegian Center for Study of the Holocaust and Religious Minorities, which opened to the public in the summer of 2006, has a permanent display that documents the destruction of the local Jewish community during the Nazi occupation as well as the recent cases of genocide such as ex-Yugoslavia, Rwanda, and Sudan. (The example from Norway demonstrates that a research institution does not necessarily have to carry the word 'genocide' in its name to pursue a comparative genocide studies agenda.) The situation is slightly better when it comes to learning resources. The interactive video display on genocide at Imperial War Museum in London is probably the most comprehensive of any similar resources currently available.

The issue of prevention

Prevention has been mentioned as the single most important issue in genocide studies. Charny proposed to create a genocide early warning system as early as 1982, in his book *How Can We Commit the Unthinkable? Genocide, the Human Cancer*. Many academics, including Kuper, Chalk, Fein, Totten, and George Andreopoulos, insist that an adequate typology is crucial for preventing future genocides. Scholars like Stanton, Huttenbach, and Markusen believe that by labeling one or another contemporary case of mass killing 'genocide' would help to end violence. Charny argues, for example, that the Western world would have learned a great deal more about the Stalinist terror if the latter had been labeled genocide.[74] Unfortunately, as the recent exchange at the highest political level on the current situation in Darfur, Sudan, has shown, putting a name to a particular event does not automatically bring about a solution to a problem.

In September 2004, the then US Secretary of State Colin Powell accused the government of Sudan of genocide. This announcement was based on the findings collected in Darfur by an international group of experts on behalf of the US State Department's Atrocities Documentation Team (ADT) the previous summer. The European Parliament symbolically rebutted Powell, declaring that the massive displacement of population and accompanying atrocities did not amount to genocide (though later on the European parliamentarians did adopt the US position). In December 2004 the UN sent its own Commission of Inquiry to Darfur. The UN report released in early 2005 stated that the government of Sudan and *Janjaweed* militia had not committed genocide. Since the formal declaration of genocide in Darfur by the US government, the situation on the ground has not changed for the better and the chances for a peace settlement in the region remain as illusive as ever. Totten and Markusen, who were among the 30 members of the ADT fact-finding commission, commend the precedent when one sovereign nation attempted to ascertain whether another nation was committing genocide.[75] The problem is that such a unilateral decision further undermines the influence of the UN, the organization in need of reform. Considering the unpopularity of the current US administration in the world today, it is unlikely that a political declaration like the one made by Powell will carry enough weight internationally, let alone be followed through. Finally, it raises the question of legitimacy. What if, for example, China decides to assemble its own commission and sends it to a conflict zone/area of humanitarian disaster to assess the degree of violence?

As Staub argues, distinguishing between genocide and mass killing is not especially useful from the standpoint of predicting and preventing collective violence, or even understanding its origins. Because the word genocide has an emotional appeal, by identifying an event as genocide we unwittingly downgrade mass killing, which is abundant in the world today. Indeed, there is no international treaty on mass killing similar to the UN Genocide Convention. This may be one of the reasons why the civil wars in Sudan and Democratic Republic of the Congo did not generate enough international attention until after the violence reached the level at which genocide charges could be invoked. It is practically impossible and functionally ineffective, as Staub stresses, to focus on genocide prevention to the exclusion of all other forms of mass violence.[76] Huttenbach is altogether skeptical about what he calls 'sub-industry of genocide prediction'.[77]

Ironically, the highly sophisticated level of theoretical discourse, which *JGR* has been promoting, makes prevention of genocide less feasible. To amass support at all levels of society for a collective action against genocide, one needs to exercise the power of conviction. The politicians simply do not have time to ponder the definitional muddle, while the general public apparently has difficulties assessing it. The ultimate success of comparative genocide studies will come then, when one spots a person sitting next to oneself on a subway (Underground, Metro, commuter train, bus) reading a book that has the word 'genocide' in its title. This has not happened yet. Unfortunately, not even the monumental study of Mark Levene was able to break the invisible barrier that separates academia from the rest of the world.

Some genocide scholars, particularly those with a legal training, found themselves at the forefront of the international campaign to prevent genocide. Thus, Kuper helped to establish *International Alert Against Genocide*, an organization based in London, while Stanton in 1998 founded *Genocide Watch* in the US. The latter, according to Stanton, would have been more effective if it had been part of Human Rights Watch.[78] Melson believes that genocide scholars are no different from the nineteenth-century American abolitionists and thus belong to a larger human rights movement.[79] Like historians of fascism, who are expected to take a clear stand on the resurgence of neo-Nazism, some scholars of genocide engage in politics and policy-making in order to help create conditions that would make genocide improbable. At the same time, as Huttenbach notes, scholars should be aware of the danger of joining the ranks of politicians arguing about history, even if it deals with such an unambiguous case of genocide as the destruction of the Armenians in the Ottoman Turkey. In this and similar cases, political resolutions may not be the best way of stimulating the debate.[80]

The question whether genocide scholars should actively participate in politics does not have a definite answer. The experience that Stanton has had working for the US State Department provides a good illustration to this dilemma. In spite of his invaluable contribution to the establishing of the Rwandan and Cambodian criminal tribunals, Stanton was eventually squeezed out of the US State Department as too vocal an employee. As far as political activism is concerned, it should probably be left up to individual scholars to decide. Obviously, individuals such as Power or Stanton will continue their crusade no matter what, while other students of genocide may choose to stay outside of politics. There is also no need to blame genocide studies, and effectively genocide scholars – as Christian Gerlach does – for attracting government funds and public attention at the expense of less deadly conflicts, which tend to be ignored.[81] As genocide scholars should not overestimate their abilities to change the ways national or international politics are being done, the very nature of the subject of their studies makes them descend from the ivory tower.

In the end, there is no alternative to a mass movement grounded in liberal democracy. At the time of writing (May 2006), the international community has renewed its pressure on the Sudanese government to stop violence in Darfur, mainly in response to a massive solidarity campaign in the United States and Canada. Challenging oppressive regimes and fostering democratic freedoms worldwide is the most effective deterrence against genocide. Comparative genocide studies have set themselves high targets but are they up to the task?

Future uncertain

As an interdisciplinary field, comparative genocide studies has certain advantages, which it has not explored fully. To the contrary, historians, legal scholars, and social scientists keep pulling in different directions, unable to reach a consensus on virtually any aspect of genocide. The scholarly community has failed to agree on the definition of genocide – to the detriment of the UN Genocide Convention – proposing an alternative terminology. Numerous new terms and concepts have brought little clarity to the debate. The discussion has moved to a pseudo-scientific level, at the expense of empirical research. There are few comparative studies that successfully marry theory with historical facts. Looking from the perspective of genocide prevention – which is often mentioned as the foremost objective – comparative genocide studies have failed to deliver. At the same time, the emphasis on the crime of genocide has unintentionally devalued the much more frequent occurrences of mass killing. The amount of genocide literature (of varying quality) has reached a point beyond which we may start talking about the emergence of a 'genocide industry'. The field is in crisis, which has never been acknowledged within the larger scholarly community. Instead, students of genocide have assumed a self-congratulatory tone, of which the publication of the volume *Pioneers of Genocide Studies* is just one example. I often think of genocide studies as a building constructed on unstable ground. Despite the visible cracks in the foundation, the builders keep piling one floor upon another. The danger is that one day the building will collapse under its own weight.

Notes

1. For the overview of the early scholarship on genocide see: F. Chalk, 'Redefining Genocide', in *Genocide: Conceptual and Historical Dimensions*, ed. G. Andreopoulos (Philadelphia, PA: University of Pennsylvania Press, 1994), p. 48.
2. Among the best accounts of Lemkin's life and work are the following: W. Korey, *An Epitaph for Raphael Lemkin* (New York: American Jewish Committee, 2001); S. Power, *"A Problem From Hell": America and the Age of Genocide* (New York: Basic Books, 2002), pp. 17–78; special issue of *Journal of Genocide Research* (hereafter: *JGR*), 7, 3 (2005).

3. M. Levene, 'Plumbing the Depths: Issues and Problems in Current Genocide Research', *Patterns of Prejudice* (hereafter: *PP*), 36, 4 (2002), 3.
4. *The Genocide Forum* (hereafter: *GF*), 5, 2 (1998).
5. Editorial in *JGR*, 3, 3 (2001), 345.
6. Yehuda Bauer, for example, questioned the wisdom of comparing the Holocaust to the Armenian genocide. The First International Scholars' Conference on the Holocaust, convened by Bauer in New York in 1975, promoted the view that the Holocaust was unique. Back in 1984 he distinguished between genocide and the Holocaust. Bauer has revised his views since then, though only up to a certain degree. See Bauer's Letter to the Editors, *JGR*, 8, 2 (2006), 239–41.
7. M. Zimmermann, *Rassenutopie und Genozid: Die nationalsozialistische 'Lösung der Zigeunerfrage'* (Hamburg: Christians, 1996); G. Lewy, *The Nazi Persecution of the Gypsies* (Oxford: Oxford University Press, 2000); C. Streit, *Keine Kameraden: Die Wehrmacht und die sowjetische Kriegsgefangenen 1941–1945* (Stuttgart: Deutsche Verlags-Anstalt, 1978). The book that D. Kenrick and G. Puxon published in 1972, *The Destiny of Europe's Gypsies*, received undeservedly little attention.
8. S. Stein, 'Conceptions and Terms: Templates for the Analysis of Holocausts and Genocides', *JGR*, 7, 2 (2005), 185, 200f. Presumably, Browning has been using the UN definition of genocide.
9. C. C. Taylor, *Sacrifice as Terror: The Rwandan Genocide of 1994* (New York: Berg, 1999), pp. 39–41, 46, 68–75, 94–5; C. Scherrer, *Genocide and Crisis in Central Africa: Conflict Roots, Mass Violence, and Regional War* (Westport, CT: Praeger, 2002), pp. 20–7; M. Levene, 'Creating a Modern "Zone of Genocide": The Impact of Nation- and State-Formation on Eastern Anatolia, 1878–1923', *Holocaust and Genocide Studies* (hereafter: *HGS*), 12, 3 (1998), 393–433; D. Bloxham, *The Great Game of Genocide: Imperialism, Nationalism, and the Destruction of the Ottoman Armenians* (New York: Oxford University Press, 2005), pp. 70, 74, 106–10, 173–8.
10. Scott Straus, 'Contested Meanings and Conflicting Imperatives: A Conceptual Analysis of Genocide', *JGR*, 3, 3 (2001), 359, 368.
11. L. Kuper, 'Theoretical Issues Relating to Genocide: Uses and Abuses', in *Genocide: Conceptual and Historical Dimensions*, ed. Andreopoulos, p. 31.
12. Editorial, *JGR*, 7, 2 (2005), 169.
13. AIHGS Information 2003, Constitution, p. 4, online at http://www.aihgs.com/images/InfoBooklet2003.pdf
14. Stein, 'Conceptions and Terms', 174.
15. H. Hirsch, 'Studying Genocide to Protect Life', in *Pioneers of Genocide Studies*, eds, S. Totten and S. Jacobs (New Brunswick, NJ: Transaction Publishers, 2002), p. 125.
16. W. D. Rubenstein, *Genocide* (Harlow: Pearson-Longman, 2004), p. 8.
17. The British edition of Tim Cole's first book was entitled *Images of the Holocaust: The Myth of the 'Shoah Business'*. The American publisher, however, insisted on changing the title into *Selling the Holocaust* as to make it more attractive to potential buyers.
18. Huttenbach told the students who took his summer course on comparative genocide at Richard Stockton College of New Jersey in July 2002 that Jews in interwar Poland only escaped death from starvation thanks to the food parcels that the American Joint Distribution Committee had sent them. This was supposed to contribute to the argument about famine as a weapon of genocide that Huttenbach had developed. The request for a reference has never been satisfied.
19. *GF*, 4, 1; 4, 3; 4, 7 (1997–8).
20. I. Charny, 'Toward a Generic Definition of Genocide', in *Genocide: Conceptual and Historical Dimensions*, ed. Andreopoulos, pp. 74–5, 91–2.

21. I. Charny, 'A Passion for Life and Rage at the Wasting of Life', in *Pioneers of Genocide Studies*, pp. 460–1. When *HGS* rejected Charny's article on genocide denial, the latter explained it away as the resistance to new ideas.
22. D. Chandler, *The Tragedy of Cambodian History: Politics, War, and Revolution Since 1945* (New Haven, CT: Yale University Press, 1991); N. Naimark, *Fires of Hatred: Ethnic Cleansing in Twentieth-Century Europe* (Cambridge, MA: Harvard University Press, 2001); B. Green, 'Stalinist Terror and the Question of Genocide: The Great Famine', in *Is the Holocaust Unique? Perspectives on Comparative Genocide*, ed. A. S. Rosenbaum (Boulder, CO: Westview Press, 1998), pp. 137–61; I. Hull, 'Military Culture and the Production of 'Final Solutions' in the Colonies: The Example of Wilhelminian Germany', in *The Specter of Genocide: Mass Murder in Historical Perspective*, eds, R. Gellately and B. Kiernan (Cambridge: Cambridge University Press, 2003), pp. 141–62.
23. T. Dulić, 'Tito's Slaughterhouse: A Critical Analysis of Rummel's Work on Democide', *Journal of Peace Research*, 41, 1 (2004), 85–102. See also the ensuing exchange between Rummel and Dulić.
24. R. Rummel, *Lethal Politics. Soviet Genocide and Mass Murder Since 1917* (New Brunswick, NJ: Transaction Publishers, 1990), pp. xii, xiv–xv, 241–3; idem, *Death by Government: Genocide and Mass Murder in the 20th Century* (New Brunswick, NJ: Transaction Publishers, 1994), pp. 31–42; idem, *Statistics of Democide* (Charlotte, VA: Center on National Security and Law, 1997), pp. 1–10; idem, 'Democide in Totalitarian States: Mortacracies and Megamurders', in *The Widening Circle of Genocide. Genocide: A Critical Bibliographical Review. Vol. III*, ed. I. Charny (New Brunswick, NJ: Transaction Publishers, 1994), pp. 4–7, 10, 17.
25. A. Jones, 'Gendercide and Genocide', *JGR*, 2, 2 (2002), 185–7; idem, ed., *Gendercide and Genocide* (Nashville, TN: Vanderbilt University Press, 2004), p. 2.
26. See M. Hiebert's review in *H-Genocide* (September 2005), http://www.h-net.org/~genocide.
27. R. Lindsey, 'From Atrocity to Data: Historiographies of Rape in Yugoslavia and the Gendering of Genocide', *PP*, 36, 4 (2002), 59–78 (quotation p. 68). Lindsey refers specifically to Jones' article on ex-Yugoslavia in *Ethnic and Racial Studies* (1994).
28. E. Markusen and D. Mirkovic, 'Understanding Genocidal Killing in the Former Yugoslavia: Preliminary Observations', in *Collective Violence*, eds, C. Summers and E. Markusen (Lanham, MD: Rowman & Littlefield, 1999), p. 37; F. Chalk and K. Jonassohn, eds, *The History and Sociology of Genocide: Analyses and Case Studies* (New Haven, CT: Yale University Press, 1990), p. 26; C. Scherrer, 'Towards a Theory of Modern Genocide. Comparative Genocide Research: Definitions, Criteria, Typologies, Cases, Key Elements, Patterns and Voids', *JGR*, 1, 2 (1999), 15, 20.
29. B. Harff, 'Recognizing Genocides and Politicides', in *Genocide Watch*, ed. H. Fein (New Haven, CT: Yale University Press, 1992), pp. 27–41; idem, 'A German-Born Genocide Scholar', in *Pioneers of Genocide Studies*, pp. 105–7.
30. F. Chalk, 'Redefining Genocide', in *Genocide: Conceptual and Historical Dimensions*, ed. Andreopoulos, p. 47.
31. Quoted in: N. Eltingham, *Accounting for Horror: Post-Genocide Debates in Rwanda* (London: Pluto Press, 2004), p. 57.
32. H. Huttenbach, 'Vita Felix, Vita Dolorosa: An Academic Journey Towards Genocide', in *Pioneers of Genocide Studies*, p. 57.
33. See Mironko's article: '*Igitero*: Means and Motive in the Rwandan Genocide', *JGR*, 6, 1 (2004), 47–60.
34. K. Jonassohn, 'How I Came to the Study of Genocide', in *Pioneers of Genocide Studies*, p. 135.

35. H. Fein, *Accounting for Genocide: National Responses and Jewish Victimization During the Holocaust* (New York: Free Press, 1979), pp. 4–6, 33–6, 79–92.
36. I. Charny, 'Leo Kuper: A Giant Pioneer', in *Pioneers of Genocide Studies*, pp. 267, 272–3, 282–5.
37. S. Totten et al., eds, *The History and Sociology of Genocide*; *Century of Genocide: Eyewitness Accounts and Critical Views* (New York: Garland, 1997); Gellately and Kiernan, eds, *The Specter of Genocide*.
38. R. Melson, *Revolution and Genocide: On the Origins of the Armenian Genocide and the Holocaust* (Chicago, IL: University of Chicago Press, 1992), in particular pp. 247–57. Before Melson, R. Dekmajian and F. Mazian attempted a comparative study of the Armenian and Jewish experiences in genocide in 1986 and 1990, respectively.
39. J. Winter, 'Under Cover of War: The Armenian Genocide in the Context of Total War', in *The Specter of Genocide*, eds, Gellately and Kiernan, pp. 183–95, 206–13.
40. E. Kissi, 'Genocide in Cambodia and Ethiopia', in *The Specter of Genocide*, eds, Gellately and Kiernan, pp. 307–23; idem, *Revolution and Genocide in Ethiopia and Cambodia* (Lanham, MD: Lexington Books, 2006); see also Kissi's article comparing Rwanda, Ethiopia, and Cambodia in *JGR*, 6, 1 (2004), 115–33.
41. H, Fein, 'Revolutionary and Antirevolutionary Genocides: A Comparison of State Murders in Democratic Kampuchea, 1975 to 1979, and in Indonesia, 1965 to 1966', *Comparative Studies in Society and History*, 35, 4 (1993), 796–820.
42. B. Kiernan, 'Pol Pot and Enver Pasha: a Comparison of the Cambodian and Armenian Genocides', in *Studies in Comparative Genocide*, eds, L. Chorbajian and G. Shirinian (New York: St. Martin's Press, 1999), pp. 165–78.
43. See Kiernan's article in *The Specter of Genocide*, eds, Gellately and Kiernan, pp. 29–51.
44. E. Weitz, *A Century of Genocide: Utopias or Race and Nation* (Princeton, NJ: Princeton University Press, 2003); F. Hirsch, 'Race Without the Practice of Racial Politics', in *Slavic Review*, 61, 1 (2002), 30–43.
45. See my review of Weitz's book in *HGS*, 19, 1 (2005), 140–3.
46. N. Naimark, *Fires of Hatred* (quotation p. 16).
47. B. Valentino, *Final Solutions: Mass Killing and Genocide in the Twentieth Century* (Ithaca, NY: Cornell University Press, 2004), pp. 1–29, 91–151.
48. Rubenstein, *Genocide*.
49. M. Levene, *Genocide in the Age of Nation State* (London: I. B. Tauris, 2005), Vols. 1–2.
50. V. Dadrian, 'Patterns of Twentieth Century Genocides: The Armenian, Jewish, and Rwandan Cases', *JGR*, 6, 4 (2004), 487–522; idem, *German Responsibility in the Armenian Genocide: A Review of the Historical Evidence of German Complicity* (Cambridge, MA: Blue Crane Books, 1996).
51. Stein, 'Conceptions and Terms,' 174; *GF*, 6, 6 (2000).
52. *GF*, 6, 2 (1999), 6, 6 (2000).
53. P. Balakian, *Black Dog of Fate: A Memoir* (New York: Basic Books, 1997); Power, *A Problem From Hell*.
54. L. Kuper, *Genocide: Its Political Use in the Twentieth Century* (New Haven, CT: Yale University Press, 1981), p. 11.
55. K. Jonassohn, 'How I Came to the Study of Genocide', in *Pioneers of Genocide Studies*, p. 135.
56. R. Smith, 'Human Destructiveness and Politics: The Twentieth Century as an Age of Genocide', in *Genocide and the Modern Age: Etiology and Case Studies of Mass Death*, eds, I. Wallimann and M. Dobkowski (Syracuse, NY: Syracuse University Press, 2000 [1987]), pp. 21–39; K. Jonassohn and F. Chalk, 'A Typology of Genocide and Some Implications for the Human Rights Agenda', in ibid, pp. 3–20; H. Fein,

Genocide: A Sociological Perspective (London: Sage, 1993), pp. 32–50; idem, 'Scenarios of Genocide: Models of Genocide and Critical Responses', in *Toward the Understanding and Prevention of Genocide: Proceedings of the International Conference on the Holocaust and Genocide*, ed. I. Charny (Boulder, CO: Westview Press, 1989), pp. 8–22.

57. T. Dulić, *Utopias of Nation: Local Mass Killing in Bosnia and Herzegovina, 1941–42* (Uppsala: Uppsala University Press, 2005), p. 346.
58. H. Fein, 'Genocide and Gender: The Uses of Women and Group Destiny', *JGR*, 1, 1 (1999), 49.
59. E. Haberer, 'History and Justice: Paradigms of the Prosecution of Nazi Crimes', *HGS*, 19, 3 (2005), 488.
60. Y. Beigbeder, *Judging War Criminals: The Politics of International Justice* (New York: St. Martin's Press, 1999); H. Ball, *Prosecuting War Crimes and Genocide: The Twentieth-Century Experience* (Lawrence, KA: University Press of Kansas, 1999); G. Bass, *Stay the Hand of Vengeance: The Politics of War Crimes Tribunals* (Princeton, NJ: Princeton University Press, 2000); R. Kahn, *Holocaust Denial and the Law: A Comparative Study* (New York: Macmillan, 2004).
61. A. L. Hinton, 'Why Did You Kill? The Cambodian Genocide and the Dark Side of Face and Honor', *The Journal of Asian Studies*, 57, 1 (1998), 96–7, 109–18; idem, *Why Did They Kill? Cambodia in the Shadow of Genocide* (Berkeley, CA: University of California Press, 2005), pp. 26–31, 46–8, 64–9, 126–34, 185, 190–3, 241–7, 287.
62. C. Taylor, *Sacrifice as Terror*, p. 105.
63. C. Merridale, *Night of Stone: Death and Memory in Twentieth-Century Russia* (New York: Viking, 2001).
64. D. Stone, 'Genocide as Transgression', *European Journal of Social Theory*, 7, 1 (2004), 45–9, 54–9.
65. H. Hirsch, 'Studying Genocide to Protect Life', in *Pioneers of Genocide Studies*, pp. 122–3.
66. H. Fein, 'From Social Action to Social Theory and Back: Paths and Circles', in *Pioneers of Genocide Studies*, p. 228.
67. G. Stanton, 'The Call', in *Pioneers of Genocide Studies*, pp. 402–7, 410–11.
68. T. Fawthrop and H. Jarvis, *Getting Away With Genocide? Elusive Justice and the Khmer Rouge Tribunal* (London: Pluto Press, 2004), pp. 156, 192, 237–9.
69. *A Good Man in Hell: General Roméo Dallaire and the Rwanda Genocide*, DVD produced by CC/USHMM, 2003. The name of Dallaire, and his desperate attempts first to prevent and then to stop genocide, was rescued from oblivion thanks to Samantha Power's article in *The Atlantic Monthly* in September 2001. Dallaire described his experience in Rwanda and the post-traumatic stress in which it had thrown him in a memoir, entitled *Shake Hands With the Devil: The Failure of Humanity in Rwanda* (New York: Carroll & Graf, 2003).
70. Editorial, *JGR*, 7, 1 (2005), 3.
71. See exchange between Dan Stone and David Cesarani, *PP*, 34, 4 (2000), 53–66.
72. *GF*, 3, 5 and 4, 1 (1997).
73. Editorial, *JGR*, 7, 2 (2005), 170.
74. I. Charny, 'Toward a Generic Definition of Genocide', in *Genocide: Conceptual and Historical Dimensions*, ed. Andreopoulos, pp. 70, 79, 80.
75. S. Totten and E. Markusen, 'The US Government Darfur Genocide Investigation', *JGR*, 7, 2 (2005), 279, 288–9.
76. E. Staub, 'The Roots and Prevention of Genocide and Other Collective Violence: A Life's Work Shaped by a Child's Experience', in *Pioneers of Genocide Studies*, pp. 484–5; G. Prunier expresses similar sentiment in his recent book *Darfur: The Ambiguous Genocide* (Ithaca, NY: Cornell University Press, 2005), p. 156.

77. *GF*, 6, 1 (1999); M. Levene has similar concerns, in particular with the judicial aspect of genocide prevention. See 'A Dissenting Voice: Or How Current Assumptions of Deterring and Preventing Genocide May be Looking at the Problem Through the Wrong End of the Telescope, Part I', *JGR*, 6, 2 (2004), 158–60.
78. Stanton, 'The Call', pp. 408–9.
79. R. Melson, 'My Journey in the Study of Genocide', in *Pioneers of Genocide Studies*, p. 149.
80. *GF*, 3, 5 (1997), 5, 6 (1999).
81. C. Gerlach, 'Extremely Violent Societies: An Alternative to the Concept of Genocide', *JGR*, 8, 4 (2006), 455–71. By questioning the integrity and usefulness of comparative genocide studies, Gerlach had effectively reversed the conspiracy theory insinuated by Huttenbach with regard to Holocaust studies.

3
Conceptions of Genocide and Perceptions of History

David Moshman

Conceptions of genocide profoundly shape our perceptions of history. Is genocide rare or common? Which events are genocides and which, however objectionable or horrifying, are not? Which persons or groups are victims of genocide, which are perpetrators, and which are neither – or both? Our perception of historical events as genocides depends not only on what happened in the past – who did what to whom for what reasons, under what circumstances, and with what results? – but also on how we conceptualize genocide: which combinations of perpetrators, actions, victims, reasons, circumstances, and results constitute genocide and which do not?

I begin with Holocaust-based conceptions of genocide. Conceptions of genocide are often based on the Holocaust, which is commonly taken to be the exemplar of genocide. Other genocides are identified on the basis of resemblance to the Holocaust. Genocides are rare in this view.

Scholars of genocide, however, generally favour formal conceptions rooted in abstract definitions. Such definitions provide criteria for distinguishing genocides from other historical events. Following the discussion of Holocaust-based conceptions, I present and compare seven definitions of genocide. I then apply these definitions to historical events and questions associated with the dirty wars of Latin America in the 1970s and 1980s and the conquest of the Americas since 1492. These cases illustrate the many ways in which diverse conceptions of genocide generate divergent perceptions of history. They also provide important guidance in the conceptualization of genocide.

Holocaust-based conceptions of genocide

The Holocaust is routinely presented and understood by scholars, educators, and the general public as 'the most shocking event of the twentieth century,'[1] if not the 'most terrible event in modern history'[2] or 'the most extensive effort at genocide in history.'[3] It was the 'ultimate expression'[4] of genocide, 'the archetypal event of mass murder in human history.'[5] It 'stands alone in the history of the West and in the history of genocide,'[6] 'a global attack on Western civilization itself.'[7] The Holocaust was 'an unprecedented catastrophe in human civilization.'[8] 'The Nazi regime was the most genocidal the world has ever seen'[9] and 'the cruelest regime that the world has ever seen.'[10]

Steven Katz has been prominent among those scholars who argue that the Holocaust was unique in history. In an edited volume entitled *Is the Holocaust unique?*, Katz titled his chapter, 'The uniqueness of the Holocaust' and stated his thesis in the opening paragraph: 'The Holocaust, that is, the intentional murder of European Jewry during World War II, is historically and phenomenologically unique. No other case discussed in this book parallels it.'[11] Katz went on to deny that his claim was intended to suggest that the Holocaust was more evil than other terrible events of history and he acknowledged that it was not the largest mass killing in history. Thus:

> When I argue for the uniqueness of the Holocaust I intend only to claim that the Holocaust is phenomenologically unique by virtue of the fact that never before has a state set out, as a matter of intentional principle and actualized policy, to annihilate physically every man, woman, and child belonging to a specific people. A close study of the relevant comparative historical data will show that only in the case of Jewry under the Third Reich was such all-inclusive, non-compromising, unmitigated murder intended.[12]

It remains unclear exactly what Katz is claiming. Although the Holocaust was a mass killing, it cannot be regarded as unique in this respect. Mass killings are common, and the Holocaust, as Katz acknowledged, was not the largest.[13] Katz seems instead to be making a qualitative claim about the Holocaust as an act directed not just at some number of people, nor even at some number of Jews, but at Jewry itself. But acts of annihilation are often aimed at abstractly defined groups of people and such acts are often highly inclusive, uncompromising, and unmitigated. True, the Holocaust is phenomenologically distinct from every other genocide, but so is every other genocide distinct from every other. Every genocide is unique, and the Holocaust is no exception.

Alice and Roy Eckardt recognized that 'all historical events are unique, by which is meant simply that they are qualitatively different from each other.'[14] They insisted, however, that the Holocaust showed 'unique uniqueness'[15] and perhaps even 'transcending uniqueness.'[16] 'That the Holocaust of the Jews is a uniquely unique event,' they asserted, 'scarcely requires argument.'[17] What little argument they provided was focused on demonstrating that the Holocaust 'was an unprecedented event.'[18]

The claim that the Holocaust was unprecedented, however, raises the same problems as the claim that it was unique. Every historical event is qualitatively different from every previous historical event and is thus, in a trivial sense, unprecedented. An event might be said to be unprecedented in a stronger sense if no previous event resembled it, but the comparative study of genocide shows that there were many events prior to the Holocaust that resemble it in important ways, and there have been many since.

Nevertheless, Gunnar Heinsohn asks, 'What makes the Holocaust a uniquely unique genocide?'[19] His answer is that the Holocaust is uniquely unique 'because it was a genocide for the purpose of reinstalling the right to genocide. Hitler was not unprecedented in ruthlessly and massively breaking the commandment "Thou shalt not kill!"; he was irreducibly distinct from other mega-murderers by abrogating it.'[20] More specifically, argues Heinsohn, the Holocaust was a process of 'cleansing the Germans from Judaism's principle of the sanctity of life by eliminating the Jews.'[21] The commandment not to kill, according to Heinsohn, was seen by the Nazis as rooted in Jewish religious ideology. To avoid moral condemnation for the exterminations required by Nazi ideology, it was necessary to eliminate the source of the ban on killing, the Jews.

A major problem for this argument is that it runs counter to the consensus of historians that Nazi Germany targeted Jews as a race, not as a religious group.[22] Even if the Jews were indeed targeted by the Nazis for their actual or perceived religious ideology, however, this would only make the Holocaust unique, not uniquely unique. Every genocide involves unique issues of identity and ideology, and these are perceived in most cases to be of transcendent significance.[23]

Yehuda Bauer, along with most genocide scholars, acknowledges that genocide has been common throughout history regardless of which of the various current definitions of genocide one uses. He uses the term 'Holocaust' to refer to a subcategory of genocide that has precisely one instance – the Nazi killing of the Jews – but could have more in the future.[24] That is, the Nazi Judeocide is in a category of its own, not by definition, but as a matter of historical fact, and it is our moral obligation to keep it that way.

Bauer's view of the categorical uniqueness of the Nazi genocide is, by his own admission, not an outcome of his research but a bias directing it, the first of two biases that he acknowledges at the outset:

> Let me state my biases. I think that the planned total murder of a people was an unprecedented catastrophe in human civilization. ... And because it happened once, it can happen again.
>
> My second bias is that I am not neutral as between Nazism and anti-Nazism. I detest Nazism. I am against antisemitism and racism of any sort.[25]

Bauer defends the second 'bias' on moral grounds. His antiracist perspective is not a bias in the sense of being arbitrary or unjustified. It is a bias, presumably, because it is a moral perspective he brings to the study of genocide, not a conclusion based on his data. But it is a morally justifiable bias.

The first bias, however, is much more problematic. Bauer assumes that 'the planned total murder of a people' was an unprecedented – and, as yet, unrepeated – event. This is not a moral claim but an empirical one. Whether the Nazis committed 'the planned total murder of a people' and whether any other historical event can be characterized in that way are questions of evidence and interpretation.

Bauer does make some comparisons across genocides to support his claim that the Nazi Judeocide was and remains categorically unique, but, perhaps because he was guided by a bias rather than testing a theory, his analyses are perfunctory and fail to provide any serious test of his claims. He argues, for example, that the Hutu perpetrators of the 1994 Rwanda genocide were motivated by a quest for land and power, unlike the Nazis, who were motivated by an irrational ideology. But Hutu Power was also driven by an irrational ideology,[26] and the Nazis also sought land and power. Genocides have multiple overlapping sets of motives and other characteristics. If we try hard enough to distinguish a particular genocide from every other genocide we can find some way to do so, but we can do this for every genocide.

Conceptions of the Holocaust as unique in some special way lead to a perception of history in which nothing like the Holocaust had ever happened before. The familiar slogan 'Never Again!' is an exhortation to see that nothing like the Holocaust ever happens again. If the Holocaust is unique, we are morally obligated to see that it remains unique.

Such conceptions have been highly influential. Despite increasing awareness of other genocides, the Holocaust remains for many the prototypical genocide against which all others are recognized and understood.[27] If there were genocides before the Holocaust, such as the Armenian genocide, they were relatively few and are best seen as predecessors to that ultimate genocide – the Holocaust. If there have been genocides since, such as those in Cambodia or Rwanda, they have been relatively few and are best seen as reminders of what can happen if we forget that ultimate horror of the past. The history of genocide, in this view, centres on the Holocaust.

Early definitions of genocide

The term *genocide* was originated in 1944 by Raphael Lemkin, who defined it as 'the destruction of a nation or of an ethnic group.'[28] He made it clear that this is not limited to immediate destruction through mass killings. The term *genocide*

> is intended rather to signify a coordinated plan of different actions aiming at the destruction of essential foundations of the life of national groups, with the aim of annihilating the groups themselves. The objectives of such a plan would be disintegration of the political and social institutions, of culture, language, national feelings, religion, and the economic existence of national

> groups, and the destruction of the personal security, liberty, health, dignity, and even the lives of the individuals belonging to such groups. Genocide is directed against the national group as an entity, and the actions involved are directed against individuals, not in their individual capacity, but as members of the national group.[29]

Genocide, then, may be accomplished by mass killing but is something different from mass killing that can also be accomplished in other ways. It is something that is done to a nation, not to some number of individuals.

Consider the following hypothetical events:

1. Perpetrator A randomly chooses 100,000 people from all the people of the world and kills them instantly.
2. Perpetrator B kills all 100,000 members of an isolated tribe with a unique culture.
3. Perpetrator C provides for the health and security of all 100,000 members of an isolated tribe with a unique culture but forbids the teaching of their beliefs and practices. After several generations there are many descendants, but the culture no longer exists.

Note that case *2* resembles both *1* and *3*, but in different ways. Case *2*, like case *1*, is a mass killing. But case *2*, unlike *1*, resembles case *3* in that it involves the destruction of a human group. This is not a matter of killing on a large scale but of something different, something that exists at the level of social groups, something difficult to perceive prior to 1944 because there was no word for it. Lemkin coined the term *genocide* to help others see what he had seen in human history and was now seeing again. Not only had he seen huge numbers of mass killings, as had many others, but he had seen something else, something that overlapped with mass killing but was not the same thing. It was to highlight the destruction of social groups, as distinct from the killings of individual persons, that he coined the term *genocide*.

The key contribution of the new term *genocide*, then, was to direct attention to the destruction of groups as groups (cases *2* and *3*), not to give another name to mass killings (cases *1* and *2*). The relation of *2* to *1* is obvious, but the relation of *2* to *3* is no less important. To eliminate a way of thinking or a way of life is something different from the killing of some number of individuals. The intent of the term *genocide* was to highlight group destruction by giving it a name of its own.

In 1946, the General Assembly of the United Nations passed the following resolution:

> Genocide is a denial of the right of existence of entire human groups, as homicide is the denial of the right to live of individual human beings; such

> denial of the right of existence shocks the conscience of mankind, results in great losses to humanity in the form of cultural and other contributions represented by these groups, and is contrary to moral law and to the spirit and aims of the United Nations. Many instances of such crimes of genocide have occurred when racial, religious, political and other groups have been destroyed, entirely or in part. The punishment of the crime of genocide is a matter of international concern.
>
> *The General Assembly, therefore, Affirms* that genocide is a crime under international law which the civilized world condemns, and for the commission of which principals and accomplices – whether private individuals, public officials or statesmen, and whether the crime is committed on religious, racial, political or any other grounds – are punishable.[30]

Consistent with Lemkin's conception of genocide as a crime against groups, the General Assembly resolution begins with an explanation that genocide is not mass murder but a crime at a different level of analysis that is analogous to murder. Genocide is to a social group as murder is to an individual. It is the denial of the right to exist.

The General Assembly's conception and that of Lemkin differ in three noteworthy ways. First, Lemkin's definition appears to make intent a condition for genocide in requiring that there must be an 'aim of annihilating' the group with 'objectives of ... disintegration.' The General Assembly Resolution, in contrast, includes no reference to the aim, objective, purpose, or intent of the perpetrator.

Second, having shifted focus from the intent of the perpetrator to destroy a group to the actual destruction of the victim group, the General Assembly included, within the realm of genocide, cases in which the victim group is only destroyed 'in part.' The partial destruction of a group is presumably something more than the killing of some number of its members but something less than complete destruction. It might, for example, involve the destruction of some of the group's institutions or practices but not others.

Finally, the General Assembly provided a different list than did Lemkin of groups that could be victims of genocide. Most importantly, the Assembly list was explicitly left open to 'other' groups.

In 1948, the United Nations adopted the Convention on the Prevention and Punishment of the Crime of Genocide, generally known as the United Nations Genocide Convention. It defined genocide as follows:

> In the present Convention, genocide means any of the following acts committed with intent to destroy, in whole or in part, a national, ethnical, racial or religious group, as such: (a) Killing members of the group; (b) Causing serious bodily or mental harm to members of the group; (c) Deliberately

inflicting on the group conditions of life calculated to bring about its physical destruction in whole or in part; (d) Imposing measures intended to prevent births within the group; (e) Forcibly transferring children of the group to another group.[31]

The definition presents five 'acts' that are genocidal if they meet a set of criteria. Killing members of a group is one such act, but there are four more. Thus genocide includes more than mass killing, consistent with Lemkin and the General Assembly, but it is limited to a set of five acts. Other acts equally destructive of the indicated groups do not count as genocide. The list of potentially genocidal acts has an arbitrary quality that leads one to suspect it was the work of a committee or the product of political compromises. In fact, it was both.[32]

The definition also includes a set of criteria for determining whether an act in one of these five categories constitutes genocide. In its reference to a group 'as such,' the Convention, like the General Assembly, maintained Lemkin's core conception that genocide involves the destruction of a group as a group, not just as a collection of individuals.

With respect to the three criteria distinguishing the Resolution from Lemkin, the Convention goes along with the Resolution in one respect and is closer to Lemkin in the other two. In its reference to destruction 'in whole or in part' the Convention followed the General Assembly resolution in not requiring that the perpetrator intended or achieved total destruction.

The Convention reverts to Lemkin in its requirement of intent. Under the Convention, a perpetrator who intended to destroy one of the designated groups would be guilty of genocide regardless of whether the genocide was successful. The accidental destruction of a group, however, would not be genocide. This raises difficult questions about what constitutes an intent to destroy and when, if ever, the destruction of a group may be deemed accidental rather than intentional.

Finally, in contrast to the open-ended listing of groups in the General Assembly Resolution, the Convention is limited to four groups: 'national, ethnical, racial or religious.' This goes beyond Lemkin's original two but closes the list at four, conspicuously not including political groups, which were recognized by the General Assembly, and not allowing for any others. Some groups cannot be victims of genocide, under the Convention, no matter what is done to them.

Contemporary definitions of genocide

The Genocide Convention has not been the last word on the definition of genocide. On the contrary, although the Convention is definitive for legal purposes, virtually all scholars believe it is deeply flawed, and some have proposed alternatives. The contemporary literature is fairly represented, I believe, by

Table 3.1 Genocide: definitions and criteria

Criterion	***Definition of genocide***						
	Lemkin	**UN Res**	**UNGC**	**Fein**	**Chalk & J**	**Charny**	**Churchill**
Group destruction	Yes	Yes	Yes	Yes	Yes	No	Yes
Real group	Yes	Yes	Yes	Yes	No	No	Yes
Intent	Yes	No	Yes	Yes	Yes	No	No
Total destruction	Yes	No	No	Yes	Yes	No	No
Special groups	Yes	No	Yes	No	No	No	No
One-sided	No	No	No	Yes	Yes	Yes	No
Mass killing	No	No	No	No	Yes	Yes	No
Government perpetrator	No	No	No	No	Yes	No	No

Note: The labels of the seven definitions refer, respectively, to Lemkin (1944), the United Nations General Assembly Resolution on genocide (1946), the United Nations Genocide Convention (1948), Fein (1993), Chalk and Jonassohn (1990), Charny (1994), and Churchill (1997). Each definition does (Yes) or does not (No) require each of the eight potential criteria for genocide. These potential criteria, each of which is or is not required by each of the seven definitions, are, respectively, (1) actual or intended destruction of a group; (2) reality of the victim group outside the mind of the perpetrator; (3) intent to destroy; (4) total destruction intended or achieved; (5) finite list of specified victim groups; (6) imbalance of power in the relation of perpetrator to victim; (7) mass killing; (8) perpetrator is a governmental or other authority. See text for detail on all definitions and criteria.

what I identified in 2001 as the four most important alternative definitions – those of Fein, Chalk and Jonassohn, Charny, and Churchill.[33] These four definitions, along with the three already discussed, vary with respect to eight potential criteria for genocide, and thus enable a broad overview of the definitional options (see Table 3.1).

Helen Fein provides a thorough review and analysis of definitions of genocide culminating in a definition of her own: 'Genocide is sustained purposeful action by a perpetrator to physically destroy a collectivity directly or indirectly, through interdiction of the biological and social reproduction of group members, sustained regardless of the surrender or lack of threat offered by the victim.'[34] Following Lemkin, the General Assembly Resolution, and the Genocide Convention, Fein centres her definition on the destruction of groups. The destruction must be 'physical' but it may be achieved 'indirectly.' Thus genocide is not limited to mass killing, though the nature and scope of indirect physical destruction is unclear.

Fein does require that the perpetrator has engaged in 'sustained purposeful action ... to ... destroy.' This is close to Lemkin and the Genocide Convention, and different from the Resolution, in setting a criterion of intent. Fein does not follow the lead of the Resolution and the Convention in their acknowledgement of partial destruction as genocide. Her more stringent criterion of total destruction, however, like that of Lemkin, involves only the intent to destroy, not the actual achievement of total destruction. Consistent with the General Assembly Resolution, and contrary to Lemkin and the Convention, Fein sets no restrictions on the kind of 'collectivity' that is targeted. Any group can be a victim of genocide. Fein does, however, propose a new criterion. In an effort to distinguish genocide from most military killings, Fein specifies that genocide does not include actions against groups that pose an active threat.

Frank Chalk and Kurt Jonassohn provide an overlapping but rather different definition: 'Genocide is a form of one-sided mass killing in which a state or other authority intends to destroy a group, as that group and membership in it are defined by the perpetrator.'[35] This definition, like all the previous ones, requires the destruction of groups. Following Fein, Lemkin, and the Convention, it sets a criterion of intent. Following Fein and Lemkin, the intent is an intent to destroy in total. Following Fein and the Resolution, the Chalk/Jonassohn definition does not limit the type of group subject to genocide. And like Fein alone, Chalk and Jonassohn attempt to distinguish genocide from most military killings, in their case by specifying that mass killings do not constitute genocide unless they are 'one-sided.'

Chalk and Jonassohn's definition, however, differs from any of the previous ones in three ways. First, it limits genocide to mass killing. Not all mass killings are genocides, but only mass killings can be genocides. Destruction of groups through means other than mass killing may be objectionable, but such actions are not genocidal.

Second, Chalk and Jonassohn recognize that genocides are aimed at groups as perceived by the perpetrators. Victims may have very different perceptions regarding the groups in question and their own affiliation with them. Deadly violence may even be aimed at individuals implicated in groups such as 'demonic witches' or 'enemies of the people' that do not really exist. Chalk and Jonassohn construe an act as genocidal if it is aimed at what the perpetrators construe as a group and at those they perceive as members of that group.

Finally, Chalk and Jonassohn include in their definition a requirement that the perpetrator is 'a state or other authority.' It seems clear on empirical grounds that genocides are usually perpetrated by states or other authorities but no previous definition makes this a criterion. If a lone individual could destroy an entire nation, all but Chalk and Jonassohn would deem that an act of genocide.

This leaves us with many unanswered questions. Does the genocidal nature of an act of destruction depend on the type of perpetrator? The intent of the perpetrator? The type of target? The reality of the target? The killing of the victims? The level of destruction? The balance of power? Israel Charny laments the 'definitionalism' that insists on answering such questions:

> The predominant intellectual goal of most participants in these definitional turf battles over what is and is not genocide is generally to exclude unfavored categories from the field.
>
> For me, the passion to exclude this or that mass killing from the universe of genocide, as well as the intense competition to establish the exclusive 'superiority' or unique form of any one genocide, ends up creating a fetishistic atmosphere in which the masses of bodies that are not to be qualified for the definition of genocide are dumped into a conceptual black hole, where they are forgotten.[36]

With these considerations in mind, Charny proposed a 'generic' definition: 'Genocide in the generic sense is the mass killing of substantial numbers of human beings, when not in the course of military action against the military forces of an avowed enemy, under conditions of the essential defenselessness and helplessness of the victims.'[37] In contrast to all previous definitions, Charny does not require that the victims constitute a group in any sense. For him, the mass killing of 100,000 people is 100,000 murders, regardless of whether the victims constitute a group. Genocide is simply mass killing, nothing more. Thus there are no questions for Charny regarding the type of group destroyed, its genuine existence, or the totality of the destruction. In contrast to Fein, Chalk and Jonassohn, and the Genocide Convention, moreover, he does not require intent, and in contrast to Chalk and Jonassohn he does not require a governmental perpetrator.

Not all mass killings are genocidal, however, even under Charny's definition. He stipulates that to qualify as genocide a mass killing must involve 'conditions of the essential defenselessness and helplessness of the victims,' consistent with Fein's reference to 'surrender or lack of threat' and with the requirement of Chalk and Jonassohn that the mass killing be 'one-sided.' More specifically, mass killings associated with 'military action against the military forces of an avowed enemy' do not count as genocide. Consistent with all previous definitions, Charny construes many victims of mass killings as victims of war, not victims of genocide.

Charny's definition is inclusive in some ways but restrictive in others. In contrast to all previous definitions, it sets no criteria of group status in categorizing something as genocide. In contrast to all but Chalk and Jonassohn, however, Charny assumes that only mass killings inhabit the universe of genocide. Many group destructions that would qualify as genocidal for Lemkin, Fein, the Resolution, and the Convention are not genocidal for Charny.

Ward Churchill, dedicating his book to Lemkin, argues for a return to the original conception of genocide.[38] After recounting the political compromises leading from the 1946 General Assembly Resolution to the 1948 Convention, and analyzing the definitional debates since then, he proposes an alternative Genocide Convention. His Convention begins with a preamble taken largely from the 1946 Resolution and then proceeds to a definition rooted in that of Lemkin and the Resolution: 'In the present Convention, genocide means the destruction, entirely or in part, of any racial, ethnic, national, religious, cultural, linguistic, political, economic, gender or other human group, however such groups may be defined by the perpetrator.'[39]

Churchill, following Lemkin and the Resolution, makes clear that group destruction is genocidal regardless of whether it is accomplished by mass killing or by alternative means. Recall the three hypothetical cases presented earlier: (1) random mass killing, (2) group destruction through mass killing, and (3) group destruction by disrupting the transmission of culture across generations. Lemkin used the term *genocide* to refer to group destruction, thus highlighting the way *2* and *3* are similar to each other and different from *1*, and the United Nations initially followed his lead in its 1946 General Assembly Resolution. The 1948 Genocide Convention and Fein's definition recognize but limit the extension of the concept beyond *2*. Chalk and Jonassohn limit genocide entirely to cases of type *2*. Charny extends the concept to include *1*.

Step by step, Lemkin's concept of genocide has been lost. By the time we get to Chalk and Jonassohn, Lemkin's intent to highlight the connection of *2* and *3* is left behind. Genocide is simply a type of mass killing. Charny takes this a step further by eliminating the requirement that it targets or destroys a group. Having tied case *2* to case *1*, moreover, Charny, however inclusive he desires to be, cannot broaden the concept further to include cases like *3*. The resulting concept, in linking *1* and *3*, would be so heterogeneous as to be useless.

Churchill goes back to the origin of the concept to retrieve Lemkin's urgent vision of a dimly perceived crime against groups that must be named to be more clearly and widely seen. Genocide, in his definition, overlaps with mass killing but is neither identical to it nor a subset of it. Rather, the use of mass killing in genocide is a question for empirical examination. Consistent with Lemkin, the Resolution, the Convention, and Fein, moreover, Churchill defines genocide as the destruction of an actual group, although recognizing, consistent with Chalk and Jonassohn, that the perpetrators may perceive the group differently than its members do.

Beyond this minimum requirement of group destruction, Churchill, consistent with the General Assembly Resolution of 1946, sets no other requirements. Consistent with all definitions except that of Chalk and Jonassohn, he sets no restriction on the nature of the perpetrator. Consistent with the Resolution, Fein, Chalk and Jonassohn, and Charny, he rejects the Convention's short list of groups that can be victims of genocide as an unjustifiable political compromise. His listing of groups goes beyond the usual categories and is explicitly open.

Consistent with Lemkin, the Resolution, and the Convention, and in contrast to Fein, Chalk and Jonassohn, and Charny, Churchill sets no requirement of one-sidedness, defencelessness, or lack of threat, and makes no exception with regard to warfare. Group destruction is genocide regardless of the circumstances. Moreover, consistent with the Resolution, the Convention, and Charny, but in contrast to Lemkin, Fein, and Chalk and Jonassohn, Churchill does not require that the complete destruction of a group is either intended or accomplished.

Finally, consistent with the Resolution and Charny, but in contrast to requirements implicit or explicit in all the other definitions, Churchill does not require intent, though he does consider it important. By analogy to murder, he distinguishes four degrees of genocide, with 'premeditated intent to commit genocide' a criterion for 'Genocide in the First Degree.' Unintended group destructions may be genocides, in lesser degree, depending on whether the perpetrators were engaged in illegal actions or showed 'reckless disregard' for, or 'depraved indifference' to, the genocidal consequences of their actions.[40]

The seven definitions just discussed vary with respect to eight potential criteria for genocide (see Table 3.1). Each definition requires that at least two of these eight criteria be met and none requires more than six of them. Correspondingly, each of the eight criteria is deemed essential by at least one of the seven definitions, and none by more than six of the seven. With these definitions and criteria in mind, we now consider how conceptions of genocide shape our perceptions of history.

From *Deuteronomy* to the dirty wars

As good a place as any to start looking for genocide is the Old Testament, which includes multiple accounts of groups intentionally destroying other groups through mass killings. We cannot assume the accuracy of any of these accounts. The recurring pattern, however, strongly suggests that intentional group destructions through mass killing were sufficiently common that they were accepted as routine. In *Deuteronomy*, for instance, it is taken as a matter of course that land is attained by annihilating and displacing the previous inhabitants: 'they destroyed them ... and dwelt in their stead.'[41] With this in mind, Moses reminds the Israelites:

> And Sichon came out against us, he and all his people, to the battle at Yahaz. And the Lord our God gave him up before us; and we smote him, and his

> sons, and all his people. And we captured all his cities at that time, and utterly destroyed every inhabited city, and the women, and the little ones; we left none remaining.[42]
>
> And the Lord our God gave into our hands also Og the king of Bashan, and all his people; and we smote him until none was left to him remaining. And we captured all his cities at that time ... All these were fortified cities, with high walls, gates, and bars; besides the unwalled towns, which were a great many. And we utterly destroyed them, as we had done unto Sichon the king of Cheshbon, utterly destroying every inhabited city, the women, and the little ones.[43]

Each of these two accounts, under any of the seven definitions, describes an act of genocide consisting of a coordinated series of genocidal massacres. In each case the perpetrators, acting as a nation, intentionally destroyed another nation by killing every member of that nation. Some of the killings took place in a context of warfare but many or most were subsequent killings of defenceless women and children. The intent was not to win a war and set the terms of the peace but to destroy a nation, including all its people, and take its place.

For many historical events, however, the attribution of genocide is not so clear. Much depends on the empirical facts of the case, of course, but equally important is the definition of genocide one applies to those facts.

Consider the dirty wars of Latin America in the 1970s and 1980s. Large scale atrocities in most of the countries of Latin America around this period had enough in common that they all came to be known as 'dirty wars' but were different enough that they are not generally thought to constitute a singular 'Dirty War,' despite the active role of the United States in most of them. Thus it would be misleading to ask whether the Dirty War was an act of genocide or not. There was no Dirty War.

There were dirty wars, however, and they were, in various ways, genocidal with respect to most or all of the present definitions and criteria. The term 'dirty' reflected, perhaps, an emerging intuition that what was happening was something different, and worse, than a war. But where, when, and how we perceive genocide in the dirty wars depends on our definition of genocide.

For Charny, all victims of one-sided mass killings are victims of genocide, without distinction. The dirty wars included classic genocidal massacres in which military forces in Guatemala, El Salvador, and elsewhere destroyed hundreds of villages by killing everyone, including children of all ages.[44] They also included what came to be called disappearances, in which military units in Argentina, Chile, and elsewhere abducted tens of thousands of people, tortured them to death, and denied any knowledge of their fate.[45] From Charny's point of view, the dirty wars were genocidal through and through, adding hundreds of thousands of new victims to the historical accounting of genocide.

Chalk and Jonassohn, like Charny, limit genocide to one-sided mass killings but, in contrast to Charny, restrict it further to those that are perpetrated by 'a state or other authority' with intent to destroy what it perceives to be a group. This definition requires us to identify governmental perpetrators of mass killings and consider their perceptions and intent. In the case of the dirty wars, the vast majority of killings were perpetrated by governmental agents against individuals who were perceived as subversives, with the intent of eliminating subversion. In most of the countries of Latin America during this period, governmental authorities intended to destroy what they perceived as a group. From the perspective of the Chalk and Jonassohn definition, the dirty wars included multiple genocides.

The other five definitions, however, refer to the destruction of actual groups, requiring us to identify, country by country, the group or groups destroyed, at least in part, or targeted for destruction. Not all those perceived by their government as subversive saw themselves as subversive, and what groups they could actually be said to belong to is a matter requiring specific empirical evidence about targeted individuals and villages in various countries. The general pattern, however, was not subtle: right-wing military governments were targeting the political left.

The significance of this political dimension depends on one's definition of genocide. The General Assembly Resolution and Churchill explicitly include political groups in their open-ended lists of potential victims of genocide, and Fein, like Chalk and Jonassohn, makes no distinctions between types of groups. From this point of view, the dirty wars included multiple genocides against multiple groups, especially political groups, though there is room for disagreement, depending in part on the definition one applies, about specific events and perpetrators in particular countries.

Lemkin, however, defined genocide as 'the destruction of a nation or of an ethnic group,' and the Convention limited it to groups that are 'national, ethnical, racial, or religious,' deliberately rejecting the Resolution's inclusion of political groups. From this point of view the destruction of political groups does not qualify as genocide. What would draw the attention of the Lemkin/Convention perspective is that in Guatemala, the epicentre of genocidal massacres of entire villages, all of the destroyed villages were Mayan.[46] For Lemkin there might be an empirical question of whether the complete destruction of the Guatemalan Mayans – or a discrete subgroup thereof – was intended or achieved. Under the Convention, which requires only an intent to destroy the Mayan people 'in part,' it is clear that the government of Guatemala, with the assistance of the United States, was guilty of genocide.[47]

There is a further complication, however. The Maya were targeted largely on the basis of actual or perceived association with leftist subversion. This might include community organizing, human rights activism, material or ideological support for leftist guerrillas, or affiliation with a community deemed subversive in these ways. The targeting of the Maya arguably had at least as much to do with what was perceived as their leftist or subversive politics as with their ethnic status. Does this mean their destruction was not genocide? I take it instead as showing that a sharp distinction between ethnic and political groups and motives is meaningless and misleading.[48] This may explain why neither the Resolution nor any of the four contemporary scholarly definitions – those of Fein, Chalk and Jonassohn, Charny, and Churchill – excludes political groups from the realm of genocide.

In summary, depending on definition, we see genocide primarily in the targeting of Mayans (Lemkin, Convention), political leftists and Mayans (Resolution, Fein, Churchill), those deemed subversive regardless of their actual political or ethnic views and affiliations (Chalk and Jonassohn), or defenceless people, regardless of why they were targeted (Charny). Thus we have multiple construals of the dirty wars.

The conquest of the Americas

On a much larger scale, consider now the centuries-long conquest of the Americas.[49] Beginning in 1492, Columbus encountered a variety of Taino and other Arawak societies on the islands of the Caribbean.[50] The Taino typically lived in large multi-family wooden houses in densely populated villages. They engaged in agriculture, fishing, canoeing, swimming, handicrafts, music, dancing, ball games, and ceremonies. Consistent with their social customs, they greeted Columbus with hospitality and gifts.

On the island of Hispaniola (now divided between Haiti and the Dominican Republic), Columbus established a fort, Europe's first military outpost in the New World. The Taino were seen as a source of slave labour as Spain ransacked Hispaniola in a mostly futile search for gold. The Taino villages were burned and their way of life destroyed. Those who were not massacred outright were worked to death, died of starvation, succumbed in massive epidemics to European diseases to which they had no immunity, or were so devastated psychologically that they refused to procreate, or even killed their newborn children. The depopulation was dramatic and total. From a 1492 population currently estimated to be as great as 8 million,[51] the Taino population of Hispaniola declined by 1496 to 3 million and by 1500 to 100,000. According to Spanish census figures, they became extinct over the next few generations, with 22,000 recorded in 1514, 200 in 1542, and none subsequent to that.[52]

The destruction of the Taino of Hispaniola appears to meet all eight of the criteria for genocide specified in Table 3.1 and thus to qualify as genocide under any of the seven definitions discussed in this chapter. The Taino of Hispaniola were destroyed as a cultural group. The acts of destruction were deliberate and included mass killings. The perpetrators were agents of a government and had power over the victims. The destruction was total.

Other considerations, it might be noted, complicate the picture. Columbus did not set out from Spain for the purpose of finding and destroying new cultural groups. The Taino, in addition to being massacred, died from pestilence, enslavement, famine, despair, and moral collapse. It is open to question, moreover, whether the Taino of Hispaniola are best seen as a single culture, a set of related cultures, or a subculture of a larger Taino or Arawak culture.

Questions of this sort, however, can be raised with respect to any genocide. All genocides involve multiple motives, complex interactions of causal factors, and groups that can be divided and defined in multiple ways.[53] Genocidal processes always interact with other sorts of historical processes.[54] A purist definition of genocide requiring unmixed motives, singular causes, and discrete groups would render the concept irrelevant to the actual social worlds of human beings. For a definition of genocide to be applicable to the real world, it must be interpreted in such a manner that it potentially refers to real events.

The destruction of the Taino of Hispaniola, then, qualifies as genocide under any reasonable interpretation of any of the seven definitions considered in this chapter. This genocidal process, in many tragic variations, was to be repeated across the Caribbean and then throughout the Americas for centuries to come. Regardless of definition, the conquest of the New World included a series of genocides that were aimed at, and succeeded in eliminating, hundreds of cultures and nations. The perpetrators had multiple perceptions, motives, and methods, but their intent, and effect, was genocidal.

Nevertheless, definition does matter. In particular, although mass killing and cultural destruction often co-occur, they are not the same. The conquest of the Americas looks different depending on whether one sees genocide as mass killing or cultural destruction.

In the United States, as in most of the Americas, a definition of genocide as mass killing suggests a picture of genocide as a dwindling phenomenon. There have been many mass killings of Indians in what is now the United States, both before and after the attainment of nationhood. Such killings became less frequent and less severe over the course of the 1800s, however, and ended with the genocidal massacre of several hundred Minneconjou at Wounded Knee, South Dakota, in 1890.[55] Treatment of the indigenous people of what is now the United States may continue to be objectionable, but it has not involved mass killings in more than a century and thus is no longer genocide.

A definition of genocide as group destruction, on the other hand, provides a very different picture. The destruction of indigenous groups clearly continued well into the twentieth century and arguably continues in the twenty-first century. The contrast between these definitional alternatives – mass killing and group destruction – is perhaps most clearly seen with respect to the institution of residential schools. One way to eliminate a culture is to remove its children and socialize them into a different culture. When the adults of the targeted culture die off, their way of life dies with them. Even if no one is literally killed, a cultural group is destroyed (recall case *3* above).

Such processes were implemented on a large scale in the United States and Canada from the late-nineteenth century to the mid-twentieth century.[56] Children from dozens of tribes were taken to boarding schools where they lived isolated from their families and communities, often for years at a time.[57] Boys had their long hair cut, often to their great dismay, and all children received clothing suitable for their gender in 'civilized' society. Indian names, usually rich with cultural meanings, were replaced with names deemed more appropriate. Students were expected to learn English not as an additional language but as a replacement for their native tongue, which they were strictly forbidden to speak. As they learned English, they learned the ways and beliefs of the mainstream culture. They learned to be good Christians, good workers, and good citizens of the nation into which they were being assimilated.

Although the schools were physically and psychologically brutal, and many children succumbed to disease or died trying to escape, they were not intended to kill. They were intended to eliminate cultural groups. From the point of view of genocide as mass killing, the residential schools were alternatives to genocide, intended to assimilate native youth. From the point of view of genocide as group destruction, in contrast, this process of cultural assimilation, separating children from their parents and traditions, is precisely a process of genocide.

Genocide as mass killing is perhaps most directly illustrated by pictures of dead bodies massed as far as the eye can see. Genocide as group destruction may be a more subtle concept, but it has pictures of its own. The residential schools, which were genuinely intended to be in the best interests of all concerned, proudly illustrated and publicized their achievements through before-and-after pictures of individual children, intended to show their transformation from Indians to young Americans.[58] The changes in dress and appearance correspond, presumably, to deeper transformations of identity. From the point of view of genocide as mass killing, these pictures show children who have been spared genocide. Instead they have been socialized to function as productive members of the society in which they will live their lives. From the point of view of genocide as group destruction, in contrast, the pictures are chilling images of genocide in its purest form, stripped of mass killing. They show children who have been taken from their parents and transformed with the specific intent that they will no longer be part of the cultural group into which they were born, and that the group in question will thereby cease to exist.

The last Indian boarding schools in the United States and Canada have now been closed for decades. The destruction of native cultures, however, arguably remains a work in progress throughout the Americas. From the point of view of genocide as mass killing, the genocidal conquest of the New World is largely complete, a matter of history. Even the mass killings of Mayans during the dirty war in Guatemala, it might be argued, had less to do with their indigenous status than with their being perceived, rightly or wrongly, as subversive. From the viewpoint of genocide as group destruction, on the other hand, the genocidal destruction of indigenous groups may be seen as an ongoing process that relies less on physical killing than it did in the past but continues to destroy native groups throughout the Americas. This perspective is less reassuring, but for that reason more useful, in that it challenges us to identify and resist genocides in progress.

Genocide as group destruction

Definitions are matters of convention, not empirical propositions, and thus cannot be true or false. A definition can be enlightening, however, if it directs our attention to a set of apparently diverse phenomena that turn out to have important similarities. Alternatively, a definition can be misleading if it encompasses too large or heterogeneous a set of phenomena without making necessary distinctions.

Genocide was originally defined by Lemkin as 'the destruction of a nation or of an ethnic group.'[59] His intent was to alert the world to a crime different from the murder of an individual or even the mass murder of many individuals. Genocide is the elimination of higher-order social entities, of entire ways of life. It is the destruction of groups *as groups*, not as large numbers of individuals. Such destruction, we now know, has been very common in all regions of the world and has persisted across thousands of years of human history.[60] Thus Lemkin's conception of genocide as group destruction has brought, or at least has the potential to bring, an important phenomenon into focus. With regard to the eight potential criteria for genocide listed in Table 3.1, there is good reason to see group destruction as a necessary criterion for genocide.

Human groups are destroyed in many ways, however. Their members may be massacred, starved, enslaved, sterilized, terrorized, or dispersed. They may be denied medical care, access to religious sites, or use of their native language. Their villages, crops, schools, churches, or libraries may be burned. Their political and economic institutions may be dismantled. Their children may be socialized into other cultures. No convincing rationale has been provided for excluding some means of group destruction from the realm of genocide, nor is there any consensus in the literature as to where to draw the line between genocidal and non-genocidal processes of group destruction. This is not surprising, given the accumulating evidence that the means of group destruction are not only diverse but, in most cases, thoroughly intertwined. Thus it seems most useful to classify group destruction as genocide regardless of the means of destruction.[61] This does not prevent us from distinguishing mass killings from other historical phenomena, but it suggests that mass killing should be neither a necessary nor a sufficient criterion for genocide.

Another potential criterion that turns out to be unhelpful or misleading is the type of group destroyed. It might be reasonable, for example, to limit the term *genocide* to 'national, ethnical, racial or religious' groups – the four types named in the Genocide Convention – if such groups could be sharply distinguished from other sorts of groups and were often destroyed in ways unique to these four types of groups. That does not appear to be the case, however. On the contrary, as illustrated above with respect to the allegedly subversive Maya, distinctions among types of groups are often less meaningful than one might expect. Thus the four contemporary definitions appear to be justified in following the original UN Resolution rather than the Genocide Convention in choosing not to limit genocide to the destruction of certain types of groups.

It seems reasonable, then, to define genocide as group destruction without regard to the means of destruction or the type of group destroyed. Moreover, although genocide is usually perpetrated by governmental or quasi-governmental authorities, there is no apparent reason to make this a criterion of genocide. Thus group destruction is genocide regardless of the type of perpetrator, the means of destruction, or the type of group destroyed.

There remain difficult definitional questions with regard to the intent of the perpetrator, the defencelessness of the victim group, the extent of destruction, and the possibility that the victims are a collection of individuals who constitute a group only in the deluded minds of the perpetrators. Efforts to address such considerations are complicated by the fact that we have multiple purposes in defining genocide. Are we aiming to describe historical events? Recognize victims? Punish perpetrators? Understand genocidal behaviour? Prevent future genocides? Different purposes may best be served by definitions differing with respect to some criteria.

In acknowledging diverse conceptualizations of genocide, however, we should not lose sight of the core phenomenon Lemkin brought to our attention: human groups destroy each other. In labeling such destruction *genocide*, Lemkin pressed the world to see group destruction as a phenomenon in its own right, multifaceted in means but with a common end, intertwined with but distinct from other historical processes. Now we have research on many genocides, but we have yet to see genocide whole, as Lemkin saw it. Our need to do so has never been greater.

Notes

1. D. J. Goldhagen, *Hitler's Willing Executioners: Ordinary Germans and the Holocaust* (New York: Knopf, 1996), p. 4.

2. J. Weinberg, 'From the Director', in *The World Must Know: The History of the Holocaust as Told in the United States Holocaust Memorial Museum*, ed. M. Berenbaum (Washington, DC: United States Holocaust Memorial Museum, 1993), p. xiv.
3. S. Solomon, J. Greenberg, and T. Pyszczynski, 'Pride and Prejudice: Fear of Death and Social Behavior', *Current Directions in Psychological Science*, 9 (2000), 200.
4. M. S. Strom and W. S. Parsons, *Facing History and Ourselves: Holocaust and Human Behavior* (Watertown, MA: Intentional Educations, 1982), p. 1.
5. I. W. Charny, 'Toward a Generic Definition of Genocide', in *Genocide: Conceptual and Historical Dimensions*, ed. G. J. Andreopoulos (Philadelphia, PA: University of Pennsylvania Press, 1994), p. 72.
6. F. Chalk and K. Jonassohn, *The History and Sociology of Genocide* (New Haven, CT: Yale University Press, 1990), p. 325.
7. Y. Bauer, 'The Impact of the Holocaust', *Annals of the American Academy of Political and Social Science*, 548 (1996), 14.
8. Y. Bauer, *Rethinking the Holocaust* (New Haven, CT: Yale University Press, 2001), p. 2.
9. M. Mann, 'Were the Perpetrators of Genocide "Ordinary Men" or "Real Nazis"? Results from Fifteen Hundred Biographies', *Holocaust and Genocide Studies*, 14 (2000), 331.
10. Bauer, *Rethinking the Holocaust*, p. 61.
11. S. T. Katz, 'The Uniqueness of the Holocaust: The Historical Dimension', in *Is the Holocaust Unique? Perspectives on Comparative Genocide*, ed. A. S. Rosenbaum (Boulder, CO: Westview Press, 1998), p. 19.
12. Ibid., pp. 19–20.
13. Both Stalin and Mao far outdid Hitler in mass killing. R. J. Rummel, *Death by Government* (New Brunswick, NJ: Transaction, 1994); B. A. Valentino, *Final Solutions: Mass Killing and Genocide in the 20th Century* (Ithaca, NY: Cornell University Press, 2004).
14. A. L. Eckardt and A. R. Eckardt, 'The Holocaust and the Enigma of Uniqueness: A Philosophical Effort at Practical Clarification', *Annals of the American Academy of Political and Social Science, 450* (1980), 166.
15. Ibid., 167.
16. Ibid., 168.
17. Ibid., 167.
18. Ibid., 167.
19. G. Heinsohn, 'What Makes the Holocaust a Uniquely Unique Genocide?', *Journal of Genocide Research*, 2 (2000), 411–30.
20. Ibid., 424–5.
21. Ibid., 421.
22. Bauer, *Rethinking the Holocaust*; Valentino, *Final Solutions*.
23. E. D. Weitz, *A Century of Genocide: Utopias of Race and Nation* (Princeton, NJ: Princeton University Press, 2003); D. Moshman, 'US and Them: Identity and Genocide', *Identity*, 7 (2007), pp. 115–135.
24. Bauer, *Rethinking the Holocaust*.
25. Ibid., pp. 2–3.
26. M. Mamdani, *When Victims Become Killers: Colonialism, Nativism, and the Genocide in Rwanda* (Princeton, NJ: Princeton University Press, 2001); A. Des Forges, *Leave None to Tell the Story: Genocide in Rwanda* (New York: Human Rights Watch, 1999); P. Gourevitch, *We Wish to Inform You that Tomorrow We Will be Killed with Our Families: Stories from Rwanda* (New York: Picador, 1998); D. Moshman, 'Theories of Self and Theories as Selves: Identity in Rwanda', in *Changing Conceptions of Psychological Life*, eds, C. Lightfoot, C. Lalonde, and M. Chandler (Mahwah, NJ: Erlbaum, 2004), pp. 183–206.

27. D. Moshman, 'Conceptual Constraints on Thinking about Genocide', *Journal of Genocide Research*, 3 (2001), 431–50; S. D. Stein, 'Conceptions and Terms: Templates for the Analysis of Holocausts and Genocides', *Journal of Genocide Research*, 7 (2005), 171–203.
28. R. Lemkin, *Axis Rule in Occupied Europe* (Washington, DC: Carnegie Endowment, 1944), p. 79.
29. Ibid.
30. United Nations General Assembly Resolution 96 (I), 'The Crime of Genocide', Fifty-fifth plenary meeting, 11 December 1946.
31. Adopted 9 December 1948.
32. L. Kuper, *Genocide: Its Political Use in the Twentieth Century* (New Haven, CT: Yale University Press, 1982); W. Churchill, *A Little Matter of Genocide: Holocaust and Denial in the Americas, 1492 to the Present* (San Francisco, CA: City Lights Books, 1997).
33. Moshman, 'Conceptual Constraints'.
34. H. Fein, *Genocide: A Sociological Perspective* (London: Sage, 1993), p. 24; see also Fein, 'Genocide, Terror, Life Integrity, and War Crimes: The Case for Discrimination', in *Genocide*, ed. Andreopoulos, pp. 95–107.
35. Chalk and Jonassohn, *History and Sociology of Genocide*, p. 23; K. Jonassohn with K. S. Björnson, *Genocide and Gross Human Rights Violations* (New Brunswick, NJ: Transaction, 1998), p. 10.
36. Charny, 'Toward a Generic Definition', pp. 91–2.
37. Ibid., p. 75.
38. Churchill, *A Little Matter of Genocide.*
39. Ibid., p. 432.
40. Ibid., pp. 434–5.
41. *Deuteronomy*, 2: 12
42. Ibid., 2: 32–4.
43. Ibid., 3: 3–6.
44. M. Danner, *The Massacre at El Mozote* (New York: Random House, 1994); V. Sanford, *Buried Secrets: Truth and Human Rights in Guatemala* (New York: Palgrave Macmillan, 2003); Archdiocese of Guatemala, *Guatemala: Never Again!* (Maryknoll, NY: Orbis, 1999); B. Manz, 'Terror, Grief, and Recovery: Genocidal Trauma in a Mayan Village in Guatemala', in *Annihilating Difference: The Anthropology of Genocide*, ed. A. L. Hinton (Berkeley, CA: University of California Press, 2002), pp. 292–309.
45. I. Guest, *Behind the Disappearances: Argentina's Dirty War Against Human Rights and the United Nations* (Philadelphia, PA: University of Pennsylvania Press, 1990); M. J. Osiel, *Mass Atrocity, Ordinary Evil, and Hannah Arendt: Criminal Consciousness in Argentina's Dirty War* (New Haven, NJ: Yale University Press, 2001); R. Arditti, *Searching for Life: The Grandmothers of the Plaza de Mayo and the Disappeared Children of Argentina* (Berkeley, CA: University of California Press, 1999).
46. Sanford, *Buried Secrets.*
47. Ibid.; Manz, 'Terror, Grief, and Recovery'.
48. Kuper, *Genocide.*
49. D. E. Stannard, *American Holocaust: The Conquest of the New World* (New York: Oxford University Press, 1992); Churchill, *A Little Matter of Genocide*; M. A. McDonnell and A. D. Moses, 'Raphael Lemkin as Historian of Genocide in the Americas', *Journal of Genocide Research*, 7 (2005), 501–29.
50. B. de Las Casas, *The Devastation of the Indies: A Brief Account* (Baltimore, MD: Johns Hopkins University Press, 1992, originally published 1552); I. Rouse, *The Tainos: Rise*

and Decline of the People who Greeted Columbus (New Haven, CT: Yale University Press, 1992); Churchill, *A Little Matter of Genocide*; Stannard, *American Holocaust*; H. Zinn, *A People's History of the United States* (New York: Harper & Row, 1980).

51. Churchill, *A Little Matter of Genocide*; Stannard, *American Holocaust.*
52. Churchill, *A Little Matter of Genocide.*
53. E. Staub, *The Roots of Evil: The Origins of Genocide and Other Group Violence* (Cambridge: Cambridge University Press, 1989); D. Moshman, 'Genocidal Hatred: Now You See It, Now You Don't', in *The Psychology of Hate*, ed. R. J. Sternberg (Washington, DC: American Psychological Association, 2005), pp. 185–209; Moshman, 'Us and Them'.
54. D. E. Stannard, 'Uniqueness as Denial: The Politics of Genocide Scholarship', in *Is the Holocaust Unique?*, ed. Rosenbaum, pp. 163–208; Valentino, *Final Solutions.*
55. R. K. Andrist, *The Long Death: The Last Days of the Plains Indian* (New York: Macmillan, 1993); D. Brown, *Bury My Heart at Wounded Knee: An Indian History of the American West* (New York: Holt, Rinehart, & Winston, 1971); W. S. E. Coleman, *Voices of Wounded Knee* (Lincoln, NE: University of Nebraska Press, 2000).
56. D. W. Adams, *Education for Extinction: American Indians and the Boarding School Experience, 1875–1928* (Lawrence, KA: University Press of Kansas, 1995); W. Churchill, *Kill the Indian, Save the Man: The Genocidal Impact of American Indian Residential Schools* (San Francisco, CA: City Lights Books, 2004); K. T. Lomawaima, *They Called it Prairie Light: The Story of Chilocco Indian School* (Lincoln, NE: University of Nebraska Press, 1994).
57. Tribes included the Apache, Arapaho, Bannock, Cahuilla, Cherokee, Cheyenne, Chickasaw, Choctaw, Comanche, Cree, Creek, Crow, Dakota, Delaware, Havasupai, Hopi, Kiowa, Klamath, Laguna, Lakota, Lower Brule, Maricopa, Menominee, Mohave, Navajo, Nez Percé, Ojibwa, Omaha, Osage, Papago, Pawnee, Pima, Ponca, Potawatomi, Pueblo, Quapaw, Santee Sioux, Serrano, Shawnee, Shoshone, Ute, Walapai, Wichita, Winnebago, Yankton, Yavapai, and Yuma (each named in one or more of works ibid.)
58. Adams, *Education for Extinction,* pp. 104–105; Churchill, *Kill the Indian*, p. 20.
59. Lemkin, *Axis Rule*, p. 79.
60. Chalk and Jonassohn, *History and Sociology of Genocide*; Fein, *Genocide*; Jonassohn with Björnson, *Genocide and Gross Human Rights Violations*; Kuper, *Genocide*; Hinton, ed., *Annihilating Difference*; Rummel, *Death by Government*; Stannard, *American Holocaust*; Churchill, *A Little Matter of Genocide*; Valentino, *Final Solutions*; Weitz, *A Century of Genocide*; Andreopoulos, ed., *Genocide*; McDonnell and Moses, 'Raphael Lemkin as Historian of Genocide in the Americas'.
61. Churchill, *A Little Matter of Genocide*; Moshman, *Conceptual Constraints.*

4

Collective Violence and the Shifting Categories of Communal Riots, Ethnic Cleansing and Genocide[1]

Veena Das

Forms of collective violence such as riots and ethnic cleansing pose an analytical challenge to social science for the political plenitude inherent in categories of collective violence makes it very difficult to separate facts and values. In political theory wars are distinguished from other forms of collective violence on the principle that states, which are recognized collective entities in international law, declare war on each other and are expected to conduct these wars under the rubric of contractual rules. This formulation reflects the privileged position that states apportion to themselves as entities that have control over legitimate violence. In the course of this chapter I will argue that there is a slippage between the various categories that we use to describe collective violence.[2] However, instead of trying to delineate which kind of discrete reality each category corresponds to I suggest we shift our attention to the conditions under which one or the other term comes to signal a state of crisis. I argue that indeterminacy of reference is not incidental to the slippage between different terms such as riots, ethnic cleansing, or even genocide but is a result of the way that assemblages of actors, institutions and discursive forms are actualized. One important corollary of this formulation is that we need to pay close attention to all forms of collective violence and the related practices of the state since these carry the potential of being transformed into ethnic cleansing and into genocide. An alarmist perspective, as Lawrence Langer has argued, is better than 'business as usual' in addressing forms of violence that can acquire lethal forms if not addressed critically and in a timely fashion.[3]

Events of collective violence have grown exponentially since the 1990s, along with new legal categories that have been coined to deal with such violence.[4] It is not the purpose of this chapter to provide a detailed listing of the various kinds of conflicts that have been variously named as low intensity wars, insurgencies, terrorism, genocide, democide, ethnic cleansing or communal riots, though everyone knows that the cost in terms of human lives and suffering from these forms of violence have been momentous. Instead, the chapter takes various historical and contemporary examples of collective violence to argue that even when the discussion on violence follows what appear to be objective criteria, the description always encodes particular subject positions. It is only by careful delineation of the implicit narrative contracts in a text that we can begin to understand what is at stake in the descriptions. In other words, the indeterminacy of reference is part of the very nature of collective violence. Thus it is imperative to pay close attention to the social actors and the practices through which the language of collective violence comes to refer or is placed in the world. Another way of saying this is that the fact/value distinction is hard to maintain in generating descriptions of collective violence, not because violence is against human nature or because it is naturally repugnant but rather because the very acts of naming and describing are part of a moral language. One cannot assume that acts of violence are somehow transparent and independent of these moral languages or that there is a straightforward linear narrative within which we can place acts of violence. Elsewhere, I have formulated this as a problem in which the body of language joins the body of the world.[5] I hope my analysis will show that the historical and ethnic record on forms of collective violence provides not only information about patterns of such violence but also the values that are encoded in the descriptions. In this sense, one needs to see the relation between different categories of collective violence ranging from communal riots to ethnic cleansing and genocide, and to be alive to the possibility of how, what seem less, lethal forms of violence might mutate into more grievous ones. I begin with a consideration of communal riots in South Asia – the region in which most of my own research has been located.

Communal riots and colonial governmentality

Historians of South Asia have debated whether 'communal' riots (referring to publicly enacted violent conflict between Hindus and Muslims) were a part of the historical and social landscape of India from at least the seventeenth century or whether they represented a particular kind of pathology generated by modes of governance instituted by British colonial rule.[6] This debate is not very useful if our concern is to fix historical antiquity. Indeed, conflicts between different kinds of communities, including that between local formations of Hindus and Muslims, find mention in travelers' accounts or court chronicles in the Mughal period prior to British rule. From this fact some scholars make the somewhat unhelpful assumption that communal riots observed today are an expression of these ancient hatreds. For example, sociologist Ghanshyam Shah starts his description of a communal riot in the city of Ahmedabad in 1969 with the following preamble: 'Hindu and Muslim communities have deep rooted prejudices against each other and tension between the two has been persisting in one form or another for several centuries. The extent of tension, however, varies from time to time. Often it is at low ebb and members of both the communities interact in socio-economic or political spheres. ... But occasionally tension reaches a high pitch, turning into mad fury.'[7] Similarly Marc Gaborieu writing in 1985 states that religious communities in South Asia are very exclusive – they coexist rather than co-operate. He then cites the conflict between Hindus and Sikhs in Indian Punjab, between Hindu Tamils and Buddhist Sinhalas in Sri Lanka as examples of this state of affairs and suggests that riots in Bhiwandi, Bombay and Hyderabad during 1984 were 'the latest instances of this recurring conflict'.[8] Analysis offered by Suranjan Das on communal riots in Bengal and Chris Bayly on the prehistory of communalism are more careful in their claims but, nevertheless, they do not quite engage the question of what was new in the social configurations of what came to be called riots in the colonial official documents.[9]

A close attention to the colonial archive shows that the interesting question is not one of origins but of the salience that communal riots acquired in the practices and discourses of government under colonial rule. Colonial governments had a great stake in representations of colonized societies as if they were prone to communal or sectarian violence almost with the force of nature. Gyanendra Pandey refers to the 'communal riot narrative' as a master narrative to indicate that one can detect a template in official documents in the colonial period which comes to be applied to instances of publicly enacted violence in such a manner that the specificity of issues or of different local histories of conflict are deleted in colonial reports.[10] Roma Chatterji and Deepak Mehta argue that comparison with epidemics served to 'naturalize' communal riots.[11] Thus legislative and administrative measures to secure public order and safety mention both communal riots and epidemics within the same framework of explanation and action.

One of the most interesting features of the communal riot narrative, as described by social historians, is that instances of violence in public places come to be termed 'communal' whether the issue was protest over taxes, anti-plague measures or fights between different segments of a community to establish their rights over use of public spaces, as in the right to determine the route of a religious procession. For instance, in her work on Kanpur textile workers in the early twentieth century, Chitra Joshi shows the multiple causes of unrest among mill workers, including the widespread suspicion of new legislative measures to control outbreaks of plague. Yet official descriptions of this unrest assimilated it to the category of communal conflict.[12] Communal conflict came to be perceived as somehow natural to India and the communal riot as the natural expression of this recurring conflict. Indians were seen as incapable of any kind of 'politics' whether of rational accommodation or of enlightened protest on the basis of political alliances. As Pandey says, 'In a colonial reading of history that had become dominant by the end of the nineteenth century, "communalism" was seen as the special mark of the Indian section of the "orient."'[13]

Pandey's careful reconstruction of official documents shows that these were not a record of simple facts. For instance, the account of numbers killed in riots were inflated as accounts moved from lower level documents to higher level ones so that in some cases (for example, the Banaras riots in 1809) numbers got escalated from 'twenty-eight to twenty-nine people killed' in earlier documents to 'hundreds' killed in later ones. Further, the specificity of the issues in any particular local context was lost as riots came to characterize the *general* condition of public order in the country and thus any one riot could be substituted for another. This diagnosis of the situation did not remain confined to official documents but came to characterize later academic writing as well as nationalist accounts of communal violence so that a seamless continuity was posited between one local situation and another as well as between the present and the past.

While the discursive form and their implications for denying that Indians were capable of normal politics are interesting in themselves, what is even more striking is the practices of governmentality that were instituted to control what was now rendered as a particular pathology of Indian society. In the colonial archive, the period from the turn of the century till the 1920s appeared as a period of relative peace. Beginning from 1928, however, there was at least one communal riot reported every year until 1944. In the city of Bombay itself, riots were reported in 1923, 1928, 1929, 1931, 1932, 1934, 1936, 1937, 1938, 1939, 1940, 1941 and 1944. In their remarkable work on collective violence Chatterji and Mehta argue convincingly that the measures taken by the colonial government for dealing with this problem contributed to the idea of communal riots as some kind of 'epidemic'.[14] Every riot in the colonial period produced an array of documents such as Inquiry Committee Reports, daily briefings of the Commissioner of Police as well as Riot Prevention Schemes to show that disputes, whatever their origin, were likely in India to turn into communal riots. For instance, in 1929, violence between Hindu millhands who were on strike in Bombay and Pathan temporary workers hired to replace them was described as a communal riot within the framework of police language. It is only through a careful reading of notes made by various officials and side remarks that one learns that in some cases even murders committed on side lanes were assimilated within the category of deaths during riots.[15] Thus though riots were short-lived and did not escalate into ongoing violence, the ever-present possibility that riots might break out over any issue and take a communal turn gave the government the power to institute surveillance of the city, especially over so-called bad characters or rowdy-sheeters. This was a useful strategy for the government to control all kinds of political dissent.

It is not my argument that tensions between Hindus and Muslims did not prevail or that the colonial discourse on communal riots was conjured though the colonial imagination out of thin air. My point is that we cannot understand the nature of communal riots in this period without paying close attention to governmental practices. This perspective leads us to consider the following points. First, in the colonial imagination, the communal riot served as an index of a particular pathology of Indian society – viz. that it was incapable of politics of association since primordial loyalties were seen as 'natural' to the Indians. Second, riots were expected to be limited in time – like any disease they passed through natural phases and thus had a beginning and an end. However, though a particular riot might end, there was an anticipation of a future occurrence – hence the government had to arm itself with various administrative measures to deal with this recurring problem. Third, following from the above points, riots were seen as primarily a matter of securing public order and peace. Though a particular riot was seen as transitory, the policing practices put in place allowed a continuous surveillance of cities and especially of these who were seen as habitual offenders. Of particular interest is the fact that individuals defined as dangerous (hooligans, rowdy-sheeters) could be turned out of the territories of British India to neighbouring princely States under the amended Police Act of 1902 and later under the amended Foreigners Act so that the anticipation of riots and the imperative to keep public peace allowed all kind of dissent to be dealt with as a problem of policing rather than of politics.[16]

On the side of various Hindu and Muslim communities who were becoming city dwellers, the right to claim public spaces was an important stake in building communities. Jim Masselos analyzed the conflict between different *mohallas* (neighbourhoods) during a riot in 1911 over the routes of processions to be followed by the Muslim residents of the different *mohallas*.[17] The *Police Commissioner's Inquiry Report* on the disturbances in which police had to resort to firing does not mention Hindu–Muslim conflict but rather the rivalries between different *mohallas* in which various castes of Shias and Sunnis lived. The rivalries related to precedence and to the challenges by new caste groups that were now living in the same city spaces as the old well-established Muslim castes or *biradaris*. The point I want to make is that these fights were about claims over *urban spaces* and not over controlling the resources of the state as the term 'ethno-nationalism' used in the later literature to refer to ethic conflicts would imply.[18] It seems, therefore, necessary that we do not assume a complete overlap between the term communal riots as it is applied in the practices of the colonial and post-colonial state. While the imperatives to maintain public order continue and riots continue to be treated as intimately linked with problems of policing, there is also a shift in the values attached to the riot as an expression of political action within the frame of the nation state.

From public order to nation building

There seems a fairly wide consensus among scholars that post-colonial ethnic conflicts can be traced to the colonial legacy of the arbitrary processes of drawing boundaries between States and subsequent failures in nation building.[19] Peter Kloos expresses this clearly for Sri Lanka when he states that 'The Sri Lankan civil war is a fairly typical example of the kind of civil war flowing from the construction of a colonial State and failing nation building after independence.'[20] I shall argue in this section that many of these arguments are based upon a level of aggregation that ignores specific regional histories and thus the routes through which ethnicity and collective identity in general have come to acquire the force that they do today. Even more important, these theories assume that persons were attached to territory in the same way in pre-colonial societies as in the later colonial and national social formations.

Let us take the example of Africa. A major argument explaining the role of ethnic conflict in the independent nation states of Africa runs as follows. The Congress of Berlin held in 1884 carved the region into different parts to be controlled by different European powers. The aim was to regulate the rivalries between the colonists for the control of resources. Though there was no movement of populations involved in this division, it cast a shadow into the future as the later divisions of the continent carved out nation states that reflected a particular nation's relation to a spatially distant European power rather than to its own regional environment.[21]

Scholarly work on the African crisis written within this frame of analysis argues that with the departure of the colonial states in the 1960s, nation states were created by the drawing of artificial borders that broke apart ethnic groups or artificially fused them, thus violating the homogeneity assumed to be natural to these groups. What was specific to the colonial projects of partitioning was that the borders that were created came to be invested with a solidity in legal terms – yet the geopolitical considerations of the Cold War led to very limited sovereignty for the new states. Much of the literature on failed states and the failure of nation-building projects in the post-colonial period attributes this phenomenon to the presence of ethnic conflict in Africa that undermines the unity and integrity of the nation, but this literature seems to bracket any discussion of the geopolitical context in which the newly independent states were embedded. It has been argued, for instance, that the association of particular regions within the nation state with particular ethnic groups – for example, in the case of Nigeria, the Hausa-Fulani with the North, the Yorubas with South West and the Igbos with South East – led to sub-nationalism since these ethnicities got politicized in the process of nation making and democratic mobilization.[22] In the influential volume on ethnic conflict in Africa edited by Harvey Glickman, for instance, threats to the project of nation building in Africa were attributed to the persistence of ethnicity, and the instrumental character it acquired in the struggle for power sharing.[23]

The failing state thesis and its relation to political diversity, however, has a long history in political theory. The influential thesis of Glazer and Moynihan that argued that plural societies are subject to terrible strains of competitive ethnic politics was formulated in the 1970s.[24] This particular formulation is repeated in the recent work of Gross who argues that the possibility of conflict is exacerbated by the size and degree of ethnic cleavage in heterogeneous societies.[25] Clifford Geertz, one of the major contributors of new nation projects in the 1960s, continued to assume throughout his illustrious career that nation-building projects were fraught with the possibility of failure in the new nations because these states could not manage internal conflict.[26] Explanations for this state of affairs ranged from holding that the culture of these nations was incompatible with the project of the nation to positing that institutions of governance in the region were underdeveloped and hence could not assure a smooth transition to modern forms of statehood. What was hardly ever put into question was the legitimacy of the national project itself and even a teleology of human history in which the nation state was simply waiting in the wings to make its appearance in world history.[27]

There are four important criticisms of this position that I would like to consider. These criticisms have not resulted in dissolving the framework of ethnonationalism and nation building as appropriate for understanding ethnic conflict but they have compelled those who took the project of nation building as an unquestioned value to deepen their analyses.

The first criticism of the new nation state thesis I consider is the formulation that the boundaries that the colonial states created were entirely arbitrary. As Achille Mbembe has shown boundaries in Africa had multiple geneses. Several factors such as natural barriers, histories of wars, annexations and exchanges by imperial powers; as well as routes of trade, missionary activities and memories of traditional kingdoms have to be taken into account in understanding the history of boundaries.[28] Thus to argue that an ethnic group's association with a particular territory as a relation stemming from time immemorial, and that the colonial state disrupted this long standing relationship, is to overlook the multiple forms of territory that are folded into the same space.[29]

The second criticism of the framework that places ethnic conflict squarely within the nation-building project is that it takes the self-proclaimed statement of the nation state as a neutral mediator of conflicts as if it were a description of the facts on the ground rather than an expression of value. Just as the representation of communal riots as somehow *natural* to the colonies provided legitimacy to the colonizer's own self-image as providing 'law and order' to a previously unruly society, so the post-colonial state represents itself as a neutral manager of communal and ethnic conflicts. However, empirical studies of communal riots and ethnic conflicts have shown that the state, at best, occupies an ambiguous position vis-à-vis the groups in conflict. Many scholars have been led to question the ethical pronouncements made by the state as if it alone were the entity bestowed with reason while ethnic groups were acting out of passion.[30]

The third criticism of the nation-building thesis in relation to ethnic conflict is that it does not explain the geographic variations in the incidences of communal or ethnic violence. This variation may be observed at several levels ranging from that between states, between different regions within a state and even at the micro-level of different localities within a city. The attention to variation has proved to be very important in questioning the level of generality and aggregation assumed in many studies of ethnic conflict and violence. In the following section I explore how the geography of ethnic violence provides a corrective to general theories of ethno-nationalism.

Finally, theories that rely upon the failed state thesis to explain ethnic violence assume that these conflicts are internal to the nation state. However, considerable research now exists to show that geopolitical considerations have played a major role in escalating violence in many countries. Ranging from the organization of training camps for militants that fuels violent conflict to the supply of arms and money, the international dimension of ethnic conflicts cannot be ignored. The impact of globalization especially in escalating the stakes that diasporic communities have developed in the conflicts of their homelands, the increasing reach of global media in transmitting images of violence across the globe and in some regions the erosion of the sovereignty of the state require that the boundaries of ethnic conflicts are not seen as coterminous with the boundaries of the nation state.[31]

In the following sections, I wish to develop these criticisms through examples of actual conflicts as well as new ways of theorizing these issues that have emerged in the social science literature.

Borders and boundaries

As mentioned earlier, some authors have questioned the general idea that most ethnic conflict in post-colonial societies can be traced to the colonial legacy of drawing arbitrary boundaries. Nugent and Asiwaju, for example, have both argued in different ways that in the case of Africa the colonial powers were more aware of the pre-colonial units than many scholars have assumed.[32] They suggest that colonial formations were sometimes in direct continuity with earlier political alliances. Further, borders in Africa are considered to be exceptionally permeable as networks of trade cut across formal borders and many of the conflicts within a state are directly related to the movements of people and arms across borders.[33] In other regional cases the pre-colonial political formations are mapped on the territory of the nation in other complex ways. For instance, Farhana Ibrahim shows that in the region of the Kutch and Sindh border between India and Pakistan, there is a long history of alliances and circulations between different political entities and one can detect multiple boundaries as a result of these processes. So, for instance, rather than being opposed, the princely state of the Jadejas, a Rajput kingdom and the British colonial authorities cooperated in containing marauding tribes in the large and poorly inhabited areas of the desert that surrounded the kingdom.[34] Ibrahim tracks various kinds of circulations in the region and shows that instead of clearly divided religious and ethnic groups what marked the border regions was a market place of religious ideas and a multiplicity of identities that groups could slip into. Thus while the boundaries between India and Pakistan are clear on maps, in practice even today the memories of different routes continue to guide people into various border crossing practices. The work on close historical detailing of the relation between different kinds of borders, boundaries and frontiers destabilizes what was considered to be a fairly secure thesis on the causes of ethnic conflict in post-colonial societies.

More than the boundaries between states, it might be much more instructive to look at the manner in which space is carved up within the new nation states. The most obvious example of the racial appropriation of resources and redistribution of ethnic groups within poor enclaves is provided by the apartheid regime of South Africa which had the consequence that membership in a race or ethnic group became the basis of claims over resources.[35] Similarly the divisions into provinces or municipalities which might be on the basis of political movements, or administrative convenience in many cases led to crystallization of ethnic identities. The most troubling examples of internal relocations through forced deportation of whole populations are to be found in the Soviet Union in which the category of 'enemies of the state' was used in the 1920s to place 'kulaks' in this category and then to deport them *en masse* to the Far North, Central Asia and Siberia.[36] Amir Weiner argues that in 1936 the rhetoric of enemies of the state was displaced from class to ethnicity and used to identify nationalities that were considered dangerous to the Soviet project.[37] Thus, deportation came to focus on enemy peoples rather than on class enemies. At that time many smaller national units and subunits were eliminated as reactionary. Large nationalities such as Koreans, Chinese, Poles and Germans were removed from the borderlands on grounds of national security in the late 1930s while in 1944 the Soviet army descended on the south and southwest region of Georgia and according to some sources, 300,000 of its mostly Muslim residents were herded into cattle trains and deported to Central Asia.[38]

A related move of population displacement was the securing of the nation as an ethnically homogeneous nation leading to the expulsion of populations from Niger, Ghana and Uganda – to take early and late examples. Mamdani suggests that what we see in these expulsions is the conflict between populations regarded as indigenous and those regarded as settlers.[39] In his formulation the crisis of ethnic conflict and violence is a crisis of citizenship which is racialized, whereas for Mbembe, Mamdani's analysis relies on old legal and political categories which fail to capture the complex interweaving of various forces which have established multiple sovereignties in the region.[40] Ethnic violence for Mbembe cannot be understood through a single dichotomy such as the conflict between indigenous groups or natives versus the settlers but instead has to be mapped on the different processes through which territoriality is being produced as a heterogeneous entity in Africa in which overlapping temporalities are folded.

The 'neutrality' of the state

Let us come to the second criticism of the claims of the state as neutral manager of ethnic conflicts. Some scholars question whether the state can act as a neutral arbitrator in communal conflicts since the ideology of the nation which provides the glue to link state and nation together emphasizes the importance of the culture or language or religion of the majority community within the nation. Arjun Appadurai gives an impressive array of examples in which the fear of minorities is expressed in public debates and becomes part of the popular culture in many countries across the globe.[41] For instance, in India the Hindu right has repeatedly questioned the loyalty of Muslims to India. Despite the constitutional allegiance to secularism, Muslims are asked to publicly perform their loyalty to the nation by the groups propounding the ideology of a cultural nationalism based on Hindu values. Hindus on the other hand are not obliged to demonstrate their loyalty to the nation; it is simply taken for granted. In Sri Lanka, the measures taken by the Sri Lankan Government to establish Sinhala as the national language and Buddhism as state religion in the 1980s served to crystallize the sense of alienation on the part of Tamils.[42] In Pakistan, the suspicion of sects such as the Ahmadis led not only to anti-Ahmadi riots but also to the declaration of Ahmadis as a non-Muslim minority.[43] In the cases of Rwanda and Burundi, the colonial policies of placing the Tutsi minority in elite positions in government and politics is said to have fueled Hutu resentment.[44] The debates over immigration in various European countries and the suspicion under which Muslims have come to be viewed within the post-security scenarios in the USA, all point to the fact that nations, however advanced, tend to see themselves as unfinished projects. While identifying the source of the fear of minorities as inherent in the nation state project is useful as a starting point, it paints the problem with too broad a brush. There are subtle ways in which specific regional histories not only point to differences in the manner in which identities come into being and are sustained – but also in the way that these ideas translate into actual practices of governmentality.

Let us take two examples to demonstrate the importance of specific regional and national histories for understating collective violence. In the case of Pakistan which came into being at the Partition of India in 1947 as a homeland for the Muslims of the subcontinent, the definition of minorities such as the Ahmadis has shifted over a period of time. While the Ahmadis were always seen as a problematic sect by the more orthodox theologians such as Maualana Madoodi, it was only with the birth of Pakistan that the question of defining whether they were Muslim became a matter for the state. The Munir Report (1954) produced by an Inquiry Commission set up to inquire into the anti-Ahmadi riots in the Pakistani Punjab in 1953 submitted its report in 1954. Justice Munir who headed this Commission decided that in order to determine whether Ahmadis were apostates, it was necessary to determine the criteria for establishing who was a Muslim. The Commission invited the prominent *ulama* to give their views on the matter and on the basis of their responses decided that it was impossible to find any agreed criteria to determine who was a Muslim. This was the ground on which it rejected the demand of the *ulama* that Pakistan be declared an Islamic State[45] and that Ahamdis be declared a non-Muslim minority.

Justice Mohamad Munir and Justice Kiyani, the authors of the report had this to say on the issue:

> Keeping in view the several definitions given by the *ulama*, need we make any comment except that no two learned divines are agreed on this fundamental [*sic*]. If we attempt our own definition as each learned divine has done and that definition differs from that given by all others, we unanimously go out of the fold of Islam. And if we adopt the definition given by one of the *ulama*, we remain Muslims according to the view of that *alim* but *kafir* according to the definition of everyone else.[46]

Twenty years after this report was submitted, the Ahmadis were declared to be a non-Muslim minority in Pakistan on the basis of a Supreme Court decision. Naveeda Khan's excellent analysis of this development details how the legal reasoning used for arriving at this decision was not derived from Islamic theology but from copyright laws used in commercial case law.[47] Ahmadis were forbidden to use certain religious insignia or to call their house of worship a *masjid* through an analogy with copyrights over particular names. These practices came to be classified as punishable by prison sentences of up to three years according to the Ordinance XX (1984) of the Pakistan Penal Code. Case law and appeals by prominent Ahmadis continue to challenge the constitutionality of these measures that have also received international attention through the efforts of various human rights and Ahmadi organizations.

My point in drawing attention to this case is that while Appadurai's formulation on the fear of minorities which are seen to be threatening to the formation of modern nation states remains valid, the actual legal and governmental technologies used vary across nations and over time. One must not underestimate the fact that the vision of the nation as culturally homogeneous is contested by many groups within the nation so as to not end up by 'naturalizing' the ways states behave in these matters.

The second case I want to discuss is the violence against Muslims in Gujarat, India, which has been variously characterized as 'riots', 'pogroms' and 'genocidal violence'.[48] At stake here is the question of what it means for such communal or ethnic violence to be effectively sanctioned by the state. I argue that the idea of a cultural nationalism based upon notions of Hindutva or a cultural Hinduism not only has an impact upon distribution of resources since the majority community comes to be seen and sees itself as having natural links with the nation whereas the minorities are asked to prove their loyalty; it directly affects the way that street level functionaries such as policemen behave towards members of the minority community in everyday situations as well as in extreme circumstances. Often the composition of the police force is skewed in favour of the majority community.

Many empirical studies provide evidence that street level bureaucrats such as policemen fail to act as neutral keepers of peace. In closely studied communal riots in India, for instance, it has been shown that decisions to impose curfew in violent areas often take into account the strategic moment when considerable harm has already been done to the minority community in any riot. Further, police firing during riots disproportionately targets members of the minority communities. Thus more Muslims than Hindus have died in communal riots in India from police firing.[49] Second, in many cases it is not only the lower level policemen, but the higher functionaries of the government who have been shown to be actively involved in instances of communal violence – often to use these occasions to teach members of the minority community a 'lesson' for a previous act of violence. In the case of the anti-Sikh violence in 1984 in North India which followed the assassination of the then Prime Minister Indira Gandhi at the hands of her Sikh body guards, survivor accounts clearly pointed to the active encouragement to crowds by both police officers and certain members of the Congress Party.[50] Similarly in the case of the lethal violence against Muslims in Gujarat in 2002, scholars and civil rights groups have demonstrated the active compliance of important political figures including the Chief Minister who along with many other leaders of the Hindu right attributed the violence to the natural anger of people against Muslims because of an earlier and controversial incident of a fire in a train in which right-wing Hindus activists were travelling. Thus the neutrality of the state has been put into question on grounds of the very ideology of the nation state within which minorities are seen as threats to the imagined purity of the nation and also by demonstrating how such an ideology translates into actual practices of policing.

Let me return to the Gujarat case in order to see how the local practices of policing are influenced by the extra legal considerations. After all, the Narendra Modi government that was in power in Gujarat in 2002, however great their allegiance to the ideology of Hindutva, could not use any mechanism of the court to hold Muslims as a whole responsible for the previous so-called trigger event, in which a train carrying Hindu *kar sevaks* was burnt when it made an unscheduled stop at a small town (Godhra).[51] Opinions vary as to how the train caught fire but explanations have ranged from enraged local Muslims setting the train on fire in response to offensive slogans being shouted by the Hindus in the train to the explanation that the fire was accidental. So what practices on the ground were initiated on behalf of the Modi government which show that the state did not act as a neutral actor in this conflict? Some of the best evidence in this case is provided by bureaucrats who refused to comply with the demands of the politicians and other senior officials for partisan implementation of the law or downright illegal violence against Muslims under the guise of preserving public order.

A remarkable analysis of the work of one such bureaucrat is offered by Shiv Visvanathan on the basis of four affidavits that the official, Sreekumar, who was the Head of the Intelligence Unit in the state government of Gujarat, filed before the Nanavati Commission of Inquiry into the Gujarat riots of 2002.[52] Visvanathan believes that the affidavits provided by Sreekumar stand as testimony to the fact that the police was prevented from acting in a way to control the violence. Sreekumar was asked by senior officials and by the Chief Minister at several points of time to take action that he (Sreekumar) considered unconstitutional and against the law. What was most interesting in the Sreekumar case was that he decided to keep a diary of the daily orders he received and the actions he took during the riots. Notings from these diaries were made available to the Nanavati Commission that was set up to conduct an inquiry into the causes of the riots and to fix responsibility. I produce one extract below from Visvanathan's account to show how the state works in violation of its own laws.

> On 30th April, the DGP [Director General of Police] informed him [Sreekumar] that CM [Chief Minister] had instructed him to book Congress leaders for their alleged involvement in instigating Muslims to boycott the ongoing examination and that he had told the CM that action could only be taken on the basis of specific complaints. On 1 May in a person to person

> meeting, the DGP informed Sreekumar that the Chief Secretary was being persuaded to 'eliminate' Muslim extremists disturbing communal peace in Ahmedabad. Sreekumar replied that this would be premeditated murder and the DGP agreed.

It is worth reflecting on the implications of the diary entries made by Sreekumar, for his experience was not unique. Unlike the formal legal technologies through which the Ahmadi sect was declared to be a non-Muslim minority in Pakistan the Muslims in India have full legal rights to citizenship, including the right to follow their religion. The state cannot initiate an open policy of discrimination, yet the manner in which administrative measures are implemented allow the state to act in violation of its own laws. Thus while the official representation of riots continues to draw from the colonial vocabulary of crowds maddened by passions of all kinds going out of control, in fact, the state actively connives in 'punishing' minorities by allowing crowds to engage in killing and looting.

It is not that the state has its own way without any resistance. The very fact that Sreekumar was repeatedly able to point to the illegality of the actions that were being proposed by the Chief Minister and the Chief Secretary and to refuse to comply with orders that were disguised as suggestions, should alert us to the difference between the covert subversion of the law at the administrative level and the situation in which the law itself embodies the ideology of ethnic or racial cleansing at the level of legal rules. There are, of course, several tactics that parties in power use to secure compliance from civil servants, including police officers, such as large scale transfers of police officials who refuse to follow illegal orders. These measures reveal a continuity between everyday practices of corruption in the nexus between politicians and civil servants and the open flouting of law during communal riots. The negotiation between legality and illegality is an important feature of the state in everyday life but it becomes most visible during communal or ethnic riots. I am hesitant to simply classify this as the sovereign right to declare a state of exception since we have seen that officials such as Sreekumar, in their refusal to obey orders show that the law is not fully suspended.

The geography of violence

Even if we assume that ethnic conflicts are related primarily to the failure of nation building in post-colonial states, how do we account for the variations in space and time in the prevalence and course of such conflicts? I consider three different formulations of this issue. The first theory frames the answers within a modified rational action theory and argues that conflicts between ethnic groups and the state are primarily conflicts over territory mediated by the settlement patterns historically inherited within a given state. However, there is an important caveat to this theory which is that territory is defined not as a material resource but as endowed with symbolic value for the ethnic group which makes it non-negotiable. The second theory explains variation in ethnic group conflicts in terms of the strength of civil society and cross-ethnic or cross-religious networks in building an associational politics. The third theory does not deal with presence or absence of ethnic conflict but instead asks why do some conflicts spread from one place to another while others have a short life time and remain confined to the local society in which they emerged?

Many political scientists have used existing data sets, such as the Minorities at Risk data set, to argue that a significant correlation exists between settlement patterns and the likelihood of tensions between an ethnic group and a state turning into violent conflict. In a magisterial study using both statistical data sets and case studies from the Soviet Union during and after its break up, Monica Toft renders the relation between ethnic violence and settlement patterns in the following terms: 'First, a group's concentration in a region of a state serves as practically a necessary condition for violence, whereas urbanism and dispersion are practically sufficient conditions for nonviolent political activity ... Second, the richness of resources in a region is negatively associated with violence.'[53] Toft goes on to argue that the first finding provides rigorous proof to what many scholars intuitively believe to be true. The second, however, is counter-intuitive since states and ethnic groups do not simply fight over resource rich regions but also over regions that might be poor in material terms but might have great symbolic significance. For the state, the refusal to grant sovereignty to an ethnic group fighting over territory is related to the fear of a domino effect; for the ethnic groups, Toft argues, the issue is that of fighting over the territory as homeland associated with the survival of the group as a group. This great symbolic value that the group attaches to territory, she argues, makes it non-negotiable.

While such exercises are interesting in generating pictures of conflict between state and ethnic groups in macro terms, they rest upon certain assumptions that need to be interrogated. First of all, the concentration of an ethnic group in one region as a taken-for-granted fact in this theory renders the relation between ethnic groups and territory in static terms. It neglects the processes through which such relationships come to be established. It also ignores the fact that in pre-colonial polities people owed multiple allegiances to different kinds of territories and thus territory had much more of an itinerant character than it developed under colonialism and in modern polities.[54] Where nation states have emerged as a result of colonial processes of boundary making, the conflict between the ethnic groups and the state may result from the fact that groups that had developed traditional patterns of movement over a territory that cuts across the newly created boundaries between two states are now restricted to the boundaries of a nation state to which they might not owe allegiance. This was the case, for example, of tribal groups such as the Nagas in the northeast of India whose traditional territory spread between India and Burma (now Myanmar) and who, after independence, were divided between these newly created nation states.[55] It was, however, not simply a matter of symbolic significance of territory but the repressive police and military practices that exacerbated the conflict between the Nagas and the Indian state for more than five decades. Second, some ethnic groups have come to be concentrated into a territory by previously experienced violence such as religious minorities fleeing persecution who receive sanctuary in a different state, for example, the concentration of Huguenots in Germany or Sweden. In still other cases, the particular connection between land and ethnicity is result of state-propagated ideologies. It is not an expression of primordial loyalties and sentiments. A very good example is the attempt by the Hindutva parties in India to propagate the ideology that India belongs to Hindus alone.[56] The fact that these parties have needed to use all kinds of means, including violence against Muslims, to make such sentiments stick shows that the link between territory and ethnic or religious group is not some kind of primordial given.[57] Such processes of social engineering appear only retrospectively to reflect the 'natural' attachment of an ethnic group to a territory as in the examples cited by Toft in support of her argument.

I hope the above discussion establishes the danger of explanations that resort to the taken-for-granted relation between territory and ethnicity that naturalizes the connection. Such explanations are flawed because they obscure the processes through which such 'natural' attachments are sought to be created. When translated into policy, such conceptions of ethnicity lead to a totalization of group identities eclipsing serious intra-group differences in the process. Most significantly, the role of violence in forcibly making the individual feel that he or she belongs to an ethnic or sectarian identity rather than to more diverse or diffused identities must be taken into account. Instead of thinking of violence as the act committed by previously fully constituted groups, one needs to think of violence as producing the particular form that such identifies take by solidifying them. There are many examples and testimonies of this process but the sense of disappointment and a loss of faith in values of secularism (in the case of religious conflict) or in the nation (in the face of separatist demands) produced by violence is reflected in this poignant example of a moving lament by the journalist Saeed Naqvi after the terrible Gujarat carnage against Muslims:

> Oh, how I used to show off the fact of my being an Indian Muslim. Statesmen, politicians, journalists, diplomats of every conceivable country (particularly from Pakistan) were constantly subjected to my original

> mantra: Indian secularism protects, among a billion others, the world's second largest Muslim population and every issue, including Kashmir, must be addressed keeping this fact in mind. ... Just look what you have gone and done. In Gujarat you robbed me of my mantra. How will I cope with all those people I once confronted with rare self-assurance when they now fix me in a questioning, pitying gaze?[58]

To think of violence as carrying the potential of recreating identities by making them more solid and less porous, allows us to question the *givenness* of ethnic groups as collective actors simply because they have proper names.[59] Instead of looking primarily at *fully realized acts* in the course of which one entity such as an ethnic group engages in violence against another such as the state or another ethnic group – each of which is assumed to be fully formed – we are encouraged to look at how the juxtaposition of the actual and the virtual in the case of violence itself shapes agents.[60] Glenn Bowman argues for this position theoretically by suggesting that 'intransitive violence' might be thought of as a force which operates prior to being manifested itself in action and thus, 'serves to create the integrities and identities which are in turn subjected to those forms of violence which seeks victims'. 'Violence', he says, 'rather than being a performance in the course of which one integral entity (person, community, state) violates the integrity of another – may as well serve to generate integral identities by inscribing borders between something in the course of becoming an entity and its surroundings'.[61]

It is not my argument that theories of ethnic conflict that try to explain the conditions of possibility under which 'ethno-nationalism' flourishes and becomes a potent source of conflict with the state have nothing to offer. What I am trying to argue, instead, is that when we base our explanations of why ethnic groups fight for territory on the grounds that ethnic groups, unlike states, have a sentimental attachment to territory since the latter is treated as essential to the identity of the group, we short-circuit the process through which such sentiments are, in fact, mobilized. Toft, for example, summarizes the differences in the manner in which states and ethnic groups are attached to territory in the following words: 'Thus, the state's focus on physical survival often overrides subjective or sentimental attachments to land. The perspective contrasts with that of ethnic groups who view territory as intricately bound with their identity and, ultimately, their survival as a group.'[62] The examples offered by Toft of orthodox Jews who, as she sees it, put their physical safety at risk in 'order to save Jews from a fate worse than death', or Serbs, who even under the threat of destruction from NATO refused to consider Kosovo as lost are problematic precisely because the place of memories of violence, not to speak of global actors, in creating such sentiments is left unexamined.

The second theory that is on offer to explain the variation in the incidence of ethnic and sectarian violence looks for explanations, not in some abiding sentiment in defining identity but rather at the strength of associational life, especially that which cuts across ethnic or sectarian ties. As compared to the first kind of explanation of ethnic conflict that looked at ethnic group versus state, this theory is primarily interested in explaining the spatial variation in the incidence of violence between two groups such as Hindus and Muslims. Ashutosh Varshney, who proposed this formulation, used existing data sets and supplemented these with carefully compiled records of Hindu–Muslim violence from newspaper reports in the post-independence period.[63] It is interesting to note that while Toft argues that urban dispersion is a very strong indicator of the *absence* of conflicts between states and ethnic groups since urban groups do not have an attachment to land, an opposite relationship holds in the case of communal riots in India. Thus Varshney and several other scholars have argued that villages constitute a remarkably small portion of communal rioting in India. Between 1950 and 1995, only 3.6 per cent of deaths in communal riots occurred in villages. Hindu–Muslim riots thus seem to be primarily urban phenomena. However, even in cities there are considerable variations in the frequency of riots. Varshney examines three sets of cities juxtaposing one peaceful city with one riot prone one in each set. The proportion of Muslims resident in the cities in all cases is roughly similar. The variations in the incidence of communal violence are remarkable. Calicut [now Kozhikode] in Malabar, Kerala, for instance, has not witnessed a single communal riot in the last hundred years while Aligarh in Uttar Pradesh is a site of frequent riots. Varshney is not arguing that Hindus and Muslims live harmoniously in these peaceful cities but he is interested in asking why sectarian or religious conflict does not get transformed into violence. His explanation is that there are networks of various kinds among the trader associations in Calicut which foster ongoing relationships between Muslims and Hindus. In Aligarh, he argues, there is a dearth of such associations making ties between Hindus and Muslims extremely fragile. This explanation has merit to the extent that it does not treat the ethnic or sectarian categories as if they were destined to produce violence against each other. His question as to why ethnic conflict or antagonism is contained in some places while in others it is transformed into violence would remain even if one found the explanation somewhat overdetermined as some critics have claimed.

Varshney's work has been appreciated for the careful compiling of macrolevel data and his attention to civil society. However, there is a curious neglect of the role of the state and especially of the role of policing in escalating the level of violence in the riots in his work. Second, there is no attempt to link issues at the local level with changes in national politics and especially with the role of the Hindu right in recent years (especially in the Gujarat riots) in mobilizing hatred against Muslims. But even if we took all these factors into account, the puzzle would remain as to why the police in some cities is less partisan than in others.[64] Finally, there is the question of temporality. As I suggested earlier, violence is not simply the expression of conflict or hostility between two groups – it can, in fact, *produce* the boundaries between groups. Thus what Varshney takes to be the cause of violence – viz., the absence of associational forms that cut across religious identities – might well be the result of violence. Chatterji and Mehta's work cited earlier, clearly shows that a series of events – the demolition of the Babri mosque, bomb attacks in Dharavi in Bombay, followed by riots in the city – led to an estrangement not only among neighbours and people tied in various kinds of economic relations but also among the members of community-based organizations who had worked on social issues affecting the neighbourhood prior to the riots. The authors also show, however, that it is the possibility of re-engaging in neighbourhood associations such as NGOs and other community-based organizations to work for such causes as housing rights that re-established social exchange, however shot with ambivalence this resumption proved to be.

The third question that I posed with regard to variation is about duration and intensity. Why do some acts of ethnic and sectarian violence get contained within the local context in which they arise and others gain momentum and spread to other places? Paul Brass's classic study of incidences of communal violence that range from the theft of an idol to the alleged rape of a woman addresses this issue with the help of carefully crafted empirical examples.[65] Brass opines that when local acts of violence are pushed into larger political contexts by political actors who might have had nothing to do with the original conflict but who can now manipulate it for their own ends, these local acts acquire national salience. As he says, local conflicts provide a fertile ground for 'meddling' by regional politicians and media. Thus some conflicts get resolved within the local worlds in which they arise while others can become magnified involving new networks of actors and interests. Brass's case studies are by necessity constructed long after the event, so he has to rely upon *post factum* construction through interviews, but the cases provide fascinating insights into these processes. He is perceptive in the weight he places on uncertainty about the origins and spread of violence and the role played by rumour.[66] Arguing that it is not truth *per se* that is at stake but the 'storyness of truth', he shows how different versions of a story come to be believed among different social groups. All this sounds like a postmodern dismantling of metanarratives of ethnic violence, but questions of narrative and truth telling are oversimplified in this text as are questions of time and of memory. Any communal riot produces conflicting versions of the truth but for Brass, the story one comes to believe in is determined completely by one's collective identity. So, for instance, in a conflict involving inter-caste rivalry between backward castes (Lodhas in this case) and upper caste Brahmins or communal conflict over a stolen idol, people place credence only in the versions circulating in their own groups which ignores the fact that stories do not map onto social morphology in such neat ways.[67] Brass fails to realize that his method of eliciting a version from informants much after the event gives these accounts far more coherence than is ever found during a riot. My own work on the role of panic rumours shows that there are considerable conflicts over interpretation even in a single community. The circulation of panic rumours and the fact that people are singled out for killing on the basis of an ascribed identity do lead to a considerable hardening of stories along communal lines, but during every riot there are people who provide protection to those from other communities, and also those who mobilize for reducing the level of the violence or brining it to an end.[68] It is also somewhat curious that while Brass is willing to read ambiguity in the accounts of violence in some contexts he is completely certain about facts in other contexts. For instance, the role of local politicians, the police and other state actors, who, he claims, form a riot machine, does not receive the same methodological treatment nor does this formulation allow space for those like Sreekumar mentioned earlier, who do not become a part of the machine.[69]

Ethnic cleansing: a new form of violence?

The term ethnic cleansing emerged in the international arena in the summer of 1992 during the first stages of the war in Bosnia during the tragic events of the dissolution of Yugoslavia and the establishment of new nations.[70] The Serbs, the ethnic group from which perpetrators were largely drawn in this case had themselves used the term to refer to the violence done to other Serbs in Kosovo by Kosovar Albanians in the early 1980s.[71] Although the composite term 'ethnic cleansing' came to be used extensively only in the 1990s, the idea of cleansing to refer to the removal of a group that was considered alien from the body politic was used in the rhetoric of racial hygiene by prominent Nazi leaders.[72] As a military tactic the idea of cleaning a territory by killing the local inhabitants and making it safe for military occupation was known and used extensively in Latin America with reference to undesirable groups such as prostitutes, enemy collaborators and the vagrant poor.[73]

While there are some continuities in the kinds of ethnic conflicts we have been discussing earlier and the operations against minorities that have been characterized as ethnic cleansing since the ideology of the nation state requires purification of all elements defined as 'alien', there are also significant differences. Three of these differences are worth considering. First, there is an intimate relation between war and ethnic cleansing. All the recent instances of ethnic cleansing happened in the shadow of war. Norman Naimark considers several cases in twentieth-century Europe – from the Nazi atrocities against Jews to the ethnic cleansing operations against Bosnian Muslims – and argues that war provided a cover for atrocities since war habituated people to brutalities and mechanisms of censorship silenced any dissenting voices. Second, the ideology of ethnic cleansing espouses a totalistic vision – very few exceptions are tolerated since the goal is to kill every person of the defined minority. A corollary of this is that women become targets of systematic sexual and reproductive violence since they are seen as the biological and cultural repositories of the nation. Third, ethnic cleansing has generated new legal mechanisms involving juridical concepts and transnational institutions to deal with the consequences. It is not that legal issues were absent in the case of the kinds of communal riots and ethnic violence discussed earlier but that they occupied a different region of the law since violence was treated as a problem of policing rather than that of war crimes or crimes against humanity.

War and ethnic cleansing

The cases of ethnic cleansing in Europe that Naimark discusses in his masterly compilation of cases all happened in the shadow of war. In fact the term 'cleansing' is itself derived from military tactics as I noted earlier. The projects of eliminating a minority can be more easily accomplished in the shadow of war as in the cases of atrocities committed against Jewish populations and later against Bosnian Muslims, since civil law is suspended and military exigency is often evoked to impose censorship. Naimark cites the cases of Greek expulsion as a direct result of the Greco-Turkish war, the intensification of ethnic cleansing when NATO bombing started in March 1999 in Kosovo, and the brutal dealings with the Chechen–Ingush and Crimean Tartar by Stalin during the Second World War. While regular armies play an important role in campaigns of pacification that were often a euphemism for ethnic cleansing, perhaps the most important factor was the emergence of paramilitary units that were used by political leaders to eliminate minorities that were seen as a danger to military success.[74] The Latin American and Mexican cases are particularly illuminating in this regard for the experiences of violence in these regions is not usually included in discussions of ethnic violence – yet the mechanisms through which violence against groups described as undesirable are remarkably similar.[75]

I want to emphasize that while the term ethnic cleansing is relatively new, it not only bears a discursive relation to other terms such as communal violence but more importantly to practices that are not entirely new. Many modern scholars of ethnic cleansing emphasize the events within Europe but place relatively less importance on the experience of violence that was gained in the colonies. Mahmood Mamdani makes a strong case for considering these connections.[76] He argues that the techniques of annihilation that were later applied with such absolute brutality in the Holocaust had some precedent in the way that

Germans 'managed' any signs of rebellion against their colonial rule in Africa.[77] Mamadani calls the killing of the Herero people in 1904 in Southwest Africa the first genocide of the twentieth century. This territory that was later to become Namibia was the home of the Herero who had taken up arms in the early twentieth century to defend their land and cattle against the German settlers. The General (Lothar von Trotha) who was designated by Kaiser Wilhelm II to quell the rebellion believed that the nation of the Herero should be eliminated. Mamdani cites the following quote from the General:

> ... the views of the Governor and also a few old Africa hands on the one hand, and my views on the other, differ completely. The first wanted to negotiate for some time already and regard the Herero nation as necessary labour material for the future development of the country. I believe that the nation as such should be annihilated, or, if this was not possible by tactical measures, they have to be expelled from the country by operative means and further detailed treatment. This will be possible if the water-holes ... are occupied. The constant movement of our troops will enable us to find the small groups of the nation who have moved back westwards and destroy them gradually. ... My intimate knowledge of many central African tribes (Bantu and others) has everywhere convinced me of the necessity that the Negro does not respect treaties but only brute force.[78]

Certainly the techniques of deportation, long marches in which the deportees were likely to die of hunger and disease as well as detention in camps to use the subordinated people as mere bodies for extraction of labour were part of the way that colonial powers ruled so that in terms of sheer numbers as well as techniques of brutal elimination of targeted populations the fate of European minorities was not unrelated to the fate of colonial subjects earlier. The question of how appropriate it is to think of the colonial scenario as ethnic cleansing or genocide when the terms did not have legal or administrative weight is important, but I am proposing that one might look for a genealogical rather than a lineal relation between ethnic cleansing or genocide and other forms of collective violence such as riots or violence targeted against groups defined as undesirable because of their class rather than ethnicity. In other words while ethnic cleansing or genocide are not direct descendants of colonial wars; nor can the legal mechanisms to deal with them be traced in a straight line to earlier practices of colonial governments to deal with riots or rebellions by colonial subjects, there is a shifting pattern of convergence and dispersal of contingent elements across these various formations that can be fruitfully brought to light by the use of a genealogical method.

While the association of war and ethnic cleansing is important in the European cases, in the colonies it was the process of independence and the partitioning of the country that was associated with large-scale ethnic or religious violence. Partitioning was always a solution imposed by the departing colonial power on the territory it previously ruled as in the cases of India and Pakistan or Rwanda and Burundi. In some cases the issue of division was left to an outside agency, as in the case of the division of Palestine and the creation of Israel when responsibility for the actual division of the country was passed on to the UN.[79] In the case of the breakdown of the Soviet Union some commentators have noted that the only communist states that broke part were those characterized by ethno-federal institutions.[80] Whatever the differences it is obvious that making a territory coterminous with one group can never be accomplished by peaceful means. Thus the very imagination of a space as the exclusive container of one type of group generates the need for population transfer which can merge into ethnic cleansing despite the talk of peaceful transfer of population.[81]

Finally, it is important to consider the changing nature of warfare today. Most contemporary wars depart from the classical model in that they increasingly involve civilian populations, child soldiers and paramilitary organizations so that the distinction between soldiers and civilians has become very porous. Thus it is increasingly becoming difficult to separate war from other forms of collective violence within the fabric of the social. The relation of war to underground shadow economies of arms and drugs makes it imperative to think of these forms of violence as related and to think of analytical tools that emphasize emergent forms of violence that cannot be neatly categorized into existing categories.

Annihilating the other

An important aspect of ethnic cleansing, as Naimark contends, is its totalistic character. Naimark attributes this to the ideology of the nation combined with the technology of the modern state.[82] The Nazi regime's attempts to annihilate the Jews treated them as a unified category regardless of their nationality, class or any other attribute. The technology of the state was combined with theories of racial hygiene to reduce the Jews to the status of vermin who were polluting the body politic. As Naimark puts it:

> The goal is to remove every member of the targeted nation; very few exceptions to ethnic cleansing are allowed. In premodern cases of assaults of one people on another, those attacked could give up, change sides, convert, pay tribute, or join the attackers. Ethnic cleansing, driven by the ideology of integral nationalism and military and technological power of the modern state, rarely forgives, makes exceptions, or allows people to slip through the cracks.[83]

The central idea of Naimark and several others who have tried to distinguish between ethnic cleansing and other kinds of pre-modern ethnic or religious conflicts that took a heavy toll on populations is that in the modern era the killings are organized, using the particular nexus between knowledge and power that characterizes the modern state.[84] This is relevant in two ways. First, technologies of information are used in organizing collective violence against a targeted group even when the state seems not to be directly involved Thus voters lists have been used in communal violence in India; in the case of Rwanda, there is evidence that death lists were being drawn up by the Hutu power militias using similar voting lists. The extreme case of administrative, efficient organization of killing, however, remains that of the Nazi camps. Second, the modern state's imperatives to fix identities have led to a crystallization of identities. For instance, Belgian administrative measures in 1933 to fix Hutu, Tutsi and Twa identities by tracing these only through the male line and fixing one identity on one person contradicted the complex ways in which social identities were constructed over time and could draw upon multiple sources in earlier times.[85] However, one needs to track the lines of actualization by which such potentialities are transformed into ethnic cleansing, for nation states are not inevitably fated to produce ethnic violence. This is why social science research needs to take specific historical conditions as well political choices that are explicitly made to account for the way ethnic violence comes to be executed.

Feminist scholars considering ethnic violence and genocide have suggested that the fundamental idea underlying both these forms of collective violence is that of social death.[86] Centering on social death, they argue, allows us to recognize that genocidal acts or acts of ethnic cleansing are not always homicidal. Thus, forced sterilization of women or men from a targeted group, forcibly separating women from their children for reeducation, as happened to children in indigenous groups in Australia, or even forcibly assimilating them into another group as has been alleged for Chinese policies, with regard to Tibet, could all be considered as forms of social death and hence forms of genocide or ethnic cleansing. This would explain why policies of ethnic cleansing or genocide specifically target women and direct both sexual and reproductive violence towards them, for women are seen as the cultural and biological repositories of ethnic or religious groups.[87] However, in this, as in other cases, context is imperative for defining the meaning of such actions. Though sexual and reproductive violence is associated with most if not all forms of collective violence there are differences of underlying perspective. In some cases, reproductive violence is part of an ideology of eugenics translated as, say, racial or religious 'improvement' of the targeted populations. In other cases, sexual violence becomes part of the disorder when the social contract is completely loosened or abandoned; and thus, other views of what it is for men to be within an imaginary that is akin to a state of disordered nature come to the fore. Thus, for instance, sexual or reproductive violence against Bosnian Muslim women was framed by a discourse of revenge and humiliation related to some kind of 'Serbization' of the Muslim population. Many feminist scholars have spoken of the 'rape regime' in which Bosnian women were forcibly interned in camps and made to carry their pregnancies to term. Beverley Allen has argued that mass rape of Muslim women took place primarily for the purpose of impregnating Muslim women who the Serbs felt were originally Serbs who had been forcibly converted to Islam. Their babies would be salvable for the Serb nation.[88] Similarly Pakistani soldiers who raped women during the war of liberation in Bangladesh in 1972 participated in a discourse of the effeminate Islam in Bangladesh which needed to be invested with more muscular and purer Islam.[89] Although wide-spread sexual violence occurred during the Partition of India in 1947, the discourse of reproductive violence was not in circulation. Rather, the emphasis on the part of both India and Pakistan was to 'recover' women who had been abducted and to restore them to their families as almost a condition for both the social contract and the sexual contract to be in place for the new nation sates to be inaugurated.[90]

While I think the differences in the social and cultural imaginaries behind the two situations I describe cannot be completely mapped on to each other, the common thread is the imagination of the state as a masculine state and the sexualization of the social contract.[91] Both in theoretical and empirical terms this directs us towards considering the connections between the manner in which the sexualization of the social contract occurs in everyday life at the level of banal nationalism (for example) and its refiguration into mass rape in times of war, genocide and ethnic cleansing.

Ethnic cleansing and genocide: the other life of legal concepts

It is now well known that the term 'ethnic cleansing' entered the scholarly and popular media in 1992 during the first stage of the war in Bosnia to refer to the practices of mass killing, torture, rape and forcible confinement into labour camps. As we noted earlier, the idea of cleansing has often been deployed in the context of military tactics to make a region safe for military operations by forcible removing or killing civilians defined as dangerous for an occupying force. However, in the 1990s the term was first popularized in the international media and only later acquired judicial meaning as a category distinct from genocide through the proceedings of the war crimes court in The Hague.

The essential judicial distinction between ethnic cleansing and genocide is seen by many scholars to lie in the question of intentionality. Naimark puts across this point in the following quotation:

> A new term was needed because ethnic cleansing and genocide are two different activities and the differences between them are important. As in the case of determining first-degree murder, intentionality is the critical

> distinction. Genocide is the intentional killing off of part or all of an ethnic, religious, or national group; the murder of a people or peoples ... is the objective. The intention of ethnic cleansing is to remove a people and often all traces of them from a concrete territory.[92]

Other scholars who disagree with this distinction argue that, first, ethnic cleansing is a perpetrator's term while genocide privileges the perspective of the victims and survivors.[93] Second, they argue that though Raphael Lemkin who proposed the term genocide in his writings during World War II was speaking primarily of Nazi Germany, the United Nations Convention on the Prevention and Punishment of the crime of Genocide of 9 December 1948 used the idea of genocide as a general category which provided the framework within which all crimes of mass atrocities should be addressed. Martin Shaw, for example, proposes that a sociological rather than a strictly legal definition of genocide would be much more effective in preventing mass atrocities.

Recent events have made abundantly clear that despite new juridical developments in the field of international law, intentionality remains one of the most difficult things to prove even in genocide when strict legal standards are applied.[94] While individuals have been tired and convicted for the crime of genocide, states cannot easily be shown to have intentionality as in the recent decision of The Hague court when Bosnia failed to get damages against Serbia in a civil suit. In the case of mass atrocities such as ethnic cleansing, apartheid and other kinds of crimes against humanity, even when the evidence is overwhelming, either the scale is so large that only a few people responsible for the crimes can be actually convicted, or the emphasis shifts to reconciliation rather than punishment. For instance, in the case of Rwanda where 120,000 persons are awaiting trial for crimes committed during the mass killings of Tutsis, the legal system is simply not able to cope with crimes of this magnitude and sometimes local communities cultivate forgetfulness as a way of learning to live together again.[95] In other cases, as in South Africa, the imperatives of creating a new polity shifted the emphasis on reconciliation and public telling of 'truth' rather than punishment of the perpetrators of the hateful apartheid regime. While it is true that some individuals have been punished for the crime of genocide and others for crimes against humanity in international courts, no single state has been indicted for its role in genocide or ethnic cleansing. It seems, therefore, that simply defining all facts of collective violence within the larger framework of genocide is not likely to make it easier to get convictions against states implicated in such acts. What seems at stake then is whether naming events of collective violence as genocide is likely to lead to earlier international action that would prevent such conflicts from escalating into mass atrocities. For example, some scholars have argued that talking of the mass killing or rape of black tribal groups by the Janjaweed in Darfur as a humanitarian crisis leads to the false assumption that humanitarian aid will solve the crisis. Much seems to be at stake here in the actual language deployed. This is not pure nominalism for the power to name indicates the ability of particular groups within the international arena to control the definition of a situation. And on this issue geopolitical interests rather than referential certainty seems to dictate whether international institutions will intervene to prevent killing. In the case of Yugoslavia, Kumar and Woodward have effectively argued that it was the eagerness to give recognition to break-away states in which various west European states were implicated that resulted in the escalation of conflict and the dissolution of Yugoslavia.[96] Similarly the role of the diaspora and the shadow economies of illicit drug and small arms trade have international dimensions that feed into ethnic conflicts.[97]

A second consideration that one might keep in mind is the stakes various kinds of groups have developed in revisiting past events and claiming the legal status of genocide for them. Indeed, historical reference has become an important part of mobilization of affect in conditions that lead to collective violence. For example, the massacres of Hutu in Burundi in 1972 are considered to have been of genocidal proportions and the mobilization of sentiment around this for the mass killing of Tutsis seems to have used cultural symbols of sacrifice.[98] The Serbian ultra-nationalist rhetoric expressed, for instance, in the now infamous 'Memorandum of the Serbian Academy of Sciences' issued in 1996, claimed that Serbs in Kosovo had been the subject of a 'genocide'.[99] Hindu nationalists in India claim that past Muslim conquests of Hindu kingdoms were genocidal in their systematic killing and targeting of Hindu groups and some point to the violence against Hindus in Bangladesh or forcible conversions through marriage of Hindu girls in Pakistan as examples of ethnic cleansing or of genocide. No one would deny that violence of massive proportions did take place in the past but the question is whether one can read these as 'genocidal' since the term is used by many of the proponents to institute a politics of hatred and vengeance.[100] Hayden's concern that the model of the Holocaust is seen to be automatically applied to all kinds of collective violence deserves some sympathetic consideration.[101] Scholars of secular persuasion in India dismiss such claims on the part of Hindu right as mere propaganda and, indeed, one must be careful of the way in which such claims have been used to mobilize hatred against Muslims. However, unless one can find ways of talking about past violence in a manner that does not mechanically assume that a politics of vengeance is justified, I see great dangers in expanding the concept of genocide, however good the intentions on any side might be.

Concluding reflections

Considerations of collective violence understandably raise difficult ethical questions for those studying these events and the pressure to translate research into policy and prevention quickly. My intention in this chapter has been more in the diagnostic spirit in that I am interested in seeing how the forms of collective violence constitute the social rather than being a rupture or a break from commonly held agreements at the level of the social and the political. From this perspective, I offer the following reflections.

A long term perspective on the manner in which collective violence is represented seems to suggest that at the level of global politics, collective violence is closely tied to Europe's self-definition. Thus in the colonies, collective violence was seen as a pathology of the colonized rather than pathology created by the mutual implication of local politics with the coercive forms of governance instituted by the colonizers. As we saw, the communal riot was seen as a pathology of that part of the orient and signified the inability of Indians to engage in rational politics of self-interest. I believe that the reason why the dissolution of Yugoslavia was seen as traumatic and generated so much research and reflection is because it came to stand for a particular failure of the European project. Though explanations were constantly sought in the specific characteristics of the Balkans, as Todorova has shown, ethnic stereotyping or forms of sociality said to be specific of the Balkans were in fact common in different parts of Europe.[102] The routine way in which the expression 'in the civilized world' is used by politicians and academics alike to refer to Western civilization shows how unreflective academic and popular writing is on the interconnected histories of Europe and its colonies.

An unfortunate outcome of the languages we use to refer to collective entities such as ethnic groups as agents is that we pay somewhat less attention to tensions within an ethnic or religious group and the role of violence in making boundaries more solid. One assumes consent of all the constituent units of an ethnic group whereas actions that show one's distance from the events taking place are rarely described. I find it particularly illuminating to see how dissent is silenced within a group and the role that such dissent plays in countering the violence.[103]

Finally, a longer-term perspective should help us to see how everyday forms of violence, the close embrace of the legal and the illegal and the way that the state is both undone and remade at the margins, at borders and in the lives of those whose mode of laying claims on the right to survive institute multiple sovereignties. There is constant play between the urge to fix the meaning of particular terms such as genocide to enable law to act and the politics of becoming that generate new entities and modalities in social life. One of the implications of such a view of violence is to study the manner in which everyday life might be both – the site of violence and a turn towards reconciliation and peace.

Notes

1. I am grateful to my friends and colleagues Roma Chatterji, Jane Guyer, Naveeda Khan, Deepak Mehta, Deborah Poole and Pamela Reynolds for conversations and comments on the issues discussed in this chapter. I thank Dan Stone for his patience and as always, Ranendra Das for his amazing insights.
2. J. Spencer, 'Collective Violence', in *The Oxford India Companion to Sociology and Social Anthropology*, ed., V. Das (Delhi: Oxford University Press, 2003), pp. 1564–81.
3. L. L. Langer, 'The Alarmed Vision: Social Suffering and the Holocaust Atrocity', in *Social Suffering*, eds, A. Kleinman, V. Das and M. Lock (Berkeley, CA: University of California Press, 1997), pp. 47–67.
4. The references cited in this chapter make a cut into the extensive literature on collective violence in order to present a particular argument here. It is simply not possible to do a comprehensive survey within the scope of an essay.
5. V. Das, 'Trauma and Testimony: Implications for Political Community', *Anthropological Theory*, 3, 3 (2003), 293–307.
6. See C. A. Bayly, 'The Pre-History of "Communalism"? Religious Conflict in India, 1700–1860', *Modern Asia Studies*, 19, 2 (1985), 177–203; R. Chatterji and D. Mehta, *Living with Violence* (Delhi: Routledge, 2007); I. Copeland, 'The Further Shores of Partition: Ethnic Cleansing in Rajasthan, 1947', *Past and Present*, 160 (1998), 203–31; S. Das, *Communal Riots in Bengal, 1908–1947* (Delhi: Oxford University Press, 1991); G. Pandey, *The Construction of Communalism in North India* (Delhi: Oxford University Press, 1990).
7. G. Shah, 'The 1969 Communal Riots in Ahmadabad: A Case Study', in *Communal Riots in Post-Independence India*, ed., A. A. Engineer (Delhi: Sangam Publications, 1984), p. 175.
8. M. Gaborieu, 'From Al-Baruni to Jinnah: Idiom, Ritual, and Ideology in the Hindu-Muslim Confrontations in South Asia', *Anthropology Today*, 13 (1985), 7–14.
9. Das, *Communal Riots in Bengal*; Bayly, 'The Pre-History of "Communalism"?' It is worth noting that the term 'riot' is a category taken from police manuals though it has proved to be a very portable term to describe violence between religious communities in South Asia. The local terms such as *danga* or *fasad* owe their origin to Persian sources and refer to a different semantic domain for these include public disturbances as well as forms of insurgency. The connotations of race riots in the United States and the recent use of ethnic riots to refer to events in France would similarly need to be spelt out in the context of race relations in these countries.
10. Pandey, *The Construction of Communalism*.
11. Chatterji and Mehta, *Living with Violence*.
12. C. Joshi, 'Bonds of Community, Ties of Religion: Kanpur Textile Workers in the early Twentieth Century', *Indian Economic and Social History Review*, 22, 3 (1985), 251–80. Joshi notes that there was widespread resistance to the anti-plague measures and resentment at the colonial state's intrusion into sacred spaces. Unfortunately, Joshi too slips into the colonial language of rendering this resistance as simply superstition. For another acute analysis of the conditions of industrialization under which communal riots took place, see D. Chakrabarty, 'Communal Riots and Labour: Bengal's Jute Mill-Hands in the 1890s', in *Mirrors of Violence: Communities, Riots and Survivors in South Asia*, ed., V. Das (Delhi: Oxford University Press, 1990), 146–85.
13. Pandey, *The Construction of Communalism*.
14. Chatterji and Mehta, *Living with Violence*.

15. Ibid. For a subtle analysis of the way one might track the processes through which bureaucratic regulation relates to law by looking at file notings, see A. Mukhpadhyay, 'File Notings and Governmentality', *Seminar*, 569 (2007), online at: www.india.seminar.com/2007.
16. Chatterji and Mehta, *Living with Violence*.
17. J. Masselos, 'Power in the Bombay "Mohalla", 1904–1915: An Initial Exploration into the World of the Indian Urban Muslim', *South Asia*, 6 (1975–76), 75–95; idem., *The City in Action: Bombay Struggles for Power* (Delhi: Oxford University Press, 2007).
18. Cf. S. Freitag, *Collective Action and Community: Public Arenas and the Emergence of Communalism in North India* (Berkeley, CA: University of California Press, 1989).
19. See P. Brass, *The Production of Hindu–Muslim Violence in Contemporary India* (Seattle, WA: University of Washington Press, 2003); S. J. Tambiah, *Leveling Crowds: Ethnonationalist Conflicts and Collective Violence in South Asia* (Berkeley, CA: University of California Press, 1996).
20. P. Kloos, 'A Turning Point? From Civil Struggle to Civil War in Sri Lanka', in *Anthropology of Violence and Conflict*, eds, B. E. Schmidt and I. W. Schroder (New York: Routledge, 2001), pp. 176–97.
21. A. G. Hopkins, 'Quasi States, Weak States, and the Partition of Africa', *Review of International Studies*, 26 (2000), 311–20; M. Mamdani, *When Victims Become Killers: Colonialism, Nativism, and the Genocide in Rwanda* (Princeton, NJ: Princeton University Press, 2001).
22. D. Abubakar, 'Ethnic identity, democratization and the Future of the African State: Lessons from Nigeria', *African Issues*, 29, 1–2 (2001), 31–6; E. I. Odugu, 'The Issue of Ethnicity and Democratization in Africa: Towards the Millennium', *Journal of Black Studies*, 29, 6 (1999), 790–808.
23. H. Glickman, ed., *Ethnic Conflict and Democratization in Africa* (Atlanta, GA: The African Studies Association Press, 1995).
24. N. Glazer and D. P. Moynihan, *Beyond the Melting Pot* (Cambridge, MA: MIT Press, 1963).
25. M. L. Gross, 'Restructuring Ethnic Paradigms: From Premodern to Postmodern Perspectives', *Canadian Review of Studies in Nationalism*, 23, 12 (1996), 51–65.
26. C. Geertz, ed., *Old Societies and New States* (New York: The Free Press, 1963); idem., 'What is the State if it is not a Sovereign?', *Current Anthropology*, 45 (2004), 577–93.
27. V. Das and D. Poole, 'State and its Margins: Comparative Ethnographies', in *Anthropology in the Margins of the State*, eds, V. Das and D. Poole (Santa Fe, NM: School of American Research Press, 2004), pp. 3–35.
28. A. Mbembe, 'At the Edge of the World: Boundaries, Territoriality and Sovereignty in Africa', *Public Culture*, 12, 1 (2000), 259–84.
29. See especially A. I. Asiwaju, 'Borderlands in Africa: A Comparative Research Perspective with General Reference to Western Europe', *Journal of Borderland Studies*, 8, 2 (1993), 1–12, and P. Nugent and A. I. Asiwaju, eds, *African Boundaries: Barriers, Conduits and Opportunities* (London: Printer Publications, 1996) for the diverse ways in which the notion of boundaries operates in African societies.
30. See A. Appadurai, *Fear of Small Numbers: An Essay on the Geography of Anger* (Durham, NC: Duke University Press, 2006); A. Basu, 'When Local Riots are Not Merely Local: Bringing the State Back In. Bijnor 1988–92', *Economic and Political Weekly*, 26 (1994), 2605–21; Brass, *The Production of Hindu–Muslim Violence*; Das, ed., *Mirrors of Violence*; T. B. Hansen, *Wages of Violence: Naming and Identity in Postcolonial Bombay* (Durham, NC: Duke University Press, 2001).

31. See Appadurai, *Fear of Small Numbers*; R. M. Hayden, 'Imagined Communities and Real Victims: Self-Determination and Ethnic Cleansing in Yugoslavia', *American Ethnologist*, 23, 4 (1996), 783–801; L. Malvern, *A People Betrayed: The Role of the West in Rwanda's Genocide* (London: Zed Books, 2000); S. Woodward, *Balkan Tragedy: Chaos and Dissolution after the Cold War* (Washington, DC: Brookings Institute, 1995).
32. P. Nugent, 'Introduction', in *African Boundaries*, eds, Nugent and Asiwaju, pp. 1–32; Asiwaju, 'Borderlands in Africa'.
33. M. C. Ferme, 'Deterritorialized Citizenship and the Resonances of the Sierra Leonean State', and J. Roitman, 'Productivity in the Margins: The Reconstitution of State Power in the Chad Basin', both in *Anthropology in the Margins of the State*, eds, Das and Poole, pp. 81–117 and 191–225.
34. F. Ibrahim, *Boundaries, Sovereignty, and the Margins of the State: Producing a Region in Western India* (Delhi: Routledge, forthcoming).
35. Mbembe, 'At the Edge of the World'.
36. A. Nekrich, *The Punished Peoples: The Deportation and Fate of Soviet Minorities at the End of the Second World War* (New York: W. W. Norton, 1978).
37. A. Weiner, 'Nature, Nurture and Memory in a Socialist Utopia: Delineating the Soviet Socio-Ethnic Body in the Age of Socialism', *American Historical Review*, 104, 4 (1999), 1114–55.
38. K. Ray, 'Reparation and De-territorialization: Maeskhetian Turks' Conception of Home', *Journal of Refugee Studies*, 13, 4 (2000), 391–414.
39. Mamdani, *When Victims Become Killers*.
40. Mbembe, 'At the Edge of the World'.
41. Appadurai, *Fear of Small Numbers*.
42. Spencer, 'Collective Violence'; Tambiah, *Leveling Crowds*.
43. A. R. Gualiteri, *Conscience and Coercion: Ahmadi Muslims and Orthodoxy in Pakistan* (Ontario: Guernica Editions, 1989); A. M. Khan, 'Persecution of the Ahmadiyya Community under International Law and International Relations', *Harvard Human Rights Journal*, 16 (2003), 217–44.
44. G. Prunier, *The Rwanda Crisis: History of a Genocide, 1959–1994* (New York: Columbia University Press, 1995).
45. It is important to keep the difference between a homeland for Muslims and an Islamic State for both theological and legal purposes in mind. The Munir report did not deny that Pakistan was created as a homeland for Muslims.
46. *Report of the Court of Inquiry Constituted to Enquire into the Anti-Qadai Riots of 1953* (Lahore: Government Printing Press, 1954), p. 215.
47. N. Khan, 'Trespasses of the State: Ministering the Copyright to Theological Dilemmas', *Bare Acts: Sarai Reader*, 5 (Delhi: Center for the Study of Developing Societies, 2005), pp. 178–89.
48. A. A. Engineer, *The Gujarat Carnage* (Delhi: Orient Longman, 2003); S. Vardarajan, ed., *Gujarat: The Making of a Tragedy* (Delhi: Penguin, 2002).
49. Das, ed., *Mirrors of Violence*; Tambiah, *Leveling Crowds*.
50. V. Das, *Life and Words: Violence and the Descent into the Ordinary* (Berkeley, CA: University of California Press, 2006).
51. The ideology of Hindutva refers to an aggressive form of political Hinduism and is primarily supported by the Hindu party, Bharatiya Janata Party (BJP) which was in power at the time of the Gujarat riots in 2002. *Kar sevaks* refers to Hindu volunteers recruited by the Bharatiya Janata Party and its front organizations in the movement for the demolition of the Babri mosque in 1992 which led to an escalation of

conflict between Muslims and Hindus in various parts of the country. The official website of the BJP glosses Hindutva as cultural nationalism.

52. Visvanathan, 'The Wages of Dissent'.
53. M. D. Toft, *The Geography of Ethnic Violence: Identity, Interests and the Indivisibility of Territory* (Princeton, NJ: Princeton University Press, 2003), p. 34.
54. Mbembe, 'At the Edge of the World'; Nugent and Asiwaju, eds, *African Boundaries*.
55. S. Haokip, *Identity, Conflict and Nationalism: The Naga and Kuki Peoples of Northeast India and Northwest Burma* (Liverpool: Liverpool University Press, 2003).
56. D. E. Ludden, *Making India Hindu: Religion, Community and the Politics of Democracy in India* (Delhi: Oxford University Press, 1996).
57. For a subtle analysis of the way that Hindu mythic symbols provide the resources for critiquing the propaganda of the Hindutva parties and the violence unleashed in Gujarat see M. S. Singh, 'Religious Iconography, Violence, and the Making of a Series', *Domains*, 3 (2007), 38–66.
58. S. Naqvi, 'Caught in a pitying gaze', available online at: http://www.onlinevolunteers.org/Gujarat/news/articlaes/saeed.htm.
59. We might call this the myth of the given as in critiques of bald naturalism in philosophy.
60. On the relation between the virtual and the actual in the constitution of an event formed by violence, see Das, *Life and Words*.
61. G. Bowman, 'The Violence in Identity', in *Anthropology of Violence and Conflict*, eds, Schmidt and Schroder, p. 27.
62. Toft, *The Geography of Ethnic Violence*, p. 20.
63. A. Varshney (with A. I. Wilkinson), *Ethnic Conflict and Civic Life: Hindus and Muslims in India* (New Haven, CT: Yale University Press, 2002).
64. Another piece of the puzzle is that princely states in India, as compared with cities in British India, were relatively peaceful. Ian Copland attributes this to ideas of kingship since the rulers of princely states were patrons of religious places sacred to different communities. Paradoxically it was only in the context of mobilization of religious sentiment before independence by the followers of the reform sects of Hindus that led to violence in an earlier peaceful state of Bharatpur in Rajasthan. See Copeland, 'The Further Shores of Partition'.
65. P. Brass, *Theft of an Idol: Text and Context in the Representation of Collective Violence* (Princeton, NJ: Princeton University Press, 1997).
66. Stanley Tambiah, in *Leveling Crowds*, proposed the pair – focalization and transvaluation – to refer to the manner in which chains of events lose their local reference and become retrospectively into macro events. He opposed this to the pair of nationalization and parochialization to refer to the way in which a national event radiates outwards towards the local. Such spatialized concepts of scale have some limited use but fail to consider the question of perspective that is crucial for defining what comes to count as an event of violence. See Das, *Life and Words*.
67. See P. B. Mehta, 'Ethnicity, Nationalism and Violence in *South Asia: Review Article, Pacific Affairs*, 36 (2003) for an elegant critique of this view.
68. See especially Das, *Life and Words*; S. Kakar, *The Colors of Violence: Cultural Identities, Religion and Conflict* (Chicago, IL: University of Chicago Press, 1996); A. Nandy, S. Trivedi, S. Mayaram and A. Yagnik, *Creating a Nationality: The Ramjanmabhumi Movement and the Fear of the Self* (Delhi: Oxford University Press, 1998).

69. I have argued throughout this chapter that the police are often complicit with the crowds and more members of the minority communities die through police firing than members of the majority community but this does not mean that there are no complex stories that would need to be understood in the case of police actions which does not just unfolds mechanically. See Das, *Life and Words* and Das and Poole, 'State and its Margins' to see the complex interweaving of the local and the extra-local in the workings of the state on the margins.
70. A. Bell-Fialkoff, 'A Brief History of Ethnic Cleansing', *Foreign Affairs*, 72, 3 (1993), 110–20; idem., *Ethnic Cleansing* (New York: St. Martin's Press, 1996).
71. Naimark, *Fires of Hatred*. The question of earlier injustices done to Serbs is a vexed one and has generated much controversy; see R. M. Hayden, 'Schindler's Fate: Genocide, Ethnic Cleansing and Population Transfers', *Slavic Review*, 55, 4 (1996), 727–48; idem., 'Imagined Communities and Real Victims'; S. Woodward, 'Genocide or Partition: Two Sides of the Same Coin', *Slavic Review*, 55, 4 (1996), 755–61. Since the Serbs used the rhetoric of historical injuries to Serbs to mobilize sentiments against the Croats and the Bosnian Muslims, and this fed into the real escalation of atrocities against Muslims, there seems to be no moral language available to talk of the Serb loss of lives. This is one consequence of using a totalizing model to speak of ethnic identity that it leaves little room for discussing intra-group differences.
72. G. Aly, P. Chroust and C. Pross, eds, *Cleansing the Fatherland: Nazi Medicine and Racial Hygiene* (Baltimore, MD: Johns Hopkins University Press, 1994); R. N. Proctor, *Racial Hygiene: Medicine under the Nazis* (Cambridge, MA: Harvard University Press, 1988).
73. See K. Kooning, 'Armed Actors, Violence and Democracy in Latin America in the 1990s: Introductory Notes', *Bulletin of Latin American Research*, 20, 4 (2001), 401–8; M. Mann, *The Dark Side of Democracy: Explaining Ethnic Cleansing* (Cambridge: Cambridge University Press, 2005) and D. Petrovic, 'Ethnic Cleansing: An Attempt at Methodology', *European Journal of International Law*, (1994) for examples that connect military cleansing with the idea of ethnic cleansing.
74. Mann, *The Dark Side of Democracy*; M. Shaw, *War and Genocide: Organized Killing in Modern Society* (London: Polity Press, 2003).
75. Kooning, 'Armed Actors'.
76. M. Mamdani, 'A Brief History of Genocide', *Transition*, 10, 3 (2001), 26–47.
77. H. Bley, *Southwest Africa under German Rule, 1894–1914* (London: Heinemann, 1971).
78. Mamdani, 'Brief History', 29. See also Jürgen Zimmerer's chapter in this volume.
79. R. Kumar, 'The Troubled History of Partition', *Foreign Affairs*, 76, 1 (1997), 22–34.
80. P. G. Roeder, 'Soviet Federalism and Ethnic Mobilization', *World Politics*, 43, 2 (1991), 196–232.
81. Woodward, 'Genocide or Partition'.
82. The close link between modernity and the totalistic character of violence against a targeted group has been made by many scholars including most famously Z. Bauman, *Modernity and the Holocaust* (Ithaca, NY: Cornell University Press, 1989). Yet, it seems to me that the specificity of colonial wars, cold war related wars and now the war on terrorism needs to be accounted for. According to The Human Security Report (New York: Oxford University Press, 2005), the single most important factor in the decline of wars since 1942 is the end of colonial wars. The region in which the maximum death toll has happened in the 1990s is sub Saharan Africa

though it is the indirect deaths of war through disease and malnutrition that contribute to this momentous violence.

83. Naimark, *Fires of Hatred*, p. 190.
84. See Bauman, *Modernity and the Holocaust*.
85. A. Destexhe, *Rwanda and Genocide in the Twentieth Century* (London: Pluto Press, 1994); H. M. Hintjens, 'Explaining the 1994 Genocide in Rwanda', *The Journal of Modern African Studies*, 37, 2 (1999), 241–86; Mamdani, *When Victims Become Killers*; P. Uvin, 'Prejudice, Crisis and Genocide in Rwanda', *African Studies Review*, 40 (1997), 91–115.
86. C. Card, 'Genocide and Social Death', *Hypatia*, 18, 1 (2005), 63–79.
87. S. K. Fisher, 'Occupation of the Womb: Forced Impregnation as Genocide', *Duke Law Journal*, 46, 1 (1996), 91–133.
88. B. Allen, *Rape Warfare: The Hidden Genocide in Bosnia-Herzegovina and Croatia* (Minneapolis: University of Minnesota Press, 1996).
89. N. Mookherjee, *A Lot of History: Sexual Violence, Public Memory, and the Bangladesh Liberation War of 1971* (unpublished PhD dissertation, School of Oriental and African Studies, University of London, no date); Y. Saikia, 'Beyond the Archive of Silence: Narratives of Violence of the 1971 Liberation War of Bangladesh', *History Workshop Journal*, 58 (2004), 275–87.
90. U. Butalia, *The Other Side of Silence* (Durham, NC: Duke University Press, 1998); U. Menon and K. Bhasin, *Borders and Boundaries: Women in India's Partition* (New Brunswick, NJ: Rugers University Press, 1998); Das, *Life and Words*.
91. See Das, *Life and Words*.
92. Naimark, *Fires of Hatred*, p. 3.
93. See especially M. Shaw, *What is Genocide?* (Cambridge: Polity Press, 2007).
94. Department of State, 'Legal Analysis of 1994 Genocide in Rwanda', *The American Journal of International Law*, 96, 1 (2002), 258–62.
95. S. Z. Buckley, 'Remembering to Forget: Chosen Amnesia as a Strategy for Local Co-Existence in Post-Genocide Rwanda', *Africa*, 76, 2 (2006), 131–50; S. Stockman, 'The People's Court: Crime and Punishment in Rwanda', *Transition*, 9, 4 (2000), 20–41.
96. R. Kumar, *Divide and Fall? Bosnia in the Annals of Partition* (London: Verso, 1997); Woodward, *Balkan Tragedy*.
97. Mbembe, 'At the Edge of the World'; C. Nordstrom, *Shadows of War: Violence, Power, and International Profiteering in the Twenty-First Century* (Berkeley, CA: University of California Press, 2004).
98. C. C. Taylor, *Sacrifice as Terror: The Rwandan Genocide of 1994* (Oxford: Berg, 1999).
99. E. D. Gordy, *The Culture of Power in Serbia: Nationalism and the Destruction of Alternatives* (Philadelphia, PA: Penn State University Press, 1999).
100. The entry Hindu genocide on the Google search engine yields 795,000 sites. For a sampling of the kind of argument, see www.hindunet.org or www.mantra.com/holocaust. The issue here is not whether the holocaust is unique in history – many convincing arguments suggest that the theological–political nexus in the claiming of uniqueness sometimes amounts to a denial of other people's suffering or a hierarchy of suffering. The point is that such terms are inserted within different kinds of politics and as I argued earlier relate to the political plenitude of concepts that needs to be carefully attended to. The secularism debate in India has to continuously grapple with this problem, See R. Bhargava, *Secularism and its Critics* (Delhi: Oxford University Press, 1998) and L. Liang, 'The Secularism Debate in India', *Lines* (May 2003).

101. Hayden, 'Schindler's Fate'.
102. M. Todorova, *Imagining the Balkans* (New York: Oxford University Press, 1997).
103. See Das, *Life and Words*; S. Hunt, *This was Not Our War: Women Reclaiming the Peace* (Durham, NC: Duke University Press, 2004); U. Menon, 'Do Women Participate in Riots? Explaining the Notion of "Militancy" among Hindu Women', *Nationalism and Ethnic Politics*, 9, 1 (2003), 20–51.

5
Cultural Genocide in Australia[1]

Robert van Krieken

One of the continuing disputes which have marked the history of the concept 'genocide' has been the question of how narrowly or broadly it ought to be understood. A narrow conception restricts itself to the various forms of killing and physical annihilation, whereas the broader definition addresses a wider variety of ways in which human groups can be 'eliminated', including the destruction of their distinct cultural identity. A central element of this broader approach is the concept of 'cultural genocide',[2] and it is around this idea that much of the debate between the two understandings revolves.

The arguments *for* carving out a moral, political and legal space for 'cultural genocide' began with Raphael Lemkin's original concerns in formulating the new concept of genocide. He wanted to capture an essential dimension of Nazi Germany's colonizing legal and administrative practices in its occupied territories, well before Auschwitz. The foundations of his orientation were laid as the National Socialists came to power in 1933, when Lemkin used the concept of the crime of 'barbarity' to capture 'oppressive and destructive actions directed against individuals as members of a national, religious, or racial group', and that of 'vandalism' to refer to 'malicious destruction of works of art and culture'.[3] His formulation of the crime of 'genocide' combined these two into one.

Subsequently, Lemkin distinguished three 'forms' of genocide: physical, biological and cultural. The first captures what became the common-sense and most widely used understanding of the term, actions leading to death. The second concerns techniques of preventing biological reproduction: sterilization, abortion and so on. The third 'consists, not in the destruction of members of a group, nor in restrictions on birth, but in the destruction by brutal means of the specific characteristics of the group'.[4] Lemkin argued that 'a racial national or religious group cannot continue to exist unless it preserves its spirit and moral unity'. Cultural genocide was more than forced assimilation, it constituted 'a policy which by drastic methods, aimed at the rapid and complete disappearance of the cultural, moral and religious life of a group of human beings'.[5] He saw the destruction of culture as closely linked with physical elimination, either as a prelude or as causally related. Samantha Power reports how Lemkin was fond of saying, 'First they burn books and then they start burning bodies'.[6]

The arguments *against* incorporating the destruction of culture in the definition of genocide include, first, the practical-political one that the UN Genocide Convention (UNGC) was simply not the most appropriate or effective instrument for dealing with the problems being identified, which are better addressed elsewhere, with international law instruments dealing with the protection of minorities. As the Dutch jurist Pieter Drost argued:

> Genocide is collective homicide and not official vandalism or violation of civic liberties. It is directed at the life of man and not against his material or mental goods. The protection of culture belongs primarily to the province of human rights and, perhaps to a lesser degree also to the department of minority rights. It is foreign to the field of criminal law. In a convention on group murder it is completely out of place.[7]

Keeping the definition focused on mass killing was always a practical concern in securing sufficient support for the Convention within the UN – the broader the definition, the bigger the target for opposition, the more reasons there could be found to reject the whole project.[8]

A second argument has been that the inclusion of harm, damage or suffering other than mass killing constitutes a conceptual inflation which undermines the term's meaningfulness and political effectiveness. Samantha Power has outlined the costs associated with what she calls 'Holocaustization', the overuse of the Holocaust analogy in establishing the horror of some particular event.[9] They include distracting arguments over the aptness of the parallel, backlash from those who see the Holocaust as unique, setting an essentially absurd level to the 'standard' of horror, and restricting our understanding of contemporary crimes against humanity to their connections with the Holocaust. Similar points can be made about 'genocidization' – a great deal of time and energy gets diverted to definitional disputes, effective practical action gets tied up in a backlash from those attached to a particular understanding of genocide, and the standard for an acknowledgement of harm and suffering is set at an inappropriately high level.

From another perspective, Michael Ignatieff has characterized what he sees as the occasionally excessive political enthusiasm for calling something seen as destructive in some way or another 'genocidal' as a tendency towards banalization, and therefore a weakening of the concept's practical effectivity. Rather than operating as a 'validation of every kind of victimhood,' it should, he suggests, be reserved for 'genuine' horrors and barbarisms.[10] In other words, as the Danish delegate to the United Nations, Per Federspeil, said during the debate on the draft convention, in a sense responding to Lemkin's 'burning books' comment, 'it would show a lack of logic and a sense of proportion to include in the same convention both mass murders in gas chambers and the closing of libraries'.[11]

The example to which I would like to relate this these arguments is the reference to the UNGC in the debates surrounding the Australian 'stolen generations', those Aboriginal people who were removed from their families in the course of the twentieth century. Two of the focal points of this attempt to mobilize the concept of cultural genocide were the Australian Human Rights and Equal Opportunity Commission's (HREOC) 1997 report on the history of the removal of Indigenous children from their families, *Bringing them Home* (*BTH*), and the High Court *Kruger* case concerning the legislation empowering the Aboriginal child removal.[12] The argument put in both contexts was that the removal of Aboriginal children from their families constituted acts defined as genocide by Article II of the Convention, 'acts committed with intent to destroy, in whole or in part, a national, ethnical, racial or religious group', including clause (e) 'Forcibly transferring children of the group to another group'.

What makes this example especially significant is that, unlike most debated cases of genocide, there are also active defenders of the policy whose position extends beyond the insistence that the policies and practices should not be seen as genocide, to encompass the even stronger argument that the removal of Aboriginal children in fact *improved* the condition of the children concerned, enhancing both their physical condition and their social prospects in the broader Australian society. An important part of its significance in the historiography of genocide is, then, that it appears to straddle the distinction between 'welfare' and 'genocide' in a unique way, and raises some important conceptual issues concerning how easily and clearly the two can be kept separate from each other.

In law, the pursuit of a broader understanding of genocide has indeed fallen on very stony ground,[13] with the Australian High Court in the *Kruger* case rejecting the argument that the legislation concerning Aboriginal child removal was characterized by any intent to 'destroy' Aboriginal groups. Heavily influenced by this legal outcome, the argument has also had a similarly rocky passage in broader societal and political terms. Four years after the *BTH* Report, Sir Ronald Wilson, the President of HREOC who co-authored the report with Mike Dodson, admitted that '[w]ith hindsight, I think it was a mistake to use the word genocide ... once you latch onto the term "genocide", you're arguing about the intent and we should never have used it.' The most widely shared 'common-sense' position was nicely captured by historian Inga Clendinnen, who wrote, also in 2001:

> I am reasonably sophisticated in various modes of intellectual discussion, but when I see the word 'genocide' I still see Gypsies and Jews being herded

> into trains, into pits, into ravines, and behind them the shadowy figures of Armenian women and children being marched into the desert by armed men. I see deliberate mass murder: innocent people identified by their killers as a distinctive entity being done to death by organised authority.[14]

For Clendinnen, like everyone on that side of the debate, 'to take the murder out of genocide is to render it vacuous'.[15]

However, the often triumphalist insistence on the virtues of the narrower conception of genocide has constituted an odd kind of deafness to what is being said on the other side, and in itself does nothing towards responding to the claims based on the broader approach. Acknowledging that 'cultural genocide' does not fall within the scope of the UNGC does not mean that we cannot remain alive to the concerns which that concept is invoked to address, as well as recognizing that there may still be a problem requiring some other sort of engagement, both conceptually and practically. As Larissa Behrendt has emphasized, the legal ineffectiveness of cultural genocide has done 'nothing to dispel the feeling Indigenous people have that this is the word that adequately described our experience as colonized peoples'.[16] The support for an understanding which goes beyond outright killing is particularly strong among Indigenous peoples subjected to settler-colonialism, where there remains such a heartfelt and persistent sense of inflicted violence, pain and suffering at the heart of the settler-colonial project,[17] that it may be ill-advised to stand too stubbornly on the conceptual purity of a 'correct' definition.

Rather than simply dismissing the claims regarding cultural genocide and ethnocide because they are ineffective for legal purposes, in this chapter I would like to work towards returning from an engagement with those claims with a deeper and broader understanding of exactly what is at issue when people speak of cultural genocide. After outlining the obstacles facing the cultural genocide argument in relation to the 'stolen generations' in Australia, the chapter will move on to taking a closer look at the arguments surrounding cultural genocide in the drafting of the convention, as well as the biography of the 'forcible removal' clause. These debates indicate the instability of a key principle underpinning the arguments against cultural genocide, that it is possible to distinguish clearly between cultural and physical destruction. The essential point made by those who reject the concept of cultural genocide is that destroying people's culture doesn't destroy them as people. For example, Russell McGregor argues as follows:

> A culture, in the 'thick' anthropological sense, can be destroyed without destroying the group that formerly lived and thought according to that cultural framework; the group can continue to maintain its existence as a group, even if its cultural heritage has been reduced to a 'thin' folkloric residue.[18]

People actually subjected to such compulsory cultural weight-reduction programs might, of course, come to a different assessment,[19] but in any case the salience of this argument is weakened if the distinction between culture and biology is itself essentially contested.

This is followed by an examination of the kinds of arguments put forward by those seeking to 'protect' Aboriginal people earlier in the twentieth century, in order to highlight the ways in which many of the issues being addressed with the concept 'cultural genocide' in fact took the form of a concern for Aboriginal 'welfare'. Finally, I will reflect on how it might be possible to move beyond a 'one size fits all' approach to the concept of genocide – it ought to be possible to distinguish between the understanding we rely on to attribute criminal responsibility, and the one we use to approach our history and our sense of what it means to be a settler-colonial subject.

The aim is to recognize the types of coercion characterizing the emergence of modern societies up to the present day, in their most apparently 'benign' as well as their explicitly destructive forms, in order to contribute to the identification of ways in which current social institutions and practices might at least address the effects of the various forms of 'founding violence'[20] underpinning settler-colonial state formation and nation building.

Aboriginal child removal and genocide law

By the last quarter of the nineteenth century, it had become widely accepted among European Australians that the Aborigines were a 'dying race', and this was based on the notion of the essential 'fragility' of Aboriginal culture in contact with Europeans.[21] Extinction was thus simply a matter of time, so that the most Europeans could do was to 'smooth the dying man's pillow'.[22] Around the turn of the century, however, it turned out that 'traditional' Aborigines were not dying as quickly as anticipated, and as European settlement spread across the continent, so did contact between Europeans and Aborigines, including sexual contact, which of course had its inevitable consequence – children. The resultant mixed-blood population was itself very fertile, so that by around the 1890s European Australians were becoming increasingly concerned about what came to be defined as the 'half-caste problem'. 'There was a growing realisation', writes Russell McGregor, 'that the descendants of a dying race might continue to haunt a White Australia for generations'.[23]

One key element to the resultant 'civilizing offensive' on the part of both State and Church, which aimed to protect as well as advance civilization by eliminating this hybrid form of Aboriginality from a 'White Australia', was to turn to an existing social technology designed to deal with problems of social discipline, revolving around the concept of 'rescuing the rising generation'.[24] A policy of removing mixed-blood Aboriginal children was introduced in all the Australian states in order to address the dangers of the *hybridity* of mixed-bloods, their threat to the boundaries between the civilized and the savage. The state was made the legal guardian of all children of Aboriginal descent, overriding Aboriginal parents common-law rights over their children, who were to be removed at official will and sent to a mission or a child welfare institution, or to be fostered with a white family if sufficiently light-skinned. The legislation enabling this was introduced in relatively weak form between 1886 and 1909 in all Australian states, strengthened around 1915, and further reinforced in the 1930s, by which time, in legal terms, the state had become the custodial parents of virtually all Aboriginal children.[25]

The actual number of Aboriginal children removed from their families is unclear, partly because the records kept were patchy, with no accounting for Aboriginal children sent to homes not specifically designated for Aborigines; some were removed 'unofficially' and placed in the care of church agencies or individuals. Also difficult to quantify, as Peter Read reminds us, were 'those who went away to white people for a "holiday" and did not return'.[26] Rowena MacDonald suggests that in the period 1912–62, 'probably two out of every three part-descent children spent some of their lives away from their parents as a result of the policy of removal'. The *BTH* Report sums up its estimation as lying between one in three and one in ten in the period between 1910 and 1970, and points out both that 'not one indigenous family has escaped the effects of forcible removal' and that 'most families have been affected, in one or more generations, by the forcible removal of one or more children'.[27]

This assertion of legal guardianship by the state over all Indigenous children only ceased in the 1960s. The primary and overarching concern was to 'solve' the 'half-caste problem' by breeding out the colour of both body and mind through this programme of social engineering, and in this sense the removal of Aboriginal children meshed with the first strategy of controlling sexual relations and reproduction among adult Aborigines. This was certainly the most strongly articulated argument in the writings of the politicians, administrators and anthropologists central to the development of the various forms of legislative and administrative action. 'Merging', 'absorption' and 'assimilation' into the ways of 'civilization' were the key concepts around which this discourse was organized. In 1936 a conference of the leading authorities in Aboriginal affairs declared its belief 'that the destiny of the natives of aboriginal origin, but not of full blood, lies in their ultimate absorption by the people of the Commonwealth'.[28]

In 1989, the Royal Commission into Aboriginal Deaths in Custody focused attention on how many Aboriginal prisoners had a long history of institutionalization, beginning with their removal from their families. Commissioner J. H. Wootten, in his report on the suicide, of one particular Aboriginal prisoner, Malcolm Smith, spoke of 'a life destroyed, not by the misconduct of police and prison officers, but in large measure by the regular operation of the system of self-righteous and racist destruction of Aboriginal families that went on under the name of protection or welfare well into the second half of this century.'[29] Commissioner Wootten went on to draw attention to the fact that 'the attempt to 'solve the Aboriginal problem' by the deliberate destruction of families and communities ... is seen by many Aborigines as falling squarely within the modern definition of genocide.'[30]

By the time the HREOC was requested by the Attorney-General, Michael Lavarch, in August 1995, *inter alia*, to 'trace the past laws, practices and policies which resulted in the separation of Aboriginal and Torres Strait Islander children from their families by compulsion, duress or undue influence, and the effects of those laws, practices and policies', the concept of genocide had already become part of the vocabulary used to understand Aboriginal child removal. The HREOC Commissioners, Sir Ronald Wilson and Michael Dodson, developed its utilization still further in their *BTH* Report, released on 27 May 1997.

The fact that the legislation allowed for the removal of Aboriginal children without parental consent[31] meant that such removals could be seen as constituting acts identified as one of the possible acts of genocide – the second leg of the Convention's definition – that is, clause (e) of Article II of the UNGC, 'forcibly transferring children of the group to another group'. The first leg of the definition, that of the relevant acts being committed 'with intent to destroy, in whole or in part, a national, ethnical, racial or religious group, as such' was also satisfied, argued the *BTH* Report, by the overall objective of assimilationist Aboriginal policy among all State and Commonwealth Governments up until the 1970s: the effective disappearance of Aboriginal culture as a distinct basis of individual and collective identity, its 'swallowing up' by a European way of life.

This objective had been clearly articulated in 1937, when A. O. Neville, Chief Protector in Western Australia, posed the rhetorical question, 'Are we going to have a population of 1,000,000 blacks in the Commonwealth, or are we going to merge them into our white community and eventually forget that there ever were any aborigines in Australia?'[32] It continued, in language of liberal citizenship, in the thinking of Paul Hasluck, later to become Commonwealth Minister for Territories (1951–63), who told the House of Representatives in 1950 that '[t]heir future lies in association with us, and they must either associate with us on standards that will give them full opportunity to live worthily and happily or be reduced to the social status of pariahs and outcasts living without a firm place in the community'.[33]

It was the absence of *recognition* of Aboriginal culture underlying assimilationist policies that led the *BTH* Inquiry to conclude that 'the predominant aim of Indigenous child removals was the absorption or assimilation of the children into the wider, non-Indigenous, community so that their unique cultural values and ethnic identities would disappear'. The 'principal aim', said the Inquiry, was 'to eliminate Indigenous cultures as distinct entities', and the removal of

Aboriginal children with this objective was genocidal 'because it aims to destroy the "cultural unit" which the Convention is concerned to preserve'.

The Report concluded that the policy of removing Aboriginal children from Aboriginal groups 'for the purpose of raising them separately from and ignorant of their culture and people could properly be labelled "genocidal" in breach of binding international law from at least 11 December 1946', when the UN General Assembly adopted its resolution declaring genocide a crime under international law. The *BTH* Report did not seek the remedy for this breach in litigation: its 'finding' of genocide has instead operated more to structure the stolen generations debate and to lend support to arguments for various forms of reparation and compensation,[34] and the term 'genocide' has since remained a central element of the way in which many critics frame their understanding of the illegitimacy of Aboriginal child removal.

These arguments were paralleled in a High Court case in which six Aboriginal plaintiffs sought legal redress against the Commonwealth on the basis of a challenge to the validity of the *Aboriginals Ordinance* 1918 (NT). Five had been removed themselves, and the sixth was the mother of a child who had been removed. The removals took place between 1925 and 1949, and the latest detention ended in 1960. The point of contention in relation to the question of genocide was 'intent', and whether the Ordinance conferred powers which *aimed* at the destruction or harming of Aboriginal people, or at their protection and welfare.

If the Aboriginal Ordinance were to be construed as manifesting an intention to destroy Aboriginals as a human group, this purpose would have to be explicitly and unequivocally indicated by its wording. As Justice Toohey explained it,

> The notion of genocide embodied in the definition in Art II of the Genocide Convention is so fundamentally repugnant to basic human rights acknowledged by the common law that, by reason of well settled principles of statutory interpretation, an intention to authorise acts falling within that definition needs to be clear beyond doubt before a legislative provision can be construed as having that effect.[35]

All of the High Court found that it was impossible to put such a construction on the relevant sections of the Ordinance, which granted the Chief Protector the power to 'undertake the care, custody, or control of any Aboriginal or half-caste', on the condition that he had formed the opinion that 'it is *necessary or desirable in the interests* of the Aboriginal or half-caste for him to do so', as well as the power to take Aboriginal people into custody for *that* purpose, and that purpose only. As Justice Gaudron put it:

> Although it may be taken that the Ordinance authorised the forcible transfer of Aboriginal children from their racial group, the settled principles of

> statutory construction ... compel the conclusion that it did not authorise persons to remove those children 'with intent to destroy, in whole or in part, ... [their] racial ... group, as such'. It follows that the Ordinance did not authorise acts of genocide as defined in the Genocide Convention ...[36]

The arguments questioning the validity of the Ordinance in relation to international law norms regarding genocide thus collapsed on the need to demonstrate clear and unambiguous 'intent to destroy'.[37] The materials drawn upon by the *BTH* Report to argue this intent – the 1937 Conference, assorted writings by Neville, Cook, Spencer, Bleakley and various other public officials and commentators – simply have no legal effect.

The underlying problem is that the pursuit of an argument backed by the authority of law, in this case the application of the UNGC to the question of the removal of Indigenous children, demands an individualized and detailed (that is, substantiated with evidence), case by case analysis, rather than the broad-brush account provided by the *BTH* Report. Since genocidal aims were not stated in the legislation, the 'crime' of genocide could only be committed, as Hal Wootten has pointed out, by individuals who appeared to be being judged without any opportunity to defend themselves against the charges.[38]

In referring to the fact that there were a *variety* of ways in which children were removed, Wootten distinguishes between two different types of purposes in analyzing the history of the stolen generations; if the aim is understanding of the destructive effects of removal practices, the reasons for removal are only peripherally relevant as is the question of the applicability of the UN Genocide Convention. However, for the purpose of the attribution of criminal responsibility and the finding of an intent to destroy Aboriginals as a group, the reasons for removal are highly relevant, and Wootten feels that 'the failure to investigate individual circumstances makes problematic any finding that the removals were all carried out with intent to destroy a group, as such'.[39] Wootten regards the *BTH* Report's 'finding' of genocide a 'quite unnecessary legal ruling' which has generated 'pointless controversy':

> The enormity of what was done speaks for itself through the lips of those to whom it was done, and the lips of self-righteous administrators of the past whose ideas would today be seen as genocidal.[40]

Interestingly, we still circle back to the concept of 'genocide' which, despite its ineffectiveness in the legal arena, seems to retain conceptual force in addressing this aspect of the history of relations between Indigenous and non-Indigenous Australians.

The question I would like to turn to, then, is whether it is possible or useful to make distinctions between different conceptions of genocide, perhaps between gradations of genocide,[41] approaching an understanding which can do justice *both* to the concept's limited application in law, *and* to its continuing attraction to Indigenous peoples as a means of capturing an essential dimension of their experience of settler-colonialism. In order to engage with this issue, it is useful to turn the analysis of purpose and intent to the UNGC itself. What was its underlying purpose? What 'mischief' was it designed to correct, and what was the precise role played by the clause concerning the forcible removal of children from one group to another? Is the UNGC a reliable guide for a useful understanding of genocide, or do the attempted mobilizations of the UNGC actually constitute a *critique* of it, as well as an argument for a new and different approach to the whole question of cultural genocide within modern state-formation?

What is genocide? Culture and biology

The mechanisms of colonialism were central to Lemkin's conception of genocide, which was not confined simply to 'obvious' examples of killing. The dynamics of genocide included the whole German colonizing regime in the occupied countries, a very particular kind of legal order based on a variety of 'techniques of occupation' constituting 'a gigantic scheme to change, in favour of Germany, the balance of biological forces between it and the captive nations for many years to come', aiming 'to destroy or cripple the subjugated peoples in their development' so that Germany would be placed in a position of 'numerical, physical and economic superiority' regardless of the military outcome of armed conflict. The concept of genocide was intended by Lemkin to capture this 'new technique of occupation aimed at winning the peace even though the war itself is lost',[42] a 'practice of extermination of nations and ethnic groups' that is 'effected through a synchronized attack on different aspects of life of the captive peoples', in the realms of politics, society, culture, economics, biology, physical existence (starvation and killing), religion and morality.[43] In his words:

> Generally speaking, genocide does not necessarily mean the immediate destruction of a nation, except when accomplished by mass killings of all members of a nation. It is intended rather to signify a coordinated plan of different actions aiming at the destruction of essential foundations of the life of national groups, with the aim of annihilating the groups themselves. The objectives of such a plan would be disintegration of the political and social institutions, of culture, language, national feelings, religion, and the economic existence of national groups, and the destruction of the personal security, liberty, health, dignity, and even the lives of the individuals belonging to such groups. Genocide is directed against the

national group as an entity, and the actions involved are directed against individuals, not in their individual capacity, but as members of the national group.[44]

It is clear, then, that Lemkin was prompted to speak of genocide by his observations of a multi-faceted political rationality and a multi-dimensional set of legal and administrative forms and practices, of which outright killing was one, but not the only part, and he was keen to point out the heterogeneity of ways in which the destruction of human groups could take place.[45]

This analysis was the starting point, then, for the United Nations' attempts to develop an instrument of international law which might help prevent such conduct on the part of governing authorities in the future. At Lemkin's urging, and with the strong support of the US delegation,[46] the United Nations General Assembly passed a resolution on 11 December 1946 that a convention aimed at the prevention of genocide should be drafted for discussion at the UN, and after some to-ing and fro-ing, in April 1947 the Secretary-General requested the Human Rights Division, together with three external experts, to draw up a draft convention.[47] This first Secretariat's draft, issued on 26 June 1947,[48] contained the seeds of most of the debates, disagreements and divergences which have characterized varying approaches to genocide ever since.

First, the Secretariat's draft insisted that the literal definition of genocide as 'the deliberate destruction of a human group ... must be rigidly adhered to; otherwise there is a danger of the idea of genocide being expanded indefinitely to include the law of war, the right of peoples to self-determination, the protection of minorities, the respect of human rights, etc.'[49] Second, the draft explicitly excluded 'the policy of compulsory assimilation of a national element' from its definition, even if such acts 'may result in the total or partial destruction of a group of human beings'.[50] A policy of forced assimilation 'does not as a rule constitute genocide'.[51] It was '[t]he system of protection of minorities, if applicable' which was seen as relevant to 'the protection of minorities against a policy of forced assimilation employing relatively moderate methods'.[52]

Nonetheless, thirdly, the draft *did* retain Lemkin's three-fold typology of physical, biological and cultural genocide, albeit under protest from de Vabres and Pella.[53] In the face of this opposition, Lemkin maintained that 'a racial, national, or religious group cannot continue to exist unless it preserves its spirit and moral unity' and insisted that his conception of cultural genocide constituted something *more* than 'forcible assimilation', it was 'a policy which by drastic methods, aimed at the rapid and complete disappearance of the cultural, moral and religious life of a group of human beings'. The boundary between the two remained unclear.[54]

Fourth, the committee included the act of the forcible transfer of children within its definition of *cultural* genocide:

> The separation of children from their parents results in forcing upon the former at an impressionable and receptive age a culture and a mentality different from their parents. This process tends to bring about the disappearance of the group as a cultural unit in a relatively short time.[55]

Lemkin, Pella and de Vabres 'agreed that this point should be covered by the Convention on Genocide' but we are also told, tellingly, that 'their agreement did not go further than that'.[56]

In the second draft, the tripartite division into physical, biological and cultural genocide was again retained, but the 'forcible transfer of children' clause was omitted. In the subsequent discussions in the 6th Committee, both these points were reversed. The 'forcible transfer of children' clause was re-introduced by re-framing the idea of 'forcible transfer of children' as being about *physical* rather than cultural genocide. 'There could be no doubt,' declared the Greek delegate, Mr Vallindas, 'that a forced transfer of children, committed with the intention of destroying a human group as a whole, or at least in part, constituted genocide'. It could be 'as effective a means of destroying a human group as that of imposing measures intended to prevent births, or inflicting conditions of life likely to cause death'.[57] In supporting the amendment, the US delegate, John Maktos, asked the Committee rhetorically 'to consider what difference there was from the point of view of the destruction of a group between measures to prevent birth half an hour before the birth and abduction half an hour after the birth'.[58]

In the battle surrounded the push to remove cultural genocide, Johannes Morsink has pointed out that the UN divided essentially into three blocs: the Communist and Arab delegations in favour of retaining a cultural genocide article, the North and South American delegations opposing it and the Western European delegations wavering between the two positions.[59] The first bloc, in favour of retention,[60] were all countries which either had experienced the worst of the National Socialists 'population' policies, being to Germany's East, or had other reasons to be responsive to the protection of cultural diversity against social and political forces aimed at cultural homogeneity – at this particular time, at least, even if they were later to take up different attitudes. One major argument was that there was an intimate relationship between the destruction of culture, especially when *linked* to biological arguments about racial inferiority or degeneracy, and physical or biological annihilation.

The Pakistani delegate, Mr Bahadur Khan, appreciated that 'new countries' needed to assimilate immigrants 'in order to create a powerful national unit', but also believed that the genocide convention should still be used to prevent those forms of assimilation which were 'nothing but a euphemism concealing measures of coercion designed to eliminate certain forms of culture.'[61]

The member states most strongly opposed to the cultural genocide article were those composed of a large proportion of immigrants, and/or settler-colonies with a minority or majority Indigenous population: the USA and Canada, most of the Latin American states, Australia, New Zealand, South Africa. Mr Reid (New Zealand) pointed out that the United Nations itself, in the Trusteeship Council, was busy attempting to 'advance' Indigenous peoples beyond their tribal forms of social organization, so that the Council was in fact 'opposed to the maintenance of a distinctive cultural trait of the local population', producing the embarrassing situation of the UN's own organs being subject to its Genocide Convention.[62] It was clear that Lemkin's conception of the cultural dimensions of genocide actually overlapped significantly with a type of pursuit of cultural homogeneity characterizing 'the civilizing mission' that had become a normalized aspect of modern state-formation and nation-building, particularly in relation to immigrants and to Indigenous populations attached to pre-industrial forms of social cohesion and interaction.[63] The removal of Article III dealing with cultural genocide was supported by 25 votes to 16, with 4 abstentions.[64]

There were two aspects of the genocide question, then, which remained essentially disputed, even if a dominant position on both did ultimately emerge: how and where we should place the boundaries, first, between 'biology' and 'culture' and, second, between legitimate and illegitimate organized violence. The passage of the 'forcible transfer of children' clause shows that the distinctions between 'biology' and 'culture' were by no means clear. The practice of child removal was originally understood by Lemkin as part of the cultural dimension of genocide, and this is how it first entered the convention, but it was subsequently re-defined as 'really' an element of physical or biological genocide, and it was on this basis that agreement was secured on its place in the convention. However, this construction of child removal as biological and as having little to do with forcible assimilation and the pursuit of cultural homogeneity remained disputed, with the Venezuelan delegate using the inclusion of the clause as a 'lever' for the argument in favour of cultural genocide, re-framing it again in cultural rather than biological or racial terms.[65]

Similarly the arguments surrounding cultural genocide indicate a varying sensitivity to the cultural dimensions of genocide and a disputed understanding of what it means to 'destroy' a human group: whether it is necessary to physically kill them, or whether they can be 'killed' in more subtle and apparently civilized ways. It is useful here to recall Alexis de Tocqueville's observations on the destruction of the North American Indians, and the difference between the approaches of the Spanish and the Americans:

> The Spanish unleash their dogs on the Indians as on ferocious beasts; they pillage the New World like a town taken by assault, without discrimination

> and without pity; but one cannot destroy everything, fury has a limit: the remnant of the Indian populations escaping the massacres in the end mixes with those who have defeated it and adopts their religion and mores.
>
> The conduct of the Americans of the United States towards the natives, on the contrary, breathes the purest love of forms and legality. Provided that the Indians stay in the savage state, the Americans do not mix at all in their affairs and treat them as independent peoples; they do not permit themselves to occupy their lands without having duly acquired them by means of a contract; and if by chance an Indian nation can no longer live on its territory, they take it like a brother by the hand and lead it to die outside the country of its fathers.[66]

This distinction between different modes of destruction remained the one splitting the debates in the UN, and continues to divide our understanding of genocide between a 'narrow' and a 'broad' view to this day. On the one side were the arguments that genocide should be narrowly conceived, restricted to the approach adopted by the Spanish in South America, and on the other were the proposals that we should understand genocide more broadly, and recognize what is problematic about the techniques adopted by the Americans in North America, what remains violent and destructive about the apparently civilized management of the process of settler-colonization within the rule of law.

Lying underneath this division is a related one concerning the character of legitimate force and violence within processes of state-formation, particularly in a settler-colonial context in relation to Indigenous populations, as well as the relationship between nation-building and cultural homogeneity or diversity. The arguments against the workability of the inclusion of attempts to address cultural genocide within the same convention dealing with killing and mass murder were not trivial, and there is force to the point that it might make more sense to engage with this kind of question in the sphere of human rights. Perhaps we would have all ended up voting against the inclusion of Article III. Nonetheless, along the way a very interesting bedfellow has been acquired, namely the proposition that states really have the right to do more or less as they please regarding cultural and behavioural uniformity as long as they do not actually murder anyone. As Patrick Thornberry has put it:

> The Nazi experience impelled States to support the criminalization of genocide and give some promise of protection to groups as such, but this criminalization has its limits. These limits, characteristically, are reached when the law might be seen to function as a barrier to nation-building, to the 'civilizing mission' of States.[67]

Indeed, Leo Kuper has his doubts about the restriction on murder, saying that the modern state has 'as an integral part of its sovereignty, the right to commit genocide ... against peoples under its rule' and that 'the United Nations for all practical purposes defends this right'.[68] There was also a strong argument being put, both in these particular debates on the Convention, but also on the issues of 'minority' (as opposed to 'individual') rights and throughout the UN in this period,[69] that particular eggs simply had to be broken in making the omelette of modern progress, and that it is acceptable, desirable and entirely consistent with the lofty ideals of humanitarian liberalism, to construct some ways of life as not constituting 'culture' at all, but merely misery, poverty, backwardness, savagery, illiteracy, ill health, inequality, oppression and social disorganization. It is, of course, about precisely this world view that Indigenous peoples have expressed most dismay.

Welfare versus genocide?

In addition to the polarization between narrow and broad conceptions of genocide, one of the significant features of the Australian debates around Aboriginal child removal is the stand-off between those who argue that it should be seen in terms of 'welfare' on the one hand, or 'cultural genocide' on the other. The Commonwealth Government's response to the *BTH* Report,[70] for example, concentrated on contesting what proportion of the Aboriginal population was in fact removed from their families, complaining about the semantic accuracy of the word 'generation', protesting that Aboriginal children were treated no *more* appallingly than white children and, above all, insisting that the underlying intent, and often the actual effect of child removal policies was always the 'welfare' and 'interests' of Aboriginal people. The categories 'welfare' and 'genocide' are generally treated as mutually exclusive, so that one can only argue for one by completely denying the validity of the other.

One of the problems with attempting to pursue this debate within the context of a welfare–genocide distinction is, as we have seen, that the different sides have divergent understandings of 'genocide' (narrow versus broad), so that these two categories overlap rather than oppose each other. Another is that there is certainly little correspondence between our current understandings of the distinction between welfare and genocide, and the ones which were operative at the time of the relevant legislation being passed and the relevant policies being formulated and translated into administrative practice.

Looking back at the political forces which produced the laws, policies and practices of child removal around the turn of the century, they aligned themselves along different lines from the current welfare–genocide distinction. If the broader understanding of 'genocide' effectively operates as a synonym for 'colonization', it may be useful to recall that state formation is also a process of social and cultural formation which should not be equated with 'government', so that we might need to distinguish between genocidal actions and policies on the one hand, and a genocidal structuring of social relations on the other. One of the reasons it is even possible to debate whether particular organized interventions (by Church as well as state agencies) were 'genocidal' or pursuing Aboriginal 'welfare' is that we are observing an *assembly* of *interactions* between government action (via legislation, interventions and support of Church agency interventions) and extra-governmental social, demographic and economic processes with their own logic and dynamic. Tony Barta has pointed out, for example, that it is true to say that Australian governments have consistently spoken not of eliminating the Aboriginal people, but of *saving* them, from an essential genocidal society, a mode of structuring social relations and ordering the disposition of land which could have no effect other than destroying Aboriginal social life.[71]

The *Aboriginals Ordinance* (NT) 1911, on which the 1918 Ordinance was based, had been drafted in large part by Atlee Hunt (1864–1935), secretary and permanent head of the Department of External Affairs (1901–15), and the anthropologist and public servant W. Baldwin Spencer. Spencer's views were much respected by Hunt,[72] and he was relied upon by the government to rebuild its Aboriginal legislation and policy.[73] The very broad powers granted to the Chief Protector were those which Spencer had sought to render what was, from an administrator's point a view, a very unruly state of relations between Indigenous and non-Indigenous people in the Northern Territory more amenable to governance and regulation. The problem facing Spencer, as Mulvaney and Calaby point out, was

> how to reconcile paternalism with indigenous initiative, or compulsion in humanitarian interests with civil liberties. ... how to implement government decisions relating to the black majority, when the white minority effectively controls administration and regards both the laws and the native population with contempt. ...[74]

His solution fell very much on the side of paternalism, giving the Chief Protector enormous powers over the Aboriginal population, powers which could be deputed to any other official designated a Protector, which included all police officers, and from a contemporary perspective constitutes an extraordinary governmental intrusion into the everyday lives of a particular section of the population.

However, although Mulvaney and Calaby agree that 'there was an element of racial arrogance, which enabled him to ignore the emotional, personal problems, resulting from his rational legal solutions',[75] they also argue that this needs to be placed within the particular ideological and material context from which this racial arrogance emerged. They point out that the racist overtones of Spencer's writings and policy developments 'should be compared with the naked and aggressive racism of tropical Australian contemporaries, rather than with the United Nations Charter'.[76] Equally important was the fact that the arguments *against* such government paternalism, supposedly in support of the civil liberties of the Aboriginal population, came from precisely those individuals and groups hoping to most ruthlessly exploit Aboriginal labour and to retain unlimited sexual access to Aboriginal girls and women.[77]

The reasoning of the Commonwealth Member of Parliament who spoke up most frequently 'on behalf of' Aboriginal interests, Dr Charles Carty Salmon (1860–1917),[78] also tells us a little more about the liberal political rationality underlying this concern better to govern Indigenous affairs. Salmon insisted that 'The aboriginals of Australia have, in the past been shamefully treated', and that this 'is one of the greatest blots on the history of the States'.[79] He felt, the House of Representatives was told,

> a personal responsibility towards those people who were the original owners of the soil. We have dispossessed them, taking from them their birthright; and although there are those who believe that Australia was pre-ordained as a home of the white race, I feel sure that the extinction of the aboriginals in the fashion that prevails was not pre-ordained.[80]

However, Salmon was also an active supporter of the White Australia policy, and clearly supported Spencer's 'stern paternalism' in order to improve the governance of the racial composition of the Northern Territory. The particular problem there, in Salmon's view, was that part-Aboriginal children were being born of Asian rather than European fathers.

> I am sorry to notice ... the admixture of races that is going on. We have been accustomed to look upon the half-caste as being partly a European product, but a reference to the reports will show that it is with the Eastern aliens that the admixture is taking place. Chinese and Japanese have been using the native women against their will, and against the will of their natural protectors ... I do not know what the Minister of External Affairs has done in order to deal with this matter, but I hope he will use the enormous powers with which he is invested to issues Ordinances for the Northern Territory, and also for Papua, which will properly protect the chastity of the native women. The admixture of European with aboriginal blood is bad enough, but the admixture of the blood of Chinese, Japanese, and Malays of low caste with the blood of the aboriginal race is too awful to contemplate. If we are to have a piebald Australia, let it be by the admixture of European blood with the blood of another race, not by the mixture of alien blood with the

> blood of the aboriginal race, which would be more degrading and lowering to our status as a nation.[81]

Salmon's declared sensitivity to his position as a colonizer did not prevent him from continuing to see Aboriginal people, unlike the more war-like Papuans and Maoris, as 'more degraded', as 'lower in the scale of intelligence', as 'more susceptible to evil influences and most likely to be imposed upon', and thus in need of 'immediate and sympathetic attention',[82] such as precisely the 'stern paternalism' embodied by ss 6 and 16 of the *Aboriginals Ordinance*.

It is clear, then, that what the broader approach might wish to identify as the genocidal element in the child removal policies lay less in an unambiguous 'intent to destroy' a human group, than in the presumption that there was not much *to* destroy. Aboriginal culture and its way of life, especially once it had encountered European civilization, was presented by Paul Hasluck and almost every other administrator in Aboriginal affairs as inherently flawed, fragile and basically worthless, producing only illness, disease, drunkenness, filth and degeneracy in the 'thousands of degraded and depressed people who crouch on rubbish heaps throughout the whole of this continent'.[83] Aboriginality was constructed simply as a 'primitive social order' composed of 'ritual murders, infanticide, ceremonial wife exchange, polygamy',[84] so that for Hasluck and most white Australians, the permanent elimination of Aboriginality from the fabric of Australian social life was self-evidently synonymous with civilization and progress itself, a crucial element of the truth that 'the blessings of civilization are worth having'. 'We recognise now', said Hasluck, 'that the noble savage can benefit from measures taken to improve his health and his nutrition, to teach him better cultivation, and to lead him in civilised ways of life . ... We know that the idea of progress, once so easily derided, has the germ of truth in it.'[85]

The concern was rather with some 'thing' which was not meant to have a legitimate existence, namely racial and cultural hybridity, the combination of Aboriginal with European and Asian culture/blood/skin, so that there was no ethical problems raised by the construction of the destruction of that hybridity as being consistent with promoting the welfare of Aboriginal people. Pierre Clastres prefers the concept 'ethnocide' to 'cultural genocide', and he emphasizes that 'ethnocide, from the perspective of its agents, does not recognize itself as a destructive enterprise: on the contrary, it is a duty, demanded by the humanism inscribed at the heart of Western culture'.[86] It was in this sense that the practices of settler-colonization were able, in the minds of their executors, to escape from the concerns normally attached to an abhorrence of the narrow conception of genocide, and for the destructive dimensions of nation-building, what Strickland calls 'genocide-at-law',[87] to take place 'tranquilly; legally, philanthropically, without spilling blood, without violating a single one of the great principles of morality in the eyes of the world'.[88]

Many usages of the concept of 'genocide' have revolved around whether there are parallels between the Australian practices of colonization and the annihilation of Jewish, Gypsy and otherwise 'marginal' peoples in the Holocaust. However, it is more meaningful in a broader sense to compare the assimilation of the Aboriginal people in Australia, not with the Holocaust, but with the processes, structures and political rationalities of assimilation of 'outsiders' and 'strangers' in the modern state generally, both in the centuries prior to the Holocaust and continuing after it. The distinction between eugenicist forms of assimilation based on *race* – possibly leading to 'real' genocide – and forms based on *culture* – leading not to genocide, but perhaps to violations of human rights, is inherently problematic because culturally based discourses of colonization *preceded* those organized around racial distinctions, rather than the other way around. As Robert Williams puts it in his analysis of medieval discourses of conquest and colonization, in medieval Christian jurisprudence the central focus was on 'the deficient cultures and religious customs of normatively divergent races of people, rather than with their racially distinctive biological features'.

> When the Christian European legal tradition justifying cultural racism against normatively divergent peoples finally encountered the indigenous tribal cultures of the New World, Christian Europeans had already accepted the rights and responsibilities belonging to a superior race to exercise its lawful privileges of power and aggression over such inferiorly-regarded human beings.[89]

The difference between the narrow and broad conceptions of genocide, or as Clastres puts it, between genocide and ethnocide, is not that one is based on race and the other on culture, because we find a reliance on *both* race *and* culture in each.[90] It is more that the former is *pessimistic*, in the sense that all that can be done with the (racial and/or cultural) Other is to destroy them physically, whereas the latter is *optimistic*, in the sense that it is seen as possible to lead barbarians and savages to civilization,[91] that it is indeed possible to 'kill the Indian and save the man'.

Conclusion: civilizing the settler-colonial state

One of the central concerns of this chapter has been to draw attention to the inherent instability of the concept of 'genocide', but also of all the concepts which surround, underlie and oppose it, such as 'welfare', 'race' and 'culture', and the heterogeneity in the ways in which they can be assembled in relation to each other. The question of the forced transfer of children, for example, straddled biology/race and culture, and was capable of being moved to either side of the divide between them, depending on the political purposes being addressed. This means that the utilization of any of these concepts according to their current meaning in relation to the past – to 1911, when the *Aboriginals Ordinance* (NT) was introduced, or to 1948, when the UNGC appeared – has to take place in different ways for differing purposes.

To the extent that the UNGC emerged from a narrow conception of genocide, the *BTH* Report's reliance on it to address the question of genocide in the history of Australian settler-colonialism was probably a misjudgment. The United Nations which produced the UNGC was, at that time, no real friend of Indigenous peoples, and the New Zealand delegate pointed out during the debates on the convention how central concepts of assimilation and integration – if need be, forced – were to the UN's own understanding of the place of Indigenous peoples within processes of progress and social improvement.[92] The *BTH* Report turned to the 'forced transfer of children' clause in the Convention as an ally in its engagement with a central dimension (child removal) of the experience of settler-colonialism, but the problem is that this was not the way in which the UN itself approached that clause and the acts it was intended to deal with, and it is a construction of the UNGC which is actually alien to its overall intent, particularly its concern to exclude the question of 'cultural' genocide. In this sense, then, it is clear that 'genocide' has a particularly restricted range of application in law.

However, if we agree that cultural genocide should, for particular purposes – especially that of identifying legally cognizable responsibility – be distinguished from physical genocide, and that this distinction is a central feature of the UNGC, this has still done nothing to deal with the question of what continuity there, nevertheless, remains, what they continue to have in common with each other, what general 'spirit' they share, and what might be done in response to that continuity.[93]

After all, what was the most important distinction between mass murder *tout court* and the actions that Lemkin wanted to create a new word for and constitute as a distinct crime? It was the intent, indeed the desire to see a distinct cultural group removed from the pages of history, to make way for whatever was defined as progress, civilization, real humanity, which was constitutive of settler-colonialism. The fact that this homogenizing, erasing desire, deeply embedded in Western political rationality, can as often take the form of enlightened concern for a group's welfare and well-being obviously makes it impossible to see it as coextensive with mass killing. And yet, the reason the term 'cultural genocide' continues to resonate is because it is one of the few ways in which it is possible to capture what Veracini calls the 'founding violence' of settler-colonial nation-states.[94] The Australian discussions of the 'forced transfer of children' clause in the Convention is precisely a telling illustration of how problematic the opposition of biology to culture remains, and how problematic and unsatisfactory the distinction between 'destruction as killing' and destruction as cultural 'euthanasia'[95] actually is.

The recognition that genocide has limited legal application also does not change the fact that there remain significant problems of *legitimacy* surrounding colonization and all its attendant practices, including child removal. This is why the stolen generations debate generates so much heat, emerging from the collision of the two central ways of dealing with this issue – how to be a legitimate colonizer? We should be uneasy, then, about agreeing with the idea that any proportion of this heat, of the resistance to the moral and political questions raised by the stolen generations debate is attributable to 'anger at that charge being leveled promiscuously against individuals who perhaps were less informed or less imaginative than they might have been, but who in many cases acted in good faith'.[96] It may be more plausible to see the public resistance to the mobilization of the idea of genocide as being primarily a reaction to the suggestion that white Australians' self-image might be tarnished, that our 'civilization' has a dark side to it, and that European Australians are indeed colonizers. Albert Memmi, in his book *The Colonizer and the Colonized,* has pointed out that the problem with being a colonizer is that ones identity is essentially that of a usurper, and that colonizers are constantly concerned with trying to legitimate their usurpation – of land, of space, of power and of bodies.

> In other words, to possess victory completely he needs to absolve himself of it and the conditions under which it was attained. This explains his strenuous insistence, strange for a victor, on apparently futile matters. He endeavours to falsify history, he rewrites laws, he would extinguish memories – anything to succeed in transforming his usurpation into legitimacy.[97]

The history of the stolen generations is a particularly close and proximate manifestation of the destructive and violent dimensions of the European presence in Australia, and the resistance to a recognition of its problematic nature is perhaps a result of its being a little 'too close for comfort'. Massacres are almost 'easier' for colonizing populations to deal with, because they can still be relatively easily placed in the past, and liberal non-Aboriginals can see themselves as 'better' than those blood-thirsty settlers. But this is more difficult to achieve in relation to the removal of Aboriginal children, partly because the practices took place closer in time, but also because they were more central to ideologies we currently continue to hold to, such as welfare, civilization and assimilation/integration.

It is important to take account here of the different forms which can be taken by liberal political rationality institutions and practices, depending on how the relationships between individuals, intermediate collectivities (culture and civil society) and the state are conceived. If they are understood in ways which seek simply to detach individuals from communal ties and reconstruct them as abstract universalized and infinitely interchangeable 'citizen-isolates' in relation to the state and the nation,[98] they generate the kinds of institutions and practices which the human beings being acted upon, especially Indigenous people under settler-colonialism, are highly likely to experience as essentially genocidal, no matter how well-intentioned the architects of those institutions and practices might be.

Liberal models of individual rights can never really detach themselves from an accompanying conception of 'society as a whole' to which individuals are to be 'assimilated'. Indeed, the rhetoric of liberal democracy tends to draw attention away from the models of society and community which are in fact being drawn upon, making their problematic effects that much harder to perceive, let alone respond to. On the other hand, when combined with an organic, mono-cultural and unitary conception of citizenship and community, individualistic liberalism has a strongly normalizing edge to it which can, in situations where the boundaries between the 'normal' and the 'pathological' communities are drawn strongly enough (as with racial divisions), have effects very similar to more authoritarian regimes based on quite different political philosophies. Russell McGregor suggests that post-1945 assimilation policies should be seen in terms of 'governance' rather than 'genocide',[99] but the problem being raised with the idea of cultural genocide is precisely the extent to which the two overlap.

One of the earliest applications of the concept of 'cultural genocide' in the Australian context was in 1959, in a memo by a Department of External Affairs officer, Phillip Peters, on Hasluck's address to the Anthropology section at the 1959 ANZAAS Congress.[100] Peters observed that Hasluck's statement suggested 'that cultural genocide is a prerequisite of full assimilation of the Aborigines into the non-Aboriginal community', making 'no reference to the wishes of the Aborigines as regards their future' and failing to 'envisage any alternative which might allow Aborigines to preserve some of their customs and culture'.[101] The 1960s thus began a confrontation between Hasluck's liberalism and an ethical orientation which conceived assimilationist monoculturalism, given its construction of 'welfare' as concerned to transcend/eliminate cultural difference, as inherently 'despotic',[102] to the point of at least verging on the political, if not legal, conception of 'genocide'. An important manifestation of this confrontation was the on-going tension between Hasluck and his main competitor as the leading 'theorist' of assimilation A. P. Elkin, professor of anthropology at the University of Sydney between 1934 and 1951. 'Assimilation, however,' wrote Elkin in the 1950s, 'does not mean, or necessarily involve, the extinction of the Aboriginal race, that is, swallowing it by social processes and intermarriage',[103] nor that 'to be citizens, Aborigines must give up all their kinship customs and their beliefs and rites, or that local groups must no longer think of themselves as closely knit communities.'[104] Elkin felt that 'although scattered in groups across Australia, and increasing in numbers, the Aborigines will have their own sense and experience of solidarity, of possessing a common history, – in short, of being a people.'[105]

Respect for 'the laws of humanity', such as those surrounding genocide, is clearly significant, but it does not guarantee that we avoid inflicting violence and pain on each other. If human beings are conceived as 'disembodied, defamilialized, and degendered',[106] this prevents a comprehension of individuals as socially located, inter-generational, inter-subjective beings, their essentially communal identities 'stretched' over time both backwards and forwards.[107] A mono-cultural and organicist conception of 'society', also allows only for assimilation to a single, individualized and de-communalized 'way of life'. It is only to extent that both these aspects of liberal political rationality are addressed, and a form of liberalism is nourished which instead conceives individuals as integral parts of collectivities, with their communal identity an essential rather than expendable element of their relationship to the state, that we can hope that similar histories might not re-emerge, and that people might cease experiencing themselves as the objects of one or other form of organized violence, regardless of whether it is appropriate to call it 'genocide'.[108]

Notes

1. This chapter draws extensively from an earlier version published as 'Rethinking Cultural Genocide: Indigenous Child Removal and Settler-Colonial State-Formation', *Oceania*, 75 (2004), 125–51.
2. 'Ethnocide' is often proposed as an alternative – see P. Clastres, 'On Ethnocide', *Art & Text*, 28 (1988), 51–8 and A. Palmer, 'Ethnocide', in *Genocide in our Time: An Annotated Bibliography with Analytical Introductions*, eds, M. N. Dobkowski and I. Wallimann (Ann Arbor, MI: Pierian Press, 1992), pp. 1–21 – but the concerns are more or less the same.
3. R. Lemkin, *Axis Rule in Occupied Europe: Laws of Occupation, Analysis of Government, Proposals for Redress* (Washington, DC: Carnegie Endowment for International Peace, 1944), p. 91.
4. United Nations Economic & Social Council (UNESC), *Draft Convention on the Crime of Genocide*, (New York: United Nations, UN Doc E/447, 1947), p. 26.
5. Ibid., p. 27.
6. S. Power, *"A Problem from Hell": America and the Age of Genocide*, (New York: Basic Books, 2002), p. 530.
7. P. N. Drost, *Genocide: United Nations Legislation on International Criminal Law. Vol. 2 of Crimes of State* (Leiden: A. W. Sythoff, 1959), p. 11.
8. P. Thornberry, *International Law and the Rights of Minorities* (Oxford: Clarendon Press, 1991); J. Morsink, 'Cultural Genocide, the Universal Declaration, and Minority Rights', *Human Rights Quarterly*, 21 (1999), 1009–60; W. A. Schabas, *Genocide in International Law: The Crime of Crimes* (Cambridge: Cambridge University Press, 2000).
9. S. Power, 'To Suffer by Comparison?', *Daedalus*, 128 (1999), 31–66.
10. M. Ignatieff, 'The Danger of a World Without Enemies. Lemkin's World', *The New Republic*, 224 (2001), 27. See H. Fein, *Genocide: A Sociological Perspective*,

(London: Sage, 1993), p. 17; R. McGregor, 'Governance, Not Genocide: Aboriginal Assimilation in the Postwar Era', in *Genocide and Settler Society: Frontier Violence and Stolen Indigenous Children in Australian History*, ed., A. D. Moses (New York: Berghahn Books, 2004), p. 291; for the full range of counter-arguments, see Thornberry, *International Law and the Rights of Minorities*; Morsink, 'Cultural Genocide, the Universal Declaration, and Minority Rights'; Schabas, *Genocide in International Law*.

11. 3rd Session, 6th Committee, 83rd Meeting, 25 October 1948: UN General Assembly, *Summary Records of Meetings*, (Paris: United Nations, 1949), p. 199.
12. Human Rights and Equal Opportunity Commission (HREOC), *Bringing Them Home: Report of the National Inquiry into the Separation of Aboriginal and Torres Strait Islander Children from their Families* (Sydney: Sterling Press, 1997); *Kruger, Bray & Ors v Commonwealth* (1996–1997) 190 CLR 1.
13. B. Saul, 'The International Crime of Genocide in Australian Law', *Sydney Law Review*, 22 (2000), 527–84.
14. I. Clendinnen, 'First contact', *The Australian's Review of Books*, 6, 4 (2001), 25–6.
15. Ibid., p. 26.
16. L. Behrendt, 'Genocide, the Distance Between Law and Life', *Aboriginal History*, 25 (2001), 132.
17. K. Bischoping and N. Fingerhut, 'Border Lines: Indigenous Peoples in Genocide Studies', *Canadian Review of Sociology & Anthropology*, 33 (1996), 481–506; W. Churchill, 'Genocide: Toward a Functional Definition', *Alternatives*, 11 (1986), 403–30; W. Churchill, *A Little Matter of Genocide: Holocaust and Denial in the Americas, 1492 to the Present* (San Francisco, CA: City Lights Books, 1997); W. Churchill, 'Genocide By Any Other Name: North American Indian Residential Schools in Context, in *Genocide, War Crimes and the West: History and Complicity*, ed., A. Jones (London: Zed Books, 2004); D. E. Stannard, *American Holocaust: The Conquest of the New World*, (New York: Oxford University Press, 1992); G. E. Tinker, *Missionary Conquest: The Gospel and Native American Cultural Genocide* (Boston: Augsburg Fortress, 1993).
18. McGregor, 'Governance, Not Genocide', p. 304.
19. For example, R. Strickland, 'Genocide-at-Law: An Historic and Contemporary View of the Native American Experience (The Langston Hughes Lectures)', *University of Kansas Law Review*, 34 (1986), 721.
20. L. Veracini, 'The Evolution of Historical Redescription in Israel and Australia: The Question of the "Founding Violence"', *Australian Historical Studies*, 34 (2003), 326–45.
21. P. Brantlinger, '"Dying races": Rationalizing Genocide in the Nineteenth Century', in *The Colonization of Imagination: Cultures, Knowledge and Power*, eds, J. Nederveen Pieterse and B. Parekh (London: Zed, 1995), pp. 43–56; P. Brantlinger, *Dark Vanishings: Discourse on the Extinction of Primitive Races, 1800–1930* (Ithaca, NY: Cornell University Press, 2003); R. McGregor, *Imagined Destinies: Aboriginal Australians and the Doomed Race Theory, 1880–1939* (Melbourne: Melbourne University Press, 1997).
22. D. Bates, *The Passing of the Aborigines* (London: John Murray, 1944).
23. McGregor, *Imagined Destinies*, p. 134.
24. R. van Krieken, *Children and the State: Social Control and the Formation of Australian Child Welfare* (Sydney: Allen & Unwin, 1992).
25. A. Haebich, *For Their Own Good: Aborigines and Government in the Southwest of Western Australia, 1900–1940* (Perth: University of Western Australia Press, 1988), p. 350.

26. P. Read, *The Stolen Generations: The Removal of Aboriginal Children in New South Wales, 1883 to 1969* (Sydney: Ministry for Aboriginal Affairs, 1983), p. 8.
27. HREOC, *Bringing them Home*, p. 37.
28. Commonwealth of Australia, *Aboriginal Welfare: Initial Conference of Commonwealth and State Aboriginal Authorities* (Canberra: Government Printer, 1937), p. 3.
29. Royal Commission into Aboriginal Deaths in Custody 1989, p. 1.
30. Ibid., p. 5.
31. *Cubillo & Anor v Commonwealth (No 2)* (2000) 103 FCR 1 at 88. For a discussion of this case, see R. van Krieken, 'Is Assimilation Justiciable? Lorna Cubillo and Peter Gunner v The Commonwealth', *Sydney Law Review*, 23 (2001), 239–60.
32. Commonwealth of Australia, *Aboriginal Welfare*, p. 11.
33. P. Hasluck, *Native Welfare in Australia: Speeches and Addresses* (Perth: Paterson Brokenshaw, 1953), p. 6.
34. C. Cuneen, 'Reparations and Restorative Justice: Responding to the Gross Violations of Human Rights', in *Restorative Justice and Civil Society*, eds, H. Strang and J. Braithwaite (Cambridge: Cambridge University Press, 2001), pp. 83–98.
35. *Kruger* at 105; *Potter v Minahan* (1908) 7 CLR 277, 304–5 (O'Connor J); *Ex parte Walsh & Johnson; In re Yates* (1925) 37 CLR 36, 93 (Isaacs J); *Sorby v The Commonwealth* (1983) 152 CLR 281, 289–90 (Gibbs CJ); 309, 311 (Mason, Wilson & Dawson JJ); *Balog v Independent Commission Against Corruption* (1990) 169 CLR 625, 635–6; *Bropho v Western Australia* (1990) 171 CLR 1, 18 (Mason CJ, Deane, Dawson, Toohey, Gaudron & McHugh JJ); *Corporate Affairs Commission (NSW) v Yuill* (1991) 172 CLR 319, 322 (Brennan J); 331 (Dawson J); 338 (Gaudron J); 348 (McHugh J); *Coco v R* (1994) 179 CLR 427, 437–438 (Mason CJ, Brennan, Gaudron & McHugh JJ); 446 (Deane & Dawson JJ).
36. *Kruger*, at 107.
37. Contrary to the interpretation in M. Storey, '*Kruger v Commonwealth*: Does Genocide Require Malice?' *UNSW Law Journal*, 4 (1998), repeated in C. Tatz, 'Genocide in Australia', *Journal of Genocide Research*, 1 (1999), 315–52 and in the *BTH* Report.
38. H. Wootten, 'Ron Brunton and *Bringing Them Home*', *Indigenous Law Bulletin*, 4 (1998), 6.
39. Ibid., 7.
40. Ibid., 6.
41. Churchill, 'Genocide'.
42. Lemkin, *Axis Rule*, p. 81.
43. Ibid., p. xi–xii.
44. Ibid., p. 79.
45. For Lemkin's analysis of colonial genocide in the Americas, see M. A. McDonnell and A. D. Moses, 'Raphael Lemkin as Historian of Genocide in the Americas', *Journal of Genocide Research*, 7 (2005), 501–29.
46. R. Lemkin, 'Genocide as a Crime under International Law', *American Journal of International Law*, 41 (1947), 149.
47. The drafting committee consisted of two members of the UN Division of Human Rights: Prof Humphrey (Director), Prof Giraud (Chief of Research Section), Mr Kliava from the Secretariat's Legal Dept, and the three external experts invited by S-G: Professor Donnedieu de Vabres (Prof of Law, Paris), Professor Vespasion V. Pella (Romanian Law Professor, Chair of International Penal Law Association) and Professor Lemkin.
48. http://www.preventgenocide.org/law/convention/drafts/
49. UNESC, *Draft Convention*, p. 16.

50. Ibid., p. 23.
51. Ibid., p. 24.
52. Ibid.
53. Ibid., p. 27.
54. It is not entirely clear, then, why Helen Fein (*Genocide: A Sociological Perspective*) insists that cultural genocide 'was not a term used by Lemkin' (p. 9) and that he had 'never distinguished cultural genocide' (p. 11). It is true that the phrase does not appear in *Axis Rule*, but there he certainly meant 'genocide' to *include* a cultural dimension, and the first Secretariat's draft proposes a whole Article III dealing specifically with 'Cultural Genocide', to which Lemkin lent his support.
55. UNESC, *Draft Convention*, p. 27.
56. Ibid.
57. 3rd Session, 6th Committee, 82nd Meeting, 23 October 1948: UNGA *Summary Records*, pp. 186–7.
58. Ibid., p. 187; again on p. 189; There is no need, then, to regard the eventual inclusion of the 'forcible transfer' clause as 'enigmatic' (Schabas, *Genocide in International Law*, p. 175) just because it had started its life as part of the cultural genocide provisions and the UN ultimately excluded the cultural genocide Article. It is also incorrect to say that 'one aspect of "cultural" genocide, forcible transfer of children, is included in [the] list', even though 'cultural genocide generally is not prohibited by the convention: P. Starkman, 'Genocide and International Law: Is There a Cause of Action?' *ASILS International Law Journal*, 8 (1984), 5.
59. Morsink, 'Cultural Genocide'.
60. Consisting of the USSR, the BSSR, the UkSSR, Yugoslavia, Czechoslovakia, Poland – Egypt, Lebanon, Saudi Arabia, Ethiopia, Syria – China, Pakistan, the Philippines – Mexico, Ecuador.
61. 3rd Session, 6th Committee, 83rd Meeting, 25 October 1948: UNGA *Summary Records*, p. 194.
62. Ibid., p. 201.
63. Similar arguments were mobilized against the protection of minority rights, or the extension of the concept of human rights to collectivities and groups as well as individuals, for related reasons associated with state-formation (Morsink, 'Cultural Genocide'; Thornberry, *International Law and the Rights of Minorities*, p. 122).
64. For deletion: South Africa, the UK, the USA, Australia, Belgium, Bolivia, Brazil, Canada, Chile, Denmark, Dominican Republic, France, Greece, India, Iran, Liberia, Luxembourg, the Netherlands, New Zealand, Norway, Panama, Peru, Siam, Sweden, Turkey. Against: the USSR, BSSR, UkSSR, Yugoslavia, Czechoslovakia, Ecuador, Egypt, Ethiopia, Lebanon, Mexico, Pakistan, the Philippines, Poland, Saudi Arabia, Syria; Abstaining: Venezuela, Afghanistan, Argentina, Cuba.
65. This means that the *BTH* Report's usage of the Venezuelan delegate's comments (p. 271) is a little misleading, in that it gives the impression that they reflect the UN's overall position on the child transfer question. But the ultimately successful arguments for the inclusion of the child transfer clause were those based precisely on its *exclusion* from the concerns about assimilationist policies and practices, or 'cultural genocide', and its *redefinition* as an essentially biological or physical intervention. We need to recognize the Venezuelan delegate's speech, then, as an (unsuccessful) attempt to *re*-assert a 'cultural' understanding of child transfer so as to gather support for the idea of cultural genocide more broadly, rather than as based on a shared understanding that 'forced transfer of children' should be approached as an act of cultural genocide.

66. A. de Tocqueville, *Democracy in America* (Chicago, IL: University of Chicago Press, 2000), p. 325.
67. Thornberry, *International Law and the Rights of Minorities*, p. 14.
68. L. Kuper, *Genocide: Its Political Use in the Twentieth Century* (New Haven, CT: Yale University Press, 1981), p. 171; related arguments can be found in M. Levene, 'The Chittagong Hill Tracts: A Case Study in the Political Economy of "Creeping" Genocide', *Third World Quarterly*, 20 (1999), 339–69.
69. C. Tennant, 'Indigenous Peoples, International Institutions, and the International Legal Literature from 1945–1993', *Human Rights Quarterly*, 16 (1994), 1–57.
70. Commonwealth of Australia, Federal Government Submission to the Senate Legal & Constitutional References Committee Inquiry into the Stolen Generation (Canberra: Government Printer, 2000).
71. T. Barta, 'After the Holocaust: Consciousness of Genocide in Australia', *Australian Journal of Politics and History*, 31 (1985), 159.
72. D. J. Mulvaney, and J. H. Calaby, *'So Much that is New': Baldwin Spencer, 1860–1929, A Biography*, (Melbourne: Melbourne University Press, 1985), p. 277.
73. Ibid., p. 278.
74. Ibid., pp. 264–5.
75. Ibid., p. 286.
76. Ibid., p. 289.
77. Ibid.
78. Salmon was born in 1861, educated at Scotch College, Melbourne University and Edinburgh Medical School. He joined the Australian Natives Association in 1894, its Board of Directors in 1895, and became President in 1898. Salmon was a member of the Legislative Assembly between 1893 and 1901, and became Minister for Education. Between 1901 and 1913 he was a member of the House of Representatives in the Federal Parliament, and he was Speaker of the House during 1909–10.
79. *Commonwealth Parliamentary Debates*, 4th Parl, 3rd Session, Vol. LXVIII, 13 Nov 1912 p. 5462.
80. Ibid., p. 5463.
81. Ibid., p. 5462. Later A. O. Neville was to come to a different view, telling the 1937 Commonwealth Conference that '[t]he Asiatic cross, however, is not a bad one. We find that half-caste Asiatics do very well indeed; in fact, very often they beat the white cross' (Commonwealth of Australia 1937: 11).
82. *Commonwealth Parliamentary Debates*, 4th Parl, 3rd Session, Vol. LXVIII, 13 Nov 1912 p. 5463.
83. P. Hasluck, *Native Welfare in Australia: Speeches and Addresses* (Perth: Paterson Brokenshaw, 1953), p. 9; see also Read, *The Stolen Generations*, p. 20.
84. P. Hasluck, 'Policy of Assimilation', NTAC 1956/137, National Archives of Australia, p. 2.
85. Hasluck, *Native Welfare*, p. 17.
86. Clastres, 'On Ethnocide', 53.
87. Strickland, 'Genocide-at-Law'.
88. de Tocqueville, *Democracy in America,* p. 325.
89. R. A. Williams Jr, 'Columbus's Legacy: Law as an Instrument of Racial Discrimination Against Indigenous Peoples' Rights of Self-Determination', *Arizona Journal of International and Comparative Law*, 8 (1989), 60; also R. A. Williams Jr, *The American Indian in Western Legal Thought: The Discourses of Conquest* (New York: Oxford University Press, 1990), pp. 149–50.

90. Cecil Cook, for example, spoke of 'colour of the mind' and wrote, 'where the coloured individual is "white" in all but colour very little conflict is likely to take place' (in McGregor, *Imagined Destinies*, p. 162). Cook's notion of 'breeding out the colour' was thus aimed more at the *perception* of people of Aboriginal descent among Europeans, who would not accept non-whites, than at what he regarded as the real difference between Aboriginals and Europeans, which he constructed in sociological terms.
91. Clastres, 'On Ethnocide', 53.
92. See above; see also Tennant, 'Indigenous Peoples', pp. 26–7.
93. R. Gaita, 'Genocide: The Holocaust and the Aborigines', *Quadrant*, 41 (1997), 45.
94. Veracini, 'The Evolution of Historical Redescription'.
95. H. Merivale, *Lectures on Colonization and Colonies* (London: Frank Cass, 1967), p. 511.
96. Clendinnen, 'First Contact', 7.
97. A. Memmi, *The Colonizer and the Colonized* (New York: Orion Press, 1965 [1957]), p. 52.
98. T. Rowse, 'The Modesty of the State: Hasluck and the Anthropological Critics of Assimilation', in *Paul Hasluck in Australian History: Civic Personality and Public Life*, eds, T. Stannage, K. Saunders and R. Nile (St. Lucia: University of Queensland Press, 1998), p. 127.
99. McGregor, 'Governance, Not Genocide'.
100. P. Hasluck, 'Some Problems of Assimilation' (1959) *Elkin Papers*, University of Sydney, Folio no. 12/295–80.
101. National Archives of Australia (NAA) A1838 557/1; I am grateful to Susan Taffe (S. Taffe, 'Australian Diplomacy in a Policy Vacuum: Government and Aboriginal Affairs, 1961–62', *Aboriginal History*, 19 (1995), 154–72) for drawing my attention to this memo, and also for providing me with her copy of it, since I was unable to locate it personally in National Archives.
102. M. Valverde, '"Despotism" and Ethical Governance', *Economy & Society*, 25 (1996), 357–72.
103. Elkin Papers, University of Sydney, Series 17, Box 19, Item 109.
104. Elkin Papers, University of Sydney, Series 17, Box 143, Item 111.
105. Elkin Papers, University of Sydney, Series 17, Box 19, Item 109. See also the discussions in N. Thomas, *Colonialism's Culture: Anthropology, Travel and Government* (Cambridge: Polity, 1994); Rowse, 'The Modesty of the State', pp. 119–32; R. McGregor, 'Wards, Words and Citizens: A. P. Elkin and Paul Hasluck on Assimilation', *Oceania*, 69 (1999), 243–59; R. McGregor, 'Intelligent Parasitism: A. P. Elkin and the Rhetoric of Assimilation', *Journal of Australian Studies*, 50/51 (1996), 118–30.
106. J. O'Neill, 'On the Liberal Culture of Child Risk: A Covenant Critique of Contractarian Theory', *Sociological Studies of Children*, 7 (1995), 3.
107. R. van Krieken, 'Sociology and the Reproductive Self: Demographic Transitions and Modernity', *Sociology*, 31 (1997), 445–71.
108. For a discussion of these issues in relation to the USA, see the comparison of American and Nazi race laws in J. Scales-Trent, 'Racial Purity in the United States and Nazi Germany: The Targeting Process', *Human Rights Quarterly*, 23 (2001), 259–307.

6
Genocide and Modernity

A. Dirk Moses

Introduction

For the older generation of 'genocide scholars', an intimate relationship between genocide and modernity seemed so obvious as to hardly warrant investigation.[1] After all, the frequency and scale of genocides in all parts of the globe during the twentieth century suggested that modernization crises regularly resulted in the destruction of human communities. It remained to reconstruct and compare cases by mixing the ingredients of the standard recipe: a base of utopian ideology, a packet of racial enmity, plenty of state terror and some indifferent bystanders, topped off by an uncaring global community. These scholars also had an activist agenda, more interested in predicting and preventing genocide in the contemporary world by exhorting the United States, where they lived, to 'humanitarian intervention', than in reflecting on the deeper causes of civil wars and regional conflicts.[2] There seemed little point in pondering the nuances of such concepts when people were being displaced and killed *en masse* today.

There is no denying it, academic discourse can seem futile when even the meanings of 'genocide' and 'modernity' are subject to permanent dispute, as in the following:

> 'Modernity' stems from anthropocentric thought! Or is it instrumental reason? Belief in science? Rationality? The rise of nation-states? A shift from a static to dynamic ideal ('make it new') or reflective consciousness? All have singly or in combination been praised or blamed for Modernity which, everyone knows, started with Gutenberg, Machiavelli, Erasmus, Luther, Montaigne, Bruno, Galileo, Descartes, Roussseau, American or French revolutionaries, or Hegel; or is it Nietzsche? One author's Modernity starts circa 1500 then also, again, with the French Revolution...[3]

And so on. Other scholars dispute whether it makes sense to speak about a single 'modernity' or the 'enlightenment' at all, because these terms suggest the existence of monolithic entities that were in fact heterogeneous.[4] Definitional imprecision seems to preclude scientific certitude let alone political action.

And yet, intellectuals and scholars outside the field of 'genocide studies' have been convinced that much is at stake in these academic debates for the national group, religion or political ideal to which they belong or are committed. Consider both optimistic and pessimistic analyses of modernity.[5] As a byword for material and intellectual advancement, national liberation and international peace, individual freedom and enlightenment, modernity promises a utopia realizable in the rational unfolding of history as the scientific method supplants religious obscurantism, and the public use of reason dissolves the unexamined assumptions of encrusted traditions and the arrogant claims of absolutist authority. By contrast, pessimists wonder whether the Promethean attempt to master the circumstances of existence by fetishizing reason and material production has imprisoned humanity in systems and structures of its own making. Far from signifying emancipation, modernity has issued in racist utopias and totalizing visions of purity, soulless bureaucracy and the omnipotent state, global capitalism and rapacious industrialism, advanced weaponry and inhuman technology, the 'culture industry' and 'the last man'.

We are dealing then, really, with the question of theodicy: how can evil, above all the undeserved suffering of innocents, be squared off with historical progress? Has the fantastic growth in human productivity over the past three centuries resulted in greater human happiness? Indeed, is 'historical progress' a coherent or morally defensible concept any longer? Or, are there still grounds for secular hope in human affairs? What is the link between the global spread of 'civil society' and destruction of Indigenous peoples since the sixteenth century? If modernity promises human improvement over time, does it also accept the terrible human cost exacted by the epochal transformation from premodernity?

Given the underlying issues of theodicy and group survival, it is no surprise that rhetorical excess is sometimes a feature of the discourse. Thus the Jewish Studies scholar Steven T. Katz is ambivalent about modernity because he thinks it hastens the assimilation of Jews, especially in countries with little anti-Semitism, leading to 'an invisible though far less painful Holocaust'.[6] Jews are fated to suffer a Holocaust in all conditions it seems, whether at the hands of fanatical anti-Semites or by those for whom ethnic identity is irrelevant when choosing a marriage partner. The Nazi and the secular liberal are equally perpetrators of genocide, the one physical, such as the Edomites supposedly attempted, the other spiritual, represented by the Moabites. For someone who has devoted his career to forbidding use of the descriptor 'genocide' for the large-scale destruction of other national groups, Katz's claim reveals more about his ethnic anxieties than the subject matter he seeks to examine.[7]

If verbal hyperbole is a problem for some, explanatory over-determination is a temptation for others, especially social scientists who vie with one another to identify the 'essential' or 'underlying' meaning of modernity. Noted sociologist Zygmunt Bauman, for instance, writes of the 'modern era' that it 'has been founded on genocide, and has proceeded through more genocide', basing this generalization more on an ideal typical model of modernity than the empirical examination of genocides through the ages.[8] Equally sweeping is the opposite claim that attributes genocide solely to anti-modern or counter-enlightenment movements and ideologies, conveniently equating modernity with liberalism and benign social progress.[9] These polarized positions, which have characterized the tensions within German historiography for one, are difficult to reconcile.[10]

Still another approach questions whether the genocide–modernity couplet obscures more than it reveals. The stark distinction between modernity and premodernity, civilization and barbarism, historian Dan Stone points out, ignores the fact that genocidal violence may be intrinsic to all human societies at all stages of history. And characteristic of modernity is neither the genocidal potential of a cool instrumental reason, nor the anti-genocidal prophylactic of the liberal rule of law advocated by Raphael Lemkin, but the barbaric behaviour modern societies can produce because they stifle non-rational modes of expression.[11]

Going even further, the postcolonial perspective criticises modernity as an irreducibly Eurocentric construct requiring unmasking. Non-Europeans experience the category of modernity as a European license to dominate them because it implies their own backwardness. Marxism is as much the culprit as liberalism, justifying forced 'development' to 'overcome backwardness' at the cost of millions of lives lost in contrived famines and coerced population movements. As if working in concert with modernity, the concept of genocide then obscures from view the ultimately western source of these fatalities and cultural disasters because, as a western invention as well, its preoccupation with individual and state intentions to consciously destroy human groups precludes problematizing the equally destructive effects of authoritarian modernization programmes.[12]

Plainly, these debates do matter for scholars of genocide but so far philosophers and social theorists have been their main contributors.[13] 'Genocide studies' can learn from this literature by examining how it answers the central questions of the discipline: why does genocide occur, and do the social upheavals of the past two to five hundred years constitute a qualitatively different 'genocidal context' than earlier periods? We will see that the most influential theories of modernity since the middle of the twentieth century were produced by German Jews whose focus was not genocide per se but, understandably enough, the Holocaust and either totalitarianism, fascism or Nazism. Any consideration of the relationship between genocide and modernity, then, has to work through this foregrounding of Europe and the Holocaust, and consequent marginalization of colonialism and non-European genocides.

For all their Eurocentrism, however, these theories' assumption that *any* society can descend into genocide remains an important antidote to 'exighophobia', the substitution of explanation for the emotionally satisfying but intellectually and morally questionable ascription of genocidal potential solely to certain, stigmatized peoples.[14] Due to its historiographical remit, this chapter proceeds in a nominalist fashion, eschewing the attempt to define either keyword conclusively, and focusing on the key thinkers who have defined the terms of discussion.

Civilization, progress and genocide

If liberals were inclined to equate historical progress and civilization, they also associated genocide with barbarism. Raphael Lemkin, the Polish Jewish lawyer who coined the concept of genocide in 1944, regarded the development of national and international law as a civilizational advance because such legal codification inhibited the militarization of social norms. For him, the Nazis represented a reversion to the barbarism of premodern wars in which combatants and civilians were not distinguished.[15] The work of the German Jewish historical sociologist Norbert Elias provides an influential theoretical and empirical elaboration of this common paradigm. The belated discovery of his works from his days as an assistant to Karl Mannheim at the University of Frankfurt in the 1930s has led to a cottage industry of commentary and application of his approach since the 1980s.[16] Like the other key thinkers of genocide and modernity examined here, Elias's ideas developed out of personal experience of Nazism. Witnessing the paramilitary violence of the Weimar Republic, and having fled to Great Britain, Elias was acutely conscious of the fragility of those norms underlying social life. *The Civilizing Process* highlights the historical contingency of such norms by reconstructing the process of their development since the Middle Ages. Drawing on Freud, Elias postulated an anthropology of violent and egoistic drives, represented historically by the 'warrior' ethos of the aristocracy. The epochal development was the absolutist state, whose monopoly on force diminished capricious violence in everyday life and the anti-civilizational ethos of the warrior caste. Over time, the subjects of early modern Europe internalized the new external constraints with the help of etiquette manuals. Knives and forks came into use.

The Civilizing Process is primarily about the French case because of that country's paradigmatic constellation of social forces. The aristocracy eventually accepted its reduced status by the crown, swapped the 'warrior' ethos for 'courtly' rituals and then socialized the rising middle class in the art of modern manners and self-restraint. The court at Versailles became the school of the nation. Like the maturation of children, the civilization of a society is the gradual replacement of external social or state authority with the individual super-ego. At the summit of this process stands parliamentary democracy, whose functioning requires the anthropologically remarkable ability of individuals and groups to delay or forgo gratification in the name of compromise. Civilization is the habitus of self-control.[17]

How did Elias apply his theory to Nazism and the Holocaust? In *The Germans*, he explained Germany's descent into barbarism by reference to its divergence from the west, especially France and Great Britain. Germans became enthralled by Nazism and they perpetrated the Holocaust because they were never fully civilized in the first place.[18] Their vulnerability to Nazism was the result of a German tradition that had retained the cultural hegemony of the warrior ethos represented by the Junker elites, whose power and influence had never been entirely tamed. Indeed, dueling fraternities and the army became the school of the nation, and bourgeois Germans spared no effort to associate themselves with these institutions, which inculcated 'a pitiless human habitus'.[19] The strong emphasis on ritual in this milieu inhibited the development of internal behavioural and moral restraints. Consequently, Germans did not develop the self-control or conscience that could inhibit their national delusions when the rule of law was removed. [20] They were civilizational children.

If the defeat in 1918 and the rise to power of the despised Social Democrats traumatized the bourgeois German habitus, the 'humiliation of Versailles' was felt by all Germans. Unlike Britain after the Second World War, Germans were unable to come to terms with their national decline because their insufficiently developed individual egos required a commensurately strong group national ideal as compensation. Consequently, they opposed the Weimar Republic and its policy of international co-operation, eventually following the man who promised to fulfill their dream of historical greatness. The Nazis merely generalized the anti-civilizational habitus that hitherto had been limited to middle class and aristocratic Germany.[21] When they began to implement their ideologically driven plans of genocide, there was little within Germans to prevent their enthusiastic participation.

Although Elias was an unashamed proponent of the *Sonderweg* thesis, he was, nonetheless, offering a theory of universal application. The originality of the analysis lies in the attention to the dynamic relation between the macro-level of state formation and the micro-level of personality structure. The static categories of 'the individual' and 'society' are historicized and situated within an overarching theory of modernization. Thus the 'lust for submission' of middle-class

Germans is explained by reference to centuries of national development rather than by recourse to specious national character arguments in the manner of Robert Vansittart.[22]

Even so, Elias's theory is open to a number of objections. If he defines civilization as a functional matter of self-control (such as eating with knives and forks), it is less clear how the normative component of social equality and mutual recognition evolves.[23] This tension is evident in the seeming paradox that the Nazis ate with knives and forks and that Himmler, in his infamous 'Posen Speech', took pride in the 'decency' of his men because they had not robbed the Jews they had just shot. Were not Germans very civilized in many respects? Was not an aspect of their racism towards 'Ostjuden' and Slavs that they were seen as uncivilized? It seems unsatisfactory to conclude that German behaviour under Nazism can be fully captured by thinking they had relapsed into barbarism.

Elias's interpreters have amended his stark contrast between barbarism and civilization by attending to processes of 'dycivilization'.[24] Barbarism and civilization can co-exist when the former is 'compartmentalized', that is, demarcated in separate social spaces. Acting as a psychic defence mechanism, such compartmentalization allows, say, concentration camp guards to cordon off their conduct in their minds, and behave like any other person. Violent ghettos are perfectly compatible with liberal societies because they are normalized as 'off-limit' zones for the majority of citizens.

For all that, if Elias's argument has been nuanced to the extent that the state's monopoly on violence does not necessarily entail complete social civilization, it still implies that those pockets, such as ghettos, are uncivilized because the state's writ does not extend to them. But what if the state is the perpetrator? Elias's interpreters have considered this possibility: for genocide to occur the violent targeting of marginalized groups of people needs to escalate and be extended: 'a radical and annihilationist regime [must] complete the shift in the direction of a dycivilizing process'.[25] But *why* does this extension and escalation happen? What drives the state to persecute and even destroy certain categories of people? How and why such a regime comes to power is left open. Here are lacunae in Eliasian civilization theory that other traditions have pondered.[26]

Pessimism, civilization and genocide

Writing at roughly the same time as Elias, Max Horkheimer and Theodor W. Adorno came to very different conclusions. Although also German Jews of the same generation who worked in Frankfurt, and likewise indebted to Freud, their disciplinary and ideological backgrounds set them apart. As philosophers, Horkheimer and Adorno did not feel as obliged to offer detailed explanations for specific phenomena as the historical sociologist Elias, even if applied social research was central to the mission of Critical Theory.[27] As Marxists, they did not privilege any existing state as ideal, least of all liberal capitalist ones. And yet, their question was largely the same: what was the source of the German fascism that made refugees of them all, and what did the Nazi regime and its crimes mean for 'civilization'?

The key text is *Dialectic of Enlightenment*, published in 1944 but only read widely years later. Although Horkheimer and Adorno did not thematize modernity per se – they placed the entire span of western civilization in the dock – their supposed thesis that 'instrumental reason' was the defining and most dangerous feature of the modern age has achieved classic status.[28] Even if they went well beyond Max Weber's famous definition of rationalization as the 'disenchantment of the world', Horkheimer and Adorno agreed that the 'nationalist, pagan and other modern mythologies' of the age were not a counter-Enlightenment reversion to barbarism, as Elias and Lemkin maintained. 'Enlightenment itself' culminated in fascism 'when paralyzed by the fear of truth'. Enlightenment tended to myth if confined to the 'factual mentality' of British empiricism, positivism and the technological mastery of nature. People forgot that the humanly created apparatus had become autonomous and was dominating both them and nature.[29]

In laying the blame for the genocide of European Jewry at the feet of the Enlightenment, Horkheimer and Adorno were not referring only to the intellectual movement and cultural changes of the seventeenth and eighteenth centuries. The process of enlightenment commenced with the socio-psychological constitution of the self at the dawn of western civilization. Their book, then, is as much a philosophical anthropology as a reconstruction of a historical process.[30] We need to understand both aspects of the argument.

They found clues to the pathological construction of the self in ancient literature, specifically in Homer's epic poem, *Odyssey*. Their starting point was the assumption that human survival initially depended on a mimetic relationship to nature, which was thought of in animist or magical terms. Because nature was also feared, the imperative of survival eventually led to the constitution of the self through its separation from and domination of nature.

This diremption had a number of fatal consequences. One was that selfhood was based not only on the human alienation from nature but also on the universalization of domination. 'The awakening of the self is paid for by the acknowledgement of power as the principle of all relations'.[31] Another consequence was that the self, in resisting the duty of propitiary sacrifice to nature, sacrificed its own 'inner nature' – the capacity to experience sensual pleasure and, ultimately, happiness.[32] The development of the self, then, paradoxically undermined the possibility of a fulfilling life.

> Man's domination over himself, which grounds his selfhood, is almost always the destruction of the subject in whose service it is undertaken; for the

> substance which is dominated, suppressed, and dissolved by virtue of self-preservation is none other than the very functions of which the achievements of self-preservation find their sole definition and determination.[33]

Horkheimer and Adorno drew on Nietzsche, Freud and the French surrealist intellectual Roger Caillois to maintain that this renunciation of natural instincts was pathological.[34] Odysseus exemplified this renunciation. In order to resist the Sirens' songs, he had to block the ears of his sailors and tie himself to the ship's mast, signalling the proto-bourgeois subject's atrophied imagination and diminished capacity to enjoy beauty.[35] The origins of totalitarianism lay here:

> The irrationalism of totalitarian capitalism ... [that] makes the satisfaction of needs impossible and tends towards the extermination of mankind, has its prototype in the hero who escapes from sacrifice by sacrificing himself.[36]

Simultaneously, the management of the world required the development of universally applicable systems of logic and science abstracted from natural objects themselves. Reason no longer meant self-legislation but substanceless technique at the service of any power. Emotion was treated as irrational, although the worship of this truncated reason was itself irrational.[37] Unlike Marx's optimistic faith in the historical process of 'self-enriching alienation' – humanity's dialectical recovery of its historical products in the economy, culture and religion – Horkheimer and Adorno postulated a pessimistic historical process one might call 'self-impoverishing alienation': 'the submission of everything natural to the autocratic subject finally culminates in the mastery of the blindly objective and natural.' This process was 'the self-destruction of the Enlightenment'.[38]

If Horkheimer and Adorno thought fascism perfected methods of domination and brandished them nakedly, how did they account for its emergence out of the liberal Enlightenment? The answer lay, again, in the dystopian unfolding of human subjectivity. Unable to encounter nature itself, the instincts sought gratification in illusion, projecting desires outward. As before, the *Odyssey* provided a clue to this phase of the dialectic of Enlightenment. The episode of the lotus-eaters showed that illusory pleasure was meaningless, leading not to the enjoyable experience of nature but to the conformity of the culture industry. Illusions replaced reality and became a surrogate for utopia. What is more, the culture industry made even its pleasure 'an object of manipulation', thereby effectively extinguishing it.[39]

Such an impoverished subject was prone to destructive episodes of paranoid projections against scapegoated minorities. The world, evacuated of pleasure, was experienced solely as dangerous and fearful. Security demanded the imposition of uniformity, leading ultimately to the impulse to destroy external reality.[40] Minorities were targeted because, in their weakness and vulnerability, they reminded the majority of the nature from which it was alienated and that it oppressed: 'since he cannot allow himself the pleasure of following his own instincts, he attacks other individuals in envy or persecution just as the repressed bestialist hunts or torments an animal'.[41] Horkheimer and Adorno linked the fate of all vulnerable minorities, as well as women, because patriarchy was also the will to domination.

> And since the victims are interchangeable according to circumstances – gypsies, Jews, Protestants, Catholics, and so on – any one of them may take the place of the murderers, with the same blind lust for blood, should they be invested with the title of the norm. There is no genuine anti-Semitism, and certainly no such thing as a born anti-Semite.[42]

Their point was that such prejudices did not posses ontological status. They were not pre-given, 'independent variables', as Daniel J. Goldhagen theorized in his controversial study *Hitler's Willing Executioners*. These prejudices were referable, ultimately, to a flawed society. 'The Jews today are the group which calls down upon itself, both in theory and practice, the will to destroy born of a false social order'.[43] The Holocaust was not just a large hate crime.

Christianity was an important cultural precondition for fascism. Having never totally exorcized magic from its religious imaginary, unlike Judaism, Christianity postulated two realms: the spiritual realm that offered the pleasure of modulated mimesis in pseudo-magical practices; and the earthly one that was emptied of moral law and, therefore, available for domination.[44] Fascism continued this tension by trying to recover pleasure through its symbols and mass events – 'the organized imitation of magic practices' – while simultaneously perfecting modes of domination. 'The new German pagans and warmongers', Horkheimer and Adorno observed, 'want to set pleasure free once more'.[45]

For all that, the fate of the Jews in European modernity was particular. They were attacked not only because they represented a 'provocative image of powerless happiness'. Jews also suffered for the sins of rapacious capitalism for which they were held responsible. A double victim, Jews represented both nature and civilization.[46] The 'Jewish question', Horkheimer and Adorno wrote, 'would prove in fact to be the turning point of history', because it represented the most acute crisis experienced by the capitalist system. Germany had not embarked on a divergent path of development, as Elias supposed, but incarnated all the pathologies of western civilization in its most acute form. 'By raising the cult of strength to a world-historical doctrine, German Fascism also took it to an absurd extreme.'[47] Anti-Semitism was the most extreme case of paranoia and false projection, the culmination of the dialectic of Enlightenment.[48]

As might be expected, *Dialectic of Enlightenment* has been criticized by many commentators for various sins of commission and omission. It does not adequately explain why Germany should have perpetrated the Holocaust.[49] It focuses too much on individual psychology at the expense of mass psychology.[50] It lacks any grounding in historical events, identifying the process of Enlightenment over a millennium rather than the specific events of leading to National Socialism, let alone the Enlightenment of the seventeenth and eighteenth centuries.[51] It conflates the disaster of German development with the west as a whole, unjustifiably denouncing the Enlightenment.[52] All these objections are sustainable, and more could be added, such as the book's virtual conflation of liberalism and fascism. *Dialectic of Enlightenment* is also astonishingly Eurocentric, totally ignoring the effects of European colonialism that Marx and Engels had noted in considerable detail. Subaltern writers, some of them Marxists, were much more sensitive to the global context of European fascism, which they felt non-European peoples had been enduring for centuries.[53] It would seem that no general theory of genocide is to be extracted from Critical Theory unless the thesis that civilization culminates in total domination in the form of fascism is to be counted as one. Moreover, it goes without saying that many elements of their analysis are now of historical interest only. The philosophy of history to which they subscribed, with its Marxist anthropology of the human subject rationally controlling its creations, is not one to which even Horkheimer and Adorno held fast after the Second World War.

And yet, looking for elements that are not in the book is to miss its point. *Dialectic of Enlightenment* was not intended as a work of history, sociology or political science. In its idiosyncratic blend of philosophy and psychology, this Hegelian Marxist account of civilization and, ultimately, modernity attempted to ground the origins of murderous prejudice in a bigger story than the analytically fruitless fables of 'ancient hatreds', 'ethnic conflicts' or even the rise of integral nationalism. Horkheimer and Adorno sensibly rejected the tautological and circular argument that one group targeted another simply out of hate.

In its stead, they proposed a general theory in which any minority could be victim, any group a perpetrator. Societies produced prejudice, and social crises were the backdrop to genocides. Consequently, they did not think paranoid false projection ceased with the defeat of Nazism. It lingered even in liberal democracies like the USA, where they had seen out the war, in the form of the stereotypical thinking ('ticket mentality') that affected the 'Jewish masses', as they put it, as much as any other. 'The anger against all that is different is teleologically inherent in the [ticket] mentality, and, as the dominated subjects' resentment of natural domination, is ready to attack the natural minority – even when the social minority is threatened first.'[54]

Was there an antidote? The survival of Jewish minorities provided a model of resistance. After effectively ignoring anti-Semitism in the 1930s, Horkheimer and Adorno came to see the refusal of Jews to assimilate as the salutary resistance of the non-identical – of human variety and plurality – to the steamrolling conformism of modern civilization.[55] The presence of any minority in a population, they were effectively arguing, preserved social and political freedom by challenging the tendency of the unhappy majority to cast reality in its own impoverished image.

Their aspiration to join psychology and philosophical anthropology to explain the unprecedented events of the 1940s was intellectually courageous. So was the insistence that paranoid false projections persisted in all societies after fascism's defeat. That was the conclusion to which Adorno and his collaborator came in their famous study on the 'authoritarian personality'.[56] After all, post-war genocides have been driven by such paranoia. Horkheimer and Adorno help researchers today by locating the origins of genocide in social crises rather than only in the crises of the perpetrators themselves.

Hannah Arendt and the 'rise of the social'

Horkheimer and Adorno's bleak portrait of modernity became an inspiration for cultural pessimists on the left who were appalled by the arms race of the Cold War and possible nuclear Armageddon. The German writer Hans Magnus Enzensberger expressed such anxieties in his book, *Politik und Verbrechen* (Politics and Crime), which became the subject of a celebrated exchange with the political philosopher Hannah Arendt, one of a brilliant generation of German émigré scholars who analyzed totalitarianism.[57] Declining to review Enzensberger's book, she objected to his claim that Auschwitz had discredited the western political tradition, which he held accountable for the possibility of future 'Holocausts' by producing the technological capacity for global nuclear annihilation. Such a generalization of Auschwitz's meaning, she complained, was 'a highly cultivated form of escapism', because it diluted German national responsibility for the crime.[58] Enzensberger replied that his future-oriented construction was in fact necessary to prevent further catastrophes. While assuring Arendt that he had never sought to diminish Germany's culpability, the real escapism, he retorted, was to consign the Holocaust solely to the German context and to the past, and fail to draw pressing, more general, conclusions about the present. Such a conclusion highlighted the destructive trajectory of a technologically driven western civilization, of which Auschwitz was hitherto its most extreme instance.

Arendt remained unconvinced. While not disagreeing with the imperative to avoid future disasters, the question remained regarding the correct lessons the Holocaust taught. The 'equation' of Auschwitz and the 'megadeath' of nuclear war, she insisted, obscured the anti-Jewish specificity of the former, and this distinction issued in very different political implications than those urged by

Enzensberger. 'The fatal dimension of Auschwitz [unlike nuclear war], of course, is that a repetition is possible without catastrophic consequences for all participants.' She concluded by warning against an 'apparent radicalism' that subsumed particular cases under general categories, and she urged commentators to forsake abstractions and constructions in favour of the 'concrete'.[59]

That Arendt's own account of modernity and genocide, or 'megadeath', was concrete would surprise those detractors who have criticized her for supposedly downplaying the specificity of Jewish victimhood in and German responsibility for the Holocaust.[60] In fact, like her own complex German-Jewish identity, she tried to mediate particularism and universalism, in this case accounting for the Holocaust neither in terms of its perpetrators' intentions alone, nor as the unintended product of blind, anonymous forces. To understand her position, we need to attend to the special notion of judgement, to which she was referring Enzensberger.

Modernity conspired against the judgement necessary for political life. The modernizing process had eroded the customs, habits and life-worlds – the 'common sense' – by which people assessed moral and political issues. Totalitarian ideologies offered substitute categories to such disoriented people; their widespread popularity represented 'total moral collapse'. Drawing on Kant's *Critique of Judgement*, she saw the antidote in 'reflective judgement' that permitted objects to reveal themselves in moments of 'exemplary validity'.[61] Such judgements illuminated an object's universal significance while retaining its particularity, rather than reducing it to an instance of some global process or a universal category. This epistemology shared ground with Critical Theory, which also retained the difference between subject and object so that neither dominated the other.[62] The act of judging thus resisted totalizing philosophies of history that categorized people under the aspect of their teleology.[63] In practice, this meant that those Germans who helped Jews during the Second World War judged them as victimized individuals rather than in terms of the regime's propaganda. These Germans were able to distinguish right from wrong.[64]

Modernity was also a problem because of the decline of 'the political' and the 'emergence of the social realm'. The concern with the material reproduction of human existence (the social) was supplanting the possibility of 'spontaneous action or outstanding achievement' (the political) by demanding that everyone conform to 'only one opinion and one interest'.[65] Such uniformity tended to totalitarianism, but this epochal transformation was characteristic of bourgeois society generally. Arendt echoed Luxemburgian themes in her depiction of capitalist modernity.[66] The imperialist phase before totalitarianism was brought about by 'the political emancipation of the bourgeoisie', because this class sought to use politics to transcend the limits of the nation state for the global spread of capital.[67] Contrary to Elias and other theorists of the *Sonderweg* who thought the under-development of the German middle class was the problem of German political culture, Arendt saw its gradual increase in political and economic power after the mid-nineteenth century as the key issue.[68] The bourgeoisie was the bearer of the social, as was the consequent labour movement, whose concern was, of course, the 'social question'.

Arendt had to draw on a variety of intellectual traditions to reconstruct the decline of the political. Like conservative observers, she noted the rise of the 'mob', the proletarian and petty bourgeois masses dislodged from traditional lifeworlds; it eventually joined forces with the German middle class in National Socialism.[69] Heidegger's analysis of inauthentic modern speech went into her theory of political communication.[70] But whether the source of her analysis was leftwing, conservative or reactionary, the bourgeois man, concerned only for his own well-being and that of his family, was the main culprit responsible for genocide.

Contrary to the widely held view, Arendt was not fascinated by bureaucracies because they distanced administrators from the genocidal consequences of their actions, or because the interchangeability of their personnel meant they functioned smoothly irrespective of individual intentions. In fact, she was more interested in how the prosaic careerism of the bourgeois individual drove policies and processes, having witnessed the opportunism of Germans when the Nazis came to power in 1933.[71] People without previous ideological commitments quickly and avidly adjusted themselves to the prevailing norms in the name of getting on and fitting in. Arendt's much-discussed and much-misunderstood concept of the 'banality of evil' must be set against this background. Evil prevailed with the ordinary motivations of careerist bureaucrats who espoused the party line.[72] She did not think that even someone like Adolf Eichmann possessed a subjective criminal intent, because his actions were lawful in the criminal regime of Nazi Germany, and because he had convinced himself that his actions were just. His was not a conscious choice for evil, a willed transgression. He participated in the deportation and killing process with a good conscience. 'The deeds were monstrous, but the doer ... was quite ordinary, commonplace, and neither demonic nor monstrous.' A wicked heart was unnecessary to cause tremendous evil. 'Thoughtlessness', the inability or unwillingness to judge, was the essential precondition.[73]

What about the question of destructive intention central to the crime of genocide? Its source was not to be found in Nazis like Eichmann, Arendt insisted, because his banality bore no relationship to the scale of the enormity being perpetrated. The Holocaust was 'beyond the pale even of solidarity in human sinfulness', and could not be ascribed to the usual 'promptings of interest or volition'.[74] Because the intention to render people superfluous was not humanly willed, she wrote in *The Origins of Totalitarianism*, Nazi crimes represented a form of 'radical evil'.[75] Radical evil and banal evil complemented one another. If the former was ontologically distinct from human intentions because it was driven by a humanly created but uncontrollable historical process, it required 'banal' agents – 'thoughtless' people who had lost their convictions and ability to judge – to blindly expedite its imperatives.[76] The meaning of the Nazi genocide could not be grasped by reading back from the motives of the perpetrators but by paying regard to the deeper significance of their persecution in relation to the trajectory of modern history.

For that reason, she thought that fixating on the Nazis' anti-Semitism obscured what was really going on. It was wrong to regard the Holocaust 'as not much more than the most horrible pogrom in Jewish history'. Nazi anti-Semitism was a historically contingent manifestation of pathological modernization, not pathological Jew-hatred: 'only the choice of victims, not the nature of the crime, could be derived from the long history of Jew-hatred and anti-Semitism'.[77] The actual crime, then, was the decision to erase *any* people from the human community, not just the Jews. This was a crime against that community as well as against the victims. For all that, she did not think Jews were accidental targets of the Nazis. They were isolated and persecuted because they were neither permitted to assimilate successfully nor be accepted as Jews in an environment increasingly dominated by integral nationalism. Germany's pathological modernity had no place for them.

Still, the problem remained the broader crisis of modernity: the simultaneous rise of the social and the social disintegration of political-ethical categories and judgement. This process had culminated in the totalitarian regimes of Stalin and Hitler, being 'the invention of a system in which all men are equally superfluous'. Their concentration camps were the sites where the 'logic of total domination' was perfected. 'The camps are meant not only to exterminate people and degrade human beings, but also to serve the ghastly experiment of eliminating, under scientifically controlled conditions, spontaneity itself...'.[78] Totalitarianism manifested a crisis of world-historical proportions: a 'system' that rendered people superfluous, perfected total domination and extinguished spontaneity.

If the inhuman potential of the world-historical process of modernization (the 'system') was revealed in totalitarianism, it persisted fatally into the post-war period.[79] 'The danger of the corpse factories and holes of oblivion', she wrote in 1951, 'is that today, with populations and homelessness everywhere on the increase, masses of people are continuously rendered superfluous if we continue to think of our world in utilitarian terms'.[80] Human nature itself continued to be threatened after the war: by effacing plurality and inhibiting spontaneity, the system was creating a uniform 'human species' bereft of the regenerative capacities she called 'natality'. Like Horkheimer and Adorno, then, Arendt thought the paramount problem was much broader than radicalized moments like the Holocaust.

What can scholars of genocide learn from this analysis? Certainly, her methodology is difficult to emulate. Arendt consciously eschewed a narrative, structural or psychological account of Nazism and totalitarianism because she thought that history viewed in terms of cause and effect violated the postulate of human freedom and responsibility.[81] Accordingly, she could morally condemn Nazi criminals like Eichmann, however banal, while also proclaiming the ultimate reasons for his deeds a mystery.[82] The social sciences, she complained, failed to appreciate the novelty of totalitarianism because they interpreted all phenomena through their conventional disciplinary lenses. Though indebted to Luxemburg, she opposed Marxist and social science history because they purported to uncover the hidden significance of historical phenomena instead of attending to their patent meaning or connections. She was a political philosopher writing a phenomenology of modernity and totalitarianism, not a social scientist or conventional historian constructing models or crafting narratives of particular events. She had little time for Weber, whether on bureaucracy or charisma.[83]

This is difficult advice to follow, and Arendt did not do so herself. After all, her rendering of 'the social's' rise could be read off 'the facts' only with her particular blend of Marxism, German Idealism and Heideggarian cultural pessimism. Would genocide scholars be content to refer to specific group destructions under the aspect of a global process that supposedly renders people superfluous, culminates in total domination, and extinguishes spontaneity? Is it possible to discount ideology in the way she did because it permitted agents to kill with a good conscience? Can we talk any longer of the 'mob'?

For all that, her attention to imperialism as a precursor to Nazism is yielding important insights in genocide research. If Arendt was not the first thinker to make this connection, she was at least less Eurocentric than the émigrés from Frankfurt.[84] And her attempt to chart the course of modernity as a material and cultural totality that radicalizes in certain circumstances is equally valuable, even if elements of her analysis are no longer tenable. To register her impatience with sociology's penchant for typologization is to understand why much of genocide studies need revamping: sociological abstractions do not explain why events unfold.[85] Like Critical Theory, she did not take anti-Semitism, or any other racism, as an ontologically given starting point for the explanation of genocide. Like Critical Theory, then, Arendt challenges genocide studies to make its unit of analysis a global social system rather than a nation state or ethnic group.

Marxism, genocide and modernity

Given Marxism's dialectical epistemology, it is no coincidence that both Arendt and the Frankfurt School inspire the work of Enzo Traverso, the Italian political scientist and historian who has been modifying Marxism to meet the challenge of Holocaust scholarship.[86] Following Arendt, he wishes to uncover the 'European roots of National Socialism', because focusing solely on Germany misses the broader crisis of modernity.[87] He disagrees with François Furet, Ernst Nolte, Arno Mayer and Goldhagen that Nazism can be explained monocausally as a species of either anti-Communism, anti-modernism or anti-Semitism. And like Arendt, he wants to highlight the formative and radicalizing effect of European colonial violence that liberal scholars like George L. Mosse and Zev Sternhell ignored. At the same time, with Adorno, he does not want to dissolve the 'crime in a long historical process' as other Marxist historians have.[88] The aim of his *The Origin of Nazi Violence* is to mediate the proposition that the Holocaust of European Jewry is rooted deeply in the traditions of liberal Europe – there was no German *Sonderweg* – as well as maintain its particularity by avoiding reductionist arguments. Finally, he adopts Arendt's phenomenological approach as a source of methodological inspiration. In her introduction to Walter Benjamin's *Illuminations*, he notes, Arendt used felicitous imagery to distinguish the approach from orthodox historical ones: 'Like a pearl diver who descends to the bottom of the sea, not to excavate the bottom and bring it to light but to pry loose the rich and the strange, the pearls and the coral in the depths, and bring them to the surface.'[89]

What, then, are the pearls and coral that the author brings to the surface? The origins of Nazi extermination are generally European rather than specifically German, and they begin in the late eighteenth century. The material preconditions emerge with the rise of industrial civilization. In particular, the guillotine and industrial factory, and especially Taylorism and bureaucratic procedures, are the innovations of modernity that permitted humans to be slaughtered impersonally en masse. Another element is the European penetration of the world through conquest and colonization, above all, in Africa. Combining the growing literature on social Darwinism, eugenics and imperialism, Traverso shows how European elites regarded the colonies as spaces for their fantasies of modernization. In the colonies, the European powers learned practices of racist exclusion and exercised the right to decide the fate of entire peoples, many of whom disappeared from the face of the earth. The notion of 'living space' was developed there long before German eyes looked eastwards, just as colonial wars demonstrated the murderous power of the machine gun to mow down thousands of 'natives' well before the First World War.

Presumably relying on Foucault, Traverso highlights the 'biologization' of the proletariat by bourgeois elites. Beginning with the Paris Commune in 1871, they linked leftist insurrection and degeneracy as a dangerous threat to the capitalist order.[90] This marriage of class and racial hygiene became even more significant as Jews came to be regarded as purveyors of political subversion, a view that was pan-European rather than distinctly German. Winston

Churchill, for instance, was one of many who saw Jews as 'the force hidden behind every subversive movement of the nineteenth century'.[91]

The 'Nazi synthesis', as Traverso describes its ideological 'magma', was to link class racism and modern anti-Semitism; the 'biologization of political subversion' was the distinctive feature of German fascism.[92] The Nazis also congealed the preceding features of European modernity: the striving for a racial state and living space, anti-liberalism and anti-Bolshevism based on a mysticism of nature and a 'redemptive myth of a return to the land', 'to produce a unified anti-Jewish crusade'. Drawing on Saul Friedländer, Traverso concludes that Nazism was driven by a 'regenerative anti-Semitism' that functioned as a 'political religion', a characteristic that defines Nazism as 'unique'.[93]

For all its synthetic virtues, *The Origins of Nazi Violence* does not help us explain why colonial and other genocides occurred. And despite its teleological focus on the Holocaust, it cannot answer the question about its causes because, like Arendt, his method explicitly eschews causal analysis. Instead, he deploys an ensemble of metaphors to capture the relationship between the Holocaust and its antecedents, technology, industry, and eugenics: they were a 'forerunner', a 'laboratory', an 'analogy', they 'led ultimately' to Auschwitz, 'prepared the way' or were an 'anteroom'. The Nazis 'integrated and developed' them. The basic argument is that these general European developments were a necessary precondition for the genocide, a conclusion reached by scholars discussed here some time ago. In attempting to marry Marxism and the Holocaust's uniqueness, Traverso has abandoned the most interesting feature of theories that inspired him, namely that a *process* drives historical change.[94]

Bureaucracy, technology and biopolitics

The difficulty of reconciling the contingency of specific cases of genocide with overarching processes such as modernization is evident in the influential work of the Polish-born sociologist, Zygmunt Bauman. An outsider in his own discipline, he sees himself working in the critical tradition of 'solitary writers such as Theodore [sic.] Adorno or Hannah Arendt'. Reflecting on the background to his famous book, *Modernity and the Holocaust* (1989), he reported that

> It was my intention to pick up where Adorno and Arendt had left a blatantly unfinished task: to exhortate [sic.] fellow social thinkers to consider the relation between the event of the Holocaust and the structure and logic of modern life, to stop viewing the Holocaust as a bizarre and aberrant episode in modern history and think through it instead as a highly relevant, integral part of that history.[95]

The debt to Arendt and Critical Theory is indeed heavy. Like these thinkers, he rejected the proposition that the Holocaust could be explained by referring to anti-Semitism alone. As Arendt had excoriated sociology for failing to identify the radical novelty of totalitarianism, so Bauman criticized his colleagues for ignoring the Holocaust's challenge to the assumptions of their discipline.[96] He drew on her theory of morality and judgement for his 'postmodern ethics', which counter-posed an autonomous conscience to the norms that sociologists usually regarded as a functional, and presumably healthy, product of social reproduction.[97] Far from contradicting modern society, as the social sciences generally presumed, the Holocaust brought its destructive potentials to the surface. Like Horkheimer and Adorno before him, Bauman pointed out that since modernity regards people in terms of abstract categories, rather than as concrete others, people are killed by virtue of the category to which they belong.[98] He also followed their thesis that enlightenment (or modernity) seeks to control, if not obliterate, everything outside its compass, because untamed reality is a source of fear and frustration.[99] From Arendt, he also took the notion that the Holocaust was conducted with 'ethically indifferent efficiency' – i.e., its perpetrators were 'banal' – and thus indifference rather than racism was the real danger of modernity.[100]

However extensive his reliance on these thinkers, Bauman remains a sociologist, given to generalizing about 'modernity' as an ideal type. Such modelling, though rich in insights, also has the shortcomings identified by Arendt decades earlier. What, then, does his model look like? Bauman posits that modernity is a temporal modality, a never-ending drive of modernizing the premodern, an 'order making zeal', a 'perpetually unfinished project' of removing 'weeds' from the social garden, a process that is thereby 'transgressive' and potentially genocidal. States are gardeners, the minorities who stand in the way of its plans are 'weeds'. Hitler was, in his own way, 'keeping order'. Genocide occurs when fantasies of order conflict with the messiness of reality.[101] We are speaking, then, of an 'authoritarian high modernism'.[102]

Unlike Arendt, Bauman thinks bureaucracy, that emblem of modernity, was elemental to the Holocaust, propelled by an instrumental reason whose only criteria of success were efficiency and economy.[103]

> [T]here is hardly any doubt that however vivid was Hitler's imagination, it would have accomplished little if it had not been taken over, and translated into routine process of problem-solving, by a huge and rational bureaucratic apparatus [...] bureaucracy made the Holocaust. And it made it in its own image.[104]

Because of such statements, Bauman's name has become synonymous with the thesis that instrumental reason and bureaucracy are modernity's contribution to genocide.[105] That does not mean he has succeeded in convincing all. Consider the criticism of the Polish intellectual historian Andrzej Walicki, remembering the Nazi-occupied Warsaw of his youth.

> I agree that people of all countries are capable of committing horrendous crimes but, nonetheless, the holocaust was not a problem of soulless modern bureaucracy. It involved genuine hatred, genuine cultural repulsion. I vividly remember the Nazi posters in the occupied Warsaw: all of them mobilized popular hatred by portraying Jews as vermin, lice, dirty bearers of typhus, definitely non-human beings. It would be impossible to launch such a campaign against, say, the Danish minority – even if a Danish minority were numerous and disliked by the Germans. And it was typical that German soldiers began to hate Jews even more when they saw the masses of poor 'Ostjuden' in Poland. This, I think, shows the power of spontaneous hatreds towards people seen as cultural alien, 'oriental', etc. Modern bureaucracy could mobilize and employ these feelings but could not create them.[106]

In reply, Bauman would contend that the antagonistic identities at odds here are themselves products of 'liquid modernity', as imagined national communities replace premodern social bonds dissolved by secularization and urbanization. Still, there is an air of inevitability here that sidesteps the production of extreme affects in moments of social and political crisis: 'Categorical murder is nowadays a by-product, side-effect, or waste of their production', he writes.[107] So although Bauman is aware that bureaucracies do not initiate genocide themselves, he prioritizes the moment of social engineering. Thus he thinks that the Armenians were murdered by the Young Turks in 1915 'for being the wrong people in a wrong place'.[108]

The limitations of model building when applied to factual circumstances are readily apparent in such statements. The Armenian genocide cannot be explained in terms of the utopian schemes of Ottoman modernity. The most important context is the contingent two-front invasion of the country when the Armenians were accused of collaborating with the enemy.[109] Such explanatory lacunae are also evident in Bauman's belief that genocide could occur

> whenever an *accelerated construction of a new and improved order happened to be undertaken* by some resourceful and overwhelmingly strong powers of the modern state, and whenever that state exercised full and undivided, non-interfered with rule over the population of its sovereign territory.[110]

Nowhere does he attempt to explain why states feel compelled to engage in accelerated development, nor why its elites become enthralled by utopian ideologies. An account of modernity that claims genocide lies at its heart, as Bauman does, must attend to these issues. Just as significantly, his belief that genocide is most likely when a state is most sovereign flies in the face of research that shows genocides are usually undertaken by revolutionary regimes in countries of failed modernization that feel extremely weak and vulnerable and, indeed, are at war with foes that they fear will destroy them.[111] Bauman's picture of an all-powerful bureaucracy exterminating hapless victims in radically asymmetric encounters occludes the fact that paranoia as well as frustration is the operative emotion in the perpetrator, and that conquest and occupation, which are colonial in nature, are the common circumstances of genocide rather than nation-building exercises. Here, counter-insurgency and security imperatives, intrinsic to empires in all epochs, are as much a factor as any specifically modern attributes.[112]

Similarly general is the hugely influential work of Michel Foucault. Most relevant for the question of modernity and genocide has been his identification of a new form of power in the eighteenth century: 'biopower'. In terms strikingly similar to Arendt's notion of the 'rise of the social' also occurring at this time, Foucault observed that European states began to make the physical welfare of their populations the objects of policy in order to increase the productivity of the economy. 'Biopower' brought human life, at the level of both the individual body and body politic, 'into the realm of explicit calculations'. Governing was replaced by 'governmentality', characterized by the administration of material life.[113] Henceforth, the state and its agencies became preoccupied with measures to improve health, life expectancy and the birthrate.

Such measures did not necessarily have sinister outcomes, as historians of the modern welfare state have pointed out.[114] At the same time, optimizing life was not the only potential policy outcome of biopolitics. The state could incarcerate or destroy elements in the population – the unproductive, the mentally ill, for instance (Arendt's 'superfluous people'?) – that were thought to endanger public health or 'racial fitness'. Foucault rarely used the term 'genocide', but when he did its implication with the modern regime of governmentality was clear.[115] The inverse of biopolitics was 'thanatopolitics'.

> If genocide is indeed the dream of modern powers, this is not because of a recent return of the ancient right to kill; it is because power is situated and exercised at the level of life, the species, the race, and the large-scale phenomena of population.[116]

These theoretical insights contributed to a wave of research into eugenics, racial hygiene and demographic discourses in the nineteenth and twentieth centuries. This now massive body of work has yielded important insights into the nature of modern societies, highlighting the policies of 'population

improvement' common to both liberal and totalitarian states, including the use of sterilization in progressive, supposedly liberal societies.[117] At the same time, the literature concurred in regarding fascist societies, above all Nazi Germany, as taking the logic of 'negative eugenics' to its disastrous, logical conclusion.[118]

For all the influence in these branches of historiography, Foucault's approach has not been as useful to scholars of genocide who must attend as much to government as to governmentality. They need to understand the workings of the conventional sovereignty – the agency of government actors – that Foucault expressly sought to supplant with his focus on subjectivity formation through discipline and regulation. What is more, many scholars of the Holocaust contest the proposition that anti-Semitism and the genocide of European Jewry can be regarded as by-products of biopower. They were not an outcome of the modernity paradigm, but had specifically German roots.[119] Are we left, then, with the stark polarization of a homogeneous modernity on the one hand, and a German *Sonderweg* on the other?

Supplementing modernity

Critics of both approaches have supplemented them by drawing on anthropology and psychoanalysis, thereby following in the footsteps of Critical Theory. Dan Stone has advanced the discussion by drawing attention to the importance of the French surrealist thinker Georges Bataille for understanding the relationship between fascism and modernity, while Dominick LaCapra has highlighted the social-psychological mechanism of 'scapegoating' and, like Bataille, sacrifice, common to all genocides, and most extreme in the Holocaust.[120]

Bataille helps us theorize the source of the powerful affects that accompany genocide – the 'social madness' of the carnivalesque intoxication experienced by many killers while committing atrocities. With Roger Caillois, who, we will recall, Horkeimer and Adorno read with profit, Bataille founded the *Collège de sociologie* in the 1930s to replace surrealism's focus on the individual with a 'sociology of the sacred', a study of social rituals and myths. This group of intellectuals was particularly interested in how traditional societies reproduced themselves by permitting the periodic expression of excessive emotions in carnivals, festivals and other manifestations of semi-controlled ritual violence.[121] In critical sympathy with Bataille, Stone posits that societies have permanent violent propensities that historically have been safely dissipated in various social rituals. Modernity's potential for barbarism lies in its taboos that increase the desire for non-rational forms of behaviour but do not allow for its release.[122] Elias's civilizing process is Bataille's pressure cooker.

Can one interpret National Socialism and the Holocaust as irrational outbursts of pent-up social energies? Yes and no. Bataille thought bourgeois society enslaved people to the 'homogeneous', the utilitarian calculus that reduced human life to the pursuit of material profit. If for Arendt freedom from the utilitarianism of 'the social' inhered in political action, Bataille thought that human 'sovereignty' lay in non-instrumental behaviour, indeed with the Dionysian unleashing of emotions and the transgression of social norms. He esteemed the role of sacrifice as the pinnacle of sovereignty, because the purposeless killing of a creature created an 'ecstatic community' by enabling contact with the sacred.[123]

Did he think the Holocaust was an authentic expression of the 'heterogeneous' rather than its opposite, instrumental reason? Apparently not. Fascism and the Holocaust were in fact the perversion of social energies by a hyper-exploitative state capitalism, although it undoubtedly harnessed affects pent-up by bourgeois society. Neither could the Holocaust be seen as a purposeless sacrifice, Stone points out, because Jewish bodies and goods were actually exploited by the Nazis who justified their actions in terms of eradicating vermin, that is, on instrumental grounds. The Holocaust was the murder of Europe's traditional scapegoats in a society whose affective life had been distorted and channeled in a pathological, pseudo-productive manner. The petty bourgeois character of the genocidal crime was sealed by Himmler's taboo on excess and emotion, and invocation of restraint.

Even so, Bataille's celebration of excess as an expression of sovereign freedom is hard to follow, Stone continues, when the law against murder is precisely that prohibition which is supposed to be transgressed in the name of sacrificial freedom. Although he is well aware of Arendt's argument that European morality was corrupted in its racism and imperial exploitation, Stone believes that Auschwitz was the ultimate transgression because, as Horkeimer and Adorno pointed out, Jews represented the monotheistic prohibition on killing, they rejected sacrifice, and they simultaneously incarnated modern and premodern characteristics.[124]

Dominick La Capra also thinks the modernity literature underplays the religious and chiliastic dimension of the Nazis worldview. In showing that there is more to National Socialism and the Holocaust than instrumental reason, he draws on French thought as well, adapting René Girard's notion of sacrifice. In the theory of modernity he advances, anti-Semitism figures as the manifestation of a scapegoating mechanism that is the return in a secularized form of religious impulses repressed in the modernizing process.[125] Mediating the universal and particular, LaCapra sees anti-Semitism as an irreducible component of Nazism while also embedded in a broader schema of modernization. To make his point, he focuses on the simultaneous presence of radical transgression and social norms in Heinrich Himmler's infamous 1943 Posen speech.[126]

Because so much is made of the speech by many commentators, it is worth quoting the relevant section in full.

> Most of you must know what it means to see a hundred corpses lie side by side, or five hundred, or a thousand. To have stuck this out and – excepting cases of human weakness – to have kept our decency – that is what has made us hard. In our history this is an unwritten and never-to-be-written page of glory, for we know how difficult we would have made it for ourselves if today – amid the bombing raids, the hardships and the deprivations of war – *we still had the Jews in every city as secret saboteurs, agitators, and demagogues. If the Jews were still ensconced in the body of the German nation, we probably would have reached the 1916–17 stage by now.*[127]

I submit that this quotation can be interpreted without suggestive but ultimately ahistorical theories of sacrifice and scapegoating. If we accept Arendt's advice to attend to the actual events and statements of historical subjects, we should take seriously what Himmler openly declares. He is saying that Jews were an internal security threat and needed to be dealt with accordingly, lest Germany be betrayed and undermined from within yet again, as in the final stages of the First World War when strikes crippled German industry. Protracted theoretical throat-clearing is not necessary to understand the juxtaposition of the proclaimed 'decency' and mass murder. There is no paradox. The sharp distinction between cold-blooded (or bureaucratic 'desk') murderers and sadistic killers presented by Goldhagen and his critics does not account for a third possibility: men and women who convinced themselves that their deeds were necessary rather than gratuitous.[128] However fantastical Himmler's linkage of Jews and subversion in 1916–17 and the 'danger' of Jewish partisans in 1939 or 1941, and however useful concepts of trauma are to comprehend how he could view events in this way, the key variable here, as in virtually all genocides, is the fear of internal subversion at a time of existential crisis. The questions raised by Stone and LaCapra – and by Critical Theory 60 years before them – are the right ones: how to explain this paranoia. Seen in this light, the answer of scholars such as Saul Friedländer and Dan Diner that anti-Semitism is the causal starting point seems insufficient.[129] We need to dig deeper. Why the vehement anti-Semitism in the first place?

Colonialism and the rise of the West

If the bureaucratic focus of Bauman's and Foucault's model of modernity needs to be supplemented by the insights of surrealism, anthropology and psychology, their attention to the temporal consciousness of modernity is more fruitful for genocide studies. Bauman is interested in how modernity – postcolonial theorists would say 'the west' – 'managed to recast as inferior and doomed all those forms of life which did not harness their own plan to the chariot of reason'.[130] Less Eurocentric scholars have pointed out that such a philosophy of history licensed Europeans to commit violence against non-Europeans because the metanarrative of progress divided humanity along the lines of modernity–tradition, civilization–savagery, science–magic and nation state–non-state spaces. These differences were then essentialized, such that the male European was inevitably superior to his non-European other. In other words, the revolutionary social logic of modernity was inherently colonial.[131] Not for nothing were the new weapons of modernity – the cylindro-conoidal bullet, the machine gun, even artillery – perfected in the dozens of colonial wars in the nineteenth century.[132] Bauman implicitly acknowledges the colonial and imperial application of his theory when he admits that most genocides occurred *without* modern bureaucracy. His singular focus on the Holocaust participates in the Eurocentrism of much writing on modernity.[133]

It is important, therefore, to pay regard to non-European thinkers who have examined the colonial essence of modernity. Rather than locating the apogee of what Achille Mbembe calls 'necropolitics' in Nazi Germany, like Foucault and others, he finds it much earlier in European colonies. Drawing on Carl Schmitt's notion of the 'state of exception' via Giorgio Agamben, Mbembe identifies these colonial spaces as 'the site where sovereignty consists fundamentally in the exercise of a power outside the law (*ab legibus solutus*) and where "peace" is more likely to take on the face of a "war without end"'. As a 'formation of terror', then, the colony was not a space in which the usual distinction between enemy and criminal obtained. The European rulers could decide upon matters of life and death absolutely: 'the sovereign right to kill is not subject to any rule in the colonies.'[134] The destruction of colonialism did not just inhere in cultural assimilation or even the violence of 'pacification', Mbembe avers, but in the Europeans' arrogation of the right to dispose of their subject peoples in any manner they wished.

An important though neglected voice is that of the Argentine philosopher, Enrique Dussel who, unlike many South Asian postcolonial theorists, does not place himself in the postmodern camp, which he regards as equally Eurocentric.[135] Drawing on the world-systems theory of Immanuel Wallerstein, he identifies the origins of modernity with Spain's foundation of the first world-system late in the fifteenth century. Hitherto, Europe had been at the periphery of the Eurasian landmass dominated by China and other powers, and only geographical contingencies enabled the Iberian maritime states to gain a comparative advantage over the far more advanced eastern economies. The point is that modernity did not originate solely in Europe as modernization theorists suppose, but that it evolved in the European relationship with non-Europe, initially with Amerindia. The 'Eurocentric fallacy in understanding modernity' forgets its non-European anchoring.[136] Like Horkeimer and Adorno, Dussel thinks modernity is blind to its own mythic quality; it 'carries out an irrational process that remains concealed even to itself'.[137]

This blindness, to be sure, did not obtain at the outset. In the first phase of modernity, Europeans like Bartolomé de Las Casas questioned the genocidal consequences of European empire, inaugurating an important international debate about the morality of foreign occupation.[138] These scruples were forgotten by philosophy, however, during the second phase of modernity that commenced with capitalism in the late eighteenth century and that was dominated by north-western Europe. Henceforth, European reflection centered on managing the burgeoning world, capitalist system rather than questioning its impact on the non-Europeans with whom modernity had originated. Only with this forgetting of its non-European roots and blindness to its impact could philosophy think that modern subjectivity developed solely in the Renaissance, Reformation, Enlightenment and French Revolution.[139]

This erasure had grave consequences for non-Europeans. The theodicies of Kant, Hegel and others, Dussel continues, posited dramas of reason and emancipation overcoming backwardness and tyranny that made the West the culmination of world history. The bearers of the world spirit were the 'Germanic peoples' before whom 'every *other people* have no rights'. Spreading civil society became their right and duty, and conquest became integral to the modern ego, whose first exponent was the notorious conquistador Fernando Cortes. Northern military power to conquer and colonize was thereby sacralized, and 'sacrificial violence' became the essence of western modernity. The European philosophical tradition became complicit in the 'saving sacrifice' of indigenous people.[140]

Dussel does not want to abandon modernity, only to overcome its mythic development. The 'transmodernity' he enjoins includes non-Europe in its consciousness, and thereby overcomes the justification of developmental violence. If his approach adds much needed historical and non-European flesh to the bones of the mid-century theorists of modernity, Mark Levene's recent contribution provides the clothes for this body of thought. For over a decade, he has been developing an approach that takes the international states' system, above all, the rise of the west, as its object of analysis rather than individual nation states.[141] Distinctive in the twentieth century, he thinks, is the supplanting of the multi-national empire by the nation state as the normative form of political organization. Like Michael Mann in the *Dark Side of Democracy*, Levene recognizes that the empires were racist, hierarchical and often practiced retributive genocide when challenged, but were inclusive if subject nations, peoples and cities towed the line.[142] They were not inherently genocidal. Extermination or the effacement of otherness was not essential for their reproduction.

The replacement of such empires with a global system of competitive nation states led to inevitable problems. The imperative to establish sovereign autonomy collided with reality as the leaders of ethnically heterogeneous states mobilized their demographic and natural resources to survive in the competitive environment. The rise of the west, then, led to unprecedented state-driven modernization that often destroyed domestic obstacles, like ethnic or national minorities. Far from being a return to barbarism as Lemkin thought, the twentieth century marked a very new phase in world history, the distinctively modern paradox of progress and destruction.

> Only after the Second World War and, more specifically, in the era of European post-colonial retreat did genocide become a truly global phenomenon, most obviously facilitated through the extension of the Western-created concept of the nation-state to all hemispheres, and with it of the embrace of the entire world's population as citizens of such states within its international nation-state framework.[143]

We have here, then, a *Sonderweg* of the West, an anti-theodicy that inverts the celebratory rise of the West in the pro-imperial encomia fashionable today. The European origins of the nation state lie in the unique combination of political power and religious uniformity of the small starts that emerged from the disintegration of the Roman Empire in the middle ages.[144] With Christianity as the official religion of small feudal entities, the inevitable conflicts were met with declarations of war on schismatics and heretics, who were scapegoated in a phobic way. This phobic reaction, a pattern and term Levene uses in relation to twentieth century totalitarian regimes, started here.

Given that the master narrative is the rise of the West, the world historical turning point is not 1492 – the spread of European power abroad in blue water empires – but the French Revolution of 1789 with its militarized nationalism. The first modern genocide occurred in the *Vendée* against royalist rebels whom republicans regarded as evil opponents of the reason and progress embodied by the new nation. This new ideology knew no internal limits against the extirpation of such opponents, nor was there a chance of conversion that Christian Europe at least offered heretics and non-Christians. Here was a totalizing agenda of statist people-making – Heather Rae calls it 'pathological homogenization' – engendering the new religion of patriotism and a mass politics that elites would later find difficult to contain, as conservative German historians like Friedrich Meinecke and Gerhard Ritter feared long ago.[145] Unlike liberals such as Eric Weitz and Norman Naimark, however, Levene does not think the ideology of integral nationalism can account for genocide.[146] It is the modernizing process, rather than modernity per se, that forces insecure states to catch up to the core, often liberal, states in the system. The system produces what he calls a 'political environment of almost perpetual crisis' that issues in illiberal, sometimes genocidal polities.[147]

These are the preconditions of genocide. What triggers genocide is a confluence of factors: when modernizing elites perceive that their attempts to secure political and economic sovereignty are hampered by national minorities, such as Armenians in the Ottoman Empire or Jews in Germany; when they regard these minorities as proxies for foreign enemies; and when these minorities are held responsible for the failure of previous bids for sovereignty, for instance, the perceived Armenian disloyalty in the late nineteenth century, and the perceived Jewish and leftist betrayal of the army between 1917 and 1920. Never again would these national elites permit such minorities to undermine national security and progress by representing foreign influence and causing domestic mayhem.

At the same time, these elites fantasized about a 'powerful and resplendent past' that they contrasted with a 'diminished and enfeebled present' for which these minorities were to blame.[148] Such ideologies compensated such enervated elites (or would-be elites), driving them to vain attempts – with genocidal shortcuts – to establish national sovereignty. These traumatic memories, then, are a contingent cultural dimension that account for the vehemence phobic reaction to perceived minority disloyalty. Even in this short explication, it is clear that Levene's combination of world systems theory and cultural factors is a tremendously impressive advance in our understanding of how and why genocides have occurred in long twentieth century.

Conclusion

The disputes of Holocaust historiography may seem peripheral in light of such a global perspective. After all, one of the great contributions of genocide studies has been to inform scholars and the public that the Holocaust is far from the only case of group destruction in the past century, even if its status as the most extreme case is widely acknowledged. And yet, debates within this field remain of general interest because its particular intensity continues to yield insights. The reception of Götz Aly's book *Hitlers Volksstaat: Raub, Rassenkrieg und nationaler Sozialismus* (Hitler's People's State: Theft, Racial War and National Socialism) is a case in point. Aly, a former leftist activist turned journalist-historian, is the author of a number of ground-breaking works on the Holocaust that link its unfolding to administrative and material factors rather than to antisemitism alone.[149] Over the years, his materialism has been roundly condemned by German-Jewish historians like Dan Diner for playing down the independent variable of ideological Jew-hatred. Diner, it should be noted, is also dissatisfied with Arendt who he thinks mischievously argues that 'while the crimes had indeed been committed by Germans, others were capable of perpetrating similar criminal acts'. The problem with the historiography, he complains, is that too often Germans are tempted to regard the Holocaust as a 'human-historical problem' rather than a particularly German one.[150]

Aly's *Volksstaat* advances a case in terms of the modernity paradigm that certainly violated Diner's precepts. It argues that the Nazi state won the considerable support of the German population less for its racism than by the distribution of plunder from Jews ('Aryanization') and the occupied territories. Nazi German was a racist social democratic welfare state populated by banal figures who could have been drawn by Arendt: 'Without stature, or much of a brain', opportunists, profiteers, mercenaries and politically irresponsible. He topped off the argument by adapting Horkheimer's famous quip about anti-Semitism, capitalism and fascism: 'He who won't speak about the advantages of millions of simple Germans should keep silent about National Socialism and the Holocaust'.[151]

Reviewers of the book made the usual kinds of academic objections about the sources used, the methodological underpinnings and so forth.[152] Because of the high identity stakes associated with the Holocaust, and because the generalizing dimension of the modernity paradigm challenges the 'Nazism as aberration' thesis that Diner and many others advance, *Volksstaat* also attracted exighophobic criticisms – replacing explanatory strategies based on the assumption of a common humanity with national character 'arguments' – mentioned at the outset of this chapter. As this problem is not uncommon in the literature, it is important to briefly examine Natan Sznaider's symptomatic discussion of the book, which demonstrates the emotional affect and problems of exighophobia.

> The brouhaha [about Aly's book] has erupted because, underneath all the numbers, readers find a unique argument that Germans have seemingly been waiting to hear for sixty years. Just as they always suspected, every one of them was guilty – but not of hating the Jews. It turns out what they were guilty of was of giving into their baser instincts and robbing the Jews. For Aly, this judgment makes the Germans – if anything – even more guilty; such greed makes the crime more base. But in terms of the German public, exoneration of the crime of racism is a dream come true. According to Aly, the Germans did not hate the Jews more than any other Europeans. There was no *Sonderweg*. Germany was a 'normal' country. People have tried to make this argument intermittently for years.
>
> He says that Nazi Germany was an ethnically based, social-democratic state. It followed the same logic as all other such states – it simply took it

farther. Of course, non-ethnic Germans lived worse, to put it mildly. But, Aly argues, what is that condition but the logic of the ethnically homogenous welfare state carried out to its logical conclusion? European welfare states have always been based on ethnic solidarity.

> ... it is all the fault of 'ordinary Germans'—but they are just the same as everybody else. They are not racist. Just greedy. They responded to the same incentives that everyone else did. There were just more of them. Clearly, the idea that Nazi Germany was no more racist than any other country is on its face absurd.[153]

Consider what Sznaider is asking the reader to believe. First, that Germans were (are?) ontologically different from other human beings because they did (do?) not respond to the same incentives as the rest of the human race. Second, that Germans were (are?) more racist than other Europeans. Both propositions are untenable; if the first is sociological nonsense, the second is historically questionable. Nazi Germany may have been the most racist of states, but most Europeans at the time thought in national if not racist terms. Ukrainians and Poles fought an extremely vicious ethnic war in the 1940s, as did Croats, Serbs and other nationalities; many Europeans turned on their Jewish and Roma neighbours, betraying them to the Nazis and callously stealing their property. The fighting in Palestine in 1948 was no less barbaric, as was the partition of India at the same time.[154] After the war, the so-called liberal powers of France and Great Britain tortured and killed tens of thousands of Arabs, Africans and Asian to maintain their profitable empires.[155]

Given the blindness to these realities in Sznaider's review, the validity of the modernity paradigm, whatever its limitations, remains a necessary, indeed humanistic antidote to exighophobia. Seen in this light, it is to the lasting credit of the cosmopolitan German Jews Elias, Arendt, Horkheimer and Adorno that, despite the harrowing experience of exile from their native Germany, they resisted the exighophobic temptation, and developed critical narratives of modernity of lasting significance that addressed generally human as well as specifically Jewish concerns. Genocide scholarship would benefit from applying many of their insights about modernity and the Holocaust to other cases of genocide.

Notes

1. Members of this generation like to regard themselves as the founders of the discipline although that honour goes to the much older Raphael Lemkin (1900–1959). See S. Totten and S. L. Jacobs, eds, *Pioneers of Genocide Studies: Confronting Mass Death in the Century of Genocide* (Westport, CT: Greenwood Press, 2002). My thanks to Yehonatan Alshesh and Natasha Wheatley for helpful comments. Of course, they are neither responsible for the view expressed or any errors committed here.

2. For example, H. Fein, 'Definition and Discontent: Labelling, Detecting, and Explaining Genocide in the Twentieth Century', *Jahrbuch für Historische Friedensforschung*, special edition, *Genozid in der Modernen Geschichte*, eds, S. Förster and G. Hirschfeld, 7 (1999); S. Totten, 'The Intervention and Prevention of Genocide: Sisyphean or Doable?', *Journal of Genocide Research*, 6, 2 (2004), 229–47. For commentary, see A. D. Moses, 'Why the Discipline of "Genocide Studies" Has Trouble Explaining How Genocides End?', Social Science Research Council, http://howgenocidesend.ssrc.org/Moses/, December 2006. Prominent exceptions to this trend are the English scholars Mark Levene and Martin Shaw: Levene, 'A Dissenting Voice: Part 1', *Journal of Genocide Research*, 6, 2 (2004), 153–66, and 'A Dissenting Voice, Part 2', *Journal of Genocide Research*, 6, 3 (2004), 431–46; Shaw, *What is Genocide?* (Cambridge: Polity, 2007).
3. E. Rothstein, 'Broaching the Cultural Logic of Modernity', *Modern Language Quarterly*, 61, 2 (2000), 363.
4. B. Yack, *The Fetishism of Modernities: Epochal Self-Consciousness in Contemporary Social and Political Thought* (Notre Dame, IN: University of Notre Dame Press, 1997); J. Schmidt, 'What Enlightenment Project?', *Political Theory*, 28, 6 (2000), 734–57.
5. J. Kaye and B. Strath, 'Introduction', in Kaye and Strath, eds, *Enlightenment and Genocide, Contradictions of Modernity* (Brussels: Peter Lang, 2000).
6. S. T. Katz, *Post-Holocaust Dialogues: Critical Studies in Modern Jewish Thought* (New York: New York University Press, 1983), pp. 258–9. D. J. Goldhagen made analogous claims about the assimiliationist demands of nineteenth-century German liberals, which he described as 'eliminationist': *Hitler's Willing Executioners: Ordinary Germans the Holocaust* (New York: Knopf, 1996). A more nuanced case for the Enlightenment's complicity in the Holocaust by virtue of its hostility to particularity is advanced by B. Lang, *Act and Idea in the Nazi Genocide* (Chicago, IL: University of Chicago Press, 1990), pp. 186–95.
7. S. T. Katz, *The Holocaust in Historical Context*, vol. 1 (New York: Oxford University Press, 1994). Volume two has not appeared at the time of writing.
8. Z. Bauman, *Postmodern Ethics* (Oxford: Blackwell, 1993), p. 227.
9. W. D. Rubinstein, *Genocide: A History* (Harlow: Pearson Education Limited, 2004).
10. Good surveys of the literature are D. Stone, *Constructing the Holocaust: A Study in Historiography* (London: Vallentine Mitchell, 2003); T. Rohkrämer, 'Antimodernism, Reactionary Modernity, and National Socialism: Technocratic Tendencies in Germany, 1890–1945', *Contemporary European History*, 8, 1 (1999), 29–50; A. Beyerchen, 'Rational Means and Irrational Ends: Thoughts on the Technology of Racism in the Third Reich', *Central European History*, 30, 3 (1997), 386–402; M. Roseman, 'National Socialism and Modernization', in *Fascist Italy and Nazi Germany: Comparisons and Contrasts*, ed., R. Bessel (Cambridge: Cambridge University Press, 1996), pp. 197–229.
11. D. Stone, *History, Modernity, and Mass Atrocity: Essays on the Holocaust and Genocide* (London: Vallentine Mitchell, 2006).
12. V. Lal, 'The Concentration Camp and Development: the Pasts and Futures of Genocide', in *Colonialism and Genocide*, eds, A. D. Moses and D. Stone (London: Routledge, 2007), pp. 124–47; D. Chakrabarty, *Provincializing Europe: Postcolonial Thought and Historical Difference* (Princeton, NJ: Princeton University Press, 2000).
13. Exceptions are S. Clark, *From Enlightenment to Risk: Social Theory and Modern Societies* (New York: Palgrave Macmillan, 2006); J. Shipway, 'Modern by Analogy: Modernity, Shoah and the Tasmanian Genocide', *Journal of Genocide Research*, 7, 2 (2005), 205–19; J. Docker, 'The Enlightenment, Genocide, Postmodernity', *Journal of Genocide Research*,

5, 3 (2003), 339–60; A. Kimura, 'Genocide and the Modern Mind: Intention and Structure', *Journal of Genocide Research*, 5, 3 (2003), 405–20; M. Freeman, 'Genocide, Civilization and Modernity', *British Journal of Sociology*, 46, 2 (1995), 207–23.

14. I take this concept from G. Hage, '"Comes a Time We Are All Enthusiasm": Understanding Palestinian Suicide Bombers in Times of Exighophobia', *Public Culture*, 15, 1 (2003), 65–89.
15. See D. Stone, 'Raphael Lemkin on the Holocaust', *Journal of Genocide Research*, 7, 4 (2005), 539–50.
16. N. Elias, *Über den Prozeß der Zivilisation: soziogenetische und psychogenetische Untersuchungen*, 2 vols, rev. edn (Bern: Francke, 1969); *The Civilizing Process: State Formation and Civilization*, trans. E. Jephcott. (Oxford: Blackwell, 1982); S. Mennell, *Norbert Elias: Civilization, and the Human Self-Image* (Oxford: Blackwell, 1989); idem, *Norbert Elias: An Introduction* (Dublin: University College Dublin Press, 1998); D. Smith, *Norbert Elias and Modern Social Theory* (London: Sage Publications, 2001).
17. R. van Krieken, *Norbert Elias* (London: Routledge, 1998), chapter four.
18. N. Elias, *The Germans: Power Struggles and the Development of Habitus in the Nineteenth and Twentieth Centuries*, trans. and preface by E. Dunning and S. Mennell; (New York: Columbia University Press, 1996).
19. Ibid., 107–8.
20. E. Dunning and S. Mennell, 'Elias on Germany, Nazism, and the Holocaust: On the Balance Between "Colonizing" and "De-Civilizing" Trends in the Social Development of Western Europe', *British Journal of Sociology*, 45, 3 (1995), 339–57.
21. Ibid., 197, 374.
22. Lord Vansittart, 'The Problem of Germany: A Discussion', *International Affairs*, 21, 2 (1945), 313–24.
23. Elias, *The Germans*, 32–3, 109.
24. A. de Swaan, 'Dyscivilization, Mass Extermination and the State', *Theory, Culture and Society*, 28, 2–3 (2001), 265–76.
25. Ibid., 271.
26. Ibid., 273.
27. M. Jay, *The Dialectical Imagination: A History of the Frankfurt School and Institute for Social Research, 1923–1950* (New York: Little Brown, 1973).
28. M. Horkheimer and T. W. Adorno, *Dialectic of Enlightenment*, trans. J. Cummings (Boston, MA: Beacon Press, 1972). The section on 'Element of Anti-Semitism' was added in 1947. Commentary: J. Schmidt, 'Language, Mythology and Enlightenment: Historical Notes on Horkheimer and Adorno's *Dialectic of Enlightenment*', *Social Research*, 65, 4 (1998), 807–38; J. Habermas, 'The Entwinement of Myth and Enlightenment: Re-Reading *Dialectic of Enlightenment*', *New German Critique*, 26 (1982), 13–30; A. Honneth, 'The Possibility of a Disclosing Critique of Society: The Dialectic of Enlightenment in Light of Current Debates in Social Criticism', *Constellations*, 7, 1 (2000), 116–27; A. Hewitt, 'A Feminine Dialectic of Enlightenment? Horkheimer and Adorno Revisited', *New German Critique*, 56 (1992), 143–70; C. Rocco, 'Between Modernity and Postmodernity: Reading *Dialectic of Enlightenment* against the Grain', *Political Theory*, 22, 1 (1994), 71–97.
29. Horkheimer and Adorno, *Dialectic of Enlightenment*, pp. xiii–iv, 4, 37–8.
30. Ibid., pp. xvii, 45.
31. Ibid., p. 9.
32. See A. Rabinbach, 'Why Were the Jews Sacrificed? The Place of Anti-Semitism in *Dialectic of Enlightenment*', *New German Critique*, 81 (2000), 55.
33. Horkheimer and Adorno, *Dialectic of Enlightenment*, pp. 54–5.

34. Caillois wrote about traditional rituals of excess and chaos that he thought regenerated the collective order. See J. Clifford, 'On Ethnographic Surrealism', *Comparative Studies in Society and History*, 23, 4 (1981), 559.
35. Horkheimer and Adorno, *Dialectic of Enlightenment*, pp. 35, 105–6.
36. Ibid., p. 55.
37. Ibid., pp. 14–16, 87–92.
38. Ibid., p. xvi. On self-enriching alienation, see A. Walicki, *Marxism and the Leap into the Kingdom of Freedom: The Rise and Fall of the Communist Utopia* (Stanford, CA: Stanford University Press, 1995).
39. Ibid., pp. 62, 83, 106, 170. Y. Sherratt, 'The *Dialectic of Enlightenment*: A Contemporary Reading', *History of the Human Sciences*, 12, 3 (1999), 41–4.
40. Sherratt, 'The *Dialectic of Enlightenment*', 48–9.
41. Horkheimer and Adorno, *Dialectic of Enlightenment*, p. 192.
42. Ibid., pp. 110–12, 171, 187. 'The thought of happiness without power is unbearable because it would then be true happiness': 172.
43. Ibid., p. 168. D. J. Goldhagen, *Hitler's Willing Executioners: Ordinary Germans and the Holocaust* (New York: Knopf, 1996).
44. Ibid., pp. 177–8, 190.
45. Ibid., pp. 31, 184–9.
46. Ibid., pp. 60, 173–4.
47. Ibid., p. 100.
48. M. Jay, 'The Jews and the Frankfurt School: Critical Theory's Analysis of Anti-Semitism', *New German Critique*, 19 (1980), 147.
49. Rabinbach, 'Why were the Jews Sacrificed?', 62.
50. E. Bahr, 'The Anti-Semitism Studies of the Frankfurt School: The Failure of Critical Theory', *German Studies Review*, 1, 2 (1978), 137.
51. R. Rorty, 'The Overphilosophication of Politics', *Constellations*, 7, 1 (2000), 128–32.
52. J. Herf, *Reactionary Modernism: Technology, Culture, and Politics in Weimar and the Third Reich* (Cambridge: Cambridge University Press, 1984), pp. 9–10.
53. K. Marx, *Colonialism and Modernization*, ed. and intro. S. Avineri (Garden City, NY: Doubleday, 1968); R. H. King, *Race, Culture, and the Intellectuals, 1940–1970* (Washington, DC and Baltimore, MD: Woodrow Wilson Center Press/The Johns Hopkins University Press, 2004).
54. Horkheimer and Adorno, *Dialectic of Enlightenment*, p. 207.
55. Jay, 'The Jews and the Frankfurt School', 148f.
56. T. W. Adorno, Else Frenkel-Brunswick, Daniel Levinson, and R. Nevitt Sanford. *The Authoritarian Personality* (New York, Harper, 1950).
57. *Politik und Verbrechen* (Frankfurt am Main: Suhrkamp, 1964). For a contextualisation of her work on totalitarianism with that of other émigré scholars, Ernst Fraenkel, Franz L. Neumann, Sigmund Neumann, Carl Joachim Friedrich and Zbigniew Brezinski, see A. Söllner, 'Hannah Arendt's *The Origins of Totalitarianism* in its Original Context', *European Journal of Political Theory*, 3, 2 (2004), 219–38.
58. *Merkur*, 205 (April 1965), 380–1.
59. Ibid., 384.
60. E. Gellner, *Culture, Identity, and Politics* (Cambridge: Cambridge University Press, 1987), pp. 89–90; M. Marrus, 'Hannah Arendt and the Dreyfus Affair', *New German Critique*, 66 (1995), 147–61; S. E. Aschheim, 'Nazism, Culture and *The Origins of Totalitarianism*: Hannah Arendt and the Discourse of Evil', *New German Critique*, 70 (1997), 117–39; W. Laqueur, 'The Arendt Cult: Hannah Arendt as Political Commentator', *Journal of Contemporary History*, 33, 4 (1998), 483–96; R. Wolin, 'Operation Shylock: Arendt,

Eichmann, and the "Unheimlichkeit" of Jewish Identity', *History and Memory*, 8, 2 (1996), 9–34. Sympathetic studies are R. J. Bernstein, *Hannah Arendt and the Jews* (Cambridge, MA: MIT Press, 1996), S. Benhabib, *The Reluctant Modernism of Hannah Arendt* (Thousand Oaks, CA: Sage Publications, 1996); N. Curthoys, 'The Politics of Holocaust Representation: the Worldly Typologies of Hannah Arendt', *Arena Journal*, 16, (2001), 49–74. See also D. R. Villa, *Politics, Philosophy, Terror: Essays on the Thought of Hannah Arendt* (Princeton, NJ: Princeton University Press, 1999).

61. H. Arendt, *Lectures on Kant's Political Philosophy*, edited with an interpretive essay by R. Beiner (Chicago, IL: University of Chicago Press, 1982), chapter eight, 'Evil, Thinking, and Judging', 154–78.
62. Jay, 'The Jews and the Frankfurt School', 147.
63. See Beiner in Arendt, *Lectures on Kant's Political Philosophy*, p. 127.
64. H. Arendt, *Eichmann in Jerusalem: A Report on the Banality of Evil*, rev. edn (New York: Penguin, 1965), p. 295.
65. H. Arendt, *The Human Condition* (Chicago, IL: University of Chicago Press, 1958), pp. 27, 39–40. See H. F. Pitkin, *The Attack of the Blob: Hannah Arendt's Concept of the Social* (Chicago, IL: University of Chicago Press, 1998).
66. P. Spencer, 'From Rosa Luxemburg to Hannah Arendt: Socialism, Barbarism and the Extermination Camps', *The European Legacy*, 11, 5 (2006), 525–40.
67. H. Arendt, *The Origins of Totalitarianism*, 2nd edn. (London: George Allen and Unwin, 1958), 125. Contrary to Lenin, she thought (p. 138) that 'Imperialism must be considered the first state in political rule of the bourgeoisie rather than the last stage of capitalism'.
68. B. Moore, Jr., *Social Origins of Dictatorship and Democracy* (Boston, MA: Beacon Press, 1966); R. Dahrendorf, *Society and Democracy in Germany* (London: Weidenfeld and Nicolson, 1968). See the fundamental critique of D. Blackbourn and G. Eley, *The Peculiarities of German History* (Oxford: Oxford University Press, 1984).
69. Arendt, *The Origins of Totalitarianism*, p. 124.
70. A. N. Flakne, 'Beyond Banality and Fatality: Arendt, Heidegger and Jaspers on Political Speech', *New German Critique*, 86 (2002), 3–18.
71. She explicitly rejected the 'cog in the machine' argument because it ignored human responsibility: Arendt, *Eichmann in Jerusalem*, p. 289.
72. Y. Lozowick, *Hitler's Bureaucrats: The Nazi Security Police and the Banality of Evil* (New York: Continuum, 2002); M. T. Allen, 'The Banality of Evil Reconsidered: SS Mid-Level Managers of Extermination Through Work', *Central European History*, 30 (1997), 253–94.
73. H. Arendt, *The Life of Mind – Thinking – Willing* (New York and London: Harvest/HJB Book, 1978), p. 4; idem, *Eichmann in Jerusalem*, p. 287. See Lang, *Act and Idea in the Nazi Genocide*, for an attempt to argue that the Nazis were consciously committing evil.
74. H. Arendt, 'Thinking and Moral Considerations: A Lecture', *Social Research*, 38, 3 (1971), pp. 418, 437.
75. Arendt, *Origins of Totalitarianism*, pp. 459.
76. Ibid., pp. 459, 468.
77. Arendt, *Eichmann in Jerusalem*, pp. 267–8, 282.
78. Arendt, *Origins of Totalitarianism*, p. 438.
79. Ibid., p. xxx; idem, 'On Humanity in Dark Times', in *Men in Dark Times* (New York: Harcourt Brace, 1968), pp. 3–31.
80. Arendt, *Origins of Totalitarianism*, p. 459.

81. H. Arendt, 'The Concept of History', in *Between Past and Future: Eight Exercises in Political Thought* (New York: Viking, 1961), pp. 41–90; S. E. Aschheim, 'Against Social Science: Jewish Intellectuals, the Critique of Liberal-Bourgeois Modernity, and the (Ambiguous) Legacy of Radical Weimar Theory', in *In Times of Crisis: Essays on European Culture, Germans and the Jews* (Madison, WI: University of Wisconsin Press, 2001), pp. 23–43.
82. H. Arendt, 'The History of a Great Crime', *Commentary*, 13, 3 (1952), 304.
83. P. Baehr, 'Identifying the Unprecedented: Hannah Arendt, Totalitarianism, and the Critique of Sociology', *American Sociological Review*, 67, 6 (2002), 804–31.
84. For example, R. H. King and D. Stone (eds), *Hannah Arendt and the Uses of History: Imperialism, Nation, Race and Genocide* (New York: Berghahn Books, 2007).
85. Symptomatic is H. Fein, 'Revolutionary and Antirevolutionary Genocides: A Comparison of State Murders in Democratic Kampuchea, 1975 to 1979, and in Indonesia, 1965 to 1966', *Comparative Studies in Society and History*, 34, 4 (1993), 796–823.
86. E. Traverso, *Understanding The Nazi Genocide: Marxism after Auschwitz* (London: Polity Press, 1999); idem, *The Marxists and the Jewish Question* (New Jersey: The Humanities Press, 1994).
87. E. Traverso, *The Origins of Nazi Violence*, trans. J. Lloyd (New York: The New Press, 2003), p. 4.
88. See the critique of N. Geras, *The Contract of Mutual Indifference: Political Philosophy after the Holocaust* (London: Verso, 1998), and P. Spencer, 'The Shoah and Marxism: Behind and Beyond Silence', in *Re-Presenting the Shoah for the Twenty-First Century*, ed., R. Lentin (New York: Berghahn Books, 2004), pp. 155–77.
89. H. Arendt, 'Introduction', in W. Benjamin, *Illuminations*, trans. H. Zohn (London: Jonathan Cape, 1970), pp. 50–1.
90. M. Foucault, *Society Must be Defended: Lectures at the Collège de France 1975–76*, trans. D. Macey (London: Penguin, 2004).
91. Traverso, *Origins of the Nazi Violence*, p. 103.
92. Ibid., p. 121.
93. Ibid., p. 143.
94. Norman Geras likewise wants to reconcile Marxism with Holocaust uniqueness: Geras, 'In a Class of its Own?', in *Moral Philosophy and the Holocaust*, eds, E. Garrard and G. Scarre (Aldershot: Ashgate, 2003).
95. Z. Bauman, 'The Duty to Remember – But What?', in *Enlightenment and Genocide*, eds, Kaye and Strath, pp. 31–2.
96. Z. Bauman, 'Sociology after the Holocaust', *British Journal of Sociology*, 39, 4 (1988), 469–97. On Arendt, see Baehr, 'Identifying the Unprecedented'.
97. Z. Bauman, *Modernity and the Holocaust* (Cambridge: Polity Press, 1989), pp. 177–78.; idem, *Postmodern Ethics*, pp. 249–50.
98. Z. Bauman, 'Categorical Murder, or: How to Remember the Holocaust', in *Re-Presenting the Shoah for the Twenty-First Century*, ed., Lentin, p. 24.
99. Z. Bauman, *Modernity and Ambivalence* (Ithaca, NY: Cornell University Press, 1991), p. 16.
100. Bauman, 'The Duty to Remember', 37; idem, 'The Holocaust's Life as a Ghost', in *Social Theory after the Holocaust*, eds, R. Fine and C. Turner (Liverpool: Liverpool University Press, 1999), p. 16.
101. Ibid., pp. 38–40; idem, *Postmodern Ethics*, p. 123; idem, *Modernity and the Holocaust*, p. 92.

102. J. C. Scott, *Seeing Like a State: How Certain Schemes to Improve the Human Condition Have Failed* (New Haven, CT: Yale University Press, 1998).
103. Arendt thought Nazi Germany was anything other than an orderly bureaucratic state: Arendt, *Origins*, p. 361.
104. Bauman, *Modernity and the Holocaust*, p. 105. For a lucid discussion of the issue in general, see D. Bloxham, 'Bureaucracy and Mass Murder: a Comparative Historical Analysis', *Holocaust and Genocide Studies*, 22, 1 (2008).
105. He is not, of course, the first to draw the link. Hilberg, his teacher Franz Neumann, and Hans Gerth, had done so much earlier. See Söllner, 'Hannah Arendt's *The Origins of Totalitarianism* in its Original Context'.
106. A. Walicki, personal communication, 14 January 1999.
107. Bauman, 'Categorical Murder', 37.
108. Ibid., 24; idem, *Modernity and the Holocaust*, p. 105: 'True, bureaucracy did not hatch the fear of racial contamination and the obsession with racial hygiene. For that it needed visionaries, as bureaucracy picks up where visionaries stop'.
109. D. Bloxham, *The Great Game of Genocide: Imperialism, Nationalism and the Destruction of the Ottoman Armenians* (Oxford: Oxford University Press, 2005).
110. Bauman, 'Categorical Murder', 36. Emphasis added.
111. M. Levene, *Genocide in the Age of the Nation State*, 2 vols (London: I. B. Tauris, 2005); R. Melson, *Revolution and Genocide: On the Origins of the Armenian Genocide and the Holocaust* (Chicago, IL: University of Chicago Press, 1992); T. Skocpol, *States and Social Revolutions: A Comparative Analysis of France, Russia and China* (Cambridge: Cambridge University Press, 1979).
112. A. D. Moses, 'Empire, Colony, Genocide', in *Empire, Colony, Genocide: Conquest, Occupation, and Subaltern Resistance in World History*. ed., A. D. Moses (New York: Berghahn Books, 2008); Freeman, 'Genocide, Civilization and Modernity'.
113. M. Foucault, 'Governmentality', in *The Essential Works of Foucault, 1954–1984*, vol. 3, ed., J. D. Faubion (New York: The New Press, 2000), pp. 201–22. Cf. Arendt, *The Human Condition*, pp. 28, 46: 'the body of peoples and political communities in the image of a family whose everyday affairs have to be taken care of by a gigantic nationwide administration of housekeeping'. Society becomes 'the form in which the fact of mutual dependence for the sake of life and nothing else assumes public significance and where the activities connected with sheer survival are permitted to appear in public'.
114. E. R. Dickinson, 'Biopolitics, Fascism, Democracy: Some Reflections on Our Discourse about "Modernity"', *Central European History*, 37, 1 (2005), 1–48.
115. N. Rose, 'The Politics of Life Itself', *Theory, Culture & Society*, 18, 6 (2001), 1–30.
116. M. Foucault, *The History of Sexuality, vol. 1. An Introduction*, trans. R. Huxley (Harmondsworth: Penguin, 1984), pp. 137, 143.
117. A small sample: A. Bashford, *Imperial Hygiene: A Critical History of Colonialism, Nationalism, and Public Health* (Basingstoke: Palgrave Macmillan, 2004); W. Schneider, *Quality and Quantity: The Quest for Biological Regeneration in Twentieth-Century France* (Cambridge: Cambridge University Press, 1990); M. S. Quine, *Population Politics in Twentieth-Century Europe: Fascist Dictatorships and Liberal Democracies* (London: Routledge, 1996); D. G. Horn, *Social Bodies: Science, Reproduction, and Italian Modernity* (Princeton, NJ: Princeton University Press, 1994); C. Ipsen, *Dictating Demography: The Problem of Population in Fascist Italy* (Cambridge: Cambridge University Press, 1996); R. A. Soloway, *Demography and Degeneration: Eugenics and the Declining Birthrate in Twentieth Century Britain* (Chapel Hill, NC: University of North Carolina Press, 1990); P. Weindling, *Health,*

Race and German Politics between National Unification and Nazis, 1870–1945 (Cambridge: Cambridge University Press, 1989).

118. G. Eley, 'Introduction 1: Is there a History of the *Kaiserreich*?' in *Society, Culture, and the State in Germany, 1870–1930*, ed., G. Eley (Ann Arbor, MI: University of Michigan, 1996), p. 28; D. Padovan, 'Biopolitics and the Social Control of the Multitude', *Democracy and Nature*, 9, 3 (2003), 473–94.
119. S. T. Katz, 'The Uniqueness of the Holocaust: The Historical Dimension', in *Is the Holocaust Unique? Perspectives on Comparative Genocide*, ed., A. S. Rosenbaum (Boulder, CO: Westview Press, 1996); D. Diner, *Beyond the Conceivable: Studies on Germany, Nazism, and the Holocaust* (Berkeley, CA: University of California Press, 2000).
120. This literature also emphasizes fantasy and redemption in Nazism, or Nazism as a political religion. See A. Confino, 'Fantasies about the Jews: Cultural Reflections on the Holocaust', *History and Memory*, 17, 1–2 (2005), 296–322; M. Burleigh, *The Third Reich: A New History* (New York: Hill and Wang, 2001); see also his *Sacred Causes: The Clash of Religion and Politics, from the Great War to the War on Terror* (New York: HarperCollins, 2007).
121. F. Peace, 'Introduction: The *Collège de sociologie* and French Social Thought', *Economy and Society*, 32, 1 (2003), 1–6; M. Richman, 'Myth, Power and the Sacred: Anti-Utilitarianism in the *Collège de sociologie*, 1937–9', ibid., 29–47.
122. Stone, *History, Memory and Mass Atrocity*, p. 241.
123. On Bataille and sacrifice, see J. Goldhammer, *The Headless Republic: Sacrificial Violence in Modern French Thought* (Ithaca, NY: Cornell University Press, 2005), p. 11.
124. Ibid., pp. 83–6; King and Stone, *Hannah Arendt and the Uses of History*.
125. D. LaCapra, *Representing the Holocaust: History, Theory, Trauma* (Ithaca, NY: Cornell University Press, 1994), pp. 92, 99–100; idem, *History and Memory after Auschwtiz* (Ithaca, NY: Cornell University Press, 1998).
126. D. LaCapra *Writing History, Writing Trauma* (Baltimore, MD: Johns Hopkins University Press, 2000), p. 137.
127. L. Dawidowicz, ed., *A Holocaust Reader* (West Orange, NJ: Behrman House, 1976), p. 132. Emphasis added. I replace the word 'integrity' with 'decency', which is a better translation of *antständig*.
128. Cf. A. D. Moses, 'Structure and Agency in the Holocaust: Daniel J. Goldhagen and his Critics', *History and Theory*, 37, 2 (1998), 194–219.
129. S. Friedländer, *Nazi Germany and the* Jews, *vol.1, The Years of Persecution, 1933–39* (London: Weidenfeld & Nicolson, 1997). He relies on the work of U. Tal, 'On Structures of Political Theology and Myth in Germany Prior to the Holocaust', in *The Holocaust as Historical Experience*, eds, Y. Bauer and N. Rotenstreich (New York: Holmes and Meier, 1981), pp. 43–76.
130. Bauman, *Postmodern Ethics*, p. 226.
131. A. L. Hinton, 'The Dark Side of Modernity: Toward an Anthropology of Genocide', in *Annihilating Difference: The Anthropology of Genocide*, ed., A. L. Hinton (Berkeley, CA: University of California Press), 6; Shipway, 'Modern by Analogy'.
132. P. K. Lawrence, 'Enlightenment, Modernity and War', *History of the Human Sciences*, 12, 1 (1999), 3–25.
133. Bauman, *Modernity and the Holocaust*, p. 17.
134. A. Mbembe, 'Necropolitics', *Public Culture*, 15, 1 (2003), 23–4. See Agamben's discussion of Schmitt in *Homer Sacer: Sovereign Power and Bare Life*, trans D. Heller-Roazen (Stanford, CA: Stanford University Press, 1998), pp. 36–7.

135. E. Dussel, 'Beyond Eurocentrism: The World-System and the Limits of Modernity', in *The Cultures of Globalization*, eds, F. Jameson and M. Miyoshi (Durham, NC: Duke University Press, 1988), p. 19.
136. E. Dussel, *The Invention of the Americas: Eclipse of 'the Other' and the Myth of Modernity*, trans. M. D. Barber (New York: Continuum, 1995), p. 10.
137. E. Dussel, 'Europe, Modernity, and Eurocentrism', *Nepantla: Views from South*, 1, 3 (2000), 472.
138. On Las Casas and his idealization by Raphael Lemkin, see M. A. McDonnell and A. D. Moses, 'Raphael Lemkin as Historian of Genocide in the Americas', *Journal of Genocide Research*, 7, 4 (2005), 501–29.
139. Dussel, 'Beyond Eurocentrism', pp. 25–6.
140. Ibid., pp. 12, 25–6. Emphasis in the original. Dussel, 'Europe, Modernity, and Eurocentrism', 472–3.
141. E.g., M. Levene, 'The Chittagong Hill Tracts: A Case Study in the Political Economy of "Creeping" Genocide', *Third World Quarterly*, 20 (1999), 339–69; idem, 'A Moving Target, the Usual Suspects and (Maybe) a Smoking Gun: The Problem of Pinning Blame in Modern Genocide', *Patterns of Prejudice*, 33, 4 (1999), 3–24; idem, 'The Limits of Tolerance: Nation-State Building and What It Means for Minority Groups', *Patterns of Prejudice*, 34, 2 (2000), 19–40; idem, 'Why is the Twentieth Century the Century of Genocide?', *Journal of World History*, 11 (2000), 305–36.
142. M. Mann, *The Dark Side of Democracy: Explaining Ethnic Cleansing* (New York: Cambridge University Press, 2004), p. 79.
143. Levene, *Genocide in the Age of the Nation-State*, vol. 1, p. 164.
144. Ibid., p. 121.
145. H. Rae, *State Identities and the Homogenisation of Peoples* (Cambridge: Cambridge University Press, 2002); cf. H. Maier, 'Potentials for Violence in the Nineteenth Century: Technology of War, Colonialism, and the "People in Arms"', *Totalitarian Movements and Political Religions*, 2, 1 (2001), 1–27.
146. E. D. Weitz, *A Century of Genocide: Utopias of Race and Nation* (Princeton, NJ: Princeton University Press, 2003); N. Naimark, *Fires of Hatred: Ethnic Cleansing in Twentieth-Century Europe* (Cambridge, MA: Harvard University Press, 2001).
147. Levene, *Genocide in the Age of the Nation-State*, vol. 1, p. 177.
148. Ibid., p. 187.
149. The book is translated as *Hitler's Beneficiaries: Plunder, Racial War, and the Nazi Welfare State* (New York: Metropolitan Books, 2007); Earlier works are: G. Aly and S. Heim, *Architects of Annihilation: Auschwitz and the Logic of Destruction*, trans. A. G. Blunden (London: Phoenix, 2003), and G. Aly, *'Final Solution': Nazi Population Policy and the Murder of European Jews*, trans. B. Cooper and A. Brown (New York: Oxford University Press, 1999).
150. D. Diner, 'Hannah Arendt Reconsidered: On the Banal and the Evil in Her Holocaust Narrative', *New German Critique*, 71 (1997), 179. The second quotation by Diner is in T. Assheuer, 'Die Wiederkehr der Schuldfrage?', *Frankfurter Rundschau*, 10 May 1996. His critique of Aly and Heim is in his *Beyond the Conceivable*, pp. 187–200.
151. G. Aly, *Hitlers Volksstaat: Raub, Rassenkrieg und nationaler Sozialismus* (Frankfurt am Main: Fischer Verlag, 2005), p. 362: 'Wer von den Vorteilen fuer die Millionen einfacher Deutscher nicht reden will, der sollte vom Nationalsozialismus und vom Holocaust schweigen'. The Horkheimer quotation is: 'He who does not wish to speak of capitalism should also be silent about fascism'. See Jay, 'The Jews and the Frankfurt School', 138 for discussion of Horkheimer's 'Die Juden und Europa'.

152. For example, M. Wildt, 'Alys Volksstaat. Hybris und Simplizität einer Wissenschaft', *Mittelweg*, 36, 3 (2005).
153. N. Sznaider. 'Review of Götz Aly, *Hitler's Volksstaat: Raub, Rassenkrieg und nationaler Sozialismus*', H-German, H-Net Reviews, May 2005. URL: http://www.h-net.org/reviews/showrev.cgi?path=202471121350466.
154. T. Snyder, 'The Causes of Ukraine-Polish Ethnic Cleansing, 1943', *Past and Present*, 179 (2003), 197–234; M. Hogan, 'The 1948 Massacre at Deir Yassin Revisited', *Historian*, 63, 2 (2001), 309–33.
155. For one notorious episode, see D. Anderson, *Histories of the Hanged: Britain's Dirty War in Kenya and the End of Empire* (London: Weidenfeld & Nicholson, 2004); C. Elkins, *Britain's Gulag: The Brutal End of Empire in Kenya* (London: Pimlico, 2004).

7
Religion and Genocide: A Historiographical Survey

Doris L. Bergen

The first problem in discussing the historiography of religion and genocide is to define the parameters, a difficult task, because all of the categories involved are open to interpretation. According to the definitions used, one will either find that almost nothing has been written about religion and genocide or that the body of relevant material is endless. What is Religion? Are we talking about organized, institutionalized religion: Judaism, Christianity, Islam, Hinduism, Buddhism, Baha'i and the like? Or about religious impulses: belief, tradition, spiritualism, transcendence and ethical systems linked to some notion of divinity? Are we talking about a communal phenomenon or an individual matter? This discussion focuses on institutionalized religion but also pays attention to religion as it functions at the level of individuals and groups involved in situations of extreme violence – as perpetrators, targets/victims, witnesses/bystanders, but also as resistors/rescuers, beneficiaries and people left to deal with the aftermath. As for genocide, given the scope of this volume, I follow the legal definition associated with Raphael Lemkin and the 1948 United Nations Convention,[1] but I also consider some cases of state-sponsored, extreme violence that are not legally and formally genocide or have not been widely acknowledged as such.

Even the choice to define religion and genocide broadly nets only a handful of works that approach their intersection in a comparative, historical perspective. Indeed, a single volume stands out as having made such an attempt: *In God's Name: Genocide and Religion in the Twentieth Century*, edited by Omer Bartov and Phyllis Mack.[2] In their introduction and in the themes highlighted throughout the essays they included, Bartov and Mack emphasize the seemingly paradoxical relationship between religion and violence in the historical situations under consideration: the Armenian, Jewish, Bosnian and Rwandan cases. Religion, Bartov and Mack point out, 'has both legitimized mass murder and resisted it, repressed past crimes and tried to come to terms with them, justified the perpetuation of existing social, political, and religious structures and subjected them to scrutiny and criticism'.[3] Those insights are a point of departure for this essay, although my scope extends beyond the twentieth century and encompasses more than the four cases Bartov and Mack's contributors address.

Genocide is often deemed a disease of the twentieth century (and since),[4] and of course the term itself did not exist before World War II. But it seems useful at least to be mindful of earlier cases of extreme violence – of which there are many – where religion featured in significant ways, for example, the Crusades and the Inquisition.[5] Moreover, restricting our view to the twentieth century tends to occlude issues of religion, because many people assume that organized religion lost most or even all of its public power, at least in the West, sometime between the French Revolution and World War I. Seen this way, the category of genocide is itself a product of the so-called age of secularization: religion is present in the definition but only as one of the possible identifiers of the targets of attack. That religion might have something to do with the perpetrators of genocide is hinted at the UN definition's focus on intention, but it is not made explicit.

A practical consideration involves what kind of literature to include in a historiographical survey of religion and genocide. There is a relevant body of scholarship on specific cases by historians, but more has been produced by political scientists and other social scientists, theologians, philosophers and scholars of literature; and there are many less or non-scholarly works: accounts by journalists, memoirs and reflections by eyewitnesses and survivors. Even in the Bartov and Mack volume, only half of the twenty contributors are historians, counting the two editors and Ian Kershaw, author of the afterword. Then there is a vast body of what might be called creative work: novels, poems, short stories, art of all kinds and movies. Some of the most productive and provocative reflections on religion and mass violence have taken place here, and works of this kind often reach – and move – a wider audience than does scholarship, an audience that includes scholars and students of genocide as well as the general public. For how many readers did the challenge to think about religion and mass murder begin with Elie Wiesel's cry from Auschwitz: 'Where is God now?'[6] Other accounts echo that agony. Thirty years earlier, upon seeing a pile of corpses in Anatolia, the Armenian survivor Donabed Lulejian prayed for dirt to cover the dead: 'Let the Armenian become a fossil. Let him be the disgrace of the civilization which tore him to pieces. ... Let him be the curse of the religion which abandoned him and left him without succor. Give, God, the handful of earth requested of Thee!'[7] Such words and images are unforgettable. Although it is not possible to discuss everything here, I try, at least, to indicate some influential, non-scholarly works.

The scholarship on religion and genocide has developed unevenly. In certain cases, most notably the Holocaust, the literature is voluminous, especially on the role of the Christian churches in preparing, enabling, motivating, or failing to prevent murder of Jews.[8] The genocide in Rwanda has also generated a significant discussion on the role of the churches[9]: even the journalist Philip Gourevitch, who is not primarily concerned with religion, starts his influential book, *We wish to inform you that tomorrow we will be killed with our families*, with the premise of Christian failure.[10] In other cases, for example, the Stalinist or Maoist terrors, one is hard-pressed to find any scholarly work at all on issues of religion.[11] Rather than proceeding case by case, which would end up reproducing this imbalance, this discussion focuses on themes – various roles that religion plays or has played in genocidal situations. I identify some ways that religion and extreme violence intersect and in each regard, I discuss works that demonstrate the possibilities and provide examples from specific cases. In other words, I proceed to build categories through accretion: assembling historical and historiographical particulars, each of them different, that together form not a stable methodology, but something that can be identified as an approach.

Four varieties or types of interaction are addressed here: religion as a motivating and/or legitimating force for perpetrators of extreme violence; religion as a target of genocidal attack and identifier but also comforter of victims; religion as a brake against mass brutality; and religion as a healing or concealing factor in post-genocidal situations. Although these categories are complex composites that overlap and co-exist in specific historical situations, they provide a way to organize and analyze a bewildering array of issues, cases and studies.

Religion and the perpetrators of genocide

To many people, the link between religion and genocide seems obvious. Who has not heard the claim that more people have been killed in the name of God than for any other cause in the history of humanity? The scholarship, in contrast, includes few concerted attempts to identify and analyze such assumptions with historical specificity. Such efforts, when they have occurred, point to the elusive nature of their subjects. Take the immensely powerful volume edited by Carol Rittner, John K. Roth and Wendy Whitworth, *Genocide in Rwanda: Complicity of the Churches?*[12] This book bravely and painstakingly situates the Christian churches in the midst of the Rwandan genocide of 1994. Octave Ugirashebuja, S.J., a Jesuit priest and professor of philosophy in Rwanda, describes the Catholic Church as involved in establishing divisions and sowing conflict between Hutus and Tutsis (under the influence of European missionaries); preaching that hatred of Tutsis was in accord with love of the Church (in the decades prior to 1990); witnessing the massacre that began in April 1994 'in a kind of total paralysis'[13]; and denying the genocide after it occurred.

Fr. Ugirashebuja's countryman, the journalist and Commissioner of the Rwandan National Human Rights Commission Tom Ndahiro, underscores these points with his observation that the Catholic Church 'was the only institution involved in all the stages of genocide': creating an 'exterminationist ideology'; colluding with the powers that carried out the genocide; remaining silent during the killing and even providing killers from among its clergy.[14] A collection of photographs by James M. Smith and Carol Rittner, R.S.M. shows church buildings strewn with human remains and heaped with rotting shoes, altar cloths stained with blood. Eleven per cent of the victims of genocide were killed inside churches, the authors tell us.[15] A fascinating essay by Leon D. Saur compares the Marian apparitions in Kibeho, Rwanda in 1981 with those in Medjugorje, Yugoslavia that same year and concludes that in both cases, extreme-right, conservative and ethno-nationalist parties appropriated visions of Mary and transformed her calls for peace into an invitation to '"crush the head of the snake" and vanquish the "forces of evil"'.[16]

Together these and the other contributions in the book assemble an undeniable case against the Christian churches in the Rwandan genocide. But at the level of individual perpetrators and specific acts of killing, the findings still prove inconclusive. What exactly did Christianity mean to the killers, who attacked members of their own churches, often inside those very church buildings? Precisely how did religion, here Christianity, function in the minds and bodies of men and women hacking with machetes into the flesh of other human beings, including children, old people and neighbours – sometimes members of their own families? Some of the difficulties inherent in answering questions of this sort are hinted at in the volume, from which, John Roth informs us in the epilogue, four Rwandan priests withdrew their contributions as the book was nearing completion.[17] The one chapter that explicitly examines Catholic religious (in this case, nuns) charged with participation in genocide in a court of law is the most patently apologetic, and also one of the shortest, in the book.[18] Readers who seek to understand how religion works at the level of individual acts of violence – to motivate? numb? justify? sanctify? forgive? – find much to ponder here, but they will need to keep searching.

The personal difficulties of grasping the place of religion in extreme violence translate into practical obstacles for scholars. According to Israel Charny, a founder of the field of genocide studies, it was almost impossible to find someone to prepare a major section on religion and genocide for the 1994 work, *The Widening Circle of Genocide*.[19] Repeatedly, scholars who had agreed to the task dropped it with little explanation. 'To me,' Charny wrote, 'it seemed that what happened was that they were unable to tell the truth about the religious establishments with which they were variously connected.'[20] Charny's speculation points to one reason why studies of religion and the perpetrators of genocide are rare. As John Roth put it, religion and genocide is a very 'hot' topic, religiously and politically.[21]

If scholars hesitate to write about religion and the perpetration of extreme violence from within their own tradition, they are also reluctant to venture into the faiths of others. Since the 1980s, the rise of fundamentalisms of various kinds has prompted increased attention to religion and violence, as attested to by the works of R. Scott Appleby and others.[22] Since the attacks on the United States of 11 September 2001, scholars, like the general North American and European publics, have shown an increased interest in religion, especially Islam, as a motivating force for extreme violence, and the notion of a 'clash of civilizations,' advanced in the early 1990s by political scientist Samuel P. Huntington, has gained currency.[23] Such approaches are challenging, not the least because language itself constitutes a minefield.[24] Outsiders to the tradition in question – usually Islam, these days – can appear to be on the attack or guilty of stereotyping, and often they are.

The basic idea that religion can be a significant motivating force for perpetrators of violence, including genocide, has been approached in various ways, almost all of them abstract or indirect. Most famously, René Girard's 1972 work, *Violence and the Sacred,* argued that all religion is intrinsically violent, that ideas and practices related to sacrifice and scapegoating are at the heart of conceptions of the sacred.[25] Barbara Ehrenreich's important exploration of war, *Blood Rites,*[26] restates and refines Girard's concept as essential to a general theory of war. But neither of these works addresses genocide explicitly, so that the mechanisms that connect the violent impulses of religion they reveal to historically specific practices of organized, mass killing remain unclear.

In his 1994 reflections on 'Religion and Genocide' Leonard Glick took a different view. Religion, Glick argued, whether localized or universalist in nature, is inextricably intertwined with issues of identity and exclusion. As such it is entangled in 'universal human dispositions' to dislike, mistrust and attack those viewed to be outside one's own reference group. In other words, Glick concluded, religions are 'part of the problem' of genocidal oppression.[27] This provocative claim situates religion in the midst of extreme violence, but it does not help answer the historically specific question as to why hatred, bolstered by religion, produces extreme violence in some cases but not others. Nor does Glick's emphasis on religious difference provide a way to understand the Rwandan case, where Tutsi victims and Hutu perpetrators shared a faith tradition.

A small group of works has attempted to identify a religion–genocide nexus in the nature of specific beliefs. Monotheism, in particular, emerges as suspect in its frequent association with genocidal situations and other cases of extreme violence.[28] The four cases Bartov and Mack's volume addresses – Armenian, Jewish, Bosnian and Rwandan – all involved perpetrators (and victims) who were products of monotheistic religions. Bartov and Mack note but do not analyze this fact, and they point out that genocides have also occurred in parts of the world where Judaism, Christianity and Islam do not have a significant presence.[29] Leo Kuper's now classic article, from 1990, 'Theological Mandates for Genocide,' in contrast, argues that it is precisely the absolute truth claims of the monotheistic religions as enshrined in specific texts and traditions of Judaism, Christianity and Islam that have provided 'mandates' for genocide.[30] In a short piece titled 'A Sweet-Smelling Sacrifice: Genocide, the Bible, and the Indigenous Peoples of the U.S., Selected Examples,' Chris Mato Nunpa shows how Christian notions of 'chosenness' and use of biblical passages promising 'Christ Our Victory' and calling on the Lord to 'smite our Enemies ... and to give us their Land for an inheritance' promoted massive destruction of native peoples in the Americas.[31]

Likewise, other observers have noted the presence of extreme violence in the religious texts of the monotheistic traditions and teachings of superiority, especially as typical of the Christian position vis-à-vis Judaism and Jews.[32] Susannah Heschel's image of Christianity as a bulemic – swallowing Judaism and then out of loathing and shame trying to vomit it up – captures this dynamic in a disturbingly vivid way.[33] Yet even such powerful, and in the cases of Rosemary Ruether, James Carroll and Susannah Heschel, theologically and theoretically informed investigations cannot provide the smoking gun to link genocidal beliefs and fantasies to the practice of organized, mass killing. As Steven Katz once put it, Judaism survived almost two thousand years of Christianity. It nearly did not survive 12 years of Nazism. Something must have changed.[34]

Like the argument about Christian antisemitism as a cause of genocide, Michael Sells points to elements of Serbian Orthodox Christianity, or more specifically, Serbian religious nationalism, as the most important factor in understanding violence against Slavic Muslims. According to Sells, Christo-Slavism, enshrined in sacred texts like 'The Mountain Wreath', ritualized in ceremonies commemorating the Battle of Kosovo in 1389, characterized by the collapsing of past and present and stirred up by church leaders and self-serving demagogues, most notably Slobodan Milošević, was key in motivating the brutal 'ethnic cleansing' in Bosnia in the early 1990s and in justifying and denying those events after the fact.[35] Sells is a professor of comparative religion. His interpretation, highly influential both within and perhaps especially outside the circle of Balkan experts,[36] is revised and challenged by other scholars, among them Sabrina P. Ramet and Paul Mojzes, who place less emphasis on the independent role of religion in the Balkan conflicts of the 1990s.[37]

The notion of political religion offers a way to consider the explosion of extreme violence in recent centuries, often precisely in societies where organized religion appears to have lost ground. It was Eric Voegelin who first suggested the concept in early analyses of National Socialist Germany where, according to Voegelin, Nazism became itself a religion, complete with rituals, sacred texts, truth claims and demands for unconditional obedience and total sacrifice.[38] For the devout Roman Catholic Voegelin, this appropriation spoke to the fruits of Enlightenment secularization: as true religion lost its place in European societies, pseudo-religions like nationalism, communism, fascism and Nazism stepped into the breach. They fulfilled some of the sociological and existential functions of religion and stirred up intense religious feelings without providing any ethical boundaries. As a result, they produced horrific violence. One might sum up Voegelin's assessment of the relationship between political religions and genuine religion (he was concerned above all with Christianity) as simultaneously parasitic and vulture-like. That is, political religions both drew on the power of genuine religion, harnessing those powers to their own purposes, and they fed off its corpse. Philippe Burrin and Stanley Stowers offer reassessments and helpful critiques of the concept of political religion in light of developments since Voegelin's original discussion.[39]

Analyses based on the concept of political religion can move in various directions. In his studies of nationalism, George Mosse showed how adulation of the nation in the nineteenth and early twentieth centuries borrowed religious, especially Christian, imagery and offered new forms of sacrifice, worship and communion.[40] Emilio Gentile's important book, *The Sacralisation of Politics in Fascist Italy*,[41] made a convincing case for Mussolini's appropriation of religious/Roman Catholic beliefs and practices in the consolidation of Fascist power. Mosse and Gentile do not focus on genocide, but their works start from the premise that the combination of extreme violence and intense popularity of German Nazism and Italian Fascism require explanation. The emphasis in some of Omer Bartov's work on utopian thinking as a cause of genocide also shares theoretical ground with the concept of political religion.[42]

In *The Third Reich: A New History*, Michael Burleigh offered an extensive analysis of National Socialism as a political religion.[43] That project was not explicitly comparative, but Burleigh subsequently founded a journal, *Totalitarian Movements and Political Religions*, to investigate the phenomenon of totalitarian religion in other historical manifestations.[44] Unlike Mosse or Bartov, who parted ways with Voegelin when it came to his identification of the Enlightenment as the root of the problem, Burleigh shares the assumption that not religion but its perversion in secular forms needs to be uncovered as a major cause of violence and oppression. Burleigh has widened his scope to all of modern European history in a two-volume exploration of 'the clash of religion and politics' in modern Europe over two-hundred years.[45]

The notion of political religion, although not identified by that name, is invoked in a wide range of historical settings as one of the motivations for atrocity. In *Hadji Murad*, his posthumously published, short novel on the Russian wars in the Caucasus in the 1850s, Leo Tolstoy reflected on the dangerous linkages between religion and power. Tsar Nicholas I, Tolstoy's heartless villain, punctuates his adulterous sex with a twenty-year-old virgin and careless proclamation of death sentences on scores of people with recitation of his prayers, attendance of a church service and participation in Mass.[46] Nicholas's counterpart, the Chechen leader and Imam Shamil, pauses in his military campaign against the Russians to accept the adoration of his followers, preside over life-and-death decisions of the religious court and seek out the attentions of his favourite wife.[47] In both cases, religion reinforces the arbitrary, destructive power of a tyrant whose goals are far from spiritual. In her memoir of the Cambodian genocide, *First They Killed My Father*, Loung Ung presents a victim's view of how practices of political religion exacerbated the cruelty of people in power.[48] Ung, born in 1970, survived the Khmer Rouge as a little girl, separated for long periods of time from everyone in her family. While in a youth training camp, she witnessed and presumably participated in the pseudo-religious rituals of the Angkar, who enforced conformity to create the illusion of unanimity.

Another dimension of religion and the perpetrators involves the issue of cultural genocide. In such cases the aim is not necessarily to destroy people physically but to annihilate their communities and their identity.[49] Although recognized by Raphael Lemkin,[50] cultural genocide remains contested as a category of genocide. It is suggested in the UN charter, with its recognition that 'forcibly transferring children of the group to another group', if conducted with the aim of destroying the group in question, is a genocidal act.[51] Religion plays a crucial role here, because, along with language, its prohibition and the enforcement of the perpetrators' religion on the people transferred, is the hallmark of attempts to eradicate a culture. Studies of cultural genocides invariably assume religion to have been both a tool and a motivating force for the perpetrators. The nature of the crime – which, if pulled off, sees its victims disappear into the perpetrator population – means that studies of cultural genocide as seen through the eyes of the victims are rare.

One of the most sustained examples of this approach to the study of religion and genocide is George Tinker's *Missionary Conquest: The Gospel and Native American Cultural Genocide*.[52] In Tinker's analysis, cultural genocide implies a pattern of destruction that is both systematic and, at least to a large extent, intentional. As Marie Fleming points out in a short discussion of the missionary John Eliot, a contemporary of Thomas Hobbes, however, the erasure is even more total. From the example of Eliot, a 'good missionary', Fleming concludes that it might 'be more correct to say that under colonial rule, missionaries serving the cause of Europe do not so much set out to destroy a culture as they do not even recognize that there is one'.[53] The themes Tinker raises – in particular, the role of Christian missionaries and churches in destroying Native American family, community and social bonds – are taken up in studies of later periods, for example, dealing with abusive residential schools for First Nations children in Canada,[54] or the kidnapping of indigenous children in Australia.[55]

Missionaries as agents of cultural genocide are also a theme in some African literature examining the colonial period, most notably the Cameroonian Mongo Beti's hard-hitting 1956 novel, *The Poor Christ of Bomba*.[56] The 'poor Christ' of the title, a French priest, discovers after years in West Africa that he has brought not salvation but destruction to 'his' people. Colonial administrators have used his mission to 'soften up' the local people, and in turn his project of evangelization has been most successful in areas of intense, colonially induced suffering and deprivation, as desperate people grasp at any hope of amelioration. Right under his nose, his religious school for young women has been turned into a brothel and centre of sexually transmitted diseases. Beti's narrative reveals a point difficult to unpack in scholarly analysis: the embeddedness of religion in complex relations of power that involve race, sex and economics as well as more easily recognized issues of authority and armed might.

Such multi-dimensionality of causes in the situation of forced conversions is evident in other works that examine the subject as part of extreme violence. In his classic study of the Spanish Inquisition, Benzion Netanyahu shows a development from the 'age of conversions' to 'attacks on the conversos' and finally a 'genocidal solution to the converso question'. In Netanyahu's assessment, racial arguments emerged in the context of fifteenth-century Spain precisely because there was no evidence that the great majority of conversos were not sincere in their Christianity.[57] He draws a comparison to the rise of racist antisemitism in nineteenth-century Europe, likewise at a time when religion no longer 'sustained impassable divisions between groups'.[58] In an essay titled 'The Absorption of Armenian Women and Children into Muslim Households as a Structural Component of the Armenian Genocide', Ara Sarafian estimates that, beginning in 1915, tens of thousands of Armenians disappeared into the Muslim community through forced conversion.[59] Sarafian's discussion invites comparisons with other situations where religion is a marker of difference and where, accordingly, conversion might offer some possibility of protection. Kenneth Jacobson's study of identities in crisis is the prime example in the case of the Holocaust, [60] and Saul Friedländer's memoir, *When Memory Comes*, also provides food for thought.[61] I know of nothing comparable as a study of religious conversion or 'passing' in the cases of Bosnia or Kosovo.

In general, it seems that efforts to theorize the place of religion in extreme violence — and attempts to understand extreme violence that are attentive to religion — end up, as Leonard Glick did, pointing to the impossibility of disentangling strands of motivation, preparation and process. In the introduction to their comparative volume on genocide, Robert Gellately and Ben Kiernan stress the conflation of racism and religion in most genocidal situations.[62] Even 'atheistic' regimes, they note – the Ottoman Turks in World War I, Nazi Germany and Pol Pot's Cambodia – targeted religious minorities. Many studies, in particular of the Armenian and Bosnian cases, echo this position.

Another sub-theme here is religion and the mentality of the perpetrators: What kind of religiosity is shared by those who carry out acts of extreme violence? This question turns out to be the hardest to answer, and not surprisingly, few scholars have tackled it. The most extended effort to uncover the roots of Belgian atrocities in the Belgian Congo and to identify the role of missionaries in the deaths of an estimated ten million Africans there between 1890 and 1910 came not from a historian but a journalist, Adam Hochschild.[63] Hochschild's gripping book, *King Leopold's Ghost*, is an indictment of European greed, negligence and destruction, but for the most part, the missionaries come off surprisingly well in his analysis. Some of them energetically tried to expose atrocities in the Belgian Congo, and in general Christianity seems to have played a minor role in shaping the mindsets of men who hacked the hands off Africans they killed for failing to meet quotas of ivory or rubber, in order to prove to their superiors that they had not wasted bullets. Still, a discussion of the horrific children's colonies established under Belgian rule, many of them by Catholic missionaries, reveals that the partnership that Mongo Beti referred to – between colonizers and missionizers – appears to have functioned in the Congolese context, too. Not only did Belgian's King Leopold II subsidize the Catholics richly, Hochschild tells us; he 'sometimes used this financial power to deploy priests, almost as if they were soldiers, to areas where he wanted to strengthen his influence.'[64] Over 50 per cent of the African children packed into state and Catholic colonies died, and many more did not even live through the journey to these sites. In 1895, the mother superior of one Catholic colony for girls wrote to a state official that 'Several of the little girls were so sickly on their arrival that ... our good sisters couldn't save them, but all had the happiness of receiving Holy Baptism; they are now little angels in Heaven who are praying for our great king.'[65]

In the case of the Holocaust, it has likewise been a journalist, the remarkable Gitta Sereny, who has done the most to get into the mind of a major perpetrator – Franz Stangl, the onetime T-4 operative who became commandant first of Sobibor, then of Treblinka – and who assessed the role of religion in his descent 'into that darkness.'[66] Although readers emerge puzzled as to the precise nature of Stangl's own religiosity – he was raised Roman Catholic and claimed to have been forced to renounce his membership in the Church but to have admired his wife's piety – Sereny makes it clear that for him, the Vatican's complicity in

Nazi crimes was a crucial factor enabling his own participation. Stangl took solace in the obvious involvement of Catholic religious in the murder of people deemed handicapped, and after the war, his route of escape from Europe passed directly through Rome and the Vatican 'ratline'. James Waller, a psychologist, pays at least some attention to religion in *Becoming Evil*, his investigation of the development of perpetrators in a range of genocidal situations.[67] In contrast, in Christopher R. Browning's influential *Ordinary Men*,[68] a work by a historian of the Holocaust influenced by social science, religion plays no identifiable role in shaping the mindset of the killers. Jonathan Steinberg gets us a step closer with his discussion of the Roman Catholic Church and wartime genocide in Croatia, including a chilling description of the Ustasha officer who made the sign of the cross each night before going to sleep – after killing Serbs, Jews and Roma in Jasenovać.[69] Still, a reader has no way of knowing how widespread such cases were or what they meant.

The rare sources from perpetrators themselves raise questions of their own. In his post-war memoir, written from a Polish prison, Rudolf Hoess, former commandant of Auschwitz, emphasized his father's fanatical Catholicism and his own childhood piety. A dutiful altar boy, he claimed that his 'deep, true, childlike faith' was 'smashed' when he witnessed a priest violating the secrecy of the confession. Hoess left the Church in 1922 but remained spiritually tormented, he wrote, and in a letter to his family from April 1947, he announced that he had 'again found my faith in my God'.[70] In a book that unfortunately remains untranslated into English, Manfred Deselaers, a Catholic priest who heads the Centre for Dialogue and Prayer in Auschwitz, examined Hoess's biography through the lens of Christian theology and morality.[71]

The most detailed consideration of the role of Christianity in the mental world of major perpetrators of the Holocaust is also the least historical: Rolf Hochhuth's controversial 1963 play, *The Deputy*.[72] Act Five, titled 'Auschwitz, or Where Are You, God?', includes a long exchange between the Doctor Josef Mengele character and Riccardo, a Jesuit priest who has accompanied a transport of Jews from Rome to the killing centre, intent on dying with them. In the tradition of the temptation of Jesus in the desert and Dostoevsky's *The Grand Inquisitor*, Hochhuth's fictionalized Mengele reveals himself to be theologically informed and articulate, a former priest and fallen angel who revels in his power not to create but to 'cremate life', and who calls the SS 'the Dominicans of the technological age'.[73] 'It is no accident', he tells the horrified Riccardo, 'that so many of my kind, the leaders, come from good Catholic homes'.[74] Hochhuth's look into the soul of Mengele ventures into terrain that scholars, obliged to stick to the existing sources, restricted by training in caution and fearful, perhaps, of losing credibility with their peers, are unlikely to enter. Raul Hilberg, the pre-eminent scholar of the Holocaust for half a century, has dismissed Hochhuth's play as riddled with errors of detail as well as interpretation.

Nevertheless, Hochhuth's depiction of the radically evil Nazi killer, shaped by Christianity yet characterized by his violent repudiation of it, remains influential in many understandings of the perpetrators of genocide, not only during the Shoah.[75]

Of the many aspects of religion and genocide in need of attention, it is this question – What did religion mean to the killers? – that remains most urgent. Studies on Rwanda, so eloquent when it comes to identifying the role of the churches in creating divisions between Hutu and Tutsi, promoting hatred and sanctifying violence, fall silent on this point.[76] Examinations of individual killers, most notably, the unforgettable *Machete Season*, based on interviews conducted by the French journalist Jean Hatzfeld, situate the perpetrators of genocide in the cozy atmosphere of Christian congregations. 'Previously I was leader of the church choir', the head of a group of ten convicted murderers told Hatzfeld, 'so now I became a real leader, so to speak.'[77] Another man described how he took part in a massacre in the church in Ntarama: 'Me, I had been sincerely baptized Catholic, but I felt it preferable not to pray traditionally during the killings. There was nothing to be asked of God during that filthy business. Still, to get to sleep some nights, I could not help bowing down in secret to ease some gloomy fears with a timid "Sorry."'[78] These glimpses give the reader pause, but they remain curiosities, shocks that seem to stop analysis rather than deepening it. One is left with a sense of the dizzying range of responses among the killers. In one man's words: 'Each person satisfied his faith in his own way without any particular instructions, since the priests were gone or were up to their necks in it. In any case, religion adapted to these changes in belief.'[79]

In an essay on 'The Killing Frenzy', the historian Joanna Bourke quotes a Vietnam veteran who, as part of a SEAL team, massacred many women and children. 'After each mission', he said, 'I would vomit for hours and beg God to forgive us for what we were doing.'[80] That man's words point to another connection between religion and the perpetrators of extreme violence, perhaps the most potent one. More than direct motivation, personal accounts and scholarship show religion as a legitimating force: for perpetrators, but also for bystanders and witnesses. This function is linked to the preceding matters but less directly connected to the violence itself.

A passage in Tolstoy's *Hadji Murad* that refers to Tsar Nicholas I serves to illustrate: 'Nicholas frowned. He had done much evil to the Poles. To justify that evil he had to be certain that all Poles were rascals, and he considered them to be such, and hated them accordingly in proportion to the evil he had done to them.'[81] In calculations like this one, religion is often part of a bundle of convictions, traditions of domination and superiority. Work on military chaplains indicates that they have often embodied this legitimating role.[82] The same might be said for missionaries. The Bartov–Mack collection, *In God's Name,* emphasizes this role of religion as legitimator in all of the cases of genocide considered.

Legitimation can take active forms, such as blessing the killers, as in the Rwandan case, or providing the sacraments to them. It can also function to organize acts of violence, as in the Armenian genocide, where the Muslim call to prayer often served to signal an attack. The eastern European tradition of pogroms at Easter is comparable. Legitimation also has passive forms, usually described as 'silence', a key accusation of the failure of the Christian church leadership in the Holocaust and later in Rwanda.[83] Religion's legitimating role can precede the violence, as in the case of Christian antisemitism and the Holocaust or Orthodox contempt for Bosnian Muslims, or it can follow it, as an ad hoc justification. According to Katharina von Kellenbach, after World War II, Christian teachings of forgiveness helped Germans feel absolved of the guilt of murdering Jews and other people during the war.[84]

The study of religion and the perpetrators of violence is full of pitfalls for scholars. On the one hand, attention to religion can dead-end in an all-out attack on tradition as if religion itself were the root of all conflict. Alternately, attention to religion can end up as a reaction, as if traditional religions always represent a brake to violence whereas political religions usurp and corrupt religious powers to open up unbounded violent possibilities. It is easy enough to find evidence for both positions if they are used as self-fulfilling prophecies, but analytically neither extreme is particularly fruitful.

Religion as target and identifier

One might describe this approach to the study of religion and genocide as 'victim literature'. Not surprisingly, there is a lot of literature of this sort, often written by people themselves victimized. Some of it is scholarly, much of it is not. It starts with the assumption that genocides or at least specific cases of extreme violence, target members of particular religious groups, and their responses, both collective and individual, deserve to be considered in religious terms. What impact do persecution and murder have on the religious beliefs and practices of people and their communities? What resources does religion provide to individuals and groups under severe duress?

Readers interested in exploring such questions with regard to Jews and the Shoah can turn to a complex body of theological, philosophical, literary and historical writing, for example, by Emil Fackenheim, Steven Leonard Jacobs, David Roskies, Zev Garber[85] and Gershon Greenberg. Greenberg has been especially important in linking reflections on the world of ideas to the lives and practices of real people,[86] although even his work is not easily accessible to readers unfamiliar with Jewish thought and traditions. A short piece by Emmanuel Levinas titled 'To Love the Torah More Than God', offers a tantalizing glimpse into one religious Jew's response to the Shoah – but leaves open the question as to whether its protagonist is a historical figure or a rhetorical device.[87] In *Hasidic Tales of the Holocaust*, the historian Yaffa Eliach uses personal accounts from survivors of the Holocaust to reveal both how some Hasidim experienced the catastrophe and to demonstrate how the tradition of Hasidic story-telling could give meaning to suffering and devastation.[88]

Still, the scholarship investigating the religious impact of the Holocaust on Jews remains surprisingly small, especially when compared to the mountains of studies on the mechanics of destruction. Even widening the scope to consider relevant diaries, letters and memoirs available in English adds only a handful of titles where religion is thematized or addressed in detail, and the same few works, indeed, the same specific passages (for example, by Etty Hillesum and Elie Wiesel) are referenced repeatedly in scholarly discussions.[89] Rare and valuable are personal accounts that focus on religion, like the one by Gabor Vermes included in the Bartov and Mack volume. Vermes, a Hungarian Jew, spent January and February 1945 hiding in a basement in Buda, listening to German and Soviet gunfire and praying. He was 11 years old, and the religious polarization in his family was typical for his times: his father was secular and assimilated, his grandfather pious and observant. Curled up on a cot, a coat pulled over his head, Vermes found his own way to God. His few pages of description do not attempt to analyze that response theologically or psychologically, but they do reveal what must have been one point on a spectrum of religious responses to attack by Jews in Europe during the Shoah.[90]

Another point – more mature and sophisticated in its self-consciousness, but not so far from Vermes's reaction – is presented in the diary of the Romanian Jewish writer Mihail Sebastian. In Bucharest on 11 October 1943, Sebastian was explicit about his longing for the comfort of religion: 'Saturday was Yom Kippur. I fasted, and I went to the synagogue in the evening to hear the sound of the shofar. Reading over someone's shoulder, I tried to intone the Avinu Malkenu. Why? Do I believe? Do I want to believe? No, not even that. But it is as if, in all these unthinking gestures, there is a need for warmth and peace.'[91] By then Sebastian's once large group of prominent gentile friends – among them Mircea Eliade – had not only abandoned him to isolation and poverty; they had become involved with the extreme right-wing Iron Guard and embraced a vicious antisemitism.

The wide range of religious responses to extreme violence – even from within a targeted group – can both obstruct and shape discussion and analysis. In his classic memoir, *Survival in Auschwitz*, the Italian Jewish scientist Primo Levi describes a pious Jew in the death camp who prayed to express his gratitude for being spared from a 'selection' for the gas. 'If I were God', writes Levi, 'I would spit on his prayer.'[92] Yet Levi also remembers with admiration the spiritual and intellectual energy of one particular rabbi he encountered.[93] Judith Isaacson, a Hungarian Jew who survived Auschwitz-Birkenau as a teenager, recalls feeling comforted by Sabbath services held in the camp,[94] and Elie Wiesel insists that in all his reading and meeting with people who lived through the Holocaust, he has never found evidence of a rabbi who served as a kapo.[95]

In a brief study of Jewish resistance, *They Chose Life*, the historian Yehuda Bauer links faith with fighting back against the Nazi assault. Bauer took the title of his book from the Hebrew Bible (Deuteronomy 30:19), and he included subsections called 'Roots of Jewish Strength', 'What Makes for Survival' and 'Many Meanings', in which he speculates about the impact of Jewish tradition on forms of resistance. But this is no devotional work: Bauer's methodology is firmly secular, and his efforts to understand the roots and limits of resistance have implications beyond the specific context of the Holocaust. One of Bauer's remarks about resistance might also be taken to explain the interplay of tradition and scholarship in the historian's own trajectory: 'Men may come to similar attitudes by different roads; while dissenting from religious Judaism, a Jew will often follow a path that is Jewish by historical tradition.'[96] Unfortunately the brevity of the work means that Bauer cannot develop his insights in detail.

If historians' reticence with regard to the religious experiences of Jews in the Shoah seems surprising, the absence of a scholarly literature on religion in the genocide of the Armenians is even more noticeable. In contrast to Jews, who after all, at least officially in Nazi ideology and law, constituted a racial rather than a religious group, Armenians were incontrovertibly marked off within the Ottoman Empire by their religion. Nevertheless, my request to a specialist in the Armenian genocide for a bibliography of items on the subject netted three articles, two of them in the Bartov–Mack volume. Ara Sarafian investigates issues surrounding coerced conversions of Armenian women and children, and Maud Mandel explores the post-genocidal religious responses of Armenians in France with those of Jews there 30 years later.[97] Leo Kuper and Gary Remer's 1992 article, 'The Religious Element in Genocide', takes an even broader view.[98]

It is probably safe to assume that there is a literature in Armenian that presents individual and collective responses to the killing in religious terms and that draws on the venerable tradition of Armenian Christianity to give meaning to mass death and loss. But such works have not crossed over into the mainstream. Given the need to assert that there in fact was a genocide of the Armenians, perhaps scholars have avoided a focus on religion as something that might make their efforts appear somehow amateur or parochial. In any case, non-specialists are most likely to get their impressions of the role of the Armenian church and its leaders in coping with attack and destruction from Franz Werfel's powerful 1933 novel, *Forty Days of Musa Dagh*.[99] One of the central characters and a pillar of strength throughout is the priest Ter Haigasun, Aaron to the protagonist Gabriel Bagradian's Moses.

Casting about for studies of the religious experience of groups and individuals targeted in genocide and extreme violence turns up no established historiography, but there are some astonishing exceptions. Like many other analysts, Bartov and Mack describe the Cambodian case as one 'where the main motivation of, and reactions to, genocidal policies were largely unrelated to religious belief and institutions'.[100] A closer look, however, proves that in Cambodia too, religion formed one of many axes of persecution. As Ben Kiernan shows, targets of the Khmer Rouge included the Muslim Cham. Between 1975 and 1979, Pol Pot's forces killed an estimated 90,000 of the 250,000 Cham in Cambodia. They forced the Cham to raise pigs and eat pork, forbade Cham women to wear their hair in the traditional style, prohibited use of the Cham language, dispersed their villages and destroyed their religious texts. Kiernan's sketch of this violence is based on interviews with a small number of Cham survivors, who managed to re-assemble as a community and build a wooden mosque in Cambodia in 1980.[101]

Chanthou Boua's 'Genocide of a Religious Group: Pol Pot and Cambodia's Buddhist Monks', shows how paying attention to a religious group can reveal aspects of the wider dynamic of violence. Boua's short and poignant article is based in part on accounts from Buddhist monks and former monks and shows both how high a priority the Khmer Rouge placed on destroying the monasteries as centres of social cohesion and also how complete the destruction of Buddhism in Cambodia was.[102] Scattered references in Loung Ung's memoir echo Boua's findings at a personal, lay level. As a young girl in the midst of extreme violence, Loung tried to draw strength from Buddhism but found she knew precious little about her own religious tradition. Reunited with her older brother in a refugee camp in Thailand in 1979, she followed his lead and agreed to be baptized a Christian. She still felt herself to be Buddhist but accepted her brother's argument that Christians were more likely to find sponsors in the United States.[103]

Boua's study and Ung's remarks indicate an important challenge in the study of religion and genocide as seen by those targeted for attack. Although religious language itself sometimes disguises the fact, the experience of extreme violence changes – indeed, sometimes totally destroys – religions. In some cases, it seems religion and violence become intertwined in a dialectical process, whereby changes in one produce a response from the other that in turn sparks further transformations. Gary Hamburg shows this dynamic at work in the nineteenth-century Russian wars in the Caucasus in his commentary on Tolstoy's *Hadji Murad* and Muhammad al-Qarakhi's contemporary chronicle, *The Shining of Daghestani Swords*.[104] As Hamburg demonstrates, Russian pressure on the indigenous Muslim peoples provoked 'a series of mobilizations in defense of Islam' beginning in the 1780s. A self-proclaimed imam, Shaykh Mansur, and a Sufi confraternity known as the Naqshbandiyya, both active in Chechnia and neighbouring Daghestan, preached an Islamic lifestyle in accordance with sacred law and proclaimed a holy war against Russian 'infidels' and anyone else who threatened Muslim purity. They also taught that it was impossible to live according to Muslim law under the rule of infidels. Russians misread the campaign for godliness as an attempt to seize political power in the region and viewed evidence of what they called 'fanaticism' as a call to reinforce the brutality of their wars of conquest. By the 1830s and 1840s, the result was unconventional warfare, as the insurgents took hostages to intimidate local populations and the Russians polluted water supplies and burned villages to punish alleged collaborators. While the Russians displaced people they deemed unwanted and demeaned the leaders they captured, the insurgents rallied around imams who now claimed absolute secular as well as religious authority. Although this situation is more likely to be characterized as a case of war with attendant 'ethnic cleansing' than a genocide, the dynamic revealed is instructive for reflecting on ways that extreme violence affects the practice and even the teachings of a religion.

In their study of a case removed by one hundred years and a vast distance, Leslie Dwyer and Degung Santikarma present a different variety of religious responses to mass death that, nevertheless, also point to the ways religion, like extreme violence, is embedded in every aspect of society. The main focus of their article, '"When the World Turned to Chaos": 1965 and Its Aftermath in Bali, Indonesia', is not religion but a call for public recognition of the events of that year and their ongoing repercussions.[105] Still, a reader interested in religion will find much to ponder here. In a few months of 1965, under Suharto's rule and as part of an anti-communist campaign, as many as one million people were murdered in Indonesia. In Bali alone, Dwyer and Santikarma indicate, some 100,000 people were killed: 7–8 per cent of the island's population. Most of these people denied any affiliation with communism, but severe pressures led to the creation of victims to whom the label 'communist' was often applied after their death. Sometimes individuals who feared they would be targeted asked members of their family to kill them, hoping that someone they knew, unlike the military or paramilitary gangs, would carry out the necessary rituals to ensure reincarnation of their soul.

The violence fractured social units of all kinds, and as Dwyer and Santikarma show, the particular religious practices of Balinese Hindus shaped its effects in measurable ways. Unlike Hindus elsewhere, Dwyer and Santikarma explain, Balinese Hindus are reincarnated back into their extended families, usually within one or two generations of their death. Since 1965, however, very few of the people killed in the violence have returned to their families. Instead, in the small city of Kesiman, where Dwyer and Santikarma conducted their research, the family has become a site of 'traumatic memory or karmic retribution.' For example, one killer, who boasted of hacking his victims to pieces, had a child born without arms or legs.[106]

According to Dwyer and Santikarma, the violence in Bali built on and revitalized the traditional concept of the *leak*, a person who can change into a terrible demon that causes sickness, madness or death to his or her victims. In Balinese belief, anyone can become a *leak*, a possibility that embodies the reality of unpredictable behavior or sudden, drastic transformations, even among one's closest friends and family members. Whether intentionally or not, the military exploited the tradition of the *leak* by labeling communists the *musuh dalam selimut*, 'the enemy in the blanket'. Seen from this perspective, it becomes somewhat easier to understand how Balinese could imagine that people they knew to have had little or nothing to do with communism could be communists – and how they could brutally kill members of their own communities and families.[107]

Dwyer and Santikarma's complex, anthropological arguments are a powerful reminder of the ways that religion shapes practices and memories of extreme violence, even as religion itself is transformed in the process. They also counsel against exoticizing cultural difference – a real risk in an academic discourse that tends to assume that religion exists in some kind of 'timeless' zone or only 'primitive' peoples have religion. To this way of thinking, religion is directly relevant only in certain cases of genocide, for example, in Rwanda, but not in more 'advanced' or 'modern' genocides, such as those in Europe from the Armenian genocide, to the Holocaust, the mass murders under Stalin, or the violence in Bosnia and Kosovo in the 1990s, where it is deemed only a marker for something else: nationalism, racism or a political power grab. In his reflections on the Holocaust, Dominick LaCapra acknowledged this tendency to dismiss religion: 'We secular intellectuals', he wrote, 'are more comfortable with the notion of the aesthetic, even when we criticize its putative role, than we are with the idea of the continued importance of religion and its relations to secularization'.[108]

One instructive case where research and personal accounts of the religiosity of victims of extreme violence has begun to permeate the wider scholarly discussion involves Jehovah's Witnesses in Nazi Germany. Since the 1980s, a small but convincing body of research has argued that Jehovah's Witnesses were one of the earliest targets of Nazi aggression and that study of their experience is instructive for understanding the Nazi system as a whole. Scholars associated with universities and archives have done some of this work – Christine King and Detlev Garbe,[109] for example – and some has been conducted by Jolene Chu, Hans Hesse and James Pellechia,[110] two historical researchers and a journalist who are connected with the Watch Tower Society. In a number of significant projects, researchers of both kinds have worked together. The documentary film, 'Stand Firm', for example, was based on a conference held at the United States Holocaust Memorial Museum on Nazi persecution of Jehovah's Witnesses.[111] It brought together scholars of Nazi Germany, among them Sybil Milton, John Conway and Susannah Heschel, and Jehovah's Witnesses who lived through the Nazi era or had become experts on that history. The result is a compelling account of a small religious minority that withstood Nazi German assault and retained its integrity.

The 'Stand Firm' project demonstrates both the necessity of the 'victims' approach' to studying religion and extreme violence and some of the dangers or at least challenges of doing so. Only insiders to a group have access to the kind of information necessary to comprehend what a massive assault means to the religious lives of individuals and communities. And only adherents are likely to care enough to make sure that what might seem from the outside to be marginal experiences of suffering are not forgotten. The result of such research – and it is evident in the 'Stand Firm' film and some of the other Jehovah's Witnesses scholarship[112] – is a kind of historical work of inspiration that presents suffering as martyrdom and uses it to galvanize followers and gain moral standing in the eyes of outsiders.

Similar kinds of work, though rarely marked by such careful scholarship and almost never presented in conjunction with secular historians, can be found in many other contexts. During the Spanish Civil War of 1936–39, torrents of literature described in lurid detail the persecution and killing of Roman Catholic nuns and priests by 'Reds', and the wave of beatifications of Spaniards 60 years later has revived and reproduced parts of that tradition.[113] Under Communist rule, Christians and other discriminated religious groups in the Soviet Union, Eastern Europe and China produced (and in the Chinese case, continue to produce) publications documenting their suffering and publicizing it abroad.[114] Sometimes such inspirational literature serves devotional purposes.

It is easy to discredit such accounts as special pleading, biased, one-sided and even propaganda. And some of them undoubtedly are. Historians of the Spanish Civil War have shown that claims of mass slaughter of priests and nuns by the forces of the Republic, although based on some real incidents early in the war, were wildly exaggerated.[115] Even the heroic view of the Jehovah's Witnesses in the Third Reich has come under attack by M. James Penton, a former member whose research indicates that the official picture has ignored evidence of engrained antisemitism within the group and concealed the leadership's early enthusiasm for Hitler and National Socialism.[116] Such correctives are valuable, indeed essential. Still, any attempt to take seriously the presence of religion in times of extreme violence, as experienced and seen by the victims, cannot dismiss research (or memories) as invalid just because the researcher or person doing the remembering has an interest in presenting certain things and not others. Such sources, selective as they often (always) are, are sometimes all we have.

Equally unavoidable when addressing religion and violence with what I have termed the victims' perspective is the implication of the author her or himself in the discussion. If writers from the 'inside' have to earn credibility with a wider readership, writers from the outside are open to charges of either being prejudiced (if they are too critical) or being duped (if they are not). In societies obsessed with identity politics and often naively convinced that identity and bias are the same, authors risk being dismissed if they disclose their personal religious position and accused of masking their prejudices if they conceal it. For this reason too, explorations of religion and genocide turn out to be fraught with difficulties.

Religion as a force for good

As Bartov and Mack remind us, religion is found not only among the perpetrators and victims of extreme violence but also on the side of the heroes: those who rescue, resist and bring healing. This role, too, is evident in the literature, both scholarly and popular. Usually but not always accounts that focus on religion as a force for good are written or created by insiders to the religious group in question. In their popular form, they present religiously motivated heroes as role models and inspirations for others; as scholarship, they emphasize the sincerity, integrity and insight of their subjects. One need only think of depictions of the sixteenth-century priest Bartolomé de Las Casas, who insisted that the indigenous peoples of the 'new world' had souls and should not be enslaved and slaughtered;[117] of studies showing Christian missionaries as champions of the downtrodden, for example, in Puritan New England;[118] of accounts of the lives of religious figures who shone as 'lights in the darkness': Leo Baeck,[119] Bernhard Lichtenberg,[120] Dietrich Bonhoeffer,[121] Edith Stein,[122] Maximilian Kolbe,[123] Oscar Romero,[124] Desmond Tutu[125] and many others.

One can capture the impact of popular literature of this type with the example of Corrie ten Boom's *The Hiding Place*.[126] The daughter of devout Dutch Reformed parents, ten Boom described how her family provided shelter to a group of Dutch Jews during the German occupation in World War II. Matter-of-fact and accessible, the book has been translated into numerous languages and made into a movie.[127] Church groups and schools all over North America, and presumably elsewhere, have used both forms to educate and enlighten audiences, including many children and young people. The message is clear: true Christianity was not implicated on the side of the Nazis: instead it risked everything in solidarity with the victims.

Scholarly works cannot – and should not – duplicate such simplicity, but some do present religion in comparable ways, especially in the context of World War II and the Holocaust. Peter Hoffmann's standard work on Claus Schenk von Stauffenberg, the would-be assassin of Hitler in July 1944, points to his 'sincere Catholicism' as central to his motivations (although Hoffmann does not analyze exactly what Stauffenberg's Catholicism meant to him).[128] Tatjana Blaha develops the connection in detail in her examination of the Roman Catholic Willi Graf and the White Rose, a group of students in Munich who spoke out against the crimes of Nazi Germany.[129] Philip P. Hallie's moving study of André and Magda Trocmé and the French Protestant rescuers of Jews in Le Chambon-sur-Lignon, *Lest Innocent Blood Be Shed*,[130] and Pierre Sauvage's beautiful movie tribute to the same community, 'Weapons of the Spirit',[131] situate religious motivations at the heart and soul of that remarkable rescue in rural France of some 5000 Jews – among them, Sauvage himself. Such incidents, we can assume, were rare but not anomalous. The important sociologist of genocide Helen Fein pointed out that in the case of the Holocaust, wherever leaders of the dominant church spoke out against murder of Jews, many Jews were spared.[132]

Comparable literature on religion as a brake against extreme violence in cases of genocide other than the Holocaust is scarce. The Rittner, Roth and Whitworth volume on Rwanda is dedicated to the memory of three Rwandans, including one Catholic priest and a nun, 'who laid down their lives for their friends, and for all Christians in Rwanda, known and unknown, who before, during, and after the 1994 genocide in Rwanda, defended humanity, stood firm against a tide of unprecedented atrocities, and who did not leave God without witnesses'.[133] Some of the contributions allude to individual Christians who acted heroically, but an analysis of how their religiosity motivated their acts is not included. The Bartov and Mack volume includes one study of Christian rescuers in the Holocaust (Jessica A. Sheetz-Nguyen, 'Transcending Boundaries: Hungarian Roman Catholic Religious Women and the "Persecuted Ones"'),[134] but no investigations of religion on the side of good in the other cases of genocide that are considered.

It is possible that a literature of religious rescuers exists in the original languages somewhere: for example, on individual Muslims who were inspired by their religion to show mercy towards Armenians or shelter them from harm; or on Serbs who, mindful of Jesus' blessing of the peacemakers, protected their Muslim neighbours. Accounts from survivors of massacres indicate that such individuals existed, although their motives were not usually described to those they helped. It seems safe to assume, however, that little information of this kind has been recorded or distributed in societies where the genocides and/or mass killings themselves have not been officially acknowledged – and where complicity on the part of the dominant religions is not even under discussion.[135] Works like ten Boom's *The Hiding Place* are easily criticized as one-sided, idealized and selective, but their existence itself attests to a recognition that Jews were murdered and that Christianity has something for which to answer.

There are obvious problems with the literature of rescue as a way to get at the intersections of religion and extreme violence. By definition it draws our attention to the exceptions, often without asking, how did the situation get to that point, and where were religious institutions as a whole? Here Michael Phayer's careful study of the Catholic Church and the Holocaust is instructive.[136] As Phayer argues, we need to recognize heroic individuals, but doing so cannot answer the urgent question as to how genocide and extreme violence can occur in the first place, nor can it explain why we need extraordinary individuals to try, usually without much success, to stop it. The impact of extraordinary individuals is immense in terms of their moral significance (and their import for co-religionists), but as a historical force at the time of violence, they are often sadly negligible.

Religion and post-genocidal legacies

A fourth way to approach issues of religion and extreme violence is to consider religion as a force for reconciliation and healing. What is left for the survivors, for those who carried out and witnessed terrible crimes? How do their relationships with their faith traditions change, if they do? The Holocaust prompted much theological grappling, most markedly among Jews, and to a lesser extent and beginning later, among Christians. Many of the formative works are excerpted in the volumes co-edited by Richard L. Rubenstein and John K. Roth,[137] and Roth and Michael Berenbaum.[138] Other cases of genocide do not seem to have sparked similar re-thinking, or at least not on a comparable scale, and here too, one can assume that recognition of atrocities, acceptance that religion was involved and the existence of some survivors with an awareness of their religious traditions are preconditions for such a discourse.

Religion has provided a basis for building relations between Jews and Christians after the Holocaust, and it is no surprise that the most concerted efforts to find points of contact beyond the old Christian triumphalism have begun here. One remarkable effort was the publication during September 2000 of 'Dabru Emet: A Jewish Statement on Christians and Christianity', signed by over 150 rabbis and Jewish scholars, most of them from the United States, but some from Canada, the UK and Israel.[139] Beginning with a recognition that Christianity had changed dramatically in recent years, *Dabru Emet* offered eight points around which Jews and Christians might relate to one another. Among them were the statements that 'Jews and Christians worship the same

God'; 'Nazism was not a Christian phenomenon'; and 'a new relationship between Jews and Christians will not weaken Jewish practice.'[140]

Dagmar Herzog's work, notably the book *Sex after Fascism*, shows that Christianity, particular Protestant church leaders in Germany, played some less constructive roles after the Holocaust.[141] Herzog analyzes how Christian leaders in the post-war Germanies helped shift the subject of moral approbation from those who murdered Jews and others to those who transgressed narrow notions of sexual propriety.[142] In general, in post-genocidal situations, leaders of religions associated with the perpetrators tend to struggle with what might be considered the easier questions, such as the role of bystanders or sins of omission, rather than confront the existence of religious killers. There is evidence of this tendency in the 1998 papal statement 'We Remember the Shoah' and in the remarks of Pope Benedict XVI at Auschwitz in 2006, but also in post-genocidal statements by the Rwandan Catholic hierarchy and responses from Christians to the trials of Roman Catholic nuns and a Seventh Day Adventist clergyman.

Attention to religion in post-genocidal situations serves to highlight both the totality of destruction and the comfort of tradition – even if invented or improvised – for subsequent generations. Chris Mato Nunpa's article on 'Dakota Commemorative March: Thoughts and Reactions' provides a moving illustration.[143] Nunpa, a Wahpetunwan Dakota and professor of Indigenous Nations and Dakota Studies at Southwest Minnesota State University, describes a trek he organized in memory of the forced removal of Dakota people in 1862 from Minnesota to Nebraska and South Dakota. Religion, although not explicitly analyzed in the piece, features in various contexts. Spiritual leaders were important sources of solace at particular moments of the march, and a number of participants lamented the lack of a proper burial for their ancestors. Some Christian church groups helped feed and shelter the marchers along the 150-mile route, but then resented the bitter tone of Nunpa's remarks and expected to be thanked for their charity, as if coffee, scarves and gloves could make up for the loss of land, homes, community, tradition and loved ones. In areas where they sensed that some of their people had been killed, Nunpa and the other participants decided it would be a good idea to hang prayer ribbons and offer tobacco.

Religion plays other roles post-genocide, too, at least in specific cases. Individual religions can be the beneficiaries of genocide and extreme violence, as Richard Rubenstein has pointed out regarding Islam in Turkey benefiting from the eradication of Christian Armenians and Christianity profiting from the Holocaust and destruction of its Jewish rivals. In Rubenstein's words, 'Without Christianity, the Jews could never have become the central victims.'[144] The flip side of this equation is that when religion is manipulated and exploited by the executioners of mass violence, it can end up losing credibility afterward. John Conway has made this argument about Christianity in World War I and after,[145] and it could also be true of those religious elements who sided with communism in the Soviet Union.[146]

It may be that the post-genocide discrediting of religion is itself an illusion, an indication that religion was not really very significant during the events in question. Some of the most influential works on extreme violence hint at this position. Norman Naimark's work on 'ethnic cleansing' shows little interest in religion,[147] and Isabel Hull's brilliant study of German military culture in the early twentieth century, *Absolute Destruction*, does not need religion for its analysis.[148] Jürgen Zimmerer's account of the German genocide in Southwest Africa draws on missionary sources but gives little independent agency to religion,[149] and even the important collections edited by Frank R. Chalk and Kurt Jonassohn,[150] and Samuel Totten, William S. Parsons and Israel W. Charny have relatively little to say about religion.[151] Samantha Power's much-quoted *'A Problem from Hell': America and the Age of Genocide* says practically nothing at all about the subject.[152]

Still, Power's book draws our attention to a final role of religion in studies of extreme violence. With her title's reference to 'hell' (embedded in a quotation from United States Secretary of State Warren Christopher),[153] Power reminds us that religious language and religious images persist in even the most secular analyses as a way of making sense, or at least talking about, extreme violence. Power's choice is duplicated in numerous other works on massacres and genocide. It is not surprising that studies focusing on religion use such allusions in their titles: for example, Sabrina Ramet's *Balkan Babel*; Hugh McCullum's *The Angels Have Left Us: The Rwandan Tragedy and the Churches*; and Mark Juergensmeyer's *Terror in the Mind of God: The Global Rise of Religious Violence.*[154] What is noticeable is that many works with nothing explicit to say about religion do the same thing. Peter Maass, *Love Thy Neighbor* and Ed Vulliamy, *Seasons in Hell* are two examples from the war in Bosnia.[155]

A high-profile case is Romeo Dallaire, *Shake Hands with the Devil,*[156] and the documentary movie with the same name.[157] Dallaire, a Canadian general who had charge of the United Nations forces stationed in Rwanda in 1994, watched the preparations for mass slaughter and found himself unable either to rouse international action or to stop the violence. His memoir recounts his observations and experiences. With the exception of the opening segment, it reveals little about the role of the churches or about his own religious predilections. Nevertheless, Dallaire frames his recollections with a verse from the Christian Bible, Matthew 5:9: 'Blessed are the peacemakers: for they shall be called the children of God.' In the preface, he explains his title by referring to a Canadian Forces chaplain who asked how he could still believe in God. 'Because in Rwanda I shook hands with the devil,' Dallaire tells us. 'I have seen him, I have smelled him and I have touched him. I know the devil exists, and therefore

I know there is a God.'[158] Later Dallaire adds that 'we watched as the devil took control of paradise on earth and fed on the blood of the people we were supposed to protect.'[159] Such religious language serves to give meaning and familiarity to what defies comprehension – to sort human experience into good and evil, two binary opposites. But as Dallaire's title indicates, in a manner that reflects his humility and intense self-scrutiny, it is not always easy and comforting to resort to those patterns; that handshake implies Dallaire's sense of his own failure, too.

There are many challenges in the study of genocide, and in particular in the study of genocides comparatively. How does one master the necessary languages and often vast and dispersed literatures? How can one deal with the overwhelming sadness and suffering or accept the criticisms and attacks that are so often dealt out as audiences 'shoot the messenger'? All of those problems are compounded when one adds the hot-button issue of religion to the mix. There are accusations of disloyalty if one talks about one's own religious tradition and charges of prejudice, theological ignorance or failure to appreciate complexities if one focuses on another religion. As interest in both religion and extreme violence increases, we can hope for production of more, nuanced, informed studies of individual cases – and for publication of more general and comparative works.[160] Nevertheless, I am not optimistic that there will be a large amount of scholarship on issues of religion and genocide, broadly conceived. The stakes are too high and the rewards probably too few.

Notes

1. Reproduced in C. Rittner, J. K. Roth and W. Whitworth, eds, *Genocide in Rwanda: Complicity of the Churches?* (St. Paul, MN: Paragon House, 2004), pp. 279–80. I gratefully acknowledge the students in my class at the University of Notre Dame on 'Religion and Violence in Comparative Perspective' (fall 2006) who helped me think through many of the issues discussed in this essay.
2. O. Bartov and P. Mack, eds, *In God's Name: Genocide and Religion in the Twentieth Century* (New York: Berghahn, 2001).
3. Bartov and Mack, 'Introduction,' in ibid., p. 17.
4. Two influential studies – one of genocide, one of the phenomenon that has become known as 'ethnic cleansing' – as twentieth-century phenomena are E. D. Weitz, *A Century of Genocide: Utopias of Race and Nation* (Princeton, NJ: Princeton University Press, 2003) and N. M. Naimark, *Fires of Hatred: Ethnic Cleansing in Twentieth-Century Europe* (Cambridge, MA: Harvard University Press, 2001). Neither focuses on religion, but both acknowledge its relevance.
5. On the Crusades, see the useful overview by T. F. Madden, *A Concise History of the Crusades* (Lanham, MD: Rowman and Littlefield, 1999). An in-depth analysis of the Inquisition is B. Netanyahu, *The Origins of the Inquisition in Fifteenth Century Spain* (New York: Random House, 1995).
6. E. Wiesel, *Night*, trans. S. Rodway (New York: Penguin, 1981), p. 77.

7. Quoted in P. Balakian, *The Burning Tigris: The Armenian Genocide and America's Response* (New York: Harper Collins, 2003), pp. 248–9.
8. Some influential older and newer works available in English include J. S. Conway, *The Nazi Persecution of the Churches, 1933–45* (New York: Basic Books, 1968); E. C. Helmreich, *The German Churches under Hitler: Background, Struggle, and Epilogue* (Detroit, MI: Wayne State University Press, 1979); R. P. Ericksen, *Theologians under Hitler: Gerhard Kittel, Paul Althaus and Emanuel Hirsch* (New Haven, CT: Yale University Press, 1985); K. Scholder, *The Churches and the Third Reich. Vol. 1: Preliminary History and the Time of Illusions, 1918–1932; Vol. 2: The Year of Disillusionment: 1934, Barmen and Rome*, trans. J. Bowden (Philadelphia, PA: Fortress, 1987–8); D. L. Bergen, *Twisted Cross: The German Christian Movement and the Third Reich* (Chapel Hill, NC: University of North Carolina Press, 1996); R. P. Ericksen and S. Heschel, eds, *Betrayal: The German Churches and the Holocaust* (Minneapolis, MN: Augsburg Fortress, 1999); W. Gerlach, *And the Witnesses Were Silent: The Confessing Church and the Persecution of the Jews*, trans. and ed. V. J. Barnett (Lincoln, NE: University of Nebraska Press, 2000); C. Rittner and J. K. Roth, eds, *Pope Pius XII and the Holocaust* (Leicester: Leicester University Press, 2002); B. A. Griech-Polelle, *Bishop von Galen: German Catholicism and National Socialism* (New Haven, CT: Yale University Press, 2002); and R. Steigmann-Gall, *The Holy Reich: Nazi Conceptions of Christianity, 1919–1945* (Cambridge: Cambridge University Press, 2003).
9. See most importantly, the chapters in Rittner, Roth and Whitworth, eds, *Genocide in Rwanda*. There are two relevant chapters in Bartov and Mack, eds, *In God's Name*: T. Longman, 'Christian Churches and Genocide in Rwanda,' pp. 139–60; C. de Lespinay, 'The Churches and the Genocide in the East African Great Lakes Region,' pp. 161–79. Also significant are A. Des Forges, *Leave None to Tell the Story: Genocide in Rwanda* (New York: Human Rights Watch, 1999); and H. McCullum, *The Angels Have Left Us: The Rwandan Tragedy and the Churches* (Geneva: World Council of Churches Publications, #66 in Risk Book Series, 1995).
10. P. Gourevitch, *We wish to inform you that tomorrow we will be killed with our families* (New York: Farrar, Straus and Giroux, 1998).
11. A notable and valuable exception is the eyewitness account of L. L. S. Braun, *In Lubianka's Shadow: The Memoirs of an American Priest in Stalin's Moscow, 1934–1945*, ed., G. M. Hamburg (Notre Dame, IN: University of Notre Dame Press, 2006).
12. Rittner, Roth and Whitworth, eds, *Genocide in Rwanda*.
13. Fr. Ugirashebuja, 'The Church and the Genocide in Rwanda,' in ibid., pp. 49–63.
14. Ndahiro, 'The Church's Blind Eye to Genocide in Rwanda,' in ibid., pp. 229–49.
15. Smith and Rittner, 'Churches as Memorial Sites: A Photo Essay,' in ibid., pp. 181–205; statistic on p. 181.
16. Saur, 'From Kibeho to Medjugorje: The Catholic Church and Ethno-Nationalist Movements and Regimes,' in ibid., pp. 211–27.
17. Roth, 'Epilogue,' in ibid., p. 270.
18. M. (Francois) Neyt, 'Two Conflicted Rwandan Nuns,' in ibid., pp. 251–8.
19. I. W. Charny, ed., *The Widening Circle of Genocide: Genocide: A Critical Bibliography*, 3 vols. (New Brunswick, NJ: Transaction Publishers, 1988–99).
20. Charny, 'A Passion for Life and Rage at the Wasting of Life,' in *Pioneers of Genocide Studies*, eds, S. Totten and S. L. Jacobs, (New Brunswick, NJ: Transaction Publishers, 2002), p. 447.

21. Roth, 'Epilogue: What Should be Remembered,' in *Genocide in Rwanda*, eds, Rittner, Roth, and Whitworth, p. 270.
22. R. S. Appleby, *The Ambivalence of the Sacred: Religion, Violence, and Reconciliation* (Lanham, MD: Rowman and Littlefield, 2000).
23. S. P. Huntington, *Clash of Civilizations and the Remaking of World Order* (New York: Simon and Schuster, 1996). A more nuanced and informed analysis is M. Ruthven, *A Fury for God: The Islamist Attack on America* (London: Granta Books, 2002).
24. See B. Weisbrod, 'Religious Languages of Violence. Some Reflections on the Reading of Extremes,' in *No Man's Land of Violence: Extreme Wars in the 20th Century*, eds, A. Lüdtke and B. Weisbrod (Göttingen: Wallstein, 2006), pp. 253–81.
25. R. Girard, *Violence and the Sacred*, trans. P. Gregory (Baltimore, MD: Johns Hopkins University Press, 1977).
26. B. Ehrenreich, *Blood Rites: Origins and History of the Passions of War* (New York: Henry Holt, 1997).
27. L. Glick, 'Religion and Genocide,' in *Widening Circle*, ed., Charny, pp. 43–74.
28. See R. M. Schwartz, *The Curse of Cain: The Violent Legacy of Monotheism* (Chicago, IL: University of Chicago Press, 1998); and J. Kirsch, *God against the Gods: The History of the War Between Monotheism and Polytheism* (New York: Viking, 2004).
29. Bartov and Mack, 'Introduction,' in *In God's Name*, eds, Bartov and Mack, p. 2.
30. L. Kuper, 'Theological Mandates for Genocide,' *Terrorism and Political Violence*, 2, 3 (1990), 351–79.
31. Nunpa, unpublished manuscript. For additional discussion of the concept of 'chosenness' and its uses in nationalist contexts in the late nineteenth and early twentieth centuries, see the essays in *Many Are Chosen: Divine Election and Western Nationalism*, eds, W. R. Hutchison and H. Lehmann (Minneapolis, MN: Fortress, 1994). Although nationalism in general, not genocide or violence in specific, is the focus of the volume, related matters are addressed in a number of the pieces.
32. Most influential are probably R. Ruether, *Faith and Fratricide: The Theological Roots of Antisemitism* (New York: Seabury Press, 1974); J. Carroll, *Constantine's Sword: The Church and the Jews: A History* (Boston, MA: Houghton Mifflin, 2001); D. J. Goldhagen, *A Moral Reckoning: The Role of the Catholic Church in the Holocaust and Its Unfulfilled Duty of Repair* (New York: Alfred A. Knopf, 2002).
33. S. Heschel, *The Aryan Jesus: Christians, Nazis, and the Bible* (Princeton, NJ: Princeton University Press, forthcoming).
34. See discussion in S. T. Katz, *The Holocaust in Historical Context: The Holocaust and Mass Death Before the Modern Age* (Oxford: Oxford University Press, 1994).
35. M. Sells, 'Kosovo Mythology and the Bosnian Genocide,' in *In God's Name*, eds, Bartov and Mack, pp. 180–205; also idem., *A Bridge Betrayed: Religion and Genocide in Bosnia* (Berkeley, CA: University of California Press, 1996).
36. See also B. Anzulovic, *Heavenly Serbia: From Myth to Genocide* (New York: New York University Press, 1999).
37. See the chapters on religion in S. P. Ramet, *Balkan Babel: The Disintegration of Yugoslavia from the Death of Tito to the War for Kosovo*, 3rd edn (Boulder, CO: Westview Press, 1999); P. Mojzes, *Yugoslavian Inferno: Ethnoreligious Warfare in the Balkans* (New York: Continuum, 1994).
38. E. Voegelin, *Die politischen Religionen* (Munich: W. Fink, 1993; first ed. 1938).
39. P. Burrin, 'Political Religion. The Relevance of a Concept,' *History & Memory*, 9, 1–2 (1997), 321–49; S. Stowers, 'The Concepts of "Religion," "Political Religion," and the Study of Nazism,' *Journal of Contemporary History*, 42, 1 (2007), 9–24.

40. See G. L. Mosse, *The Nationalization of the Masses: Political Symbolism and Mass Movements in Germany from the Napoleonic Wars Through the Third Reich* (New York: 1975).
41. E. Gentile, *The Sacralization of Politics in Fascist Italy* (Cambridge, MA: Cambridge University Press, 1996).
42. O. Bartov, *Mirrors of Destruction: War, Genocide, and Modern Identity* (New York: Oxford University Press, 2000).
43. M. Burleigh, *The Third Reich: A New History* (New York: Hill and Wang, 2001).
44. See first issue, 1, 1 (2000), with articles by Peter Calvert, Emilio Gentile, Michael Burleigh and Desmond King.
45. M. Burleigh, *Earthly Powers: The Clash of Religion and Politics in Europe, from the French Revolution to the Great War* (New York: Harper Collins, 2005); idem., *Sacred Causes: The Clash of Religion and Politics from the Great War to the War on Terror* (New York: Harper Press, 2006).
46. L. Tolstoy, *Hadji Murad*, trans. A. Maude (New York: Modern Library, 2003), pp. 85–94.
47. Ibid., pp. 108–14.
48. L. Ung, *First they Killed My Father: A Daughter of Cambodia Remembers* (New York: Perennial, 2001).
49. See some of the cases in F. Chalk and K. Jonassohn, eds, *The History and Sociology of Genocide: Analyses and Case Studies* (New Haven, CT: Yale University Press, 1990).
50. R. Lemkin, *Axis Rule in Occupied Europe: Laws of Occupation, Analysis of Government, Proposals for Redress* (Washington, DC: Carnegie Endowment for International Peace, Division of International Law, 1944), pp. 84–5.
51. Quoted in Appendix 1 in *Genocide in Rwanda*, eds, Rittner, Roth and Whitworth, p. 279.
52. G. Tinker, *Missionary Conquest: The Gospel and Native American Cultural Genocide* (Minneapolis, MN: Fortress, 1993).
53. M. Fleming, 'Gender and the Body Politic in the Time of Modernity,' in *The Specter of Genocide: Mass Murder in Historical Perspective*, eds, R. Gellately and B. Kiernan (Cambridge: Cambridge University Press, 2003), pp. 111–12.
54. See E. Barkan, 'Genocides of Indigenous Peoples: Rhetoric of Human Rights,' in ibid., pp. 117–39.
55. See A. D. Moses, ed., *Genocide and Settler Society: Frontier Violence and Stolen Indigenous Children in Australian History* (New York: Berghahn, 2004), although the essays in this volume do not focus on religion nor do they approach the issue in terms of cultural genocide.
56. M. Beti, *Poor Christ*, trans. G. Moore (London: Heinemann, 1956).
57. Netanyahu, *The Origins of the Inquisition*, p. 1052.
58. Ibid., p. 1053.
59. A. Sarafian, 'The Absorption of Armenian Women and Children into Muslim Households as a Structural Component of the Armenian Genocide,' in *In God's Name*, eds, Bartov and Mack, pp. 209–21.
60. K. Jacobson, *Embattled Selves: An Investigation into the Nature of Identity Through Oral Histories of Holocaust Survivors* (New York: Atlantic Monthly Press, 1994).
61. S. Friedländer, *When Memory Comes*, trans. H. R. Lane (New York: Farrar, Straus & Giroux, 1979).
62. R. Gellately and B. Kiernan, 'The Study of Mass Murder and Genocide,' in *The Specter of Genocide*, eds, Gellately and Kiernan, pp. 7, 9, 16.

63. A. Hochschild, *King Leopold's Ghost: A Story of Greed, Terror and Heroism in Colonial Africa* (New York: Houghton Mifflin, 1999).
64. Ibid., p. 134.
65. Quoted in ibid., p. 135.
66. G. Sereny, *Into That Darkness: An Examination of Conscience* (New York: Vintage Books, 1983).
67. J. Waller, *Becoming Evil: How Ordinary People Commit Genocide and Mass Killing* (Oxford: Oxford University Press, 2002).
68. C. R. Browning, *Ordinary Men: Reserve Police Battalion 101 and the Final Solution in Poland* (New York: Harper Collins, 1992).
69. J. Steinberg, 'The Roman Catholic Church and Genocide in Croatia, 1941–1945,' in *Christianity and Judaism: Papers Read at the 1991 Summer and the 1992 Winter Meeting of the Ecclesiastical History Society*, ed. D. Wood (Oxford: Blackwell, 1992), p. 463.
70. R. Hoess, *Death Dealer: The Memoirs of the SS Kommandant at Auschwitz*, ed. S. Paskuly, trans. A. Pollinger (New York: Da Capo Press, 1996), pp. 49–53, 72, 192.
71. M. Deselaers, *Und Sie hatten nie Gewissensbisse? Die Biografie von Rudolf Hoess, Kommandant von Auschwitz, und die Frage nach seiner Verantwortung vor Gott und der Menschen* (Leipzig: St. Benno Verlag, 1997, 2nd edn, 2001). Also of interest in recent German-language scholarship on religion and the perpetrators of the Holocaust is W. Dierker, *Himmlers Glaubenskrieger. Der Sicherheitsdienst der SS und seine Religionspolitik, 1933–1941* (Paderborn: Ferdinand Schoeningh, 2002).
72. R. Hochhuth, *The Deputy*, trans. R. and C. Winston (New York: Grove Press, 1964; German original 1963).
73. Ibid., p. 248.
74. Ibid.
75. See, for example, Costa-Gavras's 2002 movie *Amen*, based on Hochhuth's *The Deputy*. Also of interest for the Latin American context are works by Ariel Dorfman: see *Resistance Trilogy: Widows; Death and the Maiden, Reader* (London: Nick Hern Books, 1998).
76. See, for example, Longman and de Lespinay in *Genocide in Rwanda*, eds, Rittner, Roth and Whitworth.
77. J. Hatzfeld, *Machete Season: The Killers in Rwanda Speak*, trans. L. Coverdale (New York: Farrar, Straus and Giroux, 2003), p. 12.
78. Ibid., p. 141.
79. Ibid., p. 143. For a powerful fictional exploration of the varying roles of religion in the Rwandan genocide, see U. Akpan's short story, 'My Parents' Bedroom,' *The New Yorker* (12 June 2006), 130–45.
80. Quoted from S. Dicks, *From Vietnam to Hell: Interviews with Victims of Post-Traumatic Stress Disorder* (Jefferson, NC, 1990, p. 30), in Bourke, 'The Killing Frenzy,' in *No Man's Land of Violence*, eds, Luedtke and Weisbrod, 119.
81. Tolstoy, *Hadji Murad*, p. 91.
82. See the contributions in D. L. Bergen, ed., *The Sword of the Lord: Military Chaplains from the First to the Twenty-First Century* (Notre Dame, IN: University of Notre Dame Press, 2003).
83. For discussion, see V. J. Barnett, *Bystanders: Conscience and Complicity During the Holocaust* (Westport, CT: Greenwood Press, 1999).
84. K. von Kellenbach, 'The Forgiveness of Sins: Prison Chaplains Work with Nazi Perpetrators 1945–1970,' lecture at Vanderbilt University, October 2005; also

'Vanishing Acts: Perpetrators in Postwar Germany,' *Holocaust and Genocide Studies*, 17, 2 (2003), 305–29. On related issues, see S. Brown-Fleming, *The Holocaust and Catholic Conscience: Cardinal Aloisius Muench and the Guilt Question in Germany* (Notre Dame, IN: University of Notre Dame Press, 2006).

85. Examples of the vast and varied output of these scholars include, E. L. Fackenheim, *To Mend the World* (New York: Schocken, 1982); S. L. Jacobs, *Rethinking Jewish Faith: The Child of a Survivor Responds* (Albany, NY: State University of New York, 1994); D. G. Roskies, *Against the Apocalypse: Responses to Catastrophe in Modern Jewish Culture* (Cambridge, MA: Harvard University Press, 1984); and Z. Garber, *Shoah: The Paradigmatic Genocide: Essays in Exegesis and Eisegesis* (Lanham, MD: University Press of America, 1999).
86. See, for example, G. Greenberg, 'Orthodox Jewish Thought in the Wake of the Holocaust: Tamim Pa'alo of 1947,' in *In God's Name*, eds, Bartov and Mack, pp. 316–41.
87. E. Levinas, 'To Love the Torah More Than God,' trans. H. A. Stephenson and R. I. Sugarman, with commentary by R. I. Sugarman, in *Judaism: A Quarterly Journal of Jewish Life and Thought*, 28, 2 (1979), 216–23.
88. Y. Eliach, *Hasidic Tales of the Holocaust* (New York: Vintage, 1988).
89. In addition to Wiesel's *Night*, see his memoir, *All Rivers Run to the Sea* (New York: Schocken, 1996) and by Hillesum, *Etty Hillesum: An Interrupted Life. The Diaries 1941–1943 and Letters from Westerbork*, trans. A. J. Pomerans (New York: Henry Holt, 1996).
90. G. Vermes, 'A Personal Account,' in *In God's Name*, eds, Bartov and Mack, pp. 259–63.
91. M. Sebastian, *Journal 1935–1944: The Fascist Years*, trans. P. Camiller, introduction by R. Ioanid (Chicago, IL: Ivan R. Dee, 2000); excerpted as 'Diary. Friends and Fascists,' *The New Yorker* (2 October 2000), 107–13; entry from 11 October 1943 on 113.
92. P. Levi, *Survival in Auschwitz* (New York: Simon and Schuster, 1993), p. 130.
93. Ibid., p. 68.
94. J. Magyar-Isaacson, *Seed of Sarah: Memories of a Survivor* (Urbana, IL: University of Illinois Press, 1990), pp. 80–2.
95. Wiesel's remarks during keynote address at Lessons and Legacies Conference on the Holocaust, Dartmouth University, 1994.
96. Y. Bauer, *They Chose Life: Jewish Resistance in the Holocaust* (New York: American Jewish Committee, Institute of Human Relations, 1973), p. 57.
97. M. Mandel, 'Faith, Religious Practices, and Genocide: Armenians and Jews in France following World War I and II,' in *In God's Name*, eds, Bartov and Mack, pp. 289–315.
98. L. Kuper and G. Remer, 'The Religious Element in Genocide,' *Journal of Armenian Studies*, 4, 1–2 (1992), 307–29.
99. F. Werfel, *Forty Days of Musa Dagh* (New York: Viking, 1934).
100. 'Introduction,' in *In God's Name*, eds, Bartov and Mack, p. 2.
101. See B. Kiernan, *The Pol Pot Regime: Race, Power and Genocide in Cambodia under the Khmer Rouge, 1975–79* (New Haven, CT: Yale University Press, 1996), pp. 460–3; and for more detail, B. Kiernan, 'Orphans of Genocide: The Cham Muslims of Kampuchea under Pol Pot,' *Bulletin of Concerned Asian Scholars*, 20, 4 (1988), 2–33. Additional reflections in a comparative perspective in E. Kissi, 'Genocide in Cambodia and Ethiopia,' in *The Specter of Genocide*, eds, Gellately and Kiernan, pp. 307–23, esp. pp. 312–15.

102. C. Boua, 'Genocide of a Religious Group: Pol Pot and Cambodia's Buddhist Monks,' in *State-Organized Terror: The Case of Violent Internal Repression*, eds, T. Bushnell, V. Shlapentokh, C. K. Vanderpool and J. Sundram (Boulder, CO: Westview, 1991), p. 235.
103. Ung, *First They Killed My Father*.
104. G. Hamburg, 'A Commentary on the Two Texts in Their Historical Context,' in *Russian-Muslim Confrontation in the Caucasus: Alternative Visions of the Conflict Between Imam Shamil and the Russians, 1830–1859*, ed. and trans., T. Sanders, E. Tucker and G. Hamburg (London and New York: Routledge Curzon, 2004), pp. 171–238.
105. L. Dwyer and D. Santikarma, '"When the World Turned to Chaos": 1965 and Its Aftermath in Bali, Indonesia,' in *The Specter of Genocide*, eds, Gellately and Kiernan, pp. 289–305.
106. Ibid., p. 297.
107. Ibid., p. 303.
108. D. LaCapra, *Representing the Holocaust: History, Theory, Trauma* (Ithaca, NY: Cornell University Press, 1994), p. 221.
109. C. E. King, *The Nazi State and the New Religions: Five Case Studies of Non-Conformity* (Lewiston, NY: Edwin Mellen Press, 1982). King is vice-chancellor of Staffordshire University. D. Garbe, *Zwischen Widerstand und Martyrium. Die Zeugen Jehovahs im Dritten Reich* (Munich: Oldenbourg, 1993). Garbe is head of the Neuengamme Concentration Camp Memorial and Museum in Hamburg.
110. For examples of their work, see J. Chu, 'Purple Triangles: A Story of Spiritual Resistance,' *Judaism Today*, 12 (1999), 15–19; H. Hesse, ed., *Persecution and Resistance of Jehovah's Witnesses During the Nazi Regime, 1933–1945* (Bremen: Edition Temmen, 2001); J. Pellechia, *The Spirit and the Sword. Jehovah's Witnesses Expose the Third Reich* (Brooklyn, NY: Watch Tower Society, 1997).
111. 'Jehovah's Witnesses Stand Firm Against Nazi Assault,' produced by the Watch Tower Society, 1997.
112. See, in particular, the useful volume edited by Hesse, *Persecution and Resistance*, which includes contributions by Jehovah's Witnesses and scholars from outside the group.
113. A ceremony on 11 March 2001 marked beatification of 233 dead from the Spanish Civil War: see 'Vatican Update,' EWTN Global Catholic Network (19 February 2001).
114. For an example of this type of literature, see the missions classic, *God's Smuggler*, by Brother Andrew, with J. Sherrill and E. Sherrill (New York: Signet, 1964).
115. For scholarship in English on the Catholic Church and its roles in the Spanish Civil War and public remembering and forgetting of the violence, see presentations by J. Casanova, H. Raguer, and A. Cazorla-Sanchez at the conference, 'Franco's Mass Graves: An Interdisciplinary International Investigation,' University of Notre Dame, October 2005; contributions by Casanova and Raguer to appear in *Unearthing Franco's Legacy: Mass Graves and the Recuperation of Historical Memory in Spain*, eds, C. Jerez-Farrán and S. Amago (Notre Dame, IN: University of Notre Dame Press, forthcoming). More details are available in H. Raguer, *Gunpowder and Incense: The Catholic Church and the Spanish Civil War*, trans. G. Howson (New York: Routledge, 2006).
116. M. J. Penton, *Jehovah's Witnesses and the Third Reich: Sectarian Politics under Persecution* (Toronto: University of Toronto Press, 2004).

117. See lecture by L. N. Rivera-Pagan, 'A Prophetic Challenge to the Church: The Last Word of Bartolomé de Las Casas,' Princeton Theological Seminar, 15 November 2004.
118. An example of a strong scholarly endeavor to rehabilitate the reputation of the seventeenth-century missionary John Eliot is R. W. Cogley, *John Eliot's Mission to the Indians Before King Philip's War* (Cambridge, MA: Harvard University Press, 1999).
119. An informed and laudatory biography by a former student and rabbi is A. H. Friedlander, *Leo Baeck: Teacher of Theresienstadt* (New York: Holt, Rinehart and Winston, 1968).
120. Useful on Lichtenberg is K. Spicer, *Resisting the Third Reich: The Catholic Clergy in Hitler's Berlin* (DeKalb, IL: Northern Illinois-University Press, 2004).
121. The definitive biography is by Bonhoeffer's close friend, colleague, student and brother-in-law, E. Bethge, *Dietrich Bonhoeffer: A Biography*, ed., V. J. Barnett (Minneapolis, MN: Augsburg Fortress, 2000).
122. There is a vast literature on Stein, but interesting in this context are the popular biography by the German Carmelite nun, W. Herbstrith, *Edith Stein: A Biography. The Untold Story of the Philosopher and Mystic Who Lost Her Life in the Death Camps of Auschwitz* (San Francisco, CA: Ignatius, 1992; first published in German in 1971); and the study by the Catholic philosopher A. MacIntyre, *Edith Stein: A Philosophical Prologue, 1913–1922* (Lanham, MD: Rowman and Littlefield, 2005).
123. See A. Frossard, *Forget Not Love: The Passion of Maximilian Kolbe*, trans. C. Fontan (San Francisco, CA: Ignatius, 1991).
124. See the influential biography by the Jesuit priest J. R. Brockman, *Romero: A Life* (Maryknoll, NY: Orbis Books, 1989).
125. See S. du Boulay, *Tutu: Voice of the Voiceless* (Grand Rapids, MI: William B. Eerdmans, 1988). Du Boulay has also written biographies of other religious figures: Teresa of Avila, Bede Griffiths, Swami Abhishiktananada and Cicely Saunders.
126. C. ten Boom, *The Hiding Place: The Triumphant True Story of Corrie ten Boom*, with J. and E. Sherrill (Old Tappan, NJ: Fleming H. Revell, 1971). See also the tribute by L. Baron, 'Supersessionism Without Contempt: The Holocaust Evangelism of Corrie ten Boom,' in *Christian Responses to the Holocaust: Moral and Ethical Issues*, ed. D. J. Dietrich (Syracuse, NY: Syracuse University Press, 2003), pp. 119–31.
127. Available on DVD as 'Billy Graham Presents: The Hiding Place,' dir. J. F. Collier (1975), 146 mins.
128. P. Hoffmann, *Stauffenberg: A Family History, 1905–1944*, rev. edn (Montreal: McGill-Queen's University Press, 2003).
129. T. Blaha, *Willi Graf und die Weisse Rose. Eine Rezeptionsgeschichte* (Munich: Saur, 2003).
130. P. P. Hallie, *Lest Innocent Blood Be Shed: The Story of the Village of Le Chambon and How Goodness Happened There* (New York: Harper and Row, 1979).
131. 'Weapons of the Spirit,' dir. P. Sauvage (New York: First Run/Icarus Films, 1986).
132. 'The majority of Jews evaded deportation in every state occupied by or allied with Germany in which the head of the dominant church spoke out publicly against deportation before or as soon as it began.' H. Fein, *Accounting for Genocide: National Responses and Jewish Victimization during the Holocaust* (Chicago, IL: University of Chicago Press, 1979), p. 67; see also chap. 4, 'The Keepers of the Keys: Responses of Christian Churches to the Threat against the Jews,' pp. 93–120.

133. Rittner, Roth and Whitworth, eds, *Genocide in Rwanda*, p. v.
134. J. A. Sheetz-Nguyen, 'Transcending Boundaries: Hungarian Roman Catholic Religious Women and the "Persecuted Ones,"' in *In God's Name*, eds, Bartov and Mack, pp. 222–42.
135. Indeed, recognition of the vulnerability of Christian rescuers of Jews in post-World War II Poland is the point of departure for J. T. Gross, *Fear: Antisemitism in Poland after Auschwitz* (New York: Random House, 2006).
136. M. Phayer, *The Catholic Church and the Holocaust, 1930–1965* (Bloomington, IN: Indiana University Press, 2000).
137. R. L. Rubenstein and J. K. Roth, *Approaches to Auschwitz: The Holocaust and Its Legacy* (Atlanta, GA: John Knox, 1987).
138. J. K. Roth and M. Berenbaum, *Holocaust: Religion and Philosophical Implications* (New York: Paragon House, 1989).
139. The phrase 'Dabru emet,' meaning 'speak the truth,' comes from Zechariah 8:16. The statement was published in the *New York Times* (10 September 2000) and the *Baltimore Sun*. Its authors were P. Ochs, D. Novak, T. Frymer-Kensky and M. Signer.
140. See text posted by National Jewish Scholars Project at www.bc.edu/research/cjl/meta-elements/texts/cjrelations/resources/documents/Jewish/dabru-emet.htm.
141. D. Herzog, *Sex after Fascism* (Princeton, NJ: Princeton University Press, 2006).
142. See also D. Herzog, 'Pleasure and Evil: Christianity and the Sexualization of Holocaust Memory,' in *Gray Zones: Ambiguity and Compromise in the Holocaust and Its Aftermath*, eds, J. Petropoulos and J. K. Roth (New York: Berghahn Books, 2005), pp. 147–64.
143. Nunpa, 'Dakota Commemorative March: Thoughts and Reactions,' *The American Indian Quarterly*, 28, 1 & 2 (2004), 216–37.
144. R. L. Rubenstein, *After Auschwitz: History, Theology, and Contemporary Judaism*, 2nd edn (Baltimore, MD: Johns Hopkins University Press, 1992), pp. 43–4.
145. For a concise presentation of some of Conway's key ideas, see J. S. Conway, 'Totalitarianism and Theology,' in *Christian Responses*, ed. Dietrich, pp. 1–11.
146. See especially E. E. Roslof, *Red Priests: Renovationism, Russian Orthodoxy, and Revolution, 1905–1946* (Bloomington, IN: Indiana University Press, 2002).
147. Naimark, *Fires of Hatred*.
148. I. V. Hull, *Absolute Destruction: Military Culture and the Practices of War in Imperial Germany* (Ithaca, NY: Cornell University Press, 2005).
149. For a look in English at some key points, see J. Zimmerer, 'Annihilation in Africa: The "Race War" in German Southwest Africa (1904–1908) and its Significance for a Global History of Genocide,' in *Bulletin of the German Historical Institute*, Washington, D.C., 37 (2005), 51–7.
150. Chalk and Jonassohn, *The History and Sociology of Genocide*; although some of the case studies included raise issues around religion, for example, J. R. Strayer and M. Ruthven's pieces on the Crusades and M. Hane's discussion of Christians in Japan.
151. S. Totten, W. S. Parsons and I. W. Charny, eds, *A Century of Genocide: Eyewitness Accounts and Critical Views*, 2nd edn (New York: Routledge, 2004).
152. S. Power, *'A Problem from Hell': America and the Age of Genocide* (New York: Harper Collins, 2002).
153. Ibid., p. 306.

154. M. Juergensmeyer, *Terror in the Mind of God: The Global Rise of Religious Violence*, 3rd edn (Berkeley, CA: University of California Press, 2003).
155. P. Maass, *Love Thy Neighbor: A Story of War* (New York: Alfred A. Knopf, 1996); E. Vulliamy, *Seasons in Hell: Understanding Bosnia's War* (New York: St. Martin's, 1994).
156. R. Dallaire, with B. Beardsley, *Shake Hands with the Devil: The Failure of Humanity in Rwanda* (Toronto: Vintage Canada, 2004).
157. 'Shake Hands with the Devil,' dir. P. Raymont, 2004, 91 mins., Canada.
158. Dallaire, *Shake Hands with the Devil*, p. xviii.
159. Ibid., p. 7.
160. Some exciting new work is included in M. Skidmore and P. Lawrence, eds, *Women and the Contested State: Religion, Violence and Agency in South and Southeast Asia* (Notre Dame, IN: University of Notre Dame Press, 2007).

8
Gender and Genocide

Adam Jones

This chapter explores how the concept of gender has been deployed to understand genocide and other mass violence. How do masculine and feminine roles shape women and men as genocide's victims, perpetrators, and bystanders? How does gender intersect with variables such as social class, age, and 'combatant' or 'civilian' status? How might an understanding of gender and genocide assist in devising more effective strategies of intervention, prevention, and reconstruction/reconciliation?

Before proceeding, some caveats are necessary. First, as Christopher Browning wrote in his survey of 'The Decision-Making Process' for *The Historiography of the Holocaust*, I too 'have been a participant in the debates' that are the subject of this chapter, and 'have decided openly to use the first person rather than third person to avoid both stylistic infelicity and any pretence that I am transcending my own involvement and offering an unengaged view.'[1]

Second, *The Historiography of the Holocaust* contained a comprehensive survey by Lisa Pine of 'Gender and the Family' in the context of the Shoah. Accordingly, I will make only passing references to the literature on gender and the Holocaust, limiting myself to more global and comparative analyses of gender and mass violence.

Lastly, I shall consider framings and insights across a broader spectrum than gender and genocide *per se*. In her *Historiography* chapter, Pine noted that only recently had the subject of gender in the Holocaust 'begun to expand with conferences and books focusing exclusively on the subject'.[2] The study of gender in comparative genocide studies is even more recent. I am not aware of any conference held on the theme, and only two edited volumes – one of them my own – have appeared at the time of writing. On the other hand, since the 1970s an extensive, mostly feminist literature has developed around themes of gender, violence, development, and humanitarian intervention. Much of this work is essential to an understanding both of the gendered dynamics of genocide, and of the framing of those dynamics in the few treatments that have so far appeared. Likewise, some studies of genocide do not focus substantively on gender, but still provide some important insights. I draw freely on such works.

The evolution of the core concept of 'gender' should now be addressed. Its origins are often linked to the publication of Simone de Beauvoir's treatise *The Second Sex* (1949), in which the author argued that 'women are not born but made'. Prior to de Beauvoir, and the 'second wave' of feminist theory that her work inspired, it was widely assumed that men's and women's behaviour was ingrained, reflecting innate and essential differences between the sexes. De Beauvoir pointed instead to the social construction of masculine and feminine identities, and how that process was shaped to marginalize women and preserve male dominance in economic, political, and domestic spheres.

Following de Beauvoir, second-wave feminists in the 1970s and 1980s distinguished between

> sex as the anatomical and physiological characteristics, which signify biological maleness and femaleness, and gender as socially constructed masculinity and femininity. Masculinity and femininity are defined not by biology but by social, cultural and psychological attributes, which are acquired through becoming a man or a woman in a particular society at a particular time. The term gender was hence used to describe those characteristics of men and women, which are socially defined, in contrast to those which are biologically determined.[3]

For feminist scholars, the 'gender system' built on these ideological underpinnings was *patriarchy*, 'a system of male dominance, legitimised within the family and society through superior rights, privileges, authority and power'.[4] (Note, however, that 'patriarchy' means rule by the fathers, not rule by men as a whole. The distinction speaks to fissures in patriarchy, and opens the way for a discussion of hegemonic versus subordinate masculinities – as in R. W. Connell's formulation, discussed later.)

Many analyses of gender and international violence, including genocide, have maintained a basic distinction between biological sex and socially constructed gender. In her chapter 'Beyond "Gendercide"' (2004), for example, R. Charli Carpenter defines 'gender' as 'refer[ring], variously, to social beliefs and institutions that direct our awareness to sex differentiation and regulate human interaction on that basis'. By contrast, 'sex', for Carpenter and many others, 'inheres biologically rather than being socially ascribed'.[5] Other scholars, however, have sought to destabilize what they see as overly neat distinctions between biological sex and socially ascribed gender. They emphasize instead the practical and conceptual areas of crossover, and often prefer to use 'gender' as something of a catch-all (as, indeed, it tends to be used in ordinary speech and media discourse). Thus, Joshua Goldstein, in *War and Gender*, rejects claims that 'sex is fixed and based in nature; gender is arbitrary, flexible, and based in culture.' For Goldstein, 'this sex-gender discourse constructs a false dichotomy between biology and culture, which are in fact highly interdependent':

> Biology provides diverse potentials, and cultures limit, select, and channel them. Furthermore, culture directly influences the expression of genes and hence the biology of our bodies. ... I see no useful border separating 'sex' and 'gender' as conventionally used. I therefore use 'gender' to cover masculine and feminine roles and bodies alike, in all their aspects, including the (biological and cultural) structures, dynamics, roles, and scripts associated with each gender group.[6]

On balance, however, it is the Beauvoirian-feminist perspective on gender that has guided most research into gender and mass violence. The earliest specific treatments were centred on two main themes: 'femicide', the selective killing of women and girls; and sexual violence against women, especially rape. In both cases, radical-feminist authors have been most prominent in the analysis.

The emphasis in the femicide literature has been diverse, ranging from individual acts of male domestic violence against women, and through the depredations of serial killings, to what I would later call 'gendercidal institutions against women and girls',[7] notably female infanticide and foeticide.[8] In all cases in the literature, female deaths were viewed as the structurally determined outcome of a patriarchal order intent on destroying females, or securing their conformity through the threat and use of violence. Jill Radford drew upon scattered usages and framings of 'femicide' in her 1992 work, *Femicide: The Politics of Woman Killing*, which concentrated heavily on domestic violence in industrialized societies.[9] A global framing of the phenomenon was Diana E. H. Russell's and Roberta A. Harmes's 2001 edited volume, *Femicide in Global Perspective*.[10] In this work, Russell expanded the framework to include cases of 'covert' (structural or social) femicide, such as

> deaths from unnecessary surgeries such as hysterectomies; genital mutilation (particularly excision and infibulation); experimentation on women's bodies, including the use of insufficiently tested methods of birth control, some of which have turned out to be carcinogenic; dangerous marriage practices such as those in which extremely young females are married to much older men, some of whom die as a result of forced sexual intercourse; and the deliberate preference given to boy children in many cultures, resulting in countless female deaths from neglect, illness, and starvation in numerous impoverished nations, such as China and India.[11]

In recent years, the term 'femicide' has gained renewed currency with feminist mobilizations against an alleged campaign of femicide in the Mexican border city of Ciudad Juárez.[12]

The longstanding taboo impeding detailed investigation of sexual violence and its gendered foundations was shattered with the publication of Susan Brownmiller's *Against Our Will: Men, Women and Rape* (1975). The book was a sweeping and passionately written study of rape in modern times, which Brownmiller defined as 'nothing more or less than a conscious process of intimidation by which *all* men keep *all* women in a state of fear'.[13] This contention – that rape permeated patriarchal society, and was essential to its perpetuation – was advanced by a number of key radical-feminist writers following Brownmiller, most notably Susan Griffin, Catharine MacKinnon, and Andrea Dworkin.[14] Dworkin went so far as to argue that 'Penetrative intercourse is, by its nature, violent', while MacKinnon contended it was 'difficult to distinguish' rape from ordinary intercourse 'under conditions of male dominance'.[15]

Whatever the ideological excesses of this line of thinking,[16] it contested much in gender relations that had been taken for granted and, in a legal sense, swept under the rug. Brownmiller's groundbreaking work also addressed the international sphere, with cogent analyses not only of rape in wartime, but during genocide – as with her study of mass rapes by West Pakistani forces in Bangladesh (1971), and the social ostracism inflicted upon female victims. MacKinnon's efforts were vital in emphasizing legal failings and potential avenues of change and redress. This buttressed subsequent initiatives at both national and international levels to confront rape and violence against women more generally.

The expansion of female and feminist influence worldwide in the 1970s and 1980s gave rise to an impressive array of international governmental and non-governmental initiatives focused on women. The United Nations Decade for Women (1975–85), with its Convention on the Elimination of All Forms of Discrimination Against Women (CEDAW) issued in 1979, was an important catalyst. A 'Women in Development' (WID) school of scholars and activists worked to analyze female experience and victimization in global development processes. The concept of 'violence against women' grew increasingly popular, both as a heuristic device and as a mobilizing agenda.

These institutional and academic developments are important for understanding the response, by feminists and the international community more generally, to the outbreak of war and genocide in the Balkans (1991–2). This conflict, or at least the part of it that took place in Bosnia-Herzegovina, became an intensely gendered one in the eyes of the world, with a heavy focus on rapes of (mostly Bosnian Muslim) women. It was alleged that Serb forces had established 'rape camps' in which Muslim women were systematically attacked and impregnated. Two widely cited books, Alexandra Stiglmayer's edited volume

Mass Rape and Beverly Allen's *Rape Warfare*, built upon MacKinnon's (and others') insights in examining how the sexual assault of women was used both to damage and subordinate women of a targeted community, and to emasculate and humiliate community men.[17]

The actual number of rapes of women in the Balkans wars is a matter of ongoing debate, with estimates ranging from the low to the high tens of thousands. Nonetheless, the assaults were on a sufficient scale, and of a sufficiently clear character, to give rise to the concept of genocidal rape. Catharine MacKinnon seems first to have deployed the concept of 'rape [as] a genocidal act' in an influential essay, 'Rape, Genocide, and Women's Human Rights', printed in both the *Harvard Women's Law Journal* (1994) and Stiglmayer's edited volume *Mass Rape*. MacKinnon argued that in the Bosnian context, rape was 'a tool, a tactic, a policy, a plan, a strategy, as well as a practice':

> In the West, the sexual atrocities have been discussed largely as rape *or* as genocide, not as what they are, which is rape as genocide, rape directed toward women because they are Muslim or Croatian. But when rape is a genocidal act, as it is here, it is an act to destroy a people. What is done to women defines that destruction. ... This is not rape out of control. It is rape under control. It is also rape unto death, rape as massacre, rape to kill and to make the victims wish they were dead. It is rape as an instrument of forced exile, rape to make you leave your home and never want to go back. It is rape to be seen and heard and watched and told to others: rape as spectacle. It is rape to drive a wedge through a community, to shatter a society, to destroy a people. It is rape as genocide.[18]

In such passages, MacKinnon sharpened what Sherrie Russell-Brown has called the 'intersectionality' of ethnicity and gender in genocidal rape.[19] Some, however, questioned this application of a genocide framework to women's rape experiences in the Balkans. The most vocal critic was Rhonda Copelon, who argued that

> The elision of genocide and rape in the focus on 'genocidal rape' ... [is] dangerous. Rape and genocide are separate atrocities. Genocide – the effort to destroy a people – based on its identity as a people evokes the deepest horror and warrants the severest condemnation. Rape is sexualized violence that seeks to humiliate, terrorize, and destroy a woman based on her identity as a woman. ... To emphasize as unparalleled the horror of genocidal rape is factually dubious and risks rendering rape invisible once again.[20]

But the outbreak of the cataclysmic genocide in Rwanda in April 1994 gave a strong spur to the concept of genocidal rape. On a scale far vaster than in the

Balkans, Tutsi women were targeted for savage sexual attack, including multiple rape, gang rape, forced concubinage, and sexual mutilation. Hundreds of thousands of them were also killed – often after rape, and sometimes by means of it. Moreover, the high prevalence of HIV among Hutu assailants meant that even women who survived rape and forced concubinage were often left not only impregnated, but infected; carrying not just a child, but a death sentence in their blood. When the world awoke, tragically late, to the scale of the Rwandan genocide, the extent and savagery of the Rwandan rapes quickly permeated the humanitarian and human rights literature. A catalyst was the 1996 Human Rights Watch report, *Shattered Lives: Sexual Violence during the Rwandan Genocide and Its Aftermath* – one of the most widely cited human rights reports of the last 20 or 30 years. Its author, Binaifer Nowrojee, strongly backed the genocidal rape framework, stating that 'during the Rwandan genocide, rape and other forms of violence were directed primarily against Tutsi women because of both their gender and their ethnicity.' According to the report,

> Acts of rape and other forms of sexual violence can fall into the categories of proscribed acts under the Genocide Convention. Where it can be shown that perpetrators committed such acts causing serious bodily or mental harm with the intent to destroy, in whole or in part, a group identified by the terms of the convention, crimes such as rape, sexual mutilation and sexual slavery may be prosecuted under subsection (b) of Article 2. As the testimonies in this report demonstrate, extremely serious bodily and mental harm was inflicted through targeted sexual violence against women. Moreover, under certain circumstances, sexual violence may be prosecuted under subsection (c) or (d) of Article 2. Sexual violence can inflict on a group conditions of life calculated to cause the group's physical destruction and can prevent births within the group. For example, women subjected to sexual violence may be left physically unable to reproduce, or, they may be denied this role by their community given the nature of the attacks they have suffered.[21]

In September 1998, the International Criminal Tribunal for Rwanda (ICTR) issued its famous judgement against Jean-Paul Akayesu, a Hutu bourgmeister charged, among many other crimes, with facilitating and supervising the rape of Tutsi women. The judgement was the first to define rape as a genocidal act, when 'in the same way as any other act' it was 'committed with the specific intent to destroy, in whole or in part, a particular group targeted as such'. The 'bodily and mental harm [inflicted] on the victim' was also emphasized. The Akayesu judgement electrified the feminist movement; the trial of Pauline Nyiramasuhuko, underway at the time of writing, promised to keep the issue front-and-centre in the literature for some years. (Like Akayesu, Nyiramasuhuko was accused of encouraging and coordinating rapes of Tutsi women.)

The Nyiramasuhuko case also highlighted in unprecedented fashion the issue of female perpetration, discussed further below. Nyiramasuhuko was the first woman ever to be tried by an international tribunal for the crime of genocide, and for genocidal rape. A certain novelty attached to her, reflecting the mass involvement of women in perpetrating the Rwandan genocide. But these were highly unusual cases from a historical viewpoint. What of the gendering of genocidal rapists and *génocidaires* more generally? Clearly, an overwhelming majority of outright killers and assailants during genocide's long history have been male, not female; often, this male dominance has bordered on exclusivity. Genocidal killing and related atrocities, like most forms of interpersonal violence, carry a strong flavour of 'macho' swagger and gendered belligerence. How have scholars and activists engaged with the figure of the male perpetrator? Two main lines of inquiry emerged from the 1970s to the 1990s.

Much feminist scholarship and activism of the 1970s and 1980s centred on the roots of male violence against women. This endeavour was roughly contemporaneous with an emphasis in the emerging genocide-studies literature on the motivations and behaviour of *génocidaires*. The result was (1) a feminist-dominated analysis that designated males as the agents of the overwhelming majority of violent acts against women and others, ascribing this to predominantly cultural, but also physiological, factors; and (2) a body of work on genocidal perpetrators that emphasized gender only rarely, but still produced some insights into men and masculinities in genocide.

To address feminist arguments first, it is worth citing Mary Daly's radical, sometimes whimsical work, with its influential motif of ogre-like males oppressing peaceful women. (Daly coined the term 'gynocide' to convey patriarchy's annihilatory intentions towards females.)[22] In formal academia, a milestone was the publication of Carol Cohn's article for *Signs*, 'Sex and Death in the Rational World of Defense Intellectuals' (1987). Cohn's work raised some of the themes then beginning to be explored in a Holocaust- and genocide-studies context, especially the phenomenon of bureaucratic and technocratic distancing from megamurder.[23] Based on her stay at a centre for defence technology, Cohn described the 'thrill of being able to manipulate an arcane language, the power of entering the secret kingdom, being someone in the know'.[24] As a feminist writer, Cohn quickly perceived 'the ubiquitous weight of gender' in the 'almost entirely male world' that surrounded her. Phallic and sexual imagery abounded: 'lectures were filled with discussion of vertical erector launchers, thrust-to-weight ratios, soft lay downs, deep penetration, and the comparative advantages of protracted versus spasm attacks. ...' This was both 'a deadly serious display of the connections between masculine sexuality and the arms race' and 'a way of minimizing the seriousness of militarist endeavours, of denying their deadly consequences'.[25]

Another groundbreaking scholar of masculinities and violence was the German Klaus Theweleit, whose doctoral dissertation appeared in two volumes in English as *Male Fantasies* (1987, 1989). Theweleit's subject was the *Freikorps*, the notorious German paramilitary force that targeted communists and others after the First World War. His rich, dense study zeroed in on the *Freikorps* persona and psyche. Theweleit identified a cult of hardness and inviolability in *Freikorps* masculinity: its erection of 'a phallus against the dissolution that surrounds them' and against the female-identified 'red tide' (communist movement) that threatened to inundate Germany. Immersion in another 'red tide', though, was liberating: 'the men we are dealing with here ... want to wade in blood; they want an intoxicant ... [They have] a desire for, and fear of, fusion, explosion.'[26]

In this heady psychological brew, women played an ambiguous role. *Freikorps* men 'vacillate[d] between intense interest and cool indifference, aggressiveness and veneration, hatred, anxiety, alienation, and desire'. A soothing, nurturing 'white nurse' figure was 'given a pre-eminent role in the psychic security system of the men ... [as] the essential embodiment of their recoiling from all erotic, threatening femininity'. The 'Red', proletarian woman, by contrast, was in *Freikorps* writing and testimony a monstrous figure, 'out to castrate and shred men to pieces'. Theweleit saw these patterns as emblematic of male psyches and gender relations under patriarchy. 'Any male reading the texts of these [Freikorps] males – and not taking immediate refuge in repression – might find in them a whole series of traits he recognizes from his own past or present behaviour, from his own fantasies.'[27]

Around the time that Cohn and Theweleit wrote, Robert Jay Lifton was publishing his study *The Nazi Doctors: Medical Killing and the Psychology of Genocide* (1986), which has served as something of a template for subsequent studies of genocidal perpetrators. Lifton reviewed the messianic aspects of access to almost incomprehensible power over others. He also touched in passing on the masculine component of the killing, notably the heavy drinking and macho posturing that accompanied it. This was evident, for example, in his lengthy profile of Dr Josef Mengele at Auschwitz. Describing Mengele's selection procedure for Jews arriving on transports, Lifton spoke of 'the Mengele style of selections performance' as 'Nazi male macho': 'immaculately clean black SS uniform with riding boots and riding crop, exaggeratedly straight posture with reserved, dignified bearing, together with a slight military swagger and an aura of absolute authority over everyone.' This attested to a 'cult of heroic hardness, always available to dominate or destroy designated others with an absolute absence of either compassion or empathy'. And it led to the resolution of existential crisis through hostility and violence:

> The Auschwitz self medicalized this overall Nazi male ideal and thereby gave it a further claim to ultimate power and symbolic immortality. In this

> combination, the Auschwitz self made especially clear how far anti-empathic male power can be mobilized to fend off death anxiety, including that associated with fear of homosexuality and of women, and with the erosion of one's ideology and ethos. This brings us to the realm of killing as a specific means of holding back death ... *a realm always inhabited by a perverse expression of maleness.*[28]

Subsequent studies of perpetrators in the Holocaust and genocide-studies canons have not advanced this gender analysis much further, however. The predominance of males among genocidal killers is regularly noted, but there has been relatively little specific probing of males-as-perpetrators in the 1990s and 2000s. In *Ordinary Men* (1992), for instance, Christopher Browning placed the emphasis squarely on the 'ordinary' rather than the 'men'. He notes 'the "macho" vision' that underpinned the actions of police-battalion killing squads on the Eastern Front, as Lifton had touched on it in describing the Nazi doctors.[29] But neither was inspired to explore this aspect more deeply. In *Machete Season* (2005), based on interviews with Rwandan Hutu men imprisoned for slaughtering Tutsis in the 1994 genocide, Jean Hatzfeld offered vivid insights into the killers' motivations. The careful reader could tease out themes of masculine pride and prestige; male bonding; the lure of material gain as a social and existential salve for men; the liberating feeling of taking sexual 'revenge' on Tutsi women. But in his commentary, Hatzfeld did not substantively analyze the role of gender. Nor has the 'gendercide' literature, discussed below, contributed much to this inquiry, focusing instead on the hitherto-unnoticed element of male victimization.[30]

One contribution, though, *did* strikingly illuminate the perpetrator mentality through gender analysis. Christopher Taylor's *Sacrifice as Terror: The Rwandan Genocide of 1994*, an anthropological study, included a chapter on 'The Dialectics of Hate and Desire: Tutsi Women and Hutu Extremism'. Taylor argued that the genocide 'was about power relations between men and women perhaps as much as it was about power relations between groups of men.' Among other things, 'to many Rwandans gender relations in the 1980s and 1990s were falling into a state of decadence as more women attained positions of prominence in economic and public life.' Genocide was an extremist backlash 'to reclaim both patriarchy and the Hutu revolution'. As for the fate of Tutsi women under Hutu Power, Taylor traced from colonial times a portrayal of Tutsi women 'as more beautiful than Hutu women', and thus objects of both attraction and resentment for Hutu males. In pre-genocidal propaganda, 'Hutu cartoonists depicted Tutsi women as prostitutes capable of enlisting Western support for the RPF [rebel] cause through the use of their sexual charms.' Accordingly, when the holocaust erupted, it was unsurprising that 'special measures of terrorism were reserved for Tutsi women by the extremists.'[31]

The Rwandan genocide points to one reason, though, why an emphasis on maleness and masculinity as factors in genocide has failed to take deep root in genocide studies. After 1994, it was rapidly and widely acknowledged that women had played a profound and apparently unprecedented role as perpetrators and supporters of the genocidal enterprise. This myth- and taboo-shattering aspect of the Rwandan holocaust resonated through the literature on gender and violence in the latter half of the 1990s. It meshed with growing nuance in the feminist-influenced discussion, as women's roles not just as victims, but as agents, began to be examined seriously.

Such examination was not entirely new. A watershed contribution to the international relations literature on gender was the 1987 publication of Jean Bethke Elshtain's *Women and War*. Elshtain's work was an intimate, clear-eyed account of the seductions of violence and militarism, one that challenged stereotypes and 'sanctimonies' of gender, such as the division of men and women into 'Just Warriors' and 'Beautiful Souls'. As far as the 'Beautiful Souls' were concerned, Elshtain stated bluntly that 'women in overwhelming numbers have supported their state's wars in the modern West': there were 'hundreds of hair-raising tales of bellicose mothers, wives, and girlfriends writing the combat soldier and requesting the sacrifice of the enemy as a tribute, or gift, to her'. She offered a six-point test to see whether 'Beautiful Soul' stereotypes of women were being 'shored up or displaced':

> (1) Does the author define all women in opposition to all men? (2) Do the author's rhetorical choices invite self-congratulatory responses and lend themselves to sentimentalist reactions? (3) Does the author open or foreclose space for debate and disagreement? ... (4) Does the author compel us to think in the absence of certainty or ensure certainty at the cost of critical reflection? (5) Do the author's formulations reassure, soothe, bring relief to, reinforce, reaffirm; or do they disturb, unsettle, take apart, make ambiguous? (6) Is the author's voice didactic, ironic, moralistic?[32]

This was a clarion call for a study of gender and conflict that was less constrained by ideological preconceptions and political agendas. Elshtain's status as a social philosopher gave it a wider circulation in the humanities and social sciences.

From the humanities, too, came Claudia Koonz's magisterial *Mothers in the Fatherland* (1987), a work of history that probed German women's multifaceted complicity in Nazism. Hitler's installation as chancellor in 1933 marked, in a real sense, the triumph of the *Freikorps* masculinity studied by Theweleit, with its hardened male persona, its visceral fear of communist and feminine 'floods'. The Nazis strictly controlled and subordinated women's organizations, but they also struck a 'patriarchal bargain' with their leaders, and with ordinary

German women. Support for the regime, and respect for the traditional female identification with home and hearth, would be rewarded with protection, a means of subsistence, and limited gender-specific attention in state policy. Amidst economic crisis and family breakdown, tens of millions of German women and adolescent girls found the bargain powerfully appealing:

> Democracy and choice had surrounded them [women] with chaos, anomie, and competition. Women demanded their right to withdraw from that world, to devote themselves to familial concerns, and to be economically secure. Authoritarian rule would, they hoped, impose order and health on the nation and tie fathers to their families. ... As fanatical Nazis or lukewarm tag-alongs, [women] resolutely turned their heads away from assaults against socialists, Jews, religious dissenters, the handicapped, and 'degenerates'. They gazed instead at their own cradles, children, and 'Aryan' families. ... Over time, *Nazi women, no less than men*, destroyed ethical vision, debased humane traditions, and rendered decent people helpless.[33]

Koonz's work won prizes and was nominated for a National Book Award; it was another milestone in perceptions of women's subaltern and subterranean agency in war and genocide.

However, apart from some lurid pop-culture portraits of female concentration-camp guards under the Nazis, there was still little to suggest that women were capable of outright 'genocidal frenzy' and bloodlust, as males demonstrably were. Events in Rwanda radically transformed this picture. An African Rights report published within a year of the genocide (1995), *Rwanda: Not So Innocent – Women As Killers*, argued that an emphasis on women as victims of the genocide had tended to 'obscur[e] the role of women as aggressors'. 'When it came to mass murder', wrote the authors, 'there were a lot of women who needed no encouragement.'[34] African Rights also found that women participated in the persecution, murder, and sexual enslavement of Tutsi women, perhaps feeling satisfaction at the 'comeuppance' of females who had for so long been presented as Rwanda's sexual elite.

In short, it seems reasonable to contend, as I did in 2002, that the 'Rwanda test' may 'substantially refute the equation of women and peace' that characterized earlier commentary on gender and mass violence. The test

> suggests that when women are provided with positive and negative incentives similar to those of men, their degree of participation in genocide, and the violence and cruelty they exhibit, will run closely parallel to those of their male counterparts. ... If women anywhere can participate in genocide on such a scale, and with such evident enthusiasm and savagery, then it seems a valid prima facie assumption that they are capable of such participation

> everywhere. The search then becomes one not for some essential 'difference' in women's approach to war and peace [and genocide], but for the range of cultural and policy mechanisms that either allow or, more frequently, inhibit the expression of women's aggressive and genocidal potential.[35]

James Waller reached a similar conclusion in a lengthy discursive footnote for his volume *Becoming Evil: How Ordinary People Commit Genocide and Mass Killing* (2002). 'The challenge for future research', Waller argued, 'is to transcend our gender expectations that women are basically innocent by nature, so that their acts of cruelty are viewed as deviant and abnormal, and approach their perpetration of extraordinary evil the same way we have men – as ordinary people influenced by dispositional, situational, and environmental factors. Only when we stop stereotyping the assumed extraordinariness of female perpetrators can we determine the applicability of this model to female perpetrators of extraordinary evil.'[36]

As noted, these comments in the genocide-studies literature were paralleled by developments in the broader feminist critique of gender and violence.[37] This was evident in a trio of works published between 1997 and 2001 by Zed Books: Ronit Lentin's edited *Gender & Catastrophe* (1997); Susie Jacobs et al.'s *States of Conflict: Gender, Violence and Resistance* (2000); and Carolyn Moser and Fiona Clark (eds), *Victims, Perpetrators or Actors? Gender, Armed Conflict and Political Violence* (2001). Each of these works challenged stereotypical assumptions, and staked out under-charted territory.

Lentin's volume is perhaps the best-known work on gender and genocide, but this is largely by default: until 2004 (when my own edited volume, *Gendercide and Genocide*, was published), no synoptic work on gender had explicitly positioned itself in the genocide-studies literature. At the outset of her introduction, Lentin called for 'the definition of genocide [to] be gendered', since 'catastrophes, genocidal or otherwise ... target women in very specific ways due to their social, ethnic and national construction.' The gender variable needed to be applied to 'the full impact of extreme situations such as genocides, wars, famines, slavery, the Shoah, "ethnic cleansing", and projects of mass rape and population control. ...'[38] But while the explicit genocide focus was new, the structure and content of the book were rather less so. For most practical purposes, 'gender' was regarded as synonymous with women/femininity. *All nineteen* chapters focused on women's experiences of genocide and other catastrophes, with an emphasis on the female as victim (indeed, the 'main' victim) of war and genocide. The result was an illuminating volume on many fronts, with particularly useful contributions by Joan Ringelheim (on the Jewish Holocaust), Urvashi Butalia (on the partition of the Indian subcontinent), and Lentin herself. But it also seemed a throwback to a previous generation of work on gender and mass violence, rather than the vanguard of a new one.

This vanguard role belonged instead to Jacobs et al.'s *States of Conflict*, which stressed at the outset its emphasis on 'women's agency, alongside men's, in both creating and challenging conflict'. The editors aimed 'for a feminist analysis which is at the same time more consistent in its treatment of *gender* than is often the case when conflict and/or violence is under examination'.[39] Especially liable to be overlooked was the role of women in using and supporting violence, a theme that feminists had found 'difficult to confront ... at both the theoretical and programmatic levels'.[40]

Two key essays were those by Judy El-Bushra and Parita Mukta. Both touched on the theme of female agency in war and conflict. In 'Transforming Conflict: Some Thoughts on a Gendered Understanding of Conflict Processes', El-Bushra rejected an understanding of gendered power relations based on 'a simplistic divide between power/men on the one hand and powerlessness/ women on the other'.[41] She also decisively discounted the 'Beautiful Soul' motifs that Jean Bethke Elshtain had first destabilized, contending that 'The association of women's "nurturing" role with the promotion of peace and compassion does not stand up to close examination, since, although women may well be active in peace-work in many contexts, they are also often in the forefront of demands for aggression in defence of their and their group's interests.'[42] Mukta's chapter, 'Gender, Community, Nation: The Myth of Innocence', starkly illustrated this female aggressiveness, providing a fascinating portrait of upper-caste women members of the Hindu extremist movement in India. Mukta showed how women had created 'a strikingly militant Hindu femaleness, where the emphasis was on the "trained, hardened, invincible female body" and where the women worshipped their weapons in particular'.[43] They had also assumed a 'central importance ... within the newly emerged politics of contemporary communalism'.[44] To truly understand that role, it was necessary to appreciate how gender was interwoven with other identities and interests:

> It is not that these women put 'caste' above 'gender' and submerge their gender interests to the cause of caste domination, but that a more complex caste-gendered politics is taking place whereby in the ideologies they espouse, the demands that they articulate and the actions that they take on their own behalf, the women are carving out a political space for themselves as a critically important and gendered section of the upper castes (and classes).[45]

This multivariate analysis represented an important advance in thinking about gender and genocide. It was displayed as well in Moser and Clark's *Victims, Perpetrators or Actors?*, the title of which reflects feminist scholarship's new preoccupation with gender complexities and female agency. The editors' introduction, along with Cynthia Cockburn's excellent framing chapter 'The Gendered Dynamics of Armed Conflict and Political Violence', offered a reasonably comprehensive 'gendered framework [that] incorporates the concepts of agency and identity in requiring policymakers and planners to recognize that women and men as actors experience violence and conflict differently, both as victims and as perpetrators, with differential access to resources (including power and decision making)'.[46] However, attention to men and masculinities in the main body of text was patchy at best. As with both Lentin's and Jacobs's collections, the emphasis in *Victims, Perpetrators or Actors?* remained squarely on women – though they were now depicted in more diverse roles, and appraised in less stereotypical fashion.[47]

The one exception, Dubravka Zarkov's 'The Body of the Other Man', was significant in exploring a theme that had surfaced only rarely, and always very briefly, in the feminist literature: the gendered vulnerability of males to mass violence and atrocity. (Zarkov studied Croatian media coverage – and lack of coverage – of male-on-male rape in the Balkans wars.)[48] By a different route, more sustained and systematic attention to the male or masculine experience was surfacing. At this point the account can usefully digress into autobiography.

Just as the Bosnian war of the 1990s had prompted the first formulations of 'genocidal rape', it also planted the seeds of an inquiry into male vulnerabilities in genocide and 'ethnic cleansing'. Reading news accounts of the violence that swept Bosnia in 1992–3, I was struck by a common strategy in the Serb campaign: the 'culling' of battle-age males from the civilian population, through execution or incarceration under severe conditions. In an article for *Ethnic and Racial Studies*, written in early 1993 and published in 1994, I suggested that while substantial attention had (justifiably) been paid to the gendered suffering of women in the Bosnian war, various gender-specific and gender-selective atrocities were also being inflicted on Bosnian men. Of these, 'the most serious ... are the gender-selective executions aimed at eliminating physical resistance to Serbian occupation and "ethnic cleansing" – up to the point of eliminating future generations of fighters.' I expressed surprise that the extraordinary vulnerability of 'battle-age' civilian males had not been widely investigated, and that in fact aid efforts seemed to be contributing to the 'culling' of this portion of the population. 'At [the] time of writing (April 1993), for example, the news from Bosnia centres on protracted attempts to secure the evacuation of civilians from the besieged town of Srebrenica. Convoys of trucks have evacuated women, children, and old people. But the Serbian requirement that no males with combat potential be carried out overland has been respected – as a glance at photographs of the evacuation convoys makes clear.' Such policies had the effect of 'leaving behind large numbers of trapped, desperate, and wounded males who feared execution or incarceration when Srebrenica fell to the Serbs'.[49]

The year following the article's publication, Srebrenica *did* fall to the Serbs, with consequences that are universally known – and almost uniquely gendered: that is, Srebrenica remains the only massacre generally acknowledged as a slaughter of 'men and boys', rather than of 'Bosnians' in general, or 'Muslims', or 'civilians'.

It was the resurgence of the Balkans conflict, in Kosovo in 1999, and events in East Timor later that year, that drove me to the systematic exploration of gender-selective mass atrocity. I recall reading news reports of the selective executions of community men in Kosovo, and saying under my breath: '*Gendercide*'. A brief moment of self-congratulation for coining the term evaporated when, after an Internet search, I learned that the feminist scholar Mary Anne Warren had been there 15 years earlier. In the introductory chapter to her book, *Gendercide: The Implications of Sex Selection* (1985), she also provided useful signposts to the *inclusive* exploration of gender and genocide. Defending her use of the term 'gendercide', Warren wrote:

> The Oxford American Dictionary defines genocide as 'the deliberate extermination of a race of people.' By analogy, gendercide would be the deliberate extermination of persons of a particular sex (or gender). Other terms, such as 'gynocide' and 'femicide', have been used to refer to the wrongful killing of girls and women. But 'gendercide' is a sex-neutral term, in that the victims may be either male or female. There is a need for such a sex-neutral term, since sexually discriminatory killing is just as wrong when the victims happen to be male. The term also calls attention to the fact that gender roles have often had lethal consequences, and that these are in important respects analogous to the lethal consequences of racial, religious, and class prejudice.[50]

This recognition that males could also be liable to 'sexually discriminatory killing' of a genocidal/gendercidal character, and that such actions were 'just as wrong' as those targeting females, were important advances. But Warren mostly sidestepped their implications, focusing in the remainder of her volume on gendercide against women and girls, such as through female infanticide and sex-selective abortion.

The genocidal targeting of males had not entirely escaped notice in the genocide-studies literature. In his field-defining book, Leo Kuper noted that cultural constructions dictated that while 'the killing of women and children arouses general revulsion ... unarmed men seem fair game.'[51] But this was only a passing observation in Kuper's discussion of the tangential Northern Ireland conflict. Ronit Lentin all but ignored the subject in her framing introduction for *Gender & Catastrophe*, but contributor Joan Ringelheim offered insights of greater substance, in the context of the Jewish Holocaust. She noted that the Holocaust 'was *one of the rare historical moments* when women and children were consciously and explicitly sentenced to death in at least equal measure to men'. She also pointed to gendered propaganda as a means of paving the way for gender-selective atrocities against males (and, subsequently, against all other Jews):

> Legitimation for targeting Jewish men was plentiful in Nazi anti-Semitic and racist propaganda and, more to the point, in Nazi policy. The decision to kill every Jew did not seem to demand special justification to kill Jewish men. They were already identified as dangerous. This was not so for Jewish women and children. ... Jewish men were always considered an objective enemy of National Socialism; they were certainly the first Jewish victims of forced labour and, in the beginning, the primary targets of the *Einsatzgruppen* [killing squads on the Eastern Front in 1941–2].[52]

Helen Fein, in her article 'Genocide and Gender' for *Journal of Genocide Research* (1999), went some distance further. She distinguished between gender-neutral and gender-specific genocide: that is, 'genocides which seek to destroy everyone regardless of gender ... and those which destroy only males (there is no record of a perpetrator of genocide destroying only females).' She argued that 'gender-neutral' genocide was on the rise, in part because the decline of slavery had reduced incentives for conquerors to preserve women and children alive.[53] Remarkably, though, for a phenomenon that was as old as recorded history (Fein cited examples of it from the Old Testament),[54] the gender-selective killing of community males had never received sustained or systematic attention, in the genocide-studies literature or outside it, apparently at any point, in any language.[55] This was the core oversight that I sought to address, with my article 'Gendercide and Genocide' (2000) and the Gendercide Watch educational initiative (www.gendercide.org) launched in the same year.

In 'Gendercide and Genocide', I provided a wealth of examples of selective mass killings of men, drawn from paradigmatic genocides of the twentieth century and contemporary campaigns of state terror. The article's core contention was that

> *the most vulnerable and consistently targeted population group, throughout time and around the world today, is noncombatant men of 'battle age'*, roughly fifteen to fifty-five years old. They are nearly universally perceived as the group posing the greatest danger to the conquering force, and are the group most likely to have the repressive apparatus of the state directed against them. The 'non-combatant' distinction is also vital. Unlike their armed brethren, these men have no means of defending themselves and can be detained and exterminated by the thousands or millions. ... The frequent and often massive correlation between male victimization and the most annihilatory genocidal

> excesses may merit a fundamental rethinking of the prevailing 'gendered' framing of many of these issues.[56]

I also proposed the term 'gendercidal institutions' to describe institutionalized forms of gender-selective killing, such as female infanticide and *corvée* (forced) labour. The Gendercide Watch website aimed to accompany the academic inquiry with an activist project to raise consciousness about gendercidal killing and generate policy attention to the phenomenon. It included 22 detailed case studies of gendercides in modern history (including gendercidal institutions).

One person attracted to the inquiry was *Journal of Genocide Research* editor Henry Huttenbach, who in addition to accepting the original 'Gendercide and Genocide' article for publication in the journal, invited me to prepare a special issue on the gendercide theme. This drew submissions from an impressively diverse group of scholars from the fields of sociology, psychology, history/political science, human rights, and queer studies. Evelin Lindner explored the role of gendered humiliation 'in honour and human-rights societies', and how such masculine humiliation played into both genocide and gendercide. Øystein Gullvåg Holter constructed a sophisticated 'Theory of Gendercide', linking the phenomenon to modern transformations in gender relations and shifting patterns of warfare. Stefanie Rixecker, a queer-studies scholar from New Zealand, evaluated the range of current and potential genetic technologies, and how they might be used to suppress particular – specifically homosexual – gender identities in the future. David Buchanan, meanwhile – a Canadian with years of experience as a human rights activist – argued for gendercide against both women and men to be integrated with the work of human rights NGOs like Amnesty International and Human Rights Watch. For his part, Stuart Stein, in an essay titled 'Geno and Other Cides: A Cautionary Note on Knowledge Accumulation', largely dismissed the relevance of the gendercide framework for genocide studies (see further below). The essays were published in *Journal of Genocide Research* in 2002, and in book form two years later, with additional essays from R. Charli Carpenter ('Beyond "Gendercide"', previously published in *International Journal of Human Rights*);[57] Augusta Del Zotto (exploring the phenomenon of 'black male gendercide in the United States'); and Terrell Carver, who placed the inquiry in the context of the burgeoning field of 'men and masculinity' studies.[58]

My subsequent work on gendercide sought to deepen understanding of gendercidal institutions,[59] and to understand gendercide against men as a 'tripwire' or harbinger of 'root-and-branch' campaigns of genocide. Under what conditions would gendercidal strategies limit the exterminatory enterprise; when would they serve as a prelude to a more sweeping assault on all members of the targeted group?[60] I also explored the gendering of humanitarian discourse during genocide, and the implications of a gendercide framework for strategies of humanitarian intervention.[61]

In the study of humanitarianism, however, the most revelatory work has clearly been that of R. Charli Carpenter. In a series of brilliant articles for leading international relations and human rights journals, Carpenter reported her findings from fieldwork in post-genocide Bosnia, and from attendance at various international symposia, concerning the gendered norms and framings of humanitarian policy and discourse. She found broad support for the argument that 'gender norms influenced both the moral framework by which the civilian protection regime developed [in Bosnia] and the manner in which civilian protection operations were carried out in the former Yugoslavia between 1991–95.' In particular, she discovered that 'gender stereotypes can inhibit effective policy', as when adult civilian males were marginalized in humanitarian efforts despite their great vulnerability to attack.[62] The field-research dimension gave Carpenter's insights added vigour, as did her insightful reading of the policy literature. She also explored the issue of gendered 'vulnerability' more deeply than I had in my gendercide work. Carpenter argued that 'there is a case to be made for conceptualizing all women as always socially vulnerable because of the gendered structure of power within war-affected communities.' But she added,

> What is problematic is the simultaneous exclusion of men's socially induced vulnerabilities from the definition. While able-bodied men, as adults, are among the least vulnerable group physically, they become far more vulnerable than women, children, and the elderly to certain forms of attack in certain situations because of socially constructed assumptions about male gender roles.[63]

In her theoretical and methodological observations, Carpenter stressed the validity of a 'nonfeminist gender theory' in studies of international politics: 'By this I mean scholarship that utilizes gender in analysis while lacking one or both other components of feminist theory: an emphasis on women and a critical/interpretive epistemology.' This allowed attention to subjects and perspectives that were largely ruled out by feminism's defining interests and presuppositions. 'Women's subordination and victimization is too often assumed by feminists rather than examined contextually, and there is little substantive work on how gender constrains the life chances of "people called men" in different contexts or affects political outcomes more generally.'[64]

Carpenter's challenging work points the way towards a nuanced and truly inclusive application of the gender variable. It suggests also that the study of gender, genocide, and mass violence holds considerable potential for the future.

How might the investigation proceed? This is a matter for both speculation and the declaration of personal preference.

First, feminist-inspired investigation of women's and girls' experiences during genocide seems far from exhausted. It can be expected – and hoped – that numerous testimonies and insightful analyses await us. This chapter has also suggested that inquiry into the psychology and sociology of male/masculine violence was somewhat attenuated after a promising start in the 1980s. Feminist framings are foundational to this inquiry, though a non-feminist standpoint may also have much to offer.

One might also expect the increasing adoption of a *relational* approach to gender. Drawing on some of groundbreaking recent work on gender and violence (such as the *States of Conflict* volume), we may see growing attention to females and males in the same text, with greater understanding of how gender identities are reciprocally constituted, and the interpenetration of much gendered experience. Among other things, a relational framework requires moving beyond the standard equation of gender with women/femininity, and an honest and reasonably empathetic attempt to incorporate the male subject in the analysis.[65] It also implies an attempt 'to understand the diverse roles and needs of women and men during and after' war and genocide, with 'such evidence ... based on what they *are* doing and not on stereotypical interpretations of gender roles and relations that presume to know what they *should* be doing.'[66] (And what 'should' be being done to them, one might add.)

Explorations of gendered discourse can produce important insights, as has been apparent since the work of Carol Cohn and Klaus Theweleit, and as is evident in R. Charli Carpenter's research today. Such examinations can also provide insights into the gendered mythologies underpinning genocidal or pre-genocidal propaganda, as Christopher Taylor showed in his analysis of gender formations and crises in Rwanda. The growing influence of anthropologists within the genocide-studies field might be significant here, producing studies of state terror based on intimate cultural observation, including attention to dominant motifs of masculinity and femininity. Likewise, communications scholars have begun to produce more work on the role of media and communications in genocide (with Rwandan 'hate radio' serving as the paradigmatic case). The gendering of media production and content could provide major insights into the dynamics of genocide. It could also assist in the development of preventive and interventionist strategies, based on the 'gender agendas' that media seem to be espousing.[67]

As the study of genocide has evolved as one of the most interdisciplinary enterprises in the social sciences, it will be intriguing to see whether it will find a space for the relatively recent contributions from the 'masculinities' school of gender studies. In 1994, R. W. Connell proposed the notion of multiple masculinities, divided broadly into 'hegemonic' identities and subordinate/marginalized ones.

The hegemonic gender order suppresses and victimizes women, but also subordinates other masculinities and their male bearers, often violently:

> Violence becomes important in gender politics among men. Most episodes of major violence ... are transactions among men. Terror is used as a means of drawing boundaries and making exclusions, for example, in heterosexual violence against gay men. Violence can become a way of claiming or asserting masculinity in group struggles. This is an explosive process when an oppressed group gains the means of violence ... The youth gang violence of inner-city streets is a striking example of the assertion of marginalized masculinities against other men, continuous with the assertion of masculinity in sexual violence against women.[68]

The masculinities literature has so far concentrated overwhelmingly on industrialized societies, where genocide is statistically less likely to occur. But it is expanding rapidly, particularly with respect to men and masculinities in the global South. This is a trend that the genocide scholar interested in gender would do well to monitor in coming years.[69]

A gender perspective is vital in understanding how hegemonic *sexualities* operate to destructive ends, through the construction of straight vs. gay, masculine vs. feminine, and active vs. passive. Among other things, such inquiries can increase empathy and interventions on behalf of those, overwhelmingly gay men targeted by other men, who suffer atrocity based on their presumed sexual identity. This inattention to the vulnerabilities of gay men and other sexual 'dissidents' represents a major gap in the genocide literature to date.[70] Research may also yield insights into the homosocial aspects of genocide perpetration – male bonding for atrocity. So far these are lacking, though there is food for thought in the work of feminists like Cohn and MacKinnon, as well as in Lifton's *Nazi Doctors*, Browning's *Ordinary Men*, and Hatzfeld's *Machete Season*.

Gender also seems a vital factor in the post-genocide processes of reconstruction and reconciliation. A growing scholarly and IGO/NGO literature examines women's needs and experiences in these contexts;[71] some attention to men and masculinities is also emerging.[72] Pursuing these themes in a balanced way will not only assist in crafting more effective international policies, but may also deepen our understanding of the psychological and emotional characteristics of post-genocidal societies.

Lastly, as several of the works surveyed in this chapter demonstrate, the complex interweaving of gender with other variables – ethnicity, religion, age, social class/caste, and political affiliation – offers wide scope for investigation. In my view, exploring gender as an analytically distinct variable will always be a valid strategy; but it is to be hoped that scholars who prefer to emphasize different aspects of genocide, or adopt a more holistic approach to the subject, will nonetheless choose to deploy a gender analysis as one useful tool among others. Until this occurs, we will not be able to speak of a true 'mainstreaming' of gendered perspectives in genocide studies.

Notes

1. C. R. Browning, 'The Decision-Making Process', in *The Historiography of the Holocaust*, ed. D. Stone (Basingstoke: Palgrave Macmillan, 2004), p. 173.
2. L. Pine, 'Gender and the Family', in *Historiography of the Holocaust*, ed. Stone, p. 364.
3. K. Mathur, *Countering Gender Violence: Initiatives Towards Collective Action in Rajasthan* (New Delhi: Sage Publications, 2004), p. 25, citing 1970s research by Ann Oakley and others.
4. Mathur, *Countering Gender Violence*, p. 43.
5. Ibid.
6. J. S. Goldstein, *War and Gender: How Gender Shapes the War System and Vice Versa* (Cambridge: Cambridge University Press, 2001), p. 2. For what it is worth, Goldstein's is the framing of 'sex' and 'gender' that I have adopted in my own work on gendercide (see below) – in part because it allows 'gender' to be deployed as a convenient catch-all: 'When I talk, for example, about the "gendering" of the victims of a mass grave (or a campaign of sexual assault, or a military press-gang), it can be assumed that I am concerned with the fate of "embodied" (biological) males and females, rather than (or prior to) more subtle elements of cultural conditioning. "Gendercide" similarly refers to the deaths of "embodied" males and females – or rather, violently disembodied ones. In gendering social phenomena and historical events, meanwhile, I should be understood as seeking to discern the explanatory power of gender (the continuum of biology and culture) in the political and sociological equation.' A. Jones, 'Problems of Gendercide: A Response to Stein and Carpenter', in Jones, ed., *Gendercide and Genocide*, p. 262.
7. A. Jones, 'Gendercidal Institutions Against Women and Girls', in *Women in an Insecure World: Violence Against Women – Facts, Figures and Analysis*, eds, M. Vlachová and L. Biason (Geneva: DCAF, 2005), pp. 15–24.
8. The application of a genocide framework to the phenomenon of female infanticide *and foeticide* was explicit, for example, in Mary Daly's analysis of 'gynocide', in which she echoed the language of the UN Genocide Convention, declaring 'the fundamental intent of global patriarchy' to be the 'planned, institutionalized spiritual and bodily destruction of women; the use of deliberate systematic measures (such as killing, bodily or mental injury, unlivable conditions, *prevention of births*), which are calculated to bring about the destruction of women as a political and cultural force, the eradication of Female/Biological religion and language, and ultimately the extermination of the Race of Women and all Elemental being.' Daly quoted in D. E. H. Russell, 'Defining Femicide and Related Concepts', in *Femicide in Global Perspective*, eds, D. E. H. Russell and R. A. Harmes (New York: Teachers College Press, 2001), p. 22 (emphasis added).
9. J. Radford, *Femicide: The Politics of Woman Killing* (Farmington Hills, MI: Twayne Publishers, 1992).
10. Russell and Harmes, eds, *Femicide in Global Perspective*. See also N. Nenadic, 'Femicide: A Framework for Understanding Genocide', in *Radically Speaking: Feminism*

Reclaimed, eds, D. Bell and R. Klein (North Melbourne: Spinifex Press, 1996), pp. 456–64.

11. Russell, 'Defining Femicide and Related Concepts', p. 19.
12. See, for example, J. Monárrez Fragoso, 'Serial Sexual Femicide in Ciudad Juárez: 1993–2001', *Debate Feminista*, 25 (April 2002), available in English at www.womenontheborder.org/sex_serial_english.pdf.
13. S. Brownmiller, *Against Our Will: Men, Women and Rape* (New York: Ballantine Books, 1993 [reprint edition]), p. 15.
14. S. Griffin, *Rape: The Power of Consciousness* (New York: Harper & Row, 1979); C. A. MacKinnon, *Toward A Feminist Theory of the State* (Cambridge, MA: Harvard University Press, 1989); idem., *Only Words* (Cambridge, MA: Harvard University Press, 1993); A. Dworkin, *Intercourse* (New York: The Free Press, 1987). See also MacKinnon's controversial article, 'Turning Rape into Pornography: Postmodern Genocide', *Ms.* (July–August 1993), 24–30.
15. Dworkin quoted at http://www.snopes.com/quotes/mackinno.htm; MacKinnon, *Toward a Feminist Theory of the State*, p. 174.
16. For a no-holds-barred critique, see M. Mullarkey, 'Hard Cop, Soft Cop: Catharine MacKinnon and Andrea Dworkin on Pornography', *The Nation* (30 May 1987); available on the Web at http://www.maureenmullarkey.com/essays/porn1.html.
17. A. Stiglmayer, ed., *Mass Rape: The War Against Women in Bosnia-Herzegovina* (Lincoln, NE: University of Nebraska Press, 1994); B. Allen, *Rape Warfare: The Hidden Genocide in Bosnia-Herzegovina and Croatia* (Minneapolis, MN: University of Minnesota Press, 1996).
18. C. A. MacKinnon, 'Rape, Genocide, and Women's Human Rights', *Harvard Women's Law Journal*, 5 (1994), 9–12.
19. S. L. Russell-Brown, 'Rape as an Act of Genocide', *Berkeley Journal of International Law*, 21 (2003), 365.
20. R. Copelon, 'Surfacing Gender: Reconceptualizing Crimes against Women in Time of War', in *The Women and War Reader*, eds, L. A. Lorentzen and J. Turpin (New York: New York University Press, 1998), p. 64. Lorentzen's and Turpin's anthology is a useful collection of second-generation feminist investigations of gender and war.
21. B. Nowrojee, *Shattered Lives: Sexual Violence during the Rwandan Genocide and Its Aftermath* (New York: Human Rights Watch, 1996), from the Web version at http://hrw.org/reports/1996/Rwanda.htm.
22. M. Daly, *Outercourse: The Bedazzling Voyage* (San Francisco, CA: HarperSanFrancisco, 1992).
23. See, for example, R. J. Lifton and E. Markusen, *The Genocidal Mentality: Nazi Holocaust and Nuclear Threat* (New York: Basic Books, 1990).
24. C. Cohn, 'Sex and Death in the Rational World of Defense Intellectuals', *Signs*, 12, 4 (1987), 704, 708–9.
25. Ibid., pp. 688, 696.
26. K. Theweleit, *Male Fantasies, Vol. 1: Women, Floods, Bodies, History* (Minneapolis, MN: University of Minnesota Press, 1987), pp. 50, 205.
27. Ibid., pp. 76, 89, 125–6. James William Gibson drew on Theweleit's insights in an American context in *Warrior Dreams: Paramilitary Culture in Post-Vietnam America* (New York: Hill and Wang, 1994). Gibson, too, saw paramilitary culture as predicated on a 'division of women into the good, "pure" sister and the bad, "impure" temptress', with communism (the 'Red Tide') once again wed to misogyny, identified with erotic and threatening women (p. 63).

28. R. J. Lifton, *The Nazi Doctors: Medical Killing and the Psychology of Genocide* (New York: Basic Books, 1986), p. 462. Emphasis added.
29. C. R. Browning, *Ordinary Men: Reserve Police Battalion 101 and the Final Solution in Poland* (New York: Harper Perennial, 1992), p. 185.
30. An exception is Ø. G. Holter's important essay 'A Theory of Gendercide', in *Gendercide and Genocide*, ed. Jones, pp. 62–97.
31. Taylor, *Sacrifice as Terror*, p. 176.
32. J. B. Elshtain, *Women and War* (New York: Basic Books, 1987), p. 145.
33. C. Koonz, *Mothers in the Fatherland: Women, the Family and Nazi Politics* (New York: St. Martin's Press, 1987), pp. 13, 17. Emphasis added.
34. African Rights, *Rwanda: Not So Innocent – Women As Killers* (London: African Rights, 1995), pp. 4, 27. See also L. Sharlach, 'Gender and Genocide in Rwanda: Women As Agents and Objects of Genocide', *Journal of Genocide Research*, 1, 3 (1999), 387–99. Joanna Bourke's book *An Intimate History of Killing: Face-to-Face Killing in Twentieth-Century Warfare* (New York: Basic Books, 1999) featured a chapter on killing by females in war that also seemed to influence thinking about female perpetrators.
35. A. Jones, 'Gender and Genocide in Rwanda', in *Gendercide and Genocide*, ed. Jones, pp. 127–8.
36. J. Waller, *Becoming Evil: How Ordinary People Commit Genocide and Mass Killing* (Oxford: Oxford University Press, 2002), p. 301 n12.
37. A significant additional factor was the growing prominence of a 'Third World' critique within feminism. Many 'Third World' feminists rejected easy claims of female global solidarity transcending social barriers, as well as stereotypical depictions of women as pacific and nurturing. Wrote Urvashi Butalia in 2001: 'Women's involvement in communal ideologies and communal conflict has raised certain important questions for women activists and has challenged various assumptions, notably that women share an overarching commonality of experience that unites them as women and transcends their caste, class and religious divisions. We now know that this most cherished article of faith for women's groups has had to be given up as a chimera.' Butalia, 'Women and Communal Conflict: New Challenges for the Women's Movement in India', in *Victims, Perpetrators or Actors? Gender, Armed Conflict and Political Violence*, eds, C. O. N. Moser, and F. C. Clark (London: Zed Books, 2001), p. 102. See also A.-M. Goetz, 'Feminism and the Limits of the Claim to Know: Contradictions in the Feminist Approach to Women in Development', *Millenium*, 17, 3 (1998), 477–96.
38. R. Lentin, 'Introduction', in *Gender and Catastrophe*, ed. Lentin (London: Zed Books, 1997), pp. 2, 5.
39. R. Jacobson, S. Jacobs and J. Marchbank, 'Introduction: States of Conflict', in *States of Conflict: Gender, Violence and Resistance*, eds, R. Jacobson, S. Jacobs and J. Marchbank (London: Zed Books, 2000), p. 1.
40. Ibid., p. 13.
41. J. El-Bushra, 'Transforming Conflict: Some Thoughts on a Gendered Understanding of Conflict Processes', in *States of Conflict*, eds, Jacobson et al., p. 79.
42. Ibid., p. 81.
43. P. Mukta, 'Gender, Community, Nation: The Myth of Innocence', in *States of Conflict*, eds, Jacobson et al., pp. 172, 174.
44. Ibid., p. 171.
45. Ibid., p. 168.

46. C. O. N. Moser and F. C. Clark, 'Introduction', in *Victims, Perpetrators or Actors?*, eds, Moser and Clark, p. 7.
47. R. C. Carpenter expresses the same criticism of the Moser/Clark volume in 'Gender Theory and World Politics: Contributions of a Non-Feminist Standpoint?', *International Studies Review*, 4, 3 (2002), 160.
48. D. Zarkov, 'The Body of the Other Man: Sexual Violence and the Construction of Masculinity, Sexuality and Ethnicity in Croatian Media', in *Victims, Perpetrators or Actors?*, eds, Moser and Clark, pp. 69–82. On this theme, see also A. Del Zotto and A. Jones, 'Male-on-Male Sexual Violence in Wartime: Human Rights' Last Taboo?', paper presented at the conference of the International Studies Association, New Orleans, March 2002; available at http://adamjones.freeservers.com/malerape.htm.
49. A. Jones, 'Gender and Ethnic Conflict in Ex-Yugoslavia', *Ethnic and Racial Studies*, 17, 1 (1994), 122–4, 131 n16.
50. M. A. Warren, *Gendercide: The Implications of Sex Selection* (Lanham: Rowman & Littlefield, 1985), p. 22.
51. L. Kuper, *Genocide: Its Political Use in the Twentieth Century* (Harmondsworth: Penguin, 1981), p. 204.
52. J. Ringelheim, 'Genocide and Gender: A Split Memory', in *Gender & Catastrophe*, ed. Lentin, pp. 21, 23.
53. H. Fein, 'Genocide and Gender: The Uses of Women and Group Destiny', *Journal of Genocide Research*, 1, 1 (1999), 43, 57.
54. Ibid., 46.
55. The claim, at least, has been on the record for several years now without being refuted.
56. A. Jones, 'Gendercide and Genocide', *Journal of Genocide Research*, 2, 2 (2000), 191–2; available at http://www.gendercide.org/gendercide_and_genocide.html.
57. R. C. Carpenter, 'Beyond "Gendercide"', *International Journal of Human Rights*, 6, 4 (2002), 77–101.
58. Jones, ed., *Gendercide and Genocide.*
59. Jones, 'Gendercidal Institutions Against Women and Girls'.
60. A. Jones, 'Why Gendercide? Why Root-and-Branch? A Comparison of the Vendée Uprising of 1793–94 and the Bosnian War of the 1990s', *Journal of Genocide Research*, 8, 1 (2006), 9–25.
61. A. Jones, 'Gendercide in Kosovo', online at: http://adamjones.freeservers.com/gendercide_in_kosovo.htm; 'Genocide and Humanitarian Intervention: Incorporating the Gender Variable', *Journal of Humanitarian Assistance* (February 2002), http://www.jha.ac/articles/a080.htm; and Jones, 'Gendercidal Institutions Against Women and Girls.' Significant empirical support for the core claim of disproportionate male victimization was supplied by two human rights reports. In 1999, the Organization for Security and Cooperation in Europe published the most detailed account of atrocities in the Kosovo war, *Kosovo/Kosova: As Seen, As Told* (OSCE, 1999, <http://www.osce.org/kosovo/reports/hr/part1/ch7.htm>). It included a chapter (15) on 'Young Men of Fighting Age', which noted that 'young men were the group that was by far the most targeted in the conflict in Kosovo ... If apprehended by Serbian forces – VJ, police or paramilitary – the young men were at risk, more than any other group of Kosovo society of grave human rights violations. Many were executed on the spot, on occasion after horrendous torture. ... Others were taken for use as human shields or as forced labour. Many young men "disappeared" following abduction.' The *Human Security Report 2005*, published by the Human Security

Center in cooperation with the United Nations, stated more broadly that 'the "gender lens" has been inconsistently applied' in studies of conflict, war, and genocide, 'creating a distorted picture of reality. ... [In fact,] it is men, not women, who "bear the brunt" of armed conflict. Both in uniform and out, men have been, and continue to be, killed, wounded and tortured in far greater numbers than women. Men are also, overwhelmingly, the major perpetrators of violence. ... We know that women are far more likely to be the victims of rape and other sex crimes, but sexual violence is only one form of "gender-based violence". Men, too, are targeted because of their gender ...' See Human Security Center, *Human Security Report 2005* (Vancouver: Human Security Center, 2005), pp. 109–10. As Charli Carpenter pointed out to me in conversation in November 2005, this concept of men as victims of 'gender-based violence' per se is something quite new in the policy literature.

62. R. C. Carpenter, '"Women and Children First": Gender, Norms, and Humanitarian Evacuation in the Balkans 1991–95', *International Organization*, 57 (2003), 688–9. See also Carpenter's book-length expansion of the argument, *'Innocent Women and Children': Gender, Norms And the Protection of Civilians* (Aldershot: Ashgate Publishing, 2006).
63. Carpenter, '"Women and Children First"', 675.
64. See Carpenter, 'Gender Theory in World Politics', pp. 155–7.
65. A 'relational' approach to gender is linked to the rise of a 'Gender and Development' school of development theory and practice, following upon (and to some degree supplanting) a 'Women in Development' approach. For an overview of this evolution, stressing 'the theoretical importance of incorporating men' (p. 22), see S. Chant and M. Gutmann, *Mainstreaming Men into Gender and Development: Debates, Reflections, and Experiences* (Oxford: Oxfam, 2000).
66. A. El Jack, *Gender and Armed Conflict: Overview Report* (Brighton: Institute of Development Studies, 2003), p. 41.
67. Recall both Christopher Taylor's work on Rwanda and Joan Ringelheim's on Nazi propaganda.
68. R. W. Connell, *Masculinities* (Berkeley, CA: University of California Press, 1994), pp. 77, 83. See also L. Bowker, ed., *Masculinities and Violence* (Thousand Oaks, CA: Sage, 1998).
69. There is also a strand of writing on men and masculinities that stresses the need to empathize with men and understand the ways in which they are selectively targeted and victimized. W. Farrell's *The Myth of Male Power: Why Men Are the Disposable Sex* (New York: Simon & Schuster, 1993) is indicative of this strand, which offers a necessary corrective to the more schematic feminist accounts, and was influential on me personally.
70. Only in rare instances might anti-queer violence rise to a genocidal level, but the intensity of anti-gay and anti-transvestite vigilantism in Colombia and several other Latin American countries suggests that the framework need not be limited to the Nazi campaign against homosexual men. See S. S. Rixecker, 'Genetic Engineering and Queer Biotechnology: The Eugenics of the Twenty-First Century?', in *Gendercide and Genocide*, ed. Jones, pp. 172–85; on the Nazi campaigns, R. Plant, *The Pink Triangle: The Nazi War against Homosexuals* (New York: Owl Books, 1988).
71. See, for example, S. Meintjes, A. Pillay and M. Turshen, eds, *The Aftermath: Women in Post-Conflict Transformation* (London: Zed Books, 2001).
72. A significant effort is the 'Gender and Displacement' special issue of *Forced Migration Review*, 9 (December 2000), available on the Web at http://www.fmreview.org/FMRpdfs/FMR09/fmr9full.pdf. See also A. Jones, ed., *Men of the Global South: A Reader* (London: Zed Books, 2006).

9
Prosecuting Genocide

William A. Schabas

The 1948 Genocide Convention recognises that 'at all periods of history genocide has inflicted great losses on humanity'. But until the second half of the twentieth century, genocide generally went unprosecuted and unpunished. Genocide is a 'crime of state', to use the term employed by one of the first to write about the *Convention.*[1] The fact that State involvement, in the form of some plan or policy, is virtually inseparable from the crime of genocide provides an explanation for this history of impunity.[2] States were not going to punish themselves, or rather their own high functionaries, for crimes that were in fact official policy in one form or another. There are two main solutions to this problem. The first is to create an international court with jurisdiction over the offence. Here, the paradigm is the Nuremberg Tribunal, which held Nazi leaders accountable for the attempted destruction of the European Jews, although the prosecutions were carried out under the rubric of crimes against humanity, rather than genocide. The second is recognition that States other than the one where the crime actually took place are entitled to prosecute genocide, a concept described as 'universal jurisdiction'. This was the basis of the first prosecution using the terms of the *Genocide Convention*, that of Adolf Eichmann before the Israeli courts after he was tracked down and abducted from Argentina, in the early 1960s.

The first recorded proposal for an international criminal justice mechanism appeared in the second half of the nineteenth century. One of the founders of the Red Cross movement, Gustav Monnier, prepared a draft statute for an international criminal court. Its intended mission was to prosecute breaches of the Geneva Convention of 1864 and other norms of the law of armed conflict.[3] The concept of international prosecution revived when, on 24 May 1915, the governments of France, Great Britain and Russia issued a joint declaration that '[i]n the presence of these new crimes of Turkey against humanity and civilization, the allied Governments publicly inform the Sublime Porte that they will hold personally responsible for the said crimes all members of the Ottoman

Government as well as those of its agents who are found to be involved in such massacres'.[4] Until that point, international law had never really concerned itself with acts perpetrated by sovereign states against their own civilian populations. Indeed, the United States did not agree that the Ottoman leaders should be held accountable. Secretary of State Robert Lansing admitted what he called the 'more or less justifiable' right of the Turkish government to deport the Armenians to the extent that they lived 'within the zone of military operations', although he added that '[i]t was not to my mind the deportation which was objectionable but the horrible brutality which attended its execution. It is one of the blackest pages in the history of this war, and I think we were fully justified in intervening as we did on behalf of the wretched people, even though they were Turkish subjects.'[5]

An international war crimes trial was apparently first mooted by Lord Curzon at a meeting of the Imperial War Cabinet on 20 November 1918.[6] The British emphasised a trial of the Kaiser and other leading Germans. There was little interest in accountability for the persecution of innocent minorities such as the Armenians in Turkey.[7] The objective was to punish 'those who were responsible for the War or for atrocious offences against the laws of war'.[8] Lloyd George subsequently explained that '[t]here was also a growing feeling that war itself was a crime against humanity ...'[9] At the second plenary session of the Paris Peace Conference, on 29 January 1919, a Commission on the Responsibility of the Authors of the War and on Enforcement of Penalties was created.[10] Composed of 15 representatives of the victorious powers, the Commission was mandated to inquire into and to report upon the violations of international law committed by Germany and its allies during the course of the war.

The Commission's report used the expression 'Violations of the Laws and Customs of War and of the Laws of Humanity'. Some of these breaches came close to the criminal behaviour now defined as genocide or crimes against humanity and involved the persecution of ethnic minorities or groups. Under the rubric of 'attempts to denationalize the inhabitants of occupied territory', the Commission cited many offences in Serbia committed by Bulgarian, German and Austrian authorities, including prohibition of the Serb language, '[p]eople beaten for saying "good morning" in Serbian', destruction of archives of churches and law courts, and the closing of schools.[11] As for 'wanton destruction of religious, charitable, educational and historic buildings and monuments', there were examples from Serbia and Macedonia of attacks on schools, monasteries, churches and ancient inscriptions by the Bulgarian authorities.[12] The Commission proposed the establishment of an international 'High Tribunal', and urged 'that all enemy persons alleged to have been guilty of offences against the laws and customs of war and the laws of humanity' be excluded from any amnesty and be brought before either national tribunals or the High Tribunal.[13]

At the Peace Conference itself, Nicolas Politis, Greek Foreign Minister and a member of the Commission on Responsibilities, proposed the definition of a new category of war crimes, designated 'crimes against the laws of humanity', intended to cover the massacres of the Armenians.[14] Woodrow Wilson protested a measure he considered to be *ex post facto* law.[15] Wilson subsequently withdrew his opposition, but he felt that in any case such efforts would be ineffectual.[16] At the meeting of the Council of Four on 2 April 1919, Lloyd George said it was important to judge those responsible 'for acts against individuals, atrocities of all sorts committed under orders ...'.[17]

Article 227 of the *Treaty of Versailles* stipulated that Kaiser Wilhelm II was to be tried 'for a supreme offence against international morality and the sanctity of treaties'. However, the Netherlands refused to extradite the German emperor, on the grounds that the prosecution would violate the principle against retroactive criminal law. Articles 228 to 230 recognised the right of the Allies to try Germans accused of war crimes before 'military tribunals composed of members of the military tribunals of the Powers'. This was, in effect, the first recognition in international law of an international criminal tribunal.[18] It was to try persons accused of violating the laws and customs of war. In deference to American objections, the *Treaty of Versailles* did not refer to 'crimes against the laws of humanity'. The new German government voted to accept the treaty, but conditionally, and it refused the war criminals clauses, noting that the country's penal code prevented the surrender of Germans to a foreign government for prosecution and punishment.[19] A compromise deemed compatible with article 228 of the *Versailles Treaty* allowed that the Supreme Court of the Empire in Leipzig would judge those charged by the Allies. Germany opposed arraignment of most of those chosen for prosecution by the Allies, arguing that the trial of its military and naval elite could imperil the Government's existence.[20] In the end, only a handful of German soldiers were tried, for atrocities in prisoner of war camps and sinking of hospital ships.[21] A Commission of Allied jurists set up to examine the results at Leipzig concluded 'that in the case of those condemned the sentences were not adequate'.[22] It was a very unsatisfying first venture in international criminal justice. Yet, as Georges Clemenceau had reminded his allies when they were initially considering the proposal, '[t]he first tribunal must have been summary and brutal; it was nevertheless the beginning of a great thing'.[23] The prosecutions did leave a small legacy in the form of case law clarifying important legal issues involved in prosecutions, such as the admissibility of a defence of superior orders.[24]

With regard to Turkey, the Allies contemplated prosecution not only for the classic war crime of mistreating prisoners (they were mainly British), but also for 'deportations and massacres', in other words, the persecution and attempted destruction of the Armenian minority.[25] The British High Commissioner, Admiral Calthorpe, informed the Turkish Foreign Minister on 18 January 1919 that 'His

Majesty's Government are resolved to have proper punishment inflicted on those responsible for Armenian massacres'.[26] Calthorpe's subsequent dispatch to London said he had informed the Turkish government that British statesmen 'had promised [the] civilized world that persons connected would be held personally responsible and that it was [the] firm intention of H.M. Government to fulfil [that] promise'.[27] Subsequently, the High Commission proposed the Turks be punished for the Armenian massacres by dismemberment of their Empire accompanied by criminal trial of high officials to serve as an example.[28]

Under pressure from Allied military rulers, the Turkish authorities arrested and detained scores of their leaders, later releasing many as a result of public demonstrations and other pressure.[29] In late May 1919, the British seized 67 of the Turkish prisoners and spirited them away to more secure detention in Malta and elsewhere.[30] But the British found that political considerations, including the growth of Kemalism and competition for influence with other European powers, made insistence on prosecutions increasingly untenable.[31] In mid-1920, a political-legal officer at the British High Commission in Istanbul cautioned London of practical difficulties involved in prosecuting Turks for the Armenian massacres, including obtaining evidence.[32] By late 1921, the British had negotiated a prisoner exchange agreement with the Turks, and the suspects held in Malta were released.[33]

Attempts by Turkish jurists to press for trial of those responsible for the atrocities before national courts were slightly more successful.[34] Prosecuted on the basis of the Turkish penal code, several ministers in the wartime cabinet and leaders of the Ittihad party were found guilty by a Court Martial, on 5 July 1919, of 'the organization and execution of crime of massacre' against the Armenian minority.[35] The criminals were sentenced, *in absentia*, to capital punishment or lengthy terms of imprisonment.[36]

According to the *Treaty of Sèvres*, signed 10 August 1920, Turkey recognised the right of trial 'notwithstanding any proceedings or prosecution before a tribunal in Turkey', and was obliged to surrender 'all persons accused of having committed an act in violation of the laws and customs of war, who are specified either by name or by rank, office or employment which they held under Turkish authorities'.[37] This formulation was similar to the war crimes clauses in the *Treaty of Versailles*. But the *Treaty of Sèvres* contained a major innovation, contemplating prosecution of what we now define as 'crimes against humanity'[38] as well as of war crimes. Pursuant to article 230,

> The Turkish Government undertakes to hand over to the Allied Powers the persons whose surrender may be required by the latter as being responsible for the massacres committed during the continuance of the state of war on territory which formed part of the Turkish Empire on the 1st August, 1914. The Allied Powers reserve to themselves the right to designate the Tribunal

which shall try the persons so accused, and the Turkish Government undertakes to recognise such Tribunal. In the event of the League of Nations having created in sufficient time a Tribunal competent to deal with the said massacres, the Allied Powers reserve to themselves the right to bring the accused persons mentioned above before the Tribunal, and the Turkish Government undertakes equally to recognise such Tribunal.[39]

The *Treaty of Sèvres* was never ratified. As Kay Holloway wrote, the failure of the signatories to bring the treaty into force 'resulted in the abandonment of thousands of defenceless peoples – Armenians and Greeks – to the fury of their persecutors, by engendering subsequent holocausts in which the few survivors of the 1915 Armenian massacres perished'.[40] The *Treaty of Sèvres* was replaced by the *Treaty of Lausanne* of 24 July 1923.[41] It included a 'Declaration of Amnesty' for all offences committed between 1 August 1914 and 20 November 1922.

Two decades later, as news of the Nazi atrocities was becoming notorious, Raphael Lemkin famously proposed the term 'genocide'. 'New conceptions require new terms', explained Lemkin.[42] Born in eastern Poland, near the town of Bezwodene, Lemkin worked in his own country as a lawyer, prosecutor and university lecturer before fleeing Poland in the face of Nazi anti-Semitism. Lemkin's interest in the subject of 'genocide' dated to his days as a student at Lvov University, where he intently followed attempts to prosecute the perpetrators of the massacres of the Armenians.[43] He made his way to Sweden and then to the United States, finding work at Duke University and later at Yale University.[44] Lemkin was present and actively involved, largely behind the scenes but also as a consultant to the Secretary-General, throughout the drafting of the *Genocide Convention*. 'Never in the history of the United Nations has one private individual conducted such a lobby', wrote John P. Humphrey in his diaries.[45]

However, the first successful international prosecution for genocide, that of the Nazi leaders at Nuremberg, did not, in fact, use the term. International lawyers opted for the somewhat more familiar concept of 'crimes against humanity' rather than the much newer one of genocide. There is no record of any debate about this issue in either the sessions of the United Nations War Crimes Commission,[46] which began meeting in late 1943 to plan the post-war prosecutions, or the London Conference, held from June to August 1945, at which the law applicable to the Nuremberg trial was adopted.[47]

The trial of the International Military Tribunal began in late 1945. A final judgment was issued on 30 September–1 October 1946.[48] Many of the participants in the trial, and of the subsequent proceedings held in the Nuremberg courthouse by United States military tribunals, have left their own recollections in published form. One of the most recent and certainly the most authoritative is that of Telford Taylor, who assisted Justice Robert Jackson as a prosecutor at the International Military Tribunal.[49] In the Pacific theatre, a broadly similar proceeding was held by the International Military Tribunal for the Far East.[50]

Trials generally leave behind a substantial archive, and there is little quarrel among historians about what actually happened at Nuremberg. The heart of the debate concerns an assessment of the overall fairness of the proceedings. Many modern students of the trials tend to judge them rather harshly in this respect,[51] and they have often been stigmatised as 'victor's justice'.[52] The credibility of the Tokyo tribunal was not helped by the dissenting judgments, which cast a shadow over some of its legal foundations.[53] But it is probably unreasonable to expect international justice in its first serious incarnation to meet the high standards of due process recognised by international law at the end of the twentieth century. One of the great apologists for the Nazis, David Irving, is Nuremberg's harshest critic. Typical of his other writings, his study of the Nuremberg trial contains isolated bits of new information and occasional insights.[54] But the more scurrilous of his criticisms are not supported by verifiable authorities, a feature of his writing already demonstrated by Richard Evans in the famous libel trial.[55] Recent scholarship has also focussed attention on the substantive shortcomings of the Nuremberg trial. Donald Bloxham's important monograph points out how marginal the issue of the Holocaust was to the trial in general.[56]

In the aftermath of the Second World War, there were many national prosecutions concerning atrocities committed in the course of the conflict.[57] The American-run trials in the Nuremberg courthouse had a thematic basis, dealing with Nazi doctors, bankers, military leaders and even judges. The so-called Justice trial[58] inspired Abby Mann's great screenplay for the film Judgment at Nuremberg. More about the story of the elderly Jew who befriends the young domestic, played by Judy Garland, has been unearthed by researchers.[59] After Nuremberg and Tokyo, international prosecution for genocide did not resume for nearly half a century. In the meantime, there were a few celebrated trials by national jurisdictions, notably that of Adolf Eichmann in Jerusalem in the early 1960s. The Eichmann trial generated great controversy in several respects, including the legality of the kidnapping that brought him to Israel in the first place, the legitimacy of the exercise of universal jurisdiction that allowed Israeli courts to undertake the prosecution, and the use of capital punishment (about which there had been no real controversy at Nuremberg). Hannah Arendt's critique of the trial has greatly influenced virtually all of the subsequent debate about accountability and impunity.[60] Rather less well known is the riposte by Jacob Robinson.[61] There are several contemporary accounts of the trial, although it took decades before scholars began to seriously assess the role of the Eichmann trial in the more general context of Israel's treatment of the Holocaust. A fascinating recent study by Hannah Yablonka published initially in Hebrew is now available in English translation.[62]

In the late 1980s, Israel judged John Demjanjuk after obtaining his extradition from the United States. Demjanjuk was believed to have been "Ivan the Terrible" at the Treblinka death camp, but he was acquitted of this charge after the Court of Appeal ruled ambiguous identification evidence entitled him to the benefit of the doubt.[63] The Attorney General of Israel refused to proceed with new charges, despite compelling evidence that Demjanjuk had in fact served as a guard in the Trawniki camp. Extradition law prevents prosecution based on charges if these were not authorised by the extraditing State which, in Demjanjuk's case, was the United States of America. The High Court of Justice was petitioned to review the Attorney General's decision, but declined to intervene.[64]

There were a few other prosecutions by national courts. An ambitious Canadian war crimes prosecution fizzled out for complex reasons. Perhaps the main thing they have shown the great difficulty in the exercise of universal jurisdiction, especially over crimes committed many decades in the past. A Cambodian show trial was held in 1979, using an idiosyncratic definition of genocide that more closely approximates the broader concept of crimes against humanity.[65] The Cambodians departed from the definition recognised in the 1948 Convention in order to encompass economic, social and political groups. French trials of Nazis and their collaborators in the 1980s and 1990s also generated great interest. In some cases they raised important legal issues, but probably the real reason for their prominence was their great political significance within France.

International criminal prosecution did not revive until the last decade of the century. In 1990 there were proposals to establish an international mechanism to bring Saddam Hussein to justice for the invasion of Kuwait, but nothing concrete ever materialised. British Prime Minister Margaret Thatcher and United States President George Bush, both evoking the precedent of the Nuremberg trials, broached the idea of an international tribunal to deal with the Iraqi invasion of Kuwait, one that might address such crimes as aggression and hostage-taking.[66] There are reports that the idea originated in the United States Department of the Army.[67] Pentagon lawyers prepared a report documenting crimes allegedly committed by Iraqi President for a possible trial. The matter was 'quietly dropped after the American-led coalition won the Persian Gulf War without capturing Mr. Hussein'.[68] Still, the concept was back on the agenda, and when war broke out in the Balkans there were several calls for international prosecution. One of the intriguing features of the proposed Iraqi tribunal concerned the subject-matter jurisdiction of the tribunal. At Nuremberg, the judges had called the waging of aggressive war ('crimes against peace') the 'supreme international crime differing only from other war crimes in that it contains within itself the accumulated evil of the whole'. But with Saddam Hussein in custody in Iraq, in 2005, a national court that was strongly influenced by the United States showed no interest in pursuing charges of aggression, focussing instead on crimes against humanity and genocide.[69]

On 16 May 1991, Mirko Klarin published an article entitled 'Nuremberg Now!' in the Belgrade newspaper *Borba*.[70] Oxford history professor Norman Stone made a similar appeal in a comment he published in *The Guardian* on 13 November 1991.[71] In early 1992, French constitutional judge Robert Badinter, who also presided over the Arbitration Commission for the former Yugoslavia that had been established by the European Commission in late 1991, raised the idea of an international criminal tribunal for Yugoslavia in discussions with the two mediators, Lord Carrington and Cyrus Vance.[72] But the legal advisor to the Quai d'Orsai, Jean-Pierre Puissochet, found Badinter's whole idea unrealistic. Puissochet felt that 'to elaborate a treaty to create a tribunal would take years' and believed it unlikely that the Security Council would contemplate such an initiative.[73] Eventually, Badinter managed to interest the French Foreign Minister, Roland Dumas, who took the matter up with President Mitterand. Mitterand was initially negative about the idea. 'That will not succeed', he told Dumas. 'What is needed, is a political solution.'[74] But subsequently, he authorised Dumas to pursue the idea.[75]

In mid-August, the Commission on Human Rights held its first ever special session in order to consider the situation in the former Yugoslavia.[76] The Commission '[c]ondemn[ed] absolutely the concept and practice of "ethnic cleansing", declared that perpetrators were individually responsible for violations of human rights, and that the international community would spare to effort to bring them to justice'.[77] The Commission on Human Rights reconvened on 30 November 1992, in a second special session, and reiterated its previous declaration. It called upon 'all States to consider the extent to which the acts committed in Bosnia and Herzegovina and in Croatia constitute genocide, in accordance with the Convention on the Prevention and Punishment of the Crime of Genocide'.[78] Presented to the Council on 3 May 1993, the report consisted of a draft statute and a detailed commentary and explanation.[79] The Security Council, without modification, on 25 May 1993, unanimously adopted the draft statute proposed by the Secretary-General.[80]

It took somewhat more than a year for the ICTY to get up and running. Observers were sceptical that it would ever function effectively. Theodor Meron of New York University, who eight years later would be elected President of the Tribunal, wrote in *Foreign Affairs* that 'despite its desirability, it is probable that the tribunal will not be very effective'.[81] Nominations for the first judges were solicited,[82] and elections were held by the General Assembly in November 1993. The Secretary-General identified a prosecutor, who was then formally appointed only to resign before ever really beginning the work.[83] A new search began, but it was not until July 1994 that consensus was reached on Richard Goldstone, a distinguished South African judge who had recently been appointed to that country's new Constitutional Court.[84] Goldstone has described his appointment, as well as certain aspects of his work at the Tribunal during its first years, in a short memoir.[85] There is also a useful account by a French journalist.[86]

The first accused to be tried by the Yugoslavia Tribunal was a 'target of opportunity', a Serb thug of no great importance to the conflict who happened to fall within the sights of the Prosecutor at a time when he was desperate for a defendant. Despite the insignificance of the accused, the trial generated a great deal of legal precedent. A somewhat journalistic account by academic Michael Scharf appeared even before the trial was complete.[87] Several subsequent monographs have described the proceedings, all of them essentially descriptive in nature.[88] A few of them have been quite negative, reflecting a view of the Tribunal that has had considerable purchase within Serbia itself.[89]

The Yugoslavia Tribunal was not even fully operational when reports hit the international media of terrible atrocities being committed within the context of a civil war in Rwanda, a former Belgian mandate in central Africa. The backdrop was an historic conflict between two ethnic groups, the majority Hutu who had governed the country since independence, and the minority Tutsi, who had dominated it during the colonial period. Since decolonisation, a series of pogroms had driven waves of Tutsi refugees into neighbouring countries. When denied their right to return, they launched a military assault, in 1990. A peace agreement, reached in August 1993, ensured repatriation for the refugees and installed a power-sharing government, with a transition to be supervised by a United Nations peacekeeping mission.[90]

The first call for an international tribunal to deal with the Rwandan genocide, similar in structure to that for the former Yugoslavia, was circulating seriously by the end of June 1994, when United States Secretary of State Warren Christopher indicated his government's support for such a project.[91] On 28 September 1994, Rwanda formally requested the United Nations to establish a tribunal.[92] Moreover, in his October 1994 address to the United Nations General Assembly, President Pasteur Bizimungu of Rwanda declared that 'it is absolutely urgent that this international tribunal be established'.[93] But although enthusiastic about the proposed tribunal in principle, Rwanda disagreed with many of the modalities.[94] 'The realization that an international tribunal is not equipped to undertake a prosecution of thousands of detainees was probably one of the reasons for which the Government of Rwanda eventually withdrew its support for the International Tribunal', observed two United Nations insiders.[95] Rwanda expressed several disagreements with the form the tribunal was taking, including the prohibition of capital punishment, the limitation on temporal jurisdiction to the 1994 calendar year, the lack of an independent prosecutor and appeals chamber, a desire to exclude nationals of 'certain countries' believed to be complicit in the genocide from nominating judges, the possibility that sentences might be served outside Rwanda, and the refusal to commit to locating the seat of the tribunal within Rwanda itself. Adoption of the Security Council resolution establishing the Tribunal was delayed by a week, as United Nations legal advisor Hans Corell travelled to Kigali to try to win the support of Rwanda.[96] He was unsuccessful, and Security Council Resolution 955 was adopted on 8 November 1994 with one dissenting vote, that of Rwanda,[97] and an abstention, from China.[98]

The tensions present at the creation did not dissipate, and over the years there were many skirmishes between the Rwandan government and the Tribunal. There are useful accounts of the work of the Tribunal from both legal and historical perspectives.[99] From another angle, there have also been sharp criticisms of those who feel the Tribunal has behaved too generously with Rwanda. They point to its failure to indict prominent Tutsi members of the Rwandese Patriotic Front with respect to allegations of crimes against humanity committed in the aftermath of the genocide.[100]

As was the case at Nuremberg and Tokyo, the judgments of the Tribunal contains a considerable amount of analysis of the factual situation that surely falls under the rubric of 'history' as well as that of 'justice'. Historians of the conflict have made frequent appearances as expert witnesses, and judges have weighed this evidence in making their own conclusions about the history of the Balkans. The first major trial judgment included a lengthy discussion of these issues, devoting some 124 paragraphs to an historical account beginning hundreds of years ago before turning to the offences with which the accused, Dusko Tadic, was actually charged.[101] The Trial Chamber said that the historical evidence presented by Prosecution and Defence was 'seldom in conflict'.[102] The Rwanda Tribunal did much the same thing: 'It is the opinion of the Chamber that, in order to understand the events alleged in the Indictment, it is necessary to say, however briefly, something about the history of Rwanda, beginning from the pre-colonial period up to 1994.'[103]

Sometimes, when accused persons have pleaded guilty, this has been taken into account by the judges as a mitigating factor because '[i]n confessing his guilt and admitting all factual details contained in the Third Amended Indictment in open court on 4 September 2003 Dragan Nikolić [...] has guided the international community closer to the truth in an area not yet subject of any judgment rendered by this Tribunal, truth being one prerequisite for peace'.[104] But plea agreements have also been criticised because they may distort the historical truth: '[n]either the public, nor the judges themselves come closer to know the truth beyond what is accepted in the plea agreement. This might create an unfortunate gap in the public and historical record of the concrete case ...'[105] One of the members of Yugoslavia Tribunal, Judge Patricia Wald, has spoken of 'truth in fact finding for history's sake'.[106] According to Judge Wald,

> Many historians as well as the relatives of victims maintain that only the adjudicated findings of an impartial international body of jurists following

> accepted rules of legal procedure will quell the doubts of future generations that the terrible things did in fact happen. To chronicle accurately for history some of the world's darkest deeds is the special responsibility of the Tribunal. Many would say it explains and even justifies the extraordinary length of the Tribunal's judgments and what sometimes appears to be the Tribunal's near-obsession with minute factual detail.[107]

Others have noted the importance of this historical role for international justice in terms of responding to 'denial' or 'revisionism'. According to Judge Gabrielle Kirk McDonald, '[t]he judgments provide an incontrovertible record of how the communities became so divided, how neighbours raped and killed neighbours, how friends forgot their friendship, and how intermarriages meant nothing when one ethnic group was pitted against another by incessant, virulent propaganda'.[108]

In a sense, it might be claimed that the Yugoslavia and Rwanda Tribunals were the institutions contemplated by article VI of the 1948 *Genocide Convention*: 'Persons charged with genocide or any of the other acts enumerated in article 3 shall be tried by a competent tribunal of the State in the territory of which the act was committed, or by such international penal tribunal as may have jurisdiction with respect to those Contracting Parties which shall have accepted its jurisdiction.' Article VI represented a partial defeat for those who had originally put forward the importance of condemning genocide. Their 1946 draft resolution in the United Nations General Assembly said: '*Whereas* the punishment of the very serious crime of genocide when committed in time of peace lies within the exclusive territorial jurisdiction of the judiciary of every State concerned, while crimes of a relatively lesser importance such as piracy, trade in women, children, drugs, obscene publications are declared as international crimes and have been made matters of international concern ...' They proposed that the General Assembly 'recommend' that 'genocide and related offences should be dealt with by national legislations in the same way as other international crimes such as piracy, trade in women, children and slaves, and others'.[109] Known as universal jurisdiction, it is posited on the fact that the State where genocide takes place will be unwilling to bring perpetrators to justice, presumably because the State itself is complicit in the crime. But there was no taste for the recognition of universal jurisdiction. Reference to the concept was dropped from the final version of the 1946 General Assembly Resolution,[110] and the General Assembly voted to exclude any mention of universal jurisdiction in the 1948 *Genocide Convention*.[111] Eichmann argued that this rejection of universal jurisdiction prevented the Israeli courts from proceeding.[112] But the District Court of Jerusalem said that even if the *Convention* did not allow for universal jurisdiction, it was authorised under customary international law.[113] Hannah Arendt didn't quarrel so much with Eichmann's legal argument, which was solid enough. She just thought that prosecuting Eichmann in Israel was unwise, and that it would be healthier if he were to stand trial in Europe, where the crimes had taken place, just as article VI required.

With rare exceptions, universal jurisdiction has always generated more heat than light. It has been a big disappointment in terms of actually holding perpetrators accountable. During the General Assembly debates France argued that the real solution to accountability for genocide lay with the establishment of a permanent international criminal court.[114] The terms of article VI suggest a treaty, which was not the mechanism used to establish the Yugoslavia and Rwanda Tribunals. When the proposed Yugoslavia Tribunal was being considered, the Secretary-General said that 'in the normal course of events' it would be established by treaty, but that this seemed unworkable, given the urgency of the project and the unlikelihood that the States concerned would sign up.[115] In fact, the treaty court for the prosecution of genocide took nearly a decade longer to establish. On 17 July 1998, the Rome Statute of the International Criminal Court was adopted, following a five-week diplomatic conference. Sixty ratifications or accessions were required for the Statute to enter into force, a target that was far more attainable than most observers ever expected. Within less than four years, nearly 70 States had joined the Court. Mexico's ratification of the *Rome Statute* in October 2005 brought the number to 100.

There is already an abundant literature on the International Criminal Court, much of it authored by participants in the process of adopting the treaty and establishing the institution.[116] These essentially legalistic accounts actually blend traditional analysis with a fair dose of anecdote. It is a principle of law that the *travaux préparatoires* of a treaty may be considered by a court as an aid to interpretation, the idea being to construe ambiguous provisions in a way that takes into account the intent of their drafters. Given that the *Rome Statute* is a tissue of diplomatic compromises, there is no shortage of ambiguity, much of it quite intentional. Those who helped draft the treaty argue that it should be interpreted in a manner consistent with what they wanted the text to mean. Strictly speaking, this is not resort to *travaux préparatoires* at all. Nevertheless, it seems likely that partial recollections and fading memories of the 1998 Rome Conference will influence the interpretation of the *Rome Statute* for many years to come, especially given that several of the negotiators themselves managed to secure election as judges in the first round of judicial selection.

The International Criminal Court can prosecute three categories of 'core crime', genocide, crimes against humanity and war crimes, with the future prospect of aggression being included. Indications within the *Rome Statute* suggest a hierarchy, with the crime of genocide at its apex. Clearly, the International Criminal Court is the institution contemplated by article VI of the 1948 Genocide Convention. Its effectiveness as a deterrent is unproven; its contribution to peace, national reconciliation and the determination of historical truth is more a matter of faith than of science. Nevertheless, at least one recent study points to a quite measurable decline in deaths as a result of armed conflict over the past decade or so.[117] Assuming the quantitative data are reasonably accurate, the question that arises is how this decline is to be explained. Perhaps the growing attention to criminal prosecution for perpetrators of genocide and other serious crimes of a similar nature provides part of the answer.

Notes

1. P. N. Drost, *Genocide, United Nations Legislation on International Criminal Law* (Leyden: A.W. Sythoff, 1959).
2. Although a State plan or policy would seem to be inherent in the crime of genocide, courts have held that it is not in fact an element of the crime. There is no reference to State plan or policy in the definition of genocide found in the Convention. See: *Prosecutor* v. *Jelisić* (Case No. IT-95-10-A), Judgment, 5 July 2001, para. 48.
3. C. K. Hall, 'The First Proposal for a Permanent International Criminal Court', *International Review of the Red Cross*, 333 (1998), 57.
4. English translation quoted in: United Nations War Crimes Commission, *History of the United Nations War Crimes Commission and the Development of the Laws of War* (London: His Majesty's Stationery Office, 1948), p. 35.
5. Quoted in V. N. Dadrian, 'Genocide as a Problem of National and International Law: The World War I Armenian Case and Its Contemporary Legal Ramifications', *Yale Journal of International Law*, 14 (1989), 228.
6. D. Lloyd George, *The Truth About the Peace Treaties*, Vol. I (London: Victor Gollancz, 1938), pp. 93–114. For a discussion of the project, see: 'Question of International Criminal Jurisdiction', UN Doc. A/CN.4/15, paras. 6–13; H. S. Levie, *Terrorism in War, The Law of War Crimes* (New York: Oceana, 1992), pp. 18–36; 'First report on the draft Code of Offences against the Peace and Security of Mankind, by Mr. Doudou Thiam, Special Rapporteur', UN Doc. A/CN.4/364, paras. 7–23.
7. Lloyd George, *The Truth About the Peace Treaties*, pp. 93–114.
8. Ibid., p. 93.
9. Ibid., p. 96.
10. S. P. Tillman, *Anglo-American Relations at the Paris Peace Conference of 1919* (Princeton, NJ: Princeton University Press, 1961), p. 312.
11. *Violations of the Laws and Customs of War, Reports of Majority and Dissenting Reports of America and Japanese Members of the Commission of Responsibilities, Conference of Paris, 1919* (Oxford: Clarendon Press, 1919), p. 39.
12. Ibid., p. 48.
13. Ibid., p. 25.
14. Dadrian, 'Genocide as a Problem', 278.
15. G. Goldberg, *The Peace to End Peace, The Paris Peace Conference of 1919* (New York: Harcourt, Brace & World: 1969), p. 151.
16. A. Walworth, *Wilson and His Peacemakers, American Diplomacy at the Paris Peace Conference, 1919* (New York: W. W. Norton, 1986), pp. 214–15, at p. 216. Also Tillman, *Anglo-American Relations*, p. 313.
17. A. S. Link, ed., *The Papers of Woodrow Wilson*, Vol. 56 (Princeton, NJ: Princeton University Press, 1987), p. 531.

18. *Treaty of Peace between the Allied and Associated Power and Germany* ('Treaty of Versailles'), [1919] TS 4. There were similar penal provisions in the related peace treaties: *Treaty of St. Germain-en-Laye,* [1919] TS 11, art. 173; *Treaty of Neuilly-sur-Seine,* [1920] TS 5, art. 118; *Treaty of Trianon,* (1919) 6 LNTS 187, art. 15.
19. Goldberg, *The Peace to End Peace,* p. 151.
20. *German War Trials, Report of Proceedings before the Supreme Court in Leipzig* (London: His Majesty's Stationery Office, 1921), p. 19. Also: 'Question of International Criminal Jurisdiction, Report by Ricardo J. Alfaro, Special Rapporteur', UN Doc. A/CN.4/15 and Corr. 1, para. 9.
21. J. F. Willis, *Prologue to Nuremberg: The Politics and Diplomacy of Punishing War Criminals of the First World War* (Westport, CT: Greenwood Press, 1982); S. Glueck, *War Criminals. Their Prosecution and Punishment* (New York: Knopf, 1944).
22. United Nations War Crimes Commission, *History of the United Nations War Crimes Commission and the Development of the Laws of War* (London: His Majesty's Stationery Office, 1948), p. 48.
23. Link, ed., *The Papers of Woodrow Wilson,* Vol. 56, p. 534.
24. Judgment in case of Lieutenants Dithmar and Boldt, Hospital Ship 'Llandlovery Castle', A.J. 95/21, b.J. 585/20., IX. 1112/21, in German War Trials. Report of Proceedings before the Supreme Court in Leipzig, Presented to Parliament by Command of His Majesty (London: His Majesty's Stationary Office, 1921), pp. 45–57.
25. Dadrian, 'Genocide as a Problem', 282.
26. FO 371/4174/118377 (folio 253), cited in ibid.
27. Ibid.
28. FO 371/4173/53352 (folios 192–3), cited in ibid., pp. 282–3.
29. Dadrian, 'Genocide as a Problem', 284.
30. Ibid., 285.
31. FO 371/4174/156721 (folios 523–4), cited in ibid., 286.
32. FO 371/6500, W.2178, appendix A (folios 385-118, 386-119), cited in ibid., 287.
33. Dadrian, 'Genocide as a Problem', 288–9.
34. Ibid., 293–317; also V. N. Dadrian, 'The Turkish Military Tribunal's Prosecution of the Author's of the Armenian Genocide: Four Major Court-Martial Series', *Holocaust & Genocide Studies,* 11 (1997), 28.
35. Cited in Dadrian, 'Genocide as a Problem', 307.
36. Ibid., 310–15.
37. [1920] UKTS 11, DeMartens, *Recueil général des traités,* 99, 3e série, 12, 1924, p. 720 (French version).
38. E. Schwelb, 'Crimes Against Humanity', *British Yearbook of International Law,* 23 (1946), 182.
39. Ibid.
40. K. Hollaway, *Modern Trends in Treaty Law* (London: Stevens & Sons, 1967), pp. 60–1.
41. *Treaty of Lausanne Between Principal Allied and Associated Powers and Turkey,* (1923) 28 LNTS 11.
42. R. Lemkin, *Axis Rule in Occupied Europe: Laws of Occupation, Analysis of Government, Proposals for Redress* (Washington, DC: Carnegie Endowment for World Peace, 1944), p. 79.
43. 'Totally Unofficial' [unpublished autobiography of Raphael Lemkin in the Raphael Lemkin Papers, New York Public Library], in United States of America, *Hearing Before the Committee on Foreign Relations, United States Senate, March 5, 1985* (Washington, DC: U.S. Government Printing Office, 1985), p. 204.

44. A. J. Hobbins, ed., *On the Edge of Greatness, The Diaries of John Humphrey, First Director of the United Nations Division of Human Rights*, Vol. I, 1948–1949 (Montreal: McGill University Libraries, 1994), p. 30.
45. J. P. Humphrey, *Human Rights and the United Nations: A Great Adventure* (Dobbs Ferry, NY: Transnational, 1984), p. 54.
46. United Nations War Crimes Commission, *History of the United Nations War Crimes Commission and the Development of the Laws of War* (London: His Majesty's Stationery Office, 1948).
47. *Report of Robert H. Jackson, United States Representative to the International Conference on Military Trials* (Washington, DC: U.S. Government Printing Office, 1949).
48. There are several monographs describing the great trial, among them: R. E. Conot, *Justice at Nuremberg* (New York: Harper & Row, 1983); E. Davidson, *The Trial of the Germans* (New York: Macmillan, 1966); A. Tusa and J. Tusa, *The Nuremberg Trial* (New York: Atheneum, 1984).
49. T. Taylor, *The Anatomy of the Nuremberg Trials* (New York: Alfred A. Knopf, 1992).
50. For a recent and quite sympathetic account of this trial, see T. Maga, *Judgment at Tokyo, The Japanese War Crimes Trials* (Lexington, KY: University of Kentucky Press, 2001).
51. M. C. Bassiouni, 'From Versailles to Rwanda in Seventy-Five Years: The Need to Establish a Permanent International Criminal Court', *Harvard Human Rights Journal*, 10 (1997), 24.
52. L. Arbour, 'Crimes against Women under International Law', *Berkeley Journal of International Law*, 21 (2003), 202; G. J. Simpson, 'War Crimes: A Critical Introduction', in *The Law of War Crimes*, eds. T. L. H. McCormack and G. J. Simpson (The Hague: Kluwer Law, 1997), pp. 1–11; R. H. Minear, *Victor's Justice: The Tokyo War Crimes Trial* (Princeton, NJ: Princeton University Press, 1971).
53. See the opinions of Judge Pal and Judge Röling: *United States of America et al.* v. *Araki et al.*, (1981) 21 *Tokyo War Crimes Trial*. See: E. S. Kopelman, 'Ideology and International Law: The Dissent of the Indian Justice at the Tokyo War Crimes Trial', *New York University Journal of International Law and Policy*, 23 (1991), 373.
54. D. Irving, *Nuremberg, The Last Battle* (London: Focal Point, 1996).
55. R. J. Evans, *Lying About Hitler, History, Holocaust and the David Irving Trial* (New York: Basic Books, 2001). On this trial, see: D. D. Guttenplan, *The Holocaust on Trial* (New York: W. W. Norton, 2001).
56. D. Bloxham, *Genocide on Trial, War Crimes Trials and the Formation of Holocaust History and Memory* (Oxford: Oxford University Press, 2001).
57. On the elaborate United States programme, see: F. M. Buscher, *The U.S. War Crimes Trial Program in Germany, 1946–1955* (Westport, CT: Greenwood Press, 1989); J. M. Greene, *Justice at Dachau, The Trials of an American Prosecutor* (New York: Broadway Books, 2003). On the half-hearted Canadian effort, see P. Brode, *Casual Slaughters and Accidental Judgments, Canadian War Crimes Prosecutions 1944–1948* (Toronto: University of Toronto Press, 1997).
58. *United States of America* v. *Alstötter et al.* ('Justice trial'), (1948) 6 Law Reports of the Trials of the War Criminals 1, 3 Trials of the War Criminals 1 (United States Military Tribunal).
59. C. Kohl, *The Maiden and the Jew, The Story of a Fatal Friendship in Nazi Germany* (Hanover, NH: Steerforth Press, 2004).
60. H. Arendt, *Eichmann in Jerusalem, A Report on the Banality of Evil* (New York: Penguin Books, 1994).
61. J. Robinson, *And the Crooked Shall be Made Straight* (New York: Macmillan, 1965).

62. H. Yablonka, *The State of Israel vs Adolf Eichmann* (New York: Schocken Books, 2004).
63. K. Mann, 'Hearsay Evidence in War Crimes Trials', in *War Crimes in International Law*, eds. Y. Dinstein and M. Tabory (The Hague: Martinus Nijhoff, 1996), pp. 321–49.
64. M. Kremnitzer, 'The Demjanjuk Case', in ibid., pp. 351–77.
65. H. J. De Nike, J. Quigley and K. J. Robinson, eds., *Genocide in Cambodia, Documents from the Trial of Pol Pot and Ieng Sary* (Philadelphia, PA: University of Pennsylvania Press, 2000). On subsequent attempts by the international community to ensure that Khmer Rouge leaders would be prosecuted, see T. Fawthrop and H Jarvis, *Getting Away with Genocide? Elusive Justice and the Khmer Rouge Tribunal* (London: Pluto Press, 2004).
66. For Thatcher, see her television interview of 1 September 1990: *British Yearbook of International Law*, 61 (1990), 602; M. Weller, 'When Saddam is brought to court ...', *The Times* (3 September 1990). For Bush, see: *US Department of State Dispatch*, Vol. I, 8 (22 October 1990), 205; *US Department of State Dispatch*, Vo. I, 11 (12 November 1990), 260. Also: L. R. Beres, 'Iraqi Crimes and International Law: The Imperative to Punish', *Denver Journal of International Law & Policy*, 21 (1993), 335; idem., 'Prosecuting Iraqi Crimes: Fulfilling the Expectations of International Law After the Gulf War', *Dickinson Journal of International Law*, 10 (1992), 425; idem., 'Toward Prosecution of Iraqi Crimes Under International Law: Jurisprudential Foundations and Jurisdictional Choices', *California Western International Law Journal*, 22 (1991), 127; idem., 'Iraqi Crimes During and After the Gulf War: The Imperative Response of International Law', *Loyola Los Angeles International and Comparative Law Journal*, 15 (1993), 675.
67. Weller, 'When Saddam is brought to court ...'.
68. E. Sciolino, 'U.S. Names Figures it Wants Charged with War Crimes', *New York Times* (17 December 1992), 1.
69. An excellent historical account of international efforts to prosecute the crime of aggression was produced by the United Nations Secretariat for the International Criminal Court in the context of ongoing work aimed at defining the concept. See: 'Historical review of developments relating to aggression', UN Doc. PCNICC/2002/WGCA/L.1.
70. English translation in *The Path to The Hague* (The Hague: ICTY, 2001), pp. 43–5.
71. N. Stone, 'Dubrovnik: the Case for a War Crime Trial – Why not Restore the Nuremberg Tribunal?', *The Guardian* (13 November 1991).
72. For Badinter's personal account, see *The Path to The Hague*, pp. 86–7.
73. P. Hazen, *La justice face à la guerre, De Nuremberg à La Haye* (Paris: Stock, 2000), p. 37.
74. Ibid., p. 38.
75. Ibid., p. 39.
76. P. Akhavan, 'Punishing War Crimes in the Former Yugoslavia: A Critical Juncture for the New World Order', *Human Rights Quarterly*, 15 (1993), 265–8.
77. 'The Situation of Human Rights in the Territory of the Former Yugoslavia', CHR Res. 1992/S-1/1, para. 2.
78. 'The Situation of Human Rights in the Territory of the former Yugoslavia', CHR Res. 1992/S-2/1, para. 10.
79. 'Report of the Secretary-General Pursuant to Paragraph 2 of Security Council Resolution 808 (1993)', UN Doc. S/25704 (1993). A detailed comparison of the various drafts is provided in V. Morris & M. P. Scharf, *An Insider's Guide to the International Criminal Tribunal for the Former Yugoslavia: A Documentary History and Analysis* (New York: Transnational Publishers, 1995), vol. I, pp. 363–462.
80. UN Doc. S/RES/827 (1993).

81. P. Lewis, 'Disputes Hamper U.N. Drive For a War Crimes Tribunal', *New York Times* (9 September 1993), A-10.
82. UN Doc. S/RES/857 (1993).
83. UN Doc. S/RES/877 (1993).
84. UN Doc. S/RES/936 (1994).
85. R. J. Goldstone, *For Humanity: Reflections of a War Crimes Investigator* (New Haven, CT: Yale University Press, 2000).
86. Hazen, *La justice face à la guerre*.
87. M. P. Scharf, *Balkan Justice: The Story behind the First International War Crimes Trial since Nuremberg* (Durham, NC: Carolina Academic Press, 1997).
88. For example, J. Hagan, *Justice in the Balkans, Prosecuting War Crimes in the Hague Tribunal* (Chicago, IL: University of Chicago Press, 2003). There is also a novel inspired by the work of the Tribunal: P. B. Robinson, *The Tribunal* (New York: iUniverse, 2004).
89. A. Fatic, *Reconciliation via the War Crimes Tribunal?* (Aldershot: Ashgate, 2000).
90. 'Letter from the Permanent Representative of the United Republic of Tanzania to the United Nations addressed to the Secretary-General, transmitting the Peace Agreement signed at Arusha on 4 August 1993', UN Doc. A/48/824–S/26915 (1993).
91. S. Greenhouse, 'U.S., Having Won Changes, Is Set to Sign Law of the Sea', *New York Times* (1 July 1994), 1.
92. 'Letter Dated 28 September 1994 From the Permanent Representative of Rwanda to the United Nations Addressed to the President of the Security Council', UN Doc. S/1994/1115.
93. UN Doc. S/PV.3453, p. 14 (1994).
94. P. Smerdon, 'PM Paints Bleak View of Rwanda', *The Guardian* (9 August 1994), 11; B. Crossette, 'Rwanda Asks Quick Start of Tribunal', *New York Times* (9 October 1994), 19; D. Beresford, 'Rwanda Dead "Need Justice"; General Warns Peace is Impossible Unless the Killers are Brought before the Courts', *The Guardian* (24 September 1994), 17; V. Brittain, 'Rwanda Threatens to Bypass UN and Start Genocide Trials', *The Guardian* (14 September 1994), 10.
95. D. Shraga and R. Zacklin, 'The International Criminal Tribunal for Rwanda', *European Journal of International Law*, 7 (1996), 504.
96. 'U.N. Delays Vote On Rwanda Panel', *New York Times* (1 November 1994), 17; Raymond Bonner, 'Rwandans Divided on War-Crimes Plan', *New York Times* (2 November 1994), A-10; 'Major Obstacles Remain Over Court', *Reuters World Service* (6 November 1994).
97. More moderate members of the Rwandan regime felt they should accept the Security Council Resolution despite disagreement with some of the conditions, but apparently the hard line vice-president and military supremo Paul Kagame prevailed. See Bonner, 'Rwandans Divided on War-Crimes Plan'.
98. The Chinese representative said it was 'an incautious act to vote in a hurry on a draft resolution and statute that the Rwanda Government still finds difficult to accept'. UN Doc. S/PV.3453, p. 11 (1994).
99. P. J. Magnarella, *Justice in Africa: Rwanda's Genocide, Its Courts and the UN Criminal Tribunal* (Aldershot: Ashgate, 2000); K. Moghalu, *Rwanda's Genocide, The Politics of Global Justice* (Basingstoke: Palgrave Macmillan, 2005).
100. C. Onana, *Les secrets de la justice internationale, Enquêtes truquées sur le génocide rwandais* (Paris: Editions Duboiris, 2005).
101. *Prosecutor* v. *Tadić* (Case No. IT-94-1-T), Opinion and Judgment, 7 May 1997, paras. 56–179.

102. Ibid., para. 54
103. *Prosecutor* v. *Akayesu* (Case No. ICTR-96-4-T), Judgment, 2 September 1998, paras. 77–110.
104. *Prosecutor* v. *Dragan Nikolić* (Case No. IT-94-2-S), Sentencing Judgment, 18 December 2003, para. 3. Similarly, *Prosecutor* v. *Sikirica et al.* (Case No. IT-95-8-T), Judgment on Defence Motions to Acquit, 3 September 2001, para. 149.
105. *Prosecutor* v. *Dragan Nikolić* (Case No. IT-94-2-S), Sentencing Judgment, 18 December 2003, para. 122.
106. P. M. Wald, 'Judging War Crimes', *Chicago Journal of International Law*, 1 (2000), 195.
107. Ibid.
108. G. K. McDonald, 'Crimes of Sexual Violence: The Experience of the International Criminal Tribunal', *Columbia Journal of Transnational Law*, 39 (2000), 1.
109. UN Doc. A/BUR/50.
110. GA Res. 96(I).
111. UN Doc. A/C.6/SR.100.
112. *A.-G. Israel* v. *Eichmann*, (1968) 36 I. L. R. 5 (District Court, Jerusalem), para. 20.
113. Ibid., para. 22 et seq.
114. UN Doc. E/623/Add.1; UN Doc. E/AC.25/SR.7, p. 9; UN Doc. A/C.6/255.
115. 'Report of the Secretary-General Pursuant to Paragraph 2 of Security Council Resolution 808 (1993)', UN Doc. S/25704 (1993), paras. 19–20.
116. See, for example, the collection assembled by Roy Lee: R. Lee, ed., *The International Criminal Court, The Making of the Rome Statute, Issues, Negotiations, Results* (The Hague: Kluwer Law International, 1999). There are several essays along similar lines in: M. Politi and G. Nesi, eds, *The Rome Statute of the International Criminal Court, A Challenge to Impunity* (Aldershot: Ashgate, 2001); A. Cassese, P. Gaeta and J. R. W. D. Jones, *The Rome Statute of the International Criminal Court, A Commentary* (Oxford: Oxford University Press, 2002).
117. *Human Security Report 2005*.

II. Case Studies

10
Genocide in the Americas

Alfred A. Cave

Introduction

Although they often differ sharply on the numbers, scholars without exception now portray the European colonization of the Americas as a monumental, perhaps unprecedented, demographic catastrophe for the continents' indigenous peoples. Rejecting earlier estimates that held that the New World was sparsely populated in 1492, demographers now provide projections that, in their highest estimates, sometimes exceed 112,000,000.[1] There is general agreement that, whatever their precise pre-contact numbers, indigenous populations within a century after contact were reduced by 90% or more. There is agreement as well on the prime agent of that decimation: infectious diseases to which native peoples had no immunity. But it is also generally recognized that atrocities against native American peoples committed by the invader–colonizers also contributed to their population decline. Did those atrocities constitute genocide? On that question there has been disagreement and controversy.

At one extreme stands a group of scholars who argue that genocide on a massive and unprecedented scale was the primary characteristic of the history of colonization in the Americas. Perhaps the most outspoken and controversial member of this group is Ward Churchill. In *A Little Matter of Genocide* he declared that 'the American holocaust was and remains unparalleled, both in terms of its magnitude and in terms of the degree to which its ferocity was sustained over time not by one but by several participating groups.'[2] Elsewhere, Churchill wrote that the perpetrators of genocide against Indians anticipated 'the behavior and the logic that have come to be associated with Hitler's SS. They defined their enemy in purely racial terms, they understood war only in terms of the sheer annihilation of the racial enemy, and they engaged in war because of a combination of abstract conceptions of "progress" on the one hand, and a related desire for pure material gain on the other.'[3]

Another notable spokesman of this school is David E. Stannard. In his *American Holocaust*, Stannard took issue with those who refuse to call 'the near-total destruction of the Western Hemisphere's native people' genocide, on the grounds that it was primarily the 'inadvertent' but 'inevitable' result of epidemic disease. 'Although at times operating independently, for most of the long centuries of devastation that followed 1492, disease and genocide were interdependent forces acting dynamically – whipsawing their victims between plague and violence, each one feeding upon the other, and together driving countless numbers of entire ancient societies to the brink – and often over the brink – of total extermination.'[4] Tzvetan Todorov, in *The Conquest of America: The Question of the Other*, found substantial support for that view in the writings of a number of contemporary historians of the Spanish invasion of the Americas, among them Fr. Toribio Motolinia, a priest not particularly sympathetic to Indians or their culture. Motolinia described 'ten plagues' which decimated the indigenous population. Only two were outbreaks of infectious disease. The others were deliberate acts of abuse and murder perpetrated by the Spanish, and included famine induced by the destruction of crops, systematic beating, starvation and overwork of enslaved Indian labourers in fields and mines, and in numerous instances, indiscriminate sadistic killing, including the widespread practice of tossing Indian babies to ravenous dogs. Motolinia's account, dating from 1534, is but one of many hundreds of contemporary records of the genocidal behaviour of conquistadores and colonists occurring in virtually every area of the American continents and extending over several centuries. Todorov, who declared the genocide in the Americas unsurpassed in its scope, dedicated his book to 'the memory of a Mayan woman devoured by dogs'.[5]

Despite the evidence of extensive abuse of indigenous peoples by colonizers, some writers have denied the validity of the concept of genocide to the understanding of the colonization of America. Historian James Axtell, to cite a leading example, has declared that 'genocide ... is historically inaccurate as a description of the vast majority of encounters between Europeans and Indians. Certainly no European colonial government ever tried to exterminate all Indians as Indians, as a race, and you can count on one hand the authorized colonial attempts to annihilate even single tribes ... [T]he vast majority of settlers had no interest in killing Indians – who were much too valuable for trade and labor – and those who did took careful aim at temporary political or military enemies.' Axtell concludes that descendents of the colonizers need not feel any particular sense of 'moral onus' surrounding the deeds of their forbearers. While recognizing that some colonists did some very bad things, he assures his readers that 'only the rare, certifiable, homicidal maniac sought to commit "genocide" against the Indians.'[6]

Others have agreed with Axtell in challenging the use of the terms 'genocide' and 'holocaust' as descriptive of the encounters of Europeans and Native Americans. Some scholars of the Nazi Holocaust in particular have argued that for atrocities to merit the name of genocide, they must involve the full and sustained use of state power driven by an intention to achieve total racial extermination. The most notable spokesman for this viewpoint is Steven T. Katz, who maintains that 'the Holocaust ... the intentional murder of European Jewry during World War II, is historically and phenomenologically unique ... by virtue of the fact that never before has a state set out as a matter of intentional principle and actualized policy, to annihilate physically every man, woman and child belonging to a specific people.' Colonial policy makers in the Americas, by contrast, according to Katz, generally sought to protect Indian lives in time of peace, as they were needed as labourers, trading partners and military allies.[7]

It is apparent that at issue here is a question of definition. While there have been many efforts over the past half century to refine and focus definitions of genocide, the 1948 United Nations Convention on Genocide remains the sole authoritative international legal definition.[8] The Convention declares, in Article II, that

> Genocide means any of the following acts committed with the intent to destroy, in whole or in part, a national, ethnical, racial, or religious group as such:
>
> (a) Killing members of the group
> (b) Causing severe bodily or mental harm to members of the group
> (c) Deliberately inflicting on members of the group conditions of life calculated to bring about its physical destruction in whole or in part
> (d) Imposing measures intended to prevent births within the group
> (e) Forcibly transferring children of the group to another group.

Katz and other scholars who argue for the uniqueness of the Nazi Holocaust insist that we must define genocide in a far more narrow and exclusionary sense than the 1948 United Nations convention permits. Their critics argue that in so doing they minimize the sufferings of many victims of racial and ethnic hatreds. They have been faulted as well for not understanding the genocidal nature of the Nazi campaign to exterminate Gypsies, or the Turkish massacres of Armenians a quarter of a century earlier.[9] Those issues lie beyond the scope of this paper. Whatever the merits of the case for the Holocaust's uniqueness, the distinctions Katz and others have drawn between twentieth-century Nazis and European colonizers are nonetheless useful, as they put in sharp focus the inadequacy of generalizations about genocide. To award or deny the label does not explain the violence, or enable us to comprehend the horrors lying beyond the words. To characterize the processes through which Native American lives and cultures were degraded and destroyed as 'genocidal' may express proper moral indignation, but it does not necessarily help us understand the complex, multi-faceted and often contradictory patterns of inter-racial and inter-cultural interaction on colonial frontiers and within colonies in the Americas.

While examples of state-sponsored extermination of indigenous populations can be found in the records of every colonial powers in the Americas, they were, as Axtell maintains, not the rule and were aimed not at all Indians but at a limited number of specific tribal groups. For that reason, Axtell advises that the term 'genocide' ought not to be used in discussions of colonialism in the Americas. But these campaigns of extermination, however limited in scope, meet the United Nations definition of genocide in that they sought to 'destroy, in whole or in part a national, ethnical, racial or religious group as such.' Granted colonial powers did not explicitly target all Indians for extermination. But the wars they waged against specific Indian nations were often genocidal in effect. Moreover, the violence visited upon tribal peoples all too often came to be justified by the growing belief that the victims no longer deserved to exist as a people. The campaigns to subdue those peoples far exceeded any rational military logic, and often led to outright mass exterminations. Axtell's dismissal of those cases in which European colonizers sought to 'annihilate ... single tribes' as actions against 'temporary military or political enemies' misses the essential point. When the killing and/or enslavement of the enemy continued after the victim group ceased to constitute any physical threat to the conqueror, those actions were acts of genocide.

Genocide, under the United Nations definition, does not require the sanction of the state. Indian fatalities in American colonies were often the result of killing campaigns mounted by colonists in apparent defiance of the will of the authorities. Colonial laws invariably forbade the slaughter of Indians in time of peace, or the murder of 'friendly' Indians in time of war. But Indians frequently fell victim to murderous settlers, who only infrequently were punished for their crimes. Were those killings genocide? While some argue that they are better described as 'massacres', the negligence and even complicity of colonial administrations in failing to protect indigenous peoples indicates that the line dividing officially sanctioned genocide and indiscriminate genocidal private killing was often far from distinct. Thus it is appropriate that the United Nations definition of genocide does not require such a distinction.

Ideological roots of racial violence in the Americas

Rabbi Abraham Joshua Herschel has declared that 'Auschwitz was built not with stones, but words.'[10] As one recent scholarly study has noted, genocide is possible only if the 'victim group' has been portrayed 'as worthless, outside the web of mutual obligations, a threat to the people, immoral sinners, and/or sub-human.'[11] In providing a background for understanding the well-documented, unprovoked and extensive physical violence visited upon Native

Americans by both explorers and colonizers, the earliest historical accounts of the conquest and colonization of the Americas are telling. Among the most influential of the builders of verbal images of Indians was Peter Martyr, an Italian humanist resident in the Spanish court. His *Decades of the New World,* first published in its entirety in 1530, provided the first comprehensive history of the founding of the Spanish colonies in the Americas. In his characterizations of Native American peoples, readers found vivid word pictures of creatures bearing resemblance to humans in form, but lacking the social, moral and intellectual qualities of civilized beings. In a strangely ambivalent invocation of a 'Golden Age', the author portrayed some of those creatures as gentle folk who lived 'simply and innocently, without enforcement of laws, without quarreling, judges, and libels, content only to satisfy nature, without further vexation for knowledge of things to come.' But the innocent child of nature is not the dominant image of Indians conveyed in Peter Martyr's writings. Many of his Indians are vicious and bestial, given to cannibalism, devil worship, human sacrifice, sodomy and bestiality. Their wars, brutal and endless, gave ongoing expression to their essentially ferocious nature. Many lived like animals, without the trappings of civilization. Those who did erect elaborate cities and found monarchies gave the superficial appearance of being 'civilized', but revealed to the knowledgeable their depravity in the sacrifice of human captives on their high altars and in the cannibalizing of the victims' bodies. The overall emotional tenor of the *Decades* is conveyed in this description of some Indian captives whom Peter Martyr, an armchair traveller who never crossed the Atlantic, visited in Spain: 'There is no man able to behold them but that he shall feel his bowels grate with a certain horror, nature hath endowed them with so terrible a menacing and cruel aspect.'[12] These deformed and monstrous peoples might be human, but even if they were, they were clearly under the control of the Devil. Belief that the New World was Satan's realm was widespread among the Spanish, and among other European explorers and colonizers, from the early sixteenth century onwards.

Despite the efforts of Fr Bartolomé de las Casas and other dissenters to promote a more humane image of the peoples of the New World, the emphasis on Indian incapacity and depravity continued to dominate Spanish thought throughout the colonial era. Spanish intellectuals, intent upon resolving the question of the crown's right to occupy and subjugate the Americas, differed on various points, including the question of whether present Indian backwardness was the product of an inborn, unchangeable incapacity. The points of difference dividing commentators such as Las Casas, Vitoria and Acosta, who affirmed the Indians' basic humanity, from others such as Oviedo, Gomara and Sepulveda, who emphasized their brutish qualities, is by no means as wide as scholars once believed.[13] Sixteenth-century Spanish writers were generally agreed that Indians of the New World, while varying in levels of savagery and barbarism, lacked fully developed rational faculties and were therefore presently (or perhaps permanently) unable to construct and maintain civil societies in harmony with natural law. The hard-core critics of Indian life saw them as equivalent to Aristotle's 'slaves by nature', unworthy of freedom. Others, following Vitoria, affirmed that with proper tutelage and care, Indians could be prepared for freedom. While only a few denied their basic humanity, virtually all regarded Native Americans as inferior peoples living in cultures that were both backward and morally depraved. The sixteenth-century Spanish debates over Indian capacity would be replicated in varying forms by other European colonizers over the next few centuries. The images, in these debates, of Indians as intellectual inferiors and moral degenerates, provided support not only to those who justified their subjugation and dispossession, but on occasion, the extermination of those regarded as most savage.

Although in promoting the 'Black Legend' the English accused the Spanish of committing atrocities against the Indians in their charge,[14] they nonetheless embraced uncritically the most negative of the Spanish characterizations of the victims.[15] The most popular English treatise on geography, published in multiple editions in the late sixteenth and throughout the seventeenth century, included these descriptions of Indians: 'a people naked and uncivil ... given to sodomy, incest, and all kinds of adultery', to 'adoration of devils', 'blind witchcraft' and 'intercourse with foul spirits'. The author concluded that while Indians appeared to possess 'reason and the shape of men', their intellectual and moral deficiencies required that they be kept under the tutelage of European Christians.[16] Early chroniclers and historians of England's first colonial ventures portrayed the New World as the Devil's realm and Indians as his slaves. Through the good offices of Christians, English writers affirmed, some might be delivered from that bondage and be led into truth and salvation. But many, perhaps most, were believed to be beyond hope. Sir Walter Raleigh, in the world history he wrote in the Tower of London, declared that all of the peoples of the Americas, North and South, had 'been brought by the devil under his fearful servitude.'[17] In his histories of the colony founded at Jamestown in 1607, Captain John Smith maintained that had God not intervened to soften the hearts of the satanic Indians, and persuaded them to defy their master the Devil and send food to aid the starving colony, the English in Virginia would have all died in agony at the hands of savages skilled in torture.[18] Smith's emphasis on providential intervention was echoed by numerous later historians of England's early colonial ventures. Governor William Bradford, in his history of the Plymouth colony, related that, upon first sighting the Pilgrims, the Indians of Cape Cod gathered in 'a dark and dismal swamp' and sought, through days of fiendish conjurations, to raise the Devil and hurl him against the Christians. But through God's intervention, His Elect remained safe. The Devil was kept at bay, and the Indians contrary to their true nature constrained to offer their friendship and aid to the newcomers.[19] Another Plymouth Governor, Edward Winslow, struck the same note in a report published in London in 1624. Had God in His mercy not 'filled the hearts of the savages with fear and astonishment', he wrote, the colony would quickly have fallen victim 'to their many plots and treacheries'.[20]

English belief in God's protection of their New World ventures was not limited to His role in restraining Indian savagery. They also maintained that the epidemic diseases which afflicted the indigenous populations soon after first contact were both a judgement against sinful Indians and an act of kindness to God's own Elect. By killing Indians He was making room for the colonizers. Thomas Hariot, the chronicler of Sir Walter Raleigh's short lived Roanoke colony noted, in 1586, that whenever the English encountered any opposition, 'within a few day's departure from such a town, the people began to die very fast apace.' God, Hariot declared, was doing 'a special work ... for our sakes' by killing Indians.[21] Comparable views of epidemic disease as divine judgement against diabolical peoples echoed through the English colonies in the early seventeenth century. They found their fullest expression in the writings of New England's Puritan historians. Edward Johnson, official historian of the Massachusetts Bay Colony, rejoiced 'at the wondrous work of the great Jehovah ... wasting the natural inhabitants with death's stroke'. By that means, the Almighty 'not only made room for his people to plant, but tamed the hearts of these barbarous Indians ... Thus did the Lord allay their quarrelsome spirits.'[22]

The early chronicles and histories of colonization are thus dominated by a world view that believed Indians to be slaves of the devil, regarded their way of life as not only primitive but depraved and diabolical, and saw Indian mortality from infectious diseases evidence as an act of God intended to clear the wilderness of evil and make room for God's own people. These writings provide important insights into the ideological roots of racial violence in the Americas.

Genocide in Virginia and New England in the early seventeenth century

The first large scale racial war in North America began at Jamestown in 1622. After a decade and a half of episodic warfare, uneasy co-existence and sporadic killings, marked by increasing conflict over land boundaries, the murder of the Powhatan Holy Man Nemattenew precipitated a surprise attack on the English settlements in Virginia. One third of the settlers perished. The response of the London-based Virginia Company was to order the settlers to mount an exterminatory war against the Powhatan Indians that was not to end until they 'were no longer a people'. The colony's Governor Edward Waterhouse was happy to comply. 'It is infinitely better', Waterhouse wrote, 'to have no heathen among us.'[23] The campaign to obliterate these particular 'heathen' was carried out with ruthless zeal. Settlers killed Powhatan tribesmen on sight. Over one-hundred Powhatans were murdered by poisoning at a dinner the English hosted, a dinner the Indians were told would lead to negotiations to end the war.[24] The tribe itself was driven out of the Virginia tidewater, as settlers complied with the 1624 resolution of the General Assembly that declared that 'the inhabitants of every corporation shall fall upon their adjoining savages.'[25] Greatly diminished in numbers, Powhatans found uncertain refuge in the interior. No historian doubts the brutality of the campaign against the Powhatans. But was it genocide? In the sense that the extermination of the Powhatan people was Virginia's objective, it is hard to answer 'no'. One scholar declares that had the early English settlers of Virginia been more numerous, they would have succeeded in satisfying their 'genocidal urges' by killing all of the Indians of Virginia.[26] Other writers, however, have argued that, despite the virulent anti-Indian rhetoric cited above, the Virginia colony's policy was never one of exterminatory war against all Indians. The English established and maintained friendly relations with several other tribes in the region, using them as trading partners and occasional military allies. The Virginia colonizers thus made a distinction between friendly and unfriendly Indians (or, as they would have it, pliant savages and vicious savages) that would reappear in other English and Anglo-American colonial areas over the centuries to come.[27] That recurrent distinction provided a rationale for genocidal actions aimed at, and officially limited to, specific presumably irreconcilably hostile groups but not at the entire Indian race. But it must be stressed once again that the singling out of any group for extermination or other specified forms of persecution based solely on group identity meets the legal definition of genocide as contained in the United Nations convention. Moreover, as we will demonstrate later, 'friendly' Indians were by no means exempted from long-term policies of subjugation and dispossession that were essentially genocidal in effect.

Among recent historians who debate the question of genocide in colonial America, the primary focus of attention has fallen, not on Virginia, but on New England, leading to a prolonged controversy over the nature of New England's first Indian war. For three centuries, beginning with the earliest Puritan accounts, historians generally portrayed the Pequots as a particularly aggressive, diabolical and dangerous tribe. Nineteenth-century historian Francis Parkman characterized Pequots as 'far worse than wolves or rattlesnakes'.[28] Alden T. Vaughan, writing in 1965, declared the tribe 'had incurred by its forced incursion into New England the enmity of its Indian neighbors and had won a notorious reputation for brutality'. The Pequot War, in Vaughan's view, was an admirable example of Indians and whites working together to deal decisively with a serious threat to their mutual security.[29]

Recent studies of Pequot history and culture have challenged the assumptions that for so long had been used by historians to justify, or at least explain, the

Puritan attack on them. Most writers now agree that the Pequots were not a real threat to the security of the English colonies in New England.[30] They do not agree, however, on the motivations underlying the English attack, with some seeing the war's origins in Puritan greed and expansionism, and others finding them in mutual cultural misunderstandings that led the Puritans to imagine a danger where none existed and Pequots to fail to perceive the probable consequences of their refusal to submit to English demands.[31] But there is no disagreement about the brutality of the Puritan campaign against the Pequots, a campaign marked by the deliberate burning alive of non-combatants in the assault on the Pequot village at Mystic, the summary execution of Pequot prisoners of war and the enslavement of their women and children. A number of scholars accordingly describe the Pequots as victims of genocide.[32]

In a provocative and controversial article published in 1991, Stephen Katz dissented, arguing that the campaign against the Pequots was a defensive war, not a genocide. Given the Pequot refusal to turn over to Puritan justice Indians suspected of killing Englishmen and their efforts to form an alliance with the Narragansetts, the English 'rightly felt, given their demographic vulnerability, that their very survival was threatened.' He acknowledges that in the course of the war the Puritans massacred non-combatants, sought to kill all adult male Pequots, enslaved other survivors and finally eliminated the Pequots as 'an independent polity'. But Katz argues that the enslavement of 'the remaining communal members – the elderly, the women, and the children – directly contradicts the imputation of any intent to commit *physical* genocide.' Countering the objection that under the United Nations resolution of 1948 such actions clearly were genocidal, Katz maintains that one should employ a 'more stringent use of the term' that defines genocide 'to mean an intentional action aimed at the complete physical elimination of a people'. Revisionist historians who termed the Pequot War 'genocidal' were, he suggested, trying to tap into 'the emotive power the notion has acquired because of its connection with Auschwitz.' Katz emphasizes that 'the number [of Pequots] killed probably totaled less than half the tribe.' Conceding, however, that Puritan measures against the Pequots were extreme, he concluded that the war might be described as an example of a 'cultural genocide' driven by a determination 'to eliminate the Pequot threat once and for all' by destroying its tribal identity. The Pequots, Katz conceded, probably were not the threat that the Puritans imagined, but their motive in attacking the tribe was self-defense and thus was not genocide.

In support of that conclusion, Katz challenged the commonplace portrayal of the massacre at Fort Mystic as genocidal. Rejecting the claim of Jennings and others that the slaughter of non-combatants there had been planned prior to the assault on the village, Katz characterized the Fort Mystic action as a spontaneous response to wartime conditions.[33] On this issue, the chronicles and histories of the war written by the Puritans themselves are of great value. The testimony of the English commanders at Mystic and of the historians who celebrated their victory tells us much about the Puritan mindset and permits us to make a judgement as to whether that mindset might be termed 'genocidal'. The Puritan writers, two of them officers who ordered the burning, made no apology and expressed no regret for the indiscriminate killing of Indian non-combatants. Instead, they represented their action as a righteous punishment of a people who, they argued, had mightily offended the Lord God. Even before the beginning of the campaign, as one Puritan historian recounted, clergy had demanded that the troops 'execute vengeance upon the heathen' by making 'the multitudes fall under your warlike weapons'.[34] That is the policy that was executed at Ft Mystic. The massacre there was a predictable outcome of the English perception of Indian adversaries. Captain John Underhill, commander of the Massachusetts Bay colony forces, admitted that both his Indian allies and the 'young soldiers' in the Puritan army were sickened by the slaughter, with some asking 'should not Christians have more mercy and compassion?' But Underhill took as his guide the military campaigns of King David in the Old Testament, and likened the Pequots to those enemies of God David slew. God in His anger allowed no compassion towards such people, 'but harrows them, and saws them, and puts them to the sword, and the terriblest death that may be.' As to the killing of innocent women and children, 'sometimes the Scripture declareth women and children must perish with their parents ... We had sufficient light from the word of God for our proceedings.'[35] Captain John Mason, the Connecticut colony's commander, portrayed God looking down on the burning village and laughing: 'his Enemies and the Enemies of his people to scorn making them as a fiery oven ... thus did the Lord God judge among the Heathen and filling the place with dead bodies.'[36] Later Puritan historians stressed the same note. Perhaps the most telling was Edward Johnson's strange report that the soldiers found it difficult to pierce the bodies of the Pequots with swords because 'the devil was in them.'[37] Puritan writers on the Pequot war leave us no reason to doubt that the Pequots were the victims of genocidal rage. Katz and others are correct in pointing out that New England's Puritan settlers did not plan the extermination of all Indians. But their identification of the Pequots, and later of other Indian tribes, as deserving of death or enslavement because of certain group characteristics (their imagined alliance with the devil, their presumed unusual treachery and brutality, etc.) certainly falls within most definitions of genocide. Neither Raphael Lemkin, who coined the term, nor the United Nations 1948 Convention on genocide foresaw the restriction of the term to the execution of a policy of total physical extermination.[38] The New England colonies at the end of the Pequot War systematically executed all Pequot warriors, and enslaved all others. Moreover, they demanded that their Indian allies do the same. No Pequot was set free.[39] These actions are a prime example of officially sanctioned genocide inflicting suffering on all of the members of a group because of their group affiliation.

The targeting of specific Indian groups and the use of extreme measures against their non-combatants as well as their warriors recurred throughout both the colonial era and the years of frontier settlement in the emergent American nation states. Ironically, some of the most powerful and warlike Indian nations were often spared. For example, both the Dutch and later the English enlisted the Iroquois as allies and trading partners. The Dutch, however, employed the veteran Indian killer John Underhill in campaigns of extermination against the more vulnerable and less useful Indians of the lower Hudson valley and Long Island. Understandably, some historians suspect that 'defensive' wars against the very vulnerable were really driven by little more than greed.[40] That is an over-simplification. Chalk and Jonassohn have proposed a typology of genocide that identifies four motives: elimination of a real or potential threat; spreading terror among real or potential enemies; acquiring economic wealth; and implementing a belief, theory or ideology.[41] Colonialist assaults on indigenous peoples were usually prompted by more than one of those motives, although it must be recognized that economic interests were often decisive in determining which groups would be the first to be targeted. In all areas, Native American groups which, for one reason or another, could not be integrated into the colonial economy were the most likely to be the earliest victims of genocide.

The mechanics of genocide in colonial America

The processes by which vulnerable indigenous peoples were driven from their lands or reduced to quasi-slavery were, in their effects, essentially genocidal. Some confusion on this point has been occasioned by the fact that the measures employed to subdue and dispossess indigenous peoples were seldom described initially as exterminatory. As we have seen, some writers have maintained that, in instances in which we lack clear evidence of intentionality to commit genocide, we ought not to describe the decimation of Native Americans and other victims of colonialism as genocide. But, as Tony Barta has argued, 'the appropriation of land' placed the colonizers in a relationship 'that implicitly rather than explicitly, in ways that were inevitable rather than intentional' fundamentally 'is a relationship of genocide'.[42] We need, as Barta emphasizes, to focus on the acts, not the stated intentions, of the expropriators. While the role of ideology in justifying and sustaining genocidal practices over the long term remains essential, the early processes of colonial subjugation of indigenous peoples contain the seeds of genocide even if the intention is usually not explicitly avowed. In understanding the origins of genocide, the emphasis on 'intent' contained in the United Nations declaration must not lead us to disregard the implications of policies genocidal in effect if not initially in avowed purpose.

Examination of the use by colonial regimes of brutal military measures often unfamiliar to European trained soldiers gives us some insight into the process by which this 'relationship of genocide' of which Barta speaks developed early in the occupation and appropriation of the territories of indigenous peoples. In their actions against resistant Indian tribes, both the French and the English in North America made use of scalp bounties that were first represented as necessary war measures but were essentially genocidal in effect and were later celebrated as such.[43] Europeans turned a ritual war practice observed by some, although not all, Native American peoples into an indiscriminate killing process, scalping not only warriors but non-combatants as well. Colonial governments paid bounties for scalps, offering payment on graduated scales that offered the most reward for adult males, but also compensated the killers of women and children at lower rates. The first bounty system was probably established by the French, who paid for the scalps of hostile Indians killed in Maine in 1688. New England relied originally on payments for body parts, usually heads or hands, demanding that their Indian allies bring in such grisly evidence that they had killed enemy Indians as ordered. In 1694, however, the Massachusetts General Court enacted a scalp bounty, and soon the colony was paying Indian killers 100 pounds for the scalp of male Indians over 10 years of age, 40 for women and 20 for children and infants.[44] These were attractive incentives, as the annual income of a New England farmer averaged around 25 pounds a year.[45] The practice soon spread to all other British colonies. Scalp taking became a popular and lucrative business venture. A Maine clergyman recorded in his journal in 1757 that he had received over 165 pounds as 'my part of the scalp money'.[46]

Enactment of scalp bounties intensified frontier violence and victimized non-combatants. Bounty hunters usually did not discriminate between children and adults, or between men and women, and sometimes murdered friendly Indians as well. To cite but one incident out of many, the scalping in Virginia in 1759 of several Cherokee warriors returning from service on the British side in the war with France helped trigger an Anglo-Cherokee war.[47] Scalping continued during and after the American Revolution and:

> turned, if anything, more sadistic and macabre, as when Ranger Colonel George Rogers Clark, during his celebrated siege of Vincennes in 1779, ordered his men to slowly scalp sixteen living captives – both Indian and white – in full view of the English garrison. The same year, during the Sullivan campaign against the Seneca, soldiers of the Continental Army weren't content with merely scalping their foes, living or dead. Not uncommonly they skinned them from the hips down in order to make leggings from the tanned 'hides'.[48]

In the nineteenth century, scalp bounties played a role in 'the winning of the west'. To cite only a few examples, in Dakota territory, Sioux who resisted dispossession and refused internment on reservations might be killed by bounty hunters, who received $200 for their scalps.[49] Texas and California offered lavish scalp bounties and thereby encouraged indiscriminate Indian killing. When California failed to renew scalp bounty legislation, private business groups stepped in to offer on-going financial support to Indian killers.[50] Texas maintained its official scalp bounties through the 1880s, leading one historian to comment that whites in Texas, Anglo and Hispanic alike, 'had no more regard for the life of an Indian than they had of a dog, sometimes less'.[51]

Another innovation in American racial wars was the creation of special, irregular ranger units that struck by stealth deep in enemy territory, taking few prisoners and inflicting maximum pain.[52] Such tactics were employed and perfected in New England during King Philip's (Metacom's) War by Captain Benjamin Church. Called out of retirement to fight Indians again during King William's War, Church exposed the genocidal nature of his activities in his description of a raid on a Christian (Catholic) Indian village in New Brunswick. Finding the men absent from the village, Church related that his rangers proceeded to club to death all the women and children they had left behind.[53] Better known are the exploits of Robert Rogers, whose most celebrated action during the French and Indian war was a raid on the Indian village of St Francis in Quebec in which, Roberts reported, his rangers killed around 200, most of whom were non-combatants.[54] Numerous witnesses to rangers' actions throughout the colonial era testified that these units killed indiscriminately. Typical is the Reverend Gideon Johnson's complaint in 1711 that Carolinians attacking Tuscarora villages did not make 'the least distinction between the guilty and the innocent ... it is vain to represent to them the cruelty and injustice of such a procedure.'[55]

Both ranger units and militia forces sometimes deliberately murdered neutral or allied Indians as well as hostiles. In the few cases in which their officers were called to account for such atrocities, punishment, if any, was invariably light. The massacre of Indian Moravian converts at Gnadenhutten and the murder of several pro-American Delaware and Shawnee chiefs, all perpetrated by American militia officers during the Revolution are prime examples. The mentality that justified such violence was exposed in the comment of frontier general George Rogers Clark who, after tomahawking five Indian captives during the siege of Vincennes in 1779, boasted that 'he would never spare a man, woman or child of them on whom he could lay his hands.'[56] Clark's sentiment was widely shared, and led to numerous atrocities. The *Kentucky Gazette* on 15 March 1788, to cite an example, reported that settlers planned to leave poison scattered in abandoned houses, hoping that Indians attempting to use or loot the premises would receive lethal doses. Whites would be warned, by signs Indians could not read, not to enter.[57] Listening to such stories, an English visitor a few years later remarked of Indians that 'nothing is more common to hear' in America 'than talk of extirpating them from the face of the earth, men, women and children.'[58]

The 1864 massacre perpetrated by Colorado militia Colonel John M. Chivington offers a particularly blatant example of the persistence of that attitude. Chivington, an erstwhile Methodist preacher, was a rabid Indian hater who demanded the killing of infants on the grounds that 'nits make lice'. During the Colorado Indian war, Chivington and his men fell upon a Cheyenne encampment that was in fact at peace with the United States. They killed, scalped and mutilated, cutting out Cheyenne genitalia for hatbands and tobacco pouches. The Sand Creek massacre was, and remains, controversial. Chivington enjoyed the encouragement and support of Colorado's territorial governor, but his actions horrified federal official concerned with Indian pacification. Three federal investigations condemned Chivington, but when a United States Senator, speaking to a Denver audience, suggested 'civilizing' the western Indians as an alternative to killing, he was shouted down by screams of 'exterminate them'.[59] Theodore Roosevelt, one of the most scholarly of the Indian haters, declared Chivington's massacre 'as righteous and beneficial a deed as ever took place on the frontier'.[60] While most historical investigations of the circumstances of the massacre fault Chivington, some writers, remarkably, still agree with Roosevelt.[61] The Sand Creek massacre was but one of many genocidal assaults on Indian villages during the western Indian wars. A California militia officer captured the spirit of those campaigns in 1849 when he described a Pomo village assaulted by his unit as 'a perfect slaughter pen'.[62]

Warfare against Indians commonly utilized 'burnt earth' tactics, sometimes called 'feedfight', intended to destroy the Indian subsistence economy and produce mass starvation. One notable example is Colonel James Grant's assault on the Cherokee in 1761 which left 5,000 without shelter or food.[63] Another is General James Sullivan's campaign against Iroquois who supported the British during the Revolutionary war, a campaign that laid waste to hundreds of square miles of once prosperous country.[64] 'Mad Anthony' Wayne's victory at Fallen Timbers in 1794 was indecisive, but his subsequent destruction of Indian villages and fields forced the Miami, the Shawnees and their allies to their knees.[65] In the western Indian wars of the following century, the destruction of the buffalo herds brought the Great Plains nations to the edge of starvation and facilitated their dispossession and confinement on reservations.[66]

Perhaps the most extreme measures of colonial genocide were experiments in germ warfare. In 1763, two Delaware chiefs visiting Fort Pitt to initiate peace discussions were given a present: two blankets. The receipt they signed, still on file, tells us that the purpose was 'to Convey the Smallpox to the Indians'. The order to do so came from the British commanding General, Lord Amherst, who had directed his subordinates to infect the Indians 'by means of blankets, as well as to try Every other method that can serve to extirpate this Execrable Race'.[67] As one historian of Pontiac's uprising notes, 'it is plain that Indians were well beyond European laws of war' which strictly forbade killing by poison.[68] It is not clear whether this was the first attempt or whether it was successful. We do know that there were later efforts to use biological agents against Indians. For example, a California newspaper in 1853 noted approvingly that local settlers, in addition to knifing and shooting Indians, were taking steps to infect them with smallpox.[69] More research needs to be done on this aspect of genocide on the western frontier.

Indian killing on frontiers and elsewhere

Colonial and national governments in both North and South America by law and decree sought to protect the lives of peaceful Indians. One of the most persistent themes in public records is complaints that efforts to make that protection a reality were ineffective, particularly in frontier regions. Often those efforts were half-hearted. But even with the best of intentions, authorities everywhere soon found their ability to restrain murderous whites driven by greed or racial hatred or both quite limited. As to the British colonies, here again contemporary historical literature is revelatory. Anti-Indian violence was not always limited to the backcountry. The writings of Daniel Gookin, the Massachusetts Bay Colony superintendent of Indian affairs, make clear his conviction that the Indian supporters of King Philip were objects of divine wrath because of their failure to embrace the Gospel. But Gookin was appalled by the clamour in Boston to kill Indian converts to Christianity as well. The genocidal fury directed at the 'praying Indians' was partly deflected, but many of their number died prematurely as a result of their internment on a barren island in Boston harbour.[70] Other Indian groups over the years were even less fortunate, falling victim to Indian haters, some of whom wore militia uniforms. As New England authorities sought to restrain indiscriminate anti-Indian violence during Metacom's War, a rebel force of Indian haters in Virginia under the command of Nathaniel Bacon deposed the royal governor, William Berkeley, who had restricted the scope of a frontier Indian war. Bacon, once regarded as a precursor or 'torchbearer' of the American Revolution for his opposition to royal authority, is now, thanks to the path breaking work of historian Wilcomb Washburn, seen as an advocate and perpetrator of genocide. Bacon's forces killed no hostile Indians on the frontier, but before their repression did rob and murder peaceful Indian communities within the colony.[71]

While Indian-hating populist elements elsewhere did not overthrow governments, those who governed often testified that their authority did not extend to the punishment of Indian killers. When a rum-seller named Frederick Stump was jailed in Carlisle, Pennsylvania, in 1768 for murdering ten Iroquois, he was freed by a mob and remained at liberty.[72] Some years later, Pennsylvania's governor declared that 'no jury in any of our frontier counties will ever condemn a man for killing an Indian. They do not consider it in the light of murder, but as a meritorious act.'[73] Mob action also freed several Indian killers in Virginia in 1767, leading General Thomas Gage to complain that the colonists generally were resolved never to punish a white man for killing an Indian.[74] After independence, territorial Governor Harrison of Indiana reported to the legislature that the task of keeping peace with the Indians was made difficult by the refusal of juries to convict 'even one of the many people who have committed murder on their people'.[75] President George Washington complained that 'frontier Settlers' too often believed that killing an Indian 'is no crime at all'.[76]

In the following century, western political leaders frequently exacerbated the problem by demagogic pronouncements against Indians. In California in the early 1850s, state officials opposed the efforts of federal agents who sought to negotiate treaties reserving some land for the state's surviving Indian groups. They secured the defeat of those treaties in the United States Senate. While some white Californians were eager to make use of Indians as slave labour, two governors advocated extermination as the solution to the 'Indian problem'. One, Peter Barnett, declared in 1851 that 'a war of extermination will continue to be waged ... until the Indian race is extinct.'[77] Western newspapers often called for Indian killing. 'Extermination', declared the San Francisco *Bulletin* in 1851, 'is the quickest and cheapest remedy' to conflicts between settlers and natives peoples.[78] Punishment of those who responded to such genocidal exhortations was often impeded not only by popular sentiment but by state laws denying Indians the right to testify in courts against whites.

How many Indians fell victim to murderous frontiersmen and other Indian haters? We will probably never know. In 1894, the United States Census Bureau estimated that between 1775 and 1890 more than 8,500 Indians were killed by individuals on their own initiative. Some authorities believe the real total was far, far higher, perhaps exceeding 100,000.[79] Some argue that only state-conducted killing should be termed genocide; but the many instances of tacit complicity by authorities who failed to protect Indians argue against that exclusion which, as we noted earlier, is not required in the United Nations declaration against genocide. Penalties for killing Indians, when imposed at all, were often ridiculously lenient. Consider, for example, the case of a sixteenth-century Indian woman burned to death in her hut by a Spaniard angered when she resisted his efforts to rape her. The Spanish governor fined the rapist/murderer five pesos![80] Similar stories can be found in every colony in the Americas.

The question of cultural genocide

In response to pressure from the United States and other major powers, the United Nations in its 1948 Convention rejected draft language that would have explicitly recognized *cultural genocide* as a crime, despite evidence that assaults on indigenous customs and mores not infrequently had the effect of meeting the standard of 'inflicting severe bodily or mental harm on members of a group'. For native American peoples, it is well documented that acute personal disorientation, depression, illness, alcoholism, suicide and consequent high mortality rates were often outcomes of presumably benevolent official programmes intended to 'civilize' them. The physical violence of Indian haters was only one aspect of the suffering of indigenous peoples under colonial rule. Preoccupation with biological extermination must not be permitted to deflect attention from the sometimes well-meaning but, nonetheless, frequently lethal efforts of the colonizers to protect and uplift their charges through changing and ultimately eliminating their cultures.

For the Americas, the most thorough investigations of increases in the death rate of peoples whose cultures were targeted for elimination have focused on the Spanish missions in upper California from their founding through their closure in the nineteenth century. Some of the first published evidence was anecdotal, but since the mid-twentieth century a number of careful statistical studies have left no room to doubt that the missions were indeed lethal places. The Spanish effort to extirpate native religion and culture, win converts and harness Indian labour through rigorous discipline and strict confinement not only inspired more resistance, passive and otherwise, than once imagined, but also was accompanied by an Indian mortality far higher than in the outside native and Spanish populations. In the missions, as Stannard notes, 'the annual death rate exceeded the birth rate by more than two to one. This is an over-all death-to-birth rate that, in less than half a century, would completely exterminate a population of any size that was not being replenished by new conscripts.'[81] The reasons remain somewhat controversial, but the best evidence attributes this abnormal mortality to a combination of psychological disorientation and despair, poor sanitation, over-crowding, inadequate diet, over work and physical abuse.[82]

Was this genocide? As the objective of the friars was not extermination but salvation, re-education and exploitation of Indian labour, that question at first glance seems very problematic. But it must be recognized that if we are to understand colonial Indian policies at all, we must be sensitive to the effects of programmes of forced assimilation on Indian survival. That is the important issue, regardless of what label we chose to affix or withhold. Some have argued that the term *ethnocide* is more appropriate in description of 'the suppression of a culture, a language, a religion' as 'it is a phenomenon that is analytically different from the physical extermination of a group'.[83] The evidence from California and elsewhere suggests, however, that a clear line cannot be drawn between 'genocide' and 'ethnocide', as the latter often leads to a slow process of partial physical extermination that, apart from the issue of intentionality, arguably meets or at least approximates the conditions of genocide specified in the United Nations convention.

Whether 'ethnocide' is seen as a form of genocide or is regarded as a separate analytical category is, I believe, of minor importance. The examination of the circumstances that have led to the reduction of indigenous populations and the demoralization and in some cases extinction of cultures cannot be, and has not been, constrained by debates over definitions. Recent investigations of inter-cultural conflicts in the Americas have produced a rich new literature on the past history and present status of matters as diverse as deprivation and mortality on Indian reservations, cultural repression in Indian boarding schools, ongoing Indian health problems, struggles over Indian land rights, Pan-Indian movements, federal Indian policies and movements of religious revitalization. Comparable topics have been pursued by Latin Americanists. Of particular interest are studies of conflicts between Hispanicized mestizo cultures and indigenous peoples. The overall thrust of current scholarship on the problems of assimilation, forced and otherwise, has been threefold: to continue the analysis of the past damage wrought by many presumably benevolent programmes of Indian uplift, to describe and evaluate various Indian resistance strategies including those involving partial assimilation (thereby challenging the once dominant image of the Indian as passive victim), and, often, to lend support to demands for policy changes that restore Indian self-sufficiency and self-determination.[84] But this is not to suggest that genocide in its starkest form has not been a part of the contemporary history of the Americas. The late twentieth century witnessed campaigns of extermination against indigenous peoples in Central America, Brazil and Paraguay, mounted both with and without, the support of the state.[85] Crimes of genocide against Native Americans are not found only in the historical record. Sadly, they remain a present reality.

Notes

1. R. Thornton, *American Indian Holocaust and Survival: A Population History since 1492* (Norman, OK: University of Oklahoma Press, 1987), p. 23.
2. W. Churchill, *A Little Matter of Genocide: Holocaust and Denial in the Americas 1492 to the Present* (San Francisco, CA: City Lights Books, 1997), p. 4.
3. Quoted in M. A. Jaimes, 'Sand Creek: The Morning After', *The State of Native America: Genocide, Colonization and Resistance*, ed. M. A. Jaimes (Boston, MA: South End Press, 1992), p. 3. Jaimes concurred, declaring 'the U.S. destruction of its indigenous population resembled the campaigns of Nazi Germany' far more closely than more recent genocides in places such as Cambodia. 'The Third Reich and the United States did what they did for virtually identical reasons.' Most other cases, she concluded, 'deviate significantly in motivation if not in method'.
4. D. E. Stannard, *American Holocaust: The Conquest of the New World* (New York: Oxford University Press, 1992), p. xii.
5. T. Todorov, in *The Conquest of America: The Question of the Other* [1984] (Norman, OK: University of Oklahoma Press, 1999), pp. 133–8. For the full text in English translation, see T. Motolinia, *History of the Indians of New Spain* (Westport, CT: Greenwood Press, 1973). J. G. Varnar and J. J. Varner, *The Dogs of Conquest* (Norman, OK: University of Oklahoma Press, 1983) provide evidence of the extensive use of 'dogging'.

6. J. Axtell, *Beyond 1492: Encounters in Colonial America* (New York: Oxford University Press, 1992), pp. 261–2.
7. S. T. Katz, 'The Uniqueness of the Holocaust: The Historical Dimension', in *Is the Holocaust Unique? Perspectives on Comparative Genocide*, ed. A. S. Rosenbaum (Boulder, CO: Westview Press, 2001), p. 49. See also D. Lipstadt, *Denying the Holocaust: The Growing Assault on Truth and Memory* (New York, Free Press, 1993). Some Holocaust scholars, however, follow Yehuda Bauer in drawing a distinction between the Jewish Holocaust, which they argue was unique, and other instances of genocide, including Nazi killings of members of other ethnic groups. See Bauer, 'The Place of the Holocaust in Contemporary History', in *Studies in Contemporary Jewry*, vol. 1, ed. J. Frankel (Bloomington, IN: Indiana University Press, 1984), pp. 213–14.
8. Of the many theoretical redefinitions in the literature on genocide, this writer follows most closely the work of Leo Kuper, who, although recognizing shortcomings in the United Nations convention, works within its parameters because of its standing international law. See, in particular, Kuper's *Genocide: Its Political Use in the Twentieth Century* (New York: Penguin, 1981).
9. For an excellent example of this criticism, see D. E. Stannard, 'Uniqueness as Denial: The Politics of Genocide Scholarship', in *Is the Holocaust Unique?*, ed. Rosenbaum, pp. 245–90.
10. Quoted in Rosenbaum, ed., *Is The Holocaust Unique? Perspectives on Comparative Genocide*, p. 211.
11. F. Chalk and K. Jonassohn, *The History and Sociology of Genocid*e (New Haven, CT: Yale University Press, 1990), p. 28.
12. The quotations above are from Richard Eden's 1555 translation reprinted in E. Arber, ed. *The First Three English Books on America* (New York: Kraus Reprint Company, 1971), pp. 70–1. For the complete text in a modern translation, see F. A. McNutt, trans., *De Orbe Novo: The Eight Decades of Peter Martyr D'Anghera*, 2 vols. (New York: G. P. Putnams's Sons, 1912.) For a corrective to the once fashionable view that Peter Martyr anticipated the eighteenth-century cult of the Noble savage, see A. Pagden, *The Fall of Natural Man: The American Indian and the Origins of Comparative Ethnology* (Cambridge: Cambridge University Press, 1982), pp. 24, 52.
13. This point is thoroughly developed in Pagden, *The Fall of Natural Man.*
14. See C. Gibson, *The Black Legend: Anti-Spanish Attitudes in the Old World and the New* (New York: Alfred K. Knopf, 1971); W. S. Mabry, *The Black Legend in England: The Development of Anti-Spanish Sentiment, 1558–1660* (Durham, NC: Duke University Press, 1971).
15. A. A. Cave, 'Richard Hakluyt's Savages: The Influence of 16th Century Travel Narratives on English Indian Policy in North America', *International Social Science Review*, 60 (1985), 3–24.
16. George Abbot, *A Briefe Description of the Whole World* [1589] (London: William Sheares, 1634).
17. Sir Walter Raleigh, *Works*, (Oxford: The University Press, 1829), vol. 4, pp. 693–4.
18. J. Smith, *A Map of Virginia* [1612], reprinted in P. Barber, ed., *The Jamestown Voyages under the First Charter, 1606–1609* (London: The Hakluyt Society, 1969), vol. II, pp. 354, 364, 372; W. Randel, 'Captain John Smith's Attitude Toward the Indians', *Virginia Magazine of History and Biography*, 46 (1939), 218–29.
19. W. Bradford, *Of Plymouth Plantation*, ed. S. E. Morison (New York: Knopf, 1976), p. 84.
20. E. Winslow, 'Good Newes from New England', [1624] in *The Story of the Pilgrim Fathers*, ed. E. Arber (New York: Kraus Reprint, 1969), pp. 513–14.
21. R. Hakluyt, *The Principal Navigations, Votages, Traffiques and Discoveries of the English Nation* [1600] (Glasgow: J. MacLeose and Sons, 1908), vol. 8, pp. 374–83.

22. E. Johnson, *Johnson's Wonder-Working Providence*, ed. J. F. Jameson (New York: Charles Scribner's Sons, 1910), pp. 41, 48–9, 79–80.
23. S. M. Kingsbury, ed., *The Records of the Virginia Company of London* (Washington, D.C.: Government Printing Office, 1905–35), vol. III, p. 672.
24. F. W. Gleach, *Powhatan's World and Colonial Virginia* (Lincoln, NB: University of Nebraska Press, 1997), pp. 148–73; A. T. Vaughan, 'The Expulsion of the "Salvages": English Policy and the Virginia Massacre of 1622', *William and Mary Quarterly*, 3rd series, 35 (1972), 57–89; W. F. Craven, 'Indian Policy in Early Virginia', *William and Mary Quarterly*, 3rd series, 1 (1944), 65–82; W. S. Powell, 'Aftermath of the Massacre: The First Indian War, 1622–1632', *Virginia Magazine of History and Biography*, 66 (1958), 44–75.
25. W. W. Hening, ed., *The Statutes at Large, being a Collection of all the Laws of Virginia, from the First Session of the Legislature, in the Year 1619* (New York: R. & G. & W. Bartow, 1823), vol. I, p. 128.
26. G. B. Nash, *Red, White and Black: The Peoples of Early North America*, 4th edn (Upper Saddle River, NJ: Prentice Hall, 2000), p. 73.
27. For a detailed analysis of tribal relations in early colonial Virginia, see J. F. Fausz, *The Powhatan Uprising of 1622: A Historical Study of Ethnocentricism and Cultural Conflict* (Ph.D. dissertation, College of William and Mary, 1977). Also of value, and more accessible, are Fausz's articles, including 'The Barbarous Massacre Remembered: Powhatan's Uprising of 1622 and the Historians', *Explorations in Ethnic Studies*, 1 (1978), 16–36; 'Profits, Pelts and Power: English Culture in the Early Chesapeake, 1620–1662', *Maryland Historian*, 4 (1983), 15–30; 'Patterns of American Aggression and Accommodation Along the Mid-Atlantic Coast', in *Cultures in Contact: The Impact of European Contacts on Native American Cultural Institutions AD 1000–1800*, ed. W. W. Fitzhugh (Washington, D.C.: Smithsonian, 1985), pp. 225–68.
28. F. Parkman, *France and England in North America*, ed. D. Levin (New York: Viking, The Library of America, 1983), vol. I, p. 1084.
29. A. T. Vaughan, *New England Frontier: Puritans and Indians, 1620–1675* (Boston: Little, Brown and Company, 1965), pp. 93–154.
30. Vaughan modified his earlier insistence of Pequot War guilt, writing in 1979 'I am less certain than I was fifteen years ago that the Pequots deserve the burden of the blame.' *New England Frontier: Puritans and Indians, 1620–1675*, 2nd edn (New York: Norton, 1979), p. xxix.
31. The notions of the Pequots as aggressive invaders of southern New England and of their terrorization of the indigenous tribes there are challenged in N. Salisbury, *Manitou and Providence: Indians, European and the Making of New England, 1500–1675* (New York: Oxford University Press, 1982), pp. 93–154 and in A. A. Cave, 'The Pequot Invasion of Southern New England: A Reassessment of the Evidence', *New England Quarterly*, 62 (1989), 27–44. The most thorough exposition of an economic interpretation of the Pequot War is F. P. Jennings, *The Invasion of America: Indians, Colonialism and the Cant of Conquest* (New York: Norton, 1976), pp. 177–227. For the argument that Puritan ideology and cultural misunderstandings were major causative factors in the war, see A. A. Cave, *The Pequot War* (Amherst, MA: University of Massachusetts Press, 1996).
32. See, for example, Chalk and Jonassohn, *The History and Sociology of Genocide*, pp. xiv, 36; Nash, *Red, White and Black*, pp. 99–102; R. Drinnon, *Facing West: The Metaphysics of Indian Hating and Empire Building* (Minneapolis, MN: University of Minnesota Press, 1980), pp. 40–5; H. Zinn, *A People's History of the United States* (New York: HarperCollins, 2003), pp. 14–15.

33. S. T. Katz, 'The Pequot War Reconsidered', *The New England Quarterly*, 64 (1991), 206–24. Katz's arguments were challenged in M. Freeman, 'Puritans and Pequots: The Question of Genocide', *The New England Quarterly*, 68 (1995), 278–93. Freeman argued that the Pequot War was one of the many cases in which nation-destruction was part of the process of nation building, a process he regarded as inherently genocidal. See also S. T. Katz, 'Pequots and the Question of Genocide: A Reply to Michael Freeman', *The New England Quarterly*, 69 (1995), 641–9.
34. Johnson, *Wonder-Working Providence*, pp. 105–6.
35. C. Orr, ed., *History of the Pequot War: The Contemporary Accounts of Mason, Underhill, Vincent and Gardiner* (Cleveland, OH: Helman-Taylor, 1897), p. 81.
36. Ibid., p. 30.
37. Johnson, *Wonder-Working Providence*, p. 168.
38. See R. Lemkin, *Axis Rule in Occupied Europe* (Washington, D.C.: Carnegie Endowment for International Peace, 1944).
39. R. D. Karr, '"Why Should You be So Furious?" The Violence of the Pequot War', *Journal of American History*, 85 (1988), 876–909 provides a useful comparative analysis that demonstrates that the slaughter of non-combatants and the killing of prisoners of war was not uncommon in European conflicts in which one side, or both, viewed the other as less than a legitimate belligerent. However, he sidesteps the genocide issue. The burden of his argument appears to be that Indians were not victims of genocide.
40. See for example, Jennings's analysis of the Puritan 'wars of conquest' in *The Invasion of America*.
41. Chalk and Jonassohn, *The History and Sociology of Genocide*, p. 29.
42. T. Barta, 'Relations of Genocide: Land and Lives in the Colonization of Australia', in *Genocide and the Modern Age: Etiology and Case Studies of Mass Death*, eds, I. Wallimann and M. N. Dobkowski, 2nd edn (Syracuse, NY: Syracuse University Press, 2000), p. 239.
43. Scalping was a war practice employed by some, but by no means all, pre-Columbian Americans. Where it was found, it operated largely as a quasi-religious ritual intended, not only to terrorize the enemy, but also to appropriate the strength and power of the fallen warrior. Scalps were given places of honour in Indian villages and sometimes formally adopted into the tribe. See J. Axtell, 'The Unkindest Cut, or Who Invented Scalping? A Case Study', and 'Scalping: The Ethnohistory of a Moral Question', in *The European and the Indian: Essays in the Ethnohistory of Colonial America* (New York: Oxford University Press, 1981), pp. 16–38 and 205–44.
44. *The Acts and Resolves of the Province of the Massachusetts Bay*, 21 vols. (Boston: Massachusetts Historical Society), vol. I, pp. 175–6; 594.
45. Churchill, *A Little Matter of Genocide*, pp. 178–88.
46. Thomas Barten, quoted in C. Van Doren and J. P. Boyd, *Indian Treaties Presented by Benjamin Franklin*, (Philadelphia, PA: University of Pennsylvania Press, 1938), pp. lxxxi–ii.
47. F. Anderson, *Crucible of War* (New York: Alfred K. Knopf, 2000), pp. 457–71.
48. Churchill, *A Little Matter of Genocide*, p. 185.
49. E. Lazarus, *Black Hills, White Justice* (New York: Harper Collins, 1991), p. 29.
50. Churchill, *A Little Matter of Genocide*, p. 187; L. Carranco and E. Beard, *Genocide and Vendetta: The Round Valley War of Northern California* (Norman, OK: University of Oklahoma Press, 1981).
51. W. W. Newcomb, *The Indians of Texas* (Austin, TX: University of Texas Press, 1961).

52. For a comprehensive view of the evolution of 'irregular war' in British North America, see J. Grenier, *The First Way of War: American War Making on the Frontier, 1607–1814* (New York: Cambridge University Press, 2005).
53. B. Church, *History of the Eastern Expeditions of 1689, 1690, and 1692* (Boston: Waggins and W. P. Lunt, 1867), pp. 11–12.
54. S. Brumwell, *White Devil: A True Story of War, Savagery, and Vengeance in Colonial America* (New York: Da Capo Press, 2004). Brumwell, drawing on Indian oral histories, concludes Rogers greatly exaggerated the number he killed at St. Francis. It tells us much about his mindset that he would do so.
55. Quoted in Grenier, *The First Way of War*, p. 46.
56. Quoted in G. B. Nash, *The Unknown American Revolution* (New York: Viking, 2005), p. 351.
57. Sword, *President Washington's Indian War*, p. 73.
58. Quoted in Nash, *Unknown American Revolution*, p. 387.
59. D. Svali, *Sand Creek and the Rhetoric of Extermination: A Case Study in Indian White Relations* (Lanham, MD: University Press of America, 1989), pp. 187–9.
60. Quoted in T. G. Dyer, *Theodore Roosevelt and the Idea of Race* (Baton Rouge, LA: Louisiana State University Press), p. 79.
61. The most authoritative and balanced study is S. Hoig, *The Sand Creek Massacre* (Norman, OK: University of Oklahoma Press, 1961). W. R. Dunn, *'I Stand by Sand Creek': A Defense of Colonel John M. Chivington and the Third Colorado Cavalry* (Ft. Collins, CO: Old Army Press, 1985) offers an example of the acceptance of Chivington's questionable claim that he found numerous scalps of white women and children at the Sand Creek encampment. Rogers had used the same argument to justify his indiscriminate killing of Indians at St. Francis a century earlier.
62. Captain Nathaniel Lyon, quoted in C. E. Trafzer and J. Hyer, eds, *Exterminate Them! Written Accounts of the Murder, Rape and Enslavement of Native Americans During the California Gold Rush* (East Lansing, MI: Michigan State University Press, 1999), p. 18.
63. D. H. King and E. R. Evans, eds, 'Memoirs of the Grant Expedition Against the Cherokees in 1761', *Journal of Cherokee Studies*, 2 (1977), 271–336.
64. B. A. Mann, *George Washington's War on Native America* (Westport, CT: Praeger, 2005).
65. Sword, *President Washington's Indian War*.
66. A. C. Isenberg, *The Destruction of the Bison* (Cambridge: Cambridge University Press, 2000).
67. Quotations from E. A. Fenn, 'Biological Warfare in Eastern North America', *Journal of American History*, 86 (2000), 1154–8.
68. G. E. Dowd, *War Under Heaven: Pontiac, the Indian Nations, and the British Empire* (Baltimore, MD: Johns Hopkins University Press, 2002), p. 190.
69. *Alta California*, 6 March 1853, quoted in Trafzer and Hyer, eds, *Exterminate Them!*, p. 67.
70. D. Gookin, 'An Historical Account of the Doings and Sufferings of the Christian Indians in New England, in the Years 1675, 1676, 1677', *Transactions and Collections of the American Antiquarian Society*, 2 (1836), 419–534.
71. W. E. Washburn, *The Governor and the Rebel: A History of Bacon's Rebellion in Virginia* (Chapel Hill, NC: University of North Carolina Press, 1957).
72. R. Downes, *Council Fires on the Upper Ohio* (Pittsburgh, PA: University of Pittsburgh Press, 1940), pp. 139–40.
73. Governor John Penn to Thomas Penn, September 12, 1766, quoted in N. B. Wainright, *George Croghan: Wilderness Diplomat* (Chapel Hill, NC: University of North Carolina Press, 1959), p. 232.

74. C. E. Carter, ed., *Correspondence of General Thomas Gage with the Secretaries of State 1763–75*, 2 vols. (New Haven, CT: Yale University Press, 1931), vol. I, p. 152.
75. W. H. Harrison, 'Message to the Legislature, 17 May 1807', in *Messages and Letters of William Henry Harrison*, ed. L. Esarey, 2 vols. (Indianapolis, IN: Indiana State Historical Society, 1922), vol. I, pp. 233–4.
76. Quoted in S. E. Miller, *An Ohio River Boundary? The Contested Ohio Country 1783–1795* (Ph.D. dissertation, University of Toledo, 2006), p. 80.
77. Quoted in B. Madley, 'Patterns of Frontier Genocide 1803–1910: the Aboriginal Tasmanians, the Yuki of California and the Herero of Namibia', *Journal of Genocide Research*, 6 (2004), 167–92. On genocide in California after 1848, see, in addition to Trafzer and Hyer, eds, *Exterminate Them!* and Carranco and Beard, *Genocide and Vendetta*, the following: S. F. Cook, *The Conflict between the California Indian and White Civilization* (Berkeley, CA: University of California Press, 1976); R. F. Heizer, ed., *The Destruction of the California Indians* (Santa Barbara, CA: Peregrine Smith, 1974); A. L. Hurtado, *Indian Survival on the California Frontier* (New Haven, CT: Yale University Press, 1988).
78. Quoted in Madley, 'Patterns of Frontier Genocide', 179.
79. Churchill, *A Little Matter of Genocide*, pp. 157–8, 188.
80. W. Sherman, *Forced Native Labor in Sixteenth Century Central America* (Lincoln, NB: University of Nebraska Press, 1979), p. 311.
81. Stannard, *American Holocaust*, p. 137.
82. For an excellent review of the evidence, see in addition to Cook (cited below) R. H. Jackson and E. Castillo, *Indians, Franciscans, and Spanish Colonization: The Impact of the Mission System on California Indians* (Albuquerque, NM: University of New Mexico Press, 1995).
83. Chalk and Jonassohn, *History and Sociology of Genocide*, p. 23.
84. For the most recent trends in Native American historiography, see D. A. Mihesuah, ed., *Natives and Academics* (Lincoln, NB: University of Nebraska Press, 1998) and R. Thornton, ed., *Studying Native America* (Madison, WI: University of Wisconsin Press, 1998).
85. The historiography of contemporary genocides in Latin America is in its formative stages. Probably the most thorough to date exposes the systematic murder of indigenous peoples by the Guatemalan military dictatorship in the early 1980s. See R. Carmack, *Harvest of Violence: The Mayan Indians and the Guatemalan Crisis* (Norman, OK: University of Oklahoma Press, 1990); C. Smith, *Guatemalan Indians and the State, 1540 to 1988* (Austin, TX: University of Texas Press, 1990); B. Manz, *Refugees of a Hidden War: The Aftermath of Counterinsurgency in Guatemala* (Albany, NY: State University Press of New York, 1988); G. Lovell, *A Beauty that Hurts: Life and Death in Guatemala* (Austin, TX: University of Texas Press, 2000); V. Sanford, *Buried Secrets: Truth and Human Rights in Guatemala* (New York: Palgrave Macmillan, 2003); G. Grandin, 'History, Motive, Law, Intent: Combining Historical and Legal Methods in Understanding Guatemala's 1981–1983 Genocide', in *The Specter of Genocide: Mass Murder in Historical Perspective*, eds, R. Gellately and B. Kiernan (Cambridge: Cambridge University Press, 2003), pp. 339–52. On other regions in Latin America, S. Davis, *Victims of the Miracle: Development and the Indians of Brazil* (Cambridge: Cambridge University Press, 1977) and R. Arens, ed., *Genocide in Paraguay* (Philadelphia, PA: Temple University Press, 1976).

11

Decent Disposal: Australian Historians and the Recovery of Genocide

Tony Barta

> One of the troubles of a colonising nation is the decent disposal of the native inhabitants of the country, of which the latter have been dispossessed.
>
> *North Queensland Register*, 11 October 1893[1]

About the dispossession of Australia's Aboriginal peoples there was no argument when the Europeans arrived. All land was claimed by the crown, which could then parcel it out to settlers in any manner the government in London, with advice from the other side of the world, saw fit. About the indigenous people themselves there would be more debate. With royal instructions 'to endeavour by every possible means to open an intercourse with the natives, and to conciliate their affections', Captain Arthur Phillip was asked to enjoin 'all our subjects to live in amity and kindness with them'. It would be a matter for punishment 'if any of our subjects shall wantonly destroy them, or give them unnecessary interruption in the exercise of their several occupations'.[2]

With these fine sentiments the trouble started. The seizing of land could not fail to interrupt the established way of life of the Aborigines, and the settlement itself would lead to both 'necessary' and 'wanton' destruction of lives. There would be Aboriginal resistance, ruthless and indiscriminate retaliation, and the rapid thinning of a population with no resistance to introduced diseases. The strangers with their strange animals could sometimes be accommodated but then came death, disruption and despair. Alcohol, venereal disease and inability to reproduce left fewer Aborigines belatedly to be 'protected'. The remnant visible to the Europeans in their thriving towns and cities bred a racism that decreed 'the nigger shall disappear'.

Disappearance was the preferred moral message, especially among those disturbed by what they saw and heard. Decent disposal came next. It was not necessary for contemporaries to go to the extreme end of possible meanings: 'Get rid of, deal conclusively with, settle; *colloq.* kill'.[3] All meanings, however, apply to the treatment historians proceeded to mete out to the issue. First the people were disposed of, then the knowledge. Australian historians, as in all the empires, were collaborators in the covering up of what took place.[4] To overcome this double sense of decent disposal required a double recovery. In the first instance, of the past so efficiently disposed of. In the second instance, of a concept that had never seemed to be appropriate in Australia, and the meaning of that concept as originally conceived.

'New conceptions' wrote Raphael Lemkin in 1944, 'require new terms'. When he coined 'genocide' the context of the time would give it an association he did not intend. He did not foresee the extent to which the Holocaust would dominate the discourse, nor the limitations its image would place on popular – and academic – imagination. It is becoming ever clearer that a careful reading of Lemkin's list of defining characteristics invites us to consider whether a 'coordinated plan of different actions aimed at the destruction of essential foundations of national groups, with the aim of annihilating the groups themselves' should be understood only as state-initiated mass murder. Genocide was first redefined for legal purposes by the United Nations and then narrowed to the kind of officially sanctioned action that could face indictment in international law. Lemkin devoted huge energy and resourcefulness to establishing this new crime and no one inspired by him would wish to weaken a regime of prosecution, judgement and punishment. While genocide so quickly became the worst of crimes the legal emphasis on official action meant a large part of human history was overlooked.

That was not Lemkin's intention. A most important advance in genocide scholarship has been the recovery of the other part of Lemkin's legacy, his own historical writing. That Australian scholars have played a prominent part is not an accident. The persistence over 20 years of a concern to connect genocide with European colonialism kept Lemkin's definition under examination and insisted its broader and less legalistic aspects be taken as seriously as the more recent horrors of twentieth-century Europe. Dirk Moses, Ann Curthoys and John Docker have shown that Lemkin was working on a more ambitious history of genocide than any undertaken since his death, and that he was more open to the diverse manifestations of genocidal relations than many guardians of his heritage believed.[5] The recovery of such diverse and complex relations has been a signal contribution of Australian genocide historiography.

Six significant advances, I will suggest, have come from the efforts of Australian historians to recover an understanding of genocide in their own country.

1. **Greater awareness of the historicity of genocide historiography.** Without the context of political activism, most importantly from the survivors of a genocidal onslaught, revisions of settlement and frontier orthodoxies would not have brought the concept of genocide into the new history.

2. **Reconsideration of intention in genocidal relationships.** An apparently radical reconceptualization, based on outcomes rather than official policy pronouncements, brought us much closer to Lemkin's own historical project and to the UN's concern with 'acts committed with intent to destroy'.
3. **Broadening of genocide historiography into new structural and dialectical perspectives.** The introduction of large-scale conceptual analysis (modern colonialism, not just the history of a colony; capitalism, not only a story of economic progress) stimulated a reconsideration of genocidal relationships within broader historical phenomena.
4. **Lengthening of historical interpretation, to comprehend the racist policies of child removal as a consequence of colonial destruction.** The twentieth-century programme of 'breeding out the colour' that followed the nineteenth-century assault on Aboriginal peoples can be understood (as it was by some at the time) as its genocidal fulfilment.
5. **Connection of European colonial genocides to the twentieth-century genocides carried out in Europe itself.** Elucidating the causes and consequences of imposing European civilization on indigenous peoples, and a continuing context of racism and imperialism, have changed our understanding of the National Socialist project and the Holocaust. (Connecting Turkish and Soviet genocides to the different legacies of Ottoman and Russian imperialism will be no less instructive.)
6. **Clarification of the way ahead in genocide studies.** New histories will combine a more determined and theoretically informed small-scale analysis of episodes, in a manner inspired by British social history and American ethnography, with the larger conceptualization of relationships between indigenous people and settlers. As in studies of the Holocaust, 'intentionalism' and 'functionalism' will be superseded by revitalized combinations of empirical and theoretical enquiry.

The six advances are not, of course, neatly linear. They criss-cross the chronological account needed to show how the historiography evolved. Connection with the Holocaust, for instance, played a key role in recovering the concept of genocide more than 20 years ago, and earlier researches into frontier history have helped impel a new campaign of revisionism. The developing historical context will continue to affect the way genocide is researched, represented and understood.

Historiography is about the marketplace of ideas. There are other relevant terms: academic life, writers and readers, the sociology of knowledge. Contingencies and idiosyncrasies are probably paramount. Not everyone with an idea can communicate it well; it might be published in the wrong place; it might never inspire discussion. Whether an idea sinks or swims depends on personality and persistence, on networking, energy and historical environment.

The last factor cannot be ranked much below the more individual ones. The success or failure of any historical proposition is historical in a thousand interlinking ways. Attached to any historiographical essay there should be a very complex map of culture, society, politics, ideology and intellectual life.

This chapter will not be able to supply that complex map. It will scarcely be able to sketch the outlines even of intellectual debate. It will not deal as fully as it should with all the individuals who have made the historiography of genocide a more interesting site of stimulus and exchange. And it will not be able to circumnavigate one of the things writers go to some lengths to avoid: repeated references to their own work. Having been in the midst of this history, I can find no way round a deal of quoting and citing to make my past positions plain and to indicate where I have addressed issues of historiography or interpretation that cannot be followed far here.

Consciousness of genocide in Australia: history and context

Before genocide in Australia could become an issue it was necessary to recover a less celebratory version of the national past. As ever, the change depended on the national present. That was evident in early Australia when a minority first questioned the 'disposal' of the Aboriginal population and it was true a century later when the first historians – Lemkin among them – used the term 'genocide' of Tasmania.[6] The disappearance of Aborigines in other settled areas was assumed by most Australians to have happened long ago. That part of the past was no one's concern or responsibility.

Change was not impelled by historical enquiry in universities. It was achieved by Aboriginal activists and a small group of mainly leftist supporters, over long years of lonely campaigning. Quite suddenly, in the 1960s, indigenous Australians attained a new visibility and a degree of sympathetic public attention.[7] A small number of senior academics – not primarily historians – were encouraged to speak out. The campaign for citizenship rights culminating in the 1967 referendum also influenced the national broadcaster and when the ABC asked the anthropologist W. E. H. Stanner to deliver its 1968 Boyer Lectures it could not have known how much effect they would have. *After the Dreaming* was an appeal to conscience connecting present conditions with past attitudes. It decisively broke what Stanner called 'the great Australian silence'.[8] From years of extensive research, published in 1970, the sociologist Charles Rowley was no less blunt in addressing past and present realities. His pioneering survey from the frontier to post-war assimilation was called *The Destruction of Aboriginal Society*. Among its original departures was one that divided the continent into 'settled' and 'colonial' Australia. The maps and tables made the somewhat idiosyncratic meaning plain. The huge area of central and northern Australia still being 'colonized', economically and culturally, contained by far the largest Aboriginal populations, with the smallest admixture (in the usage that had so long fuelled racism) of 'white blood'. In 'settled Australia', and most evidently towards the south, there were very few 'full blood' Aborigines left. In Tasmania there were none.[9]

Younger historians now began to look at racism and frontier violence with more determination. The evidence collected by Raymond Evans in Queensland was stark. *Exclusion, Exploitation and Extermination* was a compendium of atrocities against Aborigines and other racial groups that had been ignored for most of the century. It could not fail to affect anyone who read it.[10] Noel Loos published his study of North Queensland, *Invasion and Resistance.* Queensland was also the base for the most influential of the new historians, Henry Reynolds. In 1972 he published a collection of documents, *Aborigines and Settlers,* that began with frontier realities. A decade later, his short book *The Other Side of the Frontier,* with an estimate of up to 20,000 Aboriginal dead, was a sensation.[11] It did most to establish frontier conflict as an orthodoxy the country adapted to without great trauma, perhaps because the new visibility of Aboriginal activists made the idea that Aborigines actively contested European encroachment easier to accept. Very quickly indigenous *resistance* replaced passive disappearance as the dominant paradigm – with resistance to the idea of genocide as a corollary. The connotation of genocide, notably from the Holocaust but also from the Armenians in Turkey (and later the Tutsi in Rwanda) was of a passive population murdered without being able to fight back. Fighting seemed to indicate some other order of death, akin to the casualties of war.

In Australian popular culture – and historiography – Aborigines had never had the warrior status accorded by Europeans to Maori or Native American opponents. The new accounts of guerrilla warfare began to militate against the idea, even with respect to Tasmania, that genocide was at all an appropriate description. Reynolds would produce many further books looking at the realities of contact between Aborigines and settlers from all sides, some tragic, some pragmatic and some positive. Before 1987 he did not mention genocide, but he then gave the concept serious consideration. Certainly, he found, there was much talk of 'extermination' even in official circles.[12] But the question for Reynolds was: did the colonial governments *authorize* a campaign of killing? The possibilities of condoning, or turning a blind eye, did not escape him, yet when he returned to the issue more than ten years later his self-imposed criterion of formal authorization still required a question mark. *An Indelible Stain? The question of genocide in Australia's history* refers to correspondence in 1830 between Sir George Murray, Secretary of State for the Colonies, and Sir George Arthur, Lieutenant Governor of Tasmania. The feelings of the settlers could be understood, wrote Murray, but 'the adoption of any line of conduct, having for its avowed, or its secret object, the extinction of the Native race, could not fail to leave an indelible stain upon the character of the British Government.'[13]

Reynolds was aware of a developing genocide discourse, and made a balanced assessment of arguments in a chapter on the Genocide Convention. It was a basis he would not depart from: 'intent to destroy' seemed to him – as it did to almost everyone entering the field – the only secure ground on which to stand. And the intention had to come from the state. Although he reprinted article IV of the Convention – 'Persons committing genocide or any of the other acts enumerated in article III shall be punished, whether they are constitutionally responsible rulers, public officials or private individuals' – Reynolds only looked for evidence of official culpability. He did not doubt that comments made by judges in some of the highest courts in the land were also significant, even if historically misleading. 'Of equal importance' to the work done by historians and sociologists was the kind of statement made by Mr Justice Crispin in the ACT Supreme Court, finding 'ample evidence ... that acts of genocide were committed during the colonisation of Australia'. When Reynolds then laid out his own reading of the evidence he argued that while some later policies (notably the removal of children) might 'have to be seriously considered as genocidal in effect', and indeed in intention, frontier 'dispersals' (widely understood as killings) would probably have been defended, even under a 'retrospective prosecution', as legitimate. Would the actions of the Native Police, financed and directed by the Queensland Government from 1859 to 1896, make that government guilty of genocide? 'If interrogated on the question, Queensland ministers of the time would no doubt have answered that the Aborigines were killed in the course of a kind of warfare and because they threatened European life and property, and what they wanted was indigenous acquiescence, not their disappearance.'[14]

Tasmania, in Reynolds view, was no different: there as elsewhere, settler calls for 'extirpation' did not translate into the kind of government action or inaction that would amount to genocide. Even the infamous 'Black Line' of 1830, directed by Governor Arthur himself, and designed to round up all the remaining Aborigines was seen by him as having exactly the opposite intention. To Sir George Murray, who at the same time was sending his 'indelible stain' letter from London, Arthur wrote:

> I cannot ... say that I am sanguine of success, since their cunning and intelligence are remarkable; but whilst I hope His Majesty's Government will approve of my having omitted no measures which had a tendency to conciliate, or to preserve the lives of these savages, I am sure it will always be a matter of consolation to the government of the Colony, and to its respectable inhabitants, that we have made every effort in our power to save the aboriginal race from being exterminated. ...[15]

By measuring genocide strictly against the Genocide Convention, Reynolds made his own historiography a corrective to the dramatic earlier indictments of policy in Tasmania. The best-known historians – Bonwick, Turnbull, Plomley, Robson and Ryan – are lesser targets than the art historian Robert Hughes, whose best-selling history of convict Australia referred to Tasmania as 'the only true genocide in English colonial history'. There are no comments on the draft chapter about Tasmania written by Lemkin himself, by no means as strictly intentionalist as might be expected, because it was not published until four years later.[16] It might not have changed Reynolds assessment, or the impact he made on Australian readers. For all its judicious care, *An Indelible Stain?* has become Reynolds's least-noticed book. Perhaps because it was a reminder of the larger genocidal onslaught, the only book by a leading historian of Australia to confront a question so few wanted to hear disappeared into uncontroversial silence.

The controversy came two years later, and from a writer who represented Reynolds and all his works as the founder of an orthodoxy ripe for demolition. Keith Windschuttle, prominent as a conservative cultural critic rather than as an historian, launched a projected three-volume attack on the research as well as the conclusions of leading scholars by revisiting the colonial conflict in Tasmania. He claimed there was no frontier war, no Aboriginal attachment to land, and nothing remotely like genocide. The tone of his enterprise was indicated by the title: *The Fabrication of Aboriginal History*.[17] This was very much a book for the times – a context we must return to – and Windschuttle claimed it was in response to many loose claims about genocide in Australia's past, including comparisons to the Nazis. His introduction was subtitled 'The Final Solution Down Under', which served his polemical purposes even as it revealed the patchy and dated quality of his reading on genocide.[18] And in typical style he quite missed the way reference to Nazi Germany had indeed played a role in making Australian genocide a serious field of enquiry.

The discourse that passed Windschuttle by – and almost all other Australian historians as well – was opened up in the mid-1980s. When my 'Consciousness of Genocide in Australia' was published in an Australian journal it was in an issue dedicated to a conference on German Jewish refugees.[19] The setting, 'After the Holocaust', gave the argument resonance among a small constituency already engaged with genocide and although I made a point of explaining why the Holocaust was 'a unique, nowhere remotely paralleled atrocity' not every member of the audience was prepared to hear how it helped to block Australian recognition of genocide closer to home.[20]

It was not only in Australia that the exclusive association between genocide and the mass murder of Jews by Germans impeded historical understanding of Germany, Nazism and Jewish identity.[21] The instant associations of the word 'Auschwitz' – what I have elsewhere called the 'meta-image of the Holocaust' – dominated historiography and memory throughout the western world.[22] It was 'this consciousness of a uniquely terrible event', I argued, 'this distance from anything we might recognize as genocide in our own past, which is so hard to break through for Australians.'

But the chapter had another aspect as well. Whereas Reynolds was quite justifiably wrestling with the question of official intention, I thought it important to ask another question, looking at the evidence of actual events in a different way. Contrary to what has sometimes been asserted, it was not a matter of ignoring stated intentions, but I believed – in common with many colleagues influenced by both Marxism and ethnography – that the reality needed to be construed from reading actions as well as words. Every genocidal situation was more complex than the insistence on *policy*, so prominent in every attempt to define genocide, would have us believe.

> Obviously these definitions are much more appropriate to Himmler's bureaucracy of murder than to the improvisations, often contradictory in intention and effect, of the colonial frontier. Official statements towards native peoples are apt to be concerned and protective, in Australia this was consistently the case. The intentions of most settlers, as individuals were more often than not – at least until they felt threatened – sincerely benign. That their presence and everyday activities had an *effect* which was genocidal leaves us with a considerable problem. I think we have to face the fact that historically we have a *relationship* of genocide with the Aborigines which cannot be understood only in terms of a clear intention to wipe them out.[23]

Relations of genocide: intention, land and lives

The re-conceptualizing of intention was derived from the course of colonial settlement newly re-interpreted by the historians of the frontier. 'The key relation', I argued in 1985, 'was instituted by the determination of the Europeans to take over the land'. What the Aborigines still call 'country' – something to which they in many profound ways belong, rather than something which belongs to them – was rapidly claimed as private property to be exploited in the new economy brought from the other side of the world. Settlement led to resistance, resistance to reprisal. In the ensuing conflict there was open talk of genocide, 'the most certain method of getting rid of the race'. But there could be an easier way. Because of the obvious inability of the Aborigines to survive displacement, social disruption, degradation and disease, an active policy of extermination might not be necessary. For such an inferior people 'the process of their extinction' was 'the result, in a great degree, of natural causes', and thus for the settlers a matter of being realistic rather than feeling responsible.[24]

A path-breaking book *Genocide in the Modern Age* offered an opportunity to consider further the relationship between indigenous people and settlers that had such a catastrophic outcome. The reconsideration would mean reframing the question of genocide by conceptualizing historical relationships as fact.

> The basic fact of Australian history is the conquest of the country by one people and the dispossession, with ruthless destructiveness, of another ... Wherever Europeans were determined to settle, Aborigines were fated to die. Not only in Tasmania but in all the rapidly occupied south and east of Australia the processes of colonization and economic expansion involved the virtual wiping out of the Aboriginal population.[25]

This did little more than repeat the story told by Rowley in words, maps and graphs. More contentious was the assertion, 'Australia – not alone among the nations of the colonized world – is a nation founded on genocide.' Most contentious was the linking of historical processes (rather than declared policy) to genocidal outcomes. The formulation came from Marx:

> In the investigation of *political* conditions one is too easily tempted to overlook the *objective nature of the relationships* and to explain everything from the will of the persons acting. There are *relationships*, however, which determine the actions of private persons as well as those of individual authorities, and which are as independent as the movements in breathing. Taking this objective standpoint from the outset, one will not presuppose an exclusively good or bad will on either side. Rather, one will observe relationships in which only persons appear to act at first.[26]

I was careful to add that Marx did not have genocide – or Australia – in mind and that in exploring how genocide might involve objective realities I did not wish to ignore subjective factors, let alone ignore the key legal question of intent:

> I will not, I hope, beg the question of how relationships might be expressive of intentions; I expect to construe intention from action (and inaction) and from words as well. But I will assume of actions that they imply relationships, and entail consequences, which people do not always envisage clearly. Genocide, strictly, cannot be a crime of unintended consequences; we expect it to be acknowledged in consciousness. In real historical relationships, however, unintended consequences are legion, and it is from the consequences, as well as the often muddled consciousness, that we have to deduce the real nature of the relationship.

Leo Kuper, I noted, had recognized something similar in Sartre's references to Americans 'living out ... a relationship of genocide' with the Vietnamese. He also dramatically highlighted the 'genocidal process' hunting and gathering peoples had endured in the face of 'civilization'.[27] Nevertheless, my theses about a relationship 'structured into the very nature of the encounter', produced polarized responses. Only one reading was immediately positive. In an Afterword to the book, Richard L. Rubenstein took up the issues of larger historical pressures and unintended consequences.[28] His own breadth and boldness of historical view differentiated him from other commentators accustomed to a Holocaust paradigm of genocide in which policy, intentions and results were held to be clear. Few yet saw how Holocaust historiography was changing and even fewer were ready to look at the possibility that colonial genocides (should they be recognized as such at all) might require a different order of conceptualization.

A stiff adherence to the definition of genocide as explicit policy produced some rigid historical interpretations, quite removed from the realities of colonization.[29] And where the search for a more complex (and realistic) conceptualization of intention incurred any theoretical rebuttal at all, there were some odd responses. Perhaps the most disappointing was from Helen Fein, who took issue with my attempt to distinguish a genocidal state (Nazi Germany) from a genocidal society (colonial Australia). It still strikes me as strange that a sociologist would object to the kind of conceptual differentiation which is the very stuff of sociology.[30]

George J. Andreopoulos and Frank Chalk also responded critically to the perspective outlined by Wallimann, Dobkowski and myself. Andreopoulos saw some potential in a Marxian paradigm of relations: 'it is a constructive reminder of the role of impersonal forces in shaping group and individual choices.' He was right to note that it was less theoretically elaborated than Marx's economic propositions but no one – not Marx, either – was suggesting that political, social and cultural questions could be analyzed as if they were entirely economic. Though open to the possibilities of ideological and societal dialectics, Andreopoulos was drawn away from history by concern about the implications of historical analysis for current and future prevention of genocide. The eliding of history and policy was, in fact, nowhere implied, nor was 'the normalization of the genocidal process' or 'the concomitant impossibility of devising preventive measures against a policy that is part of everyday life.' Attending to the less direct expressions of intention might indeed take discussion beyond the legalistic mode but it could also bring legal proceedings closer to the realities.[31]

Frank Chalk saw 'potential gains' in attending to 'impersonal factors in capitalism conducive to genocide' but they would be gains won 'at an enormous cost in the rigor of the analysis'. There is a non-sequitur here, followed by a too easy adducing of other instances. If the conquest of Canada was less disastrous for indigenous peoples than the expansion of the United States we should most certainly follow through each case – and not just those two large categorizations – in detail.

Testing ideas of 'relations of genocide' should after all lead to a much closer analysis of each situation. My case study was focussed on Australia yet did not itself pretend to detailed comparison of different patterns of settlement across a continent, let alone between continents. Nor was there the faintest suggestion that widening the historical analysis of genocide, insisting it pay attention to factors not always expressed in commands, would 'confuse genocide with other violations of human rights and other forms of killing'.[32]

The resistance to the idea of 'relations of genocide' was trenchant with respect to official intentions and reluctant to engage with the dynamics of modernity. The scale of historical enquiry was uncongenial, or considered not feasible. It imported a kind of theory and an emphasis on history that challenged the domination of legalistic, prosecutorial definitions. It may have been the insistence on history rather than theory that caused problems for both historians and lawyers: after all, the less theorized approach of pioneering scholars already pointed in the same direction. In 1977 Stanner published a close reading of the beginnings of European settlement. He connected 'the persistent indifference to the fate of the Aborigines' with 'the structure of racial relations' established as colonization accelerated.

> In other words, there was more than an accidental correspondence between the ruin of Aboriginal, and the making of European, life in Australia. There was in fact a functional concomitance. The interdependence was more clear at some times than at others. It was particularly clear in the decades of the nineteenth century in which material development and the spoliation of the native life were most intense. The vilification of the Aborigines reached its pitch precisely over that period. Few national histories can have afforded a more blazing, and odious, rationalization of ugly deeds.

Stanner did not speak of genocide but the 'ugly deeds' left little room to make a distinction. Anthony Trollope, he thought, 'probably spoke for a majority of Australians' of his time when he said of the Aborigines: 'Their doom is to be exterminated; and the sooner that their doom is accomplished, – so that there be no cruelty, – the better will it be for civilisation.'[33]

My 'relations of genocide' thesis, then, was building on more than a century of commentary in which 'the structure of racial relations' was clearly recognized as meaning 'extermination' in the name of 'civilization'. It seems to have been the new combination of a theoretical perspective going back to Marx in the nineteenth century and a concept, genocide, from the twentieth that made it hard to accept, the more so because what Stanner called 'functional concomitance' was considered at odds with the official policy criterion loaded onto 'genocide'. It was the important first contribution of Dirk Moses, who would lead a new generation of Australian genocide scholars, to show how structural realities, policy understandings and the intentional actions of nineteenth-century settlers could be explicated as a history of genocide.

In looking afresh at 'the genocidal moment' and its origins, Moses sought to construct a more 'dynamic' analysis from what he delineated as alternatives: 'objective' structure and 'subjective genocidal policy development and implementation'.[34] 'Sartre and Barta's case about "implicit" intention and "relations of genocide" articulate the importance of structures at the expense of human agency,' he argued. Marx offered 'necessary but insufficient tools' which led to 'avoiding, rather than confronting, the problem of intention, agency, and consciousness in genocide'. There might appear to be too strong an emphasis on opposing concepts here but trying to distinguish conceptual differences is always useful, and so is an insistence on construing actions. In my view, Moses was pointing genocide studies in exactly the right direction, towards a more dialectical understanding of historical process that would bring theory to bear on the record of developments, declarations and deeds. His own demonstration of the approach with reference to the Queensland frontier showed the way and signalled a new moment of genocide awareness in Australia.

Stolen children, absorption, assimilation, reconciliation, self-destruction

Moses set his essay within the contemporary context. There had been politically contentious legal rulings in favour of Aboriginal land rights, subsequent propaganda battles over legislation, and heightened emotions over the 1996 official report of an enquiry into the removal of Aboriginal children from their families and communities.[35] The testimonies of old people who as children were snatched by police from parents they would never see again at last broke through into public expressions of sorrow, shame and – more problematically – a campaign for 'reconciliation'. Some (like me) who distrusted 'reconciliation' as the latest form of 'decent disposal' found a yet more problematical usage demanding attention in an unexpected way. For the second time an indictment of 'genocide' appeared in an Australian official document. It was not a legal prosecution, but because the accusation came from the pen of a retired High Court judge it had the possibility of carrying more authority than the case built by commentators and historians had been able to muster. Dissenting commentators – and historians – proceeded to question whether Sir Ronald Wilson really knew what he was talking about, and whether his 'rhetoric' wasn't doing more harm than good to reconciliation, but the point had been made. The main focus of writing on genocide became 'the stolen generations'.

The re-orientation of the discourse became impossible to separate from the political climate. The report was an historic breakthrough in Australian consciousness. With a new immediacy, it seemed, people in the insulated middle class heard Aboriginal people speak of what had been done to them and the consequences over many generations. Television became a medium of direct witness in a way people had experienced with Holocaust witnesses (some of them neighbours in Australia) but not with indigenous Australians (all from outside the neighbourhood). Feature films – the most successful was *Rabbit Proof Fence* – showed child removal as rationalized policy, human tragedy and courageous survival. Most affecting – they cannot be left out of the reception for academic historiography – were the songs. *Brown Skin Baby* and *Took the Children Away* remain the most compact, widely recognized and enduring histories, launched straight into the heart.[36]

The validation of oral history and victim's accounts had an immediate effect. There was palpable public sympathy. There was an equally powerful, initially less articulate, resistance to yet another revision of Australian history in the Aborigines' favour. The Prime Minister let it be known, even while the pain was still so raw, that he would not be saying sorry for wrongs committed. Instead the Commonwealth spent millions in denying responsibility.[37] The Deputy Prime Minister reassured his cattle- and sheep-raising constituency that new legislation allowing some native title to persist on pastoral leases would not affect any holding where Aboriginal rights had been 'extinguished'. The value order of white land over black lives was secure. There would be 'bucket loads of extinguishment'.[38]

In this context the unusual public prominence of a new claim of genocide made difficulties for historians as well. The opportunity to revise the freshly revealed trauma out of existence was seized by denialists, and there was often heated debate about whether removing mixed-race children from an Aboriginal environment and bringing them up to assimilate within the society of the Europeans could be classed as genocide. The historian and political commentator Robert Manne demonstrated that at the very least the idea of 'breeding out the colour' from a mixed-race population was influenced by the same genocidal racism that was current elsewhere in the 1930s, and the philosopher Raimond Gaita insisted that the use of the word gave 'a certain moral reading to what it means to intend the extinguishment of a people' which was certainly envisaged, 'with a racist contempt for them', during the time of the removal policy.[39]

When Dirk Moses edited a collection of new writing on *Genocide and Settler Society* his title explicitly linked 'Frontier violence and stolen indigenous children in Australian history'. Tracing that link remains a key challenge for historians. Essays by the foremost scholars of the removal policy (Robert Manne) and its tragic application (Anna Haebich) are examples of how the discourse on genocide can illuminate empirical research. They are given a wider context by an article on the kidnapping by the Germans of 'racially valuable' children in occupied

Eastern Europe (Isabel Heinemann) and by one of Jürgen Zimmerer's path-breaking essays on 'the archaeology of genocide' tracing the roots of the Holocaust in earlier German colonialism. The opening essay by Moses is a comprehensive introduction to the key issues in Australian genocide historiography.[40]

Whether this important historical work compels wider recognition of the link between the catastrophe of settlement sustained by indigenous people and the ongoing pressures of absorption and assimilation remains to be seen. Manne has reproduced statements by responsible officials in the 1930s and 1940s that would not have been out of place in Nazi Germany. There can be no doubt at all about a programme of absorbing 'half-caste' and other fractionally European children – by kidnapping if necessary – into the 'white race'. At a national conference on the issue in 1937 the main point of contention was not the morality of stealing children but the question of the black remainder. The Northern Territory representative, Dr Cook, worried that a too conscientious regime of protection could see numbers increase to the point where in the north of the continent there could be 'a large black population which may drive out the white.' The Western Australian official, Mr Neville, was reassuring about full-blood survival: 'No Matter what we do, they will die.' Their extinction would be accompanied by continued biological and cultural absorption so that after 50 years or so everyone would be able 'to forget that there were ever any Aborigines in Australia'.[41]

That has not happened. The turn from an overtly genocidal discourse to one of Aboriginal survival and cultural assimilation is clear in the official record.[42] That did not mean officials stopped removing children with the mixture of callousness and virtuous justification established for more than a century. Families and communities were traumatized for another heedlessly damaged sequence of generations. Only when relations with police erupted into violence, when Aboriginal deaths in custody broke into media attention, and when the stolen children were finally heard, was the national sense of satisfactory progress towards 'One Australia' disturbed. Scares about the High Court delivering the family farm – or even the family home in the suburbs – into Aboriginal hands counted for more in popular consciousness than the continuing pressure for Aborigines to embrace the standards (and opportunities) Australians should be proud of.

'Reconciliation' remains the favoured path to integration. It is less in fashion than it was. A national Sorry Day is remembered mainly among Indigenous people. Some local authorities express sympathy with low-key public observance. Meanwhile, revelations about sexual abuse in Aboriginal communities, rendered dysfunctional by alcohol, drugs and domestic violence, fill the media. A large headline points to chronic unemployment, overcrowded housing, blame being passed by Commonwealth and State politicians. Millions of dollars appear to make no impression. A small headline reads 'Mortality rate shock'. It is a report from *The Lancet* that an Aboriginal infant is three times more likely to die than a non-indigenous baby, and the gap is growing. 'Being an indigenous baby in Australia is becoming increasingly dangerous.' The relative risk rose between 1980 and 2001.[43]

Destruction has been restored to the agenda by the violent and hopeless realities of many Aboriginal lives. Whether substance abuse and violence denotes living Aboriginal communities or dying ones comes close to the nub of the issue. If the insistence on protecting abused women and children by the full force of white law also means a renewed push for full assimilation, they are likely to side with men who manipulate conceptions of 'culture' (and male power) to impede reporting of criminal acts. Once again, they feel a malevolent, indifferent, exasperated or well-meaning majority is unlikely to protect them but will exact a price – loss of identity – that Aborigines have resisted for two centuries. To Australians aware of the destruction in the past, the tragedy now is a self-destruction Aboriginal identity does not seem able to prevent.

Once again it is not only a matter of good or bad intentions, but of perspectives. In one view it is a simple matter of enforcing decent standards. Another view sees decent disposal surviving and reviving. Amidst a chorus of complaint that Aboriginal culture cannot be a shelter for child abuse, one woman's voice has turned the issue back on the majority. Hers is not the only Aboriginal voice and it is not the last word but it will serve to recall historical realities not resolved by academic debates about definition.

> Imagine how you would feel if every time you opened the newspaper your culture was denigrated and attacked. Imagine how you would respond if your self-esteem was constantly maimed and abused. When I read attacks on my Aboriginal culture, my soul is sickened to the very root.
>
> The culturally abusive stolen generations episode was a specific racist and colonial practice that sought to whiten and remove indigenous peoples from the landscape of Australia through assimilation. It is estimated that tens of thousands of indigenous children were removed from their families and raised in institutions or fostered to non-indigenous parents. Its impact continues to disrupt our families. It is one of the causes of family breakdown.
>
> The best protection we can offer any child is to give them a sense of belonging. Culture can provide that sense of belonging and, through it, resilience.
>
> The non-indigenous community appears to be suffering from collective amnesia; read your own reports, particularly the deaths in custody report. Now that there is a vast evidence base that tells us assimilation is demonstrably harmful to my people, any resurgence of assimilation policy is clearly intentionally genocidal. Please stop the abuse of our children's culture; it is killing us, it is genocide.[44]

The moment of genocide in Australia

In his first contribution to genocide scholarship in Australia, Dirk Moses sought to distinguish 'genocidal moments' within the complex of attitudes and broader historical developments fostering the extermination of Aborigines as settlement advanced. In his later work he has done much to elucidate this larger genocidal moment as well: the 150 years in which the pressures on Aboriginal societies, cultures and biological reproduction created the environment for direct killing and acceptance that the inferior indigenous race would 'disappear'. The explication of this complex remains the work before us and the two books of essays edited by Moses, with important contributions from over 20 scholars, are major advances in our understanding.[45]

Whether this new productivity will produce a more engaged interest among other Australian historians, or their audience outside the academy, remains to be seen. Living in the midst of both environments, the academic profession and the multimedia present, I have doubts. It may be that we are passing through 'the moment of genocide' in historiography as well. From its opening as a question 20 years ago (that is, a question for all of Australia, not just Tasmania) to a possible high point in the present, with a tapering off as attention shifts again, this might be as good as it gets for those of us who have hoped to establish a new consciousness of the nation's past. There is a chance that genocide might yet become part of that consciousness but it is likely – let's be realistic – that it will be sealed as safely in the past as the extinction of the Tasmanians was easily assumed to be.[46] The raw nerve of the word 'genocide' will acquire a covering of healthy growth; there will be no thanks for pointing to scar tissue. Almost everyone, including many indigenous people, will think it best to 'move on'.

It is not yet two decades since the word first appeared in an official report and a front-page headline.[47] Now it may already have lost its brief power to shock or cause resentment. Its opponents, ranging from denialists like Windschuttle to academics who contest his claims, find more 'substantive' issues to argue about: the numbers killed and the reasons for their deaths.[48] Living memory of frontier crimes did not disturb the surface; history might not succeed where memory failed. Even genocide can be interred, and acceptance of genocide in the past can be voiced within the comfortable chatter of Australian complacency. For over a century Australians have scarcely cared about references to genocide in Tasmania; will they care more if genocide becomes unexceptionable as part of the larger Australian story?

There are fewer of us willing to rub open wounds than we might think. The popularity of genocide denial in Australia and the United States and the marginalizing of genocide discourse about both countries in their academies has not encouraged many to engage either with the present issues or the elusive past realities.[49] There is, of course, a positive side. Those historians who retain the more troubled impulses of their vocation have all kinds of very interesting leads. Some of them come from the empirical and theorizing work that has appeared in genocide studies, others from empirical and theoretical work far removed from (and sometimes opposed to) genocide studies.

The problem of teasing out intentions can help us here. Genocide is both a complex historical occurrence and a crime. It is a crime with a much more adequate definition than many want to acknowledge. But the realms of crime fascinate us precisely because the precision of the law does not, in all human and narrative terms, 'cover the case'. There would be no murder mysteries, no crime genre, if we needed only to ascertain the application of the law. If it is not historically sensible (in all meanings) to treat genocide as a matter of legal terms, what historical terms are adequate? What kinds of analysis, narrative, reflection are effective for historians' purposes? These purposes are many but amount to one: to create understanding. The careful, imaginative, theoretically informed studies that are now appearing will take us well past the misguided (and sometimes mischief-making) searches for a document announcing intent to destroy a whole people.[50]

It is no coincidence that the Australian scholars most interested in using concepts of genocide to make better sense of Australian history are also historians of Germany. For some (Dirk Moses, Paul Bartrop and myself) the interest in Germany came first. For others (Colin Tatz and Andrew Markus) the trajectory was towards Germany. And the reciprocation of German scholars (Jürgen Zimmerer and Norbert Finzsch) is now completing a circle that promises to be very productive – notably more productive than the glaring lack of comparative work with American scholars and American cases of genocide. The comparisons range from parallels in discourse about inferior peoples to the contrasting ways Germany and Australia have dealt with their genocidal pasts.[51] Prospects for further exploring how both Germany and Australia developed genocidal catastrophes in the context of modernization are better now than they were 20 years ago. With the recovery of Lemkin's writing on Tasmania the research (re-search) has come full circle to the origins of the concept in Germany's most extreme colonizing episode. The war for *Lebensraum* was for a future of German settlers ruling over the inferior peoples to the east. German actions against Poles and Russians were foremost in Lemkin's mind: the Holocaust was not yet widely known.

To import the language of holocaustology into a colonial context will not always be helpful. For instance, although perpetrators, bystanders and victims were recognized from the beginning as appropriate categories as genocide was being carried out in Australia, the terms themselves lacked currency and would not have covered a very important fourth category: those who drew the attention of contemporaries to what was happening. Much of our knowledge of the hidden events, and even more of the public language of genocide, comes from the fourth category in settler society, the outraged campaigners against both the crime and its too easy acceptance by the majority. The minority who wrote official reports and public denunciations are almost our only source for the explicit nature of the crime. In private journals and in testimony to enquiries perpetrators quickly learned the conventions of obfuscation and euphemism. Outright denial was rarely necessary: they could be confident of general support for the hard methods they felt compelled to adopt. But there were enough campaigners against those methods to maintain a quiver of conscience under the complacency.[52]

In the Australian genocide, perhaps more than in any other, the voices of the victims are faint and few. Indigenous peoples in the Americas have been paid more respect in histories because their voices could be heard, often resoundingly, in the historical record. The cries of indigenous peoples in Australia were rarely recorded in documents and were long treated as unvalidated tales in oral retellings. There are enough direct accounts from perpetrators to make the obfuscatory references transparent, but documentation of deaths at the hands of settlers and their police forces is scant. There is a longer tradition of ignoring the bystanders. Australia grew up, as it were, in the fundamental belief that forebears not directly involved were innocent of any violence even though each and every atrocity was explicitly perpetrated in their name. So Australia has been weaned onto what a genocide perspective can see as a 'bystander history' for all of its 200 years – but since that history is predicated on no recognition of genocide it has never been recognized as reinforcing bystander conceptions of innocence.[53]

The problems occasioned by conventional – that is, Holocaust-loaded – understandings of genocide have prompted some of the most forthright historians of frontier violence to avoid the concept. Among the most eminent are Henry Reynolds and Raymond Evans. Reynolds confronted the question directly in his questioning book, and also encouraged Alison Palmer to explore it further in her comparative study *Colonial Genocide*.[54] Like Evans and Moses, Palmer sees Queensland as the clearest Australian case. Evans clearly shares their conviction that terrible, genocidal events occurred there but worries that 'genocide' can impede understanding. With a co-author, Bill Thorpe, he has gone so far as to offer an alternative concept, 'indigenocide'. The term is suggested as one 'which fits Australian empirical realities rather better' and 'comes closer to accounting for the Australian settler colonizing process'. I welcome the emphasis on historical process, and the inclusion of 'governments, military forces, economic enterprises or their agents, private individuals' among those 'who carry out destructive actions, policies and practices on Indigenous/Aboriginal individuals, families and groups *mainly because of their perceived indigeneity or "Aboriginality"*'. This formula has the advantage of emphasizing prior possession and the multifaceted assault of an invading colonialism. But the case that this

is something other than genocide is not made convincingly; it seems the authors would prefer 'genocide' if it could be brought back to Lemkin's full definition, and recognized in all aspects of the UN formulation.

How far have we come in 'the recovery of genocide'? For historians of Australia there is little doubt, in my view, that the most important document to surface in recent times is not the smoking gun authorization Reynolds and others have insisted on but Lemkin's own authorization of a broad interpretation of intention and historical process. The chapter on Tasmania by the main author of the Genocide Convention is the most striking example of how writing history must not to be bound by narrowly legalistic or intentionalist constraints. More than any other compact account, it demonstrates how close scrutiny of actions as well as orders, of an impersonal 'civilizing process' as well as intentional harm, will have to be pursued if we are to understand the historical actuality of genocide. The pages on the decline of the Tasmanian survivors show Lemkin coming to grips with the simplicities and complexities of genocidal process: they speak of mismanagement and misunderstanding, of intertribal quarrels and inadequate rations. Bonwick's eyewitness observations are combined with Merivale's contemporary indictment. Lemkin, too, saw atrocity and Christianity, evil and benevolence, policy confounded by intractable realities of colonisation.[55]

There has been a deal of unnecessary twisting and turning to avoid Lemkin's term in naming what took place in Australia – other candidates are 'ethnocide' and 'cultural genocide' – but the argumentation is less than convincing if Lemkin is given his due.[56] The full scope of the original conception is more than adequate to cover the differences. Scholars who use such language do not intend to appease denialists, to whom the subtleties are merely incitements to more sport, but they do – intentionally – reaffirm a hierarchy of genocides with killings by machetes, guns, forced marches and gas in a special category at the top. The most quoted formulation of this view is by Inga Clendinnen:

> I am reasonably sophisticated in various modes of intellectual discussion, but when I see the word 'genocide' I still see Gypsies and Jews being herded into trains, into pits, into ravines, and behind them the shadowy figures of Armenian women and children being marched into the desert by armed men. I see deliberate murder: innocent people identified by their killers as a distinctive entity being done to death by organised authority.[57]

This is brilliantly constructed rhetoric. It was specifically directed against the 'ill-judged' language of the *Bringing Them Home* report. But the author of *Reading the Holocaust* was also reasserting the paradigm I had sought to shift in 1985. The pre-emptive strike of the first line does not help with the issues.

It might equally have been said that failure to engage with a more sophisticated discussion of genocide was a 'moral, intellectual and (as it has turned out) a political disaster'. Martin Krygier, who has publicly wrestled with the question more than once, has most recently observed that despite the word genocide being so 'drenched with Holocaust associations that it is no longer helpful to general public conversation', 'the conceptual case for it is convincing'.[58]

The public conversation will continue to make difficulties for the conceptual case. The interaction between historians, Aboriginal activists and official enquiries that contributed to a radicalization of historical language will recurrently polarize opinion. Invasion, dispossession and discrimination – such terms caused resentment among many who were not used to Aborigines being so constantly visible and vocal. So when 'genocide' also came into currency it was too much: how could that word be used of a people loudly proclaiming their continued presence? In one of the world's most open and tolerant societies there is not much tolerance for awkward elements of the past. When Australians find themselves uncomfortably reminded that they have never negotiated their place here, they most often have the reflex that Aborigines are forever trying to negotiate too much out of a society they did nothing to create.[59]

Some Aboriginal people, coping with the destructive forces of a modernity which can now be their only way forward, will not care to pursue the argument. Bain Attwood, who knows the record of what Aborigines survived as well as anyone, is an outspoken partisan of Aboriginal accounts having a more prominent role within historiography. He knows that many of them speak of surviving a genocide; for them there is no problem about terminology or the memory of the realities. Yet he remains 'sceptical' about 'the value of "genocide" as a conceptual tool' and suggests we regard Aboriginal use of it as 'a truthful *myth*', relating to *experience*, rather than the discipline of history.[60]

So: a decent disposal. Or perhaps not yet. There is much history to write and there will be many historians to write it. They will not be hampered by hidebound disputes over definition and ownership of genocide. They will create a discipline of history that makes the most of large conceptual frameworks and close readings of actions. The range of texts – from oral to virtual – will inspire new ways of construing meaning. The conventional sources are very far from exhausted and will be combined with new styles of narrative, description and interpretation. In one of the more adventurous histories connecting past and present Ross Gibson points to a society in which there is an unaccountable or perhaps accountable unease. How can the implications be most effectively opened up? Nuanced innuendo and minute explication need not exclude each other. The poetics of history are as old as Aboriginal tradition and as new as the latest information technology. The discipline of history, praise be, is not so readily disciplined.[61]

Notes

1. N. Loos, *Invasion and Resistance: Aboriginal-European relations on the North Queensland frontier 1861–1897* (Canberra: Australian National University Press, 1982), p. 160.
2. Instructions to Captain Arthur Phillip 23 April 1787. Reproduced, with some of Phillip's observations, in S. Stone, ed., *Aborigines in White Australia* (Melbourne: Heinemann, 1974), pp. 19–25. On the first encounter see also W. Tench, *1788*, ed., T. Flannery (Melbourne: Text, 1996); W. E. H. Stanner, *White Man Got No Dreaming* (Canberra: ANU Press, 1979); and I. Clendinnen, *Dancing with Strangers* (Melbourne: Text, 2003).
3. There is almost a full column of options and nuances in *The Shorter Oxford.* This set would seem to cover the most likely understandings of the 1893 readers.
4. How this affected a historian who led in recovering the knowledge, is recalled in H. Reynolds, *Why Weren't We Told?* (Sydney: Allen & Unwin, 1998) pp. 108–16.
5. A. D. Moses, 'The Holocaust and Genocide', in *The Historiography of the Holocaust*, ed., D. Stone (New York: Palgrave Macmillan, 2004), pp. 533–55; A. Curthoys and J. Docker, 'Genocide: Definitions, Questions, Settler Colonies', Introduction to special section '"Genocide"? Australian Aboriginal History in International Perspective', *Aboriginal History*, 25 (2001), 1–15. This important set of essays should be read in full and consulted for further historiographical leads.
6. Lemkin's chapter on Tasmania appeared for the first time in *Patterns of Prejudice*, 39, 2 (2005), 171–96, Colonial Genocide issue, ed., A. D. Moses and D. Stone. See also A. Curthoys, 'Raphael Lemkin's "Tasmania": An Introduction', in ibid., 162–9. It seems (ibid., 166) that Lemkin also wrote a chapter on 'Natives of Australia' that has not been found among his papers.
7. For the successes, and setbacks, of Aboriginal activists see B. Attwood, *Rights for Aborigines* (Sydney: Allen & Unwin 2003); R. Broome, *Aboriginal Australians*, 2nd edn (Sydney: Allen & Unwin, 2003); idem., *Aboriginal Victorians* (Sydney: Allen & Unwin, 2005); H. Goodall, *Invasion to Embassy: Land in Aboriginal Politics in New South Wales 1770–1972* (Sydney 1996); and A. Markus, *Blood from a Stone: William Cooper and the Australian Aborigines' League* (Sydney, 1988). Aboriginal accounts include M. Tucker, *If Everyone Cared* (Sydney: Ure Smith, 1977); J. Miller, *Koori: A Will to Win* (Sydney: Angus and Robertson, 1985).
8. The Boyer Lectures have continued to be an important opportunity for historians. In 1980 Bernard Smith addressed the genocidal past as *The Spectre of Truganini* and in 1999 Inga Clendinnen addressed the same past – without genocide – in *True Stories* (Sydney: ABC Books, 1999). The absence of Aborigines from early historical concern is reflected in S. Macintyre and J. Thomas, eds, *The Discovery of Australian History 1890–1939* (Melbourne: Melbourne University Press, 1995).
9. C. D. Rowley, *The Destruction of Aboriginal Society* (Melbourne: Penguin, 1972). 'The Aborigines Project of the Social Sciences Research Council of Australia (1964–7) was the first independently financed and controlled survey of Aborigines throughout Australia' (p. v). Aborigines were not counted in the national census before the 1967 referendum. For the role of anthropology before this time see P. Wolfe, *Settler Colonialism and the Transformation of Anthropology* (London: Cassell, 1999).
10. R. Evans, K. Saunders and K. Cronin, *Exclusion, Exploitation and Extermination: Race Relations in Colonial Queensland* (Sydney: Australia and New Zealand Book Company, 1975).
11. H. Reynolds, *The Other Side of the Frontier* (Melbourne; Penguin, 1981). For the continuing controversy about Reynolds' 20,000 total, see R. Broome, 'The statistics of

frontier conflict', in *Frontier Conflict: The Australian Experience*, eds, B. Attwood and S. G. Foster (Canberra: National Museum of Australia, 2003), pp. 88–98. For such matters – though not for debates on genocide – this collection is a good place to start.

12. H. Reynolds, *Frontier* (Sydney: Allen & Unwin, 1987), pp. 53–7. Reynolds recounted his personal and historical journey in *Why Weren't We Told?*
13. Murray to Arthur, 5 November 1830, in H. Reynolds, *An Indelible Stain? The Question of Genocide in Australia's History* (Melbourne: Viking, 2001), p. 4; T. Barta, 'The Question Mark', *Australian Book Review* (August 2001), 32–3.
14. Reynolds, *An Indelible Stain?* pp. 117–18, 154, 174.
15. Arthur to Murray, 20 November 1830, *An Indelible Stain?* p. 70. This is also the case usually made for Victoria, most recently by R. Broome, *Aboriginal Victorians: a History since 1800* (Sydney: Allen & Unwin, 2005), p. 81. For a powerfully different view see D. Watson, *Caledonia Australis: Scottish Highlanders on the Frontier of Australia* (Sydney: Collins, 1984). In his home district of Gippsland he found a history of violence and 'acts of genocide' by which the Scots Aborigines (as Marx called them), displaced from the Highlands by capitalist sheep farmers, brought sheep around the world to dispossess the Aborigines of Australia. A historian of settlement on the other side of Victoria is careful not to allege genocide. J. Critchett, *A 'Distant Field of Murder': Western District Frontiers*, (Melbourne: Melbourne University Press, 1990). She looks for evidence that a massacre on what became known as 'The Convincing Ground' might have been something other than a clash over women rather than land. However, she concludes (p. 190) that the whole district 'was an extended Convincing Ground' to convince the remaining Aborigines they had to accept the new order. See also Critchett's chapter in *Frontier Conflict*, eds, Attwood and Foster, pp. 52–62.
16. Lemkin has a notable sub-heading: 'Intent to destroy – who is guilty, Government or individuals' and pays careful attention to the whole range of acts, including child removal, that combined individual and official responsibility. Furthermore, in terms of legal status, social position, alcohol and even clothing as a contributor to illness, 'a great many deaths may be laid to the door of the civilizing process'. Lemkin, 'Tasmania', 186–95. Apart from research in official archives, his information came largely from J. Bonwick, *The Last of the Tasmanians; or, The Black War of Van Diemen's Land* (London: Sampson Low, 1870). As Curthoys points out in her Introduction, he would not have known of Clive Turnbull, *Black War: The Extermination of the Tasmanian Aborigines* (Melbourne: F. W. Cheshire, 1948) and other major histories were published only after a considerable interval. See Curthoys, 'Raphael Lemkin's "Tasmania"', 169, n.19.
17. K. Windschuttle, *The Fabrication of Aboriginal History*. Volume One: *Van Diemen's Land, 1803–1847* (Sydney: Macleay Press 2002, corrected edn, 2003). Apart from Reynolds, his main targets were L. Ryan, *The Aboriginal Tasmanians* (St Lucia: University of Queensland Press, 1981) and L. Robson, *A History of Tasmania* (Melbourne: Oxford University Press, 1983). For the work of N. J. B. Plomley, and its importance in refuting Windschuttle, see H. Reynolds, '*Terra Nullius* Reborn', in *Whitewash: On Keith Windschuttle's Fabrication of Aboriginal History*, ed., R. Manne (Melbourne: Black Inc., 2003) pp. 109–38.
18. Windschuttle took this tag from a piece by James Morris, one Reynolds had already called 'one of the most perverse international assessments' (*An Indelible Stain?* p. 51), reprinted in Chalk and Jonassohn (see note 30, below). M. Krygier and R. van Krieken address Windschuttle's 'industrial-strength obtuseness' and the relationship between colonialism and genocide in 'The Character of the Nation', in *Whitewash*, ed., Manne,

pp. 81–108. For the contemporary Australian context see in the same volume R. Manne, 'Introduction', pp. 1–13, and, for a comparative perspective, A. D. Moses, 'Revisionism and Denial', pp. 337–70.

19. T. Barta, 'After the Holocaust: Consciousness of Genocide in Australia', *Australian Journal of Politics and History*, 31, 1 (1985), 154–61, special issue, eds, K. Kwiet and J. A. Moses.
20. This may have been the 'surreal' effect Australia's leading genocide scholar later referred to. I remain less confident that the essay was 'the first to penetrate the membrane that locked or blocked out the unthinkable notion of genocide having occurred in this moral country'. C. Tatz, 'Confronting Australian Genocide', *Aboriginal History*, 25 (2001), 19. The recollection is reprinted in C. Tatz, *With Intent to Destroy: Reflecting on Genocide* (London, Verso, 2003), pp. 102–3, where the important 1999 discussion paper 'Genocide in Australia' is also republished.
21. For an insightful sorting out, and many apposite references, see A. D. Moses, 'Conceptual Blockages and Definitional Dilemmas in the "Racial Century"', *Patterns of Prejudice*, 36, 2 (2002), 7–36.
22. T. Barta, 'Consuming the Holocaust; Memory Production and Popular Film', *Contention*, 5, 2 (1996), 161–75.
23. Barta, 'After the Holocaust', 154–61.
24. The *Geelong Advertiser* 1846, in Barta, 'After the Holocaust', 157. For different interpretations of the way these sentiments fit into the 'extinction discourse' of the nineteenth century see R. McGregor, *Imagined Destinies: Aboriginal Australians and the Doomed Race Theory, 1880–1939* (Melbourne: Melbourne University Press, 1997) and P. Brantlinger, *Dark Vanishings: Discourse on the Extinction of Primitive Races, 1800–1930* (Ithaca, NY: Cornell University Press 2003). McGregor does not see a genocidal dimension; Brantlinger most forthrightly does. He also recognizes the influence of Darwin, who did not avoid the question of one people displacing another: see T. Barta, 'Mr Darwin's Shooters: On Natural Selection and the Naturalizing of Genocide', *Patterns of Prejudice*, 39, 2 (2005), 116–36.
25. T. Barta, 'Relations of Genocide: Land and Lives in the Colonization of Australia', in *Genocide and the Modern Age: Etiology and Case Studies of Mass Death*, eds, I. Wallimann and M. N. Dobkowski (Westport, CT: Greenwood Press, 1987), pp. 237–51. The following quotations are from the same source.
26. K. Marx, 'The Defense of the Moselle Correspondent: Economic Distress and Freedom of the Press' (1843), in *Writings of the Young Marx on Philosophy and Society*, eds, L. D. Easton and K. H. Guddat (New York: Doubleday Anchor, 1967), pp. 144–5.
27. Barta, 'Relations of Genocide', p. 239; L. Kuper, *Genocide: Its Political Use in the Twentieth Century* (New York: Penguin, 1981) was in turn quoting E. R. Wolf, 'Killing the Achés,' in *Genocide in Paraguay*, ed., R. Arens (Philadelphia, PA: Temple University Press, 1976) and J.-P. Sartre, *On Genocide* (Boston, MA: Beacon Press, 1968).
28. Rubenstein returned to these large dynamics in 'Modernization and the Politics of Extermination', in *A Mosaic of Victims: Non-Jews Persecuted and Murdered by the Nazis*, ed., M. Berenbaum (London: I. B. Tauris, 1990), pp. 3–19. For the larger canvas that made Rubenstein a uniquely bold pioneer in connecting the Holocaust with other genocides see *The Age of Triage: Fear and Hope in an Overcrowded World* (Boston, MA: Beacon Press, 1983).
29. Paul Bartrop, for instance, applies the exonerating yardstick of no official declaration impartially to murderous settlements in America and Australia. P. R. Bartrop, 'Punitive Expeditions and massacres: Gippsland, Colorado, and the Question of Genocide', in *Genocide and Settler Society*, ed., Moses, pp. 194–214; idem., 'The Powhatans of Virginia

and the English Invasion of America: Destruction without Genocide', *Genocide Perspectives*, 1 (1997), 66–108.

30. H. Fein, 'Defining Genocide as a Sociological Concept', in *Genocide: A Sociological Perspective* (London: Sage, 1990), reprinted in S. Gigliotti and B. Lang, eds, *The Holocaust: A Reader* (Oxford: Blackwell, 2005), pp. 318–419. We know from her *Imperial Crime and Punishment: the Massacre at Jallianwalla Bagh and British Judgement, 1919–1920* (Honolulu: University Press of Hawaii, 1977), that Fein engaged early with the less than straightforward expressions of colonial policy, but in a guidebook she co-edited, *Teaching about Genocide* (New York: Institute for the Study of Genocide, 1992), the treatment of colonial genocide, even in the Americas, was thin and dated. Another critic, Frank Chalk, who also has trouble with state and society, is quoted with approval by Fein because a case study of Australia fails to explain the significance of Germany's 'devastation of the Herero'. (Several comparisons have since appeared, including A. Palmer, *Colonial Genocide*, London: Hurst, 2000; and B. Madley, 'Patterns of Frontier Genocide 1803–1910: the Aboriginal Tasmanians, the Yuki of California, and the Herero of Namibia', *Journal of Genocide Research*, 6, 2, 2004, 167–92.) F. Chalk and K. Jonassohn, *The History and Sociology of Genocide: Analyses and Case Studies* (New Haven, CT: Yale University Press 1990) had, even for its time, a narrow conceptual framework and a woefully out-dated piece on Tasmania. Scholars or general readers interested in Australia will see an urgent need to update I. W. Charny, ed., *Encyclopedia of Genocide* (Santa Barbara, CA: ABC-Clio, 1999). For a more balanced and thoughtful overview see R. K. Hitchcock and T. M. Twedt 'Physical and Cultural Genocide of Various Indigenous Peoples', in *Century of Genocide: Eyewitness Accounts and Critical Views*, eds, S. Totten, W. S. Parsons and I. W. Charny (New York: Garland, 1997), pp. 372–91. Among interesting attempts to lay out a larger analysis see P. Stoett, 'Shades of Complicity: Towards a Typology of Transnational Crimes against Humanity', in *Genocide, War Crimes and the West: History and Complicity*, ed., A. Jones (London: Zed Books, 2004), pp. 31–55.
31. G. J. Andreopoulos, ed., *Genocide: Conceptual and Historical Dimensions* (Philadelphia, PA: University of Pennsylvania Press, 1994), pp. 7–9.
32. F. Chalk, 'Redefining Genocide', in ibid., esp. pp. 55–7.
33. W. E. H. Stanner, 'The History of Indifference Thus Begins', *Aboriginal History*, 1, 1 (1977). Originally drafted in 1963 and reprinted in *White Man Got No Dreaming*, pp. 165–97. Trollope quoted from his *Australia and New Zealand*, 2 vols, London 1872.
34. A. D. Moses, 'An Antipodean Genocide? The Origins of the Genocidal Moment in the Colonization of Australia', *Journal of Genocide Research*, 2, 1 (2000), 89–106.
35. *Bringing them Home. National Inquiry into the Separation of Aboriginal and Torres Strait Islander Children from their Families* (Canberra: Commonwealth Printer, 1996). The issues had been opened up during the 1980s by the organisation Link-up. Some of the stories were told in C. Edwards and P. Read, *The Lost Children* (Sydney: Doubleday, 1989). Other influential memoirs were S. Morgan, *My Place* (Fremantle: Fremantle Arts Centre Press, 1988) and the documentary film *Lousy Little Sixpence*, dir. Alex Bostock 1983.
36. Very soon, all modes of history – original documents, books, films, pictures, museum exhibitions, songs – will be opened with a click as electronic notes. But not in this edition, not yet.
37. Two removed children, Lorna Cubillo (aged nine in 1947) and Peter Gunner (aged eight in 1956) lost their case against the Commonwealth of Australia in 2000. Judgment at *Australian Indigenous Law Reporter*, http://www.austlii.edu.au/au/

journals/AILR/2000/29.html. This was a significant decision, asserting legality over morality, individual damage and historical wrong.

38. H. Reynolds, *Why Weren't We Told?* (Melbourne: Penguin, 1999), pp. 217–25.
39. R. Manne, 'In Denial: the Stolen Generations and the Right', *Australian Quarterly Essay*, 1 (2001), and R. Gaita, *A Common Humanity* (Melbourne: Text, 1999). The quotation is from correspondence in *The Australian Book Review* (September 2001). See also S. Gigliotti, 'Unspeakable Pasts as Limit Events: the Holocaust, Genocide, and the Stolen Generations', *Australian Journal of Politics and History*, 49, 2 (2003), 164–81.
40. A. D. Moses, ed., *Genocide and Settler Society: Frontier Violence and Stolen Indigenous Children in Australian History* (New York: Berghahn, 2004). The essays, notes and bibliography make this, like the *Aboriginal History* volume on genocide, an essential text. See also the major histories by A. Haebich, *For their Own Good: Aborigines and Government in the South West of Western Australia, 1900–1940* (Nedlands, 1992) and *Broken Circles: Fragmenting Indigenous Families* (Fremantle: 2000).
41. R. Manne, 'Aboriginal Child Removal and the Question of Genocide, 1900–1940', in *Genocide and Settler Society*, ed., Moses, pp. 217–43. The most widely read of the new histories from the 1980s, R. Broome, *Aboriginal Australians* (Sydney: Allen & Unwin, 1982), p. 161, was the first to characterize the absorption policy as 'an attempt at benign genocide'.
42. R. McGregor, 'Governance, Not Genocide: Aboriginal Assimilation in the Postwar Era', in *Genocide and Settler Society*, ed., Moses, pp. 290–311.
43. *The Age*, Melbourne, 26 May 2006. There is also an escalating dispute about the role of customary law in sentencing; it is portrayed as allowing an excuse for child abuse.
44. M. Bamblett, 'Culture makes us what we are', *The Age*, 3 June 2006. Muriel Bamblett is CEO of the Victorian Aboriginal Childcare Agency and chairwoman of the Secretariat of National Aboriginal and Islander Child Care.
45. Moses, ed., *Genocide and Settler Society*; idem., ed., *Empire, Colony, Genocide* (New York: Berghahn, 2008).
46. Ryan, *The Aboriginal Tasmanians* attracted attention from all sides (then and again recently) not only for reopening the genocide question but also for recovering indigenous Tasmanians from assumed extinction.
47. 'Past policy genocide; inquiry QC', *The Age*, 21 September 1989. The report was on the Royal Commission on Aboriginal Deaths in Custody – another area where improvements mandated have not been maintained.
48. As to the kind of history, and the kind of status it gives the historian, I can't improve on Martin Flanagan: 'Windschuttle mounted what I would liken to a legal argument. The argument was clever and glib, like a Japanese historian writing a history of the Burma railway entirely from Japanese newspaper reports and military records. But such an inadequate history about a war crime committed against our people would be howled down. Windschuttle was howled up. Keith Windschuttle was the historian John Howard's Australia had to have. Now he's advising us on policy.' [Windschuttle had just been appointed to the Board of the ABC.] M. Flanagan, 'Is reconciliation dead? Or will white Australia finally listen? *The Age*, 2 June 2006. For more detailed arguments confronting the denialist turn in Australian history, see Manne, ed., *Whitewash*, and Attwood, below.
49. At an extraordinary national 'summit' on teaching Australian history there was no one representing the 'Black Armband' view of Australia's past decried by the Prime Minister and several of the participants. Newspaper commentary was extensive, generally in favour of a basic narrative with room for different interpretations.

One editorial perhaps summed up the Prime Ministerial view when it quoted Winston Churchill: 'History will be kind to me for I intend to write it.' *The Age*, 17 August 2006.

50. The parallel to David Irving and his fixation on the missing Hitler order is evoked by Windschuttle's Irvingesque insistence on being the umpire of what will count as evidence.
51. T. Barta, 'Discourses of Genocide in Germany and Australia: a Linked History', *Aboriginal History*, 25 (2001), 37–56; N. Finzsch, 'It is scarcely possible to conceive that human beings could be so hideous and loathsome: discourses of genocide in eighteenth- and nineteenth-century America and Australia, *Patterns of Prejudice*, 39, 2 (2005), 97–115; A. D. Moses, 'Coming to Terms with Genocidal Pasts in Comparative Perspective: Germany and Australia', *Aboriginal History*, 25 (2001), 91–115. Also A. Dirk Moses and Dan Stone, eds, *Colonialism and Genocide* (London: Routledge, 2007).
52. H. Reynolds, *This Whispering in our Hearts* (Sydney: Allen & Unwin, 1998) and *Why Weren't We Told*, pp. 104–12.
53. There is a parallel to Germany here, too, often better addressed on the screen than on the page. T. Barta, 'Recognising the Third Reich: "Heimat" and the Ideology of Innocence', in *History on/and/in Film*, eds, T. O'Regan and B. Shoesmith (Perth: History and Film Association of Australia, 1987), pp. 131–9. Important television productions before the bicentenary of settlement included John Pilger *The Secret Country* (ABC); Alex Bostock and others, the *Rainbow Serpent* series (SBS); discussion forum *Is there anything to celebrate in 1988?* (ABC); Four Corners' *Black Death* (ABC); and the still unsurpassed historical drama *Women of the Sun* (SBS). On film and historiography more broadly see my 'History Since the Cinema', in *Screening the Past: Film and the Representation of History*, ed., T. Barta (Westport, CT: Praeger, 1998), pp. 1–17.
54. Palmer, *Colonial Genocide*.
55. Lemkin, 'Tasmania', 188–95.
56. On ethnocide see A. Markus, 'Genocide in Australia', *Aboriginal History*, 25 (2001), 57–69; on cultural genocide R. van Krieken, 'The Barbarism of Civilization: Cultural Genocide and the "Stolen Generations"', *British Journal of Sociology*, 50, 2 (1999), 297–315.
57. I. Clendinnen, 'First Contact', *Australian Review of Books*, 7, (May 2001), 26, quoted by B. Attwood, 'The Stolen Generations and Genocide: Robert Manne's *In Denial: The Stolen Generations and the Right*', *Aboriginal History*, 25 (2001), 163–72. Attwood here agrees with Clendinnen that using the term in this context has been a 'political disaster' but adds that 'the concept of genocide ... *might* still be useful in to us in the historical task of imagining and so understanding the past of our forbears (and therefore, in time, it might have beneficial political outcomes).'
58. M. Krygier 'The Rhetoric of Reaction', *Australian Financial Review*, 1 July 2005, reprinted in *Civil Passions* (Melbourne: Black Inc., 2005). Krygier recognizes that avoiding the word does not dispose of the issue: 'we are simply left with the need to find some other word and idea.'
59. Many people will have gained insight into the ideological origins of this attitude, and the genocidal impulses of early settlers, through Kate Grenville's novel *The Secret River* (Melbourne: Text, 2005) but the cavalier transpositions of 'actual events' in time and place make it exasperating for historians. Should all fictions be excluded from historiography? Compare K. Grenville, *Searching for the Secret River* (Melbourne: Text, 2006) and I. Clendinnen, *The History Question* (Melbourne: Black Inc., Quarterly Essay 3, 2006).

60. B. Attwood, *Telling the Truth about Aboriginal History* (Sydney: Allen & Unwin, 2005), pp. 87–105, and notes (with many further references) on pp. 218–28. This view is criticized by R. Kennedy, 'Stolen Generation Testimony: Trauma, Historiography and the Question of "Truth"', *Aboriginal History*, 25 (2001), 116–31. Attwood's chapter, like the book as a whole, concentrates first on demolishing arguments made by Keith Windschuttle, whose references to genocide scholarship are polemically of a piece with his primitive reading of the historical record.
61. R. Gibson, *Seven Versions of an Australian Badland* (St Lucia: University of Queensland Press, 2002). Gibson has made one of the most interesting films about indigenous and settler ways of seeing (*Camera Natura,* 1986) and has recreated settlement history as multimedia installation (Museum of Sydney). On the poetics and conventions of history see G. Dening, *Performances* (Melbourne: Melbourne University Press, 1996).

12

Colonial Genocide: The Herero and Nama War (1904–8) in German South West Africa and Its Significance[1]

Jürgen Zimmerer

> A century ago, the oppressors – blinded by colonialist fervour – became agents of violence, discrimination, racism and annihilation in Germany's name. The atrocities committed at that time would today be termed genocide – and nowadays a General von Trotha would be prosecuted and convicted. We Germans accept our historical and moral responsibility and the guilt incurred by Germans at that time. And so, in the words of the Lord's Prayer that we share, I ask you to forgive us our trespasses.[2]

With these words the German Minister for Development and Economic Cooperation, Heidemarie Wieczorek-Zeul, officially apologized on 14 August 2004 in Omahakari, Namibia for the atrocities committed a century earlier by German imperial troops. Hundred years after the genocidal warfare conducted by the *Schutztruppe* in German South West Africa, in which the German colonial army deliberately killed thousands of Herero and Nama men, women and children; let even more die of thirst in the Omaheke desert; and murdered thousands more by deliberate neglect in concentration camps, the German government officially acknowledged these crimes. To my knowledge it is the first and only apology by a high-ranking member of the government of a former colonial power referring to genocide for colonial crimes. This acknowledgement of historical guilt and the application of the term genocide[3] not only changed the landscape of memory in Germany but can also be considered a landmark event in dealing with genocides in the colonial context.[4]

It is no accident that the first official apology for genocide in a former colony was delivered by a German politician. Had it not been for the Holocaust and a specific German popular culture of Holocaust remembrance – which led to a more distanced and critical relationship to the German national past as such – accepting historical responsibility in such a grave matter as colonial mass atrocities would not have been possible. The case of the Herero proves that acknowledging a colonial genocide – as indeed any other – is not necessarily apologetic of the Holocaust, it does not diminish German guilt and/or responsibility. To the contrary: the public acknowledgement of the existence of a racist and oppressive Germany prior to the Third Reich disproves the apologetic assumption of Hitler and his racist Third Reich as a mere 'freak accident in German history'.[5] If Hitler was only a derailment from an in other respects positive track, then these 12 'dark years' can easily be exorcised from German national history.

Not least for this reason, the debate about the Herero and Nama genocide possesses deeper significance and, as a result, Omahakari 2004 is seen by many observers as in line with Willy Brandt's famous knee-bending in Warsaw in order to honour the victims of German crimes. Furthermore Wieczorek-Zeul's speech sets a precedent, with which other governments and both the descendants of former victims and perpetrators alike will have to deal. Not least for this reason, the Herero case is closely observed internationally. Furthermore the manifold problems of researching and writing on colonial genocide can be seen in this case like in a prism. Analyzing the Herero and Nama genocide therefore also means reflecting on the historiography of colonial genocide more generally.

This historiographical exercise proves to be somewhat awkward for me, as I have myself been involved in the debate for more than a decade now. The apology and the current debate, in particular, originate to some extent from publications to which I have contributed or scholarly endeavours of which I was part. To pretend utter impartiality seems therefore a false pretence, and I would therefore like to follow a much more prominent example in a predecessor to this book, where Christopher Browning refers to his own active involvement in the debates he was about to summarize, and concluded:

> I have decided openly to use the first person rather than third person to avoid both stylistic infelicity and any pretence that I am transcending my own involvement and offering an unengaged view. I have tried, of course, to be fair in summarizing and evaluating the contributions of others, but what follows, none the less, is an inextricable mix of analysis, academic memoir and advocacy.[6]

I will restrict the following observations to scholarly publications only. As I will briefly discuss at the end of these considerations, it comes as no surprise that there exists quite a number of memoirs and accounts of the war by contemporaries, which celebrate colonial or military nostalgia. The fact that non-historians of German descent in Namibia – like farmers or craftsmen – now confront academic historians actively and aggressively with their own 'truth', using their knowledge of the country as an argument to dismiss out of hand any insights by 'outsiders/foreigners' is an interesting phenomenon, which would merit closer attention in the future.

The war (1904–8)

Let me begin with a very short summary of the events, which unfolded from 12 January 1904 in German South West Africa and which soon turned into arguably one of the most brutal colonial wars ever fought in history.[7] Together with the Maji-Maji War in German East Africa (1905–7)[8] the Namibian War symbolizes both the hubris and the utter failure of the German colonial project. What was supposed to prove to the world the superior colonizing skills of Germans fell to pieces within the first 20 years of Germany's colonial adventure.[9]

Germany was a colonial latecomer. Of the four African colonies that it acquired in 1884–5, German South West Africa (today Namibia) fuelled contemporary Germans' fantasies more than any other. Since it was the only possession deemed suitable for large-scale German settlement it served as a screen for all sorts of colonial fantasies.

After a slow start German colonial administration gradually intensified its grip on people and territory and governor Leutwein (1893–1904) established a system of indirect rule in order to buy time for his large scale plans for social engineering. According to him and his young assistants the African population was to be transformed into a workforce suitable for German economic demands. Since Leutwein did not have the military power to subjugate them, he hoped that by maintaining the traditional rulers formally in office, the profound effects of political and social changes being implemented would remain hidden. Of course, the assumption that the Africans would accustom themselves to the foreign power was illusionary from the beginning. The officially endorsed plans for the immigration of more and more Germans, which was part of the development programme for the settler colony, was bound, in the long run, to aggravate problems with the indigenous population. This was especially the case as some of the new arrivals revealed a blatant sense of racist superiority and behaved like members of a master race. Above all, rapes which could no longer be punished by the traditional African elites, not only raised the people against the Germans but simultaneously undermined the position of the African rulers. They could do nothing to protect their people, as the 'dual legal system' did not permit African authorities to pass judgement on 'whites', whereas German courts hardly ever punished crimes committed against African men and women. In 1897 a natural disaster further eroded African social systems, diminishing not only African ability to defend against increasing encroachments of 'Whites', but also forcing an increasing number of Africans to sell their labour to white farmers, businessmen and the colonial administration, thereby intensifying direct contact with their new colonial masters.[10]

After provocations by subaltern German officers war finally broke out on 12 January 1904, rudely waking German officials and the military from their dream that the Africans would submit to their fate and would offer no resistance to the increasing loss of their land, the limits placed on their autonomy and the attacks on their men and women, mothers and daughters. But equally, nobody expected that it would end in genocide. There had been conflicts before, but they normally ended with a peace treaty, the cession of land in favour of the colonial government and the like. This time the Africans were too successful. Within a few days they killed 123 German settlers on their farms, and looted their premises. Only the larger settlements and fortifications could be defended by the Germans. It is noteworthy, that in contrast to the rumours at the time, the Herero did not kill women, children, foreigners or missionaries.

Since the Herero failed to gain a final victory, the Germans won the opportunity to send reinforcements from Germany. Command of these reinforcements was passed from the governor to General Lothar von Trotha, a protégé of the highest military circles in Berlin. He was a highly appraised colonial warfare veteran, who had gained notoriety for his brutality in German East Africa and as a member of the German expeditionary force to crush the so-called Boxer Rebellion in China in 1900–1. If one is to ask in what respect war against the Herero and Nama differed from earlier campaigns, where the path to a war of extermination and genocide was entered on, it can be found in the decision to deprive Leutwein of his power and to have the campaign run by von Trotha.

Whereas Leutwein intended to use this opportunity to crush once and for all Herero political structures, to make them 'politically dead', von Trotha was influenced by his vision of an ongoing race war, which would end only with the complete destruction of either the 'white' or the 'black' race. In his opinion, Africans would only 'give way to brute force', which had to be used with 'gross terror and even with cruelty'. To that end, he was willing to exterminate 'the rebellious tribes in streams of blood'.[11] After all, in his opinion war in Africa couldn't be fought 'according to the laws of the Geneva Convention', as he later put it.[12] Strictly following a military fantasy of total victory he was not inclined to take any economic considerations seriously, including those which pointed to the need for African labourers in the development of the colony after the war.

There had been massacres of Africans from the beginning. But whereas those were still single events as opposed to a systematic policy of extermination, von Trotha soon ordered mass murder. Already in June, before he even arrived in the colony, he empowered his officers to have all Africans 'who were to be found engaging in treacherous acts against German troops, for example all armed rebels who were found at wartime acts, to be shot without prior trial [...].'[13] That basically meant that all enemy soldiers were to be killed.

While the massacres at the beginning of the war can perhaps be attributed to a certain 'heat of battle', of panic or a desire for revenge for personal losses, von

Trotha's orders must be seen as a rational tactical choice. With them, von Trotha transformed massacre and terror into deliberate aspects of German warfare; without doubt a major step towards genocide.

After the 'Battle' at the Waterberg, the German army started to implement their genocidal programme in earnest. The encircled Herero had managed to escape eastwards towards the desert areas of the Omaheke. German troops pursued the fugitives and deliberately drove them into the waterless areas, which they then sealed off against the return of fugitives, in order to let them die of thirst. In his infamous genocide order of 2 October 1904 von Trotha decreed:

> The Hereros are no longer German subjects.
>
> They have murdered and stolen, have cut off the ears and noses and other body parts from wounded soldiers, and in cowardice no longer want to fight. ... [T]he Herero people must leave the country. If the people does not do that, then I will force it to with the Groot Rohr [big cannon].
>
> Within the German border every Herero, armed or not, with cattle or without, will be shot, I will not take up any more women or children, will drive them back to their people or let them be shot at.

Women were not to be shot directly but the shots were 'to be fired above them, to force them to run.' As he cynically wrote, he assumed that his proclamation would 'not lead to cruelty against women and children'.[14] The only place that they could run to, though, was the desert, where thousands died of thirst as a result of this order.

This order did not initiate genocide, the practice was already well under way, but it lent further legitimacy to it. And it proves the genocidal intent of the various measures which we have already discussed above.

When the order was finally cancelled – against von Trotha's will – genocide had already been committed. And the change of mind in Berlin was not humanitarian in origin, but resulted from a growing fear that news about German atrocities could be used in Europe for propaganda against the German government. High circles in Berlin supported von Trotha's policy in principle, approved his 'intention to annihilate or expel the entire nation', since, as von Schlieffen, the General Chief of Staff, wrote, the 'race war, once commenced, can only be ended by the annihilation or the complete enslavement of one party.' In his eyes 'von Trotha's intentions can therefore be approved of', and it was regrettable, von Schlieffen continued, that von Trotha did not have the power to carry out his plans.[15]

But it was not only international public opinion that made the German government force von Trotha to change his strategy. Developments in South West Africa also made a change of policy necessary: the Nama under their *kaptein* Hendrik Witbooi, who had supported the *Schutztruppe* with a small detachment of soldiers as late as the Battle of Waterberg, had now also entered the war against the Germans. As a result, the attempt to seal off the Sandveld had to be cancelled. The troops were needed elsewhere.

Now, with the help of the missionaries, holding camps were set up to gather the Herero survivors. They were then sent to concentration camps, which had been set up in the meantime next to all major settlements. From these concentration camps, military and government institutions, but also private companies, were supplied with forced labourers. They also fulfilled an important function in the war against the Nama. Since the latter, in contrast to the Herero, avoided any large-scale battles and waged a guerrilla war that almost defeated the German army, the *Schutztruppe* used the camps as holding camps for civilians who had been forcibly moved out of the battle zone in order to prevent them supporting the guerrilla fighters.

Where Nama were not deported, the German army indulged in a strategy of destroying the Nama's food and particularly their sources of water. As with German strategy after the Battle of Waterberg, the Germans deliberately aimed at cutting the enemy off from the essential means of life, hereby deliberately targeting women and children, too. In so doing this became a war of extermination as well.

The concentration camps served – among other things – as labour camps, which lent out prisoners to local businesses, the army or the colonial administration for work. In some of them, most notoriously Shark Island near Lüderitzbuch, inmates were deliberately killed through neglect.

Finally, Germany unilaterally declared the end of war on 31 March 1907. But captivity continued until January 1908, when it was brought to a close in celebration of the Kaiser's birthday and the last Herero and Nama were released. In the meantime a tight system of control had been set up so that the freedom of the released prisoners was a very limited one. With the introduction of the 'Native Ordinances' of 1907 a system of quasi total control was intended, which subjected the Africans directly to German norms, codified a society based on racial privilege and introduced a labour market based on modified serfdom. All Africans had to carry pass-badges and were entered in 'native registers'. They had no freedom of movement and it was forbidden for more than ten families to reside together. They were forced to work on European premises. Since the Herero and Nama had already been dispossessed of all their lands and their political organizations had been disbanded there was now no alternative for them than to sell their labour to the white colonial masters.[16]

The colonial state may not have succeeded in exterminating the Herero and Nama and the system of total control never worked perfectly. Nevertheless, these policies together with the preceding genocide fundamentally altered the social and power structure in German South West Africa.

Historiography of a war

Given the importance of the genocide in German South West Africa – symbolized among other things by the very fact of the aforementioned official apology – it is surprising how little scholarly attention it received until recent years. If German colonialism was already a widely neglected field, this was even more so for the question of colonial mass violence or genocide. In the following sections, I will briefly summarize the major contributions to our understanding of the Namibian War and link them to the current discussion about genocide, before touching on the intriguing question of its historical place both in Namibian and German history.[17] I will focus my attention on the question of the war and of the occurrence of genocide, dealing with the broader issues of Namibian history and its development over the last decades only in passing.

Until very recently, German colonialism has never attracted much scholarly attention. The early loss of its colonial empire spared Germany the post-World War II frictions that decolonization imposed on other countries such as Great Britain, France, the Netherlands or Portugal, and both the public and the scholarly community forgot about the very existence of a German colonial empire. Where traces of collective remembrance existed, it was in line with a positive heroic master narrative of a generally benevolent German colonialism, which echoed both imperial ideology in Wilhelmine Germany and pro-colonial propaganda during the Weimar Republic and the Third Reich. German colonialism was seen as more caring about 'natives' and less violent than its English or French counterparts. Whereas exploitation characterized British and French colonial design, so the story went, development and education stood at the forefront of the German endeavour.

In general, historiography in the Eastern part of divided Germany was more critical than in the West. And it was from there that the first critical scholarly accounts of German colonialism originated. This comes as no surprise, first, because the former colonial archives were situated in Potsdam, and could easily be accessed, and second, because the GDR claimed, in accordance with its socialist ideology, to support decolonization and national liberation movements all over the world. Writing anti-colonial history was part of that programme. Third, the GDR saw itself as distanced from the history of Imperial Germany, which was regarded as a precursor to the West German Federal Republic, whereas by definition the GDR stood for a new Germany.

With regards to South West Africa, the first major account was published by Horst Drechsler in 1966, followed three years later by West German historian Helmut Bley.[18] Both books marked, with a few notable exceptions, the state of our knowledge until the late 1990s, and they can still be read and used with great profit. Drechsler was also the first German historian, who – to my knowledge – applied the term genocide to the war of 1904–7/8. As recent scholarship has discovered, already a decade earlier the Polish-Jewish lawyer Raphael Lemkin, who coined the term 'genocide' after the experiences of the Jews in World War II and the Armenians in the Ottoman empire a generation earlier, and who is regarded as the founder of the UN Genocide convention, had also included the Herero in his unfinished multi-volume 'History of Genocide', but this had no effect on the discussion in Germany – or internationally for that matter.[19]

Drechsler's analysis suffered, however, from the absence of any critical reflection on the terminology he used. Far from being a theoretically informed discussion of whether or not the concept of genocide can be applied to the events in South West Africa or what genocide meant exactly, Drechsler used it as a synonym for brutality and a large number of casualties. In many respects this obscured more than it enlightened, since without a theoretical discussion of the genocide concept, critics could easily dismiss it as a mere strategy to attract public attention.

And criticism there was and still is plenty, coming mainly from the wider public both in Germany and in Namibia. The fact that Drechsler was a 'communist' historian, writing at the height of the Cold War, served and still serves as a convenient reason to dismiss his findings altogether,[20] displaying in the process complete disregard for recent scholarship, which has largely confirmed Drechsler's perspective. Of course his findings and explanations can be challenged and have to be modified – as I have done myself extensively[21] – but dismissing it as mere 'communist' propaganda, as even established scholars have sometimes done, does not do justice to his work. There surely is a lot of lip service in his book to the prevailing ideology of his country, but that does not diminish Drechsler's lasting achievement: to have pointed to the large scale and even endemic violence in German colonialism.

From the perspective of genocide history, however, his book possesses two major weaknesses, which have haunted scholarship to this day. First of all, his aim of constructing German imperialism as a precursor to the Third Reich, as well as his methodological dependence on a rather crude Marxism-Leninism, made him paint a black and white picture of a monolithic German administration which from the very beginning had a grand plan for the total disappropriation of the indigenous population and carried it through with its almost unlimited power. No alteration or adaptation to the changing fortunes of war were necessary, it seems. Even the Herero escape from German encirclement at the Waterberg was not attributed by Drechsler to Herero leadership, but was explained by a sinister plan by von Trotha, who allegedly left one escape route open so that the Herero would flee towards the desert. In Drechsler's narrative the image of an almost all-powerful German army corresponded with the image of a victimized, rather passive African population. Despite Drechsler's attempts to construct a – equally misleading – picture of a unified African struggle as a precursor to the later liberation struggle against the South African occupiers, African agency is largely missing in his account. According to Drechsler the Germans decided the course of war, once the Herero had started it. Furthermore, since he was primarily interested in analyzing German capitalism and its disastrous consequences, he dealt at length with the causes of the war of 1904–8, and devoted only a few precursory pages to post-war events and developments. This absence further enhances the image of passivity on the part of the Herero and Nama. 'The peace of the graveyard', Drechsler called his chapter dealing with the post-war period of German rule, thereby grossly neglecting both African reconstruction processes and frictions within the white settler community with regard to the implication of the new native policy based on almost total control. Drechsler confuses German plans and ordinances for the political reality and takes their implementation for granted, thereby leaving no room either for African strategies of resistance or alternative German approaches to 'native policy'.[22]

Helmut Bley's major study was published three years after Drechsler's and complements the latter in many important ways. Whereas Drechsler's perspective on German colonialists is too simplistic, Bley adds a nuanced description of the early German administrators. Bley, like Drechsler, acknowledges the violent character of German colonialism and the destructive nature of the war of 1904–8. However, in contrast to Drechsler, he engages in a much more detailed analysis of the various German interest groups. Not seen as a monolithic entity, the German community is split up into administrators, settlers and soldiers, with different agendas of their own. Furthermore Bley puts considerable emphasis on the post-war period, but whereas Drechsler sees an almost automatic escalation from the early colonial days to genocide, with quasi-totalitarian German rule thereafter, Bley strictly separates post-war developments from pre-war German politics under Theodor Leutwein. In his (far too positive) description, Theodor Leutwein compares favourably with the Prussian-style military dictatorship of the war era as well as the almost totalitarian state control after 1907. Like Drechsler, Bley is mainly concerned with the German colonialists, leaving aside African developments during and especially after the war. By making Leutwein the positive antithesis of von Trotha he not only overlooks Leutwein's destructive and even proto-genocidal plans,[23] but also suggests that an alternative model of German colonization in South West Africa had existed, but was destroyed by the Herero decision to revolt. Although this was by no means Bley's or Drechsler's intention, their emphasis on Herero agency in declaring war on Germany was gratefully welcomed by revisionist authors, whether they were academic or amateur historians, extremist right-wing German authors or representatives of Namibian 'settler historiography'.[24] The apologetic message, some of these authors concluded, was that if the colony was quiet until the Herero deliberately and without provocation decided to 'rebel', then they only had themselves to blame for their fate. Had they not then risen, they could have lived under the benevolent German colonial government.

Drechsler and Bley marked the state of knowledge about German colonial crimes in Namibia for almost 30 years, the notable exception being only Brigitte Lau's criticism of the genocide concept in 1989[25] and the debate this caused,[26] as well as Henning Melber's attempt to systematize the continuities between German colonialism and the later racial regimes of Apartheid South Africa and Nazi Germany,[27] connections that both Drechsler and Bley had alluded to without specifying them in detail.

To deal with Brigitte Lau is a rather thankless task. In 1989 she caused a short but ferocious debate, when she challenged the very notion that genocide had taken place in German South West Africa. In an often-quoted article she attacked the general application of the concept of genocide to the South West African case as Euro- and German-centric. Unfortunately not very well read in the history and theory of genocide and driven by a certain (misleading) image of the Holocaust as the quintessential role model for genocide, she mistakenly claimed that the concept of genocide would evoke the image of an all-powerful German attacker and a passive African victim. It is quite obvious how an equally incorrect perception of the almost 'clinical' murdering of the Jews by the all-powerful Nazis – erroneously denying any Jewish resistance and agency in that process – influenced her criticism. In her attempt to stress African agency she unfortunately downplayed the level of German violence, thereby becoming apologetic herself. Today her article has become a work of reference for all sorts of denialists in Namibia, in Germany and internationally.[28] Unfortunately she could not defend herself against any accusations of being revisionist and apologetic, because she died in a car crash in 1996.

Rejected because of the apologetic nature of her argument by all serious scholars of the Herero and Nama War, Lau's emphasis on African agency, nevertheless, raised a valid point. With regard to the Herero, it was left to Jan-Bart Gewald and Gesine Krüger to take it up.[29] Both proved that the Herero succeeded in recovering from the consequences of the genocide and reconstructed their societies by reinventing their traditions. With his broad history of the Herero nation from the late-nineteenth century to the mid-1920s, Gewald especially managed to augment our perspective on the war. He succeeded in decentring the genocide and the German colonial period as such in Herero history, without minimizing the consequences of the traumatic war experiences. Gewald has also challenged the notion that the Herero revolted according to a pre-meditated plan. He convincingly claims that they were provoked by subaltern German officers into large-scale resistance. By doing so he refutes the often implicitly – sometimes explicitly – made claim, that the Herero were responsible for the catastrophic unfolding of events themselves.

In a detailed study of German 'native policy', I showed that the Herero war did not so much change German perceptions and plans with regards to South West Africa as accelerate their implementation. The disappropriation of Herero and Nama and the conscious attempt at social engineering in order to create a homogenized 'black' African workforce was not an outcome of the war. Rather the process had started earlier, and it was Leutwein, and especially the younger generation of administrators who assisted him, who had developed these 'utopias of planning and development', as I call them.[30] That means that even without the Herero and Nama War, traditional African political structures would have been disbanded and Herero and Nama land expropriated. Regardless of whom one sees as responsible for the war, these fundamental changes cannot be blamed on the Herero and Nama. Pointing to German administrative fantasies, however, does not reaffirm the image of the all-powerful white man: the German administration could never – even after the genocide and the establishment of a system of alleged total control – realize their plans. Both continued resistance of Africans and a lack of support on the part of the German settlers and entrepreneurs prevented the system from functioning properly. Nevertheless the envisioned utopian racial state with its emphasis on planning and social engineering – which was completed by strict racial segregation[31] – foreshadowed later German history in a rather frightening manner.

Recently, Isabel Hull has offered her own interpretation of the Herero and Nama War, in which she makes a certain Prussian/German military culture responsible for the escalation from war to annihilation. The German military, so her story goes, had developed the dogma of a fast and decisive victory to win any conceivable war. Therefore they failed to pay enough attention to the logistical support their troops required. As a result they ran into problems after the Herero refused to take up the challenge and fight a battle at the Waterberg. As is well established, the Herero fled instead into the Omaheke desert, pursued by German troops. These troops were poorly supported and supplied. Desperate to end the campaign as fast as possible, they took up ever more radical measures.

Compelling as this analysis may sound, explaining the radicalization of the German campaign as a result of German weakness rather than of strength, and offering an explanatory framework whereby an isolated colonial conflict is placed into wider developments of German military history up to World War I – thereby putting the Herero and Nama War firmly in the context of German history – leaves some questions open and prompts others.[32] The most striking feature of her story is the absence of ideology, namely racism and race war fantasies, which were so important for General von Trotha. Explaining the mass murder of women and children as a result of mere logistical problems overlooks the fact that even in pre-war planning, Herero society was envisaged as not to survive as an entity in its own right. Furthermore, and here the timing is crucial, the first steps towards annihilation warfare were taken before the so-called Battle at the Waterberg. Von Trotha ordered the shooting of any armed prisoner of war while he was still travelling to South West Africa (far away from any logistical problems), and when von Trotha and Leutwein first met, Leutwein failed to convince von Trotha to spare the Herero from annihilation. Von Trotha did not want to concede at all to any economic reason and responded that since South West Africa was supposed to be a white settler colony, the Whites should work for themselves. This is not the talk of a concerned soldier trying to cope with the hunger and thirst of his troops or frightened by an invisible guerrilla enemy. This is a cold-blooded mass murderer speaking; a man for whom annihilation and destruction was the aim from the very beginning. As valuable as the emphasis of a certain military culture of absolute destruction is, blaming it all on certain institutional features typical of the German army alone, misses the point of how the annihilation fantasies of a von Trotha developed and why and how he could climb to his high rank in the German army. Race war fantasies, of course, link colonialism with later German history.

However before we address the question of German continuities, which in many ways lies at the heart of current debates, a brief reflection on the scholarship on the Nama is necessary. They never attracted as much attention as the Herero and it took until 2003–4 to get a more detailed account of the Nama, the second nation subjected to genocide in the Namibian war. This fact mirrors in many respects intra-Namibian disputes on victimhood during colonialism and genocide, in which almost the sole focus lay on the Herero, with the result that other groups such as the Damara and the Nama were marginalized. Andreas Heinrich Bühler[33] and especially Reinhart Kößler[34] filled this gap with regards to the latter, Kößler also dealing with the politics of memory. Open questions still remain, though, especially since both German-Namibian revisionists and Herero erroneously deny the fact that Nama were subjected to the same genocidal principles as the Herero. But, 100 years after the conflict, at least we now have accounts of the war for all three major groups, the Nama, the Herero and the German military.

Genocide and the question of continuities

The debate about the justification of labelling this colonial conflict as a war of annihilation and/or genocide has now more or less been settled. What remains to be discussed, and what seems to be the more controversial subject, is the question of whether there is any continuity between the events that unfolded in German South West Africa and Nazi policies later on. As already mentioned, both Bley and Drechsler made this claim, though neither investigated it any further. This lack of theoretical and methodological reflection has helped critics who attack the hypothesis altogether. Lau, for example, ferociously attacked the existence of any link with the Third Reich, because she felt that drawing these lines meant a further downplaying of African history.

It was Henning Melber who, after Tilman Dedering's intervention in the debate with Lau, attempted for the first time a systematic analysis of the connections between German policies in South West Africa and both the later apartheid policy and the Third Reich. At the time, nobody took up the lead, and it is worth considering why historians of Germany were so reluctant to engage with this question. The German *Historikerstreit* (historians' debate) of 1986, which centred, among other things, around the uniqueness of the Holocaust, and had ended with an implicit ban on comparative research on mass violence, cast its shadow even on Africa. The Fischer controversy, which in the 1960s had sent shockwaves through the historical profession, should also receive a mention.[35] Fritz Fischer confronted German historians with continuities in German expansionist aspirations, which destroyed the convenient image of the Third Reich as mere 'accident' and as completely disconnected from earlier German national history. Even in 2004 discussing possible continuities evoked an image of this earlier battle among some historians, which the conservative German historians had 'lost'. Like Pavlov's dog they dismiss any such argument out of hand as soon as they hear the word 'continuity'. In a strange alliance, with regard to the Herero genocide and its significance for later German history, both 'camps' – the liberal and the conservative – ignore Germany's brutal colonial past: the liberal camp for fear of challenging the dogma of Holocaust uniqueness, the conservative one for fear of finding even more shocking parallels or continuities than Fischer had unearthed.

In many ways these reactions are typically German, due as they are to a certain academic provincialism, which still prevails in many quarters. Many participants in this discussion are deeply grounded in German national history of the metropolitan kind and simply do not know that the question of genocide and colonialism is part of an international debate, which rages from Australia to the Americas, from Africa to Eastern Europe.[36] Most of them have never done research on any kind of colonial history or regions outside of Germany, let alone Europe. Nevertheless almost all historians have a strong and – as they believe – educated opinion about German colonial history. Nevertheless, although they do not know much about the life of the colonial subject in Windhoek or Dar-es-Salaam, they 'know' that it was less brutal than in British Africa. They don't know about colonial warfare or racial segregation laws, but they know, that – of course – no similarities exist with the Third Reich. They have never been in a Namibian or a colonial archive, but they know that of course von Trotha did not attempt the annihilation of the Herero. They in general feel able to comment on non-European history or the history of Europeans outside Europe, whereas historians working on Africa and Asia are not allowed to comment on 'proper' German history. One wonders why that is.

Besides an obvious attempt to defend one's turf and the already mentioned historiographical taboos in dealings with the Nazi past, traces of a certain Eurocentric contempt with regards to non-European regions and their history also seem to be shining through; a flicker of the notion that Africans have to no history or at least no proper one, dating back to Hegel or the nineteenth century more generally. Some seem still influenced by a crude exoticism, which in itself is more a legacy of the colonial age than an intellectual engagement with it: Idyllic fantasies and images prevent critical analysis.

In several articles I have tried to provide a theoretically informed framework for the question of continuity. In an attempt to sketch an archaeology of genocide I analyzed the Herero and Nama case as an important link between the less bureaucratized incidents of mass violence in the colonial context and the extremely bureaucratized violence of Nazism.[37] Binary encoding and the vision of one's own superiority, combined with viewing the original population as superfluous, inferior and vanishing, which prevailed in the colonial context, were also prone to von Trotha's concept of a race war and to the Nazis' Social-Darwinian *Lebensraum* ideology. The genocide in South West Africa marks the point where colonial violence 'met' German history and is therefore of prime importance for twentieth-century German history.[38] Following this claim, I have interpreted the war of annihilation (1941–4) in eastern Europe and the related occupation policies as a colonial war and part of the German imperial project, identifying personal experience, institutional memory and public perception as major trajectories of German colonial fantasies, knowledge and experiences.[39] Since both colonial history and Nazism were not only about genocide, in a separate series of articles I have traced the history of developmental fantasies and the racial segregationist state, thereby establishing an even firmer link.[40]

Challenging one of the core beliefs in German history about the distinct and peculiar German position of the Third Reich naturally provokes criticism. As yet, no detailed scholarly engagement with my hypothesis or a convincing counter-narrative has been offered. It might still be too early for that. Rather than offering detailed counter-arguments, criticism mostly took the form of general rejections often employing a circular argumentation – stating, for example, the uniqueness of the Holocaust and using this statement to refute all comparison – or propounding almost racist statements of the sort that colonial analogies were unjustified since Russians were not Africans (meaning they were 'white'). What is striking in general is the highly emotionalized responses, which the emerging continuity debate has already evoked, which led to *ad hominem* attacks, accusing proponents of the continuity thesis of diminishing the memory of Jewish victims of the Holocaust or using the emphasis on colonial mass crimes to seek personal gain.[41]

The emotions that one witnesses here cannot sufficiently be explained as responses to a mere debate about historical facts or historical underpinnings.

What seems to be at stake here is a certain perspective on German national history as such. And this is centred around the interpretation of the Holocaust and its significance for German and indeed global history. With the claim that genocide was committed in the German colonies and that this crime was linked to the Holocaust, German colonialism was drawn into the limelight and into the debate about German national identity. This centres around the Holocaust, whereby one can distinguish between two approaches. The first is what I call the 'critical–liberal' approach in which the Holocaust is seen as such a singular crime, that any comparison or search for roots appears to be obscene. A certain kind of German *Sonderweg* notion is also part of this position. In a second approach more 'conservative–revisionist' historians try to disconnect the Holocaust from German history. Whereas the first group would reject any notion of continuity because it sees it as a trivialization of the Holocaust, that is the murder of European Jewry, the second group upholds a rather positive image of German national history which it therefore does not want to become 'contaminated' by establishing precursors to the crimes that were to come. Proponents of an idyllic image of benevolent German colonialism would belong here as well. Attempts at safeguarding the national honour of German colonialism seem to be gaining momentum again at present, with the result that nobody seems to be bothered that many of these ideas closely resemble the struggle against the 'colonial guilt lie' during the Weimar Republic.[42] In many respects the debate about German colonialism, its character and its meaning for later history is a debate about German national identity. What people don't dare to discuss with regard to the Third Reich, they dare to utter with respect to the Herero: not only Germans were racists, British and French histories have their dark spots as well, and one must not always indulge in the negative aspects of one's history – enough is enough – and so on and so forth. The debate on German colonialism has therefore to be seen as part and parcel of the debate about the Allied bombing campaign and the discussion of the expulsion of ethnic Germans from eastern Europe at the end of World War II. However, whereas the latter issues emphasize the role of the Germans as victims, the colonial genocide debate runs counter to this. Safeguarding the national honour of German colonialism therefore also has implications for this wider debate.[43] It is that fact which causes emotions to run high in this debate.

But German colonialism in Namibia in general and the question of genocide in particular are not only topics of German national identity, but also of Namibian, and are, some argue, even more important for the latter.[44] Since there is still in Namibia a considerable minority of citizens of German descent, who have preserved a distinct cultural identity, the debate about Germany's colonial legacy is still unresolved business. The matter is complicated by the fact that although descendants of the Herero and Nama live in Namibia, they are also not the majority of the population. The Ovambo, however, who are the dominant group, both demographically and politically, did not participate in the war of 1904–8.[45] Their decisive anti-colonial experience was the liberation struggle against the colonial South African regime, and in many ways they downplayed the role of the genocide, since it would put the Herero and Nama experience on to centre stage.

All three groups share the fact that no scholarly account has so far been produced out of their midst, which is itself a legacy of colonialism and Apartheid. So despite all the blaming of foreign historians for getting involved and claims to have a privileged access to the truth due to their Namibianness – a strange argument for a scholarly discussion anyway – the academic debate is and has to be an international one. Especially from the side of the settler historiography a naïve, empiricist pseudo-Rankean perspective is proposed, which claims that only White-eyewitness accounts can be taken seriously as sources. Any theoretical approach is dismissed as left-wing, biased historiography, which distracts from the task of simply showing 'how it really was'. Sources that contradict the picture of a benevolent German colonialism are simply ignored. These writings are neither of academic quality nor do they possess any value as source, other than for analyzing memory politics in modern Namibia.

In terms of reconciliation and the demand for reparations, which is pending, if not yet in terms of historical scholarship, it seems that the division within the African communities in Namibia with respect to the colonial war is gradually being overcome.[46] In autumn 2006 the Namibian parliament for the first time endorsed, with support from Ovambo votes, the motion brought by Herero chief Riruako for reparations. And in October 2006 the Nama were also demanding reparations.[47]

This, of course, does not change scholarly perception of the events more than a century ago, but since attempts to come to terms with a genocidal and traumatic past and the memory politics surrounding them are part of genocide studies, these recent developments should be noted, although no statement about their outcome can yet be made. The same is true about German plans for recognition and reconciliation, which seem to have gained new impetus since a proposal and a workshop by the party 'Die Linke' put the Herero and Nama issue back on the agenda.[48]

The example of the Namibian War shows why genocide studies, and even questions of colonial genocide which point back at least a century, remain emotionally charged. Just as genocide itself is about identity, so is debate about it linked to identity politics. Genocides in the colonial context are no exception.

Notes

1. The war has been known over time by many names. New post-colonial and post-independent perspectives demand that Herero or Nama should be named first, or that we should use the plural 'wars' to indicate that both the fighting between Herero and

the German army and Nama and the German army are being referred to. I use the singular form in the sense in which one uses the term World War for a series of distinct, yet intrinsically linked conflicts. What is important, however, is that the Eurocentric terms 'rebellion', 'uprising', 'insurrection' or 'revolt' are put to rest once and forever. These only perpetuate the colonial perspective. The implicitly made – yet fundamental – assumption behind such a labelling is to criminalize the Africans' war, since it implies that German colonial rule was legitimate, that the Kaiser was the lawful sovereign against whom the Herero illegitimately rose up. The Herero are put into the position of criminals, of lawbreakers. This might be the colonialist's perspective at the time and even today, it is however not an unbiased one and it is certainly not that of Herero and Nama. There is plenty of evidence to suggest that Herero and Nama leaders understood the Germans in the early days of colonialism as a partner and ally in their wars and struggles, not, however, as their sovereigns. Terminology shapes perception, and by using terms such as rebellion, the colonial ideology of Europeans as rightful masters of the world is perpetuated. Talking about rebellions and uprisings should therefore be avoided, and the conflict named as what it was: a war and/or a genocide. In most of the literature, the war is seen as lasting from 1904 to 1907. I prefer to use 1908 as the end of the war, because it was then that the concentration camps were dissolved and most prisoners released. Some historians even prefer 1912, when the last Nama returned from their imprisonment in other colonies, at least the few that had survived.

2. Speech of Heidemarie Wieczorek-Zeul, Omahakaris, Namibia, 14 August 2004 (http://www.bmz.de/de/presse/reden/ministerin/rede20040814.html; accessed 10.11.2006) [my translation].
3. In a semi-official conference aimed at reconciliation in Germany a few months later she was referring directly to the genocide in Namibia, without the qualifying words 'what would nowadays be called'. 'The German Herero War – One Hundred Years After. 1904–2004: Realities, Traumas, Perspectives', Bremen, 18–21 November 2004.
4. I am reluctant to use the term 'colonial genocide', because as I have discussed elsewhere, it includes the danger of creating an essentialist distinction between colonial genocides and 'proper' ones by creating a new category. Colonial genocide in this context means genocide in the colonial context. See J. Zimmerer, 'Kolonialer Genozid? Möglichkeiten und Grenzen einer historischen Kategorie für eine Globalgeschichte der Massengewalt', in *Enteignet-Vertrieben-Ermordet. Beiträge zur Genozidforschung,* eds. D. J. Schaller, R. Boyadjian, H. Scholtz and V. Berg (Zürich: Chronos, 2004), pp. 109–28.
5. This is a classic apologetic interpretation, which recently found new expression in the context of the new-found patriotic feeling which some German publicists discovered at the time of the Football World Cup in 2006. See, for example, M. Matussek, *Wir Deutschen. Warum uns die anderen gern haben können* (Frankfurt am Main: S. Fischer, 2006).
6. C. Browning, 'The Decision-Making Process', in *The Historiography of the Holocaust,* ed. D. Stone (Basingstoke: Palgrave Macmillan, 2004), p. 173.
7. See, for a summary of the events, J. Zimmerer 'Krieg, KZ & Völkermord. Der erste deutsche Genozid', in *Völkermord in Deutsch-Südwestafrika. Der Kolonialkrieg (1904–1908) in Namibia und seine Folgen*, eds, J. Zimmerer and J. Zeller (Berlin: Ch. Links 2003), pp. 45–63. See also J.-B. Gewald, 'Imperial Germany and the Herero of Southern Africa: Genocide and the Quest for Recompense'; in *Genocide, War Crimes & the West: History and Complicity*, ed., A. Jones (London: Zed Books, 2004), pp. 59–77; D. Schaller, 'Ich glaube, dass die Nation als solche vernichtet werden muss: Kolonialkrieg und

Völkermord in Deutsch-Südwestafrika 1904–1907', *Journal of Genocide Research*, 6, 3 (2004), 395–430; D. Schaller, 'Kolonialkrieg, Völkermord und Zwangsarbeit in Deutsch-Südwestafrika', in *Enteignet-Vertrieben-Ermordet*, eds, Schaller, Dominik, Rupen Boyadjian, Vivianne Berg, Hanno Scholtz, pp. 147–232; R. Kössler and H. Melber, 'Völkermord und Gedenken. Der Genozid an den Herero und Nama in Deutsch-Südwestafrika 1904–1908', *Jahrbuch zur Geschichte und Wirkung des Holocaust* (Frankfurt am Main: Campus, 2004), 37–75.

8. For an overview of the Maji-Maji see now F. Becker and J. Beez, eds, *Der Maji-Maji-Krieg in Deutsch-Ostafrika, 1905–1907* (Berlin: Ch. Links, 2005).
9. For an overview of German utopian plans and the problems with enacting it in the colonial context, see J. Zimmerer, 'Der koloniale Musterstaat? Rassentrennung, Arbeitszwang und totale Kontrolle in Deutsch-Südwestafrika', in *Völkermord in Deutsch-Südwestafrika*, eds, Zimmerer and Zeller, pp. 26–41. For a more detailled account see J. Zimmerer, *Deutsche Herrschaft über Afrikaner. Staatlicher Machtanspruch und Wirklichkeit im kolonialen Namibia*, 3rd edn (Münster: LIT, 2004). For German imperial fantasies more general see B. Kundrus, *Moderne Imperialisten. Das Kaiserreich im Spiegel seiner Kolonien* (Cologne: Böhlau, 2003). pp. 219–79.
10. For a detailed account of the Herero before and after the war, see J.-B. Gewald, *Herero Heroes: A Socio-Political History of the Herero of Namibia 1890–1923*, (Oxford: James Currey, 1999); G. Krüger, *Kriegsbewältigung und Geschichtsbewusstsein. Realität, Deutung und Verarbeitung des deutschen Kolonialkrieges in Namibia 1904 bis 1907* (Göttingen: Vandenhoeck und Ruprecht, 1999).
11. Trotha to Leutwein, 5 November 1904, quoted in H. Drechsler, *Südwestafrika unter deutscher Kolonialherrschaft: Der Kampf der Herero und Nama gegen den deutschen Imperialismus 1884–1915*, 2nd ed. (Berlin [East]: Akademie, 1984), p. 156.
12. Trotha in *Der deutschen Zeitung* (3 February 1909), quoted in G. Pool, *Samuel Maharero* (Windhoek: Gamsberg Macmillan, 1991), p. 293.
13. Proclamation by Trotha, On Board the Steamer 'Eleonore Woermann', June 1904, Namibian National Archives, Windhoek, Zentralbureau des Gouvernements (ZBU) Geheimakten IX.A. Bd. 1, Bl. 1b.
14. Proclamation by Trotha, Osombo-Windhuk (copy), 2 October 1904, Bundesarchiv Berlin-Lichterfelde (German Federal Archive, Berlin Lichterfelde), R 1001/2089, p. 7af.
15. Schlieffen to Bülow, 23 November 1904, quoted in Drechsler, *Südwestafrika*, p. 166.
16. See for an overview of the attempted control state and the reasons for its failure (not least due to African resistance) J. Zimmerer, 'Der Wahn der Planbarkeit: Vertreibung, unfreie Arbeit und Völkermord als Elemente der Bevölkerungsökonomie in Deutsch-Südwestafrika', *Comparativ*, 13, 4 (2003), 96–113.
17. For a summary of my own position see J. Zimmerer, *Von Windhuk nach Auschwitz? Beiträge zum Verhältnis von Kolonialismus und Holocaust* (Münster: LIT, 2007).
18. Drechsler, *Südwestafrika*; H. Bley, *Kolonialherrschaft und Sozialstruktur in Deutsch-Südwestafrika 1894–1914* (Hamburg: Leibniz, 1968).
19. D. Schaller, 'Raphael Lemkin's View of European Colonial Rule in Africa: Between Condemnation and Admiration', *Journal of Genocide Research*, 7, 4 (2005), 531–8 (Special issue: 'Raphael Lemkin: the "founder of the United Nation's Genocide Convention" as a historian of mass violence', eds, D. Schaller and J. Zimmerer).
20. See, for example, the introduction by Andreas Eckl of his edition of soldier diaries. A. E. Eckl, *'S' ist ein übles Land hier'. Zur Historiographie eines umstrittenen Kolonialkrieges. Tagebuchaufzeichnungen aus dem Herero-Krieg in Deutsch-Südwestafrika 1904 von Georg Hillebrecht und Franz Ritter von Epp* (Cologne: Rüdiger Köppe, 2005). As with the defamation of Drechsler, Eckl also accuses younger German historians of being

overly tendentious and leftist, without properly substantiating his claim or offering a counter-analysis. Not surprisingly he soon became a star in revisionist Deutsch-Südwester circles.

21. See Zimmerer, *Deutsche Herrschaft über Afrikaner.*
22. Ibid.
23. I have explained in detail that Leutwein's colonial aims would have also led to the destruction of African culture and tradition. Africans would have been transformed into a 'black' working class, devoid of any memory of their cultural origins or the Herero, Nama or Ovambo identity. See Zimmerer, *Deutsche Herrschaft über Afrikaner.* In many respects the war just sped things along. The cultural destruction at which Leutwein aimed could also be termed genocide, as cultural genocide is increasingly understood as a form of genocide, as in Lemkin's explanation: genocide does not necessarily mean 'the immediate destruction of a nation, except when accomplished by mass killings of all members of a nation. It is intended rather to signify a coordinated plan of different actions aiming at the destruction of essential foundations of the life of national groups, with the aim of annihilating the groups themselves. The objectives of such a plan would be disintegration of the political and social institutions, of culture, language, national feelings, religion, and the economic existence of national groups, and the destruction of the personal security, liberty, health, dignity, and even the lives of the individuals belonging to such groups.' R. Lemkin, *Axis Rule in Occupied Europe* (Washington, D.C.: Carnegie Endowment for International Peace, 1944), p. 90.
24. The term 'settler historiography', as coined by Andreas Eckl, means amateurish accounts by German-Namibians living in the country today. Their main qualification seems to be a sort of Southwesterness, of being born in the country, of being socialized in a certain settler-colonial environment. 'Knowing' the country replaces all academic methods or scholarly training. In a rather ironic twist they are the living embodiment of all the exclusionary practises of the settler-colonial project. A critical analysis of this phenomenon is overdue; a first sketch can be found in C. Marx, 'Entsorgen und Entseuchen. Zur Diskussionskultur in der derzeitigen namibischen Historiographie – eine Polemik', in *Genozid und Gedenken. Namibisch-deutsche Geschichte und Gegenwart,* ed. H. Melber (Frankfurt am Main: Brandes & Apsel, 2005).
25. B. Lau, 'Uncertain Certainties. The Herero–German War of 1904', *Mibagus,* 2 (1989), reprinted in B. Lau, *History and Historiography – 4 Essays in reprint* (Windhoek: MSORP, 1995), pp. 39–52.
26. For a summary of this debate see: T. Dedering, 'The German–Herero War of 1904. Revisionism of Genocide or Imaginary Historiography?', *Journal of Southern African Studies,* 19 (1993), 80–8.
27. H. Melber, 'Kontinuitäten totaler Herrschaft. Völkermord und Apartheid in Deutsch-Südwestafrika', *Jahrbuch für Antisemitismusforschung,* 1 (1992), 91–116.
28. Her article was published, for example, on the webpage of the revisionist Traditionsverband ehm. Schutz- und Überseetruppen – Freunde der früheren deutschen Schutzgebiete e.v., [Society for the Upholding of the Tradition of the Former German Colonial Army and Friends of the Former German colonies] www.traditionsverband.de (accessed 26 August 2006).
29. Gewald, *Towards Redemption*; G. Krüger, *Kriegsbewältigung und Geschichtsbewusstsein.*
30. Zimmerer, *Deutsche Herrschaft über Afrikaner.*
31. For a more detailed argument about continuities of segregationist policies, see J. Zimmerer, 'Deutscher Rassenstaat in Afrika. Ordnung, Entwicklung und Segregation in "Deutsch-Südwest" (1884–1915)', in *Gesetzliches Unrecht. Rassistisches Recht im 20. Jahrhundert* (=*Jahrbuch zur Geschichte und Wirkung des Holocaust,* 2005)

(Frankfurt am Main: Campus, 2005), pp. 135–53; idem., 'Von Windhuk nach Warschau. Die rassische Privilegiengesellschaft in Deutsch-Südwestafrika – ein Modell mit Zukunft?', in: *Rassenmischehen – Mischlinge – Rassentrennung. Zur Politik der Rasse im deutschen Kolonialreich,* ed., F. Becker (Stuttgart: Steiner, 2005), pp. 97–123.

32. See, for an overview, the debate between Hull and myself in *Bulletin of the German Historical Institute,* Washington, D.C., 37 (2005).
33. A. H. Bühler, *Der Namaaufstand gegen die deutsche Kolonialherrschaft in Namibia von 1904 bis 1913. Facetten der europäisch-überseeischen Begegnung,* (Frankfurt am Main: IKO, 2003).
34. R. Kößler, *In Search of Survival and Dignity. Two Traditional Communities in Southern Namibia under South African Rule* (Frankfurt am Main: IKO, 2006).
35. For an overview on German historiographical controversies see K. Große Kracht, *Die zankende Zunft. Historische Kontroversen in Deutschland nach 1945,* (Göttingen: Vandenhoeck und Ruprecht, 2005).
36. See, for an overview, Zimmerer, 'Kolonialer Genozid'. For the Australian example, together with the Herero and Nama case probably the most intensely debated example at the moment, see A. D. Moses, ed., *Genocide and Settler Society: Frontier Violence and Stolen Indigenous Children in Australian History* (New York: Berghahn, 2004). For a more general introduction see *Patterns of Prejudice,* 39, 2 (2005), special issue, 'Colonial Genocide', eds, A. D. Moses and D. Stone; and A. D. Moses, ed., *Empire, Colony, Genocide* (New York: Berghahn, 2008).
37. J. Zimmerer, 'Colonial Genocide and the Holocaust. Towards an Archeology of Genocide', in *Genocide* and *Settler Society,* ed., Moses, pp. 49–76.
38. I have further emphasised this point in J. Zimmerer, 'Das Deutsche Reich und der Genozid. Überlegungen zum historischen Ort des Völkermordes an den Herero und Nama', in *Namibia-Deutschland. Eine geteilte Geschichte. Widerstand, Gewalt, Erinnerung,* eds, L. Förster, D. Henrichsen and M. Bollig (Cologne: Edition Minerva, 2004), pp. 106–21.
39. J. Zimmerer, 'The Birth of the "Eastern Land" out of the Spirit of Colonialism: A Postcolonial Perspective on the Nazi Policy of Conquest and Extermination', *Patterns of Prejudice,* 39, 2 (2005), 197–219.
40. Zimmerer, *Von Windhuk nach Auschwitz.*
41. For an overview, see Marx, 'Entsorgen und Entseuchen'. See also the debate between Henning Melber, Birthe Kundrus and Reinhart Kößler in *Africa Spectrum,* 40 (2005).
42. This conclusion must be drawn from the sudden interest of public and private TV in German colonial history. See, for example, the mini-series 'Die Wüstenblume', which uses German South West Africa as background for its love story. Or the TV documentary 'Deutsche Kolonien', which was the first documentary screened on prime time TV. See for 'Die Wüstenblume', W. Struck, 'The Persistence of (Colonial) Fantasies' (paper presented at the conference *War, Genocide and Memory. German Colonialism and National Identity,* Sheffield, 11–13 September 2006. For the TV documentary see my review 'Warum nicht mal nen Neger'?, *Süddeutsche Zeitung* (23 November 2005). As a third example, from literature, one could name *Herero* by Gerhard Seyfried, highly praised in German reviews. See my review 'Keine Geiseln der Geschichte', *Die Tageszeitung* (taz) (10 January 2004). Most of these productions claim to have an anti-colonial impetus, but this is mainly restricted to the surface. Beyond this lip service they use all the usual colonial stereotypes. As interesting as the works themselves are the debates among the literary and film critics, which tend to be quite positive, bar all understanding of the mechanisms of colonialism. They show that colonial nostalgia is restricted neither to a few authors or film directors, nor to the so-called uneducated classes.

43. This attempt could most prominently be seen in the TV documentary 'Deutsche Kolonien' mentioned above, in which under the guidance of historian Horst Gründer, an exoticized image of German colonial adventure was shown, explicitly rejecting the fact the a 'real' genocide had taken place in Namibia or that any connection existed with later Nazi history. When I criticized the film for that statement and even more so for reaffirming colonial stereotypes about black savages by including film shootings from colonial and Nazi propaganda film without indicating this, I was immediately attacked by Professor Gründer in a letter to the editor accusing me of paranoia and a guilt complex. A discussion of my arguments did not take place.
44. See, for an overview, *Genozid und Gedenken*, ed., Melber.
45. For details about the (minor) role of Ovambo in that conflict see D. Schaller, 'Am Rande des Krieges. Das Ovambo-Königreich Ondonga', in *Völkermord in Deutsch-Südwestafrika*, eds, Zimmerer and Zeller, pp. 134–41.
46. For an overview of the reparations claim see J. Böhlke-Itzen, *Kolonialschuld und Entschädigung. Der deutsche Völkermord an den Herero 1904–1907* (Frankfurt am Main: Brandes&Apsel, 2004). For the discussions since 2004 see J. Zimmerer, 'Entschädigung für Herero and Nama', *Blätter für deutsche und international Politik*, 50, 6 (2005), 658–60. For the latest development see H.- Melber, 'Genocide', *Insight* (November 2006).
47. Report by Namibia Press Agency/Associated Press/Inter-Press Services, 27 October 2006.
48. See H. Hintze, 'Pressure Mounts for Reparations', *The Namibian* (19 October 2006).

13
The Armenian Genocide

Donald Bloxham and Fatma Müge Göçek

Introduction

In September 2005, Turkish scholars and intellectuals critical of the Turkish official historiography on the Armenian deportations and massacres of 1915 convened a conference in Istanbul to analyze and discuss the fate of the Armenians at the end of the Ottoman Empire. Among the many discussions held, one in particular was noteworthy in that it focused on those individuals who produce the Turkish official historiography. It had so transpired that immediately before the conference, the nationalist opponents to the conference had employed the Social Science Citation Index, a measure indicating one's degree of influence in the international scholarly community, to criticize – albeit unsuccessfully – the international intellectual standing of the conference conveners. As one of the conveners, the historian Halil Berktay, discussed and criticized this tactic during the conference, he noted that he himself had conducted a similar citation check on the individuals who produced the Turkish official historiography only to find out that in opposition to the dozens and even hundreds of citations of conference conveners, there was not a single citation of the works of any of the major proponents of the official Turkish historiography such as Yusuf Halacoğlu and Hikmet Özdemir. Yet, even though these official proponents never get cited in the international scholarly community, they are extremely influential within Turkey where the Turkish official historiography still reigns triumphant.

Indeed, there are at the moment two totally mutually exclusive historiographies on the Armenian deportations and deaths of 1915, one that is constructed by the international scholarly community and approved by the Armenian survivors and the other assembled by the proponents of the Turkish state. It is necessary at this juncture to outline the main arguments of each historiography. According to the historiography of the Western scholarly community and the Armenian diaspora (which we will refer to in shorthand as the

'Western' historiography), the Armenian deportations and deaths of 1915 comprise one of the first genocides of the twentieth century, a crime against humanity that occurred during 1915–23 with the intent by the Ottoman state to annihilate its Armenian subjects, causing the systematic destruction of between 800,000 and 1.5 million Armenians. The Turkish official historiography contends instead that the same events did not comprise a genocide but were actually reciprocal massacres that occurred between the Turks and the Armenians with unintentional destruction due to sickness and travel of Armenian subjects deported from the warfront, resulting in about 400,000 Armenian deaths as opposed to at least 1.5 million Turkish wartime deaths during the same time period.

In terms of the historical sources each historiography employs to support its argument, the Western scholarly community refers to comparable empirical cases across time and space and employs the eyewitness accounts of mostly Western missionaries, travellers, merchants and other foreign professionals as well as the diplomatic correspondence of mostly Western European and/or American states, and oral histories and accounts of the Armenian survivors. Instead, those who support the Turkish official historiography refer primarily to the archival documents of the Ottoman state, the confiscated documents of the Armenian revolutionary committees in the Ottoman archives, and the correspondence of contemporaneous Ottoman government leaders; they also selectively employ Western sources after reformulating the information contained in such a manner that it either appears to support or at least does not challenge the official Turkish position.

It will probably not be surprising to note that the Western scholarly community finds the official Turkish historiography on the Armenian issue to be unscientific, propagandistic and rhetorical and therefore does not at all engage with it, while the proponents of the Turkish official historiography dismiss the discourse of the Western scholarly community as Eurocentric, imperialist and self-serving. Even though this unwillingness of the Western scholarly community to critically engage Turkish official historiography due to the latter's disregard of scientific criteria in research does to a certain degree delegitimate the official Turkish stand internationally in academic circles, it nevertheless fails to fully destabilize, deconstruct and obliterate it both outside and especially within Turkey. Given the hold of the Turkish official historiography especially within Turkish society and the ranks of state and government, there is thus still an urgent need to engage it critically.

The particular theoretical juncture in the humanities and social sciences has highlighted the insights attained from the field of subaltern studies where scholars successfully deconstructed the hegemony of the British colonial presence in the Indian past – and therefore in its present and future – through critical readings of texts against the grain. The historical contextualization of such texts not only revealed embedded meanings and power relations, but also destabilized the authority of the same texts. This particular theoretical insight could likewise be applied to the Turkish official historiography to historically contextualize it within Ottoman and Turkish history with the intent to eventually destabilize and disempower it. That is the first aim of this chapter. The second aim is to assess the state of the Western historiography, and attempt to thematize its main interpretative debates – some of which are also politicized – with the implicit goal of asking where we go from 'here'.

Official Turkish historiography in historical context

The analysis of the texts of approximately 200 works that comprise the Turkish official historiography on the Armenian issue reveals three insights about its construction. The first insight is that the access of both the Turkish state and society to their past centred strictly around the Republican experience so that the official starting point of history was either 1923, namely the year of the official foundation of the Turkish Republic, or 1919, which marked the commencement of the Nationalist War of Independence leading to the formation of the Republic. Both of these dates indirectly caused the previous time period including the crucial year of 1915 to be relegated to the realm of pre-history.

The second insight that also involved periodization was that the famous 36-hour long *Speech* Mustafa Kemal Atatürk gave in 1928, at the annual meeting of the Republican People's Party (RPP) he had founded, where he narrated his own version of the Turkish War of Independence, provided the blueprint of the Turkish official historiography. His narrative too commenced with the now famous sentence 'I alighted in Samsun on the 19th of May 1919.' Indeed, both historical vantage points of Mustafa Kemal, namely 1928 when he delivered his narrative and 1919 which was the latter's starting point were both after 1915, past the point at which the Armenians were both physically and symbolically out of the Republican vision of both the past and the future. Hence, according to this formulation, anything before 1919–1923 was regarded as pre-history in that the events were not contextualized, and the social actors did not have agency except in predetermined, premeditated ways that led to the establishment of the Republic; what succeeded likewise recognized the agency of only the ethnic Muslim Turks at the expense of all others.

This Republican narrative based on the accounts of Mustafa Kemal asserted, in relation to the Armenians in particular and the minorities in general, that all recognized minorities were to receive equal treatment as citizens. It all disclaimed any continuity of the past violence exercised against them, and when pressed, pointed to the Armenian alliance with other powers against Ottoman state as a reason for their deportation and occasional unintended massacres. The historical contextualization of this Republican narrative also pointed to two other narratives that preceded and succeeded it, namely the imperial and post-nationalist narratives of the same events.

The Turkish official historiography on the Armenians can thus be contextualized within a broader temporal framework into three distinct narratives, namely: (1) *The Ottoman Investigative Narrative* based on the contemporaneous accounts pertaining to the Ottoman Armenians, including the Armenian deportations and deaths of 1915, published either by the Turkish state or by opposing political groups; (2) *The Republican Defensive Narrative* based on the works written with the intent to justify, document and prove the nationalist master narrative of the Turkish state that explicitly denies the allegation that an Armenian genocide occurred in 1915, often published or kept in circulation by the Turkish state; and (3) *The Post-Nationalist Critical Narrative* found in recent works critical of the nationalist master narrative, but that do not, with some exceptions, focus specifically on 1915; their concern is much more on the silences in contemporary Turkish society pertaining to its history and also its ethnic composition. The main parameters of this critical engagement will be presented next.

The Ottoman investigative narrative on the events of 1915

The works in this category consist of the memoirs[1] of Ottoman officials such as Said, Kamil and Talat Pashas and Mehmed Asaf and Dr. Mehmed Reşid Beys, the investigation records[2] of the Ottoman military tribunals that tried those accused of perpetrating the massacres, the official reports[3] prepared by the Ottoman state such as the one by Hüseyin Nazım Pasha, the collections[4] of Ottoman documents ostensibly published by the Turkish nation-state from the State and Military Archives to deny the genocide allegations, the report[5] of the Ottoman government of the time, and the reports[6] of the Turkish negotiations of the Lausanne treaty.

The critical reading of these works reveals two distinguishing characteristics of the Ottoman investigative narrative. The first is that none of these works originally penned around the time of the events of 1915 question the occurrence of the Armenian 'massacres' (genocide was not a term then employed); they instead focus on the question of what happened and why. The second is the very strong tension revealed between two transforming world views. Some of the authors maintain a more traditional Ottoman imperial view and regard the existing structure of the empire as just and the position of the Armenian subjects within it as reformable: these also blame the events on easily manipulated Armenian subjects and corrupt Muslim officials. Other authors, however, display a more 'proto-national' state view and perceive the existing structure of the empire as inadequate, and the position of the Armenian subjects within it as problematic: while they are not quite clear about what to do about these inadequacies and problems, they give priority to the preservation of the state and its Muslims over all other concerns and justify their actions accordingly.

The central tension in the Ottoman investigative narrative emerges over the attribution of responsibility for the crimes committed against the Armenian subjects. When reviewed chronologically, the memoirs of Ottoman officials reveal a shift in the allocation of responsibility as the later ones who are increasingly imbued with proto-nationalist sentiments view the crimes they committed as a duty in service for the Turkish fatherland. The tension over responsibility mounts especially after World War I with the defeat of the Ottoman Empire when the Ottoman state acknowledges what happened, and prints the proceedings of the Ottoman military tribunals that tried some of the perpetrators as supplements to the official newspaper *Takvim-i Vekayi*. Yet the advent and eventual victory of the Turkish War of Independence destroy the Allied efforts to bring the perpetrators in front of justice; with increased nationalism, the newspaper issues that contain these military tribunal records start to slowly disappear to such a degree that currently no complete sets exist in any Turkish public library.

Soon after the military tribunals, especially with the transition from the Ottoman Empire to the Turkish nation-state, the responsibility for the crimes gradually shifts from the perpetrators to the victims. Ottoman official reports first note the seditious activities of the Armenian nationalist committees and the Armenian atrocities against the Turks in the eastern provinces to justify the Armenian deaths and massacres of 1915. Significant in this shift is the strong connection between the stance of the Committee of Union and Progress (CUP; the perpetrators of the deportations and massacres) that justifies the Armenian tragedy as an unfortunate consequence of their attempts to protect the Ottoman state, and the Nationalist movement that gradually adopts this Unionist stance as its own. The Ottoman state documents published by the recent Turkish nation-state also repeat the argument of their predecessors. And this argument in turn still subsists in more essentialized and radicalized form in the subsequent Republican defensive narrative that starts to get articulated in the 1950s.

These two concurrent narratives during the transition from the Ottoman Empire to the Turkish nation-state reconcile to produce the Republican narrative. The emergence of a Turkish 'nation-state' on the ashes of the Ottoman Empire precludes the discussion of any claims on the homeland the Turks had now identified as theirs; it is no accident that Mustafa Kemal states, and the Turkish state constantly continues to reiterate, that there is not 'a hand-span of their fatherland's soil' (*bir karış vatan toprağı*) they would give up without fighting until the last drop of their blood (*kanımızın son damlasına kadar*). The people's willingness to annihilate themselves for a vision demonstrates both the ideological strength of nationalism as well as its incredibly destructive power.

This nationalist tone dominates the Republican defensive narrative that is also coloured by two significant historical occurrences. One is the period of Russian occupation in 1914 and later 1917, as well as that of the Allied occupation after 1918 marked by the massacres of the Muslim Turkish populace by the Armenian committees. The Armenian massacres of the Turks which probably lead to the death of 40,000–60,000 Muslim Turks become central to the Republican narrative and are employed to counter the 1915 massacres. The second historical occasion is provided by the Justice Commandos of the Armenian Genocide (JCOAG) and Armenian Secret Army for the Liberation of Armenia (ASALA) murders of innocent Turkish diplomats throughout the world in the late 1970s into the 1980s to draw world attention to the Armenian genocide. These murders present Republican Turkey with the opportunity to include, in a nationalist move, the avenging of these deaths in its narrative; the murders only strengthen the Republican resolve to resist the Armenian claims, and further polarize their stand on the issue to a total denial of the Armenian massacres of 1915.

The Republican defensive narrative on the events of 1915

The works considered in this category mostly emerge as clusters of analyses within the nationalist paradigm. The first cluster consists of two works[7] published in 1953 which comprehensively cover the previous existing knowledge on the Armenians. The second cluster of works[8] written by direct or indirect state support in the 1970s and 1980s in reaction to the groups JCOAG and ASALA murders draws selectively upon the first cluster. The third cluster[9] comprising the works that emerge in the 1990s until the present either reproduces the same arguments made in the 1970s and 1980s, or attempts to bring in a new perspective while remaining within the nationalist paradigm.

The Republican nationalist narrative traces the origins of the 1915 tragedy to the intervention of the Western powers in the affairs of the Empire, and argues that the subversive acts of the Armenian committee members justify the Armenian relocations and subsequent massacres. This narrative fails to recognize either the significance of the pre-existing Ottoman structural relations between the Muslims and non-Muslim minorities as well as the subsequent naturalized Muslim superiority it produced or the fact that the Turkish nationalism was one of the many nationalisms that emerged during this time period with claims that were no more just than those made any of the other social groups, but that just happened to triumph over the others at their expense.

This non-recognition cloaked by a Turkish nationalism identifying the preservation of the Turkish state at all costs has led the Republican state to assign the entire moral responsibility for the Armenian deaths and massacres to anyone other than the Ottoman Turkish perpetrators. As a consequence of this non-recognition, the Armenian victims themselves have tragically and ironically emerged in the Republican narrative as the main perpetrators of the crimes alongside the guilty Western powers. Any feeble attempt to assign blame to the Turkish perpetrators is immediately dismissed in this narrative with the defence that what happened was a tragic but necessary act for the preservation of the 'state'.

If one reviews these works chronologically to depict patterns of meaning, no significant studies on the Armenian deaths and massacres appear until the two works in 1953 cited above and, when they do appear, they do so with the declarations of loyalty to the Turkish nation-state at every opportunity. There is then another gap in scholarship until 1976 when the scholarship that appears is even more strongly dominated by Turkish nationalism: its authors not only give their pledge of allegiance to the Turkish nation-state as citizens, but employ historical knowledge selectively to preserve Turkish state interests at all costs, including the cost of critical scholarship.

The first 30-year gap right after the foundation of the Turkish Republic might be due, in addition to the general trauma and devastation of the war years which at least everyone in Turkey must have wanted to put aside, to the close link between the Unionist leadership perpetrating the Armenian massacres that not only funded the War of Independence but also staffed it[10] and the leadership of the Turkish nation-state. Another reason was that by 1926, Mustafa Kemal had effectively pacified the Unionist leadership he regarded as a potential threat to his rule. The series of the traumatic social reforms the young Turkish Republic underwent during Mustafa Kemal's reign within the format of single-party rule also precluded the public discussion of significant social and historical issues. The subsequent promulgation of the laws of treason against the Turkish state and against the person of Mustafa Kemal rendered any mention and interpretation of the events that countered the official version subversive as well. After Mustafa Kemal's death, the same political framework dominated during the rule of his successor and close friend İsmet İnönü. During this period, Turkey also had to come to terms with the trauma of the Second World War that occurred around it. The 1948 transition to the multi-party system and the subsequent sweeping electoral defeat of the reigning RPP of Kemal and İnönü initially liberalized the censorship over the media, leading to the emergence of the works of the two authors Esat Uras and Çark.

The second gap of 23 years until 1976 was due to the 1960 military purge of the popularly elected Democrat Party from power and the reintroduction of censorship and state control over scholarship and the knowledge it produced. Yet this state of affairs changed once again in the late 1970s because of an external development, that of the assassination of Turkish diplomats by the radical Armenian group ASALA in an attempt to draw international attention to the Armenian genocide. The defensive Republican narrative became even more polarized during this period as it selectively drew on the previous Ottoman documents and the two early-Republican strands of scholarship to sustain its ascendance to this day.

In short, the official state scholars who started to research the Armenian deportations and massacres of 1915 naturalized the inherent nationalism because of their inability to historicize the pre-1919–1923 period. As a consequence they could only identify as the culprits of the Armenian tragedy the two 'others' of Turkish nationalism, namely the Western powers and the Ottoman Armenians themselves. Their interpretations of the actions of these two 'others' were so coloured by Turkish nationalism that they failed to see the actions of the Ottoman Turks had been just as destructive. As a consequence, they defended their view of the events, and not only dismissed the claims of the massacres, but argued instead that the Turks themselves had been not the perpetrators, but the victims. It was only within the current post-nationalist era that a more critical and self-reflective reading of the Turkish historiography placing the blame equally on all social groups including the Turks has become possible.

The post-nationalist critical narrative on the events of 1915

The works considered in this category again emerge in three disparate clusters in terms of the knowledge they provide on both the Ottoman and Turkish Armenians. The first cluster[11] comprises of works either written specifically on the events of 1915 with the intent to both understand the historical context within which the events occur and therefore critically analyze the contemporary Turkish denial of these events, or works with the intent to inform the contemporary Turkish reader about the historical transformation of the Armenians from the past to the immediate present.

The second cluster[12] contains studies on recent Turkish history on topics that do not directly focus on the Armenians, but which provide ample new information on the historical background of the events of 1915 because they do not silence the role of the Ottoman minorities in their accounts in the way that the Republican defensive narrative does. And the third cluster[13] includes literary works that reveal the worlds of meaning the Armenians created within both the Ottoman and the Republican periods where the Armenians emerge as cultural actors. It is important to note that none of these works are written to defend a particular thesis or are supported in their publication, in one capacity or another, by the Turkish state. They are also not coloured by Turkish nationalism, but assume instead a post-nationalist stance which leads to their characterization as the knowledge products of the emerging civil society in contemporary Turkey.

The most significant dimension of this post-nationalist critical narrative is its willingness to recognize Turkish society not as an imagined community of nationalist compatriots of Turks, but rather as a cultural mosaic that at present includes many diverse social groups such as the Kurds and Alevis, and also the much atrophied former minority groups such as the Armenians, Assyrians, Greeks and the Jews. At this particular moment, Turkish society at large is involved in an exploration of these social groups through their literature and historical narrative. If this exploration gradually transforms into a larger social and political movement around the recognition of human rights, and is then able to overcome the resistance of the nationalist elements embedded in society and especially in the military, one can conjecture that the Armenians deportations and massacres of 1915 would then be recognized in contemporary Turkey as the genocide that they were. This chapter hopes to contribute to that effort by historicizing and thereby disempowering the current hegemony of the Turkish official historiography.

Trends and dilemmas in 'Western' historiography

One result of disempowering the official Turkish historiography will hopefully be to create space for depoliticized discussion of some of the issues that that historiography has traditionally used in support of its blame and denial narratives. The Armenian genocide is certainly in need of full subjection to the range of legitimate if frequently competing historical perspectives and contextualizations, uninhibited by overtly political considerations. Thus, though in the very most important sense – regarding the approximate scale and systematization of the murders of 1915–16 – the Western historiography is on safe ground, areas of the whole have been shaped by Armenian nationalist concerns, and others have been rather marginalized because of their potential to upset smooth narratives of persecution and Armenian suffering. Despite their mutual exclusivity, the 'Western' historiography has been shaped – perhaps distorted – by its very rejection of the official Turkish historiography, just as the machinery of denial has proven itself sensitive to developments in Western scholarship and Armenian memory politics, as the peaks of political and scholarly activity on both 'sides' from the late 1970s and from the late 1990s show.

In a recent overview of the historiography of the genocide as broadly defined – historiography, that is, including more popular accounts and public debates – Hans-Lukas Kieser identified five phases. The first phase covered the period of contemporary accounts at the time of the genocide, the First World War and the Greco-Turkish war; the second phase is the period from 1923–45, involving the production of some Armenian memorial literature; the third phase is the period from the UN Genocide Convention of 1948 to the first significant commemorative activism in Armenian communities in the 1960s; the fourth phase is the awakening of more specifically scholarly interest in the subject in the light of various factors including burgeoning interest in the Holocaust and genocide more generally, but also the Justice Commandos of the Armenian

Genocide (JCOAG) and ASALA assassinations; and the fifth phase is what Kieser called the 'transnational, post-nationalist period in history writing', which had its roots in a combination of the new geopolitical circumstances of the post-Cold War period and the new moral context after ethnic cleansing in the former Yugoslavia further discredited ethno-nationalism.[14]

The final phase clearly corresponds with the aforementioned production within Turkey of the 'post-nationalist critical narrative' on 1915. It is the first time when in any substantial measure there has been cooperation between scholars of late Ottoman history and Armenologists as well as Holocaust and genocide scholars. The second half of this chapter is concerned approximately with the fourth and fifth phases of Kieser's schema – the periods of developing professional scholarship in the West and the Armenian diaspora. It does not seek to distinguish sharply between those final two phases since some of the most abidingly influential interpretations of the genocide were written during, or have been strongly influenced by, ideas current in the earlier of the two periods. In other words, more overtly nationalist interpretations, which tend to be more essentialist in their assessment of the origins and course of the events of 1915, continue to co-exist with post-nationalist interpretations.

History and politics

Perhaps the most obvious way in which politics has intruded into history-writing is in the matter of the post-World War I territorial settlement. This is particularly so in the issue of Armenian irredentist goals in eastern Anatolia, though the spectre of genocide has also been invoked (by both sides) in the Armenian-Azeri conflict over the contested region of Karabakh. There is certainly no uniform position on the issue of border revision either in the Republic of Armenia or the diaspora,[15] but the main political party of that diaspora, the Armenian Revolutionary Federation, for instance, still cites as its twin prime goals recognition of the Armenian genocide and a return to the terms of the Sèvres treaty of 1920 gifting a 'greater Armenia' in the Caucasus and the eastern provinces of present-day Turkey. The territorial question was fore-grounded in Peter Balakian's 2003 best-seller *The Burning Tigris*,[16] which is extensively concerned with the question of the abortive American sponsorship of an independent Armenian state in formerly Ottoman and Tsarist territory in the interwar period, and implicitly endorses the justness of the Sèvres terms. Neither ethical nor historical distinctions are clearly made between discussion of America's relationship to the genocide and its relationship to Sèvres, but it should be underlined that there is no necessary relationship between the two. One is a matter of historical truth and morality, the other a more overtly political question with ongoing ramifications for the huge non-Armenian groups living in Anatolia.

The question of other ethnic groups in the Ottoman Empire leads us on to a much more complicated, nuanced matter that has still to be fully addressed in the western historiography: the relationship between the Armenian genocide and other coercive state demographic policies both in and beyond the Ottoman Empire. The comparative scholarship emerging on the genocide has tended to focus above all on the Holocaust, for reasons that surely spring in part from the desire for political recognition.[17] Yet there may be at least as many similarities between the Armenian genocide and Tsarist assaults on Circassians from the mid-nineteenth century, or on the Kyrgyz of central Asia during the First World War, or in recent decades the Serbian attacks on particular inhabitants of Bosnia and Kosovo, where the perpetrators in each case were Christian, the victims were Muslim. Even if the scope is limited to the crimes of ethnic nationalism in the near east and the Balkans in the first half of the twentieth century, a full, comparative examination of crimes related to genocide would have to take into account the ethnic cleansing of Muslims from the new south-eastern European states from the 'eastern crisis' of 1875–8 through the Balkan Wars of 1912–13 and beyond.

Within the Ottoman Empire, insofar as it is possible to judge from the available scholarship, the Armenian genocide was perhaps somewhat more systematic and complete than the assaults on the Syriac-speaking Christian communities, very extensive and genocidal though these attacks were.[18] Collectively, Armenian suffering was more intense, and state intent more explicitly murderous, than was to be the case in either the post-war purge of members of the Greek Orthodox religion from Anatolia and the reciprocal purge of Muslims from Greek territory, or the prolonged Kemalist assault on the Kurds. Though these episodes are testament to the gathering strength of ethnic nationalism in the region, in the Greek case, inter-migration was the ultimate end; in the Kurdish case, assimilation, if Turkish policies frequently shaded into mass slaughter, as during the mid-1920s and late-1930s. Indeed, within the wider history of inter-group massacre and forced displacement in the chain from central Asia through the Caucasus, Anatolia, the Balkans and eastern and central Europe from the mid-nineteenth century during the crisis and collapse of the Ottoman, Qing, Romanov and Habsburg empires, the Armenian genocide constitutes an unusually complete instance of communal obliteration.[19] This is something that the even greater extremity of the Holocaust has tended to obscure, and it is why even within this broader history of dislocation and suffering there are strong justifications for examining the Armenian case in its specificity. Bearing that specificity in mind should not, however, be at the cost of losing sight of other victim groups, for reasons both ethical and historical.

If the ethical reasons should be self-evident, it is worth underlining how undesirable it would be for the scholarship of the Armenian genocide to go down the same road as so much of the historiography of the Holocaust in marginalizing the experience of non-Jewish victims, particularly the hundreds of thousands of Romanies and the many millions of Slavs who perished as a result of Nazi occupation and extermination policies. On the historical level, the fate of other groups provides a vital hermeneutical context for the murder of both Armenians and Jews in each of the World Wars. Recent scholarship based on Ottoman sources has revealed the extent to which Muslim as well as non-Muslim groups, including Lazes, Circassians, Albanian, Bosnian and Georgian Muslims; 'Gypsies'; and some Arabs and Jews, were also moved around the empire during the war for purposes of assimilation and/or punishment.[20] The CUP clearly had a broader demographic rearrangement in mind, influenced, in part, by the campaigns of ethnic homogenization then underway in the Balkan states. Indeed, though there was no definite causal relationship between the ethnic cleansing of Balkan Muslims and the coming Armenian genocide, Muslim suffering on this scale did provide a model for the 'solution' of population 'problems' and exacerbated an already brutalized ethos of state demographic policy in the region.

As to the genocide itself, the major debates revolve around the precise evolution of Ottoman policy during the First World War, and the issue of state-Armenian relations and inter-ethnic relations prior to that conflict. Three sections of the second half of this essay deal in turn, therefore, with the matters of immediate causation; change and continuity in state ideology in the late Ottoman Empire; and changes in the Ottoman social structure over approximately its final century. Prior to that, however, is a brief consideration of the organization of the genocide.

The machinery of destruction

A number of studies of the regional unfolding of the destruction process are in existence, and they amply illustrate the systematization of the deportation and killing.[21] Analysis of the development and dynamics of the deportations at an empire-wide level is limited, however, as are detailed studies of the central processes of decision-making.[22] Relatedly, there is still scope for debate about the precise extent of involvement across the regular government structure.

Though the breadth of participation in the destruction (with the Justice, Interior and War Ministries heavily involved) means that the Armenian genocide was ultimately a state project, its implementation was closely policed by the CUP. Indeed some cabinet ministers were in the first instance kept in the dark about the true course of Armenian policy.[23] In the lead-up to and during the war there was an attempt at fuller penetration of the state machinery by party representatives, as CUP emissaries were sent to the provinces and CUP members appointed to the state posts of provincial governorships. Yet this 'coordination' had reached nowhere near the levels achieved in the later 'totalitarian' states, and had to be pressed forward even during the genocide. Thus when general deportation had become policy it was rigidly enforced from the power centre, with provincial governors shadowed by watchful 'responsible secretaries' – *kâtib-i mesul* – of the CUP to ensure appropriate execution of their instructions.[24] Reluctant officials were replaced by more enthusiastic ones, and sometimes even killed;[25] while the most enthusiastic killers in the provinces, men like Dr. Mehmed Reşid Bey in Diyarbakır and Cevdet Bey in Van, who set the pace for mass murder even before the fully fledged policy of genocide was in place, combined senior party posts and state posts.[26]

The deportation orders themselves contain no explicit sanction of mass murder. Doubtless the CUP leaders did not want to leave incriminating documentary evidence, but – presumably – nor did they wish to risk potential opposition from anyone in the larger governing structure with any qualms.[27] Yet testimony from various executors of the genocide at the few post-war trials conducted under the auspices of the new Ottoman government exposes the deliberate use of euphemism and camouflage in the instructions for 'care' of the deportees. It reveals that the onus was on outright killing, and the existence of oral and secret telegraph orders from Istanbul and local CUP functionaries to this effect,[28] though regional differences in the death-tolls exacted from the deportation convoys suggests that there was not complete uniformity in this 'second track' of orders. Further to the issue of concealment, the fact that much of the killing was done by irregulars does not alleviate the responsibility of the power centre, since the deployment of irregulars for 'dirty work' was an Ottoman (and Balkan) tradition. While it played a role in the Armenian genocide,[29] the regular Ottoman army had traditionally not been used regularly in attacks on internal communities. Such work had long been the preserve of better-qualified irregular specialists, which were an integral part of the state's arsenal. Their actions had traditionally had the acceptance and tacit compliance of the Ottoman authorities and provided the latter with plausible deniability. Unlike the regular army, irregulars were expected to live off plunder.[30]

Opportunities and catalysts: debates on proximate causation

Given the above factors, it should be no surprise that, as with the historiography of the 'final solution of the Jewish question', the central question of when, and therefore under what circumstances, the chief perpetrators decided on mass murder remains open. Such matters are particularly charged in the historiography of the fate of the Armenians, given the attempts by the CUP and later nationalist historians to portray the deportations as a militarily necessary response to Armenian insurgency. In the determination to undermine what Robert Melson has called the 'provocation thesis', the precise character of and stimuli for any armed Armenian action have become matters of great sensitivity, while a premium has been put upon finding a clear indication of genocidal intent emerging independent of any Armenian insurgent behaviour. These tendencies have dovetailed with the problem, generic to the writing of any reconstructive history, of imposing a unified narrative from the perspective of posterity on complex events – the search, as it were, for a moment of origin at which it is later possible to say that an episode 'began'.

There is a point in 1915 by which traditional consensus suggested that a policy of general killing had definitely been arrived at. 'The Van uprising', which took place in the second half of April, writes Vahakn N. Dadrian, 'was a desperate and last-ditch effort to thwart the Turkish design to proceed with their matured plan of genocide by launching the massacre of that province's Armenian population as an initial step.'[31] This famous act, which ended in May with the establishment of Armenian rule in a major eastern Anatolian city, was according to this interpretation the pretext the CUP wanted to begin their predetermined, empire-wide anti-Armenian programme. The first measure in the proper enactment of this plan, so the argument goes, was the decapitation of the Armenian nation with the mass arrests of political and social elites that began on 23–4 April.

The pretext theory is intuitively appealing. One can then retrospectively identify as preparations for genocide previous discriminatory measures, such as the disarming of Armenian soldiers in the Turkish armies – in February 1915 – and their assignment to labour battalions. Other historians opt for an earlier 'decisive' moment, as for instance with the intensification of anti-Armenian sentiment after the Ottoman defeat at the battle of Sarıkamış in the Caucasus at the turn of 1914–15 by a Russian army aided by Armenian volunteer battalions comprised of Russian subjects and some Ottoman subjects.[32] Elsewhere, Dadrian has put greater emphasis on the pre-war years in the quest for genocidal intent, emphasizing variously the activation of the 'Special Organization' (Teşkılat-ı Mahsusa) – which murdered many of the deportees in 1915 – for irregular tasks during the earlier Balkan wars and even the CUP's congress of 1910 (others have focused on the 1911 congress[33]) pursuant to which measures of enforced cultural Turkification were introduced, revolving particularly around language use.[34] Taner Akçam, while emphasizing the meetings of the CUP's central committee in mid-March 1915 as the time when concrete decisions about deportation were taken, has also stressed the significance of pre-war CUP thinking (in the light of the Balkan wars of secession and, thereafter, the resurrection of the Armenian reform question on the international stage) about the ethnic homogenization of Anatolia.[35]

None of these interpretations is necessarily incompatible with the others. Everything depends upon how one interprets the idea of 'planning' and the relationship between aspiration to a 'purified' Anatolia, latent intent to act on that aspiration, and trigger moments crystallizing such intent, and, further, how one envisages the translation into state policy of ideas circulating among a relatively small elite. Any argument that the extirpation of the Armenians was *determined* before the war, however, needs to address the fact that the deportations were not enacted immediately on the outbreak of war, nor immediately after the Sarıkamış defeat, nor, indeed, immediately after the beginning of the Van rising. The idea that the CUP was simply waiting for an *opportunity* for genocide is further vulnerable given that when the major deportations from Eastern Anatolia did start, from the end of May, they did so at a distinctly awkward time in terms of orchestrating major population movements, as Russian forces were advancing into the region. This suggests that rather than thinking of moments of opportunity, the more accurate term might be a *catalyst*, in the proper sense of an element that by its introduction changes the nature of a situation.

Accordingly, there are other ways to interpret aspects of the escalation of anti-Armenian measures. One interpretation might involve putting greater stress on the paranoia that the CUP had inherited about the disruptive potential of even small revolutionary groups, in as much as they themselves had overturned the pre-1908 order of Sultan Abdülhamid II with a comparatively small number of insurgents.[36] This paranoia would only have been accentuated in World War I by the links, of which Istanbul was well aware, between the Russian Caucasus authorities and Armenian political parties with a cross-border constituency, and by the famous Armenian volunteer battalions attached to the Russian Caucasus army.[37] As for the disarmament and enslavement of Armenian soldiers in the Ottoman army, while this was certainly motivated by distrust of Armenians, it fed into a tradition of discrimination against non-Muslim soldiers in the allocation of military functions, through which Greeks also suffered, and, moreover, also initially served a practical purpose in terms of labour required for the war effort.[38] Contrary to popular belief, the Armenian military conscripts were not systematically murdered immediately upon their assignment to labour battalions but rather during the course of the general Armenian deportations themselves. Finally, the 23–4 April arrests could be seen as a reaction to the anticipated Anglo-French landings at Gallipoli on 25 April[39] and the news of the Van rising from 20 April.

Ottoman sources actually reveal uncertainty as to precise policy even at the beginning of May, more than a week after the 23–4 April arrests. On 2 May the military leadership requested of the Interior Ministry that Armenians in 'rebellious' parts of Van province either be forced over the Russian border or dispersed in Anatolia. As well as addressing the problem of insurgency, it was argued, this would provide a form of revenge for the Russian treatment of Caucasian Muslims during the war while vacating homes for those very refugees who had fled the Tsarist domains.[40] A week later the Interior Ministry issued corresponding orders for Van and parts of Erzurum and Bitlis provinces in the face of the Russian advance, formalizing a policy that had already begun with the settlement of Muslim refugees in the Mush district of Bitlis.[41] These deportations were still of a much smaller scale and a much more specific nature than those that would occur after the general deportation order of 26–7 May, however, so it seems that the combination of the events in Van and the Russian advance provided a trigger for the escalation of CUP policy.

This does not mean that contingency plans for deportations from particular areas did not exist in advance of the decision for general deportation: they did, but the very tension in the expression '*contingency* plan' perfectly encapsulates the difficulty of establishing what A. Dirk Moses has called 'radical voluntarism' among elites responsible for genocide.[42] Nor does it mean that there were not agents of the CUP who were seeking an excuse to target the Armenians – in fact, substantial massacres by the Special Organization and military units in the regions bordering Russia and Persia from the end of 1914 probably created the environment in which the Van Armenians were driven to take up arms in self-preservation. The point of emphasizing contingency is not the issue of precise 'timing' *per se*. Its weight lies in suggesting that the perpetrators' conception of the Armenians as a collective, and of what to do with them, was still being shaped until quite late in the day – and in the truth that there is still a distance to travel between persecution and even localized murder and outright genocide. Uncomfortable though it may be, some – indefinable – part of the dynamic shaping this construction was the activity of some Armenian nationalists both within and beyond Ottoman territory. More importantly, however, talking about an ongoing process of construction of 'the Armenians' during a crisis moment helps to de-essentialize the debate in that it undermines any notion of inevitability based on readings of pre-existing inter-communal relations.

It should be underlined that any claim that the murder of the Armenians when it unfolded was not a genocide, simply because there might not be unequivocal evidence of genocidal intent prior to May 1915, is as absurd as the suggestion that the Nazi 'final solution' was not a genocide because it was not inscribed before the invasion of Poland or the USSR that every Jew was to be murdered. Since the historiography of the Shoah today is more mature and less politicized than that of the Armenian genocide, the question does not now really obtain, but it would be equally controversial for a scholar of the former as one of the latter to pinpoint exactly when that genocide began (just as it would to identify precisely when the French revolution 'began'). Part of the interpretative problem is that 'genocide' is more a legal term than an historical one, designed for the *ex post facto* judgements of the courtroom rather than the historian's attempt to understand events as they develop, that is, out of non-genocidal or latently murderous situations. In this sense, the use of 'genocide' by a historian is a classic example of the past examined teleologically. As the epithet genocide perpetrator has become the major stigma under international law, the politico-legal battle between, crudely speaking, representatives of Turks and Armenians has raged around the applicability of the term, and specifically the key notion of intent. It may be said categorically that the killing did constitute genocide – every aspect of the United Nations' definition of the crime is applicable, and the inventor of the very term was strongly influenced in his thinking by the murder of the Armenians – but recognizing that fact should be a by-product of the historian's work, not its ultimate aim or underpinning.

If Turkish nationalist historiography cynically disregards the whole history of anti-Armenian ideology and action in the late Ottoman Empire, including CUP policy, up to, say, the Van rising, much of the western historiography simplistically ignores the complexities and contingencies of state policy-making in a crisis situation, and falls into the trap of determinism based on the final outcome of state policy. Finding the balance between intention and contingency – between ideology and circumstance, as it were – is the key to explaining not only the development of state policy in 1914–15, but also the longer process by which the Ottoman state came to target the Armenian community so murderously. Discussion of the broader Armenian Question in the late Ottoman state has divided analogously between, on one hand, those generally western scholars who focus more on the development of a specific anti-Armenianism among the Ottoman elites and on the negative aspects of Armenian-Muslim interethnic relations; and, on the other hand, between those generally Turkish nationalist scholars who pay little attention to the increasingly exclusivist ideologies of the elites or the suffering of Armenians and who instead focus their energies on detailing the tribulations of the embattled state and the grounds it had for mistrusting non-Muslim populations.

State ideology in the late Ottoman Empire: change and continuity

If a model of wartime radicalization towards genocide is accepted, then it logically becomes difficult to postulate a progressive continuity in state policy in the long or medium term that logically culminated in genocide. Nevertheless, at particular moments before 1914–15 the late Ottoman state could tolerate the mass murder of Armenians, as shown by the 1909 Adana massacres of around 20,000 in the CUP era and the massacres of 80,000–100,000 in 1894–6, perpetrated under the regime of the last significant sultan, Abdülhamid II (1876–1909). Given the different constitutional regime prior to 1908, the 1894–6 killings, in particular, demand explanation, assuming that we disregard as essentialist and therefore untenable explanations for repeat massacre rooted in Islamic culture.[43]

The guiding state ideology at the time of the 1894–6 killings was 'pan-Islamism', or more precisely pan-Sunniism. The doctrine sought to mobilize the empire's Muslims into a more robust political unit in the face of challenges facing the polity from outside in the form of great power encroachments and from within in the form of developing national consciousnesses among, and often therefore separatist demands from, the non-Muslim communities of

Ottomania. The sultan also appealed to Muslims beyond the empire, playing on the symbols of the Caliphate held by the Ottoman dynasty.[44]

The massacres themselves were actually comprised of three more-or-less distinct phases, each with different chronologies and proximate causes ranging in character from local to international. Quantitatively by far the most significant phase, and that which was most widespread geographically and temporally, occurred in autumn and winter 1895.[45] In this phase, many ordinary Muslims came to the fore as perpetrators, particularly Kurds, as well, notably, as Muslim religious leaders, students and brotherhoods. In terms of their function for the state, the massacres combined political elements of a 'cull' of a proto-national element, including terrorization and expropriation, with a neo-conservative religious backlash against an 'inferior', upstart religious group.

Debate is ongoing about the extent of the central direction of the massacres. Most western scholars would now agree the following as a minimum, however. Abdülhamid may not always have been precisely informed about the extent and proximate cause of the massacres in the provinces, himself believing, and frequently being told, that Armenian nationalist insurrection was responsible, while rejecting reports by European diplomats as self-interested propaganda. Yet this is not to absolve the sultan of guilt, since he bore the primary responsibility of inculcating the atmosphere of anti-Christian chauvinism in which the massacres took place. The most important factor in encouraging the actions of private citizens and communal leaders outside the state hierarchy was the sense that they were acting in accordance with the true interests of the state and with the support of its ruler.[46]

An important function of the massacres was as a warning to Armenian nationalists, and also potential great power sponsors of the Armenians, not to press the issue of reforms for the Christians. Transgressions against supposedly religiously protected dhimmis (non-Muslim monotheists) could be justified on the basis that, by appeals to the powers for reforms both before and during the massacres, Armenian leaders had rejected Ottoman rule and therefore broken their contract with the state. Jelle Verheij argues convincingly that this factor explains why the victims were predominantly Armenian males: males occupied the public sphere, and therefore were more overtly 'political', while women, huge numbers of whom were raped, kidnapped, enslaved and forcibly converted, were not. Though by no means all western scholars would agree, this factor also suggests that the killings were not strictly genocidal in the sense of attempting to destroy or cripple the group, since it implies that the Islamic religious imperative, even in its rather perverted and overtly politicized pan-Islamic form, did leave some space for the existence of a 'protected' Armenian community as long as it remained in its politically prescribed place. What cannot be debated is that any residual element of political-religious obligation would diminish to invisibility under the CUP during the World War.

The CUP coup of 1908 began when Salonika-based revolutionaries heard of Anglo-Russian moves to solve the Macedonian Question by the time-honoured method of imposing foreign control under nominal Ottoman sovereignty.[47] The latest solution to Ottoman decline, the 'second constitutional period', began theoretically as an attempt to reintroduce pre-Hamidian notions of a shared Ottomanism. But though some less ethno-centric groupings existed within Turkish revolutionary circles, formed around some of the leaders who had previously operated largely outside the empire, in Paris and Geneva, the revolution was conducted in Muslim and, increasingly, specifically Turkish interests. The real power-holders clearly did not desire reform for reform's sake for the non-Muslim groups, and had explicitly rejected the quasi-federalism of the dissident 'Society for Private Initiative and Decentralization', aligning themselves in opposition with centralizers and nationalists.[48]

As E. E. Ramsaur puts it, if the CUP movement was 'liberal up to a point', 'the nationalistic elements far outweighed the liberal.'[49] This in itself is not singular, since from the latter part of the nineteenth century onwards, the basis of nationalistic ideologies everywhere shifted from liberalism to authoritarianism, statism and ethnocentrism. Full agreement has still to be established about the precise relationship in CUP ideology between Islamism, Turkish nationalism and other elements, including pan-Turkism and even pan-Turanianism (a doctrine seeking to unite all 'Turkic' races as far across the Eurasian landmass as 'Chinese Turkestan'), though recent work by Michael A. Reynolds has argued powerfully for the very limited practical relevance of the final two strands.[50] The growing, exclusive Turkish nationalism identified by M. Şükrü Hanioğlu among the Young Turks still seems to have been informed by the notion of the Muslim community as the *millet-i hâkime*, the dominant religious community, and as such foresaw, at least in some Young Turk rhetoric, the coexistence of Muslims under a modernizing Turkish hegemony. In the comparative context again, it should be noted that blends of religious and 'racial' identity were common to almost all of the nationalisms developing in eastern and southeastern Europe at the time. As Erik Jan Zürcher has argued, the transition to a purely secular sense of Turkishness was not completed until into the lifetime of the later Republic of Turkey. At the same time, as Kieser has also pointed out, a number of key CUP leaders were personally strong secularists and social Darwinists, and for them bonds of religious obligation towards non-Muslims were an irrelevance.[51]

Contrary to common perception, the alliance-of-convenience between 'Young Turks' in opposition and the nationalism Armenian Revolutionary Federation (ARF) had been an uneasy one from the beginning. The Balkan secessions of the nineteenth century meant that the CUP suspected non-Muslim revolutionaries of having anti-state rather than anti-regime goals.[52] The CUP had not shown any real sympathy during the massacres of the 1890s, and indeed would go on to incorporate in its regional committees local notables who had actually been instrumental in organizing those massacres.[53]

The 1909 Adana massacres and their aftermath illustrated at least a chronic lack of governmental concern as both local and immigrant Muslims attacked Armenians. The CUP centre in Istanbul may not be held directly responsible since its authority for much of the time had been compromised by a countercoup as reactionaries in the military called for the restoration of Islamic law. Moreover, many CUP members and Armenians worked together to protect the constitution. Nevertheless, the orders emanating from the ministry of the interior to Adana at the beginning of the massacres were more concerned with restoring order for the purposes of preventing external intervention than of protecting Armenians. Local CUP leaders in Cilicia were also involved in instigating and ordering massacres; after all, many had been drawn from the ranks of pre-revolutionary regional elites and had past records in attacking or condoning attacks on Armenians. Finally, many of the soldiers loyal to the CUP who were sent to Cilicia after 24 April also took part in the massacres, though there is no proof that this was on senior orders.[54]

As far as longer-term developments were concerned, the quashing of the countercoup in 1909 saw further distancing of the CUP from the liberals. A law on political associations now prohibited the formation of organizations with non-Turkish national aims,[55] and the aforementioned measures of cultural Turkification were introduced. Yet consensus suggests that it was the Balkan wars of 1912–13 that sounded the death-knell for any vestiges of CUP pluralism.[56] Muslim–Christian relations were cast into the sharpest of relief in these vicious ethnic conflicts, with widespread Christian draft evasion and Ottoman Bulgarian and Greek soldiers swapping sides to fight alongside their ethnoreligious brethren.[57] Even Muslim Albania was torn away, and the loss of this constituency accelerated the shift in CUP ranks from a general Muslim consciousness to a specifically Turkish one.

If state ideologies differed on either side of the 1908 coup, the Balkan wars also highlight some vital continuities in terms of the problems confronting the successive regimes. These problems, already hinted at, included the relative decline of the empire in the face of other great powers, as manifested in territorial loss and the diminution of internal sovereignty in the face of western economic penetration, and in the threat posed to the remaining lands by the developing consciousness of subject and primarily Christian nationalities. Both Hamidian 'pan-Islamism' and CUP 'nationalism' can, in fact, be identified as differing particularist 'remedies' to these problems, and can thus be juxtaposed with the more universalist pre-Hamidian Tanzimat reform period that sought to solve the selfsame problems by recourse to greater inter-religious equality. That the 'solutions' became increasingly vicious should not obscure the fact that the problems they sought to address were very real from the perspective of the normative state, and, indeed, recurred with increasing intensity across the lifespan of the late Ottoman Empire.

The Armenian Question and the changing Ottoman social structure

Historians differ as to precisely what factors to emphasize most strongly in the emergence and exacerbation of the 'Armenian Question' in the nineteenth century. Stephan Astourian has focused on the question of contested land-ownership in Anatolia as a spur to anti-Armenian prejudice in the light of the Tanzimat reforms that changed the traditional prescriptions on the issue, and in light of the sedentarization of Kurdish tribes and the settlement of Muslim refugees to the empire – the *muhacir* – from persecution in the Tsarist domains and in the Balkans. Kieser has emphasized the destabilization inherent to the attempt to import, force-paced, a modernity *à la française* to an empire run on entirely different principles. Other interpretations place the emphasis more on the international politics of the eastern question in exacerbating Ottoman sensitivities towards subject minorities.[58]

Where there is general agreement is on the significance of the changes in the physical and political constitution of the empire in its declining decades as Ottoman geography and demography were fundamentally altered.[59] Many aspects of this immensely complex, society-wide process did not primarily concern Ottoman–Armenian relations *per se* until around the second half of the nineteenth century, and they were as much as anything else a function of the changing nature of Ottomania from early modern empire to centralizing, modernizing state and, finally, to a supposedly homogeneous republican nation-state.

One of the many pieces of evidence supporting interpretations of the origins of genocide in changing state socio-economic structure is the comparative stability of Ottoman–Armenian relations before the mid-nineteenth century. Armenians, as *dhimmis*, like other Christian groups and Jews, occupied a position in the Islamic theocracy that, if definitively subordinated and even despised, was still legally assured. Communal life, as orchestrated through the confessional order known as the *millet* system, was therefore stable, if at the individual level, particularly for Armenian peasants in eastern Anatolia, sundry exploitations and oppressions were part of everyday life.[60] This system of stability through institutionalized prejudice worked on condition that the *dhimmis* continued to accept the hierarchical *status quo* and that the state continued to enforce it.[61] Ottoman reforms (however well-intentioned) and the rise of nationalism proved fatal to it, for both affected the aspirations of the minorities and the attitudes of the Muslim elite and majority.

Pressure – from outside and from within, in whatever proportions – to reform to survive irreversibly changed the constitutional fabric of the Ottoman Empire. The Ottoman rulers sought to prevent Christian secessionism by trying to tie in the loyalties of their Christian subjects with the fortunes of the state. Reform programmes upset many Muslims with their rhetoric of inter-religious equality, while failing to safeguard significant changes on the ground for groups such as the Armenian rural population of Anatolia, or to protect them from the Muslim backlash against their 'inappropriate' aspirational behaviour. The Armenian peasantry also suffered greatly at the hands of nomadic Kurds and the *muhacir*, many of whom had themselves been brutalized at the hands of Russia or the Balkan Christian regimes. Meanwhile, Armenians and others were encouraged by spasmodic European pressure on the Porte to believe that they had reliable defenders to which to appeal in their plight: they did not. Christian separatism and great power sequestration of Ottoman lands also meant that the ethnic composition of the empire was markedly changing, and along with it the political orientation of the Ottoman elite, which came to focus increasingly, and against the trend of the mid-century reforms, on the increasingly preponderant Muslim majority in the remaining Anatolian lands of the empire – the very lands on which Armenians dwelt among many others.

If many Armenians began to experience a sense of what Astourian calls 'relative deprivation' as their hopes and aspirations were raised above the reality of the reforms, the same was true for Ottoman Muslims who saw some Christians benefiting from the changes.[62] This was particularly true for Kurdish tribal leaders and provincial notables whose only personal power bases had been challenged by the Tanzimat reforms. A powerful stereotype of Armenians began to emerge based on relative Armenian socioeconomic success in certain quarters, as Armenian social visibility increased. This stereotype was founded on urban professionals, merchants, moneylenders, middlemen and the rural traders, as well as on certain regions and elements of the agricultural economy, notably in Cilicia.[63] Furthermore, Armenian success was associated with foreign influences, based, in part, on the Armenian importation of Western technologies.[64] Finally, the prominence of Armenians as agents and brokers for European interests and the extension to individual Armenians of the extraterritorial privileges (the 'capitulations') enjoyed by citizens of the great powers living in Turkey seemed to confirm a picture of Christians not pulling together with the Muslim population in the interests of the state on whose territory they dwelled.[65]

From the perspective of the state, this association with external, Christian powers was taken to another level by the 'internationalization' of the Armenian Question at the end of the 'eastern crisis' of 1875–8. The Berlin Treaty of 1878 supplanted the victor's peace in the Russian-dictated treaty of San Stefano, and saw British lip-service paid to the future wellbeing of the Armenians in the eastern provinces as a counter to earlier Russian rhetoric about suffering Christianity. This was the first time that Armenians had been singled-out from Ottoman Christians generally in an international treaty, and, at the end of a crisis period in which the Ottomans had lost much territory in Europe and in the Russian border region, it was a vital moment in hardening Ottoman suspicion about Armenian loyalty. The failure of the European powers to enforce the reform clauses of the treaty in turn led to the formation of Armenian revolutionary parties from the 1880s onwards.

The parties owed much to radical Russian Armenian influences and pursued their interpretation of Ottoman Armenian 'national' interest without much recourse to the security of ordinary Armenians.[66] Their actions undoubtedly served the state as one of the proximate 'justifications' for the 1894–6 massacres. More important on the broad functional level, however, was that the Hamidian ideology legitimating the massacres had developed in reaction to the failure of the earlier Tanzimat reforms to keep Christian populations within the state, and in light of a suspicion of the developing Armenian national consciousness given the loss of so much Bulgarian and other territory in the eastern crisis. Further, since the empire was simultaneously haemorrhaging millions of Christians and gaining millions of Muslim refugees, the demographics of Anatolia were also changing such that there was a real functional 'sense' in Ottoman elites both in the Hamidian and CUP periods returning their attention more exclusively to the aspirations of Muslims after the Tanzimat, particularly as many of the constituency had felt an increasing alienation from the state in the course of the mid-century reforms. In circular fashion, this in turn meant that the ongoing grievances of rural Armenians would remain substantially unaddressed both up to and after the CUP coup.

The first Balkan War accentuated all of these concerns from the perspective of the state. Millions more desperate Muslim refugees flooded into Anatolia as the vast majority of the last Ottoman lands in Europe were torn away, leaving the Christian populations of Anatolia more starkly exposed as ethno-religious 'anomalies' than ever before. Further, at the close of the Balkan Wars, as in 1878, a reform plan was promoted with Russian support by the Catholicos of all Armenians. In the revised form in which it was finally foisted onto the Ottoman Empire in early 1914, the plan entailed the creation of two zones out of the six 'Armenian' provinces of eastern Anatolia, plus Trabzon/Trebizond on the Black Sea coast, to be administered by neutral European inspectors approved by the Porte. The CUP viewed Russian sponsorship of the plan as preparation of the ground for subsequent annexation of the 'Armenian' provinces, against a recent backdrop of increased Russian agitation against Armenians and Kurds, and increased control over the adjoining regions of Persia.[67]

A strong case can be made that the Ottoman Armenians had nothing more to hope for from the CUP upon the recall of the European inspectors provided for in the reform plan. On the Turkish entrance into the First World War in 1914, the plan was annulled alongside the European-run Ottoman Public Debt Administration and the capitulations. The attempt to reshape internally what was left of the Ottoman Empire by these measures of consolidation and by population policy was the other side of the coin of protecting the frontiers against further external incursion, and even re-expanding the empire at the expense of Russia. These considerations were at once ideological and functionally 'practical' in some sense of raison d'etat, given the changing social structure of the state. Accordingly, whether or not genocide was planned prior to the conflict, the future of the Armenians as a political community in the Ottoman Empire was very bleak.

Conclusion

There is always a danger when detailing structural factors in history of seeming to absolve individual actors of decision-making power and moral responsibility. It is distinctly unsatisfactory, particularly for victims of genocidal regimes, to have massive suffering attributed to anything other than a discrete, objectively repulsive and preferably overtly *ideological* hatred. The scale of the crime is directly proportionate to the strength of the human need for unequivocal accountability. As genocide is one of the ultimate crimes, so the logic goes, a monstrous and preferably personalizable perpetrator and a monstrous, indisputable motive are required to link cause and effect by a thick, straight line. Reference to general historical forces and socio-political structures cannot satisfy this need, and nor should it, for genocide is always the result of political choices, albeit at very particular, generally crisis, moments. What the foregoing may illustrate, however, is that the dichotomy of intentionality and contingency is a false one, not just in 1915 but across the span of the bloody decline of the Ottoman Empire. Recognizing this fact is not some wrong-headed attempt to find a spurious middle ground in a sharply bifurcated historiography, but instead to endorse the ongoing move away from any simplistic narratives steeped in nationalist interpretations of Ottoman anti-Armenianism or Armenian treachery.

Notes

1. See, for instance, M. Asaf, *1909 Adana Ermeni Olayları ve Anılarım* [1909 Adana Armenian Incidents and My Memoirs] (Ankara: Turkish Historical Society Press, 1982); G. Çağalı-Güven, *Kamil Paşa ve Said Paşaların Anıları: polemikler* [Memoirs of Kamil Pasha and Sait Pasha: the polemics] (Istanbul: Arba Press, 1991); M. Kasım, *Talat Paşa'nın Anıları* [Memoirs of Talat Pasha] (Istanbul: Say Press, 1986); A. Mehmedefendioğlu, *Sürgünden İntihara: Dr. Reşid Bey'in Hatıraları* [From Exile to Suicide: Memoirs of Dr Reşid Bey] (İzmir: Belge Press, 1982); S. Sait Paşa *Anılar* [Memoirs of the Grand Vezir Sait Pasha] (Istanbul: Hür Press, 1977).
2. See, for instance, *8 Mart sene 335 tarihinde irade-i seniye-i hazret-i padişahiye iktiran eden kararname ile müteşekkil divan-ı harb-i örfi muhakematı zabıt ceridesi* [Turkish military tribunal records], (Istanbul: Takvim-i Vekayi Press, 1919–1920).

3. See, for instance, H. N. Paşa, *Ermeni Olayları Tarihi* [History of the Armenian Incidents] (Ankara: Prime Minister's Press, 1994); E. Cengiz, ed., *Ermeni Komitelerinin A'mal ve Hareket-i İhtilaliyesi* [The Actions and Revolutionary Movements of the Armenian Committees] (Ankara: Prime Minister's Press, 1983).
4. See, for instance, Prime Ministry Directorate General of Press and Information, *Documents* (Ankara: Prime Ministry Press, 1989); Prime Ministry Directorate of State Archives, *Osmanlı Belgelerinde Ermeniler (1915–1920)* [Armenians in Ottoman Documents] (Ankara: Prime Minister's Press, 1994).
5. See National Congress of Turkey, *The Turco-Armenian Question: The Turkish Point of View* (Constantinople: Societé Anonyme de Papeterie et d'Imprimerie, 1919).
6. See, for instance, C. Birsel, *Lozan* [Lausanne] (Istanbul: Sosyal Press, 1933); B. Şimşir, *Lozan Telgrafları: Türk Diplomatik Belgelerinde Lozan Barış Konferansı* [The Lausanne Telegraphs: Lausanne Peace Conference through Turkish Diplomatic Documents] (Ankara: Turkish Historical Society Press, 1990).
7. Y. G. Çark, *Türk devleti hizmetinde Ermeniler (1453–1953)* [Armenians in the service of the Turkish state] (Istanbul: Yeni Press, 1953); E. Uras, *Tarihte Ermeniler ve Ermeni meselesi* [Armenians in history and the Armenian question] (Istanbul: Belge Press, 1953).
8. See N. K. Demir, *Bir Şehid Anasına Tarihin Söyledikleri: Türkiye'nin Ermeni Meselesi* [What history told a martyr's mother: the Armenian Question in Turkey] (Ankara: Hülbe Press, 1976); Atatürk Üniversitesi Yirminci Yıl Armağanı, *Ermeniler hakkında makaleler derlemeler* [Articles and selections on the Armenians] (Ankara: Kalite Press, 1978); Jamanak, *Facts from the Turkish Armenians* [Realites exprimees par les armenien turcs/Türk Ermenilerinden gerçekler] (Istanbul: Jamanak Press, 1980); Dokuz Eylül Üniversitesi Rektörlüğü, *Türk Tarihinde Ermeniler Sempozyumu* [Symposium on the Armenians in Turkish history] (Manisa: Şafak Press, 1983); N. Göyünç, *Osmalı İdaresinde Ermeniler* [Armenians under Ottoman administration] (Istanbul: Gültepe Press, 1983); N. Gülmez, *Türkiye Büyük Millet Meclisi Zabıtlarından Doğu ve Güneydoğu meselesi* [Eastern and southeastern question from the proceedings of the Turkish grand national assembly] (Istanbul: Hamle Press, 1983); K. Gürün, *Ermeni Dosyası* [The Armenian file] (Ankara: Turkish Historical Society Press, 1983); Ş. Orel and S. Yuca, *Ermenilerce Talat Paşa'ya Atfedilen Telgrafların Gerçek Yüzü* [The truth about the telegrams attributed to Talat Pasha by the Armenians] (Ankara: Turkish Historical Society Press, 1983); C. Küçük, *Osmanlı Diplomasisinde Ermeni Meselesinin Ortaya Çıkışı (1878–1897)* [The emergence of the Armenian Question in Ottoman diplomacy] (Istanbul: Istanbul University Press, 1984); B. Şimşir, *The Deportees of Malta and the Armenian Question* (Ankara: Turkish Historical Society Press, 1983), *British Documents on the Ottoman Armenians (1856–1880)* (Ankara: Turkish Historical Society Press, 1983), *The Genesis of the Armenian Question* (Ankara: Turkish Historical Society Press, 1983), and *British Documents on the Ottoman Armenians (1880–1890)* (Ankara: Turkish Historical Society Press, 1983); A. B. Birliği, *Katliam Efsanesi* [The massacre myth] (Ankara: Anatolian Press, 1987); K. Kartal, *Van'dan Erivan'a Hatıralarım* [My memoirs from Van to Erivan] (Ankara: Anatolian Press, 1987).
9. See, for instance, B. Eryılmaz, *Osmanlı Devletinde Gayrımüslim Teb'aanın Yönetimi* [The administration of the non-Muslims in the Ottoman state] (Istanbul: Risale Press, 1990); A. Süslü, *Ermeniler ve 1915 Tehcir Olayı* [Armenians and the Population Transfer Incident] (Ankara: Sistem Press, 1990); S. Sonyel, *The Great War and the Tragedy of Anatolia* (Ankara: Turkish Historical Society Press, 2000), and *Minorities and the Destruction of the Ottoman empire* (Ankara: Turkish Historical Society Press, 1983); T. Ataöv, *The Armenians in the late Ottoman Period* (Ankara: Turkish Historical Society

Press, 2001), and *The 'Armenian Question': Conflict, Trauma and Objectivity* (Ankara: Strategic Research Center Press, 1997).

10. For a full discussion, see E. J. Zürcher, *Milli Mücadelede İttihatçılık* [The Unionist Factor: The Role of the Committee of Union and Progress in the Turkish National Movement, 1905–1926] (Istanbul: Bağlam Press, 1987).
11. For examples that cover the range of works in this cluster, see for instance, T. Akçam, *İnsan Hakları ve Ermeni Sorunu* [Human Rights and the Armenian Question] (Istanbul: İmge Press, 1999), and T. Timur, *Türkler ve Ermeniler: 1915 ve Sonrası* [Turks and Armenians: 1915 and Its Aftermath] (Ankara: İmge Press, 2001) as well as H. Onur, *Ermeni Portreleri: Milet-i* (*sic*) *Sadıkadan Hayk'ın Çocuklarına* [Armenian portraits: from a loyal community to the children of hayk] (Istanbul: Burak Press, 1999).
12. For examples of this cluster, see the works of Ş. Hanioğlu, *Preparation for a Revolution: The Young Turks, 1902–1908* (New York: Oxford University Press, 2001), and *The Young Turks in Opposition* (New York: Oxford University Press, 1995); T. T. Vakfı, *75 Yılda Tebaa'danYurttaş'a Doğru* [From subject to citizen in 75 years] (Istanbul: History Foundation Press, 1999); O. S. Kocahanoğlu, *İttihat-Terakki'nin Sorgulanması ve Yargılanması: Meclis-i Mebusan Zabıtları* [The interrogation and trial of the Union and Progress: proceedings of the Ottoman assembly] (Istanbul: Temel Press, 1998); F. Dündar, *İttihat ve Terakki'nin Müslümanları İskan Politikası (1913–1918)* [The Muslim settlement policy of the Union and Progress party] (Istanbul: İletişim Press, 2001).
13. For examples of this cluster, see for instance, P. Tuğlacı, *Ermeni Edebiyatından Seçkiler* [Selections from Armenian literature] (Istanbul: Cem Press, 1982); H. Mintzuri, *Atina, Tuzun Var mı?* [Athena, have you got some salt?] (Istanbul: Aras Press, 2000); An. Özer, *Yaşamı Beklerken* [While awaiting life] (Istanbul: Aras Press, 1997); Y. Sırmakeşliyan, *Balıkçı Sevdası* [Fisherman's passion] (Istanbul: Aras Press, 2000), and K. Zohrab, *Hayat, Olduğu gibi* [Life, as it is] (Ankara: Ayraç Press, 2000); and İ. Arıkan, *Mahallemizdeki Ermeniler* [Armenians in our neighborhood] (Istanbul: İletişim Press, 2001).
14. H.-L. Kieser, 'Looking for a lost human heritage: Some remarks on recent historiographical developments concerning the Armenian genocide', unpublished manuscript.
15. 'The Struggle for Recognition: The Next Steps', *Armenian News Network/Groong*, 15 April 2001; R. G. Hovannisian, 'The Armenian Case: Toward a Just Solution' (Jerusalem: Hai Tad Committee, 1982), 14.
16. P. Balakian, *The Burning Tigris: The Armenian Genocide and America's Response* (New York: Harper Collins, 2003).
17. For example, V. N. Dadrian, 'The Convergent Aspects of the Armenian and Jewish Cases of Genocide: A Reinterpretation of the Concept of Holocaust', *Holocaust and Genocide Studies*, 3, 2 (1988), 151–69.
18. The best treatment of this topic is David Gaunt, *Massacres, Resistance, Protectors: Muslim–Christian Relations in Eastern Anatolia during World War I* (New Jersey: Gorgias Press, 2006).
19. On these broader patterns see M. Levene, *Genocide in the Age of the Nation State. Volume 2: The Rise of the West and the Coming of Genocide* (London: I. B. Tauris, 2005); M. Geyer and C. Bright, 'Global Violence and Nationalizing Wars in Eurasia and America: The Geopolitics of War in the Mid-Nineteenth Century', *Comparative Studies in Society and History*, 38 (1996), 619–57.
20. Dündar, *İttihat ve Terakki'nin Müslümanları İskan Politikası*.
21. H. Kaiser, 'A Scene from the Inferno: The Armenians of Erzerum and the Genocide, 1915–1916', in *Der Völkermord an den Armeniern und die Shoah*, eds, H.-L. Kieser and D. Schaller (Zurich: Chronos, 2003); idem., *At the Crossroads of Der Zor: Death,*

Survival, and Humanitarian Resistance in Aleppo, 1915–1917 (Princeton, NJ: Gomidas Institute, 2001), U. Ü. Üngör, '"A Reign of Terror': CUP Rule in Diyarbekir Province, 1913–1918' (MA thesis, University of Amsterdam, 2005); K. Y. Suakjian, 'Genocide in Trebizond: A Case Study of Armeno-Turkish Relations during the First World War' (PhD dissertation, University of Nebraska, 1981); Y. Ternon, *Mardin 1915: Anatomie pathologique d'une destruction* (Paris: Centre de l'Histoire Arménienne Contemporaine, 2000); R. H. Kévorkian, ed., *La Cilicie (1909–1921),* special issue of *Revue d'Histoire Arménienne Contemporaine* 3 (1999); and the series of volumes edited by Richard Hovannisian for MAZDA publishers on the individual 'Armenian' provinces of Eastern Anatolia, each of which contains a chapter on 1915.

22. For a good summary of the routes, see R. H. Kévorkian, ed., *L'Extermination des déportés arméniens ottomans dans les camps de concentration de Syrie-Mesopotamie (1915–1916): la deuxième phase du génocide* (Paris: Bibliothèque Nubar, 1998). J. Lepsius, *Der Todesgang des armenischen Volkes: Bericht über das Schicksal des armenischen Volkes in der Türkei während des Weltkrieges* (Potsdam: Tempelverlag, 1919) and *The Treatment of Armenians in the Ottoman Empire, 1915–1916: Documents Presented to Viscount Grey of Falloden by Viscount Bryce/James Bryce and Arnold Toynbee, Uncensored Edition,* ed., A. Sarafian (Princeton, NJ: Gomidas Institute, 2000) have yet to be supplanted, though they do not provide explicit and overall links between deportations, rather examining them on a case-by-case and province-by-province basis. On the involvement of the state elites, see V. N. Dadrian, 'The Complicity of the Party, the Government and the Military. Select Parliamentary and Judicial Documents', *Journal of Political and Military Sociology*, 22 (1994), 29–96; idem., 'The Documentation of the World War I Armenian Massacres in the Proceedings of the Turkish Military Tribunal', *Journal of Political and Military Sociology*, 22 (1994), 97–132. For Dadrian's influential overall treatment of the subject, see his *The History of the Armenian Genocide* (Providence, RI: Berghahn Books, 1995). The various works of Hilmar Kaiser shed important light on the central decision-making process – see particularly the chapters on the Armenian genocide – for which Kaiser acted as research assistant, in Michael Mann's *The Dark Side of Democracy: Explaining Ethnic Cleansing* (Cambridge: Cambridge University Press, 2005). Fuat Dündar is presently engaged on a study of precisely such central decision-making. Raymond Kévorkian's huge narrative *Le Génocide des Arméniens* (Paris: Odile Jacob, 2006) appeared too late for its findings to be incorporated in this chapter.
23. Dadrian, 'Documentation', 98.
24. Ibid.; Dadrian, 'The Complicity of the Party'; Annette Höss, 'Die türkischen Kriegsgerichtsverhandlungen 1919–1921' (PhD: Vienna, 1991).
25. *Osmanlı Belgeler*, 140, on the dispatch of an inspector to Marash owing to the leniency shown towards Armenians by the district governor; also Kaiser, *Der Zor*, 15–16.
26. Höss, 'Die türkischen Kriegsgerichtsverhandlungen,' on the postwar trial of these 'responsible secretaries'; also Dadrian, 'Documentation'; on 'coordination', Üngör, '"A Reign of Terror"'.
27. Dadrian, 'Documentation', 98.
28. Dadrian, 'The Complicity of the Party', 87; Höss, 'Die türkischen Kriegsgerichtsverhandlungen', 76, 78, 81–3, 96, 130.
29. See the editor's introduction to *Eberhard Count Wolffskeel Von Reichenberg, Zeitoun, Mousa Dagh, Ourfa: Letters on the Armenian Genocide,* ed. Hilmar Kaiser (Princeton, NJ: Gomidas Institute, 2001).
30. James J. Reid, 'Militarism, Partisan War and Destructive Inclinations in Ottoman Military History: 1854–1918', *Armenian Review,* 39, 3 (1986), 1–21, here 6–11; Arnold J. Toynbee, *The Western Question in Greece and Turkey: A Study in the Contact of Civilizations* (London: Constable and Co., 1923), pp. 278–80.

31. V. N. Dadrian, 'The Role of the Special Organisation in the Armenian Genocide during the First World War', in *Minorities in Wartime*, ed. P. Panayi (Oxford: Berg, 1993), pp. 50–82, here p. 64; H. Pasdermadjian, *Histoire de l'Armenie* (Paris: Librairie orientale H. Samuelian, 1971), pp. 408–9.
32. Y. Ternon, *Les Arméniens: histoire d'un génocide* (Paris: Seuil, 1977), pp. 211–12; A. Beylerian, 'L'échec d'une percée internationale: Le mouvement national arménienne (1914–1923)', *Relations internationales*, 31 (1982), 356.
33. J. H. Tashjian, 'The Truth about the Turkish Act of Genocide', *Armenian Review*, 18, 3 (1965), 41–52, here 44.
34. T. Akçam, *Armenien und der Völkermord: Die Istanbuler Prozesse und die türkische Nationalbewegung* (Hamburg: Hamburger Edition, 1996), p. 37; V. N. Dadrian, *Warrant for Genocide: Key Elements of Turco-Armenian Conflict* (New Brunswick, NJ: Transaction Books, 1999), Ch. 9.
35. Akçam, *Armenien*, pp. 39–43; idem., 'Rethinking the Ottoman Archival Material: Debunking Existing Myths/General Overview of the Ottoman Documents', unpublished paper.
36. Lepsius, *Todesgang*, p. xiv; H. Morgenthau, *Ambassador Morgenthau's Story* (Garden City, NY: Doubleday, Page & Co., 1918), p. 347.
37. D. Bloxham, *The Great Game of Genocide: Imperialism, Nationalism, and the Destruction of the Ottoman Armenians* (Oxford: Oxford University Press, 2005), Ch. 2.
38. E. J. Zürcher, 'Ottoman Labour Battalions in World War I', in *Die armenische Völkermord*, eds, Kieser and Schaller, pp. 187–98.
39. Timur, *Türkler ve Ermeniler*, p. 35.
40. *Osmanlı Belgeler*, pp. 7–8.
41. Bloxham, *The Great Game of Genocide*, p. 84.
42. A. D. Moses, 'Conceptual Blockages and Definitional Dilemmas in the "Racial Century": Genocides of Indigenous Peoples and the Holocaust', *Patterns of Prejudice*, 36, 4 (2002), 21.
43. Dadrian, *The History of the Armenian Genocide*, pp. 3–6, 121–7.
44. S. Deringil, 'Legitimacy Structures in the Ottoman State: The Reign of Abdülhamid II (1876–1909)', *International Journal of Middle East Studies*, 23 (1991), 345–59.
45. J. Verheij, 'Die armenischen Massaker von 1894–1896: Anatomie und Hintergründe einer Krise', in *Die armenische Frage und die Schweiz (1896–1923)*, ed., H.-L. Kieser (Zurich: Chronos, 1999), pp. 69–129; Dadrian, *History*; R. Melson, 'A Theoretical Enquiry into the Armenian Massacres of 1894–1896', *Comparative Studies in Society and History*, 24 (1982), 481–509; cf. S. Duguid, 'The Politics of Unity: Hamidian Politics in Eastern Anatolia', *Middle Eastern Studies*, 9 (1973), 139–55.
46. In addition to Verheij on these points, see H.-L. Kieser, *Der verpasste Friede: Mission, Ethnie und Staat in den Ostprovinzen der Türkei 1839–1938* (Zurich: Chronos, 2000), pp. 243–7.
47. E. J. Zürcher, *Turkey: A Modern History* (London: I. B. Tauris, 1998), p. 94.
48. Ibid., pp. 92–4; K. H. Karpat, 'The Transformation of the Ottoman State, 1789–1908', *International Journal of Middle East Studies*, 3 (1972), 243–81, here 280.
49. E. E. Ramsaur Jr., *The Young Turks: Prelude to the Revolution of 1908* (Princeton, NJ: Princeton University Press, 1957), p. 147.
50. M. A. Reynolds, 'The Ottoman-Russian Struggle for Eastern Anatolia and the Caucasus, 1908–1918', (PhD dissertation, Princeton University, 2003).
51. Hanioğlu, *Preparation for a Revolution*, pp. 40–1, 84; E. J. Zürcher, 'Young Turks, Ottoman Muslims and Turkish Nationalists', in *Ottoman Past and Today's Turkey*, ed., K. Karpat (Leiden: Brill, 2000), pp. 150–79, esp. p. 151; H.-L. Kieser,

'Dr Mehmed Reshid (1873–1919): A Political Doctor', in *Der Völkermord an den Armeniern und die Shoah*, eds, Kieser and Schaller, pp. 245–80.

52. Hanioğlu, *Preparation for a Revolution*, pp. 40–1, 84.
53. A. Arkun, 'Les relations arméno-turques et les massacres de Cilicie de 1909', in *L'Actualité du génocide des Arméniens*, ed. Comité de Défense de la Cause Arménienne (Paris: Edipol, 1999), pp. 55–74, here 59.
54. R. Kevorkian, ed., *La Cilicie (1909–1921)*, special issue of *Revue d'Histoire Arménienne Contemporaine*, 3 (1999), 59–82; Astourian, 'Genocidal Process', pp. 63–6; Arkun, 'Les massacres de Cilicie'.
55. R. Davison, *Turkey: A Short History* (Huntingdon: Eothen, 1988), 128–9; D. McDowall, *A Modern History of the Kurds* (London: I.B. Tauris, 1996), pp. 90–1.
56. Davison, *Turkey*, p. 132.
57. F. Adanır, 'Non-Muslims in the Ottoman Army and the Ottoman Defeat in the Balkan War of 1912/13', unpublished paper.
58. S. H. Astourian, 'Testing World Systems Theory, Cilicia (1830s–1890s): Armenian-Turkish Polarization and the Ideology of Modern Ottoman Historiography' (PhD dissertation: UCLA, 1996); cf. Kieser, *Der verpasste Friede*; cf. e.g. Bloxham, *The Great Game of Genocide*.
59. For example, Akçam, *Armenien und der Völkermord*; R. G. Suny, 'Empire and Nation: Armenians, Turks and the End of the Ottoman Empire', *Armenian Forum*, 1, 2 (1998), 17–52; M. Levene, 'Creating a Modern "Zone of Genocide": The Impact of Nation- and State-Formation on Eastern Anatolia, 1878–1923', *Holocaust and Genocide Studies*, 12 (1998), 393–433; Kieser, *Der verpasste Friede*.
60. On the dhimmi and the millet system see B. Braude and B. Lewis, eds, *Christians and Jews in the Ottoman Empire: the Functioning of a Plural Society*, 2 vols. (New York: Holmes and Meier, 1982).
61. S. Astourian, 'Genocidal Process: Reflections on the Armeno-Turkish Polarization', in *The Armenian Genocide, History, Politics, Ethics*, ed. R. Hovannisian (Basingstoke: Macmillan, 1992), pp. 53–79.
62. Astourian, 'Genocidal Process', pp. 58–60.
63. F. Ahmad, 'Vanguard of a Nascent Bourgeoisie', in *Social and Economic History of Turkey (1071–1920)*, eds, O. Okyar and H. İnalcik (Ankara: Meteksan, 1980), pp. 329–50, esp. pp. 329–31; and, in the same volume, M. Ma'oz, 'Intercommunal Relations in Ottoman Syria during the Tanzimat Era', pp. 205–10.
64. Astourian, 'Genocidal Process', pp. 61, 64.
65. Ibid., p. 65; Ahmad, 'Vanguard', p. 329; Ma'oz, 'Intercommunal Relations', p. 207.
66. On the ideology of the parties nationalism A. Ter Minassian, *Nationalism and Socialism in the Armenian Revolutionary Movement* (Cambridge, MA, 1984), pp. 4–5, 15, 18, and Part II on the Bulgarian influence on the parties; on the composition and operational bases of the parties, idem., *La Question Arménienne* (Rocquevaire: Éditions Parenthèses, 1983), pp. 74, 108, 124–34; on their development and platforms, L. Nalbandian, *The Armenian Revolutionary Movement* (Berkeley, CA: University of California Press, 1963); on the disappointments of 1878 and the background to the formation of the revolutionary parties, C. Walker, *Armenia: the Survival of a Nation* (London: Routledge, 1980), pp. 110–32.
67. R. Davison, 'The Armenian Crisis, 1912–1914', *American Historical Review*, 53 (1948), 481–505; M. Pavlovitch, 'La Russie et les Arméniens', *La Revue Politique Internationale*, 1 (1914), 470–1, 478–9.

14
The Holocaust and Its Historiography

Dan Stone

It is not true, as is often assumed, that for the first decade or so after 1945 no one had anything to say about the genocide of Europe's Jews. There were, in fact, a quite large number of testimonies and studies published, but mostly in languages that were inaccessible to English-speaking researchers and in places that were obscure to those not directly connected to the circles of survivors.[1] There were also many popular and artistic representations of the Holocaust, although the genocide of the Jews had, of course, not yet acquired that name.[2] Nevertheless, comparatively speaking, the dearth of writing in the immediate aftermath of the war is made all the more striking by the truly mind-boggling production of historical (and other) scholarship as well as popular books and films that emerged in the last quarter of the twentieth century, an outpouring that shows no sign of abating in the near future. The historiography of the Holocaust is now fragmented into numerous sub-disciplines, conducted in many languages and based on diverse methodological and epistemological assumptions. It is larger than any one person can ever hope to master. As a result, in this survey I will merely present some of the key trends in that historiography, discuss some of its achievements and shortcomings, and position the literature on the Holocaust in relation to recent trends in comparative genocide studies.

Historiographies

Early histories of the Holocaust were based largely on the documents collected by the International Military Tribunal at Nuremberg, published in 42 volumes. But apart from the works of Léon Poliakov, Gerald Reitlinger, Joseph Tenenbaum, Raul Hilberg, Nora Levin, Helmut Krausnick, and Lucy Dawidowicz there were, by the late 1950s, already numerous specialist publications, such as Israel's *Yad Vashem Studies* (volume I appeared in 1957), and many articles and books on various aspects of what was just starting to be called 'the Holocaust', especially studies of Jewish resistance and Nazi ideology. By the 1980s, the historical scholarship was already large enough to justify the publication of historiographical surveys. Michael Marrus's *The Holocaust in History* (1987) and Ian Kershaw's *The Nazi Dictatorship* (1985), both of which have become classic works, offered clear and still useful surveys of the field; and the 1983 Yad Vashem conference *The Historiography of the Holocaust Period* (published 1988), though more eclectic, also provided guides to a varied and otherwise (to English speakers) inaccessible literature, such as Soviet or Israeli historiography. More recently, a number of collections of essays, document collections, encyclopaedias and readers have appeared, and more are planned.[3] Furthermore, the Holocaust has given rise to a good deal of theoretical literature, by historians, literary theorists, philosophers, and others, on the place of the Holocaust in the twentieth century, the nature of the historical enterprise and the 'limits of representation'. The Holocaust has played a particularly important role in the context of debates about postmodernism; for some scholars, the Holocaust is, in fact, the harbinger of postmodern thought, with its rejection of 'grand narratives' and scepticism towards ideas of progress and reason.[4] The aim of what follows is not to examine these historiographical surveys; I mention them in order to indicate the size and scope of the field, and to make it clear that such a brief précis as this essay is no more than a starting point.

Explanations, old and new

The recent fragmentation of Holocaust historiography has resulted partly from the fact that the Holocaust has become central to western consciousness, a phenomenon that it is beyond the scope of this chapter to explain, and partly from the fact that since the end of the Cold War far more documents have been discovered than historians would have believed possible at the end of the Nuremberg Trial. Early historians of the Holocaust, such as Léon Poliakov, Gerald Reitlinger, and Philip Friedman, had extensive documentation at their disposal, but in nothing like the quantities and varieties that historians can now employ.[5] The collections of the United States Holocaust Memorial Museum (Washington, D.C.) and Yad Vashem (Jerusalem) now cover many miles of shelving and extraordinary numbers of microfilms. Documents relating – to take a few random examples – to the Holocaust in Romania or Romanian-occupied Ukraine (Transnistria); to Nazi occupation policies and genocide in eastern Galicia, Belarus, or Lithuania; to the Vatican and its relations with the Third Reich or its position vis-à-vis the Jews; to the involvement of major German firms such as Schering AG, Dresdner Bank, Deutsche Bank, I.G. Farben, Daimler Benz, Degussa, and others; to the extent of the German population's complicity in the crime through the 'Aryanization' process and the spreading around of expropriated property and goods; to the extensive activities of antisemitic research institutes, whether independent (that is, run by Nazi agencies) or university-based; to the Europe-wide complicity in the genocide have all gradually become available in enormous quantities.

This new archival research has several implications. The first is that historians have turned, since the 1990s, away from theoretical approaches and discussions, which is somewhat ironic given that in the theoretical literature it is often the Holocaust that is named as the event that demands renewed attention to the epistemological or methodological underpinnings of the historical discipline. As Saul Friedländer noted, 'it is precisely the "Final Solution" which allows post-modernist thinking to question the validity of any totalizing view of history, of any reference to a definable metadiscourse.'[6] Few historians have chosen to respond to Friedländer's challenge. Second, it means that on an empirical level we now know far more about the scope and operation of the crime, the way it worked, and the extent to which large numbers of non-German collaborators, whether states or individuals, were involved. Third, and as a result of the latter, while there has emerged a huge body of evidence to which historians can appeal and that has led to a certain broad consensus about basic facts of the Holocaust, renewed interpretive divisions among scholars are opening up, as I will discuss below. The question today, for most historians, is less a theoretical or quasi-philosophical one of worrying about how their discipline can represent the Holocaust, or whether history's tools are at best inadequate and at worst implicated – few historians concern themselves with Moshe Postone's claim that the Holocaust 'burst the bounds of normal history, as it were, and, hence, of any traditional mode of coping with history'[7] – but about types of explanation, especially the relative weight one should ascribe to ideology, on the one hand, and contingency, on the other. It is for this reason that a discussion of the long-standing debate between 'intentionalists' and 'functionalists' is called for first of all.

Until the 1980s most historians, with the notable exception of Hilberg, argued that the main cause of the Holocaust was Nazi antisemitism. This is an entirely understandable position – surely the murder of the Jews must have had something to do with hatred of Jews? Indeed, only with the emergence of a school of thought that doubted the correctness of this way of thinking – 'functionalism' or 'structuralism' – could it be named at all, as 'intentionalism'.[8] Intentionalists, such as Lucy Dawidowicz, Eberhard Jäckel, Andreas Hillgruber, Gerald Reitlinger, Deborah Lipstadt, or Yehuda Bauer, believed that Hitler had a plan to murder the Jews and that he implemented it at the earliest opportunity, which happened to be under cover of war, when amidst the confusion and widespread destruction a genocidal project could more easily be disguised. In the 1970s and 1980s this interpretation increasingly came under fire as historians discovered that the unfolding of the genocidal process was by no means straightforward; rather, the road to Auschwitz was, as one historian put it, 'twisted'.[9] If Hitler had always intended to murder the Jews, they argued, why was there a need for a gradual process of social exclusion, as occurred between 1933 and 1938? And after that date, why was the 'territorial solution' of deporting the Jews to Nisko in eastern Poland or to Madagascar dreamt up?[10] Furthermore, historians began to argue that the ghettos were not initially established as 'holding pens' before deportation to killing centres, and they questioned the notion (rather paradoxical anyway, if there was always a plan) that the infamous Wannsee conference of 20 January 1942 played such a pivotal role in the decision-making process as most historians believed.[11]

The debate was quite polarized, with some functionalist historians (Martin Broszat and Hans Mommsen) arguing not only that no plan existed, but that actually no single 'decision for the final solution' was ever taken by Hitler. For Mommsen, indeed, antisemitism was merely a rabble-rousing rhetorical device and the Holocaust a 'way out of a cul-de-sac' into which the Nazis had manoeuvred themselves during the war. Functionalists stressed that their claims drew attention away from only Hitler, Himmler, and Heydrich, and established the guilt of large sections of the German population and many sectors of the German state. Intentionalists, however, saw this argument as a dissipation of guilt so that the 'cumulative radicalization' that led to genocide occurred (the passive voice and the lack of agency are important) more or less by accident. This was a classic historiographical clash between those who see the world as driven by agency, and who therefore stress the role of individuals, and those who see social forces and structures as more important, since these direct and limit individual choice.[12]

However, by 1990, the debate appeared to have quietened down. With Christopher Browning declaring himself to be a 'moderate functionalist' and Philippe Burrin naming himself a 'conditional intentionalist', a consensus appeared to have been reached. The question was reignited thanks to the work of German historians who had visited the newly opened archives in the former communist countries of Europe. These historians – among them Götz Aly, Christoph Dieckmann, Thomas Sandkühler, Christian Gerlach, and Dieter Pohl – argued in their 'regional' studies of Nazi occupation policies in eastern Europe that the genocidal onslaught against the Jews certainly took place in an atmosphere fuelled by violent antisemitism, but that the immediate causes for the murder were to be found elsewhere, for example, food shortages in the region, or plans for urban and rural 'Germanization'. This 'new functionalism' convinces insofar as it is based on archival work, but is, nevertheless, flawed because it fails to recognize that what the documents say does not necessarily conform to what happened. Merely because some young, careerist statisticians, demographers, and nutritionists who accompanied the occupation produced papers arguing that the Jews should be eliminated does not establish that this is the reason why such a thing took place. In fact, although they recognize the significance of antisemitism as the broad framework within which policy decisions were taken, these historians have remarkably little to say about the SS or about what decisions were being taken in Berlin. Nor does their work satisfactorily explain the western European dimension of the Holocaust.[13]

It is for these reasons that most recently one can see a 'return of ideology' to the literature. Where the academic consensus of the 1980s was a functionalist one, now the stress on 'modernity', 'technology', or 'cumulative radicalization' has largely given way to a stress on 'violence', radical antisemitism, and fantasy.[14] This is not because of Daniel Goldhagen's book, which, if it had any positive effects, was to act as a catalyst for scholarship that was already under way, into, for example, SS ideological indoctrination, radical antisemitism in the Weimar Republic,[15] and the extent to which 'race' structured and drove so many aspects of the Third Reich (as I will discuss further below). Nevertheless, it is striking that there are now very few historians who would take either an extreme intentionalist or an extreme functionalist position, since most now recognize both that before 1941 or 1942 there was no clearly formulated blueprint for genocide and that a worldview built on mystical race thinking, especially antisemitism, lay at the heart of the regime. The debate between Christopher Browning and Peter Longerich on the timing of the decision for the final solution illustrates this: both share many assumptions, but the former places more emphasis on the circumstances of war in autumn 1941, and plays down the fact that the death camps did not begin operating until 1942, whereas the latter stresses a continuity in 'Judenpolitik' that always sought to eliminate 'the Jew' but that only became genocidal in 1942.[16] How to reconcile these two points remains unclear. Nor is it necessarily the most important question facing historians, though it remains key to the historiography.

It would be mistaken then to assume that the fierce debates between intentionalists and functionalists of two decades ago have disappeared altogether. It might be fair to say, as Christian Gerlach does, that they have subsided:

> The current absence of controversies between scholars with entirely different approaches to Holocaust research is based on the fact that many German (and of course not only German) historians no longer search for exclusive explanations – or the only true explanation – because the complexity of the roots of the Holocaust is more and more acknowledged. True, there are still different opinions, but present research is about elements of explanation and includes the attempt to actually understand the Holocaust as having had multiple causes.

Still, Gerlach goes on to admit that 'the question as to whether ideology was the prime cause of the Holocaust remains a major line of distinction between different understandings in historiography.'[17] Thus, among the 'multiple causes'

Gerlach refers to, the same question that drove the earlier intentionalist/structuralist debate remains evident: the role of ideology on the one hand, and circumstances on the other, only now in a much broader, empirically richer as well as more complex historical context.

Recent trends

The historiography of the last decade has not yet broken the boundaries of the classic distinction between victims, perpetrators, and bystanders.[18] With research driven by thematic concerns – such as gender or memory – there is the opportunity to do so, but the trend towards increasing specialization means that few historians are willing to challenge established interpretive frameworks. Within these frameworks, however, there has been an enormous amount of fresh and original research.

Let us start with perpetrators. Dan Diner has remarked that while it 'is doubtless insufficient to claim that historiographical narratives derive solely from the historian's rootedness in a given "ethnic", national, or other collective belonging', nevertheless, 'it would be excessively rationalistic to ignore the impress of traditional and group memories on historiography.'[19] Hence, it is no surprise to discover that the study of perpetrators has been led above all by German historians, and that in Germany the study of perpetrators has become a subdiscipline in its own right: *Täterforschung* (perpetrator research). Of course, there are numerous cases of non-German historians who work on perpetrators, but in general Diner's claim is borne out.

Research has focused on individuals, in an attempt to provide some meat on the bones of the social psychologists' arguments about the importance of situational factors (as opposed to individuals' inherently 'evil' nature[20]), and on institutions, surprisingly few of which had been the subject of serious study until very recently. Thus, within the RSHA umbrella (the SS empire), the *Wirtschaftsverwaltungshauptamt* (WVHA, Business Administration Main Office), which had been neglected for far too long by historians, was examined by Michael Thad Allen; the *Sicherheitsdient* (SD, Security Service of the SS) has been scrutinized in detail by Michael Wildt; and the *Rasse- und Siedlungshauptamt* (RuSHA, Race and Resettlement Main Office) has received its first scholarly monograph thanks to Isabel Heinemann.[21] The focus here ranges from high-level functionaries (the SD) to mid-level SS bureaucrats (Allen and Heinemann). And what each reveals is the importance of ideology. Allen's work, for example, notes that the SS set up numerous enterprises in order to take advantage of its predominant position within the Nazi empire, and Himmler sought to introduce 'modern' managerial techniques to make them as efficient as possible. But Allen shows how ideological motivation continually got in the way of what functionalist historians identified as bureaucratization or routinization. Rather, various SS enterprises, such as the *Deutsche Erde- und Steinwerke* (DESt, German Earth and Stone Works) were hampered, in business terms, by ideological commitments, in particular the exploitation of unskilled slave labourers, which hardly sat well with the desire for managerial efficiency. And Wildt – like Ulrich Herbert and Lutz Hachmeister before him in their biographies of Werner Best and Alfred Six, respectively[22] – shows that the men of the SD were not passionless 'desk killers' but educated ideologues, radicalized by the Great War, and devoted to the racial regeneration of Germany. Less surprisingly, in a study devoted to one of the SS's racial agencies, Heinemann shows that RuSHA was convinced that its project to classify eastern Europe's population according to racial criteria would expedite the Nazi plan to 'regermanize' the area.

A similar scenario has emerged with respect to high-ranking Nazis who have recently been the subject of new studies. Peter Longerich confirms that Himmler was a dedicated racial ideologue, and David Cesarani has argued that Adolf Eichmann was no 'cog' in the machinery of destruction but one of its main drivers.[23] Their underlings, whether in the concentration camp administration, T4 (Euthanasia Programme) apparatus, or civil administration in the occupied east, have all been exposed as ideologically motivated perpetrators. Yaacov Lozowick and Hans Safrian, for example, have brought to light cases of lesser-known 'bureaucrats of death' who turn out to have been far more emotionally and ideologically involved in the regime's genocidal project than either a traditional functionalist argument or a narrowly focussed intentionalist argument would suggest.[24]

Perhaps the most significant field of perpetrator research has been with respect to the Wehrmacht and affiliated agencies, such as police battalions, in eastern Europe. The Wehrmacht Exhibition of 1995 finally put paid to the notion of a 'clean Wehrmacht', which historians had in any case long since scotched.[25] Even the watered down revised exhibition – from which many photographs that proved impossible to identify definitively had been removed – made it clear that 'ordinary' soldiers had taken part in committing atrocities on a wide scale. And apart from the already well-known *Einsatzgruppen*, the RSHA's mobile killing squads that followed the Wehrmacht into the USSR and shot more than one million Jews, historians picked up on Browning's 1992 study *Ordinary Men* to investigate further the question of whether perpetrators such as police battalion members were simply unlucky to find themselves in a terrible situation or whether they were, in fact, more ideologically driven than Browning thought. Work by Edward Westermann, Ben Shepherd, Konrad Kwiet, Jürgen Matthäus, Wolf Kaiser, and others suggests that the Wehrmacht had a well-organized programme of ideological indoctrination, and that while Browning was more convincing (and appealingly modest) than Goldhagen in claiming that situational factors (including seemingly banal ones like the use of alcohol, careerism, or peer pressure) should also be considered, it seems that many soldiers and policemen who became Holocaust perpetrators were certainly heavily influenced by Nazi ideology.[26] All of these perpetrators were 'normal men' insofar as they were not psychopaths or otherwise mentally deranged; but they became for the most part subscribers to an ideology that now seems decidedly 'irrational'. As George Browder puts it in a helpful review article, '"Committed ideologue" versus "banal bureaucrat" may even be a false dichotomy; they are at best two extremes on a multidimensional spectrum of perpetrators.'[27] Rather, in Mark Roseman's words, 'the "intention", to follow the language of the older debate, was dispersed far more widely than historians once thought ... we should treat antisemitism not as an abstract dogma, but effectively as a lens that influenced the way other factors were perceived and evaluated.'[28]

It is thus no surprise to discover that research institutes devoted to antisemitism and race theory were numerous and influential in the Third Reich. In the immediate aftermath of the war, several key publications revealed the extent of intellectuals' and scientists' complicity in the rise of Nazism and in its criminal activities.[29] In the last decade, scholars have looked in detail at the part played by the professions, and by academics of all stripes, including, belatedly, historians.[30] Claudia Koonz argues, in *The Nazi Conscience* (2003) that the pervasive vocabulary of race – in the press, in propaganda, and in scholarly journals, such as Walter Gross's *Neues Volk* – was key in paving the way for the Holocaust: 'Words like "extermination" (*Ausrottung*), "purging" (*Säuberung*), and "elimination" (*Vernichtung*) stocked the imaginations of hardcore antisemites long before World War II created a context in which mass murder of Jews could become a reality.'[31] Like Matthäus and others, Koonz also stresses the importance of training in 'race war'. Alan Steinweis, in his *Studying the Jew* (2006) shows the prestige and influence of individuals and research institutes devoted to researching the 'Jewish question', and Patricia von Papen-Bodek, in her study of the *Institut zur Erforschung der Judenfrage* (Institute for the Study of the Jewish Question) in Frankfurt also discusses the networks of research institutes that 'provided a niche for frustrated and unaccomplished academics', which nevertheless had considerable influence thanks to the nature of the regime and the support of local antisemitic networks across Europe.[32] And the extremely prestigious and important Kaiser-Wilhelm Institutes, the forerunners of today's Max-Planck Gesellschaft, have been the subject of exceptionally thorough research, which is befitting an umbrella organization that contained some of the world's best-known anthropologists and other scholars.[33]

The networks of persecution and complicity, then, were far wider than historians thought in the first decades after the war. Apart from the RSHA, research institutes and German state agencies, the broad German population was also deeply involved. Frank Bajohr, among others, has shown how 'Aryanization' and other efforts at expropriation mean that while economics should not be seen as the Holocaust's primary driver, nevertheless, it would be wrong to regard it as 'an insignificant secondary by-product of the Holocaust', as historians were long wont to do.[34] The revelations in the 1990s about dormant Swiss bank accounts, stolen gold, and looted artworks, coupled with public debates about compensation for forced labourers, the establishment of national committees of inquiry across the world from Europe to Latin America, the opening up of major companies' archives to historians, and historical research into 'Jew markets' or the elite *Einsatzstab Reichsleiter Rosenberg*, all added up to an explosion of interest in the sensitive and emotionally trying topic of the financial implications of the persecution of the Jews.[35]

At the time of the Third Reich, and reaching its pinnacle in the high Cold War, the leftist critique of 'fascism', based on the 1935 definition of Communist leader Georgi Dimitrov, argued for a necessary connection between fascism and big business. According to Dimitrov, fascism constituted 'the open terrorist dictatorship of the most reactionary, most chauvinist and most imperialist elements of finance capital.' Since the 1970s, most western historians have rejected the argument that Hitler was a puppet of capitalists. But since the end of the Cold War, historians have reappraised the connections between business and Nazism. Few would subscribe to the 1960s' notion of 'fascism' which saw it as nothing more than 'crisis capitalism with a cudgel',[36] but many, on the basis of detailed empirical work in company archives, now believe that, from the *Gleichschaltung* ('co-ordination' with the regime's requirements) of industry, to the workings of the insurance and clearing systems to the employment of forced labourers, many German (and international) firms were involved in the Holocaust to a far greater extent than post-war West German memory, which celebrated instead the *Wirtschaftswunder* (economic miracle) admitted.[37] Studies of Deutsche Bank, Dresdner Bank, Daimler Benz, I.G. Farben, Degussa, Schering AG, Allianz, Krupp, Volkswagen, and others have been detailed and thorough, and add up to a whole new sub-discipline of Holocaust historiography, daunting to non-specialists but important in presenting a nuanced picture of the intricate and sometimes troubled relationship between industry and Nazism.[38] The former, while by no means the puppet-masters of Communist mythology, were, nevertheless, deeply complicit with Nazi crimes and, at least, until the middle of the war were for the most part willing to go along with the demands made by the Nazi regime since they continued to benefit financially from doing so. Christopher Kobrak and Andrea H. Schneider sum up the complex nature of the historiography:

> for some companies profiting from the misery of human beings, at least at some points during the Nazi regime, was a matter of business as usual; other firms preferred to keep their distance from what should have appeared to be an immoral activity that could only damage the firm's long-term international

> reputation. The studies also suggest that, even within firms, behaviour was not uniform. Progress in this area is blocked not so much by lack of evidence, but by the complexity of economic evaluation and questions about the role of intention, as opposed to result, and pain and suffering, as opposed to profit.

They end, however, with a clear statement: 'Although there are some isolated examples of company managers who strenuously resisted these trappings of power which helped the regime establish its position, collectively, business was eager to profit from Nazi economic salvation.'[39]

Research into forced labour and the SS's economic empire serves as a reminder that, most surprisingly, there existed very few detailed studies of the Nazis' concentration camps and death camps. Each of the museums located at the former camps produced camp histories, and there have of course been numerous studies, testimonies and popular accounts, but few works have incorporated the most recent historical evidence. Gradually, this anomaly is being rectified, with Sybille Steinbacher's monograph on Auschwitz as part of a four-volume history edited by Bernd C. Wagner, the Auschwitz-Birkenau Museum's own staff publications, Bogdan Musial's collection of essays on the Operation Reinhard camps (Belzec, Sobibor, Treblinka), and detailed research into the camp system in general, its structure, functioning and development.[40] Steinbacher's work meshes to some extent with that of the 'new functionalists' discussed above, since she argues that Auschwitz's emblematic status arose from the fact that 'it became an ensemble of the main elements in Germanization policy in the conquered East: a concentration camp for the people displaced; a "model city" for those supplanting them, and a massive factory where both groups, at least for a time, and on very different terms, would find employment', as Peter Hayes neatly summarizes.[41] In other words, the genocide of the Jews, while it may have been a discrete project, has to be understood in the broader context of Nazi plans for the demographic reshaping of Europe along 'racial' lines. This argument seems to make sense of the Nazis' broader ambitions, but it also suffers from the same interpretive shortcomings as the claims that food shortages drove the decision to murder the Jews: it relies too heavily on middle-level functionaries and what their fascinating and voluminous writings tell us about their ambitions, and too readily integrates the genocide of the Jews into their plans, suggesting that antisemitism *per se* was not the cause of the Holocaust but only a necessary context for it.

Further research is currently underway into the early history of the concentration camps in Germany,[42] and more detailed work into the many facets of the different camps is to be expected. A scholarly study of Reinhard Heydrich remains needed along with suitably contextualized studies of other major perpetrators. In fact, despite the scholarly work encompassed in these multi-volume publications, a single-volume synthesis on Auschwitz is yet to appear, as is an up to date survey of the camp system as such. And finally future research into the camps needs to do more to incorporate the victims into its purview. The long-awaited publication, in English, of Gideon Greif's extraordinary interviews with surviving members of the Auschwitz *Sonderkommando* (the men forced to work in the gas chamber complex) should stimulate interest in this topic beyond the sub-genre of testimony.[43] Work on medical experiments and racial science, the Post Orders and Command Orders to SS guards, the development of the camp and its 'area of interest' (*Interessengebiet*), slave labour and big business, and the SS empire in general all need fleshing out with complementary studies on the position of the camps' inmates, both Jewish and non-Jewish, including kapos, within them.

Thus, on the one hand we have a perpetrator-centred scholarship that increasingly sees the Holocaust as but one part of Nazi imperial visions for the occupied eastern territories that went hand in hand with massive 'resettlement' (read: genocide) of Slavs and the colonial settlement of the land by ethnic Germans. On the other hand, there is a more victim-centred literature that stresses the importance of ideology. Those who study the camp system and have to make sense of the competing agencies within the SS empire that ran it are more likely to favour a structuralist interpretation, precisely because in the archives they encounter a complex mass of contradictory evidence that deals with economic interests, military matters, civilian administration and aspects of colonial settlement, as well as 'racial policy' in the narrow sense. Those who work on Nazi research institutes, racial science or Nazi ideology are more likely to favour, if not an 'intentionalist' argument in the older sense, certainly a view of the Holocaust that sees a more direct link between ideas and acts. And if the bridge between perpetrators and victims has not yet been made in the historiography of the camps, it is even less prepared when it comes to the ghettos.

In the literature on the ghettos, a victim-centred historiography is most evident. There may not yet be such a thing as a Holocaust historiography 'from a Jewish perspective' (Dan Michman's desideratum), but when it comes to the ghettos, the experiences of their occupants forms the bulk of the literature. Thanks to the comparatively large number of diaries, photographs and other documents (speeches, drama, poetry, music, medical records and so on) that survived the larger ghettos, students of Jewish experience of the Holocaust have found much to support their work. And it is here – as well as in debates about the Jewish Councils (*Judenräte*), Jewish resistance, and Jews in hiding[44] – that the responses of the Jews to their persecution have been most carefully analysed. Especially in the literature on resistance, scholars have sought to show that in the ghettos 'spiritual resistance' was a reality experienced by many Jews.

We now know a good deal about the bravery of those who, going against German regulations, taught children religious and secular subjects, performed theatre and music, and conducted scholarly research in the ghettos.[45] The courage of doctors and nurses too in the ghettos deserves mention.[46] But the concept of 'spiritual resistance' has also been challenged. First, the concept of *Amidah* ('stand') employed by Israeli historians to indicate unarmed resistance runs the risk of marginalizing the large amount of armed resistance that took place. (Contrary to early post-war claims that the Jews went 'like sheep to the slaughter' there was far more armed resistance than one would have believed possible, in ghettos and camps, and by partisan units – and certainly an amount that bears comparison with national resistance movements in Nazi-occupied Europe.) Second, it in no way downplays the fact that such things occurred to suggest that it is perhaps too easy to believe that performing plays or music provided succour for those in the ghettos, providing welcome relief from an unbearable reality.

A desire for escapism was sometimes the case, as in the Vilna Ghetto theatre, but as Shirli Gilbert shows in her fine study of music and the Holocaust, different groups of prisoners in different camps used music differently, from Polish nationalist songs that mocked Nazi rule to Yiddish songs of the ghettos that mourned the destruction of communities. Most importantly, she shows that Jewish camp inmates, in particular, were often coerced into performing, and assesses the impact this type of music had on the performers, on other camp inmates, and on the guards who established the orchestras and who also had them play for their own personal entertainment. Among many moving examples of the complexities of how music appeared under Nazi rule, Gilbert's description of Szymon Laks' orchestra in Birkenau being forced to sing carols to the inmates of the camp's women's 'hospital' at Christmas 1943 is eloquent testimony to the monstrous effects that music could have.[47]

Gilbert does not deny that in certain circumstances music may have helped to keep up the spirits of inmates, especially German political prisoners in a camp like Sachsenhausen, who drew on an established repertoire of political songs. But she also convincingly argues that music may have been accepted by the Germans in the ghettos and camps not because they were ignorant of its existence but because it helped to 'keep the peace': 'In an ironic inversion of the spiritual resistance argument,' she writes with respect to the Warsaw ghetto, 'it seems that music was one of many activities tolerated by the SS precisely because by diverting their attention from what was really happening to them, it helped in deflecting any urge on the part of the victims to resist.'[48] Similarly, in Sachsenhausen, where she notes the relative freedom that political prisoners enjoyed with respect to music making and performing, 'it is important to acknowledge that the politicals would not have been granted this freedom if the SS had perceived their activities as a serious threat.'[49] Furthermore, Gilbert argues, it was not an urge to resist that 'drove people to the concert halls, but rather a desire to escape temporarily the gnawing realities of hunger and fear.'[50] She is also quite clear about the fact that in Auschwitz only the very small minority of privileged inmates could have enjoyed music, and that for most inmates such concerns were an irrelevance. Likewise, in the ghettos, while children starved on the streets, the ghettos' prominent inhabitants were enjoying musical soirées, as the remarkable photographs of Henryk Ross in the Łódź ghetto attest.

These kind of debates about resistance are still ongoing, for only in the last decade or so have historians finally found a way of discussing the topic that owes less to 'national psychologies' than to dispassionate analysis. Even with respect to the ghettos, however, for which we have many sources, it remains the case that very little is known about any other than the handful of in many ways unrepresentative large ghettos of Warsaw, Łódź, Vilna, Minsk, Lvov and Białystok, along with the unusual cases of Amsterdam, Budapest, and the in many ways unclassifiable Theresienstadt. For this reason, Martin Dean of the USHMM, an expert in local collaboration in eastern Europe, is undertaking a project to document as many as possible of the approximately 1000 ghettos that existed under Nazi rule, some tiny and lasting for only a few days. Whether this project will do more than document names and basic facts remains to be seen.

One of the themes that has energized Holocaust historiography in the last decade is that of gender. When discussing the ghettos, camps, and resistance, a gendered analysis has now become a mainstream approach, after substantial opposition to the idea when it was first mooted by pioneer scholars such as Joan Ringelheim and Sybil Milton in the 1980s. From the point of view of perpetrators, Elizabeth Harvey has shown the extent to which women were bound up with the colonization of eastern Europe; several scholars have looked at the role of female scientists and anthropologists in legitimizing and sometimes participating in genocide; and research is currently underway into the female SS, women camp guards and women in the Euthanasia programme.[51] With respect to victims, somewhat unseemly and unproductive debates about whether men or women were more successful survivors (arguments that, ironically, often subverted the feminist agenda purportedly driving them by insisting that women were better 'carers and sharers', because of their traditional control of the domestic sphere) have given way to a more sophisticated methodology. Zoë Waxman notes that ascribing only domestic, mothering and care-giving roles to women leads one to 'obscure the diversity of women's Holocaust experiences'.[52] Scholars are thus no longer surprised to find that women could be brutal or aggressive, and no longer automatically describe such women as 'deviant females'.[53] There has been little work on masculinity, however, and so far the concept of 'gender' as applied to Holocaust research has meant in practice women and, increasingly, family studies, especially in the context of Displaced Persons. Indeed, the experience of survivors in the immediate post-war context has also been something of a growth area in the last few years.[54]

Conceptual and methodological advances in applying gender to the study of the Holocaust means that research into gender is gradually being decoupled from the study of children, as scholars realize that mothering does not encompass the full range of female experiences during the Holocaust years, and as the study of children becomes more sophisticated in its own right. Perhaps no other area of Holocaust historiography has developed so quickly over the last five years. Where a decade ago there were two noteworthy studies, now the literature has mushroomed.[55] This situation no doubt owes something both to the fact that few survivors other than child survivors remain alive, as well as to the Wilkomirski scandal, in which the man who claimed to speak for child survivors, getting them heard where previously they had been overlooked, turned out to be a fraud, thus fuelling a desire for accurate information about children.[56] It means that scholarship on children and the Holocaust is as important to recent developments in literary studies as it is in historical ones, and there have also been a number of significant publications of children's diaries and testimonies.[57]

Finally, the concept of 'bystander' has also been theoretically examined and new research on 'bystanders' has appeared, especially in the context of Poland. Here the largest single spur to debate and further research was the publication of Jan Tomasz Gross' *Neighbors* (2000 in Polish; 2001 in English). Gross argued that the murder of the Jewish population of the village of Jedwabne in the region of Białystok in 1941, shortly after the end of the nearly two-year Soviet occupation and the start of the Nazi one, was the work of their Catholic Polish neighbours and not the Germans. The difficulty was not just a local one of showing that people who lived side by side could viciously murder one another (we have become familiar with this scenario thanks to Cambodia, Rwanda and Bosnia), but one of national self-image: that Poles, inhabitants of the 'Christ of Nations', the victims of World War II, could also be victimizers, was a challenge to Polish identity. The ramifications of *Neighbors* are still being felt, with a great deal of attention being paid now to the Holocaust in Poland.

Apart from the debate in Poland, much work has also been done on the 'neutral' countries during World War II. The experiences of countries such as Turkey, Spain and Ireland were of course all different, but none has emerged from the work of scholars in a particularly rosy light. But the countries whose self-image has suffered the most are Sweden and Switzerland. The latter has been at the centre of major scandals concerning its immigration policy, or lack thereof, as well as, more famously, the bank accounts and assets of murdered Jews. The former has faced revelations about its policies of trading with Germany throughout the war, which have to some extent tarnished its reputation as a safe haven for the Jews of Denmark. Finland too, though technically not neutral (it was allied to the Third Reich for the geopolitical reason of fending off the USSR), has also been the subject of research that positions it in a similar context. More work is to be expected not only on the neutral countries as such but on the notion of bystanders in general, whether individuals, NGOs such as the Red Cross or states. Whether a 'grey zone' that complicates or blurs the distinctions between perpetrators, victims and bystanders is either desired or likely to emerge at all seems, for the time being, unclear.

Holocaust and/as genocide

Hannah Arendt argued that the crimes committed by the Nazis were conceptually distinct from cases that are referred to as 'genocide'. The 'moral point of this matter is never reached,' she wrote, 'by calling what happened by the name of "genocide" or by counting the many millions of victims: exterminations of whole peoples had happened before in antiquity, as well as in modern colonization'. Although in the context of this book, Arendt's claim might seem questionable, her next points are worth considering:

> It is reached only when we realize that this happened within the frame of a legal order and that the cornerstone of this 'new law' consisted of the command 'Thou shalt kill,' not thy enemy but innocent people who were not even potentially dangerous, and not for any reason of necessity but, on the contrary, even against all military and other utilitarian considerations. The killing program was not meant to come to an end with the last Jew to be found on earth, and it had nothing to do with the war except that Hitler believed he needed a war as a smoke screen for his non-military killing operations; those operations themselves were intended to continue on an even more grandiose scale in time of peace. And these deeds were not committed by outlaws, monsters, or raving sadists, but by the most respected members of respectable society.[58]

Recent research has turned Arendt's argument on its head (while also, paradoxically, seeing her as an intellectual predecessor for arguing, in *The Origins of Totalitarianism*, that fascism had imperialism as its forerunner) by suggesting that the fact that 'exterminations of whole peoples' had happened before is relevant to understanding the Holocaust. In this final section I will consider the impact of research that connects the Holocaust to the theme of this book: genocide.

Arguments about the 'uniqueness' of the Holocaust continue, though not with the same vociferousness as in the 1980s and 1990s.[59] But increasingly we have an empirical historiography that is putting flesh on the bones of the Arendt-inspired claim that there are important links between colonial genocide and the Holocaust, as well as meaningful conceptual gains to be made by thinking of the Holocaust in terms of comparative genocide.[60]

First, Holocaust historians are increasingly referring, if only in passing, to the 'colonial' aspects of the Nazi project in general and of the Holocaust in particular. Robert Gellately, for example, notes that 'The mentality of the [Nazi] conquerors and the intellectuals who supported them reminds one of late nineteenth-century imperialists in Africa.'[61] In his recent, major study of the decision-making process for the 'final solution', Christopher Browning writes that 'Hitler's belief in the need for German Lebensraum implied that the Nazis would construct an empire in eastern Europe analogous to what other European imperial powers had constructed overseas. Not surprisingly, this also meant that the Nazi regime stood ready to impose on conquered populations in Europe, especially Slavs in the east, the methods of rule and policies of population decimation that Europeans had hitherto inflicted only on conquered populations overseas.'[62] And Robert Cribb also asserts that there is 'a clear parallel, of course, between the actions of Western settlers in the lands of indigenous peoples and the policies of Nazi Germany in Eastern Europe, where displacement and extensive killing along with disease and starvation were intended to change demographic realities.'[63] Historians have started to go beyond these casual mentions. Wendy Lower, for example, in her important study of the Holocaust in eastern Ukraine, goes to some length to fit the Holocaust into the 'colonial genocide' paradigm. The Nazi occupiers of Ukraine, she argues, 'perceived their actions as legitimately linked to Europe's history of conquest and rule', a history that routinely included 'exploration, conquest, migration, and mass destruction of peoples'. Thus the 'Nazi occupation of Eastern Europe demonstrated that such practices were not strictly overseas forms of conquest and rule, and that the worst aspects of colonialism – forced population movements, slave labor, and mass murder – could be combined and carried out on an enormous scale, in a matter of a few years, and in the heart of "civilized" Europe.'[64] These are arguments that anti-colonial writers such as Frantz Fanon, Aimé Césaire and Albert Memmi articulated many years ago, and which post-colonial theorists such as Julian Pefanis, Vinay Lal and Achille Mbembe have developed more recently.[65] Only now have historians been not only making the same argument but also providing empirical backing for it.

Second, there is a growing literature that seeks to set the Holocaust into a broader framework of the history of genocide. The work of A. Dirk Moses, Jürgen Zimmerer, Ann Curthoys and John Docker especially, has sought to show how conceptualizing the Holocaust as 'genocide' need neither diminish the Holocaust nor exaggerate the characteristics or horror of other events, the twin fears of relativization on the one hand and inflation on the other that haunt critics whose starting point is the uniqueness of the Holocaust.

Curthoys and Docker have argued, following Ward Churchill and Patrick Wolfe, that colonialism is inherently genocidal.[66] The establishment of what Alfred Crosby calls 'Neo-Europes' could not have occurred so rapidly without genocide, in this view, though it is not a view that Crosby shares.[67] Moses notes that 'The logical corollary of equating the Holocaust with genocide is to make genocide consubstantial with state-sanctioned mass murder.'[68] This, he believes, following Lemkin, is only one – and not the most common – aspect of what constitutes genocide. By criticizing this 'liberal' understanding of genocide and advocating instead a 'post-liberal' one that is not centred on the state, Moses seeks to maintain the significance of the Holocaust but to show that holding it to be paradigmatic does little to help one understand the nature of most other cases of genocide. Yet he also acknowledges that methodologies derived from Holocaust historiography have been key to the development of the historiography of other genocides. Ben Kiernan, for example, finds the Khmer Rouge's world view helpfully illuminated by considering the Nazis' 'fear of German territorial loss and national annihilation'; Donald Bloxham employs Hans Mommsen's notion of 'cumulative radicalization' to explain the development of Young Turk policy in the Armenian genocide; and Mahmood Mamdani makes comparisons between Hutu Power's race-thinking and that of the Nazis.[69] Most importantly, scholars can at last, according to Moses, study the Holocaust alongside other cases of genocide and ethnic cleansing without having 'to make pious gestures to establish their moral credentials. The enormity and distinctive features of the Holocaust are universally appreciated in the research community'.[70]

Moses's claim is backed up by the work of scholars such as Norman Naimark, Eric D. Weitz, Benjamin Valentino and Alexander Hinton.[71] But it is most clearly shown in the work of Jürgen Zimmerer, who certainly rejects the uniqueness of the Holocaust, seeks to show how Nazi genocide was prefigured in German colonial genocide, but by no means sets out to diminish the Holocaust. Zimmerer describes the German war against Poland and the USSR as 'without doubt the largest colonial war of conquest in history'.[72] He sees the Holocaust as related to the Germans' settlement policies in general, and stresses that many of the Nazis' victims were killed in face-to-face shootings, not by gas chambers (at which point the Holocaust does indeed differ from colonial genocides).[73] Zimmerer concludes by claiming that 'The structural similarity between colonialism and National Socialism went beyond the continuity from the Herero war. With its central concepts of "race" and "space", the Nazi policy of expansion and annihilation stood firmly in the tradition of European colonialism, a tradition also recognizable in the Nazi genocides.'[74] The Holocaust, in this reading, is merely an extreme variant of a well-known phenomenon already familiar to Europeans through the history of their colonial conquests.[75]

If all of this sounds rather too dispassionate, even cold, it is important to remember that those who advocate this broad, 'theory of genocide approach' are not dead to the horror of the Holocaust. Nor do they only see economic, means-ends or purposive rational actions at work in the murder of the Jews. Rather, the striking fact about colonial genocide, and about the Holocaust too, is the way in which these aspects go hand in hand with transgressive, 'irrational' or, to use LaCapra's terms, carnivalesque dimensions. As Mark Levene reminds us, in a discussion of the Holocaust in the context of his recent book on genocide, 'fantasy' goes to the heart of the Nazi project:

> The usually brutal and often wholly sadistic physical torture and annihilation of babies, their mothers, their whole families, the sequestration of their communities' valuables and property, the laying waste of a landscape in which those people lived and worked and with it the conscious obliteration of the elements most sacred to those people in that landscape, as if those communities and with them their belief-systems had never existed – not to mention the absolute denial that any such act has taken place – all these, the common ingredients of genocide, suggest something more than a simple, straightforward utilitarian calculus. Let alone the workings of a well-oiled – or alternatively, if one does not like that reading – misshapen modernity.[76]

Levene goes on to emphasize that the perpetrators' irrational ascription of unearthly power to the victims is 'not simply a convenient rationalisation but is genuinely held.'[77] Setting the Holocaust into a broader field of genocide studies does not then lead one to making genocide a normal fact of human existence, at least, not 'normal' in the sense of being tied to everyday calculations.

Conclusions

The historiography of the Holocaust is massive. Yet despite the various sub-fields and the wide breadth and depth of the historical scholarship, it remains in certain ways rather restricted. The field remains dominated by political history, and the inroads being made by social history and cultural history (such as microhistory) are still fairly small. Certain topics, such as the 'grey zones' inhabited by kapos or the experiences of DPs in the immediate aftermath of the war, are only now receiving the attention they deserve. And connecting the Holocaust to a broader theory and history of genocide is, as we have seen, only just becoming acceptable in mainstream historiography, and much of the literature is still polemical. But in other respects too the historiography is remarkably conventional. Saul Friedländer noted some years ago that there exists in the writing of Holocaust history a 'moral imperative' to talk about the Holocaust within 'certain accepted norms of aesthetic collaboration or intellectual discourse'.[78] The quiet rejection of theory is very conspicuous in the recent historical literature.

Raul Hilberg famously told Claude Lanzmann in his film *Shoah* that 'In all of my work I have never begun by asking the big questions, because I was always afraid that I would come up with small answers; and I have preferred to address these things which are minutiae or details in order that I might then be able to put together in a gestalt a picture which, if not an explanation, is at least a description, a more full description, of what transpired.'[79] There is unquestionably something special about archival research – Ricoeur calls it history's 'victory over the arbitrary'[80] – and those obsessives who spend years studying a single photograph or a single film are often the most pleasurable to listen to or to read, for the depth of their knowledge is remarkable (for example, Richard Raskin or Stig Hornshøj Møller[81]). But Hilberg was being overly modest. It would be mistaken, though it is a common enough mistake, to believe that by writing empirical history one thereby avoids theory. No historian is obliged explicitly to address theoretical issues, but that does not mean they are not there; nor does it mean that an 'explanation' or an answer to the 'big questions' is not implicitly present in the work. The explosion in empirical history has been immensely rewarding in terms of expanding and enriching our knowledge of the Holocaust. Perhaps the time will soon come again for reflection on this body of work, and for confronting it with the challenge put forward by the philosophers of history who argue that the Holocaust should generate reconsiderations of the nature of history, historiography, and historicity. Historians might once again turn more explicitly to matters of interpretation, as well as to bigger theoretical issues concerning the nature of history and the challenge that has been presented to it – and as yet most often embarrassedly shrugged off – by the Holocaust.

Notes

1. For example, S. Szende, *The Promise Hitler Kept* (London: Victor Gollancz, 1945); *YIVO Bleter*, 30, 1 and 2 (1947), devoted to 'The Years of Catastrophe' (in Yiddish); J. Billig, *L'Allemagne et le génocide* (Paris: Editions du Centre, 1950); and the numerous *Yizker-Bikher* (memorial books, also mostly in Yiddish). It is also the case that, as Judith Baumel notes, more memoirs were published in the immediate aftermath of the war by women by men, and these tended to get ignored and quickly go our print: J. T. Baumel, *Double Jeopardy: Gender and the Holocaust* (London: Vallentine Mitchell, 1998), pp. 55–6. See also A. Wieviorka, *The Era of the Witness* (Ithaca, NY: Cornell University Press, 2006). My thanks to Andy Pearce and Zoë Waxman for their comments on an earlier version of this piece.
2. L. Baron, 'The Holocaust and American Public Memory, 1945–1960', *Holocaust and Genocide Studies*, 17, 1 (2003), 62–88; H. R. Diner, 'Post-World-War-II American Jewry and the Confrontation with Catastrophe', *American Jewish History*, 91, 3–4 (2003), 439–67; A. Wieviorka, 'Indicible ou inaudible? La déportation: premiers récits (1944–1947)', *Pardès*, 9–10 (1989), 23–59; D. S. Wyman, ed., *The World Reacts to the Holocaust* (Baltimore, MD: Johns Hopkins University Press, 1996); D. Ofer, 'The Strength of Remembrance: Commemorating the Holocaust During the First Decade of Israel', *Jewish Social Studies*, n.s. 6, 2 (2000), 24–55.
3. D. Stone, ed., *The Historiography of the Holocaust* (Basingstoke: Palgrave Macmillan, 2004); S. Hochstadt, ed., *Sources of the Holocaust* (Basingstoke: Palgrave Macmillan,

2004); S. Gigliotti and B. Lang, eds, *The Holocaust: A Reader* (Oxford: Blackwell, 2004); N. Levi and M. Rothberg, eds, *The Holocaust: Theoretical Readings* (Edinburgh: Edinburgh University Press, 2004); R. Hilberg, *Sources of Holocaust Research: An Analysis* (Chicago, IL: Ivan R. Dee, 2001); D. Michman, *Holocaust Historiography: A Jewish Perspective. Conceptualizations, Terminology, Approaches and Fundamental Issues* (London: Vallentine Mitchell, 2003); R. Rozett, *Approaching the Holocaust: Texts and Contexts* (London: Vallentine Mitchell, 2004); O. Bartov, *The Holocaust: Origins, Implementation, Aftermath* (London: Routledge, 1999); D. Cesarani, ed., *The Holocaust: Critical Concepts in Historical Studies* (London: Routledge, 2004), 6 vols.; M. Berenbaum and A. J. Peck, eds, *The Holocaust and History: The Known, the Unknown, the Disputed, and the Reexamined* (Bloomington, IN: Indiana University Press, 1998); W. Laqueur and J. T. Baumel, eds, *The Holocaust Encyclopedia* (New Haven, CT: Yale University Press, 2001); R. Rozett and S. Spector, eds, *Encyclopedia of the Holocaust* (Jerusalem: Yad Vashem, 2000); I. Gutman et al., *Enzyklopädie des Holocaust: Die Verfolgung und Ermordung der europäischen Juden*, 2nd edn. (Munich: Piper, 1998); J. M. Diefendorf, ed., *Lessons & Legacies Vol. VI: New Currents in Holocaust Research* (Evanston, IL: Northwestern University Press, 2004); J. Petropoulos and J. K. Roth, eds, *Oxford Handbook to Holocaust Studies* (Oxford: Oxford University Press, forthcoming). Older collections, such as Y. Arad et al., eds, *Documents on the Holocaust* (Jerusalem: Yad Vashem, 1981), L. S. Dawidowicz, ed., *A Holocaust Reader* (West Orange, NJ: Behrman House, 1976), and J. Noakes and G. Pridham, eds, *Nazism 1919–1945, vol. 3: Foreign Policy, War and Racial Extermination* (Exeter: Exeter University Press, 1988) are all still in print and all still very useful.

4. *Inter alia*, and to list English-language works only: S. Friedlander ed., *Probing the Limits of Representation: Nazism and the "Final Solution"* (Cambridge, MA: Harvard University Press, 1992); S. Friedländer, *Memory, History, and the Extermination of the Jews of Europe* (Bloomington, IN: Indiana University Press, 1993); D. Diner, *Beyond the Conceivable: Studies on Germany, Nazism, and the Holocaust* (Berkeley, CA: University of California Press, 2000); D. LaCapra, *Representing the Holocaust: History, Theory, Trauma* (Ithaca, NY: Cornell University Press, 1994); idem., *History and Memory after Auschwitz* (Ithaca, NY: Cornell University Press, 1998); idem., *Writing History, Writing Trauma* (Baltimore, MD: Johns Hopkins University Press, 2001); B. Lang, *Act and Idea in the Nazi Genocide* (Chicago, IL: University of Chicago Press, 1990); idem., *The Future of the Holocaust: Between History and Memory* (Ithaca, NY: Cornell University Press, 1999); idem., *Post-Holocaust: Interpretation, Misinterpretation, and the Claims of History* (Bloomington, IN: Indiana University Press, 2005); B. Lang ed., *Writing and the Holocaust* (New York: Holmes & Meier, 1988); L. L. Langer, *Admitting the Holocaust: Collected Essays* (New York: Oxford University Press, 1995); idem., *Preempting the Holocaust* (New Haven, CT: Yale University Press, 1998); idem., *Using and Abusing the Holocaust* (Bloomington, IN: Indiana University Press, 2006); L. D. Kritzman, ed., *Auschwitz and After: Race, Culture, and the "Jewish Question" in France* (New York: Routledge, 1995); A. H. Rosenfeld, ed., *Thinking about the Holocaust after Half a Century* (Bloomington, IN: Indiana University Press, 1997); E. Sicher, ed., *Breaking Crystal: Writing and Memory after Auschwitz* (Urbana, IL: University of Illinois Press, 1998); J. E. Young, *Writing and Rewriting the Holocaust: Narrative and the Consequences of Interpretation* (Bloomington, IN: Indiana University Press, 1988); M. A. Bernstein, *Foregone Conclusions: Against Apocalyptic History* (Berkeley, CA: University of California Press, 1994); G. H. Hartman, ed., *Holocaust Remembrance: The Shapes of Memory* (Oxford: Blackwell, 1994); G. M. Kren and L. Rappoport, *The Holocaust and the Crisis of Human Behavior*, 2nd edn (New York: Holmes & Meier, 1994); A. Rosenberg

and G. E. Myers, eds, *Echoes from the Holocaust: Philosophical Reflections on a Dark Time* (Philadelphia, PA: Temple University Press, 1988); E. van Alphen, *Caught by History: Holocaust Effects in Contemporary Art, Literature, and Theory* (Stanford, CA: Stanford University Press, 1997); A. Reiter, *Narrating the Holocaust* (London: Continuum, 2000); J. Cohen, *Interrupting Auschwitz: Art, Religion, Philosophy* (London: Continuum, 2003); M. Postone and E. Santner, eds, *Catastrophe and Meaning: The Holocaust and the Twentieth Century* (Chicago, IL: University of Chicago Press, 2003); R. L. Rubenstein and J. K. Roth, *Approaches to Auschwitz: The Holocaust and its Legacy* (Atlanta, GA: John Knox Press, 1987); Y. Bauer and N. Rotenstreich, eds, *The Holocaust as Historical Experience* (New York: Holmes & Meier, 1981); A. Milchman and A. Rosenberg, eds, *Postmodernism and the Holocaust* (Amsterdam: Rodopi, 1998); R. Eaglestone, *The Holocaust and the Postmodern* (Oxford: Oxford University Press, 2004); D. Stone, ed., *Theoretical Interpretations of the Holocaust* (Amsterdam: Rodopi, 2001); M. Rothberg, *Traumatic Realism: The Demands of Holocaust Representation* (Minneapolis, MN: University of Minnesota Press, 2000); P. Eisenstein, *Traumatic Encounters: Holocaust Representation and the Hegelian Subject* (Albany, NY: State University of New York Press, 2003). The literature on memory, photography, literature, testimony and film is too vast to list here. A good introduction is Levi and Rothberg, eds, *The Holocaust: Theoretical Readings*. See also, on memory, D. Stone, 'Beyond the Mnemosyne Institute: The Future of Memory after the Age of Commemoration', in *The Future on Memory,* eds, R. Crownshaw et al (New York: Berghahn Books, forthcoming).

5. Yet one should not forget how important their works were. See L. Poliakov, *Harvest of Hate* (London: Elek Books, 1956 [orig. French 1951]); G. Reitlinger, *The Final Solution: The Attempt to Exterminate the Jews of Europe, 1939–1945* (London: Sphere, 1971 [first edn 1953]); P. Friedman, *Roads to Extinction: Essays on the Holocaust*, ed. A J. Friedman (Philadelphia, PA: Jewish Publication Society of America, 1980).
6. Friedlander, 'Introduction' to *Probing the Limits*, p. 5.
7. M. Postone, 'After the Holocaust: History and Identity in West Germany', in *Coping with the Past: Germany and Austria after 1945*, eds, K. Harms, V. Dürr and L. R. Reuter (Madison, WI: University of Wisconsin Press, 1990), p. 233.
8. The naming of the 'schools' occurs in T. Mason, 'Intention and Explanation', in *Der 'Führerstaat': Mythos und Realität*, eds, G. Hirschfeld and L. Kettenacker (Stuttgart: Ernst Klett, 1981), pp. 23–42.
9. K. A. Schleunes, *The Twisted Road to Auschwitz: Nazi Policy Toward German Jews 1933–1939* (Urbana, IL: University of Illinois Press, 1970). See also U. D. Adam, *Judenpolitik im Dritten Reich* (Düsseldorf: Droste Verlag, 1972).
10. See M. Brechtken, *'Madagaskar für den Juden': Antisemitische Idee und politische Praxis* (Munich: Oldenbourg, 1997).
11. On Wannsee see M. Roseman, *The Villa, the Lake, the Meeting: Wannsee and the Final Solution* (London: Penguin, 2002).
12. For an excellent discussion see A. D. Moses, 'Structure and Agency in the Holocaust: Daniel J. Goldhagen and His Critics', *History and Theory*, 37, 2 (1998), 194–219.
13. For examples of influential 'regional' studies see C. Gerlach, *Kalkulierte Mord: Die deutsche Wirtschafts- und Vernichtungspolitik in Weißrußland 1941–1944* (Hamburg: Hamburger Edition, 1999); idem., *Krieg, Ernährung, Völkermord: Forschungen zur deutschen Vernichtungspolitik im Zweiten Weltkrieg* (Hamburg: Hamburger Edition, 1998); D. Pohl, *Nationalsozialistische Judenverfolgung in Ostgalizien 1941–1944: Organisation und Durchführung eines staatlichen Massenverbrechens* (Munich: R. Oldenbourg Verlag, 1997); T. Sandkühler, *"Endlösung" in Galizien: Der Judenmord in Ostpolen und die Rettungsinitiativen des Berthold Bietz* (Bonn: Dietz, 1996); G. Aly,

"Final Solution": Nazi Population Policy and the Murder of the European Jews (London: Arnold, 1999); B. Musial, *Deutsche Zivilverwaltung und Judenverfolgung im Generalgouvernement: Eine Fallstudie zum Distrikt Lublin 1939–1944* (Wiesbaden: Harrasowitz, 1999); C. Gerlach and G. Aly, *Das letzte Kapitel: Realpolitik, Ideologie und der Mord an den ungarischen Juden 1944/45* (Stuttgart: DVA, 2002); T. Cole, *Holocaust City: The Making of a Jewish Ghetto* (New York: Routledge, 2003); A. Angrick and P. Klein, *Die "Endlösung" im Ghetto Riga: Ausbeutung und Vernichtung 1941–1944* (Darmstadt: Wissenschaftliche Buchgesellschaft, 2006).

14. S. Friedländer, *Nazi Germany and the Jews, vol. 1: The Years of Persecution 1933–1939* (London: Weidenfeld & Nicolson, 1997), with its stress on 'redemptive antisemitism', and *vol. 2: The Years of Extermination, 1939–1945* (New York: HarperCollins, 2007); U. Tal, *Religion, Politics and Ideology in the Third Reich: Selected Essays* (London: Routledge, 2004); A. Nolzen, 'The Nazi Party and its Violence Against Jews, 1933–1939: Violence as a Historiographical Concept', *Yad Vashem Studies*, 31 (2003), 245–85; P. Burrin, *Strands of Nazi Antisemitism* (Oxford: Europaeum, 2003); idem., *Nazi Antisemitism: From Prejudice to the Holocaust* (New York: The New Press, 2005); A. Confino, 'Fantasies about the Jews: Cultural Reflections on the Holocaust', *History & Memory*, 17 (2005), 296–322.
15. D. Walter, *Antisemitische Kriminalität und Gewalt: Judenfeindschaft in der Weimarer Republik* (Bonn: Dietz, 1999); C. Hecht, *Deutsche Juden und Antisemitismus in der Weimarer Republik* (Bonn: Dietz, 2003); B. Weisbrod, 'Violence and Sacrifice', in *The Third Reich Between Vision and Reality: New Perspectives on German History, 1918–1945*, ed. H. Mommsen (New York: Berg, 2001), pp. 5–21; M. Wildt, 'Violence Against the Jews in Germany 1933–1939', in *Probing the Depths of German Antisemitism: German Society and the Persecution of the Jews, 1933–1941*, ed. D. Bankier (Jerusalem: Yad Vashem, 2000), pp. 181–209; C. Hoffmann, W. Bergmann and H. W. Smith, eds, *Exclusionary Violence: Antisemitic Riots in Modern German History* (Ann Arbor, MI: University of Michigan Press, 2002).
16. C. R. Browning, 'The Decision-Making Process', in *The Historiography of the Holocaust*, ed. Stone, pp. 173–96; idem. with J. Matthäus, *The Origins of the Final Solution* (London: William Heinemann, 2004); P. Longerich, *Politik der Vernichtung: Eine Gesamtdarstellung der nationalsozialistischen Judenverfolgung* (Munich: Piper, 1998); idem., *The Unwritten Order: Hitler's Role in the Final Solution* (Stroud: Tempus, 2001).
17. C. Gerlach, 'Some Recent Trends in German Holocaust Research', in *Lessons and Legacies, Vol. VI*, ed. Diefendorf, pp. 291–2.
18. R. Hilberg, *Perpetrators, Victims, Bystanders* (London: HarperCollins, 1993).
19. D. Diner, *Beyond the Conceivable: Studies on Germany, Nazism, and the Holocaust* (Berkeley, CA: University of California Press, 2000), p. 177.
20. The social psychological literature is outside the scope of this chapter. But for useful approaches, see S. K. Baum, 'A Bell Curve of Hate?', *Journal of Genocide Research*, 6, 4 (2004), 567–77; H. C. Kelman, 'Violence Without Moral Restraint: Reflections on the Dehumanization of Victims and Victimizers', *Journal of Social Issues*, 29, 4 (1973), 25–61; J. M. Darley, 'Social Organization for the Production of Evil', *Psychological Inquiry*, 3, 2 (1992), 199–218; A. Bandura, 'Moral Disengagement in the Perpetration of Inhumanities', *Personality and Social Psychology Review*, 3, 3 (1999), 193–209; J. Lang, 'Killing the Other: The Psychology of Intimate Murder within the Context of Genocide', *Journal of Genocide Research* (forthcoming). For a strong defence of the situationalist approach see P. A. Roth, 'Hearts of Darkness: "Perpetrator History" and Why There Is No Why', *History of the Human Sciences*, 17, 2/3 (2004), 211–51.

21. M. T. Allen, *The Business of Genocide: The SS, Slave Labor, and the Concentration Camps* (Chapel Hill, NC: University of North Carolina Press, 2002); M. Wildt, *Generation des Unbedingten: Das Führungskorps des Reichssicherheitshauptamtes* (Hamburg: Hamburger Edition, 2003); I. Heinemann, *Rasse, Siedlung, deutsches Blut: Das Rasse- und Siedlungshauptampt der SS und die rassenpolitische Neuordnung Europas* (Göttingen: Wallstein Verlag, 2003).
22. U. Herbert, *Best: Biographische Studien über Radikalismus, Weltanschauung und Vernunft, 1903–1989* (Bonn: Verlag J.F.W. Dietz Nachf., 2001); L. Hachmeister, *Der Gegnerforscher: Die Karriere des SS-Führers Franz Alfred Six* (Munich: C.H. Beck, 1998). See also K. Orth, *Die Konzentrationslager-SS: Sozialstrukturelle Analysen und biographische Studien* (Munich: Deutscher Taschenbuch Verlag, 2004).
23. P. Longerich, *Heinrich Himmler: Biographie* (Munich: Sielder, 2007); D. Cesarani, *Eichmann: His Life and Crimes* (London: William Heinemann, 2004).
24. Y. Lozowick, *Hitler's Bureaucrats: The Nazi Security Police and the Banality of Evil* (New York: Continuum, 2002); H. Safrian, *Die Eichmann-Männer* (Vienna: Europaverlag, 1993).
25. See the accompanying volume: H. Heer and K. Naumann, eds, *Vernichtungskrieg: Verbrechen der Wehrmacht 1941 bis 1944* (Hamburg: Hamburger Edition, 1995).
26. E. B. Westermann, *Hitler's Police Battalions: Enforcing Racial War in the East* (Lawrence, KS: University Press of Kansas, 2005); B. Shepherd, *War in the Wild East: The German Army and Soviet Partisans* (Cambridge, MA: Harvard University Press, 2004); J. Matthäus et al., *Ausbildungsziel Judenmord? "Weltanschauliche Erziehung" von SS, Polizei und Waffen-SS im Rahmen der "Endlösung"* (Frankfurt am Main: Fischer Taschenbuch Verlag, 2003); M. Mann, 'Were the Perpetrators of Genocide "Ordinary Men" or "Real Nazis"? Results from Fifteen Hundred Biographies', *Holocaust and Genocide Studies*, 14, 3 (2000), 331–66; W. Kaiser, ed., *Täter im Vernichtungskrieg: Der Überfall auf die Sowjetunion und der Völkermord an den europäischen Juden* (Munich: Propyläen Verlag, 2002); W. Curilla, *Die deutsche Ordnungspolizei und der Holocaust im Baltikum und in Weißrußland 1941–1944* (Paderborn: Ferdinand Schöningh, 2005). See also the important study by H. Welzer, *Täter: wie aus ganz normalen Menschen Massenmörder werden* (Frankfurt am Main: S. Fischer, 2005).
27. G. C. Browder, 'Perpetrator Character and Motivation: An Emerging Consensus?', *Holocaust and Genocide Studies*, 17, 3 (2003), 495. See J. Matthäus, 'Historiography and the Perpetrators of the Holocaust', in *The Historiography of the Holocaust*, ed. Stone, pp. 197–215 for further thoughts on the need for historians to investigate in more detail 'the importance of ideology in general and antisemitism in particular for persecution and mass murder' (211).
28. M. Roseman, 'Ideas, Contexts, and the Pursuit of Genocide', *Bulletin of the German Historical Institute London*, 25, 1 (2003), 65, 83.
29. M. Weinreich, *Hitler's Professors: The Part of Scholarship in Germany's Crimes Against the Jewish People*, 2nd edn (New Haven, CT: Yale University Press, 1999 [1946]); L. Poliakov and J. Wulf, eds, *Das Dritte Reich and seine Diener* (Wiesbaden: Fourier Verlag, 1989 [1956]); idem., *Das Dritte Reich und seine Denker* (Wiesbaden: Fourier Verlag, 1989 [1959]).
30. I. Haar and M. Fahlbusch, eds, *German Scholars and Ethnic Cleansing 1919–1945* (New York: Berghahn Books, 2005); N. Berg, *Der Holocaust und die westdeutschen Historiker: Erforschung und Erinnerung* (Göttingen: Wallstein Verlag, 2003); I. Haar, *Historiker im Nationalsozialismus: Die deutschen Geschichtswissenschaft und der 'Volkstumskampf' im Osten* (Göttingen: Vandenhoeck und Ruprecht, 2000); W. Schulze and O. G. Oexle, eds, *Deutsche Historiker im Nationalsozialismus* (Frankfurt am

Main: Fischer Taschenbuch Verlag, 1999); G. Aly, *Macht Geist Wahn: Kontinuitäten deutschen Denkens* (Frankfurt am Main: Fischer Taschenbuch Verlag, 1999); P. Schöttler, *Geschichtsschreibung als Legitimationswissenschaft 1918–1945* (Frankfurt am Main: Suhrkamp Verlag, 1997). For an excellent discussion see K. Jarausch, 'Unasked Questions: The Controversy about Nazi Collaboration among German Historians', in *Lessons and Legacies, Vol. VI*, ed. Diefendorf, pp. 190–208.

31. C. Koonz, *The Nazi Conscience* (Cambridge, MA: The Belknap Press of Harvard University Press, 2003), p. 230.
32. A. Steinweis, *Studying the Jew: Scholarly Antisemitism in Nazi Germany* (Cambridge, MA: Harvard University Press, 2006); P. von Papen-Bodek, 'Anti-Jewish Research of the Institut zur Erforschung der Judenfrage in Frankfurt am Main between 1939 and 1945', in *Lessons and Legacies, vol. VI*, pp. 155–89. See also D. Rupnow, 'Between Race and Spirit: Antisemitic Research in the Third Reich', *Patterns of Prejudice* (forthcoming).
33. H.-W. Schmuhl, *Grenzüberschreitungen: Das Kaiser-Wilhelm-Institut für Anthropologie, menschliche Erblehre und Eugenik 1927–1945* (Göttngen: Wallstein Verlag, 2005), vol. 9 of a series devoted to the history of the KWI under National Socialism. Other books in the series directly relevant to the historiography of the Holocaust include H.-W. Schmuhl, ed., *Rassenforschung an Kaiser-Wilhelm-Instituten vor und nach 1933* (Göttingen: Wallstein Verlag, 2003) and C. Sachse, ed., *Die Verbindung nach Auschwitz: Biowissenschaften und Menschenversuche an Kaiser-Wilhelm-Instituten: Dokumentation eines Symposiums im Juni 2001* (Göttingen: Wallstein Verlag, 2004).
34. F. Bajohr, 'Expropriation and Expulsion', in *The Historiography of the Holocaust*, ed. Stone, p. 52.
35. A. Beker, ed., *The Plunder of Jewish Property during the Holocaust: Confronting European History* (New York: New York University Press, 2001); *Confiscation of Jewish Property in Europe, 1933–1945: New Sources and Perspectives. Symposium Proceedings* (Washington, DC: United States Holocaust Memorial Museum, 2003); H. Junz, 'Holocaust-Era Assets: Globalization of the Issue', in *Lessons and Legacies, Vol. VI*, ed. Diefendorf, pp. 431–46; M. J. Bazyler, 'The Gray Zones of Holocaust Restitution: American Justice and Holocaust Morality', in *Gray Zones*, eds, Petropoulos and Roth, pp. 339–59.
36. C. Maier, 'The Economics of Fascism and Nazism', in his *In Search of Stability: Explorations in Historical Political Economy* (Cambridge: Cambridge University Press, 1987), p. 71.
37. S. J. Wiesen, 'Public Relations as a Site of Memory: The Case of West German Industry and National Socialism', in *The Work of Memory: New Directions in the Study of German Society and Culture*, eds, A. Confino and P. Fritzsche (Urbana, IL: University of Illinois Press, 2002), pp. 196–213; V. R. Berghahn, 'Writing the History of Business in the Third Reich: Past Achievements and Future Directions', in *Business and Industry in Nazi Germany*, eds, F. R. Nicosia and J. Huener (New York: Berghahn Books, 2004).
38. C. Kobrak and A. H. Schneider, 'Big Business and the Third Reich: An Appraisal of the Historical Arguments', in *The Historiography of the Holocaust*, ed. Stone, pp. 141–72 presents a thorough survey of the field.
39. Kobrak and Schneider, 'Big Business and the Third Reich', pp. 161, 164.
40. U. Herbert, K. Orth and C. Dieckmann, eds, *Die nationalsozialistische Konzentrationslager* (Göttingen: Wallstein Verlag, 1998), 2 vols.; K. Orth, *Das System der nationalsozialistischen Konzentrationslager* (Hamburg: Hamburger Edition, 1999); W. Długoborski and F. Piper, eds, *Auschwitz 1940–1945: Central Issues in the History of the Camp* (Oświęcim: Auschwitz-Birkenau State Museum, 2000), 5 vols; B. C. Wagner, N. Frei, S. Steinbacher, T. Grotum and J. Parcer, eds, *Darstellungen und Quellen zur*

Geschichte von Auschwitz (Munich: K.G. Saur, 2000), 4 vols.; B. Musial, ed., *"Aktion Reinhard": Der Völkermord an den Juden im Generalgouvernement 1941–1944* (Osnabrück: Fibre Verlag, 2004). On Auschwitz, earlier studies include Y. Gutman and M. Berenbaum, eds, *Anatomy of the Auschwitz Death Camp* (Bloomington, IN: Indiana University Press, 1994); R. J. van Pelt and D. Dwork, *Auschwitz 1270 to the Present* (New Haven, CT: Yale University Press, 1996). And on Aktion Reinhard the only monograph remains Y. Arad, *Belzec, Sobibor, Treblinka: The Operation Reinhard Death Camps* (Bloomington, IN: Indiana University Press, 1987).

41. P. Hayes, 'Auschwitz, Capital of the Holocaust', *Holocaust and Genocide Studies*, 17, 2 (2003), 343. See also M. T. Allen, 'Not Just a "Dating Game": Origins of the Holocaust at Auschwitz in the Light of Witness Testimony', *German History*, 25, 2 (2007), pp. 162–91 for an important study that reasserts the centrality of Auschwitz to the origin of the Holocaust.
42. Under the direction of Nikolaus Wachsmann, Birkbeck College, London.
43. G. Greif, *We Wept Without Tears: Testimonies of the Jewish Sonderkommando from Auschwitz* (New Haven, CT: Yale University Press, 2005). The book appeared in Hebrew and in German a decade earlier. See also E. Friedler, B. Siebert and A. Kilian, *Zeugen aus der Todeszone: Das jüdische Sonderkommando in Auschwitz* (Munich: Deutscher Taschenbuch Verlag, 2005).
44. On hiding see especially G. Paulsson, *Secret City: The Hidden Jews of Warsaw* (New Haven, CT: Yale University Press, 2002).
45. Michman, *Holocaust Historiography*, pp. 217–48; Y. Bauer, *Rethinking the Holocaust* (New Haven, CT: Yale University Press, 2001), pp. 143–66; R. Rozett, 'Jewish Resistance', in *The Historiography of the Holocaust*, ed. Stone, pp. 341–63.
46. See the remarkable memoir by A. B. Szwajger, *I Remember Nothing More: The Warsaw Children's Hospital and the Jewish Resistance* (New York: Pantheon Books, 1990).
47. S. Gilbert, *Music in the Holocaust: Confronting Life in the Nazi Ghettos and Camps* (Oxford: Clarendon Press, 2005), pp. 183–4.
48. Ibid., p. 37.
49. Ibid., p. 119.
50. Ibid., p. 44.
51. E. Harvey, *Women and the Nazi East: Agents and Witnesses of Germanization* (New Haven, CT: Yale University Press, 2003); B. R. McFarland-Icke, *Nurses in Nazi Germany: Moral Choice in History* (Princeton, NJ: Princeton University Press, 2000); G. E. Schafft, *From Racism to Genocide: Anthropology in the Third Reich* (Urbana, IL: University of Illinois Press, 2004); S. Heschel, 'Does Atrocity Have a Gender? Feminist Interpretations of Women in the SS', in *Lessons and Legacies, Vol. VI*, ed. Diefendorf, pp. 300–21.
52. Z. Waxman, 'Unheard Testimony, Untold Stories: The Representation of Women's Holocaust Experiences', *Women's History Review*, 12, 4 (2003), 661–77; idem., *Writing the Holocaust: Identity, Testimony, Representation* (Oxford: Oxford University Press, 2006). For a broad discussion see L. Pine, 'Gender and the Family', in *The Historiography of the Holocaust*, ed. Stone, pp. 364–82.
53. Heschel, 'Does Atrocity Have a Gender?', p. 311.
54. D. Wyman, *DPs: Europe's Displaced Persons 1945–1951* (Ithaca, NY: Cornell University Press, 1998); M. Brenner, *After the Holocaust: Rebuilding Jewish Lives in Postwar Germany* (Princeton, NJ: Princeton University Press, 1999); A. Königseder and J. Wetzel, *Waiting for Hope: Jewish Displaced Persons in Post-Word War II Germany* (Evanston, IL: Northwestern University Press, 2001); A. J. Kochavi, *Post-Holocaust Politics: Britain, the United States, and Jewish Refugees, 1945–1948* (Chapel Hill, NC: University of North Carolina Press, 2001); J. H. Geller, *Jews in Post-Holocaust Germany, 1945–1953*

(Cambridge: Cambridge University Press, 2004); E. Kolinsky, *After the Holocaust: Jewish Survivors in Germany after 1945* (London: Pimlico, 2004).

55. G. Eisen, *Children and Play in the Holocaust: Games among the Shadows* (Amherst, MA: University of Massachusetts Press, 1988); D. Dwork, *Children with a Star: Jewish Youth in Nazi Europe* (New Haven, CT: Yale University Press, 1991).
56. B. Wilkomirski, *Fragments: Memories of a Childhood, 1939–1948* (London: Picador, 1996). For the fullest discussion see S. Maechler, *The Wilkomirski Affair: A Study in Biographical Truth* (London: Picador, 2001).
57. N. Stargardt, *Witnesses of War* (London: Jonathan Cape, 2005); S. Vice, *Children Writing the Holocaust* (Basingstoke: Palgrave Macmillan, 2004); A. Reiter, ed., *Children and the Holocaust* (London: Vallentine Mitchell, 2006); A. Brostoff, ed., *Flares of Memory: Stories of Childhood during the Holocaust* (Oxford: Oxford University Press, 2001); L. Holliday, ed., *Children's Wartime Diaries: Secret Writings from the Holocaust and World War II* (London: Piatkus, 1995); *Children and the Holocaust: Symposium Presentations* (Washington, D.C.: United States Holocaust Memorial Museum, 2004).
58. H. Arendt, 'Personal Responsibility Under Dictatorship', in *Responsibility and Judgment*, ed. J. Kohn (New York: Schocken Books, 2003), pp. 42–3.
59. See Stone, *Constructing the Holocaust*, Ch. 5; idem., 'The Historiography of Genocide: Beyond "Uniqueness" and Ethnic Competition' in *History, Memory and Mass Atrocity: Essays on the Holocaust and Genocide* (London: Vallentine Mitchell, 2006), pp. 236–51; G. Rosenfeld, 'The Politics of Uniqueness: Reflections on the Recent Polemical Turn in Holocaust and Genocide Studies', *Holocaust and Genocide Studies*, 13, 1 (1999), 28–61.
60. For a broader discussion of Arendt's relevance to this ongoing debate, see R. H. King and D. Stone, eds, *Hannah Arendt and the Uses of History: Imperialism, Nation, Race, and Genocide* (New York: Berghahn Books, 2007).
61. R. Gellately, 'The Third Reich, the Holocaust, and Visions of Serial Genocide', in *The Specter of Genocide: Mass Murder in Historical Perspective*, eds, R. Gellately and B. Kiernan (Cambridge: Cambridge University Press, 2003), p. 259.
62. Browning, *The Origins of the Final Solution*, p. 14.
63. R. Cribb, 'Genocide in the Non-Western World: Implications for Holocaust Studies', in *Genocide: Cases, Comparisons and Contemporary Debates*, ed. S. L. B. Jensen (Copenhagen: Danish Center for Holocaust and Genocide Studies, 2003), p. 137.
64. W. Lower, *Nazi Empire-Building and the Holocaust in Ukraine* (Chapel Hill, NC: University of North Carolina Press, 2005), pp. 6, 19–20. See also K. Berkhoff, *Harvest of Despair: Life and Death in Ukraine under Nazi Rule* (Cambridge, MA: Harvard University Press, 2004).
65. J. Pefanis, *Heterology and the Postmodern* (Durham, NC: Duke University Press, 1991); A. Mbembe, 'Necropolitics', *Political Culture*, 15, 1 (2003), 11–40; V. Lal, 'The Concentration Camp and Development: The Pasts and Future of Genocide' in *Colonialism and Genocide*, eds, A. D. Moses and D. Stone (London: Routledge, 2007), pp. 124–47.
66. A. Curthoys and J. Docker, 'Introduction: Genocide: Definitions, Questions, Settler-Colonies', *Aboriginal History*, 25 (2001), 14; J. Docker, 'Raphael Lemkin's History of Genocide and Colonialism', paper delivered at the Center for Advanced Holocaust Studies, USHMM, 26 February 2004. See also P. Wolfe, 'Settler Colonialism and the Elimination of the Native', *Journal of Genocide Research*, 8, 4 (2006), 387–409.
67. A. W. Crosby, *Ecological Imperialism: The Biological Expansion of Europe, 900–1900*, 2nd edn (Cambridge: Cambridge University Press, 2004), p. 345 n38. Crosby does, however, talk (p. 213) of a 'dismal genocidal process', and notes (p. 209) that 'Europe's overseas colonies were, in the first stage of their modern development, charnel houses.' But

he is referring to the effects of disease brought from Europe, and not to any 'intent to destroy' in the sense of the UN Convention.

68. A. D. Moses, 'The Holocaust and Genocide', in *The Historiography of the Holocaust*, ed. Stone, p. 534.
69. Ibid., pp. 547–8.
70. Ibid., p. 548. See also A. Rabinbach, 'The Challenge of the Unprecedented: Raphael Lemkin and the Concept of Genocide', *Simon Dubnow Institute Yearbook*, 4 (2005), 397–420.
71. N. M. Naimark, *Fires of Hatred: Ethnic Cleansing in Twentieth-Century Europe* (Cambridge, MA: Harvard University Press, 2001); E. D. Weitz, *A Century of Genocide: Utopias of Race and Nation* (Princeton, NJ: Princeton University Press, 2003); B. A. Valentino, *Final Solutions: Mass Killing and Genocide in the Twentieth Century* (Ithaca, NY: Cornell University Press, 2004); A. L. Hinton, ed., *Annihilating Difference: The Anthropology of Genocide* (Berkeley, CA: University of California Press, 2002).
72. J. Zimmerer, 'Colonialism and the Holocaust: Towards an Archaeology of Genocide', in *Genocide and Settler Society: Frontier Violence and Stolen Indigenous Children in Australian History*, ed. A. D. Moses (New York: Berghahn Books, 2004), p. 49.
73. Ibid., p. 59.
74. Ibid., p. 67. See also J. Zimmerer, 'The Birth of the *Ostland* Out of the Spirit of Colonialism: A Postcolonial Perspective on the Nazi Policy of Conquest and Extermination', in *Colonialism and Genocide*, eds, Moses and Stone, pp. 101–23; and, for a different perspective, I. V. Hull, *Absolute Destruction: Military Culture and the Practices of War in Imperial Germany* (Ithaca, NY: Cornell University Press, 2004).
75. For the most recent and compelling statement of this thesis, see A. D. Moses, 'Empire, Colony, Genocide: Keywords and the Philosophy of History', in *Empire, Colony, Genocide: Conquest, Occupation, and Subaltern Resistance in World History*, ed. A. D. Moses (New York: Berghahn Books, 2008).
76. M. Levene, *Genocide in the Age of the Nation State, vol. I: The Meaning of Genocide* (London: I.B. Tauris, 2005), pp. 142–3.
77. Ibid., p. 205.
78. S. Friedländer, 'On the Representation of the Shoah in Present-Day Western Culture', in *Remembering for the Future*, ed. Y. Bauer (Oxford: Pergamon Press, 1989), vol. III, p. 3097.
79. C. Lanzmann, *Shoah: An Oral History of the Holocaust. The Complete Text of the Film* (New York: Pantheon Books, 1985), p. 70
80. P. Ricoeur, *Memory, History, Forgetting* (Chicago, IL: University of Chicago Press, 2004), p. 147.
81. R. Raskin, *A Child at Gunpoint: A Case Study in the Life of a Photo* (Aarhus: Aarhus University Press, 2004); papers by S. H. Møller at http://www.holocaust-history.org/der-ewige-jude/ See also H.-J. Lang, *Die Namen der Nummern: Wie es gelang, die 86 Opfer eines NS-Verbrechens zu identifizieren* (Hamburg: Hoffmann und Campe, 2004), and A. Wagenaar, *Settela* (Nottingham: Five Leaves, 2005) for further, moving examples.

15
The Crimes of the Stalin Regime: Outline for an Inventory and Classification*

Nicolas Werth

For about 15 years now, the opening of the Soviet archives, partial though it was, has allowed historians to examine in detail the darker, repressive and criminal aspects of the Soviet regime. Until the beginning of the 1990s there had been many accounts of this (mainly from survivors of gulags), but there had also been numerous theoretical analyses, most based on the concept of totalitarianism, assumed to provide a means of understanding the 'essence' of the Soviet regime. Despite this, it is only in the last few years that it has been possible to make a real start on taking an inventory of the victims of the Soviet regime and, more particularly, analysing the mechanisms, decision-making processes and methods for implementing the various repressive policies. These were applied with an intensity that varied considerably throughout the 74 years of what, with the hindsight of historical perspective, we can today refer to as the 'Soviet period in Russian history'. It was during those years when Stalin was in power, towards the end of the 1920s and up to the beginning of the 1950s, that state violence was at its most intense in the USSR. Unlike the violence practised by the Nazis, essentially directed outwards as part of a powerful, expansionist and imperialist thrust aimed at allowing the Third Reich to rule over the whole of Europe, or indeed the world, 'for a thousand years', violence under the Stalin regime was directed, not outwards, but inwards. It was directed at Soviet society itself, at the society that the regime wanted to transform totally by 'purging' it of its socially or ethnically 'hostile elements' or 'enemies', and by turning it into a homogeneous socialist society. Space does not permit us, within the confines of this chapter, to deal with a central historical question encountered at the outset when studying Soviet state violence, namely the line of descent in this connection from Leninist Bolshevism to Stalinism. Following other historians, I have put forward certain views on this matter.[1]

---

* Translated from the French by Mike Routledge

What has been shown in the many recent studies of the 'darker side' of Stalinism has been, above all, the extraordinary *diversity* of the regime's repressive policies and the *multiplicity* of its targets. This presents a major difficulty for the historian or indeed for the jurist: the problem of *classifying* and *defining* these actions.

Before there can be any discussion of the *nature* of the crimes committed by Stalinism, it is essential to draw up a rapid inventory on the basis of the information that emerges in recent research based on access to the archives of the principal political authorities (the Politburo and the Central Committee) and the bureaucratic agencies responsible for penal matters (ministries of the Interior and of Justice, the *Prokuratura* and the political police).[2]

Outline for an inventory

The first category of direct victims of the regime covers those condemned to death and executed by special courts held by the political police or military tribunals. They relate to the crime of 'counter-revolutionary activities', as defined by the notorious Article 58 of the Soviet Penal Code, in force for thirty long years, from the middle of the 1920s until the middle of the 1950s. Between 1921 and 1953 more than four million people were found guilty by special courts; about a million of them were sentenced to death, the remainder to long spells in the camps.[3]

About 80 per cent of the death sentences were handed down during 1937–8 alone; that is, during the period that history has come to refer to as the 'Great Terror'. This huge and secret crime was a vast engineering and social 'purification' operation, with its victim groups, its 'execution quotas', its carefully calculated and coded objectives relating to 'individuals to be repressed: category one or category two', its 'ratified additions' and 'non-ratified additions'.[4] The secretive face of the Great Terror, as it appears in the top secret resolutions passed by the Politburo and the 'operational orders' of the NKVD, that is, in texts seen by only a very limited number of top party officials and political police, aimed at eradicating, once and for all, every element considered to be 'foreign' or 'harmful' to the new Soviet society.

Recent research into this frenzied stage of Stalinist repression[5] has disproved two ideas that are still widely held. The first was that it was the denunciations originating from society itself that made this 'uncontrolled outburst' permissible (a justification that Stalin smugly put forward when, in 1939, the 'excesses' of the repression were criticized). The second was that it was the Communists and party officials that were the main victims (an idea promoted by Nikita Khrushchev in his 'Secret Report' to the 20th Congress of the Soviet Union Communist Party in February 1956).

The truth is that the 'Great Terror' was, essentially, the result of secret, repressive measures carried out on a massive scale, decided and planned by Stalin himself with the help of his People's Commissar at the Interior Ministry, Nikolai Yezhov, and implemented systematically throughout a period of 16 months (August 1937 to November 1938) by the mighty State Security apparatus. In the course of these 16 months, more than a million and a half people were arrested of whom 800,000 were executed. Recent studies of the 'Great Terror' have made it possible to see who the main 'enemies' were that were targeted and how this frenzied spasm of violence was the radical and deadly culminating point of a whole series of operations in social engineering that had been undertaken since the beginning of the 1930s. The secret, mass repressive operations at the time of the 'Great Terror' were catalogued, in the administrative jargon of the political police apparatchiks, into two 'lines': the 'Kulak Line' and the 'National Line' and aimed at two major categories of 'enemies'. The 'Kulak Line', as defined in NKVD operational order No. 00447 of 30 July 1937, was intended to 'eradicate once and for all'[6] a wide range of elements described as 'socially harmful' and 'belonging to the past'. Those specifically targeted included 'Former kulaks who have returned home after serving out their sentences or who have escaped deportation', 'recidivist criminals', 'former members of non-Bolshevik parties', 'former Tsarist civil servants or gendarmerie', 'anti-Soviet elements who served in White, Cossack or clerical divisions', 'members of sects or clergy engaged in anti-Soviet activities', and so on. Each region was assigned, notionally by the Politburo, in reality by Stalin (the Politburo, the party's supreme executive body, did no more than rubber-stamp decisions taken by the 'Guide'), a quota of individuals to be shot and others to be interned in camps for a period of ten years. There very soon developed a spirit of rivalry: regional party or NKVD officials kept sending request after request to Moscow for 'additions', to such an extent that, in the course of the 16 months of the operation, the 'initial objectives' were doubled with regard to the 'Category 2 individuals' to be dealt with (ten years in the camps) and multiplied by five with regard to the 'Category 1 individuals' (the death penalty). In all, 767,000 people were arrested under the aegis of 'Operation Kulak' alone, and of these, 387,000 were executed![7] The 'National Line', as defined by a dozen or so secret operations, referred to as 'national' (the Polish, German, Harbinian, Finnish, Romanian, Latvian, Greek and Estonian 'operations') was particularly aimed at political refugees from those countries who had fled to the USSR, Soviet citizens whose origins were Polish, German, Latvian, Finnish, Greek, etc., but also at all Soviet citizens who had (or had had) any link, no matter how tenuous, whether professional, familial or merely through geographical proximity (those living in frontier areas were especially vulnerable) with a certain number of countries identified as hostile. Hostile, that is, within a context of growing international tension: Poland, Germany, the Baltic countries, Romania or Japan. In all, 335,000 people were arrested in the course of these operations, of whom 247,000 were shot.[8]

These major, secret acts of terror must, in our view, be clearly differentiated from the purges of the elite and of political, economic, military officials and intellectuals that were carried out in parallel after different extra-judicial procedures, serving different purposes and having a distinct political function. However attention-grabbing and politically significant it may have been, the public face of the 'Great Terror', given wide 'public appeal' by the 'uncovering' of countless plots and acts of sabotage, followed by the arrest and execution after public political trials with a strong 'pedagogical content' of numerous Communist officials, still represents only a small fraction of the total of those who were victims in 1937–8.[9]

Trailing far behind 1937–8, there are four years during the Stalin era in which there were more than 10,000 executions. These were 1930 and 1931, the years of forced collectivization and 'dekulakisation', together with 1942 and 1943, years of increased repression within the context of the war.[10] Aside from these years, death sentences handed down for 'political crimes' by special courts were of the order of a few thousand per year.

A second category of victims of Soviet repression is made up of those who died in labour camps.

The number of prisoners held in gulags, the subject of a vast body of writing over several decades and of bitter disputes between historians, is nowadays well known. Since the beginning of the 1990s, teams of researchers, both Russian and western have had access to a considerable body of archive material relating to this subject.[11] It appears that the estimates extrapolated in relation to the years from 1950 to 1980 and generally popularized in such 'classics' as Alexander Solzhenitsyn's *Gulag Archipelago,* were much higher than the real figures. The archives of the gulags, confirmed by several other sources (Justice Ministry, Public Prosecutions, and Supreme Court) show that, at its high point, at the beginning of the 1950s, the gulags held 2,500,000 prisoners. Those sentenced for 'counter-revolutionary activities' by a special court made up about one quarter of the total. However, the remaining detainees were by no means all 'common criminals' in the usual sense of that term. Most of them had ended up in camps after falling foul of one of the innumerable repressive laws that criminalized many kinds of social behaviour and imposed totally disproportionate punishments on the most trivial of misdemeanours. One might cite as an example the laws of 7 August 1932 or 4 June 1947 relating to 'theft of public property': under the provisions of these laws, the most trifling of thefts – a few ears of wheat from a *kolkhoz,* some trivial object in a factory, a loaf of bread in a shop – were punishable with a sentence of five to ten years in a camp, even where these were first offences.

It seems that, in the course of one generation (from 1930 to 1953), about 20 million Soviet citizens – or one adult in six – experienced a stay in a gulag. Entry to one of the camps was not a one-way ticket. Apart from 'politicals', who were invariably sentenced to a minimum spell of ten years, nearly always automatically extended, the other detainees spent on average five to six years in a camp,[12] if they survived that long.

How many people died in the gulags? The data in the archives now available lists about 1,800,000 deaths in the gulag camps and labour colonies between 1930 and 1953. 'Here, taking someone's life is not an aim, it is either a punishment and a means of inflicting terror, or else it is an insignificant loss or accident (...). It is not death which takes on any meaning here; it is simply that life is no longer seen as having any value.'[13] This observation by Tzvetan Todorov is entirely vindicated by the erratic mortality rates in the gulags, a world where administrative chaos, sloppiness, indifference, chance and neglect seem to have played a more important role than any systematic intention to exterminate. We might recall in this connection the way that Hannah Arendt characterized the Soviet camps, 'where neglect is combined with chaotic forced labour' as opposed to the Nazi camps, 'in which the whole of life was thoroughly and systematically organised with a view to the greatest possible torment'.[14] Mortality rates in the Soviet camps varied considerably both geographically and over time. Amongst the most dreadful years, 1933 had a mortality rate of almost 20 per cent because, in the country as a whole, it was a year of famine and, for the concentration camp system, it was one of radical growth. Since the administrative system could simply not keep up, one prisoner in five died from starvation or in epidemics. In 1938, 9 per cent of the detainees perished in camps that had become overpopulated because of the huge influx of those sentenced under the Great Terror. But the most terrible years of all were 1942 and 1943 (with an annual mortality rate in excess of 20 per cent). In two years, more than 400,000 detainees, abandoned to their fate in camps that were scarcely provisioned at all, died in the gulags. At the same time, however, more than a million common criminals were set free before expiry of their sentences and immediately made to enlist in the Red Army in order to make up for the terrible military losses at the beginning of the war. Such contradictory facts are a very clear reflection of the attitude of the regime towards the inhabitants of the gulags: a mixture of indifference, criminal negligence, pragmatism and cynicism. From 1948 onwards, when the regime had come to realize the need to be 'sparing' with the penal labour-force in a country that had been bled dry, the death rate in the camps dropped considerably and stabilized at about 1 per cent at the beginning of the 1950s.

Chances of surviving in the gulags varied even more in terms of the different camps: for a single year the death rate could fluctuate between one and ten per cent.[15] Climate, the type of work that the detainee was required to do, the situation with regard to provisioning, or indeed the personality of the camp commandant could be the deciding factors in the survival or otherwise of the detainees. In some agricultural camps in Kazakhstan the average mortality rate was six times lower than, for example, in the penal complex at Norilsk (Eastern Siberia), which specialized in the extraction of nickel. But in Norilsk, the chances of survival were higher than in the Dalstroi camps in the Kolyma peninsula, which were known as the 'White Hell' and wonderfully well described in the accounts by Varlam Shalamov.[16]

The third category of victims of Soviet repression is composed of those persons who died during deportation. It is now known that, between 1930 and 1953, more than six million people were deported simply on the basis of an administrative decision, most often together with their families, to inhospitable regions of the USSR that it was intended to 'settle' or to 'develop' (Siberia, Kazakhstan, the Far North, the Soviet Far East or Central Asia). An analysis of the dozens of specific deportation operations decided on and planned at the highest levels of the Party-State between 1930 and 1953 reveals the extraordinary diversity of the groups that were targeted and of the objectives to be attained: 'liquidation of the kulaks as a class' (1930–2), punitive deportation of entire peasant communities which had not 'fulfilled their obligations towards the state' (1932–3), cleansing towns of their 'socially harmful elements' (1933–8), 'cleansing and making secure frontier regions' (from 1935 onwards), deportation of 'bourgeois nationalist elements' from countries annexed following the Soviet pact with Germany (Poland, the Baltic states and Moldavia, 1939–41), complete 'preventive' deportation of entire peoples (in the case of Germans having Soviet citizenship, deportation took place from September 1941 onwards) or 'punitive deportation' (in the case of the Kalmuks, Karachais, Balkars, Chechens, Ingush and Crimean Tartars deported towards the end of 1943 and beginning of 1944, having been accused of 'collaboration with the Nazi occupying forces'). As the years went by, deportation became a real strategy for managing populations and territories. In this respect they must be distinguished from the forced displacements of population implemented by many states – including Tsarist Russia – in time of war. There are two considerations that are immediately apparent: the first that, in Soviet territory, the distinction between peacetime and wartime seems scarcely pertinent when considering that particular form of violence that consists in the massive deportation of elements considered to be 'foreign' to the social and national community. Secondly, it is possible to identify a remarkable process of evolution in the criteria for discrimination: criteria of class, dominant up to the mid-1930s, were replaced by ethnic discrimination that culminated in the huge wave of total deportations of 'punished peoples' in 1941–4.[17] What had been social engineering – 'liquidation of the kulaks as a class' – had now become 'ethno-historical excision'.[18]

Although we now know about the principal deportation operations implemented by the Soviet regime under Stalin, together with their organization and methods, the groups targeted and the number of people deported, it is nevertheless still difficult to establish precisely the number of dead: those who died in cattle-trucks during the interminable journeys across thousands of kilometres; those who died in the first months and years following the precarious 'implantation' of the deportees in the 'special settlements'[19] in Kazakhstan, Siberia, the Far North or Central Asia.

A few figures will give some idea of the scale of the massacre. In 1930–1 more than 1,800,000 'kulaks' were deported. At the beginning of 1932, the first census carried out by the OGPU Department for Special Populations produced a figure of 1,317,000 persons present at their place of house arrest. Therefore, in two years, almost 500,000 deportees had disappeared. How many had died, how many had escaped? For the years that followed, the statistics, which were by then being regularly kept up to date, reported the following losses: in 1932, 207,000 escapees, 90,000 deaths; in 1933, 216,000 escapees and 152,000 deaths – that is a death rate of 14 per cent in that year of famine. In 1934 there were 87,000 escapes and more than 40,000 deaths.[20] It should be noted that children, and babies in particular, account for the largest proportion of the deaths. In 1933, for example, the rate of infant mortality in the 'special villages' for deportees in Western Siberia reached 50 per cent.[21] Fifteen years later we find a more or less identical situation with regard to the populations deported at the end of 1943 and beginning of 1944. Thus, of the 575,000 deportees from the Northern Caucasus who arrived in Kazakhstan and Kirghizia in the spring of 1944, a count taken four years later, at the beginning of 1948, shows that 147,000 had died in the intervening period, that is, a quarter of the total and that only 28,000 births had been registered. Of the 228,000 people deported from the Crimea in 1944 (for the most part, Tartars), 45,000 (or 20 per cent) were to die in the four years that followed. In general, it was not until the end of the fifth year following the trauma of deportation that the natural balance of births and deaths was re-established. In the context of our present state of knowledge, we would hazard the following estimate: for the total number of deportees from 1930 to 1953, an excess death toll of one and a half million persons.

And finally, there is a fourth category of victims of the Stalinist system: those who died of hunger in the course of the two last great European famines, one in 1931–3 (between five and a half and six million dead) and the other in 1946–7 (at least 500,000 dead). It is undeniable that the regime bore a weighty responsibility for these two famines which went totally unmentioned and in which meteorological conditions played only a minor part.

Since the pioneering book by Robert Conquest, *The Harvest of Sorrow*, which appeared in 1986, numerous studies, both western and Russian or Ukrainian, have finally, thanks to extensive new work on documentary archives, cast light on the mechanisms that brought about the terrible famines of the years 1931–3.[22] In 1931 the famine first struck Kazakhstan, the USSR's most important region for cattle rearing, where collectivization of the herds was accompanied by a huge plan to force the nomadic and semi-nomadic herdsmen to settle. In two years, about a million and a half Kazakhs, that is, more than a third of the native population, died of hunger or in epidemics.[23] By the summer of 1932 the famine had reached Ukraine. In one year, it caused between 3.5 and 3.8 million deaths. In the Northern Caucasus, the rich plains of the Kuban, an area administratively attached to Russia but primarily inhabited by Ukrainians and Cossacks, were likewise affected (500,000 deaths) as well as the Lower and Middle Volga regions, populated by Russians (300,000 to 400,000 deaths).

Apart from a few divergences with regard to the analysis of certain chains of cause and effect or of the respective weight to be given to the various factors leading to the famines, historians agree that these tragic events were the outcome of policies implemented by the regime from the end of 1929 onwards, in particular the enforced collectivization of farmland. These policies were made even worse in the case of the ethnic Ukrainian regions because of the specific view of the situation in Ukraine taken by Stalin, from the summer of 1932 onwards.[24] This last point will be further discussed in the next, interpretative, section.

The enforced collectivization of the countryside, carried out against the wishes of the huge majority of the peasant classes, brought in its train a catastrophic fall in the total national herd (a drop of 50 per cent) and a major reduction in agricultural production. What it caused above all, once the market forces (which had worked more or less under the New Economic Policy) had broken down, was a huge increase in state quotas levied on harvests and herds. A predatory levy of this kind, which was supposed, through massive exports of agricultural produce, to provide finance to speed up the country's industrialization process, completed the disruption of the cycle of production that had been set in train by enforced collectivization. In the face of what they saw as a 'second serfdom', the peasants, forced to become part of collective farms, resisted. They slaughtered their cattle and worked in a negligent fashion in the collective fields. As production diminished, the state quotas imposed on the *kolkhoz* increased. Despite being informed by the local authorities of the serious consequences that persisting with very high obligatory quotas would have for the peasants in Ukraine and the Kuban, the USSR's two 'granaries', the Soviet leaders, with Stalin at their head, refused to reduce the plans for these exactions. Indeed, Stalin hardened his stance, convinced as he was that the Ukrainian peasantry and, more generally, all the Ukrainian party and *kolkhoz* managers, not to mention the Ukrainian 'nationalist intelligentsia', were resisting and waging a 'war of sabotage, a war to the death against Soviet power'.[25] Armed detachments of 'activists' sent from the towns, supported by political police, were sent to the *kolkhoz* to 'seize cereal crops' by force, including the seed corn for future crops and the meagre 'advances' in kind received by the collective members for their year's work. Villages not fulfilling the 'collective plan' were 'listed in the black book', all their shops closed and imports of food or manufactured products forbidden. Finally, to prevent any mass exodus of peasants towards the towns and so that news of the famine, which had been kept completely quiet, could not leak out, the sale of train tickets was suspended. Detachments of the army and political police were deployed around the famine areas to prevent anyone escaping. In the month of February 1933 alone, cordons of OGPU troops arrested 220,000 Ukrainian peasants attempting to flee their villages. Of these, 190,000 were sent back home and consequently to certain death, and the others were sent to labour camps or deported.[26] While millions of peasants were dying of hunger, the Soviet government was exporting 1,800,000 tons of cereals to honour its debts to Germany and to buy foreign machinery intended to make possible the accelerated industrialization plans. In that year of 1933, the state's strategic reserves, held in case of war, exceeded three million tons – a quantity more than sufficient to save millions of the starving population.

Fifteen years after this terrible famine, several Soviet regions experienced hunger once more. The context for this, the last famine in Europe, was unquestionably quite different. The 1946–7 famine, in which more than half a million people died, mainly in the provinces of Kursk, Tambov and Voronezh as well as in Moldavia, was the final stage in a cataclysmic cycle of demographic losses (more than 20 million dead, including 11 million civilians, during the *Great Patriotic War*). The famine occurred after large-scale destruction of economic infrastructures during the war and against a background of endemic malnutrition and epidemics. The 1946 harvest was a catastrophe, down by 20 per cent on the harvest of 1945 and by 40 per cent for 1932. A serious drought made worse the extremely weak position of Soviet agriculture as it emerged from the war. There was a radical labour shortage (in the western areas of the USSR that had been occupied by the Germans from 1941 to 1944 there were four women as against one man in the collective farms) and a shortage of horses, tractors and machinery. Despite a catastrophic harvest, the government refused to reduce the deliveries that the *kolkhoz* was forced to make to the state because Stalin had solemnly declared the end of rationing in the towns. The government also refused to touch the state reserves of cereals that had been stockpiled in the event of another war, reserves which, at the end of 1946, had risen to about ten million tons. Once again, hundreds of thousands of members of collectives were being pitilessly taxed, left without any food aid and dying of starvation.[27]

That six to seven million Soviet citizens should have died of hunger in a major European country in the 1930s and 1940s has to be seen as a most remarkable regression. It must lead historians to wonder about the specificity and the nature of the Soviet experience, given that it claimed to be the herald of modernity and progress.

An attempt at classification

Our rapid inventory of the policies of repression carried out by the Stalin regime is overwhelming. It is all the more difficult to attempt any classification given the extraordinary diversity of the programmes for repression, of the actions implemented, and the innumerable social, political or ethnic groups targeted over a quarter of a century. It is not possible to reduce it to a single overall category such as mass murder, ethnic cleansing or genocide. Thanks to recently available documentary archives, we are able to reconstruct the origin, degree of intent, preparation, implementation, execution and consequences of each programme of repression. Each of these must, however, be simultaneously replaced in its specific historical context and analyzed in its continuing development and duration. Indeed, one of the quite specific characteristics of the crimes of the Stalin regime is that they were carried out over a long period, at least by comparison with other mass murders, programmes of ethnic cleansing or genocide in the twentieth century, all of which were concentrated over a short period of two or three years (for example, the Armenian genocide or the Holocaust).

The great merit of the Soviet example is that it demonstrates how legal frameworks and painstakingly developed definitions drawn up by political scientists and historians in an attempt to 'classify' the crimes perpetrated by states, must remain unsatisfactory. This is because they come up against the extraordinary inventiveness of regimes when it comes to persecuting peoples. While acknowledging this, we shall attempt to show that some of the gravest and largest-scale crimes committed by the Stalin regime can be classified in terms of recognized definitions.

We have chosen four cases that have already been summarily reviewed in the outline inventory above. In our view, each of them raises interesting questions about classification.

'Dekulakization': class genocide?

This classification was first proposed in 1987 by Stéphane Courtois in his introduction to *The Black Book of Communism*. 'The death from starvation of the child of a Ukrainian kulak is "equivalent" to the death from starvation of a Jewish child in the Warsaw ghetto', writes Stéphane Courtois.[28] Is this process of equating 'class genocide' with 'racial genocide' really sustainable? Let us note, at the outset, the fact that two events, two policies, two very different crimes are being lumped together: the 'liquidation of the kulaks as a class', that is the expropriation and then deportation of several million peasants and individuals judged 'hostile' to the regime ('dekulakization' was applied regardless to orthodox priests, monks, former property owners, shopkeepers, country craftsmen and people with private incomes)[29] and the Ukrainian famine of

1932–3 which affected all the peasants in the collective farms in that Soviet republic and of which millions were victims. A number of factors lead us to be very doubtful about the applicability of the term 'class genocide' when applied to the 'kulaks'. It is true that we can say that the 'kulaks', as an artificially designated group, were targeted by the persecuting regime. However, the regime did, at the outset, introduce distinctions within the victim group. It distinguished three 'categories' of kulaks: the 'active counter-revolutionaries' who had to be 'sent to the camps or executed if they resisted'[30] (between twenty and thirty thousand were indeed condemned to death and executed by extra-judiciary bodies of the political police in 1930–1); the 'hostile and exploitative kulaks', who were to be deported together with their families; and lastly the kulaks deemed to be 'loyal towards the regime', who were expropriated and made to live on the edges of their areas of residence, on 'land requiring improvement'. It is clear that 'liquidation of the kulaks as a class' does not imply physical liquidation of all kulaks, even though, as we have seen, the terrible conditions in which the deportation took place and then the 'settlement' of the kulaks, who were often abandoned in the middle of the *taiga* or the desert steppes, caused a very high rate of mortality that sometimes reached 15 per cent per year (and much higher in the case of children). It is also clear that the 'sociological defining lines' for the 'kulak' group appear not merely flexible, but actually not definitions at all. A 'kulak' is not just someone who sells grain at the market, someone who owns two samovars, someone who goes to church or demonstrates openly against collective farms. The 'kulaks' are also shopkeepers, retired civil servants of the Tsarist regime, orthodox priests, nuns and 'counter-revolutionary and socially harmful elements' who appeared in the 'Others' column of the OGPU's statistical tables.[31]

Now, let us remind ourselves: genocide is said to occur when a group is targeted in terms of what essentially defines it: the criterion of the *stability* of the group must be present for the term genocide to be applicable, and here it is manifestly not the case. Moreover, in the case of the 'kulaks', it is important to note that this pariah-status was not carried forward to the next generation: from 1938 onwards, children of kulaks who reached the age of 16 were allowed to leave their place of deportation if they continued their schooling beyond the required age. Three years later, hundreds of thousands of children of kulaks were mobilized into the Red Army. Such integration into the army *ipso facto* removed all the legal discrimination measures that had been imposed on children of kulaks, even though their parents continued to be second-class citizens.[32]

How do we classify the 'Great Terror' of 1937–8?

Recent research into this event has shown that it is incorrect to place this murderous episode in the history of Stalinism in the category of 'great purges', as some historians continue to do.[33] The term 'purge' should certainly be reserved for political purges (in Russian, *chistka*). We now know that the purging of the communist political, military, economic and intellectual elites was no more than the public face of the Terror, the visible part of the iceberg, one might say: a few tens of thousands of victims out of about 800,000. The 'mass operations', involving 90 per cent of the victims, operations that were secret, planned and decided at the highest levels of the Party-State, appear as the final stage in a vast social engineering undertaking, initiated by 'dekulakization' and intended, this time, to physically eliminate, 'once and for all', all 'socially harmful elements' (*sostvrednye* was the term used in the secret operational directives) that were polluting Soviet socialist society. However, alongside these enemies that one might call 'traditional', as far as the regime that had emerged from the Bolshevik revolution was concerned (ex-kulaks, ex-Tsarist civil servants, members of former political parties opposed to Bolshevism, etc.), there were, in 1937–8, new enemies, defined not in socio-political but in ethno-political terms. These were representatives of minorities, national diasporas suspected of maintaining links with foreign powers hostile to the USSR: Poles, Germans, Finns, Latvians or Romanians. Sometimes it was specific groups on whom some artificial definition was imposed ('Harbinians', for example) and who had supposedly become, as a result of their earlier activities, or even simply because of their geographical location in some strategic frontier region, agents of a foreign power (in that particular case, of Japan).

The extreme diversity of the victims of the Great Terror makes difficult any classification of this crime, which is in a 'class' of its own – 800,000 people executed by means of a bullet in the back of the head after a hearing that was a parody of justice; this over a period of 16 months, a rate of 50,000 executions per month or 1,700 per day for nearly 500 days. Let us therefore content ourselves with a 'minimalist' classification: 'mass crime' carried out by the Stalinist state against about one per cent of its adult population.

Mass deportation of 'punished peoples': ethnic cleansing or genocide?

Unlike 'dekulakisation' or the 'Great Terror', this case concerns very clearly defined target-groups in terms of both nationality and ethnicity. Compared with the 'partial deportations' targeting various social, political or ethnic groups as implemented by the Stalin regime during the 1930s, the deportations of 'punished peoples' in the years 1941–4 have a number of special features. The most striking is that they were 'total', that is, they targeted all members of the group that was denounced, without exception. However, there is also the fact that they were intended to be 'definitive', that is, the national minority to be 'punished' was to retain its badge of shame 'in perpetuity'.[34]

The better to understand and classify them, let us look in greater detail at the largest of them: the deportation of half a million Chechens and Ingush towards the end of February 1944. Preparation for the operation, for which we now have the complete documentation, began as early as October 1943.[35] All the logistical preparations were personally supervised by Lavrenty Beria, the head of State Security, and two of his closest collaborators, Ivan Serov and Bogdan Kobulov. All three travelled to Grozny for the final stage of the preparation. Stalin was kept personally informed, on a day-to-day basis, of the progress of this operation that was so extraordinary, both in terms of the scale of the resources that were used and in terms of the size of the groups to be deported in record time: 194 rail transports and 119,000 men from the NKVD's special detachments were mobilized to arrest and deport in just six days (23–8 February 1944) more than half a million people. It had three features in common with all the major ethnic cleansing operations implemented in the twentieth century: 'a hierarchical command structure, an enclosed theatre of operations and a culture of impunity'.[36] The deportees were given less than an hour to put together a few personal effects (no more than 100 kilos) before being loaded onto lorries to take them to the nearest station, where they were transferred into rail convoys of cattle-trucks. Because of the uneven terrain, the poor state of the roads and the particularly adverse weather conditions, many lorries were held up en route with their human cargo. One sign of the extreme violence of these ethnic cleansing operations, applied to peoples who were represented as 'enemies' for having allegedly 'collaborated' with the Nazi occupiers, was that hundreds, possibly thousands, of deportees who could not be delivered to the embarkation point for the rail convoys within the brief period allowed were summarily liquidated, often under atrocious conditions, locked up inside buildings and burnt alive.[37] It is a remarkable fact that the hunt by the police for Chechens, Ingush and other representatives of the 'punished peoples' was not confined to the territories where these groups were the majority of the population. In the course of 1944, about 157,000 private soldiers, NCOs and officers belonging to one or other of the 'punished' national minorities were 'extracted' from the Soviet army units in which they were serving and immediately deported to Kazakhstan or to Central Asia.

After an exhausting journey of three to four weeks to Kazakhstan or Kirghizia, the deportees were dispersed in small groups and assigned places in isolated collectives, building sites, mines, or factories situated in the most inhospitable areas. There they had to face a way of life and working conditions that were extremely difficult, in addition to numerous forms of discrimination. In the field of education, for example, only a minority of deported children went to school, and education was only conducted in Russian. The truth was that the 'punished peoples' were condemned to losing their national identity. For example, the Autonomous Republic of Chechnya-Ingushetia was abolished, place-names were changed, monuments commemorating national heroes were toppled, and all mention of the very existence of a Chechen nationality (as also Ingush, Balkar, Kalmuk, Karachai, Tartar, etc.) was removed from the *Great Soviet Encyclopaedia*. In a particularly hostile environment, the mortality rate among the deportees remained extremely high, as we have seen. Between 20 and 25 per cent of the deportees died in the four years following their deportation and the rate was at its highest amongst children. Another special feature of the case of the Soviet 'punished peoples' was that, on 26 November 1948, a decree of the Praesidium of the Supreme Soviet of the USSR ruled that the 'peoples punished during the Great Patriotic War' were punished 'in perpetuity'. This ruling explicitly meant that every member of the 'punished' community passed on to the next generation the 'collective fault' committed by his ancestors (unlike the case of the kulaks, for example, whose children, once they reached adulthood, were freed of their deportee status). Can we deduce from this that 'elements of racial politics had surreptitiously been slipped into Stalin's ethnic cleansing'?[38] Analysis of Stalin's policies towards these nationalities suggests that the regime did not persecute this or that people because of alleged 'biological defects'. His aim was not to eliminate this or that race or ethnic group but to eradicate any form or manifestation of ethnic or national *distinctiveness* that might risk obstructing his plan to build a community of Soviet socialist nationalities or to delay the creation of the Communist Utopia, founded on the powerful urge towards homogenization of Soviet society. Justified on the basis of a conviction that nationalities, like social classes, were socio-historical structures and not racial or biological entities, the treatment inflicted on the 'punished peoples' or the 'enemy nations' had more to do with a form of 'ethno-historical excision'.[39] The Stalin regime's aim was rather to eradicate the national, cultural and historical identities of a community than to physically eliminate every member of that community. This, like the absence of any clearly articulated racial ideology, probably explains why a regime which certainly had the capacity to implement huge genocidal operations never organized extermination camps on the Nazi model.

Some historians, however,[40] consider that the ethnic deportation/cleansing of the Soviet 'punished peoples', the intention of which is securely documented, as are all the stages of planning and implementation, does constitute genocide in the sense defined by the UN Convention of 9 December 1948. They put forward the argument that, in these operations, the Soviet regime was 'deliberately inflicting on the members of the group conditions of life calculated to bring about its physical destruction in whole or in part'.

What these divergent interpretations demonstrate are both weaknesses in the definition of genocide as it was adopted in 1948 – a definition which is simultaneously too narrow and too general – and also the fact that the boundary between ethnic cleansing and genocide is far from watertight.[41]

The Great Ukrainian Famine of 1932–3: was it genocide?

In May 2003, the parliament of the Republic of Ukraine officially recognized the 1932–3 famine as an act of genocide carried out by the Stalin regime against the Ukrainian people. The term used in Ukraine today to indicate the famine, *Holodomor* is quite explicit: it is made up of the words *holod* (hunger, famine) and *morit* (to kill by starvation, to famish) and thus clearly stresses the intentional aspect of the event. Classification of the 1932–3 famine as genocide does not receive unanimous support from historians who have studied the matter, whether Russian, Ukrainian or western. We can simplify the debate by saying that there are two main interpretive trends. On the one hand, there are historians who support the genocide view and see the famine as a phenomenon, artificially organized to break the particularly strong resistance by Ukrainian peasants to the collectivization system and to destroy the national and peasant characteristics of the Ukrainian nation which constituted an obstacle on the way to transforming the USSR into a new kind of empire dominated by Russia. On the other hand, there are other historians who, whilst recognizing the criminal nature of Stalin's policies, feel it necessary to examine *all* the famines occurring in 1931–3 (in Kazakhstan, in Ukraine, the famines affecting part of Western Siberia and regions of the Lower and Middle Volga) as a 'complex phenomenon' wherein many factors, ranging from the geopolitical situation to the demands of accelerated modernization and industrialization, played an important role alongside Stalin's 'imperial intentions'.[42] For these historians, the case has not been made for classifying the Ukrainian famine of 1931–2 as 'genocide'. As Andrea Graziosi, the Italian historian specializing in the *Holodomor* has rightly suggested, it may well be possible, in the light of the most recent research, to put the case for 'stepping outside' the existing two main interpretations. According to Graziosi, who bases his views on the work of the American historian, Terry Martin[43] and the writings of the Ukrainian historians Yuri Shapoval and Vassily Vassilyev[44], there are certain quite specific features that characterize the Ukrainian famine by comparison with the general background of Soviet famines in 1931–3. The latter are the direct but unintended and unplanned consequences of the ideologically-inspired policies applied from the end of 1929 onwards: enforced collectivization (accompanied by forced sedentarization of nomadic and semi-nomadic peoples in Kazakhstan); dekulakization; the imposition of the *kolkhoz* system; and excessive levies on harvests and cattle. Until the summer of 1932, the Ukrainian famine, which was already beginning to be apparent, fell into the same category as the other famines, which had begun earlier (in Kazakhstan and Western Siberia, to mention just two such). But from summer 1932 onwards, the Ukrainian famine changed once Stalin drew up his 'national view of the famine' (Terry Martin). As the recently published correspondence between Stalin and his main collaborators during the summer of 1932 shows,[45] he was at that time convinced that a huge resistance front, ranging from simple members of the *kolkhoz* to Ukrainian communist officials, had been set up in Ukraine with the intention of refusing to deliver to the state the agricultural produce needed for the provisioning of the towns and for export. In a letter dated 11 August 1932 to Lazar Kaganovich, Stalin went so far as to write: 'We are at risk of losing Ukraine', because the Party, the state and even the Republic's political police officials 'are infested with nationalist agents and Polish spies.'[46] From that moment on, Stalin applied a ferociously repressive policy towards Ukraine and Kuban, the latter being mainly populated by Ukrainians. His two closest collaborators, Vyacheslav Molotov and Lazar Kaganovich were sent as 'plenipotentiaries' to Ukraine and Northern Caucasus, their mission being to 'purge' and to bring into line the local Communists who were, indeed, 'dragging their feet' and sometimes even refusing to implement the excessive quotas for cereal deliveries. Reinforcements of 'activists' from Russia and detachments of political police undertook actual punitive actions in the Ukrainian collective farms in order to requisition all the available wheat. A whole panoply of repressive measures was put in place, ranging from closure of shops to police questioning of any peasants trying to flee from their starving villages. Over and above this range of repressive measures, it is clear that Stalin, *from the end of the summer of 1932*, really had decided to worsen the famine that was beginning, to turn it into a weapon, to *extend it deliberately*, with a view to teaching a lesson to peasants who were refusing the 'new serfdom', to use the weapon of hunger. Whilst the peasants suffered most – the famine brought about the death, in appalling conditions, of millions of people – the repression also affected local officials and Ukrainian intellectuals, who were arrested and imprisoned. In December 1932, two secret decrees by the Politburo brought an end in Ukraine – and only in Ukraine – to the policy of 'indigenisation' of officials that had been applied since 1923 in all the federal republics; Ukrainian 'nationalism' was firmly repressed.

Recent research has shown, without any doubt, that the Ukrainian case is quite specific, at least from the second half of 1932 onwards. On the basis of these new considerations, it seems to me legitimate to classify as genocide the totality of the actions taken by the Stalin regime to punish, by means of famine and terror, the Ukrainian peasantry. These were actions that resulted in the death of more than four million people in Ukraine and the Northern Caucasus.[47]

Nevertheless, the *Holodomor* was very different from the Holocaust. It did not aim to exterminate the entire Ukrainian nation. It was not based on direct murder of its victims. It was motivated and planned on the basis of a political rationale and not on ethnic or racial bases. However, in the number of its victims, the *Holodomor*, when seen in context, is the only twentieth-century European event that can be compared to the two other generally recognized instances of genocide: the Armenian genocide and the Holocaust.

Notes

1. See N. Werth, 'A State against its People: Violence, Repression and Terror in the Soviet Union', in *The Black Book of Communism*, eds, S. Courtois, N. Werth, J-L. Panné, A. Packowski, K. Bartosek, J-L. Margolin. (Cambridge, MA: Harvard University Press, 1999), pp. 33–268; idem., 'Logiques de violence dans l'URSS stalinienne', in *Stalinisme et nazisme. Histoire et mémoire comparées*, ed. H. Rousso (Paris/Brussells, IHTP/Complexe, 1999), pp. 35–68.
2. Among the very large number of books and articles devoted to the victims of Stalinist repression since the opening of the archives, we shall mention only a few works available in English which put forward an inventory that is detailed but synthetic: Courtois, Werth et al., *The Black Book of Communism*; J. O. Pohl, *The Stalinist Penal System* (Jefferson, NC: McFarland & Co, 1997); J. A. Getty, G. T. Rittersporn, and V. N. Zemskov, 'Victims of the Soviet Penal System in Pre-War Years', *American Historical Review*, 98, 4, (1993).
3. This inventory was drawn up, towards the end of 1953, by the Statistical Section of the MVD (GARF, 9401/1/4157/201–205). For a detailed discussion of this important document see N. Werth, 'Histoire d'un pré-rapport secret', *Communisme*, 67–8 (2001), 10–38.
4. In the coded language of the top-secret resolutions of the Politburo and in the 'operational orders' of the NKVD, 'Category 1' meant the death penalty; 'Category 2' meant a sentence of ten years in the camps. 'Ratified additions' were additional quotas approved by the Politburo; 'Non-ratified additions' referred to sentences over and above the quotas.
5. For a very full bibliography on the Great Terror, see M. Junge, R. Binner and T. Martin, 'The Great Terror in the provinces of the USSR, 1937–1938. A Co-operative Bibliography', *Cahiers du Monde russe*, 42, 2–4 (2001), 679–96.
6. Such were the terms used by Nikolai Yezhov in the preamble to NKVD operational order No. 00447 of 30 July 1937.
7. On the 'Great Terror' as a convergence of two 'lines of repression', see N. Werth, 'Repenser la Grande Terreur', *Le Débat*, 122 (November-December 2002), 118–41; M. Jansen and N. Petrov, *Stalin's Loyal Executioner: People's Commissar Nikolai Ezhov, 1895–1940* (Stanford, CA: Hoover Institution Press, 2002).
8. Cf. Jansen and Petrov, *Stalin's Loyal Executioner*, pp. 99–104.
9. Let us not forget the following statistics: about 44,000 middle-ranking Communist officials were sentenced (of whom 85% to the death penalty) by the Military College of the Supreme Court, the body which dealt with most of the cases that implicated this type of accused. Out of about 1.5 million people arrested by the NKVD in 1937–1938, about 117,000 were party members. See Jansen and Petrov, *Stalin's Loyal Executioner*, p. 105.
10. Cf. GARF, 9401/1/4157/201–205.
11. Amongst the most important publications concerning the gulags, we would pick out *Istoria Stalinskovo Gulaga*, 7 vols (Moscow: Rosspen, 2004) by a collective of a dozen or so historians.
12. GARF, 7523/89/4408. The statistical data on sentences imposed, as they emerge from several Ministry of Justice reports, were published in the first volume of *Istoria Stalinskovo Gulaga*, pp. 705–30.
13. T, Todorov, 'Le totalitarisme, encore une fois', *Communisme*, 59–60 (2000), 41.
14. H. Arendt, *The Origins of Totalitarianism*, rev. edn (San Diego: Harcourt Brace & Company, 1979), p. 445.

15. On mortality rates in the gulags, see Y. Poliakov, ed., *Naselenye Rossyi v XX veke, 1920–1959*, 2 vols (Moscow: Nauka, 2000 and 2001), pp. 311–30 and 187–210.
16. V. Chalamov, *Les Récits de la Kolyma* (Paris: F. Maspéro, 1981, re-edited La Découverte/Fayard, 1986) / Varlam Shalamov, *Kolyma Tales*, trans. J. Glad (New York: Penguin, 1994).
17. Among the various studies of deportations in the USSR, see A. Nekritch, *The Punished Peoples: the Deportation and Fate of Soviet Minorities at the End of the Second World War* (New York: Norton, 1978); N. Naimark, *Fires of Hatred: Ethnic Cleansing in Twentieth-Century Europe* (Cambridge, MA: Harvard University Press, 2001); J. O. Pohl, *Ethnic Cleansing in the USSR, 1937–1949* (Westport, CT: Greenwood Press, 1999); T. Martin, 'The Origins of Soviet Ethnic Cleansing', *Journal of Modern History*, 70, 4 (1998), 813–61; P. Polian, *Ne po svoye vole. Istoria i geografiya prinuditelnykh migratsyi v SSSR* ('Against their will: History and Geography of Forced Migrations in the USSR') (Moscow: OGI-Memorial, 2001); N. Werth, 'Les Déportations de populations suspectes dans les espaces russes et soviétiques (1914-fin des années 1940): violences de guerre, ingéniérie sociale, excision ethno-historique', *Communisme*, 78–9 (2004), 15–52.
18. I am using here the expression suggested by Francine Hirsch in 'Race without the Practice of Racial Politics', *Slavic Review*, 61, 1 (2002), 40.
19. The 'special settlements' were isolated villages in particularly inhospitable zones (the Narym region in Western Siberia, the Central Kazakhstan steppes, the Southern Urals, the Kirghiz steppes, etc.) where the 'specially relocated persons' (also called 'labour settlers') were resettled and assigned dwellings. Unlike those detained in the gulags, who were individually sentenced, the 'specially relocated persons' had been deported, as families, solely on the basis of an administrative decision. They were deprived of all civil rights, forced to do very poorly paid work and were administratively dependent on one of the 2000 *komandaturas* (special administration) of the Gulag Department for Special Populations, which managed all of the 'specially relocated persons'.
20. Poliakov, ed., *Naselenye Rossyi v XX veke, 1920–1959*, vol. 1, pp. 282–5.
21. V. Zemskov, 'Kulatskaya Sylka v 1930-ye gody' ('Kulak Exile in the 1930s'), *Sotsiologicheskye Issledovaniya*, 10 (199), 4–5.
22. A. Graziosi, *Lettere da Kharkov. La carestia in Ucraina e nel Caucaso del Nord nei rapporti dei diplomatici italiani, 1932–1933* (Turin, 1991); V. P. Danilov, R. Manning, L. Viola, eds, *Tragedia Sovetskoi Derevni*, vol. 3, 1930–1933 (Moscow: Rosspen, 2001); R. W. Davies and S. G. Wheatcroft, *The Years of Hunger: Soviet Agriculture, 1931–1933* (New York, 2004); N. A. Ivnickii, *Kollektivizatsiya i raskulatsivanye* (Moscow: Airo-XX, 1996); S. V. Kul'cyckyi, ed., *Golod 1932–1933 rokiv na Ukraini: ocyma istorykiv, movoy dokumentiv* (Kiev, 1990); idem, *Golodomor 1932–1933 rr. v. Ukraini: prycyny i naslidky* (Kiev, 1993); Y. Sapoval and V. Vassilyev, *Komandiri velikovo golodu: poizdki V. Molotova i L. Kahanovitsa v Ukrainu ta na Pivnitsnii Kavkaz, 1932–1933* (Kiev, 2001).
23. K. Aldazumanov, Z. Abylhozin, M. Kozybaev, eds, *Nasilstvennaya Kollektivizatsya i golod v Kazakhstanye v 1931–1933 gg* (Alma-Ata, 1998); I. Ohayon, *Du nomadisme au socialisme. Sédentarisation, collectivisation et acculturation des Kazakhs en URSS, 1928–1945* (Paris: Maisonneuve, 2006); N. Pianciola, 'Famine in the Steppe. The Collectivization of Agriculture and the Kazakh Herdsmen, 1928–1934', *Cahiers du Monde russe*, 45, 1–2 (2004), 137–92.
24. The historian Terry Martin brought out this essential point which he refers to as the 'national interpretation' of the 1932–3 famine by Stalin in his book, *The Affirmative Action Empire: Nations and Nationalism in the Soviet Union, 1923–1939*, (Ithaca, NY: Cornell University Press, 2001).

25. This last phrase is taken from the letter sent by Stalin to the writer Sholokhov on 6 May 1933, quoted in Werth, 'A State Against Its People', p. 166–7.
26. On these measures, see the documents published in Danilov et al., eds, *Tragedia Sovetskoi Derevni*, vol. 3, pp. 215–20.
27. The most complete account of this still largely unknown famine is by F. Zima, *Golod v SSSR 1946–1947gg* (Moscow: RAN, 1996).
28. Werth, 'A State Against Its People', p. 35.
29. On the wide social spectrum covered by the label 'Kulak', see, for example, the documents published in Danilov et al., eds, *Tragedia sovetskoi derevni*, vols. 2 and 3.
30. On the definitions for the three categories of 'Kulaks' proposed by a Committee of the Politburo chaired by V. Molotov, see Ivnitskii, *Kollektivizatsiya i raskulatsivanye*, pp. 49–54.
31. See the large number of reports from the various departments of the OGPU responsible for the arrest and deportation of the Kulaks presented in works such as Danilov et al., eds, *Tragedia sovetskoi derevni*, vol. 3.
32. See V. Zemskov, *Spetzpereseletsy, 1930–1960* (Moscow: Nauka, 2002), pp. 80ff.
33. see I. Halfin, *Terror in My Soul: Communist Autobiographies on Trial* (Cambridge, MA: Harvard University Press, 2003), p. 3.
34. As stipulated by the Decree of 26 November 1948 of the Praesidium of the Supreme Soviet of the USSR.
35. Among the numerous studies of this deportation, see M. Pohl, '"It cannot be that our graves will be here": The Survival of Chechen and Ingush deportees in Kazakhstan, 1944–1957', *Journal of Genocide Research*, 4, 3 (2002), 401–30; N. Werth, 'Handling an Awkward Legacy: The Chechen Problem, 1918–1958', *Contemporary European History*, 15, 3 (2006), 347–66.
36. J. Sémelin, 'Analysis of a Mass Crime: Ethnic Cleansing in the Former Yugoslavia, 1991–1999', in *The Specter of Genocide: Mass Murder in Historical Perspective*, eds, R. Gellately and B. Kiernan (Cambridge: Cambridge University Press, 2003), p. 187.
37. One of the largest massacres took place in the *aoul* (mountain village) of Khaibakh in the Galanchozh district, where troops commanded by General Gvichiany, blocked in by bad weather and unable to deliver their human cargo in time, locked up several hundred people in a *kolkhoz* stable and then set fire to it. See Polian, *Ne po svoye vole*, p. 123.
38. As the historian, Eric Weitz wrote in 'Racial Politics without the Concept of Race', *Slavic Review*, 61, 1 (2002), 18.
39. Hirsch, 'Race without the Practice of Racial Politics', 40.
40. See in particular the work of J. O. Pohl.
41. As Norman Naimark rightly observes in his book on ethnic cleansing in the twentieth century (*Fires of Hatred*, p. 87), 'Ethnic cleansing bleeds into genocide, as mass murder is committed in order to rid the land of a people (...) as people are violently ripped from their native towns and villages and killed when they try to stay.'
42. On developments in the historiography of the Ukrainian famine, see the stimulating article by Andrea Graziosi, 'Les famines soviétiques de 1931–1933 et le *holodomor* ukrainien. Une nouvelle interprétation est-elle possible et quelles en seraient les circonstances?', *Cahiers du Monde russe*, 46, 3 (2005), 453–72.
43. Martin, *The Affirmative Action Empire*.
44. Shapoval and Vassilyev, *Komandiry velikovo golodu*.
45. R. W. Davies, O. Khlevniuk, L. Rogovaia, L. Koseleva, eds, *Stalin-Kaganovich. Perepiska, 1931–1936* (Moscow: Rosspen, 2001).

46. Ibid., pp. 273–4.
47. I am happy to acknowledge that, until very recently, it was my view that the 1931–3 famines should be analyzed as a whole, as a 'complex phenomenon', as being the result of policies that were criminal but 'not planned', put into effect through the collectivisation of farmland, dekulakisation, the predatory system of production quotas, etc. The work of Terry Martin, Andrea Graziosi, Yuri Shapoval, Vassily Vassilyev and other Ukrainian colleagues has persuaded me to change my view on certain points that I had argued, particularly in my contribution to *The Black Book of Communism*.

16
The 1947 Partition of India

Ian Talbot

The British divided and quit India in 1947. The partition of the subcontinent was accompanied by large-scale massacres which sparked off an unforeseen mass migration. The Punjab was at the epicentre of the disturbances which spread across much of North India. In all an estimated 18 million people were displaced in a chaotic two-way flight of Hindus and Sikhs from Pakistan and Muslims from India. The migrations were over within the space of three months in the Punjab, but were to continue intermittently from Bengal during periods of communal tension throughout the following decades. The total movement of population represented the greatest forced migration of the twentieth century.

The number of casualties still remains controversial.[1] The most conservative British estimates put the number of deaths at around 200,000.[2] Some Indian authors have maintained upwards of 2,000,000 died in the communal blood-letting. The exact figure will never be known, but is conventionally reckoned at around 1,000,000.[3] In addition around 100,000 women were abducted. Some writers have seen them as the 'chief sufferers' of the violence because they were believed to embody community honour.[4] Accounts exist of gang rapes, mutilations and of women being paraded naked in the streets. The cycle of female oppression and violence was completed by forcible repatriations to families who in many instances rejected them, even if they had settled and had children with their captors.[5]

Until the 1990s, little was written about the partition-related violence and its human costs. The emphasis was rather on the 'high politics' that resulted in the division of the subcontinent.[6] Official history stood at variance with both fictional representations[7] and private memory. Community histories did draw on the violence, but primarily as a resource for identity politics and to displace blame on the demonized 'other'.[8] The work of such feminist writers and social activists as Urvashi Butalia, Kamla Bhasin and Ritu Menon, however, began to give voice to the human dimension of the partition event.[9] The experiences of previously marginalized groups such as women, children and Untouchables were introduced into the historical discourse. Even more belatedly, a handful of writers such as Anders Bjorn Hansen, Paul Brass and Ishtiaq Ahmed have begun to see the partition violence not as a unique event, but bearing similarities with other episodes of genocide and ethnic cleansing in twentieth-century history.[10] Before examining these pioneering works and assessing the scope for setting the partition-related violence in the wider literature, it is necessary to reflect why it has taken so long to attempt to understand the events of 1947 in this light.

The partition violence has only recently been considered in terms of general theories. It finds no place in, for example, leading works on genocide and religion in the twentieth century.[11] This reflects the intention by official histories of the subcontinent's independence to play down its darker side in order to trumpet the achievement of freedom. Gyanendra Pandey has criticized the way in which national histories have made the violence 'non-narratable'.[12] They have achieved this by, first, reducing it to a 'local' detail that is irrelevant to the wider event of national independence, and second, by portraying it as an aberration, arising from a temporary moment of madness that does not require rational explanation.[13] Mob violence understandings of the 1947 killings ultimately look back to Gustave Le Bon's understanding of the 'collective mind' of crowd behaviour for inspiration.[14] Javed Alam is typical of the approach that understands the violence as a spontaneous irrational outburst. He further distances the violence from conceptualization in terms of genocide by declaring there was 'no involvement of large organizations or the state as the instrument of mass killings'.[15] This type of understanding transforms the 1947 violence into a phenomenon that cannot be rationally explained. It also becomes a unique occurrence that does not repay comparative analysis.

The violence is not only distanced in this way from other episodes of twentieth-century mass killing such as the Holocaust, but is seen as having nothing in common with post-independence massacres such as the *pogrom* against Sikhs in Delhi in October 1984[16] following the assassination of Indira Gandhi, and the carnage in Gujarat in 2002 in the wake of the attack on the Sabarmati Express at Godhra on 27 February.[17] Recent research, however, points to parallels between the 1947 violence and the conceptualization of contemporary violence by such writers as Paul Brass with his emphasis on planned rather than spontaneous violence in which political actors and the police play leading roles.[18]

Contemporary interpretations of the violence were unsurprisingly polemical.[19] The 'other' community was always portrayed as the instigator. Subsequent violence was thus portrayed as retaliation. Such accounts must then be treated with extreme care by the historian. The conflicting narratives are well illustrated with respect to the situation in the Punjabi city of Amritsar. It was to straddle the new international border and to serve as a transit camp for refugees from Pakistan in the weeks after independence. As early as March 1947, however, the city had suffered endemic violence. The main work on Amritsar is the Shiromani Gurdwara Parbandhak Committee[20] (SGPC) publication of 1950. It portrays the Muslim League as concentrating its energies in the city as part of a 'war' strategy to break the Sikhs' 'morale' throughout the province,[21] and draws parallels between the Muslim League 'attack' and the Nazi assault on Stalingrad.[22] The account emphasizes the organized character of the violence and the partisan actions of Muslim officials and police. It names the areas of the initial Muslim assaults as Sattowali Gali, Gokal New Abadi in Kila Bhangian, Deviwali Gali, Chhaju Misr's Gali, Islamabad, and Hall Bazaar. These localities were dominated by Hindu and Sikh businesses, so they would provide opportunities for looting and striking at the heart of the Muslim rivals' economic power. They were also vulnerable as they were surrounded by Muslim-majority areas. The SGPC account also highlights the role of such Muslim League politicians as Sheikh Sadiq Hassan[23] and the use of mosques to store weapons.[24]

The main Muslim account of the Amritsar riots is contained in Khawaja Iftikhar's popular autobiographical work *Jab Amritsar jal raha tha*[25] (When Amritsar was burning).[26] Iftikhar was vice-president of the Amritsar branch of the Muslim League and he portrays the Muslims as victims of the 6 March violence. Their assailants are described as processing from the precincts of the Golden Temple, led by the Akali[27] Udham Singh Nago and Madi Pehlewan, the son of Amritsar's 'most notorious goonda', Bijli Pehlewan. The assault was repelled, Iftikhar maintains, as a result of the valour of Ghulam Mustafa. Despite many gunshot pellet wounds he drove off the 'invaders', in the process killing a Sikh *jathedar* (leader of a military band) with his own spear. Women on the rooftops of their houses threw down their *dupattas* (scarves) in tribute as he was carried to his house on a charpoy.[28] Muslim *pehlewans* (wrestlers) such as Manto, Nasir Khan and Manna are praised for defending lives in the face of a hostile police presence.

Chaudhuri Mohammad Said, who fled to Lahore from his post as a tax superintendent for the Amritsar Municipal Committee,[29] has provided a less renowned first-hand account that was penned on 11 September 1947. He also blames the Sikhs for the eruption of the violence. His narrative begins on the night of 4 March, when Sikh drummers announced the holding of an anti-Pakistan rally. 'Provocative slogans' were raised in front of a Sikh-owned general merchants shop, 'Gol Hatti', in a densely populated Muslim area of Hall Bazaar. Angry words gave way to a fracas in which a number of Muslims and Sikhs were injured before the police intervened. The Sikh rally was followed, he continues, by a midnight procession. The first stabbing, according to Said, occurred in Chowk Phawara, Katra Ahluwalian, where a Muslim *tonga* (a horse-drawn cart) driver was killed. A day of stray stabbing cases culminated in a night of arson.

Echoing Khawaja Iftikhar's account, Said maintains that by 6 March a large part of the city was ablaze.[30]

Later nationalist accounts of the partition-related violence play down the element of organization altogether and talk instead in the generalities of 'temporary madness'. Such writers as Alam possess genuine concerns about attempting to rationalize what appear to be senseless acts. There is also some point in the understanding of Donald Horowitz that the most extreme acts of violence tend to be disorganized and spontaneous.[31] Nevertheless one should be aware of the utility for official accounts of a portrayal of the partition massacres as spontaneous acts at a unique transitional moment in the subcontinent's history. This displaces responsibility and obscures the newly independent states' ambiguous role concerning the violence. At best local officials were demonstrably unable to protect the lives of their minority citizens. At worst they may have actively participated in the 'ethnic cleansing' of minority populations. The state's absence in official histories of violence and migration is accompanied by a marked lack of public remembrance of the mass migrations and violence. There is no equivalent of the Holocaust Day remembrance of the victims, although public commemoration was being urged on the Pakistan Government from as early as March 1956.[32]

It is the apparent absence of state involvement in the 1947 violence that has made such genocide scholars as Leo Kuper and Leonard B Glick hesitant in describing it as an act of genocide.[33] Mark Levene similarly limits genocide to the involvement of the state apparatus.[34] The more inclusivist approach of Henry R Huttenbach maintains that not just states, but well armed communal groups, 'with or without the collusion or cooperation of the instruments of the state' could embark on a genocide campaign.[35] Jason Francisco, however, sticks with a state sponsored view of genocide. For this reason he prefers to term the 1947 Punjab violence as fratricide. 'The partition stands as the archetype of what I call nationalist fratricide', he declares, 'the conflict between people of a common cultural heritage'.[36]

The works of Anders Bjorn Hansen, Paul Brass and Ishtiaq Ahmed have begun to link the 1947 violence with wider theories of genocide and ethnic cleansing. Brass uses the term 'retributive genocide' to capture the mutuality of the violence in the Punjab region throughout the period March–August 1947. He forcefully argues that the killings were organized and were motivated by the desire to ethnically cleanse rival communities. Ishtiaq Ahmed also takes up this latter theme. He has utilised first-hand accounts of the violence in the Punjabi city of Lahore to reveal the economic motives that lay behind the expulsion of the Hindu capitalist class. Hansen's more generalized study draws on the work of such scholars as Robert Melson and Mark Levene to demonstrate how the preconditions for genocide were present in the late colonial Punjab.[37] He sees the March 1947 killings as a transition point from what might be termed 'traditional' consensual violence to the later genocidal phase.[38] 'Despite the absence of the state as a perpetrator in Punjab', he declares, 'a reciprocal genocide occurred through organized mass killings that aimed at annihilating the "Other" community.'[39] Hansen's interpretation of events in the Punjab implies that a state-centric approach to genocidal violence is 'inadequate'.

Hansen's attempt to locate the 1947 violence in the context of genocide studies was based on a provincial-level treatment which relied primarily on official sources. Recent studies have examined patterns of violence and quiescence at the locality level and have deployed a range of oral as well as documentary sources.[40] They provide new evidence on three areas which are crucial for the future positioning of the partition violence in the field of genocide studies: firstly, the issue of its spontaneity or planning; secondly, the role of state authorities in its deterrence and commissioning; thirdly, the role of communal organizations in the mass killings.

Swarna Aiyar has maintained that the 1947 violence in the Punjab was 'both extraordinary and unparalleled elsewhere in India'. It was not so much 'a matter of crowds and collective action, as it was about campaigns conducted in military style'.[41] She highlights the Punjab's significance as the main recruitment centre of the Indian army. Former servicemen planned attacks on refugees and were active in the private armies that were behind much of the killing. They put not only their training to good use, 'for organizing the killings', but had easy access 'to arms and ammunition'.[42] Aiyar has provided evidence especially of the detailed planning that went into the attacks on the so-called refugee specials – the trains that were packed to their rooftops with passengers fleeing their homes for safety across the border. The wholesale slaughter of many of the trains' occupants has long provided a haunting image of the partition-related violence. The material on the attacks on refugee specials is sufficiently compelling for scholars such as Donald Horowitz who generally regard violence as unplanned and irrational[43] to admit that even amidst, 'an orgy of killing' there, 'can be interludes of detached planning ... the carefully plotted Punjab train massacres during the partition of India and Pakistan illustrate the phenomenon'.[44]

Planning is in fact evident not just in these incidents, but in earlier outbreaks of violence in the Punjab from March 1947 onwards. In the three districts of Attock, Rawalpindi and Jhelum the loss of life was estimated to be between 7,000 and 8,000.[45] About 40,000 people, mainly Sikhs, took refuge in hurriedly established camps. In Rawalpindi, the destruction and looting was the greatest in the Ratta, Kartarpur and Shivala area near jamma masjid (the congregational mosque).[46] Outlying villages such as Thamial, Kahuta, Jikka Gali, Daulatala, Kuri and Thoa Khalsa witnessed shocking violence. In the last named village over 100 Sikh women committed suicide by jumping into a well to prevent their 'dishonouring' at the hands of Muslim attackers. This episode found fictional representation in Bhisham Sahni's award winning novel *Tamas*.[47] In the Gujjar Khan and Campbellpur districts, villages were completely wiped out, corpses of young children were found hanging from trees and girls as young as 11 years old were victims of gang rape.

In addition to official and newspaper reports, historical sources on the violence are provided by the reports of the tour of the President, General Secretary and Secretary of the Hindu Mahasabha[48] and of the All-India-Congress Committee (AICC). These sources are unanimous that rather than being spontaneous, the violence was carefully planned. 'It is a mistake to call what happened in Rawalpindi area communal riots.' The AICC Report records:

> These were not riots but deliberately organised military campaigns. Long before the disturbances broke out secret meetings were held in mosques under the leadership of Syed Akbar Khan ex-MLA, Captain Lal Khan of Kahuta, Tehsildar and Police Sub Inspector Kahuta, Maulvi Abdul Rehman and Kala Khan MLA in which *jihad* (an Islamic war) was proclaimed against the minorities and emissaries were sent out to collect volunteers from the rural areas. ... The armed crowd which attacked Kahuta, Thoa Khalsa, and Nara etc. were led by ex-military men on horseback ... armed with Tommy Guns, pistols, rifles, hand grenades, hatchets, petrol tins and even some carried field glasses.[49]

The report goes on to describe what can only be recognized as an organized riot system. 'The mobs were divided into (the four following categories): 1. Armed with fire arms; 2. Lock breakers; 3. Provided with Petrol and kerosene oil; 4. In charge of donkeys, camels etc. to carry away looted property.' The following strategy, the Report continues, was used wherever the mobs attacked:

> First of all minorities were disarmed with the help of local police and by giving assurances by oaths on holy Quran of peaceful intentions. After this had been done, the helpless and unarmed minorities were attacked. On their resistance having collapsed, lock breakers and looters came into action with their transport corps of mules, donkeys and camels. Then came the 'Mujahadins' with tins of petrol and kerosene oil and set fire to the looted shops and houses. Then there were Maulvis (Muslim religious leaders) with barbers to convert people who somehow or other escaped slaughter and rape. The barbers shaved the hair and beards and circumcised the victims. Maulvis recited *kalmias* (attestations of faith) and performed forcible marriage ceremonies. After this came the looters, including women and children.[50]

The parallels with accounts of the 2002 Gujarat *pogrom* on the Muslim minority in which Vishwa Hindu Parishad (Universal Hindu Society) and

Rashtriya Swayam Sevak Sangh (National Volunteer Union) (RSS) activists came equipped with gas, oxygen cylinders and petrol[51] and in which 'respectable' people[52] joined in the looting are chillingly obvious. Moreover, these episodes contradict writers such as Donald Horowitz who argue that organized riots may be less deadly than relatively spontaneous violence in which leadership 'rises to the occasion, rather than creates the occasion.'[53]

Many accounts of the partition-related violence point to the fact that the vacuum created by the transition from colonial rule enabled the largely spontaneous bloodletting to occur. This absence of the state involvement as we have already noted has led some genocide experts to overlook the violence in their theorization. In one respect the transitional state thesis does help explain the Punjab massacres of August 1947. The delays in prosecuting the perpetrators of the March violence encouraged not only criminal classes, but those who might incite them and abet them by official inaction, that they could in future act with impunity. This along with the inflamed passions because of the cycles of retaliatory killings, helps explain the widespread dereliction of duty by police and other officials.[54] In Sonepat, in the Rohtak district, for example, rich Hindus contributed a *lakh* (100,000) of rupees to finance mob attacks on the Muslims. The ring-leaders included a couple of honorary magistrates and the Sub-Inspector of Police.[55] Similar help was provided by the Sub-Inspector of Police in organizing attacks on Muslims at Jagraon in the Ludhiana district. On 24 August 1947, the Muslim policemen at Ludhiana were disarmed and replaced by ex-Indian National Army men. Shortly thereafter, the Muslim localities of Fieldganj and Abdullahpur were attacked and looted.[56]

The rot had set in at the time of the March 1947 violence. A police contingent in the city of Multan stood by while a prominent Sikh leader and President of the Minorities Board Sardar Nanak Singh was done to death. The police then abandoned the areas outside the walls where many Hindu businesses were located leaving them at the mercy of looters. Hindu residents complained to the Congress investigators in a refrain frequently repeated by the Muslim minority in independent India that the police were the main cause of their 'misfortune'. They said that they could better defend themselves if the police were removed from the scene.[57] With the exception of the Rawalpindi Central Kotwali Police Station where Muslim constables appear to have mutinied against their officers, they appear to have taken their cue from their police and civilian superiors. There are parallels again here with major episodes of communal violence in post-independence India. Significantly violence did not occur in March 1947 in such places as the Khushab district and Mianwali where local Muslim League leaders and the District Commissioner and Deputy Superintendent of police intervened to quell the large armed crowds.[58]

Violence was thus not largely the result of state collapse, but of state inaction. Where authority was exerted, it occurred on a much smaller scale. This is amply demonstrated by Pippa Virdee's recent research on the small Muslim princely State of Malerkotla. In the surrounding British districts, there were widespread killings. These resulted not just from the administrative decline, but from the partisan role of officials. But the Nawab of Malerkotla, Ahmad Ali Khan, deployed his state forces and police to maintain peace in its borders, despite an influx of 60,000 Muslim refugees who threatened to cause disorder with the state's non-Muslim residents.[59]

The Malerkotla case study reveals the importance of a functioning administration committed to law and order in inhibiting violence. Ian Copland has revealed a very different situation in the Sikh princely states of the Punjab.[60] Attacks on Muslims were instigated by rulers of such states as Patiala. This was not only retributive violence, for the earlier Rawalpindi massacres, but was part of the so-called Sikh Plan. During the closing weeks of British rule, 'ungraded' intelligence reports were filtering through to the Punjab Governor linking the neighbouring Sikh Princely States with plans for a terror campaign in East Punjab.[61] While leading Sikh politicians[62] maintained that the Sikh Plan was a fabrication of Muslim CID officers designed to discredit the community, it is clear that the attacks on East Punjab Muslims were abetted by the rulers of the Princely States.

The violence was at its greatest in East Punjab.[63] This was not because the Sikhs were more rapacious than other communities, but because the region exhibited a fatal combination of administrative collapse in the former British areas, and of Princely rulers who far from maintaining law and order, aided and abetted attacks on the Muslim minority. These were motivated not merely by the desire to revenge the earlier Rawalpindi Massacres, but by the aspiration to forge a Sikh state. Such Princes as Yadavindra Singh of Patiala were motivated by the ambition to carve out a Sikh state in the region.[64] The rulers of the states of Faridkot and Jind had dramatically increased the size of their armed forces as the British departure grew closer.[65] They also provided weapons to the irregular Sikh armed bands (*jathas*) that were being organized in the British administered territory.[66] The Princes themselves denied that they had contacts with the *jathas*, but high-ranking court state and military officers such as Bir Davinder Singh and Colonel Bhagwan Singh of Patiala along with the chief minister of Jind were widely believed to have connived at their activities.[67] The fact cannot be denied that troops from the Princely States not only attacked the Muslim inhabitants and passing refugee trains, but joined in assaults on neighbouring districts of the former British administered Punjab. Trains coming from Ludhiana and Hissar were detained at Dhuri in the Patiala State where their passengers were systematically butchered and their possessions looted. The military and the police were involved in the violence that made it almost impossible for a Muslim to pass safely through the state.[68] They also assisted *jathas* in the systematic murder of Muslim residents. Patiala witnessed horrific communal massacres in which its ruling authorities were implicated.[69] The attack on the Muslims of Barnala, for example, in which about 3,000 Muslims were killed[70] was preceded by the enforcement of a curfew only on their community. The killings followed personal assurances from the Maharaja that the Muslim minority was safe. Its removal enabled the state to receive large numbers of incoming refugees from Pakistan. Even narrowly restrictive state-centric definitions could understand the Barnala killings as an act of genocide.

The situation in the former British administered districts is, however, problematic for many genocide scholars because of the absence of state involvement. Recent research which we have drawn on above reveals the compliance and in some cases initiative by individual functionaries. This falls short of a state policy of genocide and of the direction of all of its efforts to achieve this. Nevertheless, Huttenbach is one leading theorist who argues that civil strife can turn into genocidal conflict, 'with or without the collusion or cooperation of the instruments of the state'.[71] What is required for this to occur are 'the circumstances of political disequilibrium' and 'elements within society, harbouring genocidal intentions'.[72] The former element is self-evident. The latter requirement is more contentious because it brings us back to the argument of whether the violence was spontaneous or organized, irrational or intentional.

The spontaneity argument undermines the claim for genocidal intent. Javed Alam has put this most forcefully:

> Looking at Partition ... there is something which strikes us as a particularity. There are innumerable cases of large-scale massacres indulged in by people at a moment of a loss of judgement, of a sense of proportion, at a moment of frenzy. There is no involvement of large organizations or the state as the instrument of mass killings. You can't therefore talk of these events as a general phenomena (sic).[73]

The planning that went into the Rawalpindi Massacres and attacks on refugee specials questions Alam's interpretation. Even more important is the role of 'large organizations'. Their actions not only refute his argument, but allow the partition-related killings to be conceptualized as genocidal violence in terms of Huttenbach's interpretation. The closing decades of British rule were marked by the proliferation of uniformed organizations which were organized and drilled on paramilitary lines. These were either communal volunteer organizations such as the RSS, or the military wings of political parties, as for example, the Muslim National Guards. Their leaders professed that they were social service organizations who engaged in civil defence activities. But this could not hide the aggressive intent that lay behind the military drilling and the stockpiling of weapons. The Punjab's traditions both of army service and of urban religious tension meant that these organizations were especially active within the province. The decision in January 1947 to ban the RSS and Muslim League National Guards precipitated the civil disobedience campaign which toppled the cross-community Unionist Party. It had ruled the Punjab since 1923. The resignation of the Unionist Prime Minister Khizr Hayat Khan Tiwana was followed by the March disturbances. In such cities as Lahore and Amritsar, normal life ceased with stray stabbings, arson attacks and constant curfews. Inhabitants cowered behind the large iron gates that were erected to protect localities from assault. They divided the cities into a series of no go areas for members of rival communities.

The RSS and Muslim League National Guards thrived in such circumstances. By the beginning of June 1947, they numbered 58,000 and 39,000 volunteers, respectively. They were heavily involved in the mounting urban violence. Large Sikh *jathas* were also being formed in the countryside.[74] The *jathas* led the attacks on Muslims that ethnically cleansed them from the East Punjab. From May onwards, there had been a widespread collection of funds, manufacture and import of weapons and the establishment of an organization of 'dictators', 'company commanders' and village 'cells'. Little is known about their total numbers, the second rank of leaders or their composition, save that many ex-servicemen from both the British Indian Army and the Indian National Army were in their ranks.[75] During the final days before the publication of the Radcliffe Boundary award,[76] *jathas* commenced heavy raids on Muslim villages in 'border' areas.[77] The *jathas* were ruthlessly efficient killing machines which carefully targeted their victims.[78] They were well armed with Sten guns, rifles, pistols, spears, swords and *kirpans* (steel sword/dagger) and were well organized. The largest was around 3,000 strong.[79] They later preyed on refugee foot columns and trains. An attack on a Pakistan bound Special just outside Khalsa College, Amritsar that was marked by military precision, resulted in the massacre of over 1,000 Muslims.[80]

Can such patterns of organized violence be found outside of the Punjab in 1947? Much more research is required on the killings elsewhere in India. Suranjan Das's pioneering work on Bengal, however, points to the fact that the Great Calcutta Killing of 16–19 August 1946 was not a frenzied outbreak, but had elements of organization and purpose. The episode is significant because it marks a break with previous communal riots not only in the city, but elsewhere in North India. It commenced the spiral of killings that resulted in partition. Suranjan Das highlights the brutalizing effects of wartime inflation, unemployment and population influx into the city in the wake of the 1943 famine. He points out the 'corrupting' influence of the quartering of US troops.[81] They not only encouraged a rise in prostitution, and black marketing but sold weapons to paramilitary organizations. Das also sees the ground for the violence being prepared by the mushrooming of these bodies. Most importantly he sees the violence as occasioned not by spontaneous religious passions, as in the past, but by political parties who carefully planned the assaults.

As with any major episode of communal violence, the number of casualties and the instigators remain controversial. The figure of 4,000 deaths was officially quoted as the outcome of the three days of violence from 16 August. An English official maintained that this was 'a new order in communal rioting' and described Calcutta as a 'cross between the worst of London air raids and the Great Plague'.[82] Despite the Muslim League's denials, the outbreak was clearly linked with the celebration of Direct Action Day. Muslim processionists who had gone to the staging ground of the 150-feet high Ochterlony Monument on the *Maidan* (park) to hear the Muslim League Prime Minister Suhrawardy attacked Hindus on their way back. They were heard shouting such slogans as *'Larke Lenge Pakistan'* (We shall win Pakistan by force). Violence spread to North Calcutta when Muslim crowds tried to force Hindu shopkeepers to observe the day's strike (*hartal*) call. The circulation of pamphlets in advance of Direct Action Day made a clear connection with the use of violence and the achievement of Pakistan. One which depicted Jinnah with a sword in hand declared: 'Oh! *Kafir* (Unbeliever) your doom is not far and the general massacre will come. We shall show our glory and will have a special victory.' Another proclaimed: 'We are starting a Jehad in Your (God's) name. We promise before You that we entirely depend on you. Make us victorious over the *Kafirs*, enable us to establish the kingdom of Islam in India'.[83] Posters were also prominently displayed which declared that 16 August – Direct Action Day – would bring independence and break the 'shackles of slavery'.[84] The scene was set for violence when the Hindu Mahasabha issued its own pamphlets calling on Hindus to give a 'clear answer to this act of effrontery'. 'It is the duty of every Hindu', the pamphlet *Beware* declared, 'to carry on his normal occupation. Remember that to join the *hartal* is to support the demand for Pakistan.'[85]

While three times as much Hindu property was destroyed in arson attacks as that belonging to Muslims, the casualty figures were about equal for the two communities. The Muslim League used this to counter the claim that the Suhrawardy Government had instigated the violence. It also argued why should Calcutta, where Muslims formed only a quarter of the population, be planned as a site for violence.

Women were brutally attacked unlike in the 1918 and 1926 Calcutta riots. The other new feature was the post-riot movement of population. Around 10,000 people shifted out of the city. Within Calcutta there was a movement to Hindu or Muslim enclaves from mixed localities. This consolidation of population occurred in towns and cities across North India hit by violence in the following months. In Calcutta as in such Punjabi cities as Lahore and Amritsar, 'no-go' areas emerged, hampering everyday life for all but Europeans and Indian Christians who could still freely move around everywhere.

Yasmin Khan has examined the violence in UP as part of her research on the region's transition to independence.[86] She has revealed a similar stockpiling of weapons and establishment of paramilitary organizations as in Punjab. In UP there were around 25,000 members of the Muslim League National Guards. RSS and Hindu Mahasabha volunteers between them numbered 40,000.[87] There is also clear evidence of organization in the main episode of violence which occurred at Garhmukhteshwar on 6 November 1946, a small town in the Meerut district of western UP. The violence had begun at a fair three miles outside of the town. This annual *Kartik Purmina mela* which was encamped over an area of 12 square miles drew upwards of three quarters of a million pilgrims from the surrounding areas and as far away as Punjab. Indeed it was alleged that Jats from its Rohtak district were the main aggressors. The trouble began after an alleged insult to a Hindu woman who was watching a wall of death motorcycling display. Muslim shopkeepers were attacked at their stalls on the evening of 6 November. Official reports put the number of casualties at 46. Thus far the episode had many features of the traditional North Indian communal outbreak with the eruption of violence over a 'trivial' event. The massacre[88] of Muslims in Garhmukhteshwar the following afternoon, however, bore all the features of the transition from 'traditional' communal violence. As in Calcutta and later in Punjab, the violence spread from public arenas to private spheres, accompanied by atrocities against women, including parading them naked through the streets, forced conversions and the destruction of Muslim homes and businesses that had been singled out with chalk marks.[89]

The official report declared that the attacking crowd was 'well organised'. Other accounts[90] point to the role of RSS volunteers and ex-servicemen. Mounted horsemen directed operations. The 'mob' which destroyed the Muslim quarter of Garhmukhteshwar came equipped with petrol and other chemicals. The assailants went about their deadly and brutal task without any check from the police or the military. According to the report on the disturbances by the former Indian National Army hero, Major General Shah Nawaz Khan, 'Had the police acted more vigorously and promptly, much of the destruction to life and property could have been prevented.'[91]

The events at Garhmukhteshwar were a powerful indictment of the Congress UP government. Significantly, it took a much tighter grip on violence after this tragedy. Yasmin Khan argues that the measures it introduced were an important factor in preventing violence in August 1947 spilling over from Punjab, especially after the arrival of around half a million refugees. An emergency ordinance was introduced in May 1947. This sanctioned a police shoot to kill policy for curfew breakers. Severe punishments were introduced for acts of forced conversion and marriage. In the Meerut division, tanks were even used against rioters in the absence of police reinforcements.[92]

Conclusion

There is growing evidence of the involvement of paramilitary organizations in the violence which swept parts of North India in 1946—7. Muslim war bands, Sikh *jathas* and the RSS were well armed and organized. Their military preparedness was bolstered by the presence of ex-servicemen. They carefully selected their targets. Violence was purposeful rather than the result of temporary acts of madness. On occasion it was aided and abetted by police and officials within former British India and by state troops and members of the *darbar* (court) of Princely States.

The use of the term genocide, nevertheless, remains both controversial and sensitive with respect to the partition violence. The state's role remains more ambiguous than in other historical situations of genocide. Indeed it is because many definitions assume that the state is integral to genocide that the partition violence is excluded in many analyses of case studies. Nevertheless the UN Convention on the Prevention and the Punishment of Genocide which was adopted by the General Assembly on 9 December 1948 does not mention[93] that it must be committed by the state.[94]

There is also the question of one-sidedness which is raised in the definitions favoured by such authors as Chalk and Jonassohn.[95] The killings in North India in 1947 were not one-sided, as Paul Brass's concept of 'retributive genocide' reminds us. The patterns of violence were variegated with well-planned genocidal assaults occurring alongside opportunistic killings motivated by temporary lust for loot and women. It would be historically unsophisticated to pigeonhole them under the generic term of genocide. Ian Copland, for example, while acknowledging the planning and purpose behind much of the violence in the East Punjab Princely States also identifies a 'populist violence' unleashed by 'group-psychosis reminiscent of the "great fear" which had gripped rural France in 1789'.[96] Robert Melson's concept of partial genocide may be useful. He defines this as 'mass murder in order to coerce and to alter the identity and politics of the group, not to destroy it'.[97] In this sense, the partition-related violence was a partial rather than a total genocide as there was no attempt even in East Punjab to eliminate the entire population, although violence did cause large-scale flight.

The historiographical trend is in favour of more locality-based studies of partition and its aftermath. Documentary evidence is likely to be insufficient to conclusively link the perpetrators of violence with known politicians, princes and parties. Moreover, such studies may throw up a bewildering array of motives and understandings for participants in the same outrage. Greater knowledge could thus question, as well strengthen, the current tendency to place the events of 1947 more firmly in the field of genocide studies than hitherto. Perhaps even more importantly, work produced on the partition-related violence may contribute to the ongoing debates concerning the definition of genocide.

Notes

1. For a discussion see, G. Pandey, *Remembering Partition: Violence, Nationalism and History in India* (Cambridge: Cambridge University Press, 2001), p. 88ff.
2. See P. Moon, *Divide and Quit: An Eyewitness Account of the Partition of India* (New Delhi: Oxford University Press, 1998).
3. See, P. French, *Liberty or Death: India's Journey to Independence and Division* (London: Harper Collins, 1967).
4. See A. Major, 'The "Chief Sufferers": Abduction of Women During the Partition of the Punjab', in *Freedom, Trauma, Continuities: Northern India and Independence*, eds, D. A. Low and H. Brasted (New Delhi: Sage, 1998), pp. 57–73.
5. See R. Menon and K. Bhasin, *Borders and Boundaries: Women in India's Partition* (New Delhi: Kali for Women, 1998).
6. H. V. Hodson's, *The Great Divide: Britain–India–Pakistan* (London: Hutchinson, 1969) remains a classic 'high politics' account from the British perspective. Its Indian counterpart is V. P. Menon, *The Transfer of Power in India* (London: Longmans, 1957). Ayesha Jalal produced a famous revisionist approach which question Jinnah's motives in raising the Pakistan demand, *The Sole Spokesman: Jinnah, the Muslim League and the Demand for Pakistan* (Cambridge: Cambridge University Press, 1985). A recent approach is S. Mahajan, *Independence and Partition: The Erosion of Colonial Power in India* (New Delhi: Sage, 2000).
7. S. H. Manto's classic short stories on Partition have become increasingly available to a wider audience as a result of their translation from Urdu. See S. H. Manto, *Mottled Dawn: Fifty Sketches and Stories of Partition*, trans. K. Hasan (New Delhi: Penguin, 1997).
8. The Hindu nationalist movement has used a selective replaying of the bitter memories of Partition to both fix a stereotype of the Muslim 'aggressor' and to attack the Congress's secular inheritance. Refugees from India have constructed a *mohajir* political identity in part around the sacrifices the community made for the creation of Pakistan. The exaggerated claim has been made that 2,000,000 *mohajirs* died in its achievement. See, MQM, *Background of the Mohajir Nation and a Brief History of the MQM* (London: MQM, n.d.,) p. 1.
9. In addition to Menon and Bhasin's more academic work, *Borders and Boundaries*, Urvashi Butalia produced the best seller, *The Other Side of Silence: Voices from the Partition of India* (New Delhi: Penguin Books, 1998).
10. See A. B. Hansen, *Partition and Genocide: Manifestation of Violence in Punjab 1937–1947* (New Delhi: India Research Press, 2002); P. Brass, 'The Partition of India and Retributive Genocide in the Punjab 1946–47: Means, Methods and Purposes', *Journal of Genocide Research*, 5, 1 (2003), 71–101; I. Ahmed, 'Forced Migration and Ethnic Cleansing in Lahore in 1947: Some First Person Accounts', in *People on the Move: Punjabi Colonial and Post-Colonial Migration*, eds, I. Talbot and S. Thandi (Karachi: Oxford University Press, 2004), p. 99.

11. See O. Bartov and P. Mack, eds, *In God's Name: Genocide and Religion in the Twentieth Century* (New York: Berghahn Books, 2001). Its contributions focus on the Holocaust, the 1915 Armenian Massacres, the 1994 Rwanda genocide and the Serbian ethnic cleansing and genocidal acts in Bosnia.
12. Pandey, *Remembering Partition*, p. 45.
13. Ibid., p. 46.
14. See G. Le Bon, *The Crowd: A Study of the Popular Mind* (New York: The Viking Press, 1960).
15. Cited in Pandey, *Remembering Partition*, p. 58.
16. The aftermath of the so-called Delhi riots encouraged Urvashi Butalia to collect oral accounts of the partition-related violence because she saw parallels between them.
17. See S. Varadarajan, *Gujarat: The Making of a Tragedy* (New Delhi: Penguin, 2002).
18. See P. Brass, *The Production of Hindu–Muslim Violence in Contemporary India* (Seattle: University of Washington Press, 2003).
19. See S. Gurbachan Singh Talib, *Muslim League Attack on Sikhs and Hindus in the Punjab 1947* (Amritsar: Shiromani Prabhandak Committee, 1950); G. D. Khosla, *Stern Reckoning: A Survey of Events leading up to and Following the Partition of India* (New Delhi: Oxford University Press, 1989).
20. The SGPC is the Sikh organization which controls the Sikh shrines and gurdwaras.
21. Talib, *Muslim League Attack*, p. 144. It terms Amritsar as the theatre no. 1 in the Muslim League War on the Hindus and Sikhs of the Punjab. 'The Muslim National Guards Headquarters were shifted from Lahore to Amritsar in March', the publication declares, 'as Amritsar was the most important front on which the League had to fight' (p. 141).
22. Ibid., pp. 139–40.
23. Ibid., pp. 143, 159, 163.
24. Ibid., p. 165. According to the report, Hindus and Sikhs formed three-quarters of the victims in the early stages of the violence. See pp. 139–66.
25. K. Iftikhar, *Jab Amritsar jal raha tha* (Lahore, pub. unknown, 1991).
26. V. N. Datta, the leading Indian historian and expert on Amritsar, has criticized the work for being 'one-sided, partial and perverse'. He points out that there is no reference to the protection afforded to Muslims at personal risk by such prominent citizens as Sir Buta Singh, Sohan Singh Josh, Dr Baldev Singh, Pandit Amar Nath Vidyalanker, Sant Ram Seth, Brahm Nath Data, Qasir, G. R. Sethi and Bhai Jodh Singh among many others. V. N. Datta, 'Amritsar: When Riots Shattered a Heritage,' *Sunday Tribune* (Chandigarh), 26 April 1998.
27. An Akali is a devotee of Akal (the Timeless One). In the eighteenth and nineteenth centuries it designated a warrior. In the twentieth century it signified a member of the Akali Dal, the prominent Sikh political party.
28. Iftikhar, *Jab Amritsar jal raha tha*, ch. 3.
29. This was published by the National Documentation of the Pakistan Government in the volume *The Journey to Pakistan. A Documentation on Refugees of 1947* (Islamabad, 1993), pp. 139–53.
30. Ibid., p.140.
31. See D. L. Horowitz, *The Deadly Ethnic Riot* (Berkeley, CA: University of California Press, 2001), p. 13.
32. It was suggested at an All-Pakistan Refugees Convention held in Lahore on 10 March that a three-minute silence should be observed on every Independence Day celebration. *Dawn* (Karachi), 12 March 1956.
33. See the discussion in Hansen, *Partition and Genocide*, p. 26 &ff.

34. M. Levene, 'Is the Holocaust Simply Another Example of Genocide?', *Patterns of Prejudice*, 28, 2 (1994), 4–5.
35. H. R. Huttenbach, 'Locating the Holocaust on the Genocide Spectrum. Towards a Methodology of Definition and Categorization', *Holocaust and Genocide Studies*, 3, 3 (1988), 296.
36. J. Francisco, 'In the Heat of Fratricide: The Literature of India's Partition Burning Freshly', in *Inventing Boundaries: Gender, Politics and the Partition of India*, ed. M. Hasan (New Delhi: Oxford University Press, 2000), p. 372.
37. Melson has maintained that genocides occur when state and society are in crisis. Mark Levene has developed the concept of 'zones of genocide'. They are in existence when competing national discourses clash in a context in which outside pressures impede traditional accomodationist mechanisms in multi-ethnic societies. R. Melson, *Revolution and Genocide: The Origins of the Armenian Genocide and the Holocaust* (Chicago, IL: University of Chicago Press, 1992), pp. 15–17; M. Levene, 'Creating a Modern "Zone of Genocide": The Impact of Nation and State Formation on Eastern Anatolia, 1878–1923', *Holocaust and Genocide Studies*, 12, 3 (1998), 418ff.
38. The 'consensual' violence of traditional communal conflict possessed elements of the feud and was about altering the balance of local hierarchies of power. See, for example, V. Das and A. Nandy, 'Violence, Victimhood and the language of Silence', in *The Word and the World: Fantasy, Symbol and Record*, ed. V. Das (New Delhi: Sage, 1986), pp. 177–90. The 1947 violence in contrast was designed to prevent continued interaction between communities and contained genocidal intentions regarding the obliteration of the presence of the 'other'.
39. Hansen, *Partition and Genocide*, p. 197.
40. See, for example, P. Virdee, 'Partition and Locality: Case Studies of the Impact of Partition and its Aftermath in the Punjab region 1947–61' (PhD dissertation, Coventry University, 2005); I. Talbot, *Divided Cities: Lahore, Amritsar and the Partition of India* (Karachi: Oxford University Press, 2006).
41. S. Aiyar, '"August Anarchy": The Partition Massacres in Punjab, 1947', in *Freedom, Trauma, Continuities*, eds. Low and Brasted, p. 24.
42. Ibid., pp. 26–7.
43. Horowitz has declared, for example, that perpetrators of violence are impelled not by broader aims, so much as by the desire to inflict degradation and death. 'They kill members of other groups and commit atrocities upon them, angrily yet playfully ... when and where it is reasonably safe to do the killing. None of this evidences much of a plan beyond killing.' Horowitz, *The Deadly Ethnic Riot*, p. 423.
44. Ibid., p. 124.
45. For a detailed first-hand account, see, C. Dass Dutt, *The Punjab Riots and Their Lessons*, 30 April 1947. S. P. Mukherjee Papers IV File 17, Nehru Memorial Museum and Library (NMML).
46. Report on the Recent Disturbances in the Punjab (March–April 1947) AICC File No. G-10/1947 NMML.
47. B. Sahni, *Tamas* (New Delhi: Penguin, 1990), p. 199ff.
48. 1947 Tours – Papers Regarding President, General Secretary and Honorary Secretary's Tours to Punjab. Akhil Bharat Hindu Mahasabha Papers C-154 NMML.
49. Report on the Disturbances in the Punjab (March–April 1947) AICC File No. G-10/1947 NMML.
50. Ibid.
51. K. N. Panikkar, 'The Agony of Gujarat', in *The Gujarat Carnage*, ed. A. A. Engineer (New Delhi: Orient Longman, 2003), p. 93.

52. U. Mehta, 'The Gujarat Genocide: A Sociological Appraisal' in ibid., p. 191.
53. Horowitz, *The Deadly Ethnic Riot*, pp. 257–8, 266.
54. The British instituted an enquiry into the worst cases of official negligence and threatened to relieve all those who were found guilty of their titles and grants of government land. This was an empty threat, however, in the light of their impending departure. See *Civil and Military Gazette* (Lahore) 16 March 1947.
55. R. Zafar (compiler), *Disturbances in the Punjab 1947* (Islamabad: National Documentation Centre, 1995), p. 410.
56. Ibid., p. 407.
57. Report on the Recent Disturbances in the Punjab (March–April 1947) AICC File no. G-10/1947 NMML.
58. Ibid.
59. Virdee also reflects on the way in which social disapproval could inhibit violence. The state had a long tradition of communal harmony that was in part the result of the tradition of Guru Gobind Singh's blessing on its rulers following Sher Mohammad Khan's *haa da naara* or protest at the bricking alive of his two younger sons, Fateh Singh and Zorawar Singh in 1705. Virdee, 'Partition and Locality', p. 103ff.
60. I. Copland, 'The Master and the Maharajas: The Sikh Princes and the East Punjab Massacres of 1947', *Modern Asian Studies*, 36, 3 (2002), 657–704.
61. Abott to Brockman n.d. Ungraded Intelligence Report, R/3/1/145 India Office Records (IOR).
62. See, for example, Statement of Baldev Singh on Present Situation, n.d., R/3/1/174 IOR.
63. British observers commented that refugees fleeing from Jullundur and Ludhiana experienced, 'far worse treatment than anything ... in Montgomery and Lahore'. Report of Mr Hadow's Tour of Jullundur, Hoshiarpur, Ludhiana and Ferozepore Districts. 7 January 1948. East Punjab Affairs 1947–50. G2275/80 Do. 35,3181, Dominions Office and Commonwealth Relations Office PRO.
64. Copland, 'The Master and the Maharajas', 678. Yadavindra Singh claimed he had no part in the killings which ethnically cleansed Muslims from his state. He was, it is true, residing at his summer palace at Chail at the time, but was in telegraphic communication with ministers. It is also true that from the middle of September 1947 he ordered the district *nazims* to oversee the safety of Muslim refugees, but it could be argued that by this time, the killings and lootings had already spent their course and Muslims had almost disappeared not only from his state, but throughout the East Punjab.
65. Ibid., p. 681.
66. Ibid., p. 680.
67. Ibid., p. 693. Copland in fact cites evidence that the rulers of Kapurthala and Faridkot had direct contact with the *jathas*.
68. Ibid., p. 401.
69. State troops in Patiala regularly preyed on refugee trains passing through from Delhi to Lahore. They murdered 450 Muslim railway employees and their families at Bathinda. In Barnala, 3,000 Muslims were killed by the state military and the police. Mudie Papers Mss. Eur.F. 164 IOR. For a measured analysis of the role of the Sikh Princes in the East Punjab massacres see Copland, 'The Master and the Maharajas'.
70. Copland, 'The Master and the Maharajas', p. 409.
71. Huttenbach, 'Locating the Holocaust', 296.
72. Ibid.

73. Cited in Pandey, *Remembering Partition*, p. 58.
74. Punjab FR for the second half of May 1947, L/P&J/5/250 IOR.
75. See Copland, 'The Master and the Maharajas' for a discussion of the scanty data that does exist.
76. This demarcated the new international border in the Punjab region. Its judgments were controversially delayed until after the British transfer of power.
77. Punjab FR 30 July 1947; 13 August 1947. L/P&J/5/250 IOR.
78. Copland, 'The Master and the Maharajas', 687.
79. Punjab FR 30 July 1947; 13 August 1947 L/P&j/5/250 IOR.
80. *Civil and Military Gazette* (Lahore) 19 September 1947.
81. S. Das, *Communal Riots in Bengal 1905–1947* (Delhi: Oxford University Press, 1991), pp. 162, 180. Weapons had been purchased by rich Marwari businessmen.
82. Ibid., p. 171.
83. Ibid., p. 168.
84. Ibid., p.169.
85. Ibid.
86. Y. Khan, 'India Divided: The Impact of Partition on Indian State and Society: The Case of Uttar Pradesh, 1946–52' (DPhil dissertation, University of Oxford, 2004). The United Provinces were renamed as Uttar Pradesh in 1950.
87. Note on Volunteer Organizations in UP, 9 June 1947. IOR, L/PJ/5/276.
88. As in all communal violence, casualty figures are notoriously unreliable. The provincial government put the figure at around 200, the Muslim League reckoned on 2,000. This number was also cited by Lieutenant General Francis Tuker in his memoir, *While Memory Serves: The Last Two Years of British Rule in India* (London: Cassell, 1950), p. 200.
89. See ch. 5 of Pandey, *Remembering Partition*.
90. Ibid., for an incisive analysis of the different uses made of the violence in nationalist, Muslim League, colonial and communist accounts.
91. Ibid., p. 98.
92. Y. Khan, 'Out of Control? Partition Violence and the State in Uttar Pradesh', in *The Deadly Embrace: Religion, Politics and Violence in the Indian Subcontinent 1947–2002*, ed. I. Talbot (Karachi: Oxford University Press, 2006), p. 50.
93. The text of the convention is reproduced in many places. See, for example, R. Gellately and B. Kiernan, eds, *The Specter of Genocide: Mass Murder in Historical Perspective* (Cambridge: Cambridge University Press, 2003), pp. 381–4. See especially Article IV.
94. The Resolution entered into force on 12 January 1951.
95. See Frank Chalk and Kurt Jonassohn, *The History and Sociology of Genocide: Analyses and Case Studies* (New Haven, CT: Yale University Press, 1990).
96. Copland, 'The Master and the Maharajas', 686.
97. See Melson, Revolution and Genocide.

17

Mao's China: The Worst Non-Genocidal Regime?

Jean-Louis Margolin

China under Mao Zedong, between 1949 and 1976, seems to offer all the necessary ingredients for a genocidal configuration. The number of unnatural deaths is staggering: most probably somewhere between 44 and 72 million, if one includes the mass starvation triggered by a ruthlessly utopian Great Leap Forward,[1] thus making Mao Zedong – in absolute figures – a bigger mass murderer than Hitler or Stalin.[2] Those deaths (with the possible exception of the Great Leap ones – see below) were not in any way the products of unexpected circumstances, but of a deliberate, carefully planned murderous project. The man who conceived, launched and closely scrutinized that project, Mao Zedong (1893–1976), amply possessed the megalomania, the cruelty, the pitilessness and the contempt for mankind that make good genocidal masterminds. The victims, generally speaking, belonged (or were supposed to belong) to specific societal groups, painstakingly defined and labelled, even if the primarily targeted groups changed from time to time, generally in an incremental way: new victims were targeted, but the old ones were not left aside. The eliminationist discourse was ubiquitous, especially during the numerous 'mass campaigns', and included the freak accusations, animal analogies and calls for blood letting that constitute the fare of any good *génocidaire*. Finally, the murderous process extended over a huge space and time span, without any significant period of respite, or area of refuge.

Nevertheless these mind-boggling crimes cannot be considered as genocide – except maybe in Tibet, where the fragility of a small population and the national oppression by the Han majority government compounded general policies not radically different from those inflicted on China proper.[3] The extermination of the targeted groups, indeed, was never complete; in the most severe cases – the rural landlords, the former Guomindang cadres – human losses could be in the range of 20–30 per cent (precise evaluations are sorely lacking), but probably no more.[4] Furthermore, the killings seldom extended to family members, and even less frequently to children, although they were severely victimized and discriminated against.[5] There were three main reasons for this behaviour. First, the limits of social or political groups are much more elusive and fluctuating than the limits of ethnic or religious groups.[6] In Pol Pot's Cambodia, this led to a constant widening of the targeted groups, ultimately encompassing most of the population – hence the unprecedented death rates, at least for the communist world. But, in China, it worked most of the time the other way around: the consciousness of the risk of a 'chain reaction' of murders led to periodical 'coolings' of the ever-present temptation to eliminate physically, once and for all, the 'class enemies'. Hence, as in Stalin's USSR, the huge temporal variations in the sinusoid of political crimes: most of them actually took place over a small number of years, separated by moments of relative *détente*.

Second, Mao's regime possessed an unparalleled efficiency at tightly controlling the huge population of China. Thus its victims could be trampled over again and again, with no possibility to hide, to flee and, even less, to resist. There was no obvious drawback or danger at sparing these wretched lives. They could be put to better use as a pool of defenceless scapegoats for the future 'hate' campaigns.[7] The far less efficient Khmer Rouge regime felt too insecure to act that way: its only way to terrorize the population was to kill, on a grand scale. Thirdly, China was too poor in cadres and experts, and too ambitious on the world stage not to notice that the targeted groups included many precious talents. Closely watched, periodically humiliated, they could still contribute to the glory of the regime. The technique was almost universally used: even the highest dignitaries – Mao excepted – had occasionally to deliver abject autocriticisms in front of their peers.[8] One should not forget that Mao's China has been permanently confronted with rabid external adversaries: the US, the USSR since 1960, and a Chiang Kai-shek dreaming of revenge in Taiwan. The will to survive a possible great war imposed limitations to the internal turmoil. Stalin, in face of the German invasion, calmed down the political repression, for some years. Pol Pot, unwilling or unable to moderate the killing frenzy, lost Cambodia in two weeks to the Vietnamese. Mao, significantly, left the Liberation Army, and even more the nuclear weapons industry, out of the reach of the Red Guards.

Thus political violence under Mao Zedong was almost constantly regulated and limited to specific groups, with precise goals. Humiliation, submission and terror, in most cases, were preferred to a sheer massacre. There was no strict equivalent in Beijing to the Moscow trials – but, in relative as well as in absolute numbers, communist China probably saw the most widespread and systematic use of violence in the world's history. It was in no way something accidental, or just one aspect of Mao's use of power. No, violence was the very engine of political, social and economic transformation – and that was in no sense hidden. Mao glorified and sanctified violence. And, on that point, he did exactly what he said, with a tremendous energy. This extreme case in modern history, probably outdone only by the Khmer Rouge – those faithful disciples of the Great Helmsman – should now be investigated in some detail.

Mao, a monster?

As for Stalin or Hitler, there is a large consensus on the decisive part played by the Leader in the explosion of violence he presided over. And as in Stalin's case, once Mao was dead, his murderous ways were abandoned once and for all, and most political prisoners were freed in less than three years. Several thorough biographical works agree in depicting a strange, unpredictable, deeply amoral character. Whatever its shortcomings on Mao's political face, the recent portrait drawn by Jung Chang and Jon Halliday seems well documented and convincing on his private life.[9] On most points, it confirms and completes the momentous narrative made by Mao's private doctor.[10] All through his life, Mao appears to have been a hedonist, full of his own importance, cynical and vindictive. His behaviour with his relatives and his closest political associates was especially sinister: he combined a lack of concern for their sufferings with a manipulative use of their own feelings, and occasionally a deep cruelty. In his later years, his strongest family tie appears to have been for his mischievous and ruthless nephew, arrested along with his widow, just a few weeks after his death. His companions in revolution were treated as servants, set up against each other, and periodically humiliated – including the brilliant but slavish Prime Minister Zhou Enlai, occasionally reminded of (probably fake) 1932 letters repudiating communism. Those who dared to criticize Mao's policies were invariably crushed to pieces, stripped of their titles, expelled from the Communist party, sometimes persecuted till their death. That was the fate of the prestigious commander of the Chinese 'volunteers' in Korea, Marshall Peng Dehuai, and of the President of the Republic and one time heir apparent, Liu Shaoqi. Between 1949 and 1972, Mao never bothered to attend the burial ceremony of an official.

Dr Li's book unveiled old Mao's growing taste for young, ecstatic army dancing girls or nurses, who seldom dared to say no. Chang and Halliday mention the building for him, all over China, of about 50 bunker-like big residences, complete with swimming pools (he loved swimming); they had to be permanently maintained, as the Chairman could show up without advance warning (both the central and local authorities were frequently ignorant of his whereabouts).[11] Mao only respected the most cynical political figures: the brutal First Emperor (3rd century B.C.), famous for burying alive 460 literati and for ordering the burning of most books; Napoleon, among all Western historical figures; his own long-time enemy Chiang Kai-shek (he privately mourned him in

1975); or Richard Nixon, still welcomed in China as a head of state, after his ignominious 1974 resignation.[12]

The recent historiography (including some memoirs) has exploded huge chunks of Mao's carefully established legend.[13] His initial power base was built in alliance with rural bandits, who inspired some of his methods. He used his personal relationship with the Soviets several times to push aside his adversaries in the party. The Long March was precipitated by his amazingly harsh purges in the main red zone. During most of the Sino-Japanese war, Mao did his utmost to make the Nationalists and the Imperial army weaken each other, while preserving his best troops for the subsequent civil war. When in power, his main goal was to make China reach the status of superpower, and replace the USSR as the Mecca of international revolution, at whatever cost for his own people.[14]

Mao did constantly show an uncommon degree of cynicism, an extreme lack of compassion, a craving for radical solutions. But what made him much more obnoxious than a trivial dictator was his utopianism. Mao sincerely believed in the desirability of upturning the world, for which he was ready to risk everything: the Great Leap or the Cultural Revolution cannot find any other coherent explanation (much simpler ways to industrialize China or to eliminate his adversaries inside the Party did exist). And he came progressively to assimilate his personal destiny with the arrival on earth of the communist utopia. Hence his supreme confidence in his righteousness and his own competence, and his uncompromising ruthlessness with everything and everybody that dared to stand in his way – the way of historical progress, even more than the way of the restoration of China's primacy, as nationalism was for Mao a means more than the real goal.[15] In his very first political writing (he was 23), strong strains of social Darwinism, of nihilism and even more of Nietzscheanism may be distinguished, alongside more trivial statements of love for humanity. He read Marx through Lenin, and interpreted the founding fathers as apologists of radical voluntarism: action (correctly directed) was everything, and made everything possible.

Whatever the considerable fluctuations of his thinking, along a political career extending over six decades, five characteristics are strikingly permanent. The first one is an utter contempt for established institutions and, more generally, for any structured society. That contempt includes the communist party and state themselves, once they are established in power. Such feeling is quite common among twentieth-century revolutionaries: Lenin or Stalin spent their time blaming the deep shortcomings of their own state apparatus, and they purged it liberally. But Mao was the only one who dared launch a revolutionary movement against his very own, slavishly faithful bureaucracy. The second characteristic is a taste for destruction, more common among fringe extremists than among heavyweight and seasoned politicians. That could explain the overuse of humiliation and cruelty as a principle of good government (including *vis-à-vis* his closest companions in politics), the 'bandit mentality' occasionally claimed by Mao himself,[16] and his assumed demolition of the heritage of old China.

The third feature is a deeply ingrained amoralism – very obvious in his private life – that goes along with the idea that nothing is unreachable to a strong will. This could constitute an appreciable quality in political struggle or even management, but with the reservation of being counterbalanced by the consciousness of one's own limitations – that was hardly the case for Mao. Hence several terribly devastating adventures, which never disturbed the Chairman's sleep; but could have destroyed his regime. The fourth characteristic is a fundamentally hierarchical vision of society that could surprise those who assume that communism equals egalitarianism. Unification and homogenization of the society were actual aims. But they cannot be separated from the radical exclusion of the 'unredeemables', from the establishment of widely differing status groups, according to their 'class origins', that from the late 1950s were constituted in closed castes, and from the consolidation into absolute power of a small revolutionary elite. Its submissiveness was ensured by Mao's constant, unpredictable redrawing of its hierarchy – even if one was as seldom irrevocably excluded from the elite as promoted into it. Personally, Mao did not hide his contempt for the weak – including the war victims of the Japanese: he never had a word for the victims of the 1937 Nanjing massacre. The fifth and last characteristic is the central importance of the revolutionary party – something trivial for a Communist – but a party conceived as a secret society (its functioning was more and more autocratic), and as an irreplaceable instrument for those at its head. The party was the only fountain of legitimacy, and its cadres (picked up and disposed of at will by the Leader) were stimulated into substituting themselves for the supposedly defective state structures.

Sociology or ideology?

What was the prime mover of mass violence in communist China? The official interpretation of the Chinese revolution, based on class struggle, has been adopted, with some reservations, by most mainstream historians until the 1970s.[17] As in the pre-1917 Russian empire, hatred had accumulated against the landlords and the capitalists, and against the corrupt and repressive regime that supported them. The originality of the Chinese process was distinguished in the central role of the peasantry, in contrast with the centrality of the urban working class in Russian revolution. Or, more precisely, much ado was made of Mao's oft-mentioned pretension to make China 'walk on two legs' – a rural as well as an urban one. Mao's specific contribution to Marxism-Leninism was generally recognized in the successful tapping of peasants' revolutionary energy. The enormous amount of violence that went along with the revolution was logically connected with the assumed hatred of the miserable masses for their social and political oppressors.

The problem was that reality was only remotely connected with that fairy tale. Mao actually felt utter contempt for the backward and 'materialistic' farmers, and he never hesitated pressuring them to the limit for his lofty goals: accelerated heavy industrialization (the true aim of the Great Leap Forward) or weapons building (including nuclear armament, Mao's constant obsession in the 1950s and early 1960s, according to Chang and Halliday).[18] The first rural basis for communism in rural areas consisted not of poor or lower-medium peasants, contrary to the official version, but of two widely differing groups: fractions of the rural elite, destabilized by the persistent lack of a legitimate central authority, that had been compounded from 1937 by the turmoil triggered by the Japanese invasion; and elements of the 'lumpenproletariat' – bandits, stragglers, prostitutes and impoverished artists – hoping for personal emancipation.[19] The adhesion to communism, especially among the gentry, was based on local power equilibrium, or on the protection offered by the Liberation Army against the ruthless pro-Japanese or pro-Guomindang militias, much more than on class struggle, or even on nationalism.[20] Later on, during or slightly after the civil war (1946–9), the mass of the peasantry was won over, less through the tapping of spontaneous class struggle (as in 1917 Russia) than through a thorough infiltration by professional revolutionaries, through months of careful manipulation of local antagonisms, leading to theatrical, well-rehearsed 'bitterness trials' of the landlords and (sometimes) richer peasants, that had to be concluded by one or several death sentences. The goal was the creation between the villagers of a kind of 'blood bond', compelling them to assume collectively the pre-ordained killings. But they had also to be impressed with the party's paramountcy: the farmers were usually told whom to hate and denounce; and the 'criminals' were usually not killed on the spot, but taken away by the Red soldiers, to be dealt with elsewhere. Even somebody initially as well disposed towards Chinese communism as Mark Selden had to acknowledge that the party's strong rural basis had been acquired and strengthened through political manipulation and violence.[21]

Sociology – albeit not a very Marxist one – may, nevertheless, explain one part of the Cultural Revolution's violence, at least during its first two years (1966–8), marked by a dose of spontaneity among the activists. All accounts of the period underline the deep divisions among the Red Guards, especially between the 'Conservatives' – connected with the party-state regular apparatus – and the 'Rebels', enthralled by Mao's 'Rebellion is always right' motto, and sometimes connected with his personal gang. Both wings used the same political language, and largely similar terrorist methods against their real or supposed adversaries. Most of the beatings and humiliations of intellectuals (including the humblest teachers), so characteristic of the first few months of the movement, seem to have been accomplished by the supposedly 'moderate' Conservatives. Why were these groups so hateful of each other, to the point of waging devastating local wars? Jonathan Unger incriminates the rapid succession of contradictory school reforms between 1962 and 1965.[22] Just after the failure of the Great Leap Forward, Liu Shaoqi initiated some détente all over Chinese society: the children of the 'black' former upper and middle classes were re-admitted in significant numbers in the elite schools, and succeeded far better than the 'red' new cadres' children. But, in 1964, the Socialist Education Movement, ironically placed under the aegis of the same Liu Shaoqi, reduced the 'Blacks' intake to some 10 per cent of the freshmen. Then, in 1965, a degree of liberalization was once again introduced. Consequently, all students felt highly strained, successive classes had widely differing composition, and the antagonism between Reds and Blacks reached new heights. In factories, a bit on the same pattern, the majority, composed of non-permanent, unskilled workers could only feel severely discriminated: the permanent workers were the only ones to be able to unionize (with lot of perks associated: free medicine, children's care and accommodation) and to be protected against dismissal; they were much better paid. The first group, quite logically, joined the Rebels when Mao allowed them to do so (December 1966), while the second one leaned with its Conservative bosses and political patrons.[23] Among the cadres, the main divide often passed between the privileged 'red' administrative cadres and the frequently 'black' technical cadres, better skilled but always suspected of 'bourgeois expertise'; the latter rallied the Rebels.[24]

Sociology of the organizations illuminates another major factor of violence. The Cultural Revolution 'struggle between two lines' at the top may be interpreted as an attempt by Mao's central apparatus to domesticate the powerful local/regional party organizations that had played an essential role before 1949 in the winning over of the rural masses, and that in that way had built their own power bases.[25] Mao extensively used the most centralized body in China – the People's Liberation Army (PLA), controlled by Lin Biao – to replace the cadres, already greatly weakened by the Red Guards' persecutions. For a few years (1968–71), China was technically a military dictatorship, army officers filling more than a third of the party's Central Committee as well as, even more importantly, some 70 per cent of chairs of the provincial Revolutionary Committees.[26] Simultaneously, the civilian bureaucracy was greatly thinned, many government bodies (both provincial and central) being simply dissolved. The redundant cadres and civil servants were sent by the millions to country farms (the infamous 'May 7th Schools'), in a semi-penitentiary atmosphere, and initially with dim hopes of being readmitted one day inside the cities.[27] The only bodies that grew (sometimes greatly) in size were police, intelligence and propaganda, at least when they were directly subservient to Mao. Some groups of loyal 'Rebels' were increasingly used as a kind of auxiliary (and ruthless) police force, with their own more or less secret jails.[28] Ultimately, the paranoid Mao frowned over the excessive importance assumed by the PLA, and an extensive purge was undertaken, starting with the army boss and designated heir, Lin Biao, who disturbed in September 1971 the Chairman's game by not having the grace to commit suicide or to accept a lifelong exile in an obscure village.

Micro-sociology may be invoked to explain one part of the Red Guard violence.[29] As there was no procedure of conciliation, each faction, for its own security, tried to eliminate its competitors, politically or even physically. Preemptive attacks became more and more widespread – hence an amazing instability: in some cities, there was one 'seizure of power' per month in 1967 and early 1968, with an increasing use of firearms.[30] Necessity makes law: most Red Guards were very young, and had no military training; therefore, they turned increasingly to unprincipled street gangs and brawlers. Some youngsters were even paid to kill, the rates varying according to the importance of the victim.[31]

But, by and large, ideology was a much more decisive engine of terror than sociology.[32] Whatever the ordeal of the Cultural Revolution, more regular forms of repression in the 1950s caused at least as many deaths or long-term detentions.[33] Even during the more spontaneous violent outbursts of the late 1960s, the most heinous crimes were those of 'revisionism' and 'counter-revolution'. So-called bourgeois were damned, but always as 'reactionaries'. Actually, sociological qualifications ('landlord', 'rich peasant' and 'capitalist') became first and foremost insults to the enemy, the symbols not of a position in society, but of an evil nature, of a supposed hatred for communism and Mao Zedong – hence the strange hereditary transmission of those labels, whatever the reality of an individual's societal condition (see under). But what were the origins and characteristics of that murderous ideology?

The Bolshevik heritage and the constitution of an original repressive model

Anybody familiar with Soviet communism will easily spot strong similarities in Chinese communism, from the strict party hierarchy to the economic programme, based in both cases on an obsession with heavy industry, and especially with steel, elevated to the rank of a myth.[34] The contrary would be surprising, as the close connections between the two parties are now well explored.[35] China in the 1950s craved everything Soviet: all students had to learn Russian, Russian novels and films were everybody's favourite, and an often-repeated slogan was 'The Soviet Union's present shows us China's future'.[36] The USSR was nicknamed 'the Elder Brother', and everybody publicly had to show grief when Stalin died in 1953. Regarding violence, the Soviet model is obvious in three fields at least. First, Mao adhered enthusiastically to Stalin's theory of 'the accentuation of class struggle during the period of Socialist construction'. It was converted into his 'Never forget class struggle', that was perhaps Mao's most repeated sentence. Like in Russia, it was regarded as a Darwinian (more than Marxian) fight to the death,[37] the defeated classes having to be utterly destroyed, by whatever means deemed necessary, without any possibility of a compromise: a 'them or us' mentality that was to contaminate all kinds of political contests until Mao's demise. Hence the accusation made systematically against the opponent of being a 'landlord' or a 'capitalist roader': any degree of violence was then admissible, as there was an 'antagonistic contradiction', to keep up with Maoist jargon. Second – and consequently – any opposition was criminalized, while actual criminals could be deemed to be 'counter-revolutionaries', as they had 'shown their hatred' against the rule of the people's government, or attacked socialist property. Third, important repressive techniques were borrowed from Russia: the 'political campaigns' (actually huge purges), the labour camp archipelago[38] and the tight network of a secret police supported by innumerable informers, whose boss could occasionally become a central political figure (Beria, Kang Sheng).[39]

Nevertheless, Chinese communism proved creative in several ways. As early as 1930, Mao initiated large purges in the comparatively small area of South China he then controlled, *before* any similar thing happened in USSR. The Soviet Republic of Jiangxi was submitted to such a terror against the 'AB' (Anti-Bolsheviks) that it lost probably 10–20 per cent of its population in three years, through murder or flight.[40] The main early communist base was so weakened that it could not resist the central government's subsequent offensives, with the Long March as the consequence. That essential component of the Chinese communist official saga was first and foremost a flight; and recent studies have shown that the Red Army lost probably more troops through desertion – so great was the loss of morale – than through fighting or exhaustion.[41] Mao Zedong, who had been one of the main culprit of that initial outburst of mass violence, was for several years dismissed from the party's leadership, and, once firmly back into power, in the new Northwestern base of Yan'an, he resolved to find less costly, more efficient way of governing.[42] In 1942–3, he launched a new purge, which sometimes degenerated into sheer physical violence (with a massive use of torture, and subsequent suicides), but with relatively few human losses: the re-education process ('thought reform' or 'criticism/self-criticism') had been inaugurated. It required a lot of time, and a lot of (relatively) competent loyal cadres, as it meant a total immersion of the people to be 'reformed' in a 24-hour political bath, for weeks or months on end.[43] For the communist apparatus, the results were exhilarating: many were (at least externally) converted, the most hostile were mentally broken up, a minor inconvenience being the number of suicides. The experiment was progressively extended to the whole of China, up to the most remote village, and up to each cell in every prison,[44] again with apparent success. It is difficult to say where Mao found his inspiration. The Guomindang prison system included a form of re-education process, itself derived from the Confucian concept of 'rectification of the names'.[45] Since 1928, in Japan, the mass arrests of Communists had led to a careful 'thought reform' policy, that had converted more than 90 per cent of the militants to national-militarism (and sometimes to fascism); they were subsequently considered 'rehabilitated', and freed. Japanese Communists exiled in Yan'an could have informed Mao of that method.[46] Self-criticism was also practiced under Soviet communism, but only inside the party, and in a limited way. The use of repeated and highly detailed biography and confessional writing, at least, was borrowed from Russia, even if the Chinese expanded its use to the point of absorbing for months, or years, most of the time and energy of the suspects.[47]

The second main innovation was the systematic labelling of the population. Lynn T. White has described for Shanghai that painstaking effort, taking at least three years, in the early period of communist rule (1951–4).[48] Everybody had to be put into pre-arranged groups that could be based on the family's social origins, on the actual profession or on political affiliation. Hence the initial 'four black elements': the landlords, the rich peasants, the reactionaries and the 'bad elements'. Among the Reds were the industrial workers, the poor and lower-middle peasants, but also the 'revolutionary heroes'. The 'intermediate' elements – such as the upper-middle peasants, ('national') capitalists and the intellectuals – tended during the Cultural Revolution to be assimilated to the Blacks. The labelling process was highly refined, even if not very coherent: in Guangxi province, in 1968, to the four black elements were added 23 categories, largely based on the local balance of forces.[49] The consequences of that complicated classification were fundamental: as seen in the schools case, it determined the whole educational and professional destiny of an individual. Furthermore, the Blacks could not enter the Communist Party, and were consequently denied positions of responsibility, even sometimes purely technical ones. They were victims of a rampant apartheid, being physically discriminated against (in the classroom and in political meetings), and being almost unable to befriend people of 'good origins', even less to marry them. Even in hospitals, they did not always receive the same treatment, and were quickly sent away.[50] During the frequent political campaigns, they constituted pre-designated victims, systematically associated with the 'enemy' of the time, even if that led to completely contradictory 'crime confessions'. That recurrent scapegoating lasted in some cases from the early 1950s to the late 1970s.[51] In the process, many were killed or sent to the Laogai. Many could not bear their endless persecution, their complete isolation, even from their prudent neighbours, and committed suicide. In a country that had known 2000 years of open competition for the mandarinate, a full-size caste system was established, where the destitute children of the dispossessed landlords or capitalists had, moreover, to expiate their ancestors' supposed turpitude, without any hope of redemption; even marriage with someone of 'good origins' could not erase the original stain. The actual underclass was victimized, constantly, as if it was still a powerful and extremely dangerous upper class. Thus Mao's China set up an efficient system of affirmative action, but in favour of the dominant!

Actually, for the Chairman, the Communists, even when in power, were still by definition the heart of the working class; whatever their social origins, 'Once they joined the Party, they become members of the proletariat.'[52] That utter confusion between social and political criteria may already be noticed in Soviet Russia, where the party exercising the 'dictatorship of the proletariat' was, in fact, almost exclusively led by intellectuals coming from bourgeois or even aristocratic families. Chinese political tradition went along well with such a trend. Except during relatively short major crises, society, in China, was never able to organize independently from the state. Cities had no autonomy, merchant guilds remained submissive, and intellectuals were first and foremost the central component of the government machine. The state instituted social classes and groups, redrawing their shape and composition almost at will, especially in the upper strata and in the cities.[53] Quite logically, law remained much less central and developed than in Europe. Government rule had to be absolute in principle; the courts themselves were no more than instruments in the ruler's hands. The major restraining force was the compelling set of moral principles stemming from Confucianism and from the classical tradition. They were universally taught, known and accepted (at least in a simplified form). The emperor himself had to respect them, under the threat of having his 'Mandate of Heaven' withdrawn.

After 1949, the state did not stop at instituting societal structures: it penetrated them, from top to bottom. All groups had the choice between full integration into the government machine, and complete destruction. The PLA played a major role in that unprecedented centralization and integration. According to Mao's frequently quoted 1937 treatise: 'The Chinese Red Army is an armed force for carrying out the political tasks of the revolution (...) In China, war is the main form of struggle and the army is the main form of organization.'[54] That dynamic combination between the Bolshevik model, the Imperial heritage and a militarist approach to politics was the basis of what will probably remain as the most efficient brand of totalitarianism the world ever experienced. Any alleged 'enemy of the people' could be crushed as a counter-revolutionary, as a vicious and disrespectful individual,[55] or as an unruly element in that army barracks atmosphere.

Another consequence of that extreme tightening of state control was suspicion of anything or anybody with outside origins or connections. Xenophobia led to many episodes of violence. Thus, in a prison-farm of Northern Manchuria, in 1958, 'The youngest rightist was a 17-year-old typist, Dai Yujing, whose only crime – the casual remark, "The American-made shoe polish is really good!" – left her guilty of "admiring foreign things."'[56] Early party leader Li Lisan, who had married a Russian wife while in the USSR, died after being persecuted as a 'Soviet spy', his companion spent 11 years in jail or in internal exile, without any charge.[57]

At this point, any informed reader might be surprised not to have seen any mention yet of what has long been considered as the main originality of Maoism: the call to young students, and later on to workers, to fight the alleged 'capitalist roaders' inside the party-state – a freedom of action stunning for a communist country.[58] The Chairman added that the right to rebel was unconditional. That played an essential role in the lasting good image of Mao Zedong in the West. A contemporary best-selling book (in Italy and France) described him as 'anti-dogmatic and anti-authoritarian'.[59] True, Mao's innovative way of action appeared so frightening, or even crazy, to the other Communist parties in power that no one, even in Cambodia, Vietnam or North Korea, dared to follow the Helmsman's example.[60] However, the heterodoxy of the Red Guards movement should not be overemphasized. If the police or even the army, between the summer of 1966 and the spring of 1968, were repeatedly ordered not to intervene against the Rebels' actions (even the most murderous ones), and if the activists were allowed to organize freely federations of their groups, at the local or provincial levels,[61] they had to abide by strict constraints. Ideologically, the hegemony of the CP and of course Mao himself, the desirability of communism, the odiousness of capitalism, of Soviet revisionism, of American imperialism and of the Guomindang *ancien régime* could not be questioned. And they were indeed hardly called into question: Mao was right, by and large, to feel supremely secure of his ideological pre-eminence. The totalitarian environment, into which the young urbanites had been raised, had been so effective that, even when granted some leeway, they could only reproduce, from their own free will, the ideological tenets and the established modes of action of the communist regime, even if in a more anarchical way. The few groups that ultimately started (started only) to exceed those limits were mercilessly crushed. Mao himself, in January 1968, pronounced 'counter-revolutionary' the Shengwulian group, in Hunan province, for having analyzed the *whole* communist leadership as a 'red bourgeoisie'; its leader, 17-year old Yang Xiguang, was jailed for 10 years.[62]

But, for a huge majority of the boisterous Rebels – as for their adversaries – Mao's word remained sacrosanct. Any of his utterances, reproduced in red letters in dailies all over China, and saluted in style by noisy demonstrations of joy in every city, was immediately enforced as if it was a decree from Heaven. Consequently, whatever the fierceness of local fights for power, a victory could be suddenly reversed into defeat or even disappearance of the winner, through the unquestionable intervention of an unpredictable Leader, expert at playing divide and rule. After an unfavourable ruling, a huge Wuhan group stated during a meeting: 'Whether or not we are convinced, we must observe and implement the centre's decision without reservation.'[63] Thus Mao never seriously ran the risk of being outflanked. He could decide at will the fate of any leader, of any group, at any moment.

His immense prestige was his best weapon, especially among young people (most of the Red Guards were high school students) who were easy to turn into fanatics. But several recent studies have also put into light the tremendous efficiency of Mao's own network. Firstly, not satisfied enough with the twice daily *Internal Reference* bulletin (whose circulation was restricted to about 30 leaders), he created at the inception of the Cultural Revolution another independent information network. It was part of the rationale behind the formation, during the summer of 1966, of the Central Cultural Revolution Group (or Small Group) – the real central authority until the party's Ninth congress (April 1969), which ratified Mao's triumph. In September 1966, the Group created a 'Journalists' Station', with more than a thousand local correspondents. Reports were sent constantly to Mao's leading faction, sometimes one every hour. No significant event, all over the huge country, could escape Mao's knowledge for more than a day.[64] Secondly, the Chairman was the only one to have the privilege to issue Central Documents (*Zhongfa*), about a dozen a week in the mid-1960s: all the main decisions were communicated that way to party cadres.[65] Thirdly, the shadowy Central Case Examination Group, created as the Small Group's secret police, and lasting till 1978, possessed a staff of thousands, including hundreds of army officers. Jiang Qing – also the head of propaganda work – and Kang Sheng – who had already supervised the Yan'an purge in 1942–3 – were its masterminds.[66] They maintained very close ties with strategic Red Guard groups, especially in Peking. The young activists were often used as auxiliary police, to terrorize, detain or investigate Mao's own adversaries.[67] Their thuggery, seen as senseless and purely sadistic by its victims, was in fact quite frequently aroused, directed and protected by the top leadership. Almost always, official purges were prepared by 'struggles by the masses' against the targeted cadres or leaders, who were consequently already broken up before the final blow. Further evidence is the restitution, from 1975 on, of a good deal of the goods stolen from the raided families in 1966–7: they had been quite carefully stored in government warehouses, minus some precious pieces appropriated by the masterminds.[68] So much for the spontaneity and 'disorder' of the Red Guards' actions.

Finally, their very importance has commonly been exaggerated. Even if, officially, the Cultural Revolution only ended with the arrest of the Gang of Four (October 1976), just after Mao's demise, the Rebels had fallen from grace and had been massively 'rusticated' since the summer of 1968. About 4.7 million young, educated people were supposed to spend the rest of their life 'learning from the poor peasants' and helping to develop remote villages. The Red Guards should not be exonerated from the terrible sufferings they inflicted on their teachers, on the Black scapegoats, on party and government cadres or on each other, during rabid factional struggles increasingly waged with firearms.[69] Official historians, in China, emphasize only this violence, as it had been partly directed against communist cadres, later on massively rehabilitated in Deng Xiaoping's China.[70] But the government, including the 'Conservative' elements presently glorified, bears the responsibility for a huge majority of the deaths of the terrible decade. Even the so-called 50 days initial period of the Red Guard movement, that set the pace for persecutions and vandalism, had been under the control of the 'work teams', sent preventively into schools and universities by the Conservatives. Much bloodier was the suppression of the most determined groups of Rebels, in 1968: the PLA or local rural militias had to take over some cities by brute force, including using machine guns and artillery. Thousands of people were killed during or after these battles, in mass slaughters, such as in Guilin.[71] Even more deadly were the long campaigns of terror that brought back more traditional forms of state – mostly police – repression: 'Cleansing the class ranks' (late 1967–8) investigated no fewer than 790,000 persons in Inner Mongolia alone, of whom 23,000 died. All over China, the victims (including suicides) were probably in the hundreds of thousands.[72] In August 1967, an 'ultra-leftist plot' against Zhou Enlai was allegedly unearthed, which triggered nationwide investigations, first against radical Rebels, later on against the usual 'Black' suspects, to fully dismantle a 'May 16 Conspiracy', actually purely imaginary.[73] More than three million people could have been arrested, a significant percentage being executed or dying under torture or in detention. In the big industrial city of Wuhan alone, some 34,000 people were prosecuted by PLA teams, and commonly secretly detained in army barracks for six months to one year, generally without being tortured, but having to endure endless questioning. Families were kept uninformed of their whereabouts. Even though the first phase of the Cultural Revolution in Wuhan had been exceptionally rowdy, with constant and massive factional fighting, it was between 1969 and 1971 that the greatest number of people was victimized.[74] The campaign did not die out until the end of 1973.[75]

The sanctification of violence

Mao, for his 73rd birthday, on 26 December 1966, gave to his close associates a toast 'To the unfolding of nationwide all-round civil war.'[76] It was not a moment of exaltation, but a constant, considered choice. Mao, like many revolutionaries (one thinks of Georges Sorel's *Réflexions sur la violence*[77]), saw violence, not only as unavoidable, but also as something to be desired. He felt indignant when Khrushchev 'capitulated' over the Cuban missile crisis in 1962.

Had he not said, while in Moscow five years earlier: 'We are prepared to sacrifice 300 million Chinese for the victory of the world revolution'?[78] In front of the 8th Party Congress, in May 1958, he stated: 'Don't make a fuss about a world war. At most, people die ... Half the population wiped out – this happened quite a few times in Chinese history ... It's best if half the population is left, next best one-third.'[79] That frightening indifference to human life (and to suffering), as we have seen, extended also to his closest political associates and even to his family. The message was received, in its crudeness, by the 'large masses'. Years after the Chairman's death, Yi Wansheng, who had organized some of the Guangxi province cannibal slaughters (see below), could feel justified: 'To engage in revolution, my heart is red! Didn't Chairman Mao say "kill or get killed"? If I live, you must die. Class struggle!'[80]

The first years of the Communist regime – initially in huge sections of Northern China, then from 1949–50 all over the country – were characterized by outbursts of mass violence, still much minimized in most accounts, or in the testimonies of those who did not suffer them. True, for the majority, after more than ten years of foreign and civil war, and with massive aid from Soviet Union, the economic and social situation got significantly better, and quickly at that. Crime, prostitution and drug trafficking were almost wiped out. But at what cost? The Land reform (sometimes more accurately designated as 'Land revolution'), between 1946 and 1952, was less a redistribution from the rich to the poor than the elimination of rural 'class enemies', and the assumption of local power by the Communists. Violence was not a pre-condition for land redistribution; almost simultaneously with China, bold land reforms were launched in neighbouring countries, such as Japan, South Korea or Taiwan, which can be held accountable for almost no deaths. And actually, just a few years after getting their share, the poor peasants, around 1956, had to relinquish their new property, to the benefit of state-imposed collective farms. Social progress had been a pretext, not the real aim. Even in desperately poor villages where nobody could qualify as a landlord (as was the case in about half of Northern China settlements), some manufactured 'privileged' ones still had to be combatted. In Wugong village, the radicalism of a group of activists suddenly converted some 70 middle peasants (out of 387 households) into rich ones – consequently into acceptable targets for 'class struggle'. In some cases such arbitrary 'cappings' were quickly overturned. In some others, they were preludes to three decades of constant scapegoating, until Deng Xiaoping pronounced his famous statement: 'To be rich is glorious'.[81] In many cases, social labelling was only an acceptable dressing for pre-designated enemies of all kind: 'Some were made class enemies because of transgressions other than those of class: working in or sympathizing with the Guomindang, conversion to a foreign religion, collaboration with the Japanese, or bad behaviour; others, it would seem, suffered merely because they were ostracized outsiders or enemies of activist leaders or were just unlucky enough.'[82]

At least one 'class enemy' had to be eliminated in every village, to create a blood bond between the Communists and the beneficiaries of the Land reform.[83] All over China, probably two to five million were killed.[84] The proceedings were highly staged and theatrical. Even American leftist well-wishers, in their famous testimonies, have shown how long and difficult it had been for the activists to reach the required amount of 'bitterness' against the targeted adversaries.[85] According to a member of a reform work team, after finding suitable victims, 'we needed to inspire their hatred and coach them in what to say (...) We would teach the poor peasants, "Look, this is unfair, you are being exploited by the landlord". The second step was the "trial" itself: "The landlord being struggled against had to nod and reply "yes" when asked, "Is it true?" Sometimes he was beaten if he tried to deny anything, yet the policy was to treat landlords in a civilized fashion.'[86] The epilogue was the defeat of evil, but also the demonstration of an overwhelming party domination: 'I heard of landlords being beaten or stoned to death by angry peasants. There were actually guiding principles as to when to kill a landlord, and approval from county leaders was needed.'[87]

Repression in the cities was just as harsh, especially between 1951 and 1955 (but already in 1949–50 in some places, such as Tianjin, although in a more spontaneous and decentralized fashion). Successive campaigns hit hard the urban elites (especially the capitalists, the westernized intellectuals and the Christians), and even more the former Guomindang cadres, civilian as well as military, down to the lowest ranks. In Shanghai, some 38,000 'counter-revolutionaries' were arrested in four months in 1951, and six execution fields were opened.[88] In Nanjing, former civil servants were executed by the hundreds, in front of the city walls.[89] Thousands of others were sent to dig a waterway, in severe conditions: they had to travel inside the cramped and sealed hold of a small boat; they were threatened with being shot on the spot at the slightest attempt to escape; they saw one of them executed in front of the gathered prisoners, just for having a small banknote in his pack.[90] Executions could have been well over the million mark, and to them some 700,000 suicides could be added. Around 2.5 million people were sent to labour camps. All together, they amounted to some 4 per cent of the urban population, three times more as a proportion of the population than the victimized rural people.[91]

After the anti-rightist movement of 1958 and the completion of collectivization, any social or political opposition, even a virtual one, had become non-existent.[92] Nevertheless the mobilizations of the mid-1960s were staged exactly as if the civil war had never ended. Mao gave the example, with his famous big-character poster (*dazibao*) of August 1966, 'Bombard the Headquarters' – the 'enemies' being actually his faithful, often slavish seconds, who never dared to oppose him frontally, or even to reply to the most fantastic accusations.[93] Millions of Red Guards felt exhilarated taking part in these 'attacks' and 'offensives' against 'class enemies' who had neither the means nor even the will to defend themselves, at least until the Red Guard movement started to become deeply divided itself, during the spring of 1967. It was a farce, not a war – but nevertheless with many deaths for all that. Significantly, the violent political theatre associated with the Land reform was staged once again: huge dunce caps and chest placards for the paraded victims, public beatings and humiliations, well rehearsed mock trials.[94] The categorization of the accused (urban 'bourgeois' and 'capitalists', not rural landlords) should have implied a repetition of the 1952 Five-Anti movement, directed against the urban elites. But the overwhelming bureaucratic and police nature of the latter was unsuitable to a 'mass movement'. Furthermore, the initial anti-capitalist movement had confiscated much, but killed little: of one million investigated enterprise owners, only some 1,500 had been sentenced. Too benign to be used as a model ... Going back further in the revolutionary past, some devoted Red Guards engaged in their very own 'Long Marches', actually closer to a kind of revolutionary tourism, towards such holy places as Mao's native village or initial guerrilla stronghold. All of which shows that even when violence was actually no longer necessary, it was still considered an essential criterion for the selection of new Communists.

The limits to violence

Like in other communist countries, there was in China a constant ambiguity in the central tenet of the proclaimed necessity of a 'destruction of enemy classes'. Did that mean destroying the individuals (in Newspeak: 'exercising the dictatorship of the proletariat' against them), or only depriving them of their privileges and means of defence? Pol Pot was the only one consistently to give the first answer – however even he did not dare to articulate it. Elsewhere, the policy has been a strange mix of both: more (or almost only) deprivation in 'normal' periods, more destruction at the peak of the campaigns. It commonly led to arrest (and sometimes killing) quotas that show the inhumanity of a system that constantly required enemies to hate and suppress, as well as the limitation of the use of violence to a minority of the targeted groups. The figure of 5 per cent of irredeemables to be punished was often used in the whole communist world, including China, whatever the campaign.[95] It should be considered more metaphorically than literally, as evidence of a kind of lenient sternness: the real number of victims was frequently much lower than, but sometimes much higher than 5 per cent.[96] Thus, during the Five-Anti movement, only 0.2 per cent were actually punished. In a rural district of Guangxi, whose population was 206,000, 0.7 per cent were beaten to death during the Cultural Revolution – and that seems to be an uncommonly high figure.[97] Admittedly, the percentage was much higher among the 'Blacks'. But it could not amount to something even remotely similar to a holocaust. Even in a devastated county such as Binyang (Guangxi), where cannibalism was widespread (see below), the objective was to kill between one quarter and one third of the targeted groups.[98] Inside the Party and the army, the most extensive purges probably took place during the early 1930s, in the Jiangxi red base area: the 'AB' witch-hunt led to the killing (often after terrible tortures) of some 20 per cent of the communist 4th army. 95 per cent of the educated Party members were made to acknowledge connections with the AB; 3,400 were killed in just three of the 20 districts of the base. Similar events took place in the other communist-controlled areas: they can be deemed to have been the produce of central party policies, if not explicit orders. But Mao did radicalize the process to the point of inducing (and mercilessly crushing) a large-scale mutiny among one of the most desperate army units.[99]

Seldom were whole families killed, or even beaten. Yet it did happen, for example in Lingshan county (Guangxi), in 1968: some 520 families were wiped out, except sometimes infants. Slightly more commonly, all males (including small boys) were killed, while females were spared, as unimportant (and sometimes marketable) creatures.[100] However, the families of counter-revolutionaries were everywhere under pressure to 'draw the line' between themselves and their detained family members. Wives, especially, had to apply for divorce, under the threat of losing their job, of being expelled from the Party, of being 'struggled against' or even of being arrested themselves. Children were encouraged to reject their fathers publicly; otherwise they could be ejected from the mass organizations and lose any chance of joining a good school and getting a valuable job. Even doing so, they remained natural suspects, and easily joined the pool of scapegoats. For a family, being deprived of an important breadwinner also meant material difficulties, such as income reduction or even loss of housing, as the latter was usually provided by the work unit. Family members were not infrequently reduced to begging. They were exposed to malnutrition, or even to hunger in difficult times, such as the Great Leap Forward. Consequently, their life expectancy was significantly reduced. During the Land reform, landlords' wives could be pressurized to re-marry one of their husbands' persecutors.

Nevertheless, it seems impossible to uncover any attempt at a systematic physical destruction of a significant human group, be it in words or in deeds. Contrary to Stalin, or even Lenin (who exterminated part of the Cossacks), Mao probably never ordered the killing or the deportation of whole ethnic or social groups. This does not imply that the Chinese suffered less than Soviet citizens: oppression and repression were probably more widespread, more systematic in China, and suicide was widely resorted to as the only way out. The total number of executions (wars excluded) and politically-induced suicides may be conservatively estimated at between 4.5 million and 9 million, most of them taking place during the regime's first decade.[101] That compares quite closely, in percentage, with the direct victims of Russian communism. The main difference concerns the fate of the communist cadres: killed *en masse* in USSR in 1937–8, most of those persecuted survived in China, and frequently regained their former position, sometimes even before Mao's demise.

The dreadful crushing techniques

The publication of Zheng Yi's *Scarlet Memorial* (1996) caused a sensation. Recurrent rumours about the political use of cannibalism during the Cultural Revolution were thus confirmed, but the number of victims, the implication of local authorities and the associated horrors went beyond what most could have imagined. Some – including children – had been buried alive, others had been partly chopped for meat or even eaten while not yet dead, whole communities had participated in human flesh banquets. The avowed purpose, in these thousands of murders, was to make the victims suffer as much as possible. In the city of Xinbin (Guangxi), on 29 July 1968, the instructions had been: 'Don't use bullets, use fists, clubs and stones!'[102] In Hubin, the body of a woman, executed by Red guards, was left to rot for ten days 'as an example', right in the middle of the city's main gate.[103] That practice of terror, incidentally, had been adopted by the Japanese army during the war, for example in Nanjing, in 1937.[104,105] Numerous girls, from 1966 onwards, were victims of sex crimes, including sometimes awful tortures and even mutilations. Many victims of the Red Guards had to endure ridiculous haircuts, the most common being the 'ying yang' one.[106] During the Great Leap Forward famine, some activists used incredibly harsh methods against the starving farmers, accused of sabotaging the production: in Henan province, some children seem to have been killed, boiled and used as fertilizer.[107]

But these atrocities should not be overemphasized. The cannibalism wave had been initiated by local communist leaders, at the town or county level, and remained limited to a small and remote part of Guangxi province. Once informed (through letters sent to the Central Committee by a former 'rightist' ex-CP member), the Centre acted swiftly: regular troops were sent, the killings were stopped, and later on some perpetrators were judged and sentenced.[108] Torture was apparently not widespread in the Laogai system, especially before the Cultural Revolution. In the 1950s, it was even risky for a guard to insult an inmate, who in such a case could file successfully a report against him.[109] The situation deteriorated after 1966: it is significant that when Lin Biao's or Jiang Qing's military replaced agents of the Public Security in interrogation or detention centres, the brutalities and the number of executions exploded.[110] Even then, it was often safer for a 'counter-revolutionary' to be in jail than outside.[111] One should take care to avoid being mesmerized by collateral atrocities, at the risk of missing the fundamentals of state violence. Much more constant, much more extensive, much more painful and, finally, much more deadly were the 'normal', less spectacular repressive practices.

Huge segments of the Chinese population were submitted for years or for decades to constant victimization, almost without any respite, as even the parents, friends, workmates or neighbours that could have sympathized with their ordeal were themselves under pressure to spy, report on them and accuse them, and to break any kind of personal relationship with them. If those people did not comply, they knew that they could be targeted as accomplices. Even when released from detention, the ex-detainees seldom succeeded in ridding themselves of their incriminating political label, and consequently they remained deprived of any adequate employment, and sometimes of their home.[112] They were at the mercy of the smallest bureaucrat, and had to accept with a smile any kind of humiliation. They were the usual, defenceless targets of every political campaign, and had then to renew endless public confessions and promises to repent. During these extensive periods, people under attack had no right to have curtains in their homes: they had to be transparent to the eyes of the masses.[113] It is for such reasons that the Laogai inmates sometimes applied to remain in the labour camp after the end of their detention period: there, at least, they could get some solidarity, or even friendship, from people fallen as low as them.[114] Many more could not find any meaning in a life of misery without end, and committed suicide. If so, it was best not to fail: suicide was considered as an evidence of guilt, and as a refusal to repent and reform one's mind. Thus the once powerful Luo Ruiqing, PLA's chief of staff, received only ridicule from the other leaders (first of all Liu Shaoqi) when a defenestration left him crippled for life, and he was brought in a basket to further 'struggle' sessions.[115] A successful suicide was a humiliation for the Party, and disturbed the investigations against class enemies: spouse and children could expect reprisals, and eventually had to take the place of the 'escaped' criminal.[116] Hence awful dilemmas were created for many desperate suspects. Sometimes it looked easier for whole families to disappear by killing each other.[117] Ironically, many of the tormentors were themselves severely victimized when they ultimately fell out of favour. The 'ultra-leftist' Rebels were jailed in huge numbers (and not infrequently executed) in 1968, followed by Lin Biao's supposed stalwarts from 1971, and by the Gang of Four followers from 1976. The rustication movement sent some 17 millions young urbanites to villages and government (or army) farms, between 1957 and 1980 – less than one fourth having been Red Guards. As demonstrated by Michel Bonnin, the purpose was in no way economic, but entirely political: to re-educate the children of the old or new privileged urban groups, and select among them new Maoist faithfuls.[118]

Politics invaded every facet of private life and, like a tumour, it tended to corrupt and destroy all sources of joy and contentment. In an atmosphere of extreme puritanism, a young woman of 21 who had engaged in a love relationship with an older, married man was asked to 'confess' by her parents, afraid for their position *vis-à-vis* the Party; then her scared lover reported everything to his party unit, and charged her with behaving in a semi-prostitute fashion, his wife supporting his claims.[119] A young boy, deemed a model student till his father was accused of being a 'capitalist' during the Cultural Revolution, suddenly became an outcast to everybody. Other children spat on him and sang:

> Dog, dog, capitalist dog,
> The father is a big dog,
> The son is a little one.[120]

Trying (unsuccessfully, of course) to get himself reclassified, the boy turned against his father, to the point of beating and accusing him publicly of extra 'crimes'. As a result, the father was left partially paralyzed.[121] A mother was so broken and so terrified by her life in a 'reform farm' (the 'May 7 schools', catering for cadres) that, when her young daughter succeeded in visiting her, she was unable to express any affection for her, and she at once started to write an extensive self-criticism statement.[122] The unavoidable conclusion is that family units constituted important targets, spouses and successive generations being forcibly separated, or turned against each other. 'Horizontal' feelings (for parents, friends and workmates) were deeply suspect: all expressions of love had to be devoted to the 'vertical' relationship with one's superiors, to the Party and increasingly to Mao Zedong himself. Chihua Wen's collection of testimonies, among many more literary pieces, proves the depth of the trauma sustained by so many individuals: in countless cases, it left lifelong scars.

The Great Leap Forward and mass violence

Could we still call the 1959–61 great famine 'a tragedy of good intentions'?[123] A tragedy, indeed: some 38 million dead, according to serious recent estimates (but the figure is far from definitive). But what about the good intentions? Since the publication, in 1996, of Jasper Becker's book[124] – to this day the most complete on the subject – such a qualification can hardly be maintained. Hence the presence in a study of political mass violence of an event still officially attributed in China to a series of natural calamities and unfortunate management mistakes. The stakes are enormous, as, whatever the numerous uncertainties in figures, the Great Leap famine counts for at least one half, more probably around two thirds of political mortality under Mao's rule.

Joseph was right to assert that the promoters of the Great Leap in no way intended to provoke that devastating blow. They felt so confident of the proximity of the realm of abundance that, under Mao's pressure, they established in the newly created People's Communes common kitchens and refectories, where everybody would be able to eat as much as he wished, for free.[125] But it should be stressed that the welfare of the people was only conceived as a side effect of the main goal: an accelerated development, both of agriculture and of heavy industry, such as the world had never seen before. The huge grain production was first and foremost destined to allow a massive rural exodus to the new industrial areas, and the procurement of advanced industrial machines through massive sales abroad. Hence the limited care given to people's food by Mao and most communist leaders, when things started to turn sour: grain exports to foreign countries continued unabated, despite the Soviet proposal, in 1961, to suspend the repayment of the loans and to furnish emergency food deliveries – it was turned down.[126] All indications show that, for Mao, the Chinese people, and especially the farmers, were only a tool for the realization of his dreams of social utopia and national *grandeur,* and as such were expendable. He also proved ready to sacrifice millions of lives to his pre-eminence inside the party, when, at the Lushan central committee Plenum (July–August 1959), Marshal Peng Dehuai dared to criticize the Great Leap Forward for its catastrophic consequences. Refusing to acknowledge any mistake, Mao sacked the honest minister, accused of being a 'bourgeois democrat', and radicalized the line, for two more years.[127] Thus it can be said that, duly informed of the growing famine, Mao, then supported by future 'moderates' such as Deng Xiaoping,[128] chose deliberately not to do anything to stop it. It is one of the worst cases of criminal neglect in world history. It should be remembered that, during the Tokyo war crimes trial (1946–8), two of the Japanese leaders sentenced to hang had been recognized guilty of the same crime, committed during the 1937 Nanjing massacre.[129]

Furthermore, on numerous occasions, the communist leaders and cadres contributed actively to the worsening of the situation. For example, in the worst affected province – Anhui – a rule prohibited gleaning in the fields after harvest. Inequality was rampant: peasants were not allowed to eat the livestock or even their own dogs, when they were starving to death, but had to hand them over to local leaders. Consequently, in a village affected by a 60 per cent mortality rate, all the cadres survived.[130] The situation of the Laogai inmates was only slightly less disastrous: in a prison-farm in Heilongjiang province, they frequently had to work without having eaten, and those too weak to keep working were systematically refused any food. In a short period of 1960 – the worst year – about one third perished.[131] Despair led to a resurgence of cannibalism; families swapped their children to be able to kill and eat them more easily. In Anhui, many dead bodies were dismembered before burial – only the head and the chest remained.[132] When caught, the cannibal suspects were very severely dealt with. More generally, repression was savage against the starving farmers, unable to deliver to the state the fixed grain quotas (inflated by the baseless declarations of record harvests written by ambitious cadres). They were accused of deliberately sabotaging production. In just one district, more than 800 were killed, sometimes being buried alive; others were branded with red-hot irons; 12.5 per cent of the rural population was punished. The peasants trying to enter the better-supplied cities could be shot at.[133] Thus, as in Ukraine almost three decades earlier, the famine was compounded by a kind of anti-peasant war.

Conclusion

After the assessment of so many horrors, over such a long time, inflicted upon such an enormous population, it is hard to end with what could easily pass for a denial. But, whatever the endless debates about a working definition of what genocide is, one cannot get away from two very basic features: a targeted group of people, and the will to destroy it completely, or in a very large proportion. In Mao's China, several different groups were successively or simultaneously targeted: the landlords and the rich peasants, the agents of the Guomindang regime, the urban bourgeoisie, the intellectuals, the 'rightists' and finally the party and state cadres. No social or political bind whatsoever existed between those groups. Furthermore, the two last-mentioned groups included many, and probably most of the surviving perpetrators of earlier political brutalities. And no will to annihilate a whole group of individuals can be discerned. Examples were made, to terrify the other members of the group and to demonstrate to all the absolute power of the Party. But the actual killings seldom overstepped the 5 per cent mark, except probably in the initial destruction of the landlords. Most were left to live, humbled, harmless, dispossessed, transformed for life into scapegoats.

It was not a question of means: except for some months in 1967–8, the party-state had an absolute control on weapons, on information, on transportation, on organization. Dozens of millions of people could starve to death in 1959–61, in the absolute ignorance of the rest of the world, and even, in a large measure, of Chinese urbanites.[134] If Mao had decided some day to have all the Laogai inmates executed, it could have been done easily, swiftly, without any risk of widespread resistance, and the rest of the Chinese would probably not have learned of it for months or even years.[135] The main restraining factor was, strangely, the question of survival: the dividing line between friends and foes was drawn most arbitrarily, and was ever changing, to the point of being blurred. Nobody, even the reddest of communist cadres, even the proletarian with the most impeccable pedigree, could feel secure enough of never falling on the wrong side. Consequently, allowing most 'enemies' to survive was the best life insurance for the perpetrator himself. By and large, the same kind of mechanism could be discerned in Stalin's USSR. That constitutes an enormous difference between communism and Nazism: in the latter, the societal divides were much more simple and constant. If you were on the right, 'Aryan' side (and not a political opponent), you had almost nothing to fear from the regime; you could contemplate the extermination of the 'wrong' without personal apprehension. Only in one case did a communist regime undertake the general physical elimination of some of the targeted groups: Cambodia's Khmer Rouge. But, as in the other communist countries, the dividing line was awfully blurred. Therefore massacres snowballed, and everybody had to live in total insecurity. Within four years, the regime had become so weakened that it could not repel the Vietnamese invasion. Mao Zedong, in his megalomania, knew better: even for him, the most powerful man in the long history of China, there were limits not to be crossed.

Notes

I thank Philip Short for his careful reading and his numerous useful remarks on the present chapter.

1. J.-L. Margolin, 'Communismes d'Asie: entre "rééducation" et massacre', in S. Courtois, N. Werth, J.-L. Panné, A. Paczkowski, K. Bartosek, J.-L. Margolin, *Le livre noir du communisme: crimes, terreur, répression* (Paris: Bouquins-Robert Laffont, 1998), pp. 539–756. English language edition: *The Black Book of Communism: Crimes, Terror, Repression* (Cambridge, MA: Harvard University Press, 1999).
2. Of course, to appreciate fully the meaning of such figures, one has to take into account China's huge population: around 500 million people when Mao assumed power, around 800 million when he died. Relatively to the median figure (650 million), human losses are in the range of 7–11 per cent. Lenin and Stalin, together, took the lives of around 15 million Soviet citizens (plus some hundreds of thousands of East Europeans), about 8 per cent of a population then averaging 180 million. Hitler killed upwards from 20 million people (World War II combatants excluded), at least 6 per cent of occupied Europe's population, but with wide variations according to countries and ethnic groups. One should consider too the time span of these mass crimes: around 35 years for the USSR, 30 years for China, but only six years for Nazi Germany (the number of deaths before 1939 being comparatively insignificant).
3. The question of Tibet will not be developed further in the present chapter. As a kind of colonial dependency of China, it is a subject by itself. Furthermore, the historiography of post-1949 Tibet is far less advanced than the historiography of Communist China.
4. J.-L. Domenach, *Chine: l'archipel oublié* (Paris: Fayard, 1992).
5. The mass killing of women and children constitutes one of the surest signs of genocide.
6. Even in that case, there was a certain fuzziness: in Nazi-occupied Europe, the definition of who was a Jew varied from one country to another (it was more extensive in Vichy France than in Germany itself), and the Nazis hesitated to include the Karaites among the Jews.
7. The same individual, during the Cultural Revolution, could have been 'struggled against' as a 'bourgeois revisionist' in 1966, as an 'extreme leftist' in 1968, as a 'follower of Lin Biao and Confucius' in 1974, and as a 'Dengist counter-revolutionary' in 1976. One's distant 'bad origin' – for example, being the son of a long-dispossessed landlord – was enough to ensure one's permanent guilt.

8. F. C. Teiwes, *Politics and Purges in China: Rectification and the Decline of Party Norms, 1950–1965* (Armonk, NY: M. E. Sharpe, 1993).
9. J. Chang and J. Halliday, *Mao: The Unknown Story* (London: Jonathan Cape, 2005).
10. Li Z., *The Private Life of Chairman Mao* (London: Arrow Books, 1994).
11. Chang and Halliday, *Mao*, pp. 343–5.
12. Ibid., pp. 651–3; Li, *The Private Life*, pp. 122–3.
13. See especially G. Benton, *New Fourth Army: Communist Resistance along the Yangtze and the Huai, 1938–1941* (Berkeley, CA: University of California Press, 1999); M.-C. Bergère, L. Bianco and J. Domes, eds, *La Chine au XXème siècle. Vol. 1: D'une révolution à l'autre 1895–1949; Vol. 2: De 1949 à aujourd'hui* (Paris: Fayard, 1989 and 1990); L. Bianco, *Peasants Without the Party: Grass-Roots Movements in Twentieth-Century China* (Armonk, NY: M. E. Sharpe, 2001); M. Bonnin, *Génération perdue. Le mouvement d'envoi des jeunes instruits à la campagne en Chine, 1968–1980* (Paris: Editions de l'Ecole des Hautes Etudes en Sciences Sociales, 2004); Chang and Halliday, *Mao*; Chen Y.-F., *Making Revolution: The Chinese Communist Movement in Central and Eastern China, 1937–1945* (Berkeley, CA: University of California Press, 1986); Domenach, *Chine*; Li, *The Private Life*; R. MacFarquhar and J. K. Fairbank, eds, *The Cambridge History of China. Vol. 14: The People's Republic, Part 1 (1949–1965)* and *Vol. 15: The People's Republic, Part 2: Revolutions within the Chinese Revolution, 1966–1982* (Cambridge: Cambridge University Press, 1987 and 1991); R. MacFarquhar and M. Schoenhals, *Mao's Last Revolution* (Cambridge, MA: Belknap Press of Harvard University Press, 2006); T.M.-H. Ngo, Tunliu dans la tourmente de la réforme agraire 1946–1950 (Paris: Riveneuve, 2007); T. Saich and H. van de Ven, eds, *New Perspectives on the Chinese Communist Revolution* (Armonk, NY: M. E. Sharpe, 1995); P. Short, *Mao: A Life* (London: Hodder & Stoughton, 1999); Sun S., *The Long March* (London: HarperPress, 2006); F. C. Teiwes and W. Sun, *The Tragedy of Lin Biao: Riding the Tiger during the Cultural Revolution, 1966–1971* (Honolulu: University of Hawai'i Press, 1996); B. Womack, ed., *Contemporary Chinese Politics in Historical Perspective* (Cambridge: Cambridge University Press, 1991).
14. Thus Mao blamed Khrushchev, after the Cuban missile crisis, for refusing to risk nuclear war. Chang and Halliday, *Mao*, p. 488.
15. On that essential point I strongly disagree with M. Lynch, *Mao* (London: Routledge, 2004) and with Chang and Halliday.
16. It seems to have originated in his first contacts with peasants' and outlaws' practices of violence – he praised them – in Hunan around 1928. Chang and Halliday, *Mao*, pp. 41–3 and 54–9.
17. See for example: C. Johnson, *Peasant Nationalism and Communist Power: The Emergence of Revolutionary China* (Stanford, CA: Stanford University Press, 1962); F. Schurmann, *Ideology and Organization in Communist China*, 2nd edn (Berkeley, CA: University of California Press, 1968); M. Selden, *The Yenan Way in Revolutionary China* (Cambridge, MA: Harvard University Press, 1971); and the early works of John K. Fairbank or Lucien Bianco.
18. Chang and Halliday, *Mao*, pp. 396–8 and 500–6; J. Becker, *Hungry Ghosts: China's Secret Famine* (London: John Murray, 1996).
19. L. Bianco, 'Peasant Responses to CCP Mobilization Policies, 1937–1945', in *New Perspectives on the Chinese Communist Revolution* eds, Saich and van de Ven, pp. 175–87.
20. G. Benton, 'Under Arms and Umbrellas: Perspectives on Chinese Communism in Defeat', in *New Perspectives on the Chinese Communist Revolution*, eds, Saich and van de Ven, pp. 131–3; D. P. Barrett and L. N. Shyu, eds, *Chinese Collaboration with Japan,*

1932–1945: The Limits of Accommodation (Stanford, CA: Stanford University Press, 2001).

21. M. Selden, 'Yan'an Communism Reconsidered', *Modern China*, 21, 1 (1995), 8–44.
22. J. Unger, 'Whither China? Yang Xiguang, Red Capitalists and the Social Turmoil of the Cultural Revolution', *Modern China*, 17, 1 (1991), 3–37.
23. L. T. White III, *Policies of Chaos: The Organizational Causes of Violence in China's Cultural Revolution* (Princeton, NJ: Princeton University Press, 1989), pp. 245–7; Hua L., *Les années rouges* (Paris: Seuil, 1987); K. Ling, M. London and T.-L. Lee, *Red Guard* (London: Macdonald, 1972).
24. M. J. Blecher and G. White, *Micropolitics in Contemporary China: A Technical Unit During and After the Cultural Revolution* (London: Macmillan, 1979).
25. J. W. Esherick, P. G. Pickowicz and A. G. Walder, eds, *The Chinese Cultural Revolution as History* (Stanford, CA: Stanford University Press, 2006).
26. MacFarquhar and Schoenhals, *Mao's Last Revolution*, pp. 245–6 and 293.
27. C. Chen, *Come Watch the Sun Go Home: A Memoir of Upheaval and Revolution in China* (New York: Marlowe & Company, 1998), pp. 179–89.
28. H. Harding, 'The Chinese State in Crisis', in *The Cambridge History of China, Vol. 15*, eds, MacFarquhar and Fairbank, p. 168.
29. A. Chan, *Children of Mao: Personality Development and Political Activism in the Red Guard Generation* (London: The Macmillan Press, 1985).
30. S. Wang, *Failure of Charisma: The Cultural Revolution in Wuhan* (Hong Kong: Oxford University Press, 1995), p. 66.
31. Ibid., p. 198; MacFarquhar and Schoenhals, *Mao's Last Revolution*, pp. 204–5.
32. L. W. Pye, *The Mandarin and the Cadre: China's Political Culture* (Ann Arbor, MI: Center for Chinese Studies, The University of Michigan, 1988).
33. They are far less glossed over than the Cultural Revolution. There are two reasons: first, the Cultural Revolution was officially denounced as 'antiparty' in 1981, thus allowing some legal investigations on that episode; second, the general urban population had been little disturbed by the early waves of terror that focussed first on rural landlords, then on specific urban groups (the ex-Guomindang administration and sympathizers, the bourgeois, the intellectuals and the 'rightist' cadres), without spilling over too much.
34. With devastating consequences in China: steel obsession actually led to the *destruction* of most metals present in rural areas, melted to produce wasted 'steel'; and the huge work input, to no avail, played its part in the neglect of the fields and their crops, and consequently in the starvation process.
35. Chang and Halliday, *Mao*, pp. 360–80; Domenach, *Chine*.
36. Chen, *Come Watch the Sun Go Home*, pp. 59–61.
37. Many moderate socialists, such as Jean Jaurès or Léon Blum in France, did accept and use the concept of class struggle. What they rejected was the idea that the fight could only be ended by the extermination – partial or total – of one class by the other.
38. The world's two most extensive ones – both in number of inmates and in duration – have been the Soviet Gulag and Maoist Laogai. Hitler's concentration camps remained far behind, if only because most of their victims were killed immediately or did not survive more than a few months.
39. R. Faligot and R. Kauffer, *Kang Sheng et les services secrets chinois (1927–1987)* (Paris: Robert Laffont, 1987).
40. S. C. Averill, 'The Origins of the Futian Incident', in *New Perspectives on the Chinese Communist Revolution* eds, Saich and van de Ven, pp. 79–115. That episode could prove a fascinating forerunner to Pol Pot's rule over Cambodia.

41. Short, *Mao*, pp. 236–51; Sun, *The Long March*, pp. 15–40 and 83–116; Chang and Halliday, *Mao*, pp. 92–104; I. J. Kim, 'Mass Mobilization Policies and Techniques Developed in the Period of the Chinese Soviet Republic', in *Chinese Communist Politics in Action*, ed. A. D. Barnett (Seattle, WA: University of Washington Press, 1969), pp. 78–98.
42. M. Selden, 'The Yenan Legacy: The Mass Line', in *Chinese Communist Politics in Action*, ed. Barnett, pp. 99–151.
43. It is probably for that very reason that the Khmer Rouges were unable to do the same in Cambodia, and fell back to a crude and ultimately self-destructive use of ultra-violence: Margolin, 'Communismes d'Asie', pp. 741–3.
44. Bao, R. (J. Pasqualini) and R. Chelminski, *Prisoner of Mao* (London: Deutsch, 1975).
45. F. Dikötter, *Crime, Punishment and the Prison in China* (London: Hurst & Co, 2002); R. J. Lifton, *Thought Reform and the Psychology of Totalism: A Study of 'Brain-Washing' in China* (New York: W.W. Norton, 1961), pp. 388–98.
46. J.-L. Margolin, *L'armée de l'empereur: Violences et crimes du Japon en guerre (1937–1945)* (Paris: Armand Colin, 2007), pp. 105–7.
47. The biographies were sometimes hundreds of pages long. They had to be fully re-written from time to time, to show the progress in the consciousness of past 'crimes', but also to check any factual contradiction between the different versions.
48. White, *Policies of Chaos*, pp. 86–93.
49. Zheng, Y., *Scarlet Memorials: Tales of Cannibalism in Modern China* (Boulder, CO: Westview Press, 1996), p. 42.
50. Zhang, L. and C. MacLeod, *China Remembers* (Hong Kong: Oxford University Press, 1999), p. 168.
51. See, *inter alia*, Ye, T., *A Leaf in the Bitter Wind* (Toronto: Doubleday, 2002).
52. Tang, T., 'Interpreting the Revolution in China: Macrohistory and Micromechanisms', *Modern China*, 26, 2 (2000), 213.
53. Ibid., 207.
54. *On Guerilla Warfare*, quoted ibid, 215.
55. The most innocent joke about a Communist leader could send you to a labour camp for many years. The atmosphere of extreme puritanism dealt very severely with people in extra-marital relationships.
56. Zhang and MacLeod, *China Remembers*, p. 67.
57. Ibid., p. 100.
58. A huge number of Red Guard memoirs (often written in collaboration with Western historians or reporters) have now been published. Outside those already quoted, some of the most interesting are: J. Chang, *Wild Swans* (New York: Simon & Schuster, 1991); G. Yuan, *Born Red: A Chronicle of the Cultural Revolution* (Stanford, CA: Stanford University Press, 1987); Liang, H. and J. Shapiro, *Son of the Revolution* (New York: Alfred A. Knopf, 1983); A. F. Thurston, *A Chinese Odyssey: The Life and Times of a Chinese Dissident* (New York: Charles Scribner's Sons, 1991); Zhai, Z., *Red Flower of China* (New York: Soho, 1992). See also the anthology edited by M. Schoenhals, *China's Cultural Revolution, 1966–1969: Not a Dinner Party* (Armonk, NY: M. E. Sharpe, 1996); and the photographic report of the Cultural Revolution in Harbin, Li Z., *Red Color News Soldier* (Paris: Phaidon Press, 2003).
59. M.-A. Macciocchi, *Daily Life in Revolutionary China* (New York: Monthly Review, 1972).
60. On the contrary, the no less disastrous Great Leap Forward was slavishly imitated in the other Asian Communist countries, with similarly catastrophic results. And

the Thought Reform procedures were enthusiastically adopted: G. Boudarel, 'L'idéocratie importée au Vietnam avec le maoisme', in *La bureaucratie au Vietnam – Vietnam-Asie-Débat*, 1 (Paris: L'Harmattan, 1983), pp. 31–106.

61. The only significant limitation was the prohibition of any inter-provincial federation. The Communist Party – at least in principle – had to remain the only nationwide political force.
62. Yang, X. and S. McFadden, *Captive Spirits: Prisoners of the Cultural Revolution* (Hong Kong: Oxford University Press, 1997).
63. In Wang, *Failure of Charisma*, p. 158.
64. MacFarquhar and Schoenhals, *Mao's Last Revolution*, pp. 78–81.
65. Ibid., p. 19.
66. Ibid., p. 284.
67. MacFarqhuar and Fairbank, *The Cambridge History of China, Vol. 15*, p. 168.
68. Chen, *Come Watch the Sun Go Home*, pp. 228–9.
69. B. Barnouin and Yu, C., *Ten Years of Turbulence: The Chinese Cultural Revolution* (London: Kegan Paul International, 1993); E. Perry and Li, X., *Proletarian Power: Shanghai in the Cultural Revolution* (Boulder, CO: Westview Press, 1997); S. Rosen, *Red Guard Factionalism and the Cultural Revolution in Guangzhou* (Boulder, CO: Westview Press, 1982).
70. Yan, J. and Gao, G., *Turbulent Decade: A History of the Cultural Revolution* (Honolulu: University of Hawai'i Press, 1996) (First edition in Chinese, 1986).
71. Hua, L., *Les années rouges* (Paris: Seuil, 1987).
72. MacFarquhar and Schoenhals, *Mao's Last Revolution*, pp. 253–62.
73. Ma, J., *The Cultural Revolution in the Foreign Ministry of China* (Hong Kong: The Chinese University Press, 2004), pp. 251–84.
74. Wang, *Failure of Charisma*, pp. 219ff.
75. MacFarquhar and Schoenhals, *Mao's Last Revolution*, pp. 221–38.
76. Ibid., p. 155.
77. Published in 1908. The book deeply influenced left socialists and anarchists, but also early fascists, including Mussolini.
78. Chang and Halliday, *Mao*, p. 457.
79. Ibid., p. 458. The book has been (sometimes rightly) criticized for its use of obscure or misquoted sources. In this case, it seems to be on sure ground.
80. Zheng, *Scarlet Memorials*, p. 49.
81. P. C. C. Huang, 'Rural Class Struggle in the Chinese Revolution: Representational and Objective Realities from the Land Reform to the Cultural Revolution', *Modern China*, 21 (1995), 116–20.
82. Ibid., 124–5.
83. A. D. Barnett and E. Vogel, *Cadres, Bureaucracy and Political Power in Communist China* (New York: Columbia University Press, 1967), p. 228.
84. Domenach, *Chine*, p. 71; C. Aubert, 'Economie et société rurales', in *La Chine au XXème siècle*, eds, Bergère, Bianco and Domes, Vol. 2, p. 150.
85. J. Belden, *China Shakes the World* (Harmondsworth: Pelican, 1973) (first edition: 1949); W. Hinton, *Fanshen: A Documentary of Revolution in a Chinese Village* (Berkeley, CA: University of California Press, 1997) (first edition: 1966).
86. Zhang and MacLeod, *China Remembers*, p. 37.
87. Ibid., p. 38.
88. White, *Policies of Chaos*, p. 94.
89. Incidentally, just where the Japanese army had slaughtered scores of Chinese in December 1937.

90. Chen, M., *Les nuages noirs s'amoncellent* (Cadeilhan: Zulma, 2003), pp. 111–19.
91. Margolin, 'Communismes d'Asie', pp. 561–6.
92. Opposition remained rampant until 1957, both in the villages and in the factories, albeit on a purely local scale. It had led occasionally to outbursts of violence or to workers' strikes. E. J. Perry, *Challenging the Mandate of Heaven: Social Protest and State Power in China* (Armonk, NY: M. E. Sharpe, 2002), pp. 206–37 and 275–90; F. Gipouloux, *Les Cent Fleurs à l'usine: agitation ouvrière et crise du modèle soviétique en Chine, 1956–1957* (Paris: Editions de l'Ecole des Hautes Études en Sciences Sociales, 1986).
93. The only one who had dared to do so (during the Great Leap Forward famine), Marshal Peng Dehuai, had been immediately stripped of all his positions, without anybody saying a word in his favour.
94. Huang, 'Rural Class Struggle', p. 127.
95. It could have originated in Stalin's USSR.
96. A. F. Thurston, *Enemies of the People: The Ordeal of the Intellectuals in China's Great Cultural Revolution* (Cambridge, MA: Harvard University Press, 1988).
97. Zheng, *Scarlet Memorials*, p. 24.
98. Ibid., p. 12.
99. Short, Mao, pp. 237–48.
100. Zheng, *Scarlet Memorials*, pp. 17 and 58–59.
101. Figure based on Margolin, 'Communismes d'Asie' and more recent publications.
102. Quoted in Zheng, *Scarlet Memorials*, p. 13.
103. C. Wen, *The Red Mirror: Children of China's Cultural Revolution* (Boulder, CO: Westview Press, 1995), pp. 48–49.
104. Margolin, *L'armée de l'empereur*, p. 187.
105. Another feature of the prisons during the 1950s is reminiscent of Japanese practices: the forced (sometimes painful) physical postures that the detainees had to adopt for hours in their cells.
106. Hair was shaved off on one side of the head.
107. Margolin, 'Communismes d'Asie', p. 575. In 2006 Italian Prime Minister Silvio Berlusconi sparked an incident with China, when he used that fact against his domestic communist opponents. He implied, falsely, that it could have been a general policy.
108. Zheng, *Scarlet Memorials*, pp. 105–108.
109. Bao and Chelminski, *Prisoner of Mao*.
110. Unger, 'Whither China?', 31; N. Cheng, *Life and Death in Shanghai* (London: Grafton Books, 1986), Ch. 7.
111. Yang and McFadden, *Captive Spirits*, p. 283.
112. Thus university professor Chen Ming, freed in 1956 after five years of hard labour, could only get a job as a street sweeper – for the next 25 years. Constantly derided by his superiors, he again lost his right to vote in 1957, for no reason. Chen, *Come Watch the Sun Go Home*, pp. 149–50.
113. Zhang and MacLeod, *China Remembers*, p. 139.
114. Several examples in Bao and Chelminski, *Prisoner of Mao*; Yang and McFadden, *Captive Spirits*, and H. Wu, *Bitter Winds: A Memoir of My Years in China's Gulag* (Chichester: John Wiley & Sons, 1994).
115. MacFarquhar and Schoenhals, *Mao's Last Revolution*, p. 27.
116. Wen, *The Red Mirror*, p. 84.
117. Ibid., p. 141.
118. Bonnin, *Génération perdue*.
119. Wen, *The Red Mirror*, pp. 99–105.

120. There were many versions of that statement of the 'class blood line' theory, some even cruder than this one. Countless testimonies show its omnipresence. It was even posted as a talisman on the entrance gate of Red families.
121. Wen, *The Red Mirror*, pp. 140–2.
122. Ibid., pp. 22–4.
123. W. A. Joseph, 'A Tragedy of Good Intentions: Post-Mao Views of the Great Leap Forward', *Modern China*, 12, 4 (1986), 419–57.
124. Becker, *Hungry Ghosts*; see also W. Hinton, *Shenfan* (New York: Random House, 1984).
125. Li, *The Private Life*, p. 274.
126. Chang and Halliday, *Mao*, pp. 485–6.
127. Becker, *Hungry Ghosts*, pp. 89–93; Li, *The Private Life*, pp. 314–21.
128. It is probably for that reason that the Great Leap Forward has never been officially criticized, in contrast with the Cultural Revolution.
129. Margolin, *L'armée de l'empereur*, pp. 214–15.
130. Zhang and MacLeod, *China Remembers*, pp. 84–5.
131. Ibid., pp. 68–9.
132. Ibid., p. 83; Becker, *Hungry Ghosts*, Ch. 14 and p. 137.
133. Becker, *Hungry Ghosts*, pp.143–6.
134. Many Red Guards have narrated their stupefaction at the extreme poverty of most peasants. Before being allowed to travel for free in 1966, and sometimes before their own rustication, around 1968, most of them had never left their hometown, and even less visited a village.
135. At best, the detainees could receive one family visit per year. Many were kept for years in total secrecy, their loved ones not even knowing if they were alive or dead. The violent death of Vice-Chairman Lin Biao, in September 1971, was not made public for months.

18

Documentation Delayed, Justice Denied: The Historiography of the Cambodian Genocide

Ben Kiernan

Seven months after the Khmer Rouge took over Cambodia in April 1975, and forcibly emptied its capital, Phnom Penh, the Foreign Minister of neighbouring Thailand, Chatichai Choonhavan, travelled to Washington, D.C. There he met with the U.S. Secretary of State, Henry Kissinger, and his Assistant Secretary for East Asian and Pacific Affairs, Philip Habib. After an exchange of greetings, Kissinger informed Chatichai of U.S. President Gerald Ford's forthcoming visit to China. He then asked Chatichai about his recent meeting with China's Khmer Rouge ally, the new Cambodian Deputy Prime Minister and Foreign Minister, Ieng Sary, brother-in-law of Pol Pot.

> Kissinger: Did Ieng Sary impress you?
> Chatichai: He is a nice, quiet man.
> Kissinger: How many people did he kill? Tens of thousands?
> Habib: Nicely and quietly!!
> Chatichai: Not more than 10,000. That's why they need food. If they had killed everyone, they would not need salt and fish. All the bridges in Cambodia were destroyed. There was no transportation, no gas. That's why they had to chase people away from the capital.
> Kissinger: But with only two hours' notice?
> Chatichai: (Shrugs.)
> Kissinger: What do the Cambodians think of the United States? You should tell them that we bear no hostility towards them. We would like them to be independent as a counterweight to North Vietnam.
> Chatichai: Are you a member of the Domino Club?
> Kissinger: I am.
> Chatichai: The outer, most exposed belt of dominoes is Cambodia and Laos. Thailand is in the inner belt and is less exposed.
> Kissinger: We would prefer to have Laos and Cambodia aligned with China rather than with North Vietnam. ...

Almost immediately, Kissinger reiterated this point: 'We don't mind Chinese influence in Cambodia to balance North Vietnam.' Minutes later, the Secretary of State again returned to the subject:

> Kissinger: We are aware that the biggest threat to Southeast Asia at the present time is North Vietnam. Our strategy is to get the Chinese into Laos and Cambodia as a barrier to the Vietnamese.
> Chatichai: I asked the Chinese to take over in Laos. They mentioned that they had a road-building team in northern Laos.
> Kissinger: We would support this. You should also tell the Cambodians that we will be friends with them. They are murderous thugs, but we won't let that stand in our way. We are prepared to improve relations with them. Tell them the latter part, but don't tell them what I said before.[1]

The historiography of the Cambodian genocide was barely beginning. In line with Kissinger's instructions, the official record of his 1975 conversation with Chatichai remained classified, and did not become public for three decades. The Chinese government, for its part, later classified 'for domestic use only' the first-hand account of one of its diplomats in Cambodia, detailing Beijing's support for the Khmer Rouge regime.[2] As of 2006, any comprehensive documentation of the international alliances behind the Cambodian genocide is still mostly inaccessible in Chinese, Thai, and U.S. archives.

Moreover, when the Khmer Rouge came to power in 1975, there were very few international Cambodia experts, and most of them worked for the U.S. government. Just writing the history of events on the ground in Cambodia would prove difficult. Since then, the key task of historians of Cambodia has been to document as fully as possible what happened to its people under Khmer Rouge rule from 1975 to 1979. First, this research required consulting all available Cambodian sources.

The primary sources and first scholarship on the Khmer Rouge

After entering Phnom Penh on 17 April 1975, the Khmer Rouge not only deported Cambodia's urban populations to rural areas, but they also expelled all international diplomats and journalists from the country, shut down its newspapers, and cut off private postal, telephone and telegraphic communications. Until its overthrow by the Vietnamese army in January 1979, the Khmer Rouge regime, calling itself Democratic Kampuchea (DK), admitted very few foreign diplomatic missions, fewer reporters, and no unofficial guests or tourists. DK officials in the nearly empty Cambodian capital prevented any unsupervised travel outside the city. Only a handful of foreigners, mostly Chinese and North Korean technical advisors working on agricultural sites or military installations, could visit the countryside. Physical conditions there were extremely harsh, murder common, and intellectual life virtually prohibited.

So it was impossible for any surviving Cambodian historians or writers to publish inside the country, or to communicate with fellow Cambodia specialists in other countries. Khmer Rouge supervision was so close that few, if any, Cambodians managed to keep even private diaries. Memoirs could be written only after escape abroad, or after the fall of the DK regime in 1979. The Cambodian engineer Pin Yathay, who escaped to Thailand in mid-1977, provided an account of life in DK to *Le Monde* later that year, and in 1980, Yathay published a book that became one of the first refugee memoirs, *L'Utopie Meurtrière* ('The Murderous Utopia'). The more numerous Cambodian refugees who fled to Vietnam or Laos from 1974 all remained inaccessible to Western reporters until 1978, after the DK regime had attacked across both country's borders and severed diplomatic contact with Vietnam. Only then did Hanoi, abandoning its hope for cooperative relations with the Khmer Rouge regime, begin to facilitate foreign journalists' interviews with Cambodian refugees in Vietnam, as well as plan the overthrow of DK.

During the DK period, apart from the regime's occasional press releases in French, almost no documentary sources were available on the events that were occurring in this closed country isolated from the outside world. Oral sources of information fell into just two main categories. These were the accounts of escaping Cambodian refugees, and the new state's official radio station, 'The Voice of Democratic Kampuchea' (VODK). The CIA translated excerpts of VODK's daily radio broadcasts into English, and a few of the refugees spoke French, English or Chinese. Beyond those limited sources, any analysis of developments as they unfolded in Cambodia required Khmer-language skills that few international observers possessed, or an interpreter.

Even the United States Government had trained only a small circle of Khmer-speaking professional Cambodia-watchers. From 1965 to 1969, the U.S. had maintained no embassy in Phnom Penh, and from 1969 to 1975, American activities in Cambodia consisted largely of the massive bombardment of its countryside from the air and the two-month invasion of American ground troops from South Vietnam into the eastern part of the country in 1970. In contrast to the long and extensive U.S. involvement in Vietnam, few Americans visited Cambodia and fewer learned Khmer. The U.S. withdrew all its embassy staff from Cambodia in April 1975, and re-established a diplomatic mission there only in 1991.

Therefore, most of the burden of reporting on events inside the country from 1975 to 1979 fell to Western and Thai journalists, using Khmer interpreters to interview refugees who had fled to Thailand, mostly from western Cambodia, the region of the country where conditions were initially worst. The quality of the newspaper reporting varied widely, but much of it proved excellent and informative.[3] In a May 1976 assessment, for instance, Denis Gray, Bangkok bureau chief of Associated Press, wrote: 'After a year of these interviews I do get a growing sense of massive tragedy and brutality in the country, whether by central design or lack of central control I'm not sure. I would never place any casualty figures on all this. That's absurd and typical American newsmagazine style of drama. But I believe it could be staggering. I also see no evidence of Vietnamese or Soviet influence as some do in Cambodia.'[4] Historians of the country depended upon such Bangkok-based journalists and professional Cambodia watchers for all the information they could get, as did other scholars, such as the pioneering American anthropologist of Cambodia, May Ebihara, who had lived in Cambodia in 1959–60 but was unable to return there until the 1980s.

U.S. Government employees comprised the vast majority of the limited number of proficient Khmer-speaking observers closely watching events in Cambodia after 1975. However, the confidential reporting and analysis of the U.S. Central Intelligence Agency (CIA) on the Khmer Rouge had long been marred by internal dissension, political manipulation and suppression of information. Most U.S. Government officers were in no position to publish widely or at all on post-1975 developments in Cambodia. Several Khmer-speaking experts, who included a native Cambodian, worked for the CIA, which maintained a station in the U.S. embassy in Bangkok.[5] Yet even 30 years later, to my knowledge, none of the CIA's Cambodia reporting from 1975 to 1979 has yet been published, while very little has been declassified, and only after long delays.

For instance, in response to my 1980–1 Freedom of Information Act requests, in 1987 the CIA finally released eight of its documents on the pre-1975 history of the Khmer Rouge, and parts of 33 other pre-1975 documents. The Agency withheld in full a further 141 documents on the Khmer Rouge dating from 1954 to August 1980. Among these were 74 documents that, in addition, the CIA ruled 'cannot be listed', which included all relevant documents dating from January 1975 to 27 August 1980, on the grounds that, along with the 67 listed but fully-classified documents, they may be 'kept secret in the interest of national defense or foreign policy'.[6] Then, in May 1995 the U.S. Department of State officially asked the CIA to 'search for, review and declassify' U.S. intelligence documents 'relating to the issue of Cambodian genocide', but the Agency answered this request in January 1996 by declassifying less than 20 pages, some so heavily redacted as to leave only one or two sentences.[7]

One U.S. official, Timothy M. Carney, had learned Khmer when he served as political counsellor in the American embassy in Phnom Penh before 1975. Then, during a brief leave from government service, Carney translated Cambodian school inspector Ith Sarin's first-hand account of nine months among Khmer Rouge insurgents, published in Phnom Penh in 1973 as *Sronoh*

Pralung Khmaer ('Regrets for the Khmer Soul'). The book included details of the Communist Party of Kampuchea's (CPK) leadership and organization, its absolutist ideology, and its successes among the peasantry west of Phnom Penh. Carney translated half of the book, plus a shorter report Sarin had written in French, and two other pre-April 1975 CPK documents, and published them in 1977 under the title *Communist Party Power in Kampuchea*, with a thoughtful introduction.[8]

Meanwhile, State Department officer Charles Twining had become the leading official U.S. Cambodia expert after 1975, when he was stationed at the embassy in Bangkok. Some of Twining's careful reports on conditions under the Khmer Rouge regime, based on his interviews with refugees along the Thai-Cambodian border in 1975–7, were released by the U.S. State Department in July 1978, six months before the fall of the DK regime.[9] Other publications were delayed much longer. In the late 1970s, for instance, Carney and Twining both wrote detailed, seminal articles for publication, but these did not appear in print until 1989, when another U.S. official, Karl Jackson, published them in *Cambodia 1975–1978: Rendezvous with Death*, an anthology for which Jackson had commissioned their contributions a decade or so earlier.[10]

Another Khmer-speaking researcher working for the U.S. government by 1979 was Stephen R. Heder, a former freelance journalist who had written under the name 'J.D. Wilcox' in Cambodia before 1975. Afterwards Heder used the pseudonym 'Larry Palmer', and wrote articles favouring the Khmer Rouge side in the border conflicts between Cambodia and its neighbours. In late 1978, Heder obtained a rare DK visa to visit Cambodia, with a delegation of American Maoists. However, the invading Vietnamese forces took Phnom Penh on 7 January 1979, just before the delegation was to board its flight there from Beijing. The Khmer Rouge regime fell and the group's visit to DK had to be cancelled.[11] From 1979 until 1981, Heder served on the Thai-Cambodian border as a U.S. intelligence officer, but during the next 25 years, publicly denied having done so.[12] In 1980–1, he wrote several U.S. government-funded studies critical of the Vietnamese intervention that had defeated the Khmer Rouge forces, and highlighting their anti-Vietnamese resistance.[13]

In 1975, the corpus of historical work on the Khmer Rouge was still small. Carney's publication of Ith Sarin's 1973 accounts complemented several other studies of the pre-1975 Khmer Rouge movement, whose authors did not (or not yet) know the Khmer language. Three of these first appeared in print only in 1975–6. The American journalist Donald Kirk's prescient 1974 paper, 'The Khmer Rouge: Revolutionaries or Terrorists?', and my historical study of the Khmer Rouge rebellions in the late 1960s, based on French-language Cambodian sources and published in Australia, both appeared in late 1975.[14] At the American Political Science Association meeting in September of that year, State Department officer Kenneth M. Quinn presented an edited version of a long, classified report that he had cabled to Washington from his consulate in South Vietnam in 1974, entitled 'The Khmer Krahom Program to Create a Communist Society in Southern Cambodia'. Quinn had compiled this important, detailed report from the accounts of refugees who had reached southern Vietnam in 1972–3 after fleeing from areas of Cambodia's Southwest Zone, already controlled by Khmer Rouge insurgents. Quinn published an edited version of that paper in *The U.S. Naval War College Review* in 1976. He also wrote an article entitled 'Cambodia 1976', published the next year in *Asian Survey*. However, Quinn's major contribution to the literature on the 1975–9 Khmer Rouge regime, like those of Carney and Twining, remained unpublished until 1989, when Jackson's anthology appeared in print.[15]

As an Australian diplomat, Milton E. Osborne had learned Vietnamese and served in the Australian embassies in Saigon and Phnom Penh in the 1960s. He then left the diplomatic service to write a doctoral dissertation at Cornell University on the nineteenth-century French colonization of Cambodia and southern Vietnam. Osborne held academic positions in Australia and the United States before eventually returning to Canberra to take up a government post. In October 1976, his assessment, 'Reflections on the Cambodian Tragedy', appeared in the journal *Pacific Community*.[16]

Apart from the U.S. Government experts, only a few Khmer-speaking Western specialists on Cambodia continued actively to track events occurring inside the country in the late 1970s. Unlike the official Cambodia watchers they were in no position to do so systematically or full-time. Two of them were also former U.S. Government employees who had gone on to become leading historians of Cambodia. David P. Chandler had served in the U.S. embassy in Cambodia from 1960 to 1962, and later in Thailand. He then wrote a PhD dissertation on nineteenth-century Cambodian history, and took up an appointment in 1972 at Monash University, Australia, where I was an undergraduate student. Chandler later became my academic adviser, and in 1976, he, Muy Hong Lim and I published the account of a Cambodian refugee, Peang Sophi, who had escaped the country early that year. Sophi recounted a Khmer jingle circulating in the factory where he had worked: 'The Khmer Rouge kill, but never explain' (*khmaer krahom somlap, men dael prap*).[17] In 1976, Chandler also published an article on the new DK constitution, followed the next year by his analysis of the continuing Khmer Rouge revolution, entitled 'Transformation in Cambodia'. He concluded: 'Is the price for liberation, in human terms, too high? Surely, as a friend of mine has written, we Americans with our squalid record in Cambodia should be "cautiously optimistic" about the new regime, "or else shut up". At the same time, I might feel less cautious and more optimistic if I were able to hear the voices of people I knew in the Cambodian countryside fourteen years ago, telling me about the revolution in their own words.' In 1977, Chandler turned to commence the research for his major work, *A History of Cambodia*, which focused on the period from early times to 1953. After its publication in 1983, he wrote *Brother Number One: A Political Biography of Pol Pot*, which appeared in 1992.[18]

Another senior Cambodia historian, Michael Vickery, had worked for two years with U.S. military intelligence in Germany in the 1950s.[19] He then took a teaching post in Cambodia, where he lived from 1960–4 and 1970–2. Vickery learned Khmer and wrote his Yale University PhD dissertation, which he completed in 1977, on the early modern history of post-Angkor Cambodia, while holding an academic post at Universiti Sains Malaysia, in Penang. In the Australian journal *Westerly* in 1976, Vickery published a historical survey of the previous three decades, based on Khmer-language sources, entitled 'Looking Back at Cambodia'. Like Chandler, he went on to publish extensively on the DK regime after its fall.[20]

The French Catholic priest François Ponchaud, who had lived in Cambodia for 15 years until his expulsion by its new Khmer Rouge rulers in April 1975, also spoke Khmer fluently. In *Le Monde* in early 1976, Ponchaud published a critique of the DK regime, followed by several journal articles on it, and a book, *Cambodge Année Zéro*, published in Paris in March 1977 and in English translation the next year as *Cambodia Year Zero*. Ponchaud's was thus the first serious book-length assessment of the Khmer Rouge regime, and the most comprehensive analysis to appear in print during the DK period. It concluded that the traditional Khmer smile 'has frozen into a grimace of death'.[21] Soon after, Ponchaud reportedly began writing a sequel, covering the years 1977 and 1978, but it has not yet been published.

The nature of the Cambodian genocide

Ponchaud suggested in *Cambodge Année Zéro* that over a million Cambodians had died in the first two years of the DK regime, as a result of starvation, disease and executions.[22] Writing in an undergraduate publication in 1976, I questioned such figures, as did some scholars like Vickery.[23] One million deaths remains a high estimate for the period 1975–6. Yet even in those first two years of DK, the Cambodian toll was undoubtedly in the hundreds of thousands, possibly as many as 500,000. Ponchaud proved correct in his grim assessment of the nature of the DK regime. In 1977–8 it went on to inflict an even higher toll, now with an escalating proportion of outright murders, in contrast to the higher percentage of deaths from starvation in 1975 and especially in 1976. The DK leadership proved, then, quite the opposite of a government that observers could expect to constrain its own violence over time, let alone to punish its individual perpetrators. This was a key assessment of a genocidal regime.

Responsibility for the killing was a separate issue from the death toll. There had been brief indications, detectable in 1975–6, that unnamed Khmer Rouge leaders and cadres were attempting to control or limit the killing. The refugee Peang Sophi, in interviews with Muy Hong Lim and me, provided corroboration of such reports.[24] On this basis I had suggested in 1976 that the post-war killings were mostly regional or spontaneous, including local revenge violence that might be expected in the aftermath of a brutal conflict but would also be likely to diminish over time.[25] Such killings were documented, yet the violence did not decrease. Who was behind it? During 1976, some press reports suggested that a radical pro-Vietnam faction of the Khmer Rouge, supposedly led by Ieng Sary, had defeated a more 'moderate' pro-China faction in a power struggle in Phnom Penh.[26] This too proved incorrect. The group led by Pol Pot and Ieng Sary had indeed triumphed, but they led the 'pro-China' faction and their escalating violence was directed at Vietnamese as well as Cambodians.

Indications that the bloodletting might subside ended in 1977. The cause of the continued killing and dying lay in the nature of the Khmer Rouge leaders and their policies. From the second half of 1976, we later learned, Pol Pot and his circle had directed a series of brutal internecine purges of their own ruling party, the CPK. Escalating the assassinations of Party members that we now know had secretly begun in the early 1970s, the CPK's national-level authority, the 'Party Centre' (*mocchim paks*), which included Pol Pot, Nuon Chea, Ieng Sary, Vorn Vet, Son Sen, Khieu Samphan, and DK's top military commanders Mok and Ke Pauk, sent a succession of CPK purge teams fanning across Cambodia, zone by zone, to arrest and murder all suspected internal opponents, potential rivals and large numbers of their family members and associates, as well as many former soldiers of the Khmer Republic regime, which the Khmer Rouge had defeated in April 1975.

On an official visit to China in September 1977, Pol Pot strode confidently into the international public arena as Beijing's closest ally, unchallenged leader of the CPK, and Prime Minister of DK. To his death in 1998, however, Pol Pot never admitted that his real name was Saloth Sar, a name that Ith Sarin had identified in 1973 as that of the CPK's No. 1 leader.[27] The Khmer Rouge revolution, a CPK document put it in 1977, operated 'by taking secrecy as the basis'.[28] It took the penetrating journalism of diplomatic correspondent Nayan Chanda to uncover Pol Pot's real identity, which Chanda published in October 1977.[29] DK also successfully concealed the operations of its major extermination center, Tuol Sleng prison, which the Khmer Rouge code-named 'S-21', and its existence remained unknown to outside observers until after DK fell in 1979.[30]

In 1978, I began a PhD programme in Cambodian colonial history, started to learn Khmer, and also interviewed newly escaped refugees who had spent more than a year in DK. I acknowledged that Ponchaud's analysis, and the best reporting of the Bangkok press corps, had proved correct on telling points.[31] It remained true that the worst conditions, including starvation, had initially prevailed in northwest Cambodia, near the Thai border; that the worst violence had spread to the Eastern Zone, near the Vietnamese border, only from 1977 and especially in 1978; and that the information provided by refugees from the northwest who had reached Thailand before 1977 could not reveal much about conditions across the rest of the country, or later. Ponchaud's 1975–6 analyses had not taken account of these factors. Yet subsequently, the nationwide spread of mass killing through the CPK Centre's escalating purges of all Zones of DK vindicated his essential assessment of the nature of the Khmer Rouge leadership. DK was a killer regime which had demonstrated that capacity on assuming power, despite its often successful attempts to conceal its policies and actions from both Cambodians and foreigners, and despite its piecemeal progress in maximizing control.

As a centralizing regime too, DK's plans met recalcitrance and opposition in various regions of the country, even in CPK Zone party branches. Totalitarian absolute power was not an immediate reality but an ideological ambition, requiring a process of violent imposition starting in 1975 (or even before), but yet to be fully achieved even three years later. In the Eastern Zone on the Vietnamese border, the local CPK leaders were also harsh but more popular and, mostly unwittingly, they opted for more moderate policies than those prevailing in other Zones closer to the Centre, particularly the Southwest, which Kenneth Quinn had identified in 1974 as a region of harsh violence. The Centre leaders saw the East as the hardest nut to crack. With the assistance of Southwest units, they first purged all other Zones, and then attempted a full suppression of the Eastern CPK branch in May 1978. At that point, the Centre launched its most horrific killing spree, slaughtering possibly 250,000 eastern Cambodians in mid- to late 1978. That provoked remnant Eastern Zone CPK units to stage a conventional rebellion, which tied down the Centre's armed forces for several months, before most surviving rebels fled across the border into Vietnam.[32]

This key issue of central control inspired most of the debate at an international academic conference on the history of the Khmer Rouge regime, sponsored by the Social Science Research Council and held in Chiangmai, Thailand, in August 1981. My paper on the Eastern Zone stressed the ongoing process of DK centralization, and took a different view from Michael Vickery's emphasis on regional autonomy and differentiation ('Themes and Variations'), as did British writer Anthony Barnett's contribution, 'Democratic Kampuchea: A Highly Centralized Dictatorship'.[33]

From 1975 to 1978, then, the Khmer Rouge genocide spread from political mass murder, of officials and officers of the defeated Khmer Republic, then of its rank-and-file soldiers, and then of members and associates of the CPK itself, to finally, the extermination of geographic groups such as easterners. For historians trying to interpret this violence as it happened, another issue relevant to that of genocide was the class basis, if any, of the Khmer Rouge revolution, and of social groups it targeted for extermination. The CPK Centre proclaimed an ideological loyalty to the interests of the Cambodian peasantry. It sometimes used the term 'worker-peasant power', and it persecuted the deported urban populations as a subjugated class, classifying them at the bottom of the new DK social ladder as mere 'depositees', who lacked even the status of the next group above them, those considered 'candidates' for promotion upwards to join the highest-favoured group, whom the CPK termed 'full rights' members of Cambodia's population. What was the rationale for such categories? Did use of the latter two terms, Leninist labels for party members which the CPK extended to impose on Cambodia's entire population, mean that the Khmer Rouge had merely intensified the 'standard operating procedure' of other communist revolutions, to use David Chandler's words, and that the CPK was therefore simply 'the purest and most thoroughgoing Marxist-Leninist movement in an era of revolutions'?[34]

In his major work, *Cambodia 1975–1982*, published in 1984, Michael Vickery propounded the differing view that the Khmer Rouge armies had led 'a peasantist revolution of the purest sort', rather than a centralizing Communist dictatorship.[35] He argued that journalists and scholars, basing their assessments on interviews with former urban dwellers who had fled as refugees to Thailand, had missed an important explanation for Khmer Rouge success: peasant support in rural areas. Educated Cambodians speaking Western languages had provided many or most of the refugee accounts reported in newspapers, even if they did not comprise a majority of the refugees accessible in Thailand up to 1977. According to Vickery, these persecuted urban-dwellers were often unsympathetic to peasant viewpoints, while many peasants were sympathetic to the Khmer Rouge, and in some cases they could even pressure the DK leadership to meet anti-urban peasant demands, seize goods from the deportees, or force them to work on agricultural projects under the harshest conditions.

This thesis imputed too much autonomy to the peasantry and therefore understated the crimes of the Khmer Rouge and its leaders' responsibility for them. Yet Vickery also took a strong position in opposition to DK and its remnants in Thailand. Vickery saw their leadership of a 'peasant revolution' as a departure from worker-based orthodox Marxism, and he argued that it merited no support.[36] Taking a position on the opposing political side of the same interpretive issue was Douglas Pike, the former U.S. State Department officer and Vietnam War hawk. In 1979, Pike urged continued U.S. support for the Khmer Rouge remnants and Pol Pot, whom he termed 'charismatic', the leader of a 'bloody but successful peasant revolution with a substantial residue of popular support', a revolution in which, 'on a statistical basis, most' Cambodian peasants, Pike asserted, 'did not experience much in the way of brutality'.[37] Disagreement over this and official U.S. support for the Khmer Rouge against their Cambodian and Vietnamese opponents surfaced at the 1981 Chiangmai conference on the history of the DK regime. After Vickery opened his presentation by calling Pike 'a miserable propaganda hack', Anthony Barnett responded with a question, 'How do you know that he's miserable?'

With the idiosyncratic exception of Douglas Pike, most independent scholars remained opposed to DK and its remnants now ensconced on the Thai border. Yet they divided over the historical issue of whether DK had enjoyed peasant support during its period in power. Most conceded that the Khmer Rouge had gained significant peasant support, and even, that the poorer the peasants in any village or region, the more they had supported the Khmer Rouge. Yet such initial support had largely dissipated, especially in 1977–8. Moreover, some historians, such as Kate G. Frieson, remained inclined to the view that most peasants, or at least most Cambodians, had always opposed the Khmer Rouge and, in 1970–5, only went along with the revolution by force.[38]

The debate over a peasant revolution also led to further explorations of the nature of DK ideology. It was quite possible, of course, for the regime to proclaim itself pro-peasant without serving Cambodian peasant interests at all. Indeed DK policies attacked and suppressed all three basic elements of traditional peasant life: the individual farm, the family unit, and the Buddhist religion. Yet the insight that the DK leaders imagined themselves *ideologically* as pursuing a 'peasant revolution', or as Vickery put it, that they were 'petty bourgeois radicals overcome by peasantist romanticism' was not all that far from the truth.[39] A Khmer Rouge fetish for cultivation dominated DK policies, which imposed forced agricultural labour on nearly all Cambodians. Romantic agrarian images proliferated in the regime's propaganda. In April 1977, two years into the revolution, the DK Head of State Khieu Samphan proclaimed: 'In many places, water is flowing freely, and with water the scenery is fresh, the plants are fresh, life is fresh and people are smiling ... The poor and lower middle peasants are content. So are the middle peasants.' A few months later Pol Pot added: 'People from the former poor and lower middle peasant classes are overwhelmingly content ... because now they can eat all year round and become middle peasants.'[40] This was far from true (peasants made up half of DK's 1.7 million victims), but it appeared to be part of the CPK's ideological vision.

Yet that vision was racial as well as rural. In fact the victims of DK who suffered most disproportionately of all were the minority groups long resident in Cambodia. CPK persecution of the country's Islamic Cham minority, and of its ethnic Vietnamese, Chinese and Thai populations comprises the major legal grounds for the charges of genocide. Research carried out in the 1980s documented the large proportions of these groups who had perished during DK rule. The ethnic Khmer majority (over 80 per cent of the population) had suffered a massive death toll of 15–20 percent in less than four years. However, the CPK Centre exterminated virtually all of the 10,000–20,000 ethnic Vietnamese who remained in DK after 1975, while half of Cambodia's 500,000 Chinese and one-third of the 250,000 Chams also died during DK.[41] By the 1990s a scholarly consensus had emerged that the term 'genocide' covered these cases, as well as DK's victimization of Cambodia's majority Khmer Buddhist religious orders. As two legal scholars wrote: 'The existing literature presents a strong prima facie case that the Khmer Rouge committed genocide against the Cham minority group, the ethnic Vietnamese, Chinese and Thai minority groups, and the Buddhist monkhood. While some commentators suggest otherwise, virtually every author on the subject has reached this conclusion.'[42] In 1999, a UN-appointed group of legal experts concluded again that surviving Khmer Rouge leaders should face trial for these specific cases of genocide, and for other crimes against humanity.[43]

The international context of the Cambodian genocide

In his November 1975 meeting with Thai Foreign Minister Chatichai, Henry Kissinger had asked Chatichai to tell those 'murderous thugs', the Khmer Rouge leaders, that 'we will be friends with them' and seek to 'improve relations with them'. A week later, Kissinger accompanied U.S. president Gerald Ford to Jakarta, to visit Indonesia's President Suharto. Ford told Suharto:

> The unification of Vietnam has come more quickly than we anticipated. There is, however, resistance in Cambodia to the influence of Hanoi. We are willing to move slowly in our relations with Cambodia, hoping perhaps to slow down the North Vietnamese influence although we find the Cambodian government very difficult.

Kissinger then explained Beijing's parallel strategy:

> The Chinese want to use Cambodia to balance off Vietnam ... We don't like Cambodia, for the government in many ways is worse than Vietnam, but we would like it to be independent. We don't discourage Thailand or China from drawing closer to Cambodia.[44]

Almost immediately, trusted press sources reflected the U.S. tilt in favour of the Khmer Rouge regime. The December 1975 issue of the *Reader's Digest* magazine, which had a circulation of 30 million, featured an article entitled 'Showdown over Southeast Asia', whose author, conservative journalist Joseph Alsop, was up to date on regional U.S. policy. Alsop described the ruling Khmer Rouge as 'passionate nationalists' and defended their evacuation of Cambodia's cities the previous April. He focused instead on the threat of 'Hanoi's expansion', and added that 'the Chinese will eventually have to make the fearful choice between preventive military measures in South-East Asia – with all the risks of Soviet intervention – and acceptance of paralyzing encirclement by Soviet power to the north and North Vietnamese power to the south.' Unless China could stop Vietnam, Alsop added, 'the whole hard-won American position in the Western Pacific will begin to founder.' Thus, he wrote, 'a wholly new political game – begun soon after the fall of Saigon – is under way in Asia.'[45] Unfortunately for the Cambodian people, victims of the Khmer Rouge genocide, they were on the wrong side of this 'game'.

For such geopolitical reasons, while DK ruled Cambodia and the genocide progressed, Washington, Beijing and Bangkok all supported the continued independent existence of the perpetrator regime. Like the thousands of Vietnamese civilians killed in Khmer Rouge cross-border attacks, the domestic victims of DK received no practical support from the world's most powerful regime. Even the 1977 *Readers' Digest* book, *Murder of a Gentle Land: The Untold Story of Communist Genocide in Cambodia,* failed to divert the U.S. government from its support for China's geopolitical goal 'to use Cambodia to balance off Vietnam', as Kissinger had approvingly described it. When the Carter Administration took office in 1977, the mass killings in Cambodia were escalating dramatically. Yet in September 1977, the CIA incorrectly reported a decrease: 'In the past year there have been few reports of executions other than those related to attempted escapes across the Thai border or political discord within the communist organization.'[46]

This support continued after the Vietnamese army overthrew Pol Pot's regime and ended the genocide in January 1979. The next year the CIA even published a 'demographic report' which explicitly denied that DK was guilty of any killings during the two worst years, 1977 and 1978, when the regime had in fact murdered around half a million people. This 1980 CIA report asserted that the 'final executions' of the DK period had already come to an end in late 1976.[47]

Thus, as Beijing maintained its alliance with the exiled Khmer Rouge forces based in Thailand, Washington continued its support for that alliance under three Presidents: Jimmy Carter, Ronald Reagan and George H. W. Bush. For instance, Carter's national security advisor Zbigniew Brzezinski recalled Kissinger's earlier policy when he revealed that in 1979, 'I encouraged the Chinese to support Pol Pot. Pol Pot was an abomination. We could never support him, but China could.' According to Brzezinski, the USA therefore 'winked, semi-publicly' at Chinese and Thai aid to the Khmer Rouge forces, while U.S. officials pushed through additional U.N. and other international aid to their camps on the Thai border.[48]

After Carter's election defeat, the CIA's former deputy director Ray Cline, an associate of the incoming Reagan Administration, made a secret visit to a Khmer Rouge camp inside Cambodia in November 1980.[49] American intelligence officer Stephen Heder argued in 1982 that the Khmer Rouge regime 'became murderous' while it was in power not by premeditation, but because of its unrealistic policies and its leaders' dictatorship and corruption. In Heder's view, 'deaths caused by starvations, illness, executions, etc., originated from the internal problems of the Pol Pot regime, but they were not organized or planned.'[50]

President Reagan's Secretary of State, George Shultz, opposed efforts to investigate or indict the Khmer Rouge for genocide or other crimes against humanity. Shultz described as 'stupid', Australian Foreign Minister Bill Hayden's efforts in 1983 to encourage dialogue over Cambodia, and in 1986 Shultz refused to support Hayden's ground-breaking proposal for an international tribunal to judge the crimes of the Khmer Rouge. On a visit to Thailand, Shultz also warned against peace talks with Vietnam, telling ASEAN 'to be extremely cautious in formulating peace proposals for Kampuchea because Vietnam might one day accept them'.[51]

However by now, contrary to U.S. policy, Kissinger's 1975 diplomatic partner, former Thai Foreign Minister Chatichai Choonhavan, had changed his mind about supporting the Khmer Rouge against Vietnam. In 1988, Chatichai became Thailand's first elected Prime Minister in 12 years. He quickly adopted a new foreign policy, based on 'turning Indochina into a marketplace rather than a battlefield', and of engagement with Vietnam and its allied regime in Cambodia, instead of isolating them. The next year, seeing this new Thai policy as a defection from the positions of Washington and Beijing, the first Bush administration moved to take a hard line against Thailand. The *Far Eastern Economic Review* reported that in 1989, U.S. 'officials warned that if Thailand abandoned the Cambodian resistance and its leader Sihanouk for the sake of doing business with Phnom Penh it would have to pay a price.'[52] Secretary of State James A. Baker instead proposed that the Khmer Rouge be included in the future government of Cambodia.[53]

Washington's support for a Khmer Rouge role in Cambodia's future continued to protect Khmer Rouge interests, as did U.S. opposition to peace talks with Cambodia and Vietnam. After the breakdown of the 1989 Paris Peace Conference on Cambodia, *Asiaweek* reported: 'The only sign of settlement is a conference of the four factions along with ASEAN and Vietnam, suggested by Thailand's fence-mending Prime Minister Chatichai Choonhavan ... Washington, whose say-so is important, has indicated that it disapproves. That has put a damper on the plan.'[54] The next year the U.S. again opposed Thai proposals for a cease-fire, and for the establishment of neutral camps to protect Cambodian refugees from the depredations of the Khmer Rouge and their allies.[55] Before cease-fire talks in Tokyo in mid-1990, the U.S. Assistant Secretary of State for East Asian and Pacific Affairs, Richard Solomon, made a secret trip to deliver another warning to the Thais.[56]

On 14 June 1990, Thai Prime Minister Chatichai again visited Washington, this time to meet President George H. W. Bush. They disagreed on Cambodia. Chatichai called for U.S. pressure on China to reduce its support for Pol Pot's forces, but Bush favoured a 'comprehensive solution' that included the Khmer Rouge. China and the U.S. successfully demanded the inclusion of the Khmer Rouge in the 1991 U.N. Plan for Cambodia.[57] That February, Chinese and U.S.

officials barely concealed their satisfaction when a military junta overthrew Chatichai's democratic government in Bangkok.[58] Visiting there the next month, U.S. Assistant Secretary of State Richard Solomon also criticized a Japanese proposal to establish a commission to investigate the Khmer Rouge, saying that such a historical investigation would be 'likely to introduce confusion in international peace efforts'.[59] The new Thai strongman, Army Commander Suchinda Krapayoon, told a visiting U.S. senator that he considered Pol Pot a 'nice guy'.[60]

This was the international context, from 1975 to 1991, in which the historiography of the Cambodian genocide first emerged. The initial task was, of course, to document what had happened under the Khmer Rouge, but the international alliances facilitating and concealing the genocide were also crucial. Yet China's archives still remain closed in 2006, and the pro-Chinese U.S. policy that favoured the Khmer Rouge regime during and long after its period in power, despite its murderous record, could be documented only after the transcripts of Kissinger's diplomatic conversations with the leaders of Southeast Asian countries neighbouring Cambodia began to be declassified a quarter-century later, in 2001.

Meanwhile, a new generation of Khmer-speaking scholars emerged in the 1990s to pursue the documentation of the Cambodian genocide. Few of these were trained as historians, but political scientists and anthropologists, such as Kate G. Frieson, Alexander Laban Hinton, Caroline Hughes, Justin Jordens, Judy Ledgerwood, John Marston and David Roberts have done excellent work with new primary sources. Quality comparative work is also appearing in Susan Cook's *Genocide in Cambodia and Rwanda*, and historian Edward Kissi's *Revolution and Genocide in Ethiopia and Cambodia*.[61]

Since the demise of DK, the available Cambodian documentation has expanded exponentially as well. Approximately 100,000 pages of DK's Tuol Sleng (S-21) prison and execution records, made accessible to scholars by the Cambodian government since 1980, have been microfilmed by Cornell University. Chandler published his *Voices from S-21*, and British journalist Nic Dunlop wrote *The Lost Executioner*, a biography of the prison's commandant, Deuch, who is himself now in jail awaiting trial for his crimes.[62] By 1991 the National Archives of Cambodia had opened up tens of thousands more pages of Khmer Rouge documents, mostly trade and economic records of the DK Commerce Ministry.

Since 1994, Yale University's Cambodian Genocide Program[63] (CGP) has published 22,000 Khmer Rouge biographic and bibliographic records and 6,000 photographs of victims, along with texts and translations of DK documents, and an interactive geographic database detailing Cambodia's 13,000 villages, the 231,000 U.S. bombing sorties flown over its rural areas, 158 DK prisons, 309 DK-era mass-grave sites with an estimated total of 19,000 grave pits, and 76 sites of memorials to victims.

In 1996, the CGP and its then field office, the Documentation Centre of Cambodia, uncovered the archives of the CPK Centre's *Santebal*, or Security forces. Yale's Sterling Library has microfilmed the 100,000-page *Santebal* archive, and this collection is expected to play an important part in the joint UN/Cambodian tribunal of surviving senior DK leaders. Trials are scheduled to commence in 2007, despite the Bush Administration's denial of previously appropriated U.S. Congressional funding for the tribunal.

After 30 years of justice delayed, the Khmer Rouge trials, and continuing historical research, should finally bring to light a comprehensive documentary record of Khmer Rouge responsibility for the Cambodian genocide. However, historians have yet to fully document or address the complicity of foreign powers such as China, Thailand and the United States.

Notes

1. Memorandum of Conversation, 'Secretary's Meeting with Foreign Minister Chatichai of Thailand', 26 November 1975, declassified 27 July 2004, 19pp., at pp. 3–4, 8: (www.gwu.edu/~nsarchiv/NSAEBB/NSAEBB193/HAK-11-26-75.pdf).
2. Yun Shui, 'An Account of Chinese Diplomats Accompanying the Government of Democratic Kampuchea's Move to the Cardamom Mountains', in *Guoji Fengyunzhongde Zhongguo Waijiaoguan* [Chinese Diplomats in International Crises] (Beijing: Shijie Zhishi Chubanshe [World Knowledge], 1992), pp. 85–112; trans. P. Marks, in *Conflict and Change in Cambodia*, ed. B. Kiernan, special issue of *Critical Asian Studies*, 34, 4 (2002), 496–519; reproduced in *Conflict and Change in Cambodia*, ed. B. Kiernan (London: Routledge, 2006), pp. 1–25.
3. For different views, see N. Chomsky and E. S. Herman, 'Cambodia', in their *After the Cataclysm: Postwar Indochina and the Reconstruction of Imperial Ideology* (Boston, MA: South End Press, 1980), pp. 135–294; W. Shawcross, 'Cambodia: Some Perceptions of a Disaster', in *Revolution and Its Aftermath in Kampuchea: Eight Essays*, eds, D. Chandler and B. Kiernan (New Haven, CT: Yale University Southeast Asia Studies, 1983), pp. 230–58; M. Vickery, *Cambodia 1975–1982* (Boston, MA: HarperCollins, 1984), Ch. 2; E. S. Herman and N. Chomsky, *Manufacturing Consent: The Political Economy of the Mass Media* (New York: Pantheon Books, 1988), pp. 280–96.
4. Letter to the author from Denis Gray, Bangkok, 10 May 1976.
5. S. Adams, *War of Numbers: An Intelligence Memoir* (South Royalton, VT: Steerforth Press, 1994), pp. 191–204; M. Vickery, 'Democratic Kampuchea: CIA to the Rescue', *Bulletin of Concerned Asian Scholars*, 14, 4 (1982), 45–54, at 47.
6. Letter to the author from R. M. Huffstutler, Chairman of the CIA's Information Review Committee, 26 June 1990.
7. Letter to the author from Debbie Kingsland, Cambodia Country Officer, U.S. Department of State, 16 February 1996.
8. T. M. Carney, *Communist Party Power in Kampuchea (Cambodia): Documents and Discussion* (Ithaca, NY: Cornell Southeast Asia Program, 1977).
9. See U.S. Department of State, letter to the U.N., July 1978.
10. T. Carney, 'Cambodia: The Unexpected Victory', and 'The Organization of Power in Democratic Kampuchea', in *Cambodia 1975–1978: Rendezvous with Death*, ed. K. D. Jackson (Princeton, NJ: Princeton University Press, 1989), pp. 13–35 and 79–107.

11. S. R. Heder, 'Thailand's Relations with Kampuchea: Negotiation and Confrontation Along the Prachinburi-Battambang Border', unpublished paper, Cornell University, December 1977, 77pp.; idem. ('Larry Palmer'), 'Thailand's Kampuchea Incidents', *News from Kampuchea*, 1, 4 (1977), 1–31; idem., 'Kampuchea's Armed Struggle: The Origins of an Independent Revolution', *Bulletin of Concerned Asian Scholars*, 11, 1 (1979), 2–24; idem., 'Origins of the Conflict', *Southeast Asia Chronicle*, 64 (September–October 1978), 3–18; idem., 'The Kampuchean-Vietnamese Conflict', *Southeast Asian Affairs 1979* (Singapore: Heinemann, 1979); idem., interview in *The Call*, organ of the Communist Party of the USA (Marxist-Leninist), 5 March 1979, 11.
12. S. Heder, letter to Dr. David Roberts, 5 March 1998, taking issue with Roberts' article in *Covert Action Quarterly* (August 1997): 'The article is defamatory because it suggests that there are grounds for suspecting that I am or have been a CIA operative or United States government agent.' Heder added: 'I must therefore ask you to make, as soon as is practicable, a complete attraction [sic] and apology, in terms to be approved by me beforehand, making it perfectly clear I am not now nor have ever been a member of the CIA or agent of the United States government.' Roberts refused, and in a communication to Cambridge University Press, dated 18 December 2003, Heder acknowledged: 'I have researched the CPK [Communist Party of Kampuchea] for 30 years, as a journalist, intelligence officer, human rights advocate, historian, UN official, legal scholar and political scientist, which is my most recent professional reincarnation.' See also David Roberts, *Political Transition in Cambodia*, 1991–99 (Richmond, Curzon, 2001), 69–71.
13. S. Heder, *Kampuchean Occupation and Resistance* (Bangkok: Institute for Asian Studies, Chulalongkom University, January 1980); idem., 'Kampuchea October 1979–August 1980, The Democratic Kampuchean Resistance, The Kampuchean Countryside, and the Sereikar', unpublished paper (Bangkok, November 1980).
14. D. Kirk, 'Revolution and Political Violence in Cambodia, 1970–1974', in *Communism in Indochina: New Perspectives*, eds, J. J. Zasloff and M. Brown (Lexington, MA: Lexington Books, 1975), pp. 215–30; B. Kiernan, *The Samlaut Rebellion and Its Aftermath, 1967–70: The Origins of Cambodia's Liberation Movement* (Monash University, Centre of Southeast Asian Studies, *Working Papers* nos. 4, 5, 1975).
15. K. M. Quinn, 'Political Change in Wartime: The Khmer Kraham Revolution in Southern Cambodia, 1970–1974', *U.S. Naval War College Review* (Spring 1976); idem., 'Cambodia 1976: Internal Consolidation and External Expansion', *Asian Survey*, 17, 1 (1977), 43–54; idem., 'The Pattern and Scope of Violence' and 'Explaining the Terror', in *Cambodia 1975–1978*, ed. Jackson, pp. 179–208 and 215–40.
16. M. E. Osborne, 'Reflections on the Cambodian Tragedy', *Pacific Community*, 8, 1 (1976), 1–3.
17. D. P. Chandler, B. Kiernan and M. H. Lim, *The Early Phases of Liberation in Northwestern Cambodia: Conversations with Peang Sophi* (Monash University Centre of Southeast Asian Studies, *Working Paper* no. 11, 1976, 9); reprinted in B. Kiernan and C. Boua, eds, *Peasants and Politics in Kampuchea, 1942–1981* (London: Zed Books, 1982), pp. 318–29, at 323.
18. D. P. Chandler, 'Transformation in Cambodia', *Commonweal* (1 April 1977); idem., *A History of Cambodia* (Boulder, CO: Westview Press, 1983), p. xiii; idem., *Brother Number One: A Political Biography of Pol Pot* (Boulder, CO: Westview Press, 1992).
19. Letters from S. Heder and M. Vickery, *Phnom Penh Post* 4/6 (August 1995), 4/22-23 (November 1995).
20. M. Vickery, 'Looking Back at Cambodia', *Westerly* (December 1976), and 'Looking Back at Cambodia, 1942–76', in *Peasants and Politics in Kampuchea, 1942–81*, eds, Kiernan and Boua, pp. 89–113.

21. F. Ponchaud, *Cambodge Année Zéro* (Paris: Julliard, 1977); *Cambodia Year Zero* (London: Penguin, 1978), p. 215.
22. Ponchaud, *Cambodia Year Zero*, p. 92.
23. Ben Kiernan, 'Cambodia in the News, 1975–76', *Melbourne Journal of Politics*, 8 (August 1976); for Vickery's account of his views during 1975–9 see his *Cambodia 1975–1982* (Boston: South End Press, 1984), pp. 47ff.
24. *Bangkok Post*, 25 June and 23 July 1975; Chandler, Kiernan and Lim, 'The Early Phases', and other sources noted in B. Kiernan, *The Pol Pot Regime: Race, Power and Genocide in Cambodia under the Khmer Rouge, 1975–1979*, 2nd edn (New Haven, CT: Yale University Press, 1996, 2002), pp. 92–3, and in Vickery, *Cambodia 1975–82*, pp. 98–9, 112; N. Chanda, 'Cambodia: When the Killing Had to Stop', *Far Eastern Economic Review* (29 October 1976), cover story, pp. 21–3.
25. B. Kiernan, 'Social Cohesion in Revolutionary Cambodia', *Australian Outlook*, 30, 3 (1976), 371–86.
26. E. Lenart, *Far Eastern Economic Review* (7 May 1976), 22–3.
27. Ith Sarin, in Carney, *Communist Party Power in Kampuchea*, p. 44.
28. D. P. Chandler, B. Kiernan and C. Boua, *Pol Pot Plans the Future: Confidential Leadership Documents from Democratic Kampuchea, 1976–1977* (New Haven, CT: Yale University Southeast Asia Studies, 1988), p. 220.
29. N. Chanda, 'Cambodia's Big Five', *Far Eastern Economic Review* (21 October 1977), 23.
30. C. Boua, B. Kiernan and A. Barnett, 'Bureaucracy of Death', *New Statesman* (2 May 1980); D. Chandler, *Voices from S-21: Terror and History in Pol Pot's Secret Prison* (Berkeley, CA: University of California Press, 1999).
31. B. Kiernan, 'Why's Kampuchea Gone to Pot?', *Nation Review* (Melbourne) (17 November 1978), and 'Vietnam and the Governments and People of Kampuchea', *Bulletin of Concerned Asian Scholars*, 11, 4 (1979), 19–25, and 12, 2 (1980), 72.
32. B. Kiernan, 'Wild Chickens, Farm Chickens, and Cormorants: Kampuchea's Eastern Zone under Pol Pot', in *Revolution and Its Aftermath in Kampuchea*, eds, Chandler and Kiernan, pp. 136–211.
33. *Revolution and Its Aftermath in Kampuchea*, Chs 4–6.
34. Chandler, *Brother Number One*, pp. 3–4, 49.
35. Vickery, *Cambodia 1975–1982*, p. 287.
36. Vickery, *Cambodia 1975–1982*.
37. D. Pike quoted in *St. Louis Post-Dispatch* (29 November 1979), and *Christian Science Monitor* (4 December 1979).
38. K. G. Frieson, *The Impact of Revolution on the Cambodian Peasants, 1970–1975* (PhD dissertation, Monash University, 1991).
39. Vickery, *Cambodia 1975–1982*, p. 287.
40. K. Samphan, 15 April 1977, quoted in Kiernan, *The Pol Pot Regime*, p. 204; Pol Pot, 27 September 1977, in U.S. CIA, Foreign Broadcast Information Service, *Daily Report*, Asia-Pacific (29 September 1977), H4.
41. B. Kiernan, 'The Ethnic Element in the Cambodian Genocide', in *Ethnopolitical Warfare: Causes, Consequences, and Possible Solutions*, eds, D. Chirot and M. E. P. Seligman (Washington, D.C.: American Psychological Association, 2001), pp. 83–91.
42. S. Ratner and J. Abrams, *Accountability for Human Rights Atrocities in International Law: Beyond the Nuremberg Legacy* (Oxford: Oxford University Press, 1997), p. 244. See also Donald Reid, "In Search of the Communist Syndrome: Opening the Black Book of the New Anti-Communism in France," *International History Review* XXVII:2 (June 2005), 295–318.

43. United Nations, AS, General Assembly, Security Council, A/53/850, S/1999/231, 16 March 1999, Annex, *Report of the Group of Experts for Cambodia established pursuant to General Assembly Resolution 52/135*, pp. 19–20.
44. Text of Ford–Kissinger–Suharto discussion, US Embassy Jakarta Telegram 1579 to Secretary State, 6 December 1975 (declassified 26 June 2001), in *East Timor Revisited: Ford, Kissinger and the Indonesian Invasion, 1975–76*, eds, W. Burr and M. L. Evans National Security Archive Electronic Briefing Book No. 62 (6 December 2001) (www.gwu.edu/~nsarchiv/NSAEBB/NSAEBB62).
45. J. Alsop, 'Showdown Over Southeast Asia', *Reader's Digest* (December 1975), Australian edition (January 1976), 137–42; L. Finley, 'Raising the Stakes: The Major Powers Still Play for Keeps in Indochina', *Southeast Asia Chronicle*, 64 (September–October 1978), 19–30, at 26.
46. Memorandum, 'Human Rights Violations in Cambodia', 21 September 1977, 2 pp., declassified by the CIA, 25 January 1996.
47. *Kampuchea: A Demographic Catastrophe*, National Foreign Assessment Center, Central Intelligence Agency, May 1980. For critiques of this document, see M. Vickery, 'Democratic Kampuchea: CIA to the Rescue', *Bulletin of Concerned Asian Scholars*, 14, 4 (1982), 45–54; and B. Kiernan, 'The Genocide in Cambodia, 1975–1979', *Bulletin of Concerned Asian Scholars*, 22, 2 (1990), 35–40, and references cited.
48. E. Becker, *When the War Was Over: The Voices of Cambodia's Revolution and Its People* (New York: Simon & Schuster, 1986), p. 440; L. Mason and R. Brown, *Rice, Rivalry and Politics: Managing Cambodian Relief* (Notre Dame, IN: University of Notre Dame Press, 1983), pp. 136, 139, 155; G. Evans and K. Rowley, *Red Brotherhood at War: Vietnam, Cambodia and Laos since 1975* (London: Verso, 1990).
49. 'Thais Furious at Cambodians for Disclosing Visit by Reagan Aide', *Los Angeles Times* (5 December 1980).
50. S. Heder and Yokobori, *Asahi Shimbun* (19 February 1982), quoted in A. Barnett, 'Democratic Kampuchea: A Highly Centralized Dictatorship', in *Revolution and Its Aftermath in Kampuchea*, eds, Chandler and Kiernan, pp. 212–29, at p. 228.
51. *Bangkok Post* (13 July 1985).
52. *Far Eastern Economic Review* (2 March 1989).
53. *Boston Globe* (17 April 1989).
54. *Asiaweek* (13 October 1989).
55. P. Wedel, United Press International (UPI), 'US Opposes Proposed Ceasefire in Cambodia', 14 May 1990.
56. N. Chanda, 'Japan's Quiet Entrance on the Diplomatic Stage', *Christian Science Monitor* (13 June 1990).
57. *Indochina Digest*, no. 90-23 (18 June–22 June 1990).
58. 'Thai Coup Impacts Region', and 'China, Burma Recognize Thai Junta', *Indochina Digest* 91–9 and 10 (1 and 8 March 1991).
59. *Daily Yomiuri* (5 May 1991), reporting Solomon's statement in Bangkok, 18 March 1991.
60. Senator Bob Kerrey, testimony before the US Senate Foreign Relations Committee, 11 April 1991.
61. S. E. Cook, ed., *Genocide in Cambodia and Rwanda: New Perspectives* (New Brunswick, NJ: Transaction, 2004), and E. Kissi, *Revolution and Genocide in Ethiopia and Cambodia* (Lexington, MA: Lexington Books, 2006).
62. N. Dunlop, *The Lost Executioner: A Story of the Khmer Rouge* (London: Bloomsbury, 2005).
63. www.yale.edu/cgp.

19

Mass Killings and Images of Genocide in Bosnia, 1941–5 and 1992–5

Robert M. Hayden

Bosnia and Herzegovina (hereafter, Bosnia) was the site of the first crimes in Europe after World War II to be pronounced judicially as genocide, the massacre of thousands of Bosniak (ethnic Muslim)[1] males by the forces of the Bosnian Serb Army, in July 1995.[2] This massacre came near the end of the 1992–5 conflict in which approximately 100,000 people were killed.[3] All reasonable analyses show that the majority of the victims in the Bosnian conflict were Muslims, with Serb casualties the next largest in number; in a scientific paper, an employee of the Demographic Unit of the Office of the Prosecutor of the International Criminal Tribunal for the Former Yugoslavia (ICTY) provided figures that indicate that about 50 per cent of a total of 102,000 dead were Muslims and 30 per cent Serbs.[4] However, while Serb casualties were overwhelmingly among military personnel, Muslim casualties were evenly split between military and civilian, so that the great majority of civilian casualties were Muslims. As discussed in detail below, publicizing the victimization of Muslims by Serbs was a primary public relations strategy of the Bosnian government and those who supported it, who invoked the term 'genocide' early on in the war, using imagery that drew parallels between the events in Bosnia in the 1990s and the Holocaust, a point discussed below. The 1990s genocide in Bosnia has become a *cause célèbre* internationally, as seen in the passage of Written Declaration no. 366 by the Parliamentary Assembly of the Council of Europe on 22 June 2005, and the international commemoration of the tenth anniversary of the Srebrenica massacre in July 2005.

Yet Bosnia was also the site of far greater mass killings in 1941–5, organized and effected in ways that seem much more clearly to fit the term 'genocide' than does the massacre in Srebrenica. From 1941–5, about 300,000 people were killed in Bosnia, about 65 per cent of them Serbs, and 18 per cent Muslims.[5] However, invocation of this larger set of ethnically targeted mass killings has been seen by many analysts, myself included, as part of the late 1980s and early 1990s nationalist political mobilization of Serbs in hostility to Croats and

Muslims.[6] At the same time, attempts to minimize the 1940s events by Croatian politicians, notably Dr Franjo Tudjman in his transformation from nationalist anti-communist dissident to President of Croatia, were part of the Croatian nationalist project.[7]

The greater attention given to the lesser mass killings of the 1990s, compared with that given the larger ones of the 1940s, the insistence that the 1990s events constituted genocide, and the post-1995 insistence by many international actors and some Bosnian ones that those events be a main focus of Bosnian politics, provides an opportunity for examining the process through which the term 'genocide' becomes attached to a situation of mass killing. This is not necessarily an encouraging exercise. In regard to Bosnia, the invocation of the term 'genocide' is primarily a political process that, like the 'invention of tradition', creates essentialized images of a supposed past to serve the purposes of present-day political actors. The success of such a process depends not on the accuracy with which the images reflect the events they supposedly represent, but rather with how well the images invoke an *emotional* reaction from the intended recipients. This kind of argument is the inversion of the rationality that Max Weber invokes for science: 'to state facts, to determine mathematical or logical relations or the internal structure of cultural values'.[8] Instead, they are parts of political rhetoric; to Weber 'not means of scientific analysis but means of canvassing votes and winning over others ... such words are weapons'.[9]

This chapter analyzes the ways in which the term 'genocide' has been invoked to label events of mass killing in the Balkans. In doing so, I raise questions about the effects of this labelling that many may find uncomfortable, and I will probably be called a 'genocide denier'. So let me be clear from the outset. My analysis begins with acknowledgment of the magnitude of the causalities: approximately 100,000 in the 1992–5 war, the majority of them Bosnian Muslims, and about 300,000 in the 1941–5 war, the majority of them Bosnian Serbs. In both conflicts, the casualties were inflicted in large part by organized attempts to remove the targeted populations from part of the territory in which they were living, and where their ancestors had also lived for centuries. The questions I raise are whether the application of the term 'genocide' to these events aids or distorts our understanding of them, and may possibly have made addressing the political situations in Bosnia since the late 1990s more difficult.

To presage the argument, the effort to fit the ethno-national mass killings in the former Yugoslavia into a framework defined by the Holocaust has produced systematic distortions in the ways in which the conflict has been presented. These distortions have intellectual impact – much of the material written on 'the Bosnian genocide' by those who became interested in Bosnia only after reading accounts of events there, is inaccurate about these events and the motivations of the actors who committed them, and thus is unreliable. But this intellectual failing has also had policy impact. Insofar as policy decisions are based on mistaken premises, they are unlikely to bring about the desired result.[10]

One might respond that if the political rhetoric is being used to stop genocide, so what if the images are inaccurate? Yet the very question presupposes that what is taking place *is* in fact *genocide*, thus not only obviating the need for close inquiry about whether that label is accurate but rendering the very question itself illegitimate, probably immoral.[11] In this regard, the invocation of genocide may be 'the tactical use of passion', that 'provokes feeling rather than thought ... to provoke a direct connection between feeling and action without the intervention of mind and its capacities for criticism'.[12] It may also serve as a 'God term', the ultimate point of reference of a rhetorical framework, invoked to forestall further examination by all but heretics.[13] But more troubling is the possibility that invoking what seems to be the supreme immorality of 'genocide' served as a reason for avoiding political solutions that might have ended the conflict, and even prevented greater massacres. In that case, rather than *ending* massacres, actions grounded on the emotional politics of the rhetoric of genocide may set the stage for wider slaughter.

In Bosnia specifically, decisions by international political actors, supposedly grounded in morality and informed by the rhetoric of genocide, helped structure the local configuration of civilian populations and military forces in Srebrenica in 1995 that put Bosnian Serb forces in a position to engage in what was by far the worst crime of the Bosnian conflict, the massacre of thousands of Bosnian Muslim males in the last months of the war. That mass slaughter may have put, finally, some accuracy into the charges of 'genocide' that had been made since the very start of the conflict, thus turning 'genocide' from politically inspired label to self-fulfilling prophecy.

Raising this problem, with specific reference to Srebrenica, will be extremely distasteful to many readers. It is not comfortable for me as an author. Yet avoiding an issue because it is uncomfortable is itself of dubious morality. Tzvetan Todorov may be optimistic in arguing that 'it is understanding, and not the refusal to understand, that makes it possible to prevent a repetition of the horror', but surely he is correct to say that 'the best way to allow the murders to happen again is to give up trying to understand them.'[14]

The background: competing national identities in a multi-national region

Yugoslavia was a very logical idea. As the concept of the nation-state developed in the nineteenth century and was used to inspire political actors to persuade various people to constitute themselves as Peoples and demand independence from the European empires, the idea of a single state for the speakers of the south Slavic languages made great sense. The dialects spoken in Bosnia, Croatia and Serbia were (and are) mutually intelligible, and Slovenian and Macedonian are closely related. While there were obvious differences of religion, historical tradition and culture, the differences between Serbs, Croats and Bosnian Muslims were not greater than those between, say, Bavarians and Prussians. Thus the state recognized after World War I, composed by adding Slovenia, Croatia, Bosnia and Macedonia, plus part of what had been Hungary (Vojvodina) and the until-then independent Montenegro to the Serbia that emerged as one of the victorious allies, seemed politically viable.[15] Yet the Yugoslav idea (*jug* meaning 'south' in the various languages, thus *Jugoslavija* as the land of the South Slavs) was in constant competition with the separate nationalist movements of the South Slav peoples: Serbs, Croats, Slovenes, Macedonians and Montenegrins; later Bosnian Muslims. The first Yugoslavia (1919–41) was thus a tenuous, unstable state, almost from its birth, because the competing nationalisms of these separate (and separatist) nations could not easily be accommodated to the idea of a unified state under a Serbian king. Resistance to what was regarded as Serbian hegemony was particularly pronounced in Croatia.[16]

Whether the Kingdom of Yugoslavia would have survived the 1940s is unclear, but was rendered moot when Germany invaded the country in April 1941, conquered it in ten days, and created an 'Independent State of Croatia' (hereafter NDH, after its Croatian acronym, for *Nezavisna Drzava Hrvatske*) that included Bosnia and Herzegovina, under the fascist Ustasha party, while giving parts of Serbia to its neighbours and placing the rest under occupation. What followed was a complex combination of war of resistance to Axis occupation (mainly by the Partisan army of the Communist Party of Yugoslavia under Tito and by Serbian royalist forces), attempts to establish an ethnically pure nation state (NDH, supported by the Axis powers), and a Serbian royalist attempt to eliminate non-Serb populations from eastern Bosnia, in opposition both to the NDH and to Tito's communists and in order to establish their own ethnically pure nation-state.[17] Of all of these parties, only the communists had the goal of reconstituting a multi-ethnic Yugoslavia, and they won the war, perhaps in part for that very reason (they had also attracted the support of the Allied Powers, in place of the Serbian royal regime and its Chetnik army).

Communist Yugoslavia (1945–90) also balanced national tensions, under the slogan of (compulsory) 'brotherhood and unity', before succumbing to them with the end of communism in Europe.[18] What was striking by the end of the 1980s was that with the end of communism, no political party was able to mobilize successfully on a platform of Yugoslavia as a civil society of equal citizens; what won instead, in each republic, was separate (and separatist) nationalism: Slovenia as the state of the sovereign Slovene nation, Croatia as that of the sovereign Croat nation, etc. I have elsewhere called this formulation 'constitutional nationalism' since the sovereignty of the majority nation (ethnically defined) over all other citizens of the state is enshrined in the constitutions.[19] Demands for the sovereign state of each constituent nation of Yugoslavia was incompatible with the existence of the federation, which thereby collapsed, and led to war in portions of the former country in which newly disfavoured minorities rejected inclusion in the state premised on hostility towards them.

What is striking about the demise of both Yugoslavias is that intense ethnonational conflict followed. But this conflict is a corollary of the logic of constitutional nationalism which is openly hostile to minorities and thus also tends to produce resistance from them.[20] In both cases, 1941–5 and 1992–5, the demise of the larger state that was premised on the equality and fraternity of the Yugoslav peoples (and willing to sacrifice liberty to maintain the other two) led immediately to brutal conflicts in the most ethnically mixed regions, in efforts to establish the control of one group over the territory by expelling the members of the other group.[21]

The brutal breakdown of coexistence: numbers of casualties

Since the numbers of victims of the mass killings of both decades have been manipulated heavily for political purposes, it is necessary to begin with a brief report of the findings of studies by highly qualified statisticians not in thrall to any of the nationalist parties in the ex-Yugoslav conflicts.[22]

1941–5: in the mid-1980s, two serious studies, one by a Serb and one by a Croat, found that slightly over 1,000,000 people had been killed during the war period in Yugoslavia. After a discussion of these studies and consideration of a major data source not available to these writers in the 1980s, Srdjan Bogosavljević derived minimum and maximum figures: 896,000 and 1,210,000, respectively.[23] Using results of a 1964 registration of war victims, he calculated that about 58 per cent of these victims were Serbs, 14 per cent Croats and 5.4 per cent Muslims. Of all killed in Bosnia, 72 per cent were Serbs, 16.7 per cent Muslims, 6 per cent Jews and 4.1 per cent Croats.[24]

Tomislav Dulić provides a much more detailed study, drawing on data sources not available to Bogosavljević. In Croatia and Bosnia-Herzegovina (the NDH), he finds that at a minimum, 76.5 per cent of the Jews living there in 1941 had been killed by 1945, between 15.9 and 20 per cent of the Serbs, 10 per cent of the Muslims and 5–6 per cent of the Croats.[25] His estimate of the deaths in Bosnia-Herzegovina in the period is 292,000–308,000, of whom Serbs were 216,000–229,000, Muslims 50,000–53,000, Croats 12,500 and Jews

10,500.[26] However, flaws in the data sets make it likely that Croats were severely undercounted and should be perhaps as high as 45,000.[27]

1992–5: Ewa Tabeau and Jakub Bijak drew on a variety of sources to arrive at an estimated total figure of war-related casualties in Bosnia-Herzegovina, 1992–5, of 102,622. Of *known* casualties (as opposed to estimates), 68.6 per cent were Muslims, 18.8 per cent Serbs and 8.3 per cent Croats. Of these 47,360 were estimated to be military casualties, and 55,261 civilian. However, they noted that their figures were least complete and reliable from the Republika Srpska.

Mirsad Tokača's centre responded to the initial release of the Tabeau and Bijak findings in an interview in the main Sarajevo daily, *Oslobodjenje*, that was headlined 'The total number of victims in B&H was less than 150,000!'[28] In a Reuters interview the next day, Tokača said that 'we can now say with almost absolute certainty that the number is going to be more than 100,000 but definitely less than 150,000.'[29] As the project has neared completion, Tokača has revised the total numbers downwards: in December 2005 the BBC carried a report that said that while the project would not be completed until March 2006, final figures would be about 102,000, and that of the data processed to date, 67.87 per cent of the casualties were Bosnian Muslims, 25.81 per cent Serbs and 5.39 per cent Croats. Of the Muslim casualties, 50 per cent were military and 50 per cent civilian, a ratio that holds for the far fewer Croat casualties as well. Serb casualties were overwhelmingly military: 21,399, to 1,978 Serb civilians.[30]

Thus the two most recent studies of the 1992–5 casualties agree that total killed were about 102,000. They differ mainly in that the Tokača study shows more Serb military casualties and fewer Serb civilian casualties than does the Tabeau and Bijak study (Table 19.1).

The total figures are summarized in Table 19.1, which may be compared with the machinations over numbers discussed in the section 'numbers games', below.

Table 19.1 Total casualties by ethno-national group in Bosnia (1941–5 and 1992–5)

	Serbs	**Bosnian Muslims**	**Croats**
1941–5	216,000–229,000	50,000–53,000	12,500 (unrealistically low figure due to flaws in data set)
1992–5	24,216	63,687	2,619

Sources: **1941–5**: T. Dulić, *Utopias of Nation* (Uppsala 2005), pp. 321, 323 (Croats); **1992–5**: Published interviews with Mirsad Tokača, Istraživačko dokumentacioni centar, Sarajevo, as of December 2005.

Distortions 1: competing for victimhood in the late 1980s

Communism failed as an ideology and basis for one-party government sooner in Yugoslavia than in the countries of the Warsaw Pact. In the early 1980s, analyses critical of Yugoslavia's unique system of 'socialist self-management' were openly published. Previously taboo subjects, such as the expulsion of 500,000 ethnic Germans from Vojvodina after World War II, the brutal imprisonment of those alleged to support the Soviet Union after Tito's break with Stalin in 1948 and the mistreatment of those seen as bourgeois class enemies in 1945, were explored in magazines, novels, films and other popular sources.[31] While there were attempts to develop political alternatives to state socialism based on the principles of a civil society of equal citizens,[32] they lost in each republic to the classic position of European nationalism, that each nation (e.g., Serbs, Croats and Slovenes) had the right, and need, to be sovereign in its own separate state.[33]

The need to be sovereign, however, had to be justified, with arguments about why the given nation was damaged by its inclusion within Yugoslavia. Considering the importance of 'brotherhood and unity', direct appeals to nationalist antagonism against other Yugoslav peoples were not at first possible. Instead, the original arguments about the harmfulness of Yugoslavia were economic in nature: inclusion within Yugoslavia damaged the economic interests of the given nation. However, these economic arguments were quickly transformed into positions claiming that the writer's separate nation was threatened by other nations within Yugoslavia. This form of argumentation was common to the first direct challenges to the premise of Yugoslavia as unquestioned good for all Yugoslav peoples, the Memorandum of the Serbian Academy of Sciences and Arts (SANU, from its Serbian acronym), and the Slovenian National Program.

The SANU Memorandum quickly became notorious within Yugoslav and, once the wars began, widely condemned outside of the country.[34] Whether it was read or not is another matter. As Michael Mann has noted,[35] the first part of it was a critique of the economic failings of Yugoslav self-management socialism and elements of the structure of the Yugoslav federation; however, the second part depicts Serbs as victims of 'genocide' on the grounds that they were being forced out of Kosovo – a tendentious claim, and irresponsible rhetoric that shows, however, the political attractiveness of the 'genocide' label for claims that one's own group has been victimized.

At the same time that the Serbian *Memorandum* was being drafted and leaked to the press, a 'Slovenian National Programme' was published in Ljubljana.[36] Similarly to the Serbian *Memorandum*, the Slovenian document claimed that inclusion within Yugoslavia was not only harmful to the economic interests of Slovenia, but even threatened the existence of the ethnic Slovene nation, in this case because of 'dangerously high' immigration that threatened to turn Slovenia into a multiethnic republic.[37] Unlike the authors of the Serbian Memorandum, the Slovene writers did not invoke the term genocide to cover the allegedly dire situation of their own nation, but their view of the nature of 'nation' (*narod*) clearly was based on the standard European romantic ideology of a unity of 'blood', language and culture, which would be threatened by contamination if Slovenes had to share Slovenia with others.

Distortions 2: 'The wish to be a Jew': the power of Jewish and Nazi tropes in depicting victimization[38]

Economic problems can presumably be addressed by changing economic and political systems; they are not, of themselves, threatening to the very existence of a 'nation' perceived, in the manner of classical European Romanticism, as a biological and cultural entity. 'Threatening the existence' of the nation is, of course, a phrasing that is close to that of the definition of genocide, which concerns the 'intent to destroy, in whole or in part' such a group. As noted, the *Memorandum* of the SANU saw 'genocide' in the pressures on Serbs to leave Kosovo in the 1980s, although few non-Serbs have accepted or would be likely to accept that labelling. The point was clearly to appropriate for Serbs the most terrible victimization known. The claim was thus not about acts of extermination so much as it was about the status of victimization, and 'genocide' was invoked not as a description of the kinds of actions directed against Serbs but rather of their status as victims. In this rhetorical configuration, identification as supreme victim is crucial, and in the 1980s and 1990s in Yugoslavia, at various times Serbs, Kosovo Albanians, Croats and Bosnian Muslims all claimed to be the new Jews, thus the new victims of genocide. At the same time, in this rhetorical context there are no Jewish victims without Nazi perpetrators, so claiming victim status as the new Jews also meant imposing the status of the new Nazis on another national group.

Serb intellectuals, not themselves Jewish, were the first to assert the victimization of their own nation by claiming to be the new Jews. In 1985, the writer Vuk Drašković issued a 'Letter to the Writers of Israel' that claimed that the Serbian subjugation to the Ottoman Empire had been like that of Israel to the Babylonians; that the exodus of Serbs from Ottoman territories was like the Jewish diaspora; and that the slaughter of both Serbs and Jews by fascists in World War II had completed the common identity as martyrs of Serbs and Jews.[39] But others asserted the same claim to be the real Jews. Thus in a meeting in Slovenia held to support Kosovo Albanians said to be oppressed by Serbia, the Slovenian organizers distributed traditional Albanian men's caps decorated with a Star of David, to mark the Albanians as victims and the Serbs as the new Nazis. Another Serbian writer then asserted that the Slovenes had forgotten that in the murders of World War II, 'the kinship of Jews and Serbs has been sealed forever.'[40] In the late 1980s, a 'Serbian-Jewish Friendship Society' was organized, in an attempt to gain the support of Israel and thus, it was hoped, the United States; the Jewish Community of Serbia, however, played no part in these activities.[41]

When the wars began in 1991, some attempts were made to assert that Croats, rather than Serbs, were the victims of genocide.[42] The equation of Croats with Jews and Serbs with Nazis was explicit: 'how is it that so many ... have managed not to see "the Nazis of this story" for what they are, and have hastened to embrace them as fellow Jews instead?'[43] However, it was difficult for this effort to succeed, in large part because the regime of the NDH had not only been explicitly allied with Nazi Germany, but also because it had practiced extermination policies against Jews and Gypsies and those of mass murder against Serbs.[44] This history was made relevant by Tudjman's invocation of symbols associated with the NDH and the Ustasha in his political campaigns and in the newly independent Croatia,[45] and what have generally been interpreted as anti-Semitic passages in his best-known book, *Bespuća Povijesne Zbijlnosti* (1990), published in translation as *Horrors of War*, with the objectionable parts removed or changed. A leader of the Croatian Jewish community argued in 1991 that of all the occupied countries in World War II, it was only in Croatia that the quisling regime had independent authority over concentration camps,[46] and that of the 40,000 Jews living in 1940 in what became the NDH, 'the Ustaše killed 26,000 and paid the Germans to take care of 5,000 more in Auschwitz.'[47] In 1997, Croatia issued a statement that 'completely condemns Nazi crimes of the Holocaust and genocide over Jewish people in many European states, including Croatia', as part of its establishment of relations with Israel.[48]

The best-known passages in Tudjman's book internationally were those in which he seemed to question the total of 6,000,000 victims of the Holocaust[49] (a term, 'Holokausta', that he consistently puts into quotes), and his reference to a 'long-term policy and strategy on the plan of a "final solution" of the Palestinian problem' at a time 'in the middle of the 1980s, when world Jewry still had the need to recall their victims in the "holocaust."'[50] Perhaps the most remarkable passages in Tudjman's book were those that asserted that Jews actually controlled the internal management of the largest concentration camp in Croatia, Jasenovac, up until 1944 and that it was, therefore, Jews who had inflicted sufferings at Jasenovac on Roma and Serbs.[51] As Tomislav Dulić has pointed out, the Ustasha administration of Jasenovac followed the methods of the German camps and thus used inmates (kapos) as internal administrators; since Jews were the first prisoners brought to Jasenovac, and were also better educated than most Serbs or Roma, they dominated the internal administration in the first stages of the camp, and it was in any event standard practice in the German camps for members of one nation to be the kapos for prisoners of other groups.[52]

The image problem that Tudjman's book caused for Croatia can be seen in the favourable article on *Bespuća* in the Croatian version of the reader-edited on-line encyclopedia Wikipedia, which says that the book was translated 'in a "cleansed" version because of its supposedly murky sections which offended the sensibilities of the Jewish community'. The article then notes that Tudjman cited Israeli and Jewish historians who problematized the numbers of those killed in the Holocaust, saying that the number was closer to 4,000,000 than 6,000,000, and that because of this, 'and because he opened up the uncomfortable theme of the Jewish kapos in the concentration camps (i.e. the "cooperation" between Jewish inmates with Nazi administrators ...), and leaving aside the clumsiness of some of his formulations, Tudjman struck the "sacred cow" of the new Jewish national mythology ....'[53] If Tudjman's book still has this reputation in Croatia, it is easy to see why it was hard for Croatia under his leadership to dodge the Nazi label enough to pin it on other groups.

If Croats could not easily claim to be the new Jews victimized by Serb Nazis, however, Bosnian Muslims and their supporters were able to make effective use of both parts of this polarized pair of tropes. In part their success in this effort was indeed due to the Muslims having been brutally expelled from large parts of Bosnia by the much better armed and organized Bosnian Serbs, and the disproportionately high casualties suffered by Bosnia's Muslims compared to other groups, especially at the start of the war. However, the success of the Nazi trope for Serbs and that of Holocaust victim for Muslims also benefited from the temporal coincidence of the start of the Bosnia conflict with the opening of the United States Holocaust Memorial Museum and the critical and commercial success of Steven Spielberg's film *Schindler's List*, which brought these tropes into the centre of public discourse.

The assertion of a parallel with the Holocaust was explicit: 'from Auschwitz to Bosnia'.[54] Making this case involved the frequent and explicit invocation of elements of the Holocaust as the proper frame of reference for understanding events in Bosnia, especially images of concentration camps, and even holding a contest to find a Bosnian Muslim surrogate for Anne Frank. Just before his death, Bosnian Muslim leader (and first President of Bosnia and Herzegovina) Alija Izetbegović acknowledged to Bernard Kouchner that he had known at the time that these comparisons were false, that 'whatever horrors were there, these were not extermination camps', although he acknowledged that he had used precisely that phrase in speaking with French President Mitterrand in 1993 in an attempt to precipitate bombing of the Serbs.[55]

The point, again, is not that there were not horrors in Bosnia and Croatia in the 1940s and 1990s, but rather that the depictions of them were systematically distorted to bring them into the framings set up by the Holocaust. If we are to understand events in Bosnia, the distortions caused by this framing must be clarified.

Distortions 3: numbers games

1941–5: World War II in Yugoslavia was exceptionally brutal even for that period in Europe, since it was simultaneously a war against foreign occupation, Croat and Serb attempts to create ethnic states by expelling or killing members of other nations, and communist revolution, with retribution by the communists against the various nationalist forces at the end of the war. Immediately after the war, official figures were generated, about 1,700,000 victims overall.[56] Figures were sensitive because so many Yugoslavs had been killed by other Yugoslavs, albeit of different national groups, especially Serbs murdered by Croats, Muslims murdered by Serbs and – most sensitively – non-Communists killed by Tito's Partisans. The sensitivity of all of this history is most apparent from the fate of a census of war victims that was conducted in 1964, after extensive preparation: after its completion, the census was not publicly released, and the press run of the books was destroyed in the late 1980s.[57] Briefly opened to the public in the late 1980s, the 1964 data set was unavailable during the Milošević period, though it is now available and in fact was a main data source for Dulić's study.

In the 1980s, the topic of the casualties in World War II was re-opened by Serbian and Croatian writers.[58] Serb authors stressed what they called the genocidal nature of the NDH, increasing the numbers of people supposedly killed in Jasenovac alone to 700,000 (Vladimir Dedier) and even one million (Velimir Trzič).[59] This explosion of false information provided the opportunity for responses by Croatian historians that minimized the casualties in Jasenovac, thereby attempting to discount the accusations of genocide. This was explicitly the main argument of Tudjman's *Bespuća*, the first chapter of which refers to the 'Jasenovac myth' and also the 'thesis of genocidal Croatianism'. Tudjman devotes a great deal of space to showing the impossibility of the highest figures, and on this point he is correct. However, by focusing on the 'myth of Jasenovac', he and his critics ignore the great majority of the killings in the NDH, which did not take place in 'camps', a point discussed in the next section.

1992–5: As the war developed in Bosnia, the numbers of dead were very quickly inflated. At a hearing of the U.S. Commission on Security and Cooperation in Europe (CSCE) on 'War Crimes and the Humanitarian Crisis in the former Yugoslavia' on 25 January 1993, Congressman Christopher Smith stated that a few weeks earlier, Bosnian President Izetbegović had stated that more than 200,000 had been killed and that 70,000 people were being held in detention camps.[60] The 200,000 figure was repeated at a 4 February 1993 CSCE hearing by Bosnian Foreign Minister Haris Silajdžić. This 200,000 figure was widely accepted thereafter. At a hearing of the U.S. House International Relations Committee on 18 October 1995, Secretary of Defense William Perry said that more than 200,000 people had been killed; at a hearing before the U.S. Senate Armed Services Committee on 7 June 1995, Perry had said that in 1992, there were about 130,000 civilian casualties in Bosnia. At a National Press Club press conference on 24 June 1994, Bosnian Prime Minister Ejup Ganić raised the total to 'a quarter million' killed. Silajdžić at least remained consistent, saying on the American public television news programme *Newshour* on 13 May 1997, that 200,000 people were killed. Richard Holbrooke, on the other hand, in an interview on the tenth anniversary of the Dayton Agreements, managed to raise the figure to 300,000 dead.[61] News accounts tended to keep to the 200,000 figure, used as recently as 18 December 2005 in the *New York Times*.[62]

Estimates by researchers during the war period generally tended to overstate casualties. Figures from institutions or individual researchers within Bosnia and Croatia ranged from a low of 156,824 to a high of 329,000. Those from outside of Bosnia were somewhat lower, ranging from 25,000 to 60,000 by former State Department officer George Kenney to 200,000 by Chicago law professor Cherif Bassiouni.[63] Since Kenney's figures did not include casualties from 1995, his high-end figure for casualties through 1994 (60,000) may actually have been the closest to accurate, but did not gain acceptance, and the 200,000 figure generated in 1993 became the most accepted figure.

Distortions 4: restaging the Holocaust

Looking for Auschwitz

One effect of the establishment of Holocaust imagery as the standard for genocide has been to focus attention on concentration camps as the sites of the greatest horrors. In the former Yugoslavia, this imagery was adopted by Serbs in reference to the massacres in the NDH. A highly tendentious book from the late 1980s by Vladimir Dedijer exemplifies this approach: *The Yugoslav Auschwitz and the Vatican: The Croatian Massacre of the Serbs During World War II*.[64] The 'Yugoslav Auschwitz' was said to be the concentration camp at Jasenovac, with the methods of murder described in great detail. The unreality of the numbers game is shown in this single volume. The opening article by Mihailo Marković states that 'In one huge concentration camp alone – Jasenovac – 750,000 Serbs were exterminated, together with Jews and Gypsies',[65] but the 'Foreword to the First German Edition' that follows states that 'In this infamous "death camp", over 200,000 people, mostly Orthodox Serbs, met their death.'[66]

Even if one were to accept this second figure (and Tomislav Dulić's careful 2005 study indicates that it is about twice as high as the actual death count at Jasenovac), this would be perhaps one-third of the Serb victims of the war.

As Aleksa Djilas has noted, the technology and transportation systems available to the Ustasha were not well developed,[67] and most of the deaths occurred in direct attacks on villages and in towns, which makes sense: in the early 1940s, Yugoslavia was one of the least developed countries in Europe, with over 85 per cent of the population living in villages and small towns, rather than cities. Dulić provides better figures: in the NDH, 19 per cent of the Serbs killed died in camps, 45 per cent in 'direct terror', and 25 per cent in military-related actions; on the other hand, 95 per cent of the Jews killed died in camps.[68] Thus the focus on 'concentration camps' rather than rural massacres missed the largest component of the 1941–5 war, a mistaken focus that makes sense only if the point of the exercise is not to commemorate actual victims so much as to elaborate on the symbol of the greatest victimization of the twentieth century: the Nazi concentration camps, symbolized by Auschwitz.

The images of concentration camps became firmly linked with the 1990s events in Bosnia in August 1992, when two British television journalists delivered stories, accompanied by film, of Muslim prisoners in 'detention centres' run by Bosnian Serbs in northern Bosnia.[69] Some of the films showed emaciated prisoners, one extremely so; the apparent similarity between this prisoner's condition and that of the extremely emaciated prisoners in Nazi extermination camps was seized upon by the world press the next day as evidence that the Serbs were running concentration camps like those of the Third Reich.[70] The *Daily Mirror* of London put a picture of the most extremely emaciated Bosnian Muslim prisoner on its front page, with the captions 'Belsen '92' and 'Horror of the new Holocaust'. Thereafter, 'camps' became a dominant trope for the war in Bosnia, and a focus of international activity. The very first indictment in the ICTY was that of one Dragan Nikolić, a commander of the Susica Camp, and the first trial that of a guard at the Omarska camp, Dusko Tadić. Other cases focusing primarily on criminal actions in 'camps' were those of Mejakic et al. (Omarska Camp), Sikirica et al. (Keraterm Camp), Fustar et al. (Keraterm Camp), Mucic et al. (Celebici), Kvocka et al. (Omarska, Keraterm and Trnopolje Camps), Mejakic et al. (Omarska Camp and Keraterm Camp), Banovic (Omarska Camp and Keraterm Camp), including five of the first eight indictments made public.[71]

Considering the attention paid to 'camps', one might expect them to have been major sites of extermination, as were Auschwitz and Treblinka. The ICTY, however, found that the Omarska Camp operated only from late May to late August 1992, and that about 3,000 detainees passed through it during this time.[72] The Keraterm camp, also established in late May 1992, held up to 1500 prisoners.[73]

Obviously, this is not to say that the camps were not the sites of mass criminality. There is no question but that large numbers of prisoners were mistreated, tortured, raped and murdered.[74] The Trial Chamber in *Banovic* found that

> The Keraterm and Omarska camps were operated in a manner designed to ill-treat and persecute non-Serbs from Prijedor and other areas, with the aim of ridding the territory of non-Serbs or subjugating those who remained. The detention of non-Serbs in the camps was a prelude to killing them or transferring them to non-Serb areas.[75]

To return to the words of Bosnian leader Alija Izetbegović, however, 'whatever horrors were there, these were not extermination camps.'

Finding a Bosnian Anne Frank

The parallel between Bosnia and the Holocaust produced a great commercial success, and a major publicity one as well, with the publication of *Zlata's Diary: A Child's Life in Sarajevo,* immediately hailed as the work of 'the Bosnian Anne Frank'.[76] This 'other diary of a young girl'[77] was written by a 13-year-old girl in Sarajevo, beginning just before the war (September 1991) and lasting until two months before her growing fame in Europe and America led to her evacuation with her parents, in late 1993. The young writer explicitly compares herself to Anne Frank, first in adopting a name for her diary eight months into it (the earlier entries have no salutation), and just as the war begins (30 March 1992), 'Since Anne Frank called her diary Kitty, maybe I could give you a name too.' She lists five puns on Bosnian words, then settles on 'Mimmy', which contains a doubled consonant and the letter 'y', neither of which is found in the Latin-script orthography of Serbo-Croatian she uses, but which probably work better for foreigners than the other choices would have: 'Asfaltina, Šefika, Ševala, Pidžameta, Hikmeta.'[78] Not quite six months later, she is told that 'they want to publish a child's diary and it just might be mine ... and so I copied part of you into another notebook and you, Mimmy, went to the City Assembly to be looked at. And I've just heard, Mimmy, that you are going to be published! You're coming out for the UNICEF week! Super!'[79] The book then became a bestseller in a number of languages. The diary actually ends when the author finds out that it will be published internationally: the next-to-last entry (14 October 1993) reads 'you're going to be published abroad. I allowed it, so you could tell the world.'[80] Apparently the job was done; but not quite, for one final entry three days later ends the volume with these words: 'We haven't done anything. We're innocent. But helpless!'[81]

One must be pleased for the young author of this 'Anne Frank with a happy ending',[82] yet wonder how much calculation went into the decision of whoever 'they' were in the City Assembly, to publish a child's diary, and the editorial decision to end it with the plea of innocence and helplessness, in case anyone had missed the point. The book is controversial even in Sarajevo. One review of Bosnian literature in the Sarajevo weekly *Dani* says 'this controversial piece (to some a plagiarism of the famous *Diary of Anne Frank*) in any event supercedes all other Bosnian authors combined in terms of readership.'[83] One must also wonder about the acuity of the journalists who covered this story when Janine di Giovanni's 'Introduction' to the book describes Zlata, whom she met, as having 'bright blue eyes',[84] since the girl on the cover of the Penguin edition, at least, has brown eyes. But one of the Western journalistic clichés used during the war to show that even though they are Muslims, the Bosnian Muslims are like other Europeans, was to make reference to their blue eyes.

The involvement of the U. S. Holocaust Museum

The United States Holocaust National Museum opened on 22 April 1993, at a time when the Bosnian war was a major international story. At the request of the U.S. State Department, the organizers invited the leaders of all of the newly independent Yugoslav Republics except Serbia and Montenegro (then the 'Federal Republic of Yugoslavia'), including Croatian President Tudjman. Considering the controversy over his book *Bespuća*, this invitation attracted criticism from many quarters, and Elie Wiesel said that 'his [Tudjman's] presence in the midst of survivors is a disgrace.'[85] At the event itself, Mr. Wiesel 'looked away' from Tudjman when the Croatian president took a seat near the podium, then denounced the atrocities in the Bosnian war and called for U.S. intervention.[86]

In 2001, the U.S. Holocaust Museum did, however, mount a major exhibition, now on-line, on 'Jasenovac and the Holocaust Era in Croatia, 1941–1945'. The Museum also became involved in the preservation of records and materials from Jasenovac that had been taken to the Republika Srpska in Bosnia during the 1991–5 war.[87] Both the U.S. Holocaust Museum and Israel's Yad Vashem were involved in designing a new memorial centre at Jasenovac, which produced its own controversy in late 2005 and early 2006. That is, the new monument at Jasenovac will be patterned after Yad Vashem, and list the names of about 70,000 victims, but without indicating their nationality or indeed anything else about them; it will also be included in a web of Holocaust museums in Europe linked to Yad Vashem. But representatives of the Serbs in Croatia, the Croatian Jewish Community, and the anti-fascist veterans of Croatia – that is, of the groups that represent most of the victims at Jasenovac and their descendants – have objected, saying that turning Jasenovac into simply a Holocaust museum obscures the true nature of the camp.[88] This twist in the play of representations of victimhood solves the image problems for Croatia problems caused by Tudjman's handling of the Holocaust, and also turns the Serb victims from being the central figures of Croatian massacres in World War II to being 'collateral damage' in the Holocaust. There is a certain irony in this: the earlier Serb labelling of Jasenovac as the Croatian Auschwitz has succeeded, but Jasenovac, like Auschwitz, thereby becomes best known for its role in the Holocaust even though more Serbs than Jews were murdered there.

When we recall that most Serbs were not killed in camps, the new controversy shows again the flaw in using concentration camps as characteristic of genocide. Even the Serb representatives fall into the trap of assuming that commemoration should be done at Jasenovac, the 'camp' as representation of the events of 1941–5. Meanwhile, the great majority of the non-Jewish victims of the NDH will not be commemorated, since they did not die at Jasenovac.

Back to the 1991–5 wars, the Holocaust Museum had taken at least an informal position in 1997 that genocide had occurred in Bosnia. Thus when the Museum sponsored a discussion of a paper about whether the term 'genocide' was actually appropriately applied to the ethnic cleansing campaigns in Bosnia,[89] at the last moment the Director changed the title of the event from 'Genocide in Bosnia?' to 'Ethnic Conflict in the Former Yugoslavia: Perspectives and Implications', because, he said, the Museum had already pronounced that genocide took place in Bosnia. The website devoted to responding to threats of genocide that is maintained by the Museum's Committee on Conscience has a section on the Balkans, but the only incident specifically discussed is the massacre of Muslim males in Srebrenica in 1995, to which we now turn.

Extending the law: the mass killing at Srebrenica as genocide

In July 1995 the Bosnian Serb Army took control of the 'safe area' of Srebrenica in eastern Bosnia. The judgment of the trial chamber of the ICTY in the case of General Radislav Krstić states concisely what happened next:

> Within a few days, approximately 25,000 Bosnian Muslims, most of them women, children and elderly people who were living in the area, were uprooted and, in an atmosphere of terror, loaded onto overcrowded buses by the Bosnian Serb forces and transported across the confrontation lines into Bosnian Muslim-held territory. The military-aged Bosnian Muslim men of Srebrenica, however, were consigned to a separate fate. As thousands of them attempted to flee the area, they were taken prisoner, detained in brutal conditions and then executed. More than 7,000 people were never seen again.[90]

Demographic experts employed by the Office of the Prosecutor of the ICTY have estimated that at least 7,475 persons were killed in this action, including one-third of all Muslim men enumerated in the April 1991 census of Srebrenica. Less than 1 per cent of the victims were women, and 89.9 per cent men between the ages of 16 and 60.[91] While some of these men were killed in military action, thousands were executed. The result of the operation was to drive almost all Muslims from Srebrenica, which was almost 73 per cent Muslim before the war; only a few hundred have since returned.

The criminality of these actions is clear. What may be questioned, however, is whether the application of the term 'genocide' to this action is appropriate. Since the ICTY did proclaim this mass killing to be genocide, a discussion of this question must focus on the reasoning of the Tribunal, specifically with the judgments of both the trial chamber and then the Appeals Chamber in *Krstić*.

Genocide is defined in regard to specific 'acts committed with intent to destroy, in whole or in part, a national, ethnical, racial or religious group, as such', including killing members of the group or causing serious bodily or mental harm to them; the goal of bringing about the 'physical destruction in whole or in part' is important as well.[92] It was undeniable that the Bosnian Serb Army had killed members of the group and caused bodily and mental harm to those who survived. The only question was that of intent: 'whether the offences were committed with the intent to destroy, in whole or in part, a national, ethnical, racial or religious group, as such.'[93]

In regard to Srebrenica, this definition is more problematical than non-lawyers might realize. The original 1946 UN resolution defined genocide as 'a denial of the right of existence of entire human groups', and it was said at that time that the victim of genocide was not the individuals killed but the group.[94] But what counts as 'the group' in this case? The Prosecution was inconsistent, referring at various times to the Bosnian Muslims, the Bosnian Muslims of Srebrenica and the Bosnian Muslims of Eastern Bosnia. The Trial Chamber agreed with the Defence that the proper group was the Bosnian Muslims, leaving then the question of whether the destruction of a part of that group would qualify as genocide.[95]

Having made this determination, however, the Trial Chamber then contradicted itself by saying that

> the killing of all members of the part of a group located within a small geographical area ... would qualify as genocide if carried out with the intent to destroy the part of the group as such located in this small geographical area. Indeed, the physical destruction may target only a part of the geographically limited part of the larger group because the perpetrators of the genocide regard the intended destruction as sufficient to annihilate the group as a distinct entity in the geographic area at issue.[96]

Yet even annihilation of a small local group seems unlikely to threaten the larger 'group as such', already defined as the Bosnian Muslims, that is, the group itself (rather than the individuals that comprise it), which is the party to

be protected from genocide. Further, the Bosnian Serb Army did not try to kill *all* members of the group, but rather only males between ages of 16 and 60; although they were treated appallingly, women, small children and old people were transported out of Srebrenica. In this connection, the Trial Chamber referred to 'the catastrophic impact that the disappearance of two or three generations of men would have on the survival of a traditionally patriarchal society', thus incorporating into its reasoning stereotypes about Bosnian society.[97] Strangely, the Trial Chamber also referred to the strategic location of Srebrenica and noted that by killing the men, the Serbs 'precluded any effective attempt by the Bosnian Muslims to recapture the territory'[98] – strange, because this reasoning seems to acknowledge a military strategic reason for killing the men of military age.

Through this reasoning, the *Krstić* trial chamber extended the definition of 'genocide' from acts made with the intent to cause the physical 'destruction of a group as such', to covering acts made to remove an ethnic or religious community from a specific territory, especially one of strategic importance.

A subsequent ICTY trial chamber expressed 'some hesitancy' about adopting this reasoning, 'which permits a characterization of genocide even when the specific intent extends only to a limited geographical area, such as a municipality'. This Trial Chamber was 'aware that this approach might distort the definition of genocide if it is not applied with caution'.[99] The *Stakić* court cited a law review article that had argued that if such a definition prevails, local mass killings might be taken to indicate that there was not a plan on a national level. Carrying this logic further, Tomislav Dulić notes that if local mass killings are defined as genocide, even the Holocaust becomes composed in part of many 'individual genocides', or local massacres.[100] At that stage, the possibility arises of seeing reciprocal or 'retributive' genocides when forces of antagonistic racial, ethnic or religious groups each commit a local massacre of the other's people, even of their military forces.[101] Yet at that point, what distinguishes 'genocide' from other ethnic, racial or religious mass killings?

The defense appealed the findings of the *Krstić* trial chamber that genocide had occurred, in part, because the definition of the 'part' of the protected group – men of military age in Srebrenica, as part of the Bosnian Muslims – was too narrow, and, in part, because the Trial Chamber had enlarged the definition of genocide to encompass expulsion of a group from a territory, rather than their physical destruction. The Appeals Chamber dismissed the Appeals, but in doing so made the issues less rather than more clear.

In regard to 'part' of a protected group, the Appeals Chamber simply said that all that was necessary was that 'the alleged perpetrator intended to destroy at least a substantial part of the protected group.' 'Substantial part' was left undefined, but the Appeals Chamber then introduced a purely political consideration: 'If a specific part of the group is emblematic of the overall group ... that may support a finding that the part qualifies as substantial.'[102] It then stated that Srebrenica was important *militarily* to the Bosnian Serbs, because its capture would 'severely undermine the military efforts of *the Bosnian Muslim state* to ensure its viability.'[103] Further, the Appeals Chamber said that

> Srebrenica was important due to its prominence in the eyes of both the Bosnian Muslims and the international community .... The elimination of the Muslim population of Srebrenica, despite the assurances given by the international community, would serve as a potent example to all Bosnian Muslims of their vulnerability and defencelessness in the face of Serb military forces. The fate of the Bosnian Muslims of Srebrenica would be emblematic of that of all Bosnian Muslims.[104]

This is an extraordinary statement, because it conditions 'genocide' on the purely political determination that even a relatively small portion of a protected group is either so politically prominent or so strategically located that its removal from a territory, rather than physical annihilation, would *symbolize* the vulnerability of the larger group.

Having made this determination, the Appeals Chamber then put forth the normative statement that 'the crime of genocide is singled out for special condemnation and opprobrium. The crime is horrific in its scope; its perpetrators identify entire human groups for extinction. Those who devise and implement genocide seek to deprive humanity of the manifold richness its nationalities, races, ethnicities and religions provide.'[105] Yet the same court had just decided that, in fact, 'genocide' could be found when the intent was not to destroy an entire group, nor even a large part of it, much less 'seek to deprive humanity' of a nationality, race, ethnicity or religion.

The question of whether genocide occurred in Bosnia became even more complicated with the decision of the trial chamber in the case of Momčilo Krajišnik, one of the most important political actors among the Bosnian Serbs from 1990 throughout the war. According to the indictment against him,[106] Krajišnik

> had de facto control and authority over the Bosnian Serb Forces and Bosnian Serb Political and Governmental Organs and their agents, who participated in the crimes alleged in this indictment.

He was indicted, and convicted, of crimes based on his political responsibility. The presentation of evidence lasted more than two years, involved 27,000 pages of transcripts, 3,800 Prosecution exhibits, 380 Defence exhibits and

27 Chamber exhibits.[107] Krajišnik openly argued with his defense attorneys, so the defense was not unified and the case should have been an easy win for the Prosecution. And, in fact, Krajišnik was convicted of extermination, murder, persecution, deportation and forced transfer, all as crimes against humanity, involving imposition of restrictive and discriminatory measures and the denial of fundamental rights; murder; cruel and inhumane treatment during attacks on towns and villages and within various detention centres; forcible displacement; unlawful detention; forced labor at front lines; appropriation or plunder of private property; and destruction of private property and of cultural monuments and sacred sites. Further, all of this was the result, the court found, of a 'common criminal enterprise' involving Krajišnik and other persons in the Bosnian Serb leadership. Yet despite all of this evidence, the court found that 'none of these acts were committed with the intent to destroy, in part, the Bosnian-Muslim or Bosnian-Croat ethnic group, as such', and thus that Krajišnik was not guilty of genocide or of complicity in genocide.[108]

The February 2007 decision of the International Court of Justice in the case brought by Bosnia and Herzegovina against Serbia and Montenegro[109] did nothing to make matters more clear. It simply adopted the finding of the ICTY in *Krstić* that genocide had occurred at Srebrenica, without discussing the reasoning behind that decision.[110] It also decided that Bosnia and Herzegovina had not proved that the authorities in Belgrade had ordered the massacre, and indeed that 'all indications are to the contrary: that the decision to kill the adult male population of the Muslim community of Srebrenica was taken by the VRS [Bosnian Serb Army] Main Staff, but without instructions from or effective control by' Serbia and Montenegro.[111] For this reason, the International Court of Justice (ICJ) found that Serbia had not committed genocide, incited the commission of genocide, conspired to commit genocide, or been complicit in the commission of genocide in Bosnia, but that it had violated the Genocide convention by failing to prevent genocide in Srebrenica and by not arresting general Ratko Mladić.

Thus far, then, the international legal decisions in regard to the allegations of genocide in Bosnia are ambiguous at best. The ICTY and the ICJ have held that only the mass killings of Bosnian Muslim men at Srebrenica at the very end of the war constituted genocide (ICTY *Krstić* decision, finding adopted by ICJ); that while a general of the Bosnian Serb Army who helped organize those killings was guilty of complicity in genocide, he himself had not intended to commit genocide (ICTY, *Krstić*); that a leading political authority of the Bosnian Serbs had no intent to commit genocide (ICTY, *Krajišnik*, referred to by ICJ); that Serbia neither ordered the Bosnian Serb Army to commit the murders at Srebrenica nor was it in a position to control the Bosnian Serb Army once the killings began (ICJ); but that regardless of whether it *could* have prevented the killings, Serbia *should* have tried to do so but did not. All of these judgments rest on the decision in *Krstić* to say that a massacre of men in a single location counted as genocide, because that location was important both symbolically and militarily. While genocide requires the intent 'to destroy, in whole or in part, a national, ethnical, racial or religious group, as such,' the courts have yet to find that anyone actually had that intent – not Serbia (the ICJ decision), nor the Bosnian Serb leadership (*Krajišnik*), nor even one of the generals who carried it out (*Krstić*). Presumably, General Ratko Mladić had the intent to commit genocide, but only on a local level. But then, why is a massacre at a local level considered to be 'genocide' instead of, say, persecution, extermination or mass murder? The *Krstić* decisions are certainly neither consistent nor convincing on this issue.

By broadening the definition of 'genocide' to include expulsion from territories that are important strategically or symbolically, the *Krstić* Appeals Chamber seems to endorse a definition of genocide that would fit with that of none other than Franjo Tudjman, that 'throughout history there have always been attempts at a "final solution" for foreign and other undesirable racial-ethnic or religious groups through expulsion, extermination, and conversion to the "true religion."'[112] As discussed earlier, Tudjman's work was criticized because he questioned the extent of the Holocaust; but the logical grounds on which he argues are that since 'genocide' is a universal phenomenon of history, no special guilt may be attached to those societies or nations that practice, in his words, 'final solutions' through 'expulsion' and 'conversion' as well as extermination. The *Krstić* decision seems to accept genocide as the universal phenomenon that Tudjman envisions, though unlike Tudjman it does assign guilt.

The *Krstić* definition thus relativizes the concept of genocide to the point at which it equates conceptually the strategic killing of small numbers of people with actual efforts at the extermination of entire groups. Universalizing genocide in this way, however, means, first, that the extreme evil of attempts to exterminate a people as such, which the term 'genocide' was originally coined to cover, is left without distinction from other cases. Further, this broad definition also means that most of the forced movements of population in the twentieth century count as genocide: not only the deportations and mass murders of Armenians from Anatolia in 1915, but of Greeks from Anatolia and Turks from Greece in 1923, Serbs from the 'Independent State of Croatia' in 1941–5, Germans from Czechoslovakia, Poland and Yugoslavia in 1945, Poles from Ukraine and Lithuania in 1945, Muslims from India and Hindus and Sikhs from Pakistan in 1947, Palestinians from Israel in 1948, Jews from the Arab world after 1948, Turks from southern Cyprus and Greeks from Northern Cyprus in 1974, Croats from 'Republika Srpska Krajina' in 1992, Muslims from 'Herzeg-Bosna' in 1993, Azeris from Nagorno-Karabakh in 1993, Serbs from Croatia in 1995 – this is not a complete list. Some of these movements have been viewed as 'population transfers' accepted by the international community, others 'ethnic cleansing' or even genocide, and this labelling was made on political grounds.[113] According to the *Krstić* decision, however, such political attribution is legally appropriate, since a key criterion is the symbolic importance of the presence of that community on that territory to the international community. But what is to be gained by deciding after the fact that not only Turkey but Poland, the Czech Republic, Croatia, the Republika Srpska, India and Pakistan (among others) were founded on 'genocide'?

Conclusion

> The Holocaust has raised our tolerance for ordinary evil. This forces people to make their own plight more Holocaust-like.
>
> M. Berenbaum[114]

The *Krstić* decision's adoption of political criteria for determining 'genocide' returns us to the consideration raised at the start of this paper: that the invocation of the term 'genocide' is primarily a political process that creates images of a supposed past to serve the purposes of present-day political actors. The imagery gains its power from Auschwitz: rewarding the descendants of those murdered, and penalizing the descendants of those who did the murdering, seems justified when 'genocide' is in question. But the stakes at issue are not simply remembering the fate of the victims, but rather how that remembrance can be used to benefit those who claim to be their descendants, or to penalize those said to be the inheritors of their national guilt.

With this in mind, the invocation by Serb politicians in 1990–2 of the mass killings of Serbs in the 'Independent State of Croatia' (and thus in Bosnia) 50 years earlier was indeed a call to mobilize the descendants of those Serbs against the descendants of those said to have killed them, in order to justify aggressive Serb political actions (and later, military ones) against those Others. But the invocation of the short-lived camps of northern Bosnia in 1992–3 and the mass killing at Srebrenica in 1995 as 'genocide' has equally been a call to mobilize the international community, and also Bosnian Muslims, against Serbs. The suit by Bosnia against Serbia in the ICJ is primarily a tool by which Bosniak political forces are trying to undermine the Bosnian Serbs, even to eliminate the Republika Srpska.[115] Yet the war in Bosnia was driven by the rejections by Bosnian Serbs and Herzegovinian Croats of inclusion in a unitary Bosnian state, and they still reject this.[116] It is difficult to see how a Bosnian state can be imposed on the very large portion of the population that rejects inclusion within it – the precedents of Ireland, Kosovo and Cyprus do not augur well for such an effort. Any attempt to do so would require the maintenance of a police state, a difficult position to justify on any normative grounds. Of course, it could be proposed that those putative Bosnians who reject inclusion in Bosnia could be expelled from the state that the international community has recognized against their wishes (the Sudeten German solution) but that position is an endorsement of ethnic cleansing. Proposals for the elimination of the Republika Srpska privilege Bosniaks over Serbs, which is a major point of the invocation of 'genocide' to label the events of the 1990s.

Katherine Verdery has argued that 'entire battalions of [massacre victims] served as "shock troops" in the Yugoslav breakup.'[117] While her specific reference in this passage is to the mobilization of the dead of World War II, her model includes those of the later wars: 'the concern with corpses continues, as the fighting produces even more graves. Their occupants become the grounds for mutual recrimination ... and means of a politics of blame, guilt and accountability.'[118] As this passage shows, these are dangerous politics, which produced new corpses, and not only because of the actions of ex-Yugoslavs themselves (though they were primary: my own view in 1990–1 was that those who were insisting that history of 'genocide' not be forgotten were doing so in order to repeat the conflicts that produced it). In regard to Srebrenica, a U.S. official told me that while the U.S. government knew that at the end of the war, Srebrenica would be part of the Serbian territory, they would not, 'for moral reasons', urge the Izetbegović government to evacuate the town. This 'morality' left the Muslims of Srebrenica in place,[119] where they were massacred by Bosnian Serb forces a year later. This does not exculpate the Serb forces of responsibility for the mass killing, but it is discomfiting that concerns about a 'genocide' that had not actually taken place might have helped set the stage for these larger massacres later.

Perhaps the labelling of mass killings in Bosnia as 'genocides' should give pause. The term 'genocide' may not fit all mass killings. Invoking that term may well be a tactic for inciting hostility between the descendants of putative victims and alleged victimizers. It may serve to preclude diplomatic efforts on supposedly 'moral' grounds. Finally, forcing accounts of ethnic conflict into the framework of the Holocaust distorts perceptions of the real causes and trajectories of the conflict, thus not only hindering understanding of the conflict itself, but also obstructing efforts to establish new forms of relations between the groups involved.

Notes

1. Until 1994, the term Muslim (*Musliman*) was used in general speech and in constitutional, legal and political documents in Bosnia and the rest of the former Yugoslavia to refer to peoples of Muslim heritage who speak Serbo-Croatian. In 1994, the term 'Bosniak' (*Bošnjak*) was adopted for official use for these peoples (see F. Markowitz, 'Census and Sensibilities in Sarajevo', *Comparative Studies in Society and History*, 49 (2007), 40–73). Since 'Muslim' was the term used throughout most of the war, I will use it in this chapter. I am grateful for the comments on earlier

versions of Xavier Bougarel, William Brustein, Tomislav Dulić, Ilya Prizel and Dan Stone.

2. *Prosecutor v. Radisav Krstic*, ICTY case no. Case No: IT-98-33-A, Appeals Chamber judgment of 19 April 2004, http://www.un.org/icty/krstic/ Appeal/ judgement/ index.htm.
3. E. Tabeau and J. Bijak, 'War-related Deaths in the 1992–1995 Armed Conflicts in Bosnia and Herzegovina: A Critique of Previous Estimates and Recent Results', *European Journal of Population*, 21 (2005), 187–215.
4. Ibid.
5. S. Bogosavljević, 'The Unresolved Genocide', in *The Road to War in Serbia*, ed. N. Popov (New York and Budapest: Central European University Press, 2000), p. 155; T. Dulić, *Utopias of Nation: Local Mass Killings in Bosnia and Herzegovina, 1941–42* (Uppsala: Uppsala University Press, 2005), p. 314. The actual number of dead is undoubtably substantially higher, as both Bogosavljević and Dulić worked from a 1964 census of victims of World War II that was acknowledged by its authors to encompass probably only 56–58 per cent of the total victims.
6. R. Hayden, 'Recounting the Dead: The Rediscovery and Redefinition of Wartime Massacres in Late- and Post-Communist Yugoslavia', in *Memory, Opposition and History under State Socialism*, ed. R. S. Watson (Santa Fe, NM: School of American Research Press, 1994), pp. 167–84; B. Denich, 'Dismembering Yugoslavia: Nationalist Ideologies and the Symbolic Revival of Genocide', *American Ethnologist*, 21 (1994), 367–90. The best accounts of the rise of Serbian nationalism in the 1980s are in Popov, ed., *The Road to War in Serbia* and J. Dragović-Soso, *'Saviours of the Nation': Serbia's Intellectual Opposition and the Revival of Nationalism* (Montreal: McGill-Queen's University Press, 2002).
7. See R. Hayden, 'Balancing Discussion of Jasenovac and the Manipulation of History', *East European Politics and Societies*, 6 (1992), 207–12.
8. M. Weber, 'Science as a Vocation', in *From Max Weber*, eds, H. Gerth and C. W. Mills (New York: Oxford University Press, 1946), p. 146.
9. Ibid., p. 145.
10. If, of course, policy decisions actually are meant to bring about any result greater than increasing the domestic popularity of the political actors making them – see M. Edelman, *Political Language: Words that Succeed and Policies that Fail* (New York: Academic Press, 1977) for a discouraging analysis that argues the contrary position, and is congruent with Bailey's concept of the tactical uses of passion.
11. See, for example, T. Cushman and S. Meštrović, eds, *This Time We Knew: Western Responses to Genocide in Bosnia* (New York: NYU Press 1996), which castigates intellectuals who attempt to make a balanced analysis of events in Bosnia (p. 5): 'Balance is a necessary quality of intellectual life, except when it comes ... at the expense of confusing victims with aggressors, and the failure to recognize those who are the perpetrators of genocide and crimes against humanity.' They further assert that 'it is vitally important to let the facts speak for themselves, particularly where genocide is involved' (p. 15). How one might determine 'the facts' without engaging in a balanced weighing of evidence is left unstated. Weber, of course, said ('Science as a Vocation', p. 146) that '"To let the facts speak for themselves" is the most unfair way of putting over a political position.'
12. F. G. Bailey, *The Tactical Uses of Passion: An Essay in Power, Reason and Reality* (Ithaca, NY: Cornell University Press, 1983), p. 23.
13. Some well-known works about Bosnia (for example, those by David Rieff, Norman Cigar, Noel Malcom, Michael Ignatieff) are essentially prosecutor's briefs that ground

their presentations about the putative genocide in Bosnia on the unrebuttable presumption that genocide in fact occurred. An outstanding example of this prosecutorial genre is J. Gow, *The Serbian Project and Its Adversaries* (London: Hurst & Company, 2003), which is explicitly *not* about 'the Yugoslav war as a whole' but rather only Serbian strategies and activities, because, to Gow, this Serbian project was 'the primary and defining element in the war' and thus analysis of it is 'essential both to exploring the true character of the war and to recognizing the central responsibility for what happened' (p. 9). Purposefully ignoring the complexities of a historical process is an unusual intellectual strategy, and in this case a teleological one: all evidence is presumed to lead to the predetermined conclusion. This is a good strategy for making a prosecutor's case, but it is unacceptable in social science, because evidence that might tend to disprove the predetermined conclusion is ignored. Such studies, political rhetoric in the Weberian sense mentioned above, and are not considered here.

14. T. Todorov, *Facing the Extreme: Moral Life in the Concentration Camps* (New York: Metropolitan Books, 1996), p. 277.
15. The literature on the formation of Yugoslavia is huge; recommended recent works include D. Djokić, ed., *Yugoslavism: Histories of a Failed Idea, 1918–1992* (London: Hurst, 2003) and G. Stokes, 'Yugoslavism in the 1860s?' and 'The Role of the Yugoslav Committee in the Formation of Yugoslavia', both in *Three Eras of Political Change in Eastern Europe*, ed., G. Stokes (Oxford: Oxford University Press, 1997), pp. 83–92 and 93–108.
16. Standard references on the political development of the first Yugoslavia are I. Banac, *The National Question in Yugoslavia: Origins, History and Politics* (Ithaca, NY: Cornell University Press, 1983), and A. Djilas, *The Contested Country: Yugoslav Unity and Communist Revolution, 1919–1953* (Cambridge, MA: Harvard University Press, 1991).
17. See J. Tomasevich, *War and Revolution in Yugoslavia, 1941–1945: Occupation and Collaboration.* (Stanford, CA: Stanford University Press, 2001); Djilas, *The Contested Country*; Dulić, *Utopias of Nation*; and M. Djilas, *Wartime* (New York: Harcourt, Brace 1981).
18. The masterwork on Tito's Yugoslavia is D. Rusinow, *The Yugoslav Experiment, 1948–1974* (Berkeley, CA: University of California Press, 1977). The demise of Yugoslavia is well analyzed in S. Woodward, *Balkan Tragedy: Chaos and Dissolution after the Cold War* (Washington, D.C.: Brookings Institution 1995); see also the Central Intelligence Agencies unclassified *Balkan Battlegrounds*, 2 vols. (Washington, D.C.: Central Intelligence Agency, 2002, 2003), and R. Hayden, *Blueprints for a House Divided: The Constitutional Logic of the Yugoslav Conflicts* (Ann Arbor, MI: University of Michigan Press, 1999). A good journalistic account is L. Silber and A. Little, *Yugoslavia: Death of a Nation* (New York: TV Books, distributed by Penguin USA, 1995); however, the television series that the Silber and Little book accompanies is less reliable. The literature on the last few years of Yugoslavia and the wars that followed is otherwise too vast to survey here.
19. Hayden, *Blueprints for a House Divided*; also R. Hayden, 'Constitutional Nationalism in the Formerly Yugoslav Republics', *Slavic Review*, 51 (1992), 654–73.
20. R. Hayden, 'Imagined Communities and Real Victims: Self-Determination and Ethnic Cleansing in Yugoslavia', *American Ethnologist*, 23 (1996), 783–801.
21. In many places, the violence of the 1990s was locally viewed as a continuation of the violence of the 1940s, including Srebrenica; see C. Sudetic, *Blood and Vengeance* (New York: Penguin books, 1998) and G. Duizjing, 'History and Reminders in East Bosnia', Appendix IV to Nederlands Instituut voor Oorlogsdocumentatie NIOD),

Srebrenica: A 'Safe' Area, http://www.srebrenica.nl/en/a_index.htm. A similar point is made by Mart Bax for Medjugorje; see M. Bax, *Medjugorje: Religion, Politics and Violence in Rural Bosnia* (Amsterdam: VU Uitgeverij, 1995); see also Hayden 'Recounting the Dead', and Denich, 'Dismembering Yugoslavia'.

22. The 1941–5 sources are Bogosavljević, 'The Unresolved Genocide', and Dulić, *Utopias of Nation*; those for 1992–5 are E. Tabeau and J. Bijak, 'War-related Deaths in the 1992–1995 Armed Conflicts' and the as yet unpublished findings of the Istraživaćko dokumentacioni centar of Sarajevo (http://www.idc.org.ba) as reported by its President, Mirsad Tokača, in media interviews. These 1992–5 studies were supported by the Office of the Prosector of the ICTY (Tabeu & Bijak) and the embassies of NATO countries, especially Norway (IDC), so the fact that their findings are contrary to the rhetoric of the war period serves to give them greater credibility. The 1941–5 period studies were self-funded (Bogosavljević) and funded from Swedish academic sources (Dulić).
23. Bogosavljević, 'The Unresolved Genocide', p. 157.
24. Ibid., p. 155.
25. Dulić, *Utopias of Nation*, p. 317. In an email on 1 March 2006, Dulić informed me that he has recalculated Žerjavić's figures and slightly lowered the upper range of percentage of Serbs killed, to 19 per cent; see T. Dulić, 'Mass Killing in the Independent State of Croatia, 1941–45: A Case for Comparative Research', unpublished ms.
26. Dulić, *Utopias of Nation*, p. 321.
27. Ibid., p. 323.
28. *Oslobodjenje* (9 December 2004).
29. Report carried on Justwatch listserv, 10 December 2004.
30. BBC Worldwide Monitoring, 17 December 2005; carried on Justwatch listserv, 17 December 2005. See also 'Genocide is Not a Matter of Numbers', Bosnian Institute News & Analysis (www.bosnia.org.uk) 19 January 2006, an interview with Tokača.
31. See Hayden, 'Recounting the Dead'; Dragović-Soso, *'Saviours of the Nation'*; Popov, ed., *The Road to War in Serbia*; A. Wachtel, *Making a Nation, Breaking a Nation: Literature and Cultural Politics in Yugoslavia* (Stanford, CA: Stanford University Press, 1998).
32. See, e.g., D. Tošić, 'The Democratic Alternative' and B. Horvat, 'The Association for Yugoslav Democratic Initiative', both in *Yugoslavism*, ed., Djokić, pp. 286–97 and 298–303; Woodward, *Balkan Tragedy*.
33. Woodward, *Balkan Tragedy*; Hayden, 'Constitutional Nationalism'; I. Vejvoda, 'Yugoslavia 1945–91: From Decentralization Without Democracy to Dissolution', in *Yugoslavia and After*, eds. I. Vejvoda and D. Dyker (London: Longman, 1996), pp. 9–27. The matter was more complicated in Bosnia, since the electorate *de facto* partitioned into separate Muslim, Serb and Croat electorates, each of which voted for a single nationalist party; see S. Burg and P. Shoup, *The War in Bosnia and Herzegovina* (New York: M. E. Sharpe, 1999), pp. 46–61; and X. Bougarel, *Bosnie: Anatomie d'un conflit* (Paris: Éditions La Découverte, 1996), revised edition published as K. Bugarel, *Bosna: Anatomija Rata* (Beograd: Fabrika Knjige Edicija Reč, 2004), Ch. 1; Bougarel, 'Bosnia and Herzegovina: State and Communitarianism', in *Yugoslavia and After*, eds, Vejvoda and Dyker.
34. The Memorandum was never actually adopted by the Serbian Academy; rather, a working document was 'leaked', apparently in an effort to expose its nationalist tendencies, which portrayed Serbs as victims of the machinations of other nations throughout the twentieth century (see Woodward, *Balkan Tragedy*, p. 78). The Serbian Academy did finally issue the Memorandum in an attempt to

defend itself; in K. Mihailović and V. Krestić, *Memorandum of the Serbian Academy of Sciences and Arts: Answers to Criticisms* (Belgrade: Serbian Academy of Sciences and Arts 1995). The *Memorandum* is discussed extensively in Dragović-Soso, *'Saviours of the Nation'*, pp. 177–95.

35. M. Mann, *The Dark Side of Democracy: Explaining Ethnic Cleansing* (Cambridge: Cambridge University Press, 2005), pp. 364–5.
36. See Dragović-Soso, *'Saviours of the Nation'*, pp. 189–95; Woodward, *Balkan Tragedy*, p. 94.
37. Dragović-Soso, *'Saviours of the Nation'*, pp. 189–90. Other elements of Slovenian chavinism towards other Yugoslavs are discussed in M. Bakić-Hayden and R. Hayden, 'Orientalist Variations on the Theme "Balkans"', *Slavic Review*, 50 (1992), 1–15.
38. The title of this subsection is borrowed from M. Živković, 'The Wish to be a Jew: The Power of the Jewish Trope in the Yougoslav [sic] Conflict', *Cahiers de l'Urmis*, 6 (2000), 69–84, and many of the ideas discussed in it are based on Živković's work.
39. Ibid., p. 73.
40. Matije Bečković, quoted and translated by Živković, ibid., p. 73.
41. Ibid., pp. 73, 75.
42. See I. Primoratz, 'Israel and Genocide in Croatia', in *Genocide After Emotion: The Postemotional Balkan War*, ed., S. G. Meštrović (London: Routledge, 1996), pp. 195–206.
43. Ibid., p. 205.
44. Dulić, *Utopias of Nation*.
45. See S. Kinzer, 'Pro-Nazi Legacy Lingers for Croatia', *New York Times* (31 October 1993), 6; C. Hedges, 'Fascists Reborn as Croatia's Founding Fathers', *New York Times* (12 April 1997), 3.
46. Romania, however, also controlled its own camps (Ilya Prizel, personal communication, 14 February 2006).
47. 'Antisemitizam: Jesu li Ustaše zaista bili džentlmeni?', *Globus* (23 August 1991), 14.
48. 'Croatia Apologizes to Jews for Nazi-Era Crimes', *New York Times* (23 August 1997), A-6.
49. F. Tudjman, *Bespuća Povijesne Zbilnosti: Rasprava o povjesti I filozofiji zlosilja*.(Zagreb: Naklodni Zavod Matice Hrvatske, 1990), pp. 156–8.
50. Ibid., p. 160.
51. Ibid., pp. 316–20.
52. Dulić, *Utopias of Nation*, p. 260. Dulić refutes other arguments by Tudjman about the supposed role of Jews in Jasenovac on pp. 261–3.
53. Wikipedia article URL: http://hr.wikipedia.org/wiki/Bespu%C4%87 a_povijesne_ zbiljnosti, checked 27 January 2006.
54. This parallel is explicitly drawn, with references to other uses of it at the time, by T. Cushman and S. Meštrović in the "Introduction" to *This Time We Knew*, pp. 6–13; indeed, this volume is exemplary of the rhetorical tactic of grounding assertions about events in Bosnia on supposed parallels with the Holocaust. Meštrović's role in propagating such literatures is noteworthy. A Croatian-American, he co-authored, with a Zagreb University professor who was one of Franjo Tudjman's advisors in 1990, a book that purported to differentiate Western, thus civilized Croatia from Eastern, thus barbaric Serbia (S. Meštrović and S. Letica, *Habits of the Balkans Heart: Social Character and the Fall of Communism* [College Station, TX: Texas A&M Press, 1993]). This kind of literally Orientalist rhetoric in regard to 'the Balkans' has been well analyzed; see, for example, L. Wolff, *Inventing Eastern Europe: The Map of Civilization in the Mind of the Enlightenment* (Stanford, CA: Stanford University Press, 1994); M. Todorova, *Imagining the Balkans* (Oxford: Oxford

University Press, 1997); and most recently J. Böröcz, 'Goodness is Elsewhere: The Rule of European Difference', *Comparative Studies in Society and History*, 48 (2006), 110–38; in specific regard to the former Yugoslavia, see M. Bakić-Hayden, 'Nesting Orientalisms: The Case of Former Yugoslavia', *Slavic Review*, 54 (1995), 917–31, and M. Razsa and N. Lindstrom, 'Balkan is Beautiful: Balkanism in the Political Discourse of Tudjman's Croatia', *East European Politics and Societies*, 18 (2005), 628–50. Meštrović has used the facilities of his own university's press (Texas: A&M Press) to establish a series of books on eastern Europe, several of them asserting the evil of Serbs and Serbia. One is reminded of Milan Kundera's observation that 'the spirit of propaganda ... reduces (and teaches others to reduce) the life of a hated society to the simple listing of its crimes' (Kundera, 'Paths in the Fog', in his *Testaments Betrayed* (New York: Harper Collins, 1995), p. 225.

55. B. Kouchner, *Les Guerriers de la paix: Du Kosovo à l'Irak* (Paris: Grasset, 2004), pp. 374–5.
56. Bogosavljević, 'The Unresolved Genocide', reviews these studies.
57. Ibid., pp. 152–4. Bogosavljević was one of the highest officials in the Federal Bureau of Statistics in the Ante Marković period and thus had access to the materials.
58. See Dragović-Soso, *'Saviours of the Nation'*, pp. 100–14.
59. Ibid., p. 111. It should be noted that Dedijer also was the first to raise to prominence the issue of Serb killings of Bosnian Muslims during the war.
60. Transcripts of hearings of the CSCE may be accessed at http://www. csce.gov., where they are organized by issue and by country, then listed chronologically within each category.
61. On U.S. Public Broadcasting System, 'The Charlie Rose Show', 23 November 2005.
62. 'The Civilian Toll of War', *New York Times* (18 December 2005).
63. These studies are summarized and evaluated by Tabeau and Bijak, 'War-related Deaths', p. 194.
64. V. Dedijer, *The Yugoslav Auschwitz and the Vatican: The Croatian Massacre of the Serbs During World War II* (Buffalo, NY: Prometheus Books, 1992). The American edition is a translation from the original German edition of 1988. The hostility of some segments of Serb nationalist writers to the Roman Catholic Church is beyond the scope of this paper, but this volume is by no means unique in the historiography of socialist Yugoslavia.
65. M. Marković, 'A Preliminary Note on the Historical Background of the Present Yugoslav Crisis', in V. Dedijer, *The Yugoslav Auschwitz and the Vatican*, p. 11.
66. G. Niemtietz, 'Preface to the First German Edition', in Dedijer, *The Yugoslav Auschwitz and the Vatican*, p. 23.
67. Djilas, *The Contested Country*, p. 126.
68. Dulić, *Utopias of Nation*, p. 313.
69. These stories are extensively discussed in D. Campbell, 'Atrocity, Memory, Photography: Imaging the Concentration Camps of Bosnia – the Case of ITN versus *Living Marxism*, Part 1,' *Journal of Human Rights*, 1 (2002), 1–33; part 2, *Journal of Human Rights*, 1 (2002), 143–72. The World Wide Web version, http://www.virtual-security.net/attrocity/atroindex.htm, contains links that show the original broadcasts and other relevant visual materials.
70. Ibid. Again, the web version of Campbell's articles contains links showing international television and newspaper coverage; the print version contains some of the newspaper coverage.
71. Data taken from the index of cases on the ICTY website, http://www. un.org/icty/ cases-e/index-e.htm. All of the references to 'camps' are in the index following the names of the accused, except for the Tadic case.

72. *Prosecutor v. Miroslav Kvocka et al.*, ICTY Trial Chamber I Judgement, 2 November 2001 (http://www.un.org/icty/kvocka/trialc/judgement/index. htm), paras. 17 and 21.
73. *Prosecutor v. Predrag Banovic*, ICTY Trial Chamber III Sentencing Judgement, 28 October 2003 (http://www.un.org/icty/banovic65–1/trialc/judgement/ bansj031028e.htm#II), para. 23.
74. ICTY *Kvocka Judgment*, paras. 45–108.
75. *ICTY Banovic Sentencing Judgment*, para. 22 (references omitted).
76. Z. Filipović, *Zlata's Diary: A Child's Life in Sarajevo* (New York: Viking, 1994).
77. C. Lehmann-Haupt, 'Books of the Times: Another Diary of a Young Girl', *New York Times* (28 February 1994).
78. Filipović, *Zlata's Diary*, p. 29.
79. Ibid., p. 96
80. Idid., p. 198.
81. Ibid., p. 200.
82. F. Prose, 'A Little Girl's War', *New York Times* (6 March 1994).
83. M. Stojić, 'Bosanskahercegovačka književnost i rat', *BiH Dani* no. 216 (27 July 2001).
84. *Zlata's Diary*, p. viii.
85. 'Anger Greets Croatian's Invitation to Holocaust Museum Dedication', *New York Times* (22 April 1993); see also 'A Different Guest' (editorial), *Washington Post* (4 April 1993).
86. 'Holocaust Museum Hailed as Sacred Debt to Dead', *New York Times* (23 April 1993).
87. 'Croatian WWII Concentration Camp Records Made Available for First Time by United States Holocaust Memorial Museum', U.S. Holocaust Memorial Museum Press Release, 13 November 2001.
88. 'Jasenovac opet posvađao žive zbog mrtvih', *Jutarnji.hr*, (published on-line 13 January 2006 14: 40).
89. See R. Hayden, 'Schindler's Fate: Genocide, Ethnic Cleansing and Population Transfers', *Slavic Review*, 55 (1995), 727–78. That article, like this one, did not question the extent of the atrocities but rather only the applicability of the term 'genocide' in this context.
90. *Prosecutor v. Radislav Krstić*, ICTY Trial Chamber I, Judgement, 2 August 2001, para. 1 (hereafter, *Krstić* trial judgement).
91. All figures are from H. Brunborg, T. Lyngstad and H. Urdal, 'Accounting for Genocide: How Many Were Killed in Srebrenica?', *European Journal of Population*, 19 (2003), 229–48.
92. *Krstić* trial judgement, para. 540. While the *Krstić* court uses the definition found in the ICTY's founding statute, this is drawn directly from the relevant UN treaty definitions.
93. Ibid., para. 544.
94. Ibid., para. 552.
95. Ibid., para. 560.
96. Ibid., para. 590.
97. Ibid., para. 595.
98. Ibid., para. 595.
99. *Prosecutor v. Milomir Stakic*, ICTY Trial Chamber II, Judgement, 31 July 2003.
100. Dulić, *Utopias of Nation*, pp. 18–19.
101. See, e.g., P. Brass, 'The Partition of India and Retributive Genocide in the Punjab, 1946–47: Means, Methods and Purposes,' *Journal of Genocide Research*, 5 (2003), 71–101.
102. *Prosecutor v. Radislav Krstić*, ICTY Appeals Chamber Judgement, 19 April 2004 (hereafter, *Krstić* appeal), para. 12.

103. *Krstić* appeal, para. 15, emphasis added; the depiction of the conflict as one between a Bosnian Muslim state and a Serb state was empirically accurate (though it ignored the Croatian state in Herzegovina) but contradictory to the premise that the recognized Bosnian government represented all of Bosnia's peoples.
104. *Krstić* appeal, para. 16.
105. *Krstić* appeal, para. 36.
106. *Prosecutor v. Momčilo Krajišnik*, Consolidated amended Indictment, 7 March 2002.
107. *Prosecutor v. Momčilo Krajišnik*, ICTY Trial Chamber I Judgement, 27 September 2006, para. 21.
108. *Krajišnik* judgement, paras. 867–9.
109. International Court of Justice, *Case Concerning the application of the Convention on the Prevention and Punishment of the Crime of Genocide (Bosnia and Herzegovina v. Serbia and Montenegro)*, Judgement, 26 February 2007.
110. Ibid., paras 296–7.
111. Ibid., para. 413.
112. Tudjman, *Bespuća*, p. 166.
113. Hayden, 'Schindler's Fate'.
114. Quoted in G. Kenney, 'The Bosnia Calculation', *New York Times Magazine* (23 April 1995), 43. Michael Berenbaum was at the time Director of the Holocaust Research Institute at the U.S. Holocaust Memorial Museum.
115. See 'Editorial: Looking for a Culprit', in *Transitions on Line* (7 February 2006), http://www.tol.cz/look/TOL/.
116. See R. Hayden, 'Democracy without a Demos? The Bosnian Constitutional Experiment and the Intentional Construction of Nonfunctioning States', *East European Politics & Societies*, 19 (2005), 226–59.
117. K. Verdery, *The Political Lives of Dead Bodies: Reburials and Postsocialist Change* (New York: Columbia University Press, 1999), p. 21.
118. Ibid., p. 102.
119. Actually, rather more than that: the U.S. worked to break the U.N. arms embargo on Bosnia, and sent arms specifically to the Srebrenica region, where Muslim forces used them to attack not only the Bosnian Serb Army but Serb villages; these attacks may have contributed to the Bosnian Serb Army decision to massacre so many Muslim men. See C. Weibes, 'Intelligence and the War in Bosnia 1992–1995: The Role of the Intelligence and Security Services', Appendix II to Nederlands Instituut voor Oorlogsdocumentatie NIOD), *Srebrenica: A 'Safe' Area*, http://www. srebrenica. nl/en/a_index.htm.

20
The Historiography of the Rwandan Genocide

Scott Straus

Introduction

In recent years, the Rwandan genocide has generated a large and growing academic literature. The disciplines and themes within the scholarship are diverse. History, political science, law, and anthropology are well represented in the academic literature, but some of the most prominent contributions come from human rights practitioners and journalists. Thematically, Rwanda is a paradigmatic case of ethnic conflict and central to the rapidly growing field of genocide studies. The case is also a touchstone for students of transitional justice, humanitarian intervention, violence, and contemporary African politics – in addition to a number of other themes. Rwanda also commands attention beyond the university, in particular, from policymakers and lay audiences – the latter, especially, after a series of high profile feature films and documentaries. Thus, despite its relative recentness, the Rwandan genocide already has given rise to a very large body of work.

Broadly, the existing literature on the Rwandan genocide may be divided into three primary areas. The first focuses on the origins of the genocide, in particular the history of ethnicity as well as the planning for and execution of the genocide itself. The second focuses on the international response to the genocide, in particular the decision not to intervene to halt the killing. The third focuses on the aftermath of genocide, in particular the question of how to render justice after a crime of such enormity. Each area has generated considerable interest and writing. That said, while the third area commands significant policy attention, the academic literature on post-genocide Rwanda is at a relatively early stage. In the second area, the central questions are somewhat narrow and well covered in the literature. The first area, to date, has generated the most empirical and theoretical questions and will be the centre-piece of this essay.

Given the volume of research, I impose a few parameters on the essay. By and large, the focus is on works primarily on Rwanda (as opposed to comparative analyses where Rwanda is one case among several). I also focus on English-language literature. French is the other language in which a considerable amount on Rwanda has been published. However, covering the francophone literature comprehensively is well beyond the scope of this essay, and so instead I will make reference to French-language works when there is no apparent English-language equivalent. Overall, the essay's main purpose will be to document the trajectory of scholarship and the primary questions and themes within that scholarship. In addition, where appropriate and in the interests of suggesting avenues for further research, I will draw attention to understudied areas and to areas where there remain sharp points of disagreement.[1]

From ancient hatreds to modern, planned genocide

Stereotype has shaped, to a large degree, informed commentary on the roots of the Rwandan genocide. In particular, within the public domain there is a common view that tribalism and ancient ethnic animosities drove Rwanda's violence. The idea that African politics is reducible to 'tribalism' is not peculiar to Rwanda. But given the nature of much of Rwanda's genocide – public, face-to-face violence, often committed by machetes, and often entailing neighbour killing neighbour – the idea that what happened in Rwanda was atavistic ethnic hatred run amok found particular resonance.[2] The academic literature has a corollary that also was invoked to explain Rwanda's violence: in the genocide's aftermath, some authors argued that state 'collapse' and state 'failure' were at play during the genocide.[3]

Taken together, the ideas of ancient tribal hatred and state disintegration created an image of the genocide as spontaneous, unorganized, chaotic, and senseless. That view shaped the original terms of debate of the Rwandan genocide, and that idea remains somewhat prevalent among lay audiences, at least in the United States. As a result, much informed writing and scholarship have been centrally concerned with debunking this paradigm. The product is a new consensus on the Rwandan genocide. Rather than seeing the violence as chaotic frenzy or as an explosion of atavistic animosities, scholars and human rights activists alike stress that the violence was modern, systematic, and intentional. Specific Hutu leaders planned the violence; they drew on modern, colonially manipulated ethnic categories and a modern ideology of ethnic nationalism; they used the state to execute their plans; and they deliberately attempted to eliminate a racially defined minority. What happened in Rwanda was not tribalism writ large; it was genocide.

Those are the central points in the new consensus on Rwanda. For heuristic purposes, the main points may be divided into three major areas: (1) a history of ethnicity; (2) the immediate antecedents of genocide and planning for genocide; and (3) details of the genocide itself. I discuss each area below.

A history of ethnicity

A major focus in the literature concerns Rwanda's ethnic categories. A starting point is a critique of the notion of 'tribe' in the Rwandan context. In particular, many authors and commentators argue that Hutus and Tutsis, which are Rwanda's two main ethnic categories at 84–90 per cent and 10–14 per cent of the population, respectively, are not tribes. Hutus and Tutsis speak the same language (Kinyarwanda); they live in the same regions; they belong to the same clans; they belong to the same religions; and they intermarry frequently.

To understand the meaning of Hutu and Tutsi, authors focus on the terms' history, both in pre-colonial times and especially under colonial rule. Given an absence of written sources, the history of pre-colonial Rwanda is challenging to reconstruct. Historians marshal a range of evidence, from archeology and pollen deposits to lexicostatistics and oral histories. There is a general consensus that prior to colonialism Rwanda had one of the most sophisticated and powerful monarchies in the Great Lakes region of Africa. The monarchy was expansionist, centralized, hierarchical, and militaristic. When precisely the Rwandan monarchy emerged and took the form it eventually took by the nineteenth century is subject to debate. Nonetheless, by the late-nineteenth century, on the eve of European penetration into the region, the monarchy was firmly established, especially in what is presently south-central Rwanda.[4]

By the time of European arrival, the social categories 'Hutu' and 'Tutsi' were prominent in Rwanda's monarchical system. They were not, however, singularly prominent: clan, region, relationship to royalty, and other identities mattered. Perhaps more critical is what 'Hutu' and 'Tutsi' meant as social categories. The balance of historical opinion now locates the origins of the Hutu/Tutsi categories to changes internal to Rwandan society. There would appear to be several overlapping dimensions to the categories in pre-colonial Rwanda. One relates to economic activity. Farming and animal husbandry were central practices in pre-colonial Rwanda (and in the region). By and large, 'Tutsi' referred to herders and 'Hutu' to agriculturalists. The terms also connoted status and power. 'Tutsi' in general referred to Rwandans of higher status, while 'Hutu' referred to lower status. Historian Jan Vansina argues that 'Tutsi', in fact, may initially have referred to the political elite among herders, but then later the term was extended to herders in general.[5] A final, but important point is that the terms became salient within the context of the monarchy. That is, as the Rwandan monarchy expanded, so too did the terms' relevance. All that said, there was considerable variation within the categories. Some Hutus reared cattle and goats; many Tutsis farmed. Some Tutsis were relatively poor, while some Hutus were relatively wealthy. Moreover, the social categories were not fixed; with enough status within the monarchy, a Hutu could become Tutsi.[6]

European entry and rule into the region altered the categories' meaning. Europeans viewed the categories and the social stratification in racial terms.

To wit, the first European explorers – followed in turn by Christian missionaries and colonial administrators – described Tutsis as a superior, elegant, 'Caucosoid' race. Tutsis were seen as Hamites who had descended from northern Africa and brought with them a superior system of social organization, which they had used to conquer the more numerous Hutus, who were described as shorter, stockier, less intelligent 'negroids'. This view of Tutsis and Hutus as different and differently endowed races reflected then-current anthropological and historical ideas. Particularly prominent was the so-called Hamitic Hypothesis, which saw civilization in Africa (of which the Rwandan monarchy was one example) as the product of 'Hamitic' peoples.[7] Contemporary historical scholarship now substantially calls into question these related notions of race, fixed corporate groupings, and successive large-scale population migrations.

Nonetheless, as they established colonial oversight in the region, Europeans also made race the basis for organizing and allocating power in the colonial system. First the Germans and then the Belgians (who took control of Rwanda after World War I) opted for a system of colonial governance known as indirect rule. In so doing, the Europeans backed the ruling elite that had controlled Rwanda in the pre-colonial system. But the relevant category here was less the monarchy and more Tutsis – as a race – and Tutsis were allocated positions in the colonial administration and sent on for further education. The Europeans streamlined Rwanda's complex pre-colonial system of governance, which in turn increased local Tutsi dominance. Belgian colonial officers also introduced identity cards that labeled Rwandans according to their ethnicity. The net effect, then, of the first 50 years of colonial rule was to racialize a pre-existing social hierarchy, to make race a central determinant of power, and to increase the arbitrary power of Tutsis.[8]

A new round of changes followed World War II as decolonization spread throughout the imperial world. Under pressure from the newly established United Nations to prepare Rwanda for independence, Belgium began a programme of reform in the 1950s. One key change was to increase Hutu political representation, initially at the local level. In the same period, a Hutu political elite, nurtured largely by Catholic missionaries sympathetic to their cause, began to mobilize. There followed a complex sequence of events. In brief, some Tutsi elites whose interests were at stake resisted reform and sought an early end to colonial rule. They also denied the political relevance of ethnicity, claiming that the categories were European products. The emerging Hutu counter-elite in turn insisted on ethnicity as a way of recognizing and changing their pre-existing political and economic exclusion. Independence and democracy meant ending Tutsi control, argued Hutu political aspirants. This logic in turn gave rise to an ethnic nationalist ideology: Hutu political leaders claimed at independence that democracy meant majority rule, and majority rule meant Hutu rule.

The struggle for power in the terminal colonial period culminated in violence and radical change. The period as a whole is often labelled the 'Hutu Revolution'. The violence began in 1959. In October, some Tutsi men attacked and wounded a leading Hutu political party activist. In response, there was a wave of Hutu-led violence against Tutsi civilians, as well as counter-violence by Tutsis and others associated with the monarchy against Hutu political leaders. Eventually Belgium, which at the time still held colonial power, settled the issue – in favour of the Hutu counter-elite. In short order, the Belgians abolished the monarchy, replaced hundreds of Tutsi administrative officers with Hutus, and eventually installed a Hutu president, Grégoire Kayibanda. Tens of thousands of Tutsis in turn fled the country, taking up exile in neighbouring countries. Some in turn launched armed attacks in the early 1960s. One serious but failed attempt in late 1963 spawned a reprisal massacre that took the lives of as many as 10,000 Tutsis.[9]

Many authors argue that in post-Revolution Rwanda, under the regimes of Kayibanda (1962–1973) and Juvénal Habyarimana (1973–1994), Tutsis were treated as second-class citizens. Authors use various formulations. Linda Melvern argues that Tutsis were 'marginalized' in independent Rwanda. In particular, Melvern, like others, points to ethnic quotas that limited Tutsi representation in higher education, government, and even business enterprises.[10] Peter Uvin argues that in Rwanda there was a system of 'institutionalized prejudice'.[11] Gérard Prunier emphasizes that a 'Rwandese ideology', based on the pseudo-scientific racial theories introduced under colonialism, pervaded.[12]

These paragraphs do not do justice to a complex political and social history. The main point here is to emphasize that, as they searched for the origins of the genocide and in response to the ahistorical claims of ancient tribal hatred, authors turned to this history of ethnicity. Some consumers of this history attribute too much blame, in my view, to colonialism. The Europeans did not invent the categories 'Hutu' and 'Tutsi', nor did the Europeans invent social hierarchies in Rwanda. Rwandan elites, moreover, often adopted frameworks that served their interests. Nonetheless, colonialism did have an impact. The changes that happened under colonial rule altered the meaning and salience of ethnicity. Later, in the heady days of competition for political power in the terminal colonial period, those changes morphed into ethnic nationalism. After independence, ethnic nationalism in turn became the ruling coalitions' dominant political ideology. Changes were incremental and cumulative – Europeans did not create social or hierarchical categories from thin air – but the changes that happened were significant.

Antecedents of and planning for genocide

The 'ancient tribal hatred' model implies, as does that of state collapse, that the 1994 genocide was spontaneous, leaderless, and chaotic. In response, the academic and human rights literature has argued and shown that a model of rudderless state disintegration is misleading. In particular, authors emphasize that (a) particular officials promoted and are responsible for the genocide; (b) that particular officials planned and organized the violence; and (c) that they used the state and other modern means (especially the media) to carry out the violence. In this sense, the violence was top-down, systematic, intentional, and state-driven. To demonstrate these points, the historiography focuses on two periods – the period just before the genocide (1990–March 1994) and the period of the genocide itself. I begin with the former.

Two major macro-level changes happened in the three-year period before the genocide. First, in 1990, the rebel Rwandan Patriotic Front (RPF) invaded from southern Uganda and engaged the Rwandan government, then led by Juvénal Habyarimana, in a civil war. The RPF was composed largely of Tutsi exiles, many of whom were descendents of Tutsis who had fled Rwanda during the Revolution period.[13] The second major change was that, in 1991 under pressure from France, Rwanda's principal international backer, Rwanda ended one-party rule. A vibrant, largely Hutu opposition movement quickly formed and challenged the ruling party.[14] Many observers locate the genocide's origins to this period. In particular, facing the twin threats of civil war and domestic political opposition, Rwanda's ruling elite radicalized and sought to keep power by promoting violence.

The literature focuses on several different developments. One is that ruling officials began targeting Tutsi civilians inside Rwanda and identifying them as rebel supporters. Soon after the RPF invasion, for example, the Hutu-led government arrested some 13,000 civilians, mostly Tutsis. In addition, there were a series of violent attacks against Tutsis. Some took place in 1990, just after the RPF invasion; others took place later, and sometimes in response to actual or feared RPF incursions.[15] Of particular significance is a 10-member Military Commission that the president established in 1991. That commission identified Tutsis who were 'nostalgic for power' and Tutsis sympathetic to the RPF as Rwanda's 'principal enemy'. Numerous observers, including prosecutors at the International Criminal Tribunal for Rwanda (ICTR), consider the document evidence of a plan (or the beginning of a plan) to commit genocide.[16]

In addition, Rwandan political and military officials took measures to expand the army, launch a civilian defence programme, develop irregular militia forces, and create assassination lists. Like the military commission that identified Tutsis as the enemy, the civilian defence programme and the militia training are seen as key elements in the preparations for genocide. Most militiamen were members of the '*interahamwe*'. The *interahamwe* began as a youth organization that was a wing of the ruling National Revolutionary Movement for Development (MRND) political party. Almost every political party had a youth wing in Rwanda during the period, including opposition political parties. What distinguished the *interahamwe* was that hardliners within the military and

MRND party hierarchy siphoned off some youth and trained them militarily. In this sense, some *interahamwe* became militias – military-trained young men. There is also additional evidence of radicalization, including networks of hardliners as well as assassination lists.[17] The hardliners also are seen as the progenitors of an openly racist political party, the Coalition for the Defence of the Republic (CDR), which appeared in 1992.

Another major area of attention in the historiography of this period is the promulgation of racist propaganda. The propaganda was a mix of fear-mongering about the ruthlessness of the RPF (the rebels were routinely accused of committing atrocities against Hutu civilians); of ethnic nationalism (Tutsis were labelled as 'Hamitic' foreigners, a minority, and a danger to the Hutu majority); of chauvinism (Hutus had to unite and be vigilant against the enemy); and of ethnic stereotyping (Tutsis were often called RPF 'accomplices'). The propaganda appeared in the print media, on the radio, and at political rallies. The most illustrative and infamous examples come from the weekly *Kangura* magazine and the private radio station called Radio Télévision Libre des Milles Collines (RTLM). In 1990, *Kangura* in particular published the infamous 'Hutu 10 Commandments', instructing Hutus to sever ties with Tutsis and to protect the gains of the Hutu Revolution.[18]

There were two other significant developments in 1993 that many authors believe contributed to the radicalization of hardliner Hutu elites. The first is a peace agreement signed between the government and the RPF rebels. Finalized in August 1993, and known as the 'Arusha Accords' because they were signed in Arusha, Tanzania, the peace agreement called for restructuring the military, a transitional broad-based government, and eventual elections. The terms were broadly favourable to the RPF, and many authors believe they alienated hardliners.[19] The second significant development was the assassination, in October 1993, of Burundi's first Hutu president Melchior Ndadaye. Burundi and Rwanda have similar, though not identical, ethnic demographics and colonial histories. However, in Burundi Tutsis kept power at independence (to the exclusion of Hutus). That changed with multi-party elections in June 1993 when Ndadaye was elected. It would be his assassination that gave Hutu hardliners in Rwanda further cause for concern. Indeed, after the assassination, they formed a political alliance known as 'Hutu Power'. The alliance was composed of hardliners from all political parties who called for Hutu unity in the face of a Tutsi threat.[20]

Most authors draw a connection these various measures and the genocide. Thus, those Hutu hardliners who were involved in the military preparations for the civil defence force as well as the military commission that labelled Tutsis as enemies are considered planners of the genocide. Similarly those who were involved in creating and training the *interahamwe* militia, as well as those who were involved in the anti-Tutsi media, are considered responsible for the genocide, if not planners of it. Sometimes authors refer to the key group of hardliners as 'the *akazu*', which means 'little house' in Kinyarwanda and was the nickname for Habyarimana's inner circle. Others refer to the 'Hutu Power' alliance. But the principal argument is that the genocide had specific, powerful architects.

To summarize the main elements of the new consensus: between 1990 and 1994, a core group of Hutu hardliners associated with the ruling party radicalized as they faced the twin threats of civil war and multi-party political competition. To keep power, they developed irregular militia forces trained to kill civilians; they launched a civilian defence programme; they funded and promoted private, often racist media; they fomented violence against civilians; and they prepared to do what it took to keep power. Many observers argue that these various developments amount to a plan to commit genocide (more on this below). The ideological arguments that the Hutu hardliners developed rested on a particular history of ethnicity. To wit, the hardliners supported version of ethnic nationalism that first appeared in the Revolution period. That political vision in turn was the outgrowth of a series of changes to the meaning and institutionalization of ethnicity that occurred under colonial rule. All of these items are not necessarily found in every account of the Rwandan genocide, but this basic story line in the vast majority of existing discussions of the genocide.[21]

The key Anglophone books that contributed to forming the new consensus are Gérard Prunier's *The Rwanda Crisis* (1995), which is an overview of Rwandan history and the genocide; African Rights, *Death, Despair, and Defiance* (1994, rev. 1995), which is a long collection of witness accounts and testimony; Philip Gourevitch, *We Wish to Inform You that Tomorrow We Will Be Killed With Our Families* (1998), which is a lyrically written essay on the genocide; and Alison Des Forges' *Leave None to Tell the Story*, which is a long, detailed analysis of the genocide and its origins.

The genocide

The bulk of existing literature focuses on the above areas, on the background and immediate antecedents to the genocide. Surprisingly less systematic attention is paid to the patterns and dynamics of the genocide itself. The main exception is the Des Forges publication, *Leave None to Tell the Story*, which was a landmark in providing details about the genocide itself. The book was especially strong in documenting genocide at the national level, as well as in one region, the Prefecture of Butare. Added to the Des Forges report are the judgments and ongoing trials at the ICTR. The former U.N. commander, Roméo Dallaire, has also written an account of his time in Rwanda; that memoir provides considerable details about the genocide at the national level.[22] Other existing books provide limited details, witness accounts, and anecdotes without systematic investigation of the specifics of the violence, particularly at the local level.[23] Further empirical research on the specifics of the violence is thus an imperative for future scholarship on the genocide.

There is a general consensus in the literature about a number of issues about the genocide at the national level and the event's broad outlines. There is agreement, for example, about when the genocide started. The triggering event was the assassination of President Habyarimana on April 6, 1994. Habyarimana was killed – along with several of his top advisors and the president of Burundi – as his plane descended to land in the capital Kigali. Two surface-to-air missiles struck the plane, and it landed in a ball of flame, killing all on board. Rwandans and outside observers disagree sharply on who shot down the plane (more on this below), but the assassination is what set the genocide in motion.

There is also general agreement on what happened afterwards. Broadly, the Hutu hardliners who had radicalized in the 1990–4 period moved to take control of the state. They did this in several ways. A first order of business was to kill leading opposition politicians, including Prime Minister Agathe Uwilingiyimana. The hardliners proceeded to install a government composed either of politicians sympathetic to 'Hutu Power' or who were pliable. The hardliners simultaneously unleashed systematic violence against Tutsi civilians. The violence started earliest in the capital Kigali, but it quickly began in areas sympathetic to the ruling party. There were key areas of resistance, especially in the south and central parts of the country, where the Hutu opposition was in control. However, by 21 April, systematic massacres of Tutsis had started in most parts of the country where government forces were in control. The swiftness and character of the violence is a primary reason why many observers believe that genocide was planned before the assassination.

There appears also broad consensus on the man most responsible for the violence and for taking control: Colonel Théoneste Bagosora. At the time of Habyarimana's death, Bagosora was Cabinet Director in the Ministry of Defense. But Bagosora had been for some time a key power broker in the regime; he had chaired the Military Commission that defined Tutsis as the 'enemy'; and he had served as part of the government's negotiating team in Arusha. Des Forges's research clearly pinpoints Bagosora, as does Dallaire's account. Taking their cues from both Des Forges and Dallaire, ICTR prosecutors refer to Bagosora as the 'mastermind' of the Rwandan genocide.

Bagosora, of course, did not act alone, but there is less agreement about who specifically were the other key figures at the national level. Members of the military, ruling party, media, police, and the interim government all appear to have played central roles. Arguably the most important trial at the ICTR is 'Military I'. The defendants in the case include Bagosora, Anatole Nsengiyumva (a former chief of military intelligence and head of military operations in Gisenyi in 1994), General Gratien Kabiligi (chief of military operations in 1994), and Major Aloys Ntabakuze (commander of an elite battalion in 1994). 'Military II' is another major trial, which focuses on General Augustin Bizimungu (chief of staff in the army), General Augustin Ndindiliyimana (chief of staff in the gendarmerie [the national police]), Major François-Xavier Nzuwonemeye (commander of an elite battalion), and Innocent Sagahutu (a high-ranking officer in an elite battalion). A third major trial prosecutes the former ruling party officials; the key defendants are former MRND President Mathieu Ngirumpatse, former Secretary General of the party Joseph Nzirorera, and the party's First Vice President Édouard Karemera. A fourth major case is the 'Media Trial'. In 2003, an ICTR chamber found three journalists – two associated with RTLM and the third with *Kangura* (which published the 'Hutu 10 Commandments') – guilty of inciting genocide. There are also additionally several trials of former government ministers as well as regional and local-level authorities.[24]

There is also general consensus on the beginning and endpoints of the genocide. The former is generally dated to 6 April (Habyarimana's assassination) and the latter to 17 July (when the rebel RPF finally ousted the genocidal regime from Rwanda). Many authors refer to '100 days' of genocide. During this period, there were two primary developments. On the one hand, the RPF advanced and won successively, driving the interim government and armed forces southward and westward. The RPF victories also produced massive population flows, primarily externally to Zaire (now the Democratic Republic of the Congo) and to Tanzania, but also internally as Rwandans fled their homes for other parts of the country. The second dynamic concerned state-led violence, which was directed primarily at Tutsi civilians and secondarily at Hutu opponents of the regime and those who openly refused to participate in the massacres.

The anti-Tutsi violence was exterminatory. The hardliners labeled all Tutsis as 'enemies', and men, women, and children were targeted. Killing was the primary mode of violence, although sexual violence and looting were widespread. The exact death toll is difficult to determine and somewhat contested. Several international commission reports put the number at 800,000 civilians.[25] Des Forges estimates a smaller toll of 500,000. Working from census figures, Des Forges estimates 660,000 Tutsis were resident in Rwanda just before the genocide began, and she argues that about 75 per cent of that population was killed.[26] By contrast, a post-genocide report estimated a higher toll of 934,218 dead.[27] The key issue here concerns the validity of the last census taken before the genocide, in 1991. If the census figures are broadly correct – and Des Forges argues that there is no evidence of widespread fraud – then her estimate is probably the most reliable. I use the 500,000 estimate in my work. There is less known about the number of Hutus killed by genocidal forces.

Most killing during the genocide was public and participatory. There were four main locations where civilians were killed during the genocide: (1) at roadblocks and public meeting points, such as commercial centers; (2) in or just outside homes; (3) in fields or other places where Tutsis and targeted Hutus hid;

and (4) at central congregation points, such as churches, schools, and government buildings where Tutsis and targeted Hutus fled for safety. The largest massacres – sometimes numbering in several hundred and even thousands of civilians – occurred at the central congregation points.

Soldiers, paramilitaries, and militias often played an important role in the largest massacres. However, the state deliberately encouraged and sometimes required civilian participation, and indeed the scale of that participation is a distinguishing feature of this genocide. In primary research on local dynamics, I identify three main categories of actors at the local level: (1) local elites (including government officials, political party leaders, businessmen, and others) who often led the violence; (2) very violent men (including but not limited to militia and ex-soldiers); and (3) ordinary villagers (who formed the mass of participants). The first category tended to order, authorize, and legitimize the violence; the second category committed the most violence and directly pressured others to participate; and the third category often formed the largest number of participants in groups that killed.[28] How many Rwandans took direct part in the violence is a subject of much debate. Some authors estimate as many as three million Hutus participated in the genocide (a number that would implicate the entire adult Hutu population in 1994); others estimate tens of thousands of civilian participants. Judging from a survey of 210 convicted perpetrators, I estimate about 200,000 direct participants in the killing.[29]

Understudied dimensions of the Rwandan genocide

Despite the amount written about the Rwandan genocide, there remain a number of understudied questions. As we have seen, existing literature focuses on historical background factors and broad, national-level dimensions. Much less well understood are micro-level dynamics and patterns of violence. In addition, most existing documentary evidence comes from human rights organizations or courts. There also are a number of collections of witnesses, survivors, and in some cases perpetrators. While quite valuable, the testimonies are often anecdotal. In short, there is a need for more systematic micro-level studies and for ones that are disassociated from the normative and legal imperatives that dominate the existing record.

As of this writing, Des Forges's work is the primary published analytical work on genocide at the local level. In *Leave None to Tell the Story*, Des Forges devotes hundreds of pages to genocide in Butare and Gikongoro Prefectures. The African Rights volume includes hundreds of pages of material organized by region, but the accounts in the book are anecdotal. There are a growing number of works of testimony. French journalist Jean Hatzfeld has published two books of testimony, one of survivors, the other of perpetrators. The narratives in Hatzfeld's book are stylized, but they still contain useful details.[30]

Rwandan authors also have written several English-language memoirs.[31] I also collected some transcripts of interviews I conducted with perpetrators and published them in a book along with a series of photographs by Robert Lyons.[32] Two short academic articles based on research conducted soon after the genocide also exist.[33]

That said, there is a need for more in-depth, micro-level, and systematic investigation of the genocide. Several studies are in the works. My research is in this vein. I conducted a survey of 210 convicted and self-confessed perpetrators; I also did a micro-comparative study of genocidal dynamics in five communes; and I examined regional variation in the genocide.[34] Several other promising studies are under way. Lee Ann Fujii and Omar McDoom both conducted (separate) micro-level studies of the genocide in rural locations.[35] Even with these forthcoming studies, there will be room for more research on these questions. Future research might seek to explain why some Rwandans resisted participation in the genocide. McDoom's study focuses some attention on this issue, but considering the importance of the issue more investigation will be warranted.

An absence of hypothesis testing is another, closely related weakness in the existing literature. Currently explanations significantly outpace evidence. As a result, it is difficult to adjudicate between various explanations. Authors have focused variously on material incentives, media indoctrination, ideological conviction, structural violence, ethnic antipathy, a culture of obedience, coercion, security fears, land pressure, and coercion.[36] Several authors point to simultaneous motivations; indeed, the mechanisms I just listed are neither mutually exclusive across or within individuals (that is, different perpetrators participated for different reasons, and some individuals participated for multiple reasons). Nonetheless, a critical remaining research task is to use evidence to evaluate systematically which factors were most significant. The research of Fujii, McDoom, and I are in this vein, but more research will be needed given the complexity of these issues.

Evaluating macro-level explanations also remains understudied. What were the determinants of genocide? Why did the hardliners choose genocide over a range of other possible strategies? As we have seen, authors variously stress the impact of the Arusha Accords, the assassination of Burundi's president, Rwanda's history of ethnic ideologies, the impact of the war, economic decline, overpopulation, and other structural factors. Which issues were more salient?

Comparative analysis is one approach to answering these questions, and indeed there is now a fresh crop of scholarship in which Rwanda is one case of several. Michael Mann, for example, emphasizes that organic nationalism is central to the logic of what he calls 'murderous ethnic cleansing', and he focuses, in particular, on the birth of Hutu nationalism at independence.[37] Mann also emphasizes escalation in wartime. Manus Midlarsky emphasizes loss in wartime (in particular, that the Rwandan civil war displaced hundreds of thousands of refugees) and international dimensions (in particular, France's role in backing the Habyarimana regime).[38] Benjamin Valentino emphasizes the strategic origins of genocide. He argues, in particular, that genocide emerged as a deliberate, top-down policy because earlier efforts to diminish the threat of Tutsis had failed; genocide was thus a 'final solution'.[39] Jacques Sémelin focuses on ideologies of purity and, as with Mann, the ethnic nationalism that emerged at independence in Rwanda. [40] On the other hand, even though he draws on Melson's comparative research on the Armenian genocide and the Holocaust, Lemarchand finds comparisons of Rwanda and the Holocaust, for example, to be problematic.[41]

Another area deserving further study is the sequencing of events during the genocide. Particularly significant here will be the evidence produced in the key ICTR trials, which are on-going. The key questions concern the timing, chronology, command structure, and specifics of the planning and orders to commit genocide. There is general agreement about the significance of Bagosora after April 6, 1994, but details about how the policy to commit genocide specifically formed and was issued remain vague. Journalist Linda Melvern makes use of witness statements given to the ICTR, in particular that of former Prime Minister Jean Kambanda.[42] However, the key ICTR trials, in particular Military I, are not yet concluded. Once that trial and the other major trials are complete, scholars will do well to mine the ICTR's judgments and archives (hopefully they will be accessible) to understand the details of how the genocide took shape. There will be much to learn.

The extent and patterns of sexual violence during the genocide is also need of further study. Many discussions of the Rwandan genocide cite a figure of 250,000 or more rapes during the 100-day episode. The estimate derives from a figure that a United Nations Special Rapporteur once used.[43] However, that estimate rests on a set of assumptions and limited data, and there has been little effort, as far as I know, to empirically substantiate the claims. The original calculation stems from the following logic: since, in general, there are 100 rapes per every pregnancy caused by rape and since there were an estimated 2,000 to 5,000 'rape pregnancies' in Rwanda during the genocide, then one can estimate between 250,000 and 500,000 rapes.[44] However, the 250,000 figures exceed the number of Tutsi women and girls in Rwanda at the time of the genocide (judging from 1991 census figures).

Sexual violence is clearly an important dimension of the Rwandan genocide. Numerous authors draw attention sexual violence in the genocide.[45] Moreover, the first ICTR decision highlighted sexual violence, and the judges broke new ground in international law by listing rape as a mode of genocide.[46] Given the importance of sexual violence in this case, more investigation is needed. How prevalent was sexual violence? Was the sexual violence primarily committed by individuals or groups? There is unlikely to ever be precision on the extent, prevalence, and patterns of sexual violence, given the nature of the crimes. But further study would clarify the general picture.

Points of contention

In addition to understudied issues, there are a number of quite contentious dimensions of the Rwandan genocide. Who killed President Habyarimana is chief among them. Initially Anglophone authors suggested that Hutu hardliners who carried out the genocide were responsible (though authors were careful to note that they did not know for certain). The related claims were that Habyarimana's concessions at Arusha angered the hardliners; that the hardliners decided that a radical strategy was necessary; and that the president no longer controlled extremists within his ruling camp. The speed with which hardliners acted after the assassination – setting up roadblocks, deploying elite soldiers to kill leading politicians, and initiating violence against Tutsi civilians – is an indicator, in this view of events, that the hardliners were well prepared to act.[47]

However, there is increasing evidence that the RPF rebels may be responsible. A series of RPF defectors have claimed that former RPF leader and current Rwandan President Paul Kagame planned the assassination.[48] A French magistrate investigation similarly concluded that RPF officials planned the assassination.[49] There are various pieces of evidence to support the claim. First, like their counterparts in the government, RPF rebels acted quickly after the assassination. Second, even though the RPF has controlled the Rwandan government since 1994 and even though finding evidence to implicate the previous genocidal regime would be in their interests, no concrete evidence implicating the genocidal leaders has surfaced. Third, Habyarimana was not the only one to die in the crash; other high-ranking officials were on the plane; as such, the crash left confusion at the top of the military ranks, thus dealing a blow to the hardliners. Indeed, the RPF was in an offensive position from the beginning and throughout much of the genocide period.

All that said, the issue remains unresolved – and a subject of sharp disagreement. The ICTR refuses to investigate the matter or, if it has, will not publicly release its findings. The ICTR stance in turn provides fodder to high-level defendants, such as Bagosora, to claim that the tribunal engages only in one-sided justice. The ICTR's to date refusal to charge any RPF officials gives rise to the same charge. Even Luc Marchal, the former second in command of the U.N. forces in Rwanda, recently has focused attention on the issue, claiming it is imperative to know who assassinated Habyarimana.[50] The issue is not likely to disappear.

Who killed Habyarimana is an issue that matters for clarifying the historical record. But the issue also will help clarify another contentious issue: the timing of when a genocide plan formed and thus the determinants of that genocide plan. In particular, how significant was the assassination and, if the RPF is responsible, are the former rebels in any way culpable?[51] The historiography is unclear on the timing of the genocide plan.[52] Most authors believe that a plan for genocide hatched before 1994. Melvern, for example, claims that 'plans ... for mass murder on a countrywide scale' began in October 1990 and that 'the idea that genocide of the Tutsi would solve all problems was spread in a series of secret meetings' before 1994.[53] Prunier dates the planning for genocide to 1992.[54] Des Forges's claims that by 'March 1994 Hutu Power leaders were determined to slaughter massive numbers of Tutsi and Hutu opposed to Habyarimana'.[55] In its various decisions, the ICTR has not yet pinpointed an exact date, but rather concludes that a plan for genocide did exist before the assassination.[56] An alternative account would hold that Hutu hardliners had prepared to kill Tutsi civilians and to assassinate leading politicians before April 1994. However, by this account, the hardliners did not commit to a full-scale extermination plan until after Habyarimana was assassinated and until after the RPF began to advance. In other words, the assassination and the course of the war escalated preparations for limited killing and violence to country-wide genocide.[57]

Another key piece of evidence in the chronology debate concerns the extent and purpose of militia training. In particular, in January 1994, an informant told U.N. peacekeepers that army officers were training *interahamwe* and had buried weapons throughout Kigali. According to the informant, he had been given instructions to create lists of Tutsis, which would allow the militiamen to 'exterminate' Tutsis. In fact, the informant estimated that the militiamen could murder as many as 1,000 Tutsis within 20 minutes.[58] Alarmed, Dallaire cabled to U.N. headquarters in New York, advising that he wanted to raid weapons caches that the informant had revealed. (That cable is now often called the 'genocide fax'.) U.N. officials in New York told Dallaire not to undertake the operation. The informant's claims are not conclusive evidence that the hardliners planned, before April 1994, country-side extermination. Dallaire's cable indicated that the *interahamwe* numbered 1,700 persons and were stationed in Kigali.[59] Nonetheless, at a minimum, the informant's claims – assuming they are true – show that hardliners within the ruling party and the military had well-developed plans to massacre Tutsi civilians. And they may well have had a plan to commit nationwide genocide before the assassination. Future scholarship and evidence from the ICTR will be critical to resolving the issue.

The extent of RPF atrocities also is a contentious issue that remains unresolved and understudied in the historiography. There are four distinct episodes of focus: (1) the pre-genocide, 1990–4 civil war; (2) the genocide period in which the RPF advanced and ultimately defeated the Hutu hardliner-led regime;

(3) the immediate aftermath of the war and genocide, as the RPF consolidated power; and (4) RPF invasions in Zaire (now the Democratic Republic of the Congo) in 1996 and 1997 when the RPF killed Hutu refugees who had fled Rwanda in 1994. Compared studies of the genocide, there is very little information available about the first three periods.[60] The extent of massacres that the RPF committed in Zaire has received little systematic investigation to date. A recent book, however, by a Hutu refugee indicates that RPF soldiers committed large-scale atrocities.[61] More research in this area is clearly warranted and is a priority for establishing a more balanced historical record.

International intervention

Up to this point, the essay focuses on the domestic origins of the genocide as well as the patterns of violence during the genocide. A separate stream of research concerns the international response to the genocide. In particular, the failure to respond to early warnings of mass violence and the decision not to intervene after the genocide began have received considerable attention. Rwanda is now a showcase example of international failure to halt genocide, and many monographs, working papers, and seminars have confronted the issue.

The international record on preventing and stopping genocide is quite weak, as Samantha Power makes clear (though her work centres on the United States).[62] However, three dimensions of the Rwanda case make the issue that much more salient. First, at the time of the genocide, there already was in place a United Nations peacekeeping force. Dallaire's account of his mission demonstrates that the force had serious problems of intelligence, communication, logistics, discipline, and staffing – among other problems.[63] Nonetheless, when the genocide began, the U.N. had a force on the ground and Dallaire himself advocated a more forceful intervention.

Second, much of the genocidal violence was low-tech and thus a forceful international response could have been effective. Rwandan Army soldiers were involved in some of the killing, but loosely organized militiamen and civilians committed the lion-share of violence. On occasion, militia and civilians used grenades and guns, but often machetes, knives, clubs, and sticks were the tools of murder during the Rwandan genocide. Thus, many commentators, including Dallaire, argue that a relatively small deployment of well-armed and well-disciplined international peacekeepers could have stemmed the violence.

Third, as indicated earlier, there were a number of missed opportunities to intervene before the genocide actually began. The 'genocide fax' is considered principal among these, but there were other signs of extremism. The rise of the racist private media was a public matter. In addition, there were a series of smaller-scale massacres that took place prior to the genocide. The record is one of early warnings and missed opportunities.

Taken together, as one report concluded, Rwanda's was 'the preventable genocide'.[64] Dallaire has consistently argued that he needed 5,000 well-armed troops to bring the genocide to a halt. A panel of military experts concluded much the same: the group found that an early intervention would have had a significant impact on halting the genocide: 'a modern force of 5,000 troops, drawn primarily from one country and sent to Rwanda sometime between April 7 and 21, 1994, could have significantly altered the outcome of the conflict.'[65] The consensus, in short, is that even a relatively small, but disciplined and well-commanded force could have save hundreds of thousands of lives.

A dissenting voice is Alan Kuperman. He argues that the conventional wisdom glosses over two major obstacles. First, the violence happened too quickly to mobilize an effective U.S.-led intervention force. Second, it took about two weeks before key international decision-makers realized genocide was underway. From the point of realization, it still would have taken time to deploy an effective force. At best, Kuperman, argues, only one-quarter of the Tutsi population, or 125,000 persons, could have been saved.[66] Other observers challenge Kuperman's premises, in particular about when the genocide was recognizable. They also point out that peacekeepers already were in place and only needed reinforcement.[67] In studying the dynamics of genocide, I find that the international actions would have had an interactive effect. In particular, the international withdrawal strengthened hardliners and weakened moderates resisting the violence. Thus, assumptions about the speed and course of violence cannot be made; the speed of and course of violence may well have slowed or changed had the international decisions been different.[68]

A related concern in the historiography is why key international actors took the decisions that they did. By and large, scholars agree that the killing of American soldiers in Somalia in 1993 cast a long shadow over Rwanda. The anti-American violence was a watershed not only for the Clinton Administration, but also for United Nations officials, particularly in the Department of Peacekeeping Operations (DPKO) that was then headed by Kofi Annan. In a careful study by Michael Barnett, a political scientist who was a visiting fellow at the United Nations during the genocide, he concludes that officials in the DPKO became especially risk averse following Somalia. When Dallaire cabled to raid militia caches in January 1994 and later when he wanted to intervene to stop the genocide, U.N. officials acted to preserve the organization rather than expose it to risks.[69]

The killing of 10 Belgian peacekeepers on 7 April also was significant. The Belgians were the backbone of the U.N. peacekeeping force in Rwanda. Shortly after Habyarimana's assassination, Dallaire instructed Belgian peacekeepers to guard the then prime minister, a Hutu opposition figure. However, early on the morning of 7 April, the prime minister and her bodyguards came under attack. The Belgians were eventually captured, taken back to a military camp, severely beaten, and ultimately killed. The news prompted the Belgians to withdraw and, echoing Somalia, it likely contributed to the decision not to become entangled in another distant African country.[70]

Another prominent subject in the literature is the initial international refusal to label the violence 'genocide'. Despite pressure to do so, members of the Security Council as well as State Department officials refused to conclusively call what was happening in Rwanda 'genocide'. American spokespeople were apparently specifically instructed not to use the term. Instead, even as late as mid May – more than a month into the genocide – they were authorized to use the formulation 'acts of genocide', but not to make a definitive declaration. Footage of an American spokeswoman fending off repeated questions from reporters is a central feature of several documentaries and films on Rwanda, including two popular Frontline films *The Triumph of Evil* and *Ghosts of Rwanda* as well as the HBO movie *Sometimes in April* and the BBC's *Shooting Dogs*.

The issue at stake was that some American officials feared that a genocide declaration would have required them, under the Genocide Convention, to 'do something', as Samantha Power has reported.[71] American officials keenly wanted to avoid entanglement and hence sought to avoid the term. The Rwanda experience clearly inflected various American organizations' response to the Darfur crisis in Sudan, beginning in 2003. Numerous groups pressured the Bush Administration to call the Darfur crisis 'genocide' with the hope of spurring international action. The president and his Secretary of Defense did make the determination, but little concrete action resulted.[72]

The role of the French, who were Habyarimana's principal allies, is also the subject of considerable attention in the historiography. The French role generates two areas of criticism. The first concerns the period before the genocide. French troops helped the Habyarimana government repel the RPF in 1990. They also supplied weapons, military advisors, and training to the Rwandan government, at least through 1993. French officials also allegedly provided training to *interahamwe* militias. Critics hold that at worst French officials turned a blind eye to growing extremism and at worst directly aided a plan for genocide. The second main period concerns the French intervention in June 1994 called Opération Turquoise. The purpose of the intervention was nominally to protect Rwandans, but some critics charge that the French should have done more to stop killing of Tutsis nearby. The French also allegedly provided safe haven to killers. The issue is the subject of considerable attention in France, but deserves more attention and analysis in the Anglophone literature.[73]

Post-genocide Rwanda: justice and other matters

The social consequences and aftermath of genocide is another major subject in the literature on Rwanda – and this field is growing rapidly. There are a number of related themes for post-genocide Rwanda: reconciliation, justice, lingering psychological trauma, rebuilding destroyed infrastructure, continuing insecurity fears, and questions of governance. For interests of space and the collection's primary themes, I focus here on justice, which commands the majority of scholarly attention, though I also briefly discuss other topics.

Prosecution is the principal mode of justice and accounting for the past in Rwanda. There have been three principal tracks of prosecution since the genocide. The first track is through the ICTR, whose mandate primarily covers the major planners and organizers of the genocide. The tribunal was established in late 1994 and paired to the International Criminal Tribunal for the former Yugoslavia. Although the tribunal has almost all of the highest alleged planners and executors of the genocide in custody, as we have seen, the tribunal has been marred by a number of problems. In particular, the tribunal has been criticized for its slow pace, corruption, staffing problems, weak and disorganized investigations, and expense. In addition, ICTR officials made cases against lower-level perpetrators the first ones, rather than focusing on the key military, national government, and media trials.[74]

Another major problem concerns the ICTR's contribution to Rwandan reconciliation, which is a central part of the tribunal's mandate. Many Rwandans feel detached from the tribunal, in part because of the distance between the tribunal's headquarters in Tanzania and because of the exorbitant costs, by Rwandan standards (the tribunal routinely spends more than $75 million annually). Moreover, the tribunal is widely perceived as pursuing one-sided justice by not investigating RPF crimes and relying on current government officials for contacts and information. A detailed examination of the ICTR shows how vulnerable the institution is to intimidation by the current government officials, whose cooperation is essential to the functioning of the tribunal.[75] A former ICTR official also argues that the tribunal practices 'political', not impartial justice.[76] A major issue for judging the tribunal's legacy concerns the quality of the historical record and jurisprudence in some of the major cases that, as of this writing, are ongoing.

The second principal form of justice in Rwanda is domestic trials. Soon after taking power in 1994, the RPF began arresting individuals suspected of participating in the genocide. In 1996, the government handed down a law on the genocide that was noteworthy for creating four hierarchical categories of crimes. They corresponded to degrees of responsibility, with Category 1 reserved for organizers and planners as well as rapists and Category 4 referring to property crimes. By and large, the government pursued a strategy of maximal prosecution: that is, they arrested everyone suspected of participation. Even though trials began soon after the law was passed, the process was slow. By mid-2002, a little more than 7,000 cases had been completed, with roughly 6,000 convictions. The slowness was in part due to the devastation to the judicial system during the war and genocide. New judges had to be trained, and funds were needed: by one account, donors contributed $100 million to justice projects.[77] Producing evidence to prosecute some cases also proved time-consuming, and the process was politicized.[78] Corruption and incompetence also are issues.[79]

In addition to the problems mentioned, there were two other central limitations to the domestic court proceedings. The first was the pace. Rwanda's prison population swelled to more than 100,000 detainees by the new millennium. At the rate of case completion, Rwanda would have required decades to finish the trials. Moreover, the court proceedings were formal, long, and often alienating to Rwandans who attended them. As a result, fairly quickly the Rwandan government sought an alternative to the domestic proceedings.

The chosen alternative – Rwanda's third main track of justice – was a process called *gacaca*, which is often translated as 'justice on the grass'. Traditionally, *gacaca* was an informal conflict resolution mechanism, primarily focused on property crimes and land disputes. To prosecute genocide crimes, traditional *gacaca* was overhauled to handle murder and other serious offences. The central idea is that a panel of civilian judges, meeting in front of their peers in open-air hearings, will judge and sentence genocide suspects. While to date there only have been pilot *gacaca* hearings, there are expected ultimately to be as many as 10,000 *gacaca* courts who could prosecute as many as 500,000 suspects.[80] The process is widely hailed as a major experiment in post-conflict justice and reconciliation.[81]

An issue that has received comparatively less, but increasing attention concerns politics in post-genocide Rwanda. Many international observers and authors were especially sympathetic to the RPF, in particular since the rebel forces put an end to the genocide.[82] However, RPF policies also now draw considerable criticism. Rwanda's invasion of Zaire in 1996 and 1997, followed by a series of military incursions from 1998–2004, led to large-scale direct and indirect deaths of civilians. The story is a complex one. In 1996, Rwanda invaded Zaire because much of the rump genocidal regime lay across the border in refugee camps, which received international aid. Arguing that the camps represented a security threat, Rwanda deployed troops and helped Zairian rebel leader, Laurent Kabila to power. Newly ensconced, Kabila changed Zaire's name to the Democratic Republic of the Congo. He soon turned on his former Rwandan allies, sparking the second war (from 1998–2004). That war has been devastating – more than 3,000,000 people are estimated to have died – and should receive considerably more attention than it has.[83] Inside Rwanda, the RPF has allowed very little space for political opposition and critical media. There are consistent reports of disappearances and other serious human rights abuses. Often crackdowns are done in the name of extinguishing a 'genocide ideology' or 'divisionism'. In short, the RPF-led government is stable, but authoritarian.[84]

Conclusion

Prior to the genocide, Rwanda received little international attention, especially in the Anglophone literature. The country was small; it had limited strategic and economic value outside the immediate region; and it had few cultural, historical, or commercial ties to the United States and Britain. There has been a dramatic change in visibility since 1994. Rwanda is now a touchstone for a wide range of debates, including discussions of ethnicity, violence, genocide, foreign policy, and the failures of the United Nations. Given the enormity of the crime of genocide, such attention is well deserved. That said, because the 1994 genocide is the entry point to Rwanda for many observers, a particular normative framework often frames the way that Rwandan history is perceived. In the historiography, such a normative framework has led to an emphasis on racial ideologies (versus other, more local and Rwanda-specific factors), on the colonial period (versus post-independence history), on top-down planning for extermination (versus a more dynamic process and micro-level studies), on international inaction in the face of genocide (versus Rwanda's role in the wars in the Democratic Republic of the Congo), and on justice and reconciliation (versus the RPF's post-genocide authoritarianism inside Rwanda).

This essay has traced the trajectory of scholarship since 1994 as well as pointed to areas for future research. Much remains to be known about Rwanda and the genocide. As the scholarship moves forward, it will be important to appreciate the local complexities and lineages of the violence and to suspend the strong normative context as research is being conducted. We can never forget that genocide took place in Rwanda, but that genocide took place should not necessarily be the starting point for research on historical and contemporary questions.

Notes

1. I would like to thank Dan Stone for comments on earlier drafts of this essay. By and large, the arguments in this essay are drawn, in part, from S. Straus, *The Order of Genocide: Race, Power, and War in Rwanda* (Ithaca, NY: Cornell University Press, 2006). For other, first-rate reviews on recent Rwandan historiography or the historiography of the region, see T. Longman, 'Placing Genocide in Context: Research Priorities for the Rwandan Genocide', *Journal of Genocide Research*, 6, 1 (2004), 29–45 and C. Young, 'The Heart of the African Conflict Zone: Democratization, Ethnicity, Civil Conflict, and the Great Lakes Crisis', *Annual Review of Political Science*, 9 (2006), 301–28.
2. There are many examples of this. For one typical and telling example, see the exchange quoted in S. Power, *"A Problem from Hell": America and the Age of Genocide* (New York: Basic Books, 2002), pp. 355–6.
3. For examples of scholars and commentators citing state 'collapse' or 'failure', see E. Sciolino, 'For West, Rwanda Is Not Worth the Political Candle', *The New York Times*

(15 April 1994) and I. W. Zartman, 'Introduction: Posing the Problem of State Collapse', in *Collapsed States: The Disintegration and Restoration of Legitimate Authority*, ed., I. W. Zartman (Boulder, CO: Lynne Rienner Publishers, 1994), p. 4.

4. For excellent (English-language) overviews of pre-colonial Rwanda or the Great Lakes region as a whole, see J.-P. Chrétien, *The Great Lakes of Africa: Two Thousand Years of History*, trans. Scott Straus (New York: Zone Books, 2003), Chs 1–3; D. Newbury, 'Precolonial Rwanda and Burundi: Local Loyalties, Regional Royalties', *The International Journal of African Historical Studies*, 34, 2 (2001), 255–314; D. Schoenbrun, *A Green Place, A Good Place: Agrarian Change, Gender, and Social Identity in the Great Lakes Region to the 15th Century* (Portsmouth/Oxford: Heinemann/James Currey, 1998); and J. Vansina, *Antecedents to Modern Rwanda: The Nyiginya Kingdom* (Madison, WI: University of Wisconsin Press, 2004).
5. Vansina, *Antecedents*.
6. On these points, see (in addition to the sources in note 4) C. Newbury, *The Cohesion of Oppression: Clientship and Ethnicity in Rwanda, 1860–1960* (New York: Columbia University Press, 1988).
7. On the Hamitic Hypothesis and the racialization of Rwanda's social categories, see in particular Chrétien, *The Great Lakes of Africa*, Ch. 4 and M. Mamdani, *When Victims Become Killers: Colonialism, Nativism, and the Genocide in Rwanda* (Princeton, NJ: Princeton University Press, 2001).
8. On the Belgian impact, see in particular Chrétien, *The Great Lakes of Africa*, Ch. 4 and Newbury, *The Cohesion of Oppression*.
9. For English-language accounts of the Revolution period, see in particular R. Lemarchand, *Rwanda and Burundi* (London: Pall Mall, 1970); I. Linden, *Church and Revolution in Rwanda* (Manchester: Manchester University Press, 1977); and Newbury, *The Cohesion of Oppression*.
10. L. Melvern, *A People Betrayed: The Role of the West in Rwanda's Genocide* (London: Zed Books, 2000), p. 25.
11. P. Uvin, 'Ethnicity and Power in Burundi and Rwanda: Different Paths to Mass Violence', *Comparative Politics*, 31, 3 (1999), 253–71.
12. G. Prunier, *The Rwanda Crisis: History of a Genocide* (New York: Columbia University Press, 1995).
13. For an analysis of the dynamics that led to the RPF invasion, see Mamdani, *When Victims Become Killers*, Ch. 6.
14. There exists a thorough book on the multi-party process in French: J. Bertrand, *Rwanda, le piège de l'histoire* (Paris: Karthala, 2001). See also Prunier, *The Rwanda Crisis*, pp. 121–6.
15. Des Forges, *Leave None*, pp. 49–50; Prunier, *The Rwanda Crisis*, pp. 108–10.
16. For discussion of the document, see Des Forges, *Leave None*, pp. 62–4.
17. On these points, see Des Forges, *Leave None*, pp. 99–108; Prunier, *The Rwanda Crisis*, pp. 182–6.
18. The Rwandan media have received considerable attention. In English, see, in particular, the 'media trial' in which three Rwandan journalists were found guilty of genocide: International Criminal Tribunal for Rwanda, 'The Prosecutor v. Ferdinand Nahimana, Jean-Bosco Barayagwiza, and Hassan Ngeze', ICTR Case No. 99-52-T, Judgement and Decision, December 3, 2003, available at www.ictr.org. See also Article 19, *Broadcasting Genocide: Censorship, Propaganda & State-Sponsored Violence in Rwanda 1990–1994* (London: Article 19, 1996); F. Chalk, 'Hate Radio in Rwanda', in *The Path of a Genocide: The Rwanda Crisis from Uganda to Zaire*, eds, H. Adelman and A. Suhrke (New Brunswick, NJ: Transaction Publishers, 1999), pp. 93–107; and

D. Li, 'Echoes of Violence: Considerations on Radio and Genocide in Rwanda', *Journal of Genocide Research*, 6, 1 (2004), 9–27. For an extensive treatment in French, see J.-P. Chrétien et al., *Rwanda: les médias du génocide* (Paris: Karthala, 1995).

19. An excellent analysis of the Arusha negotiations is B. Jones, *Peacekeeping in Rwanda: The Dynamics of Failure* (Boulder, CO: Lynne Rienner Publishers, 2001).
20. On Hutu Power and the Ndadaye assassination, see Des Forges, *Leave None*, pp. 134–40.
21. In addition to those works cited in the paragraph itself, this basic version of the historiography can be found in the background sections of the various judgments that have come from the ICTR; A. Destexhe, *Rwanda and Genocide in the Twentieth Century*, trans. A. Marschner (New York: New York University Press, 1995); J. Hatzfeld, *Machete Season: The Killers in Rwanda Speak*, trans. L. Coverdale (New York: Farrar, Straus, and Giroux, 2005); H. Hintjens, 'Explaining the 1994 Genocide in Rwanda', *The Journal of Modern African Studies*, 37, 2 (1999), 241–86; Jones, *Peacemaking in Rwanda*; R. Melson, 'Modern Genocide in Rwanda: Ideology, Revolution, War, and Mass Murder in an African State', in *The Specter of Genocide: Mass Murder in Historical Perspective*, eds, R. Gellately and B. Kiernan (New York: Cambridge University Press, 2003), pp. 325–38; Melvern, *A People Betrayed*; L. Melvern, *Conspiracy to Murder: The Rwandan Genocide* (London: Verso, 2004); Organization of African Unity, *Rwanda: The Preventable Genocide. The Report of the International Panel of Eminent Personalities to Investigate the 1994 Genocide in Rwanda and the Surrounding Events*, July 7, 2000, available at http://www.aegistrust.org/images/stories/oaureport.pdf; C. Scherrer, *Genocide and Crisis in Central Africa: Conflict Roots, Mass Violence, and Regional War* (Westport, CT: Praeger, 2002); A. Twagilimana, *The Debris of Ham: Ethnicity, Regionalism, and the 1994 Rwandan* Genocide (Lanham, MD: University Press of America, 2003); and P. Uvin, *Aiding Violence: The Development Enterprise in Rwanda* (West Hartford, CT: Kumarian Press, 1998).
22. R. Dallaire with B. Beardsley, *Shake Hands with the Devil: The Failure of Humanity in Rwanda* (Toronto: Random House Canada, 2003).
23. Mamdani's *When Victims Become Killers* is one illustrative example. A widely read book on the genocide, it conforms in large measure to the new consensus I describe in this article; however, details of the actual genocide occupy fairly little space in the book.
24. All ICTR indictments and judgements may be found on-line at www.ictr.org. In addition, Internews and Hirondelle reporting services provide coverage of the tribunal. The former may be found at http://www.internews.org/activities/ICTR_reports/ICTR_reports.htm; the latter may be found at http://www.hirondelle.org/arusha.nsf.
25. United Nations, 'Report of the Independent Inquiry into the Actions of the United Nations during the 1994 Genocide in Rwanda,' 15 December 1999, p. 3, available at http://www.un.org/News/dh/latest/rwanda.htm.
26. Des Forges, *Leave None*, pp. 15–16.
27. République Rwandaise, 'Dénombrement des victimes du génocide: Analyse des resultats, draft' (Kigali: Ministère de l'administration locale et des affaires sociales, 2001), p. 7.
28. Straus, *The Order of Genocide*, Ch. 3 in particular.
29. On this calculation as well as references to the other estimates cited here, see S. Straus, 'How Many Perpetrators Were There in the Rwandan Genocide? An Estimate', *Journal of Genocide Research*, 6, 1 (2004), 85–98.
30. Hatzfeld, *Machete Season*; and J. Hatzfeld, *Into the Quick of Life: The Rwandan Genocide. The Survivors Speak*, trans. G. Feehily (London: Serpent's Tail, 2005).

31. P. Rusesabagina with T. Zoellner, *An Ordinary Man: An Autobiography* (New York: Viking, 2006); L. Mushikiwabo and J. Kramer, *Rwanda Means the Universe: A Native's Memoir of Blood and Bloodlines* (New York: St. Martin's Press, 2006). For a memoir primarily about Hutu refugees in Zaire after the genocide, but one that also deals with the period during and before the 1994 violence, see B. Umutesi, *Surviving the Slaughter: The Ordeal of a Rwandan Refugee in Zaire*, trans. J. Emerson (Madison, WI: University of Wisconsin Press, 2004). For a religiously oriented book emphasizing forgiveness, see I. Ilibagiza with S. Erwin, *Left to Tell: Discovering God amidst the Rwandan Holocaust* (Carlsbad, CA: Hay House, 2006).
32. R. Lyons and S. Straus, *Intimate Enemy: Images and Voices of the Rwandan Genocide* (New York: Zone Books, 2006).
33. T. Longman, 'Genocide and Socio-Political Change: Massacres in Two Rwandan Villages', *Issue: A Journal of Opinion*, 23, 2 (1995), 18–21 and M. Wagner, 'All the Burgomaster's Men: Making Sense of the Rwandan Genocide', *Africa Today*, 45, 1 (1998), 25–36.
34. Straus, *The Order of Genocide*.
35. L. A. Fujii, *Killing Neighbors: Social Dimensions of Genocide in Rwanda* (PhD dissertation, George Washington University, 2006); O. McDoom, *Rwanda's Ordinary Killers: Interpreting Popular Participation in the Rwandan Genocide* (PhD dissertation, London School of Economics, forthcoming).
36. On structural violence, see Uvin, *Aiding Violence*; on population growth and environmental stress, see J. Gasana, 'Remember Rwanda?', *World Watch*, 15, 5 (2002), 26–35; on population growth and land scarcity, see C. André and J.-P. Platteau, 'Land Relations under Unbearable Stress: Rwanda Caught in a Malthusian Trap', *Journal of Economic Behavior and Organization*, 34 (1998), 1–47; see also S. Khan, *The Shallow Graves of Rwanda* (London: I.B. Tauris, 2000), p. 66; on material incentives, see J. Waller, *Becoming Evil: How Ordinary People Commit Genocide and Mass Killing* (Oxford: Oxford University Press, 2002), p. 69; on a 'culture of obedience', see Prunier, *The Rwanda Crisis*, pp. 57, 245; on fear, see R. de Figueiredo and B. Weingast, 'The Rationality of Fear: Political Opportunism and Ethnic Conflict', in *Civil Wars, Insecurity, and Intervention*, eds, B. Walter and J. Snyder (New York: Columbia University Press, 1999), pp. 261–301; on security fears or more specifically a 'security dilemma' see R. Lemarchand, 'Disconnecting the Threads: Rwanda and the Holocaust Reconsidered', *Idea: Journal of Genocide Research*, 4, 4(2002), pp. 499–518; online at www.ideajournal.com/articles.php?sup=11; and on ethnic antipathy and belief in anti-Tutsi ideology, see Prunier, *The Rwanda Crisis*, pp. 40, 246, 248; Destexhe, *Rwanda and Genocide*, p. 28; Gourevitch, *We Wish To Inform You*, p. 94; Khan, *The Shallow Graves of Rwanda*, p. 66; Mamdani, *When Victims Become Killers*, p. 14; Scherrer, *Genocide and Crisis*, pp. 119–22.
37. M. Mann, *The Dark Side of Democracy: Explaining Ethnic Cleansing* (New York: Cambridge University Press, 2005).
38. M. Midlarsky, *The Killing Trap: Genocide in the Twentieth Century* (New York: Cambridge University Press, 2005).
39. B. Valentino, *Final Solutions: Mass Killing and Genocide in the Twentieth Century* (Ithaca, NY: Cornell University Press, 2004).
40. Sémelin, *Purifier et détruire*.
41. Lemarchand, 'Disconnecting the Threads'.
42. Melvern, *Conspiracy to Murder*.
43. E. Neuffer, *The Key to My Neighbor's House: Seeking Justice in Bosnia and Rwanda* (New York: Picador, 2001), p. 276.

44. Human Rights Watch, 'Shattered Lives: Sexual Violence During the Rwandan Genocide and Its Aftermath', New York, September, 1996.
45. An analysis of gender and sexual violence during and before the genocide can be found in C. C. Taylor, *Sacrifice as Terror: The Rwandan Genocide of 1994* (Oxford: Berg Books, 1999), Ch. 4.
46. International Criminal Tribunal for Rwanda, 'The Prosecutor versus Jean-Paul Akayesu', Case No. ICTR-96-4-T, available at www.ictr.org.
47. See, for examples, Prunier, *The Rwanda Crisis*, pp. 222–6; Article 19, *Broadcasting Genocide*, p. 18; and African Rights, *Rwanda*, pp. 96–9.
48. See, in particular, the testimony of former RPF officer: A. Ruzibiza, *Rwanda: L'histoire secrète* (Paris: Éditions du Panama, 2005).
49. The investigation was led by Jean-Louis Bruguière; for a discussion of the report's conclusions, see S. Smith, 'L'enquête sur l'attentat qui fit basculer le Rwanda dans le génocide', *Le Monde* (9 March 2004).
50. L. Marchal, 'Il est grand temps de faire la clarté sur la tragédie rwandaise', *Le Soir* (25 October 2005), p. 15.
51. Alan Kuperman, for example, claims that the RPF 'provoked a retaliatory genocide': A. Kuperman, 'Provoking Genocide: A Revised History of the Rwandan Patriotic Front', *Journal of Genocide Research*, 6, 1 (2004), 61–84.
52. OAU, *Rwanda: The Preventable Genocide*, paragraphs 7.2 and 7.3.
53. Melvern, *Conspiracy to Murder*, p. 19.
54. Prunier, *The Rwanda Crisis*, p. 169.
55. Des Forges, *Leave None*, p. 5.
56. International Criminal Tribunal for Rwanda, 'The Prosecutor Versus Clément Kayishema and Obed Ruzindana', Case No. ICTR-95-I-T, paragraph 275, available at www.ictr.org. On a pre-assassination plan for genocide, see also Jones, *Peacemaking in Rwanda*, pp. 35, 119 and J. Pottier, *Re-Imagining Rwanda: Conflict, Survival, and Disinformation in the Late Twentieth Century* (Cambridge: Cambridge University Press, 2002), p. 31.
57. I favour this interpretation in *The Order of Genocide*.
58. This account is drawn from Dallaire, *Shake Hands*, p. 142.
59. A replica of the fax is available on-line at www.gwu.edu/~nsarchiv/NSAEBB/NSAEBB53/index2.html.
60. Existing treatments include P. Verwimp, 'Testing the Double-Genocide Thesis for Central and Southern Rwanda', *Journal of Conflict Resolution*, 47, 4 (2003), 423–42; Des Forges, *Leave None*, pp. 724–31; and Ruzibiza, *Rwanda*.
61. Umutesi, *Surviving the Slaughter*.
62. Power, *"A Problem from Hell"*.
63. Dallaire, *Shake Hands*.
64. OAU, *Rwanda: The Preventable Genocide*.
65. S. Feil, *Preventing Genocide: How the Early Use of Force Might Have Succeeded in Rwanda*, Carnegie Commission On Preventing Deadly Conflict, New York, April 1998.
66. A. Kuperman, *The Limits of Humanitarian Intervention: Genocide in Rwanda* (Washington, D.C.: Brookings Institution, 2001).
67. See, for examples, A. Des Forges, 'Shame: Rationalizing Western Apathy on Rwanda', *Foreign Affairs*, 79, 3 (2000), 141–3 and S. Power, 'Bystanders to Genocide: Why the United States Let the Rwandan Tragedy Happen', *The Atlantic Monthly*, 288 (September 2001), 84–109.
68. Straus, *The Order of Genocide*, conclusion.

69. M. Barnett, *Eyewitness to a Genocide: The United Nations and Rwanda* (Ithaca, NY: Cornell University Press, 2002).
70. For an excellent review of the literature on the international decision to withdraw troops, see B. Valentino, 'Still Standing By: Why America and the International Community Fail to Prevent Genocide and Mass Killing', *Perspectives on Politics*, 1, 3 (2003), 565–76.
71. On the genocide debate and Rwanda, see the excellent account in Power, *"A Problem from Hell"*, pp. 358–64.
72. On this issue, see S. Straus, 'Darfur and the Genocide Debate', *Foreign Affairs*, 84, 1 (2005), 123–33.
73. For discussions of the French role in Rwanda, see Melvern, *A People Betrayed*, pp. 24–38; Prunier, *The Rwanda Crisis*, especially pp. 100–108, 281–311; Des Forges, *Leave None*, pp. 654–690; and A. Callamard, 'French Policy in Rwanda', in *The Path of a Genocide: The Rwanda Crisis from Uganda to Zaire*, eds, H. Adelman and A. Suhrke (New Brunswick, NJ: Transaction Publishers, 1999), pp. 157–83.
74. For good overviews, see in International Crisis Group, 'International Criminal Tribunal for Rwanda: Justice Delayed', Africa Report No. 30 (7 June 2001); A. Des Forges and T. Longman, 'Legal Responses to Genocide in Rwanda', in *My Neighbor, My Enemy: Justice and Community in the Aftermath of Mass Atrocity*, eds, E. Stover and H. Weinstein (New York: Cambridge University Press, 2004), pp. 51–7. One of the keenest observers of the tribunal is: T. Cruvellier, *Le Tribunal des vaincus: Un Nuremburg pour le Rwanda?* (Paris: Calman-Lévy, 2006).
75. Victor Peskin, *International Justice in Rwanda and the Balkans: Virtual Trials and the Struggle for State Cooperation* (New York: Cambridge University Press, forthcoming 2008).
76. K. Moghalu, *Rwanda's Genocide: The Politics of Global Justice* (New York: Palgrave Macmillan 2005).
77. P. Uvin and C. Mironko, 'Western and Local Approaches to Justice in Rwanda', *Global Governance*, 9 (2003), 223.
78. On this latter point and for a good overview, see Des Forges and Longman, 'Legal Responses', pp. 58–62; for a more positive account than Des Forges and Longman, see W. Schabas, 'Genocide Trials and *Gacaca* Courts', *Journal of International Criminal Justice*, 3 (2005), 879–895.
79. Uvin and Mironko, 'Western and Local Approaches', 225.
80. The figures come from Schabas, 'Genocide Trials'.
81. For an outstanding overview, see L. Waldorf, 'Mass Justice for Mass Crimes', *Temple Law Review*, 79, 1 (2006), 1–87. For shorter accounts, see Uvin and Mironko, 'Western and Local Approaches', and Schabas, 'Genocide Trials'; and, for a more thorough and historical account, A. Molenaar, 'Gacaca: Grassroots Justice after Genocide. The Key to Reconciliation in Rwanda?', *Leiden African Studies Research Centre Research Report*, 77 (2005).
82. See, for example, Gourevitch, *We Wish to Inform You.*
83. Discussions of the RPF's actions in Zaire (then the Democratic Republic of the Congo) as well as the war itself may be found in Young, 'The Heart of the African Conflict Zone'.
84. On these points, see F. Reyntjens, 'Rwanda, Ten Years On: From Genocide to Dictatorship', *African Affairs*, 103 (2004), 177–210; Front Line, 'Disappearances, Arrests, Threats, Intimidation and Co-option of Human Rights Defenders 2001–2004' (Dublin: Front Line, 2005); Human Rights Watch, 'Preparing for Elections: Tightening Control in the Name of Unity', New York, 8 May 2003; and International Crisis Group, 'Rwanda at the End of the Transition: A Necessary Political Liberalisation', ICG Africa Report No. 53 (13 November 2002).

21

¡Si Hubo Genocidio en Guatemala! Yes! There Was Genocide in Guatemala[1]

Victoria Sanford

> The army came with their guns. The people they found, they killed. The crops they came upon, they destroyed. Our clothes, our dishes, our tools, they broke them or stole them. And all our animals, our cows, goats, chickens and turkeys, they killed them too. They destroyed and ate everything on the path of their persecutions against the people.
>
> Alejandro, Ixil massacre survivor[2]

Introduction

The quantitative and qualitative toll of more than three decades of internal armed conflict was largely unknown in December 1996 when the Guatemalan army and URNG[3] guerrillas signed the historic Peace Accords. Indeed, the number and severity of human rights violations had been a hotly contested issue with numbers of dead and disappeared varying widely from 40,000 to 100,000 and everywhere in between. Likewise, the number of village massacres varied from 100 to 440.[4] Regardless of whether one pointed to the high or low end of these estimates, there was no doubt that grave human rights violations had taken place in Guatemala. Ward Churchill[5] and Ricardo Falla[6] were among the first to charge genocide in Guatemala and to do so with as much data as they could gather during the conflict. Still, when the concept of genocide was used to describe what was taking place in Guatemala, in the Cold War context, this description, like any analysis focused exclusively on army atrocities, was mostly dismissed as guerrilla or indigenista propaganda. Since the signing of the Peace Accords, however, genocide is a legal term that has been used by the Commission for Historical Clarification ([CEH] truth commission) in its report, the Inter-American Commission and Inter-American Court in its 2004 ruling against the Guatemalan state, and most recently by the Spanish Court in its 2006 international arrest warrant for generals implicated in the genocide.

Thus the historigraphy of genocide in Guatemala is one in the making. In this chapter, I draw on these documents, survivor testmonies, and other primary and secondary resources to provide the reader with an overview of the Guatemalan genocide and, thus, contribute to this burgeoning historiography.

From militarization to genocide

In 1978, the Guatemalan army garnered international attention when it opened fire on a group of unarmed Q'eqchi' Maya peasants protesting for land and killed dozens of men, women and children in what became known as the Panzos massacre. That same year, the Guatemalan army also began a selective campaign of political disappearance and assassination in Guatemala City and other urban and rural centres.[7] In tandem, it accelerated construction of military bases throughout rural Guatemala. Prior to 1979, the army had divided the country into nine military zones, each with a large army base in its centre. By 1982, the army had designated each of the 22 departments as a military zone accompanied by multiple army bases in municipalities and army garrisons in villages throughout the country.[8] Forced recruitment into the Guatemalan army ensured the requisite number of troops for this extension of the military infrastructure.[9] In 1982 troops were increased from 27,000 to 36,000.[10] Some of these large army bases, such as those in Rabinal and Nebaj, are structures that have endured to the date of this writing. Other more temporary locations, such as the churches in San Andrés Sajcabajá, Acul, Sacapulas, Joyabaj, Zacualpa, San Pedro Jocopilas, Nebaj, Chajul, Cotzal, Uspantán, Chiché, Canillá and the Marist monastery of Chichicastenango, which were used by the army as jails, torture and interrogation centres, and clandestine cemeteries, no longer house the army.[11]

This expanded army presence was accompanied by an acceleration of army violence, from selective assassinations to disappearances to multiple village massacres.[12] Within the United Nations system, these army operations of disappearances, extrajudicial executions, torture, inhuman and degrading treatment and punishment, and arbitrary detention violated numerous articles of the Universal Declaration of Human Rights (UDHR), the International Covenant of Civil and Political Rights (ICPR) and the Convention Against Torture and Other Cruel, Inhuman or Degrading Treatment or Punishment.[13] Some articles of some conventions are derogable, meaning that a signatory (state party to the convention) can sign on to the convention, covenant or protocol, on the condition of not being held to the standard of particular articles which the state party identifies as derogations prior to signing. Articles 6 and 7 of the ICPR, which guarantee the right to life and freedom from torture, respectively, are non-derogable. Articles 1 and 2 of the Convention Against Torture provide for no exceptions ever permitting torture: 'No exceptional circumstances whatsoever, whether a state of war or a threat of war, internal political instability of any other public emergency, may be invoked as a justification for torture.'[14] The Guatemalan army operations also violated Articles 1, 3, 4 and 5 of the American Convention on Human Rights to which Guatemala was one of the founding signatories in 1969. Articles 3, 4 and 5, which guarantee the right to juridical personality, right to life and freedom from torture, respectively, are all non-derogable. Indeed, army operations of terror against the Maya systematically violated these international human rights contracts to which Guatemala is a signatory.[15]

When the Guatemalan army shifted its strategy of repression from selective assassination to large-scale killings, it shifted its strategy to a prolonged series of genocidal campaigns against the Maya. These genocidal campaigns began with selective massacres in Maya villages all over the country and soon shifted to massacres of entire communities. It is when this shift happens that the Guatemalan army's human rights violations are no longer limited to the above-mentioned human rights instruments.[16] It is here that the army moves to a new level of atrocity and violates the Convention on the Prevention and Punishment of the Crime of Genocide.[17]

Critical to understanding why these massacres constitute the beginning of an intentional genocidal campaign is the fact that massacres were not a singular tactic of the army. In fact, there were three planned army campaigns of genocide against the Maya. The army's first campaign of genocide combined massacres with a 'scorched earth' campaign strategy that included the complete destruction of the Maya – the people, the villages, their livestock, their homes and their sacred milpa. The army's second genocidal campaign centered on the relentless hunt for and slaughter of massacre survivors; this campaign included army helicopters dropping bombs upon displaced civilians in the mountains and ground troops encircling and firing upon those fleeing aerial attacks. The third genocidal campaign was the simultaneous forced concentration of Maya survivors into army-controlled 're-education camps' and 'model villages', and the continued hunt for massacre survivors who had fled to the mountains.

In this chapter, I demonstrate how selective massacres as a strategy of state terror systematically shifted to a tripartite, decade-long campaign of genocide against the Maya. I provide evidence to prove that (1) each of the three campaigns of genocide I have identified is a clear violation of the UN Genocide Convention; (2) each of these campaigns was designed and implemented with the intention of genocide; (3) the Guatemalan army genocide was not unique, but rather fits a pattern of genocide wherein its intellectual authors and perpetrators use code words and expressions, such as 'scorching communists', in order to detract from and neutralize their genocidal activities in their attempts to 'render them acceptable domestically and internationally';[18] and (4) former dictators Romeo Lucas Garcia and Efrain Rios Montt in collusion with General Hector Gramajo were the intellectual authors of the massacres which they designed, implemented and supervised in army campaigns against the Maya with the intention to commit genocide.

Repression and La Violencia

At the height of La Violencia, army justification of massacres in rural Maya communities rested upon its claims that the army was, in the words of former military dictator Efraín Ríos Montt, 'scorching communists'.[19] Moreover, the transnational nature of the Guatemalan army's campaign against the Maya was revealed in a 5 October 1981 Department of State Memorandum classified as **Secret**. The memorandum acknowledged that then-dictator General Romeo Lucas García believed that 'the policy of repression' was 'working', and the state department official writing the memo described the 'extermination of the guerrillas, their supporters and sympathizers' as the measure of a 'successful' policy of repression.[20] The Guatemalan army used ground troops and aerial forces to saturate the mountains with firepower in its attempt to exterminate the unarmed Maya men, women, children and elderly who had fled the massacres and destruction in their communities.

In late 1982, prior to a meeting between US President Ronald Reagan and General Rios Montt, a confidential US State Department document reported that in 'March 1982, the current President Rios Montt came to power as expected' and pointed out that 'he quickly consolidated his power' and began 'to implement a rigorous counterinsurgency offensive.'[21] Nevertheless, the State Department officer writing the memo acknowledged that 'Rios Montt does not have a strong base of power ... We would like to be able, therefore to support Rios Montt over the short term. ...'[22] At the same time, the document acknowledged 'that the military continues to engage in massacres of civilians in the countryside'.[23]

The Impact of La Violencia[24]

Known impact of violence before CEH	**Findings of CEH final report**
440 villages massacred	626 villages massacred
1.5 million people displaced	1.5 million people displaced
150,000 people fled into external refuge	150,000 people fled to refuge in Mexico
100,000–150,000 dead or disappeared	More than 200,000 dead or disappeared

Who were the Victims of La Violencia?

The Vast Majority of the Victims of Acts of Violence Committed by the State were Civilians.

83 percent of Victims were Maya	17 percent of Victims were Ladino

Who is Responsible for These Acts of Violence against Civilians?

93 percent of Acts of Violence Committed by State	3 percent of Acts of Violence Committed by Guerrilla

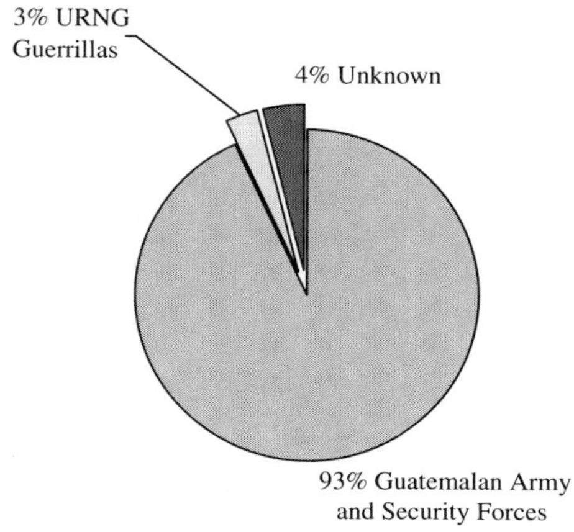

Chart 21.1 Command responsibility for acts of violence

In its final report, the CEH concluded that army massacres had destroyed 626 villages, that more than 200,000 people were killed or disappeared, that 1.5 million were displaced by the violence, and that more than 150,000 were driven to seek refuge in Mexico. Further, the Commission found the state responsible for 93 percent of the acts of violence and the guerrillas for 3 percent (See Chart 21.1).

Defining Genocide

In the Genocide Convention adopted by the United Nations General Assembly on 9 December 1948, 'genocide means any of the following acts committed with intent to destroy, in whole or in part, a national, ethnical, racial, or religious group, as such:

(a) Killing members of the group;
(b) Causing serious bodily or mental harm to members of the group;
(c) Deliberately inflicting on the group conditions of life calculated to bring about its physical destruction in whole or in part;
(d) Imposing measures intended to prevent births within the group;
(e) Forcibly transferring children of the group to another group.'[25]

Moreover, Article 1 clearly states that 'genocide, whether committed in time of peace or time of war, is a crime under international law which they [the signatories] undertake to prevent and punish.'

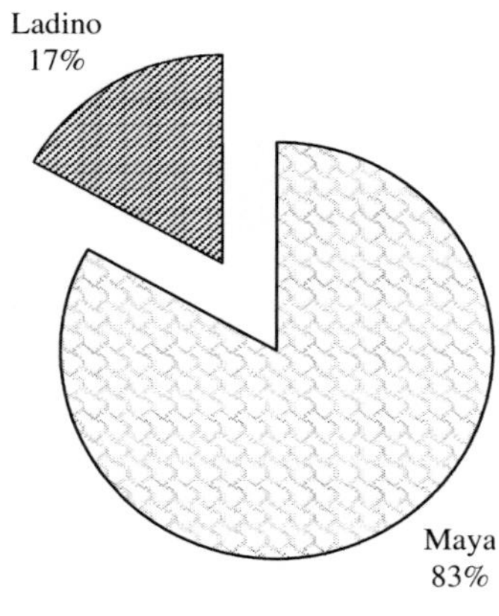

Source: CEH, 1999

Chart 21.2 Ethnicity of victims

Given that 87 percent of the victims of La Violencia were Maya (See Chart 21.2)[26] and that all 626 massacred villages were Maya, there should be no doubt that the Guatemalan army violated the United Nations Convention on the Prevention and Punishment of Genocide. In its first campaign of massacres, the army unequivocally killed members of the group, caused serious bodily and mental harm, and deliberately inflicted conditions of life calculated to bring about the physical destruction of the Maya in whole or in part. Thus, at minimum, the Guatemalan army violated Articles 2(a), (b) and (c) of the Genocide Convention. This alone, however, is not sufficient to prove genocide. Current legal debate about what constitutes genocide resides not just in determining the acts of genocide but also in proving that the acts were 'committed with intent'.[27] And, proving intent raises the question about what is acceptable as a standard of proof.

In its final report, the CEH concluded that the Guatemalan army had committed genocidal acts. However, in its discussion of genocide, the CEH wrote:

> It is important to distinguish between a policy of genocide and acts of genocide. A policy of genocide exists when the goal of the actions is to exterminate a group in whole or in part. Acts of genocide exist when the goal is political, economic, military, or whatever other such type, and the method that is utilized to achieve the end goal is the extermination of a group in whole or in part.[28]

Within the CEH interpretation, a policy of genocide has the end goal of genocide whereas acts of genocide are incidental to a plan utilizing these practices but with an end goal of something other than genocide. This CEH interpretation supports my earlier assertion that the Guatemalan army genocide fits a pattern of genocide wherein perpetrators (both individual and institutional) use code words such as 'scorching communists' and other such expressions to neutralize their activities. In this case, rather than genocide, the CEH finds genocidal acts – a finding that is, though ambiguous, nonetheless significant. In addition to pointing out the specific and varied roles of the executive, judicial and legislative branches of the Guatemalan government in violating the human rights of its citizens, the CEH attributed direct responsibility to the state and its agents for the construction of the counterinsurgency state and for the state's complete failure to comply with its obligation to investigate and prosecute human rights violations.

At the public presentation of the CEH Report in February 1998, CEH President Christian Tomuschat stated:

> On the basis of having concluded that genocide was committed, the Commission also concludes that, without prejudice to the fact that the participants in the crime include both the material and intellectual authors of the acts of genocide committed in Guatemala, State responsibility also exists. This responsibility arises from the fact that the majority of these acts were the product of a policy pre-established by superior order and communicated to the principal actors.[29]

Moreover, we can deconstruct army claims of 'scorching communists' and 'killing subversives' as the goal of the genocide by analyzing the army's own words and interpretations of the massacres. Here I offer two declassified US government documents that prove that the genocide was both a means and an end as well as under command responsibility of the hierarchy of the army.

First, a **Secret** declassified CIA document from late February 1982, states that in mid-February 1982, the Guatemalan Army has reinforced its existing forces and launched a 'sweep operation in the Ixil Triangle. The commanding officers of the units involved have been instructed to destroy all towns and villages which are cooperating with the Guerrilla Army of the Poor (EGP) and eliminate all sources of resistance.'[30] Point one of the memo claims that civilians 'who agree to collaborate with the army ... will be well treated'. Then, in point three of the memo the CIA acknowledges that 'a large number of guerrillas and collaborators have been killed.' Point three concluded with, 'COMMENT: When an army patrol meets resistance and takes fire from a town or village it is assumed that the entire town is hostile and it is subsequently destroyed. ... An empty village is assumed to have been supporting the EGP, and it is destroyed.' Point four cynically concludes that the Army High Command is 'highly pleased with the initial results of the sweep operation and believes it will be successful'. The CIA then clarifies that 'the army has yet to encounter any major guerrilla force in the area', and goes on to conclude that the army's 'successes to date appear to be limited to the destruction of several "EGP-controlled-towns" and the killing of Indian collaborators and sympathizers.' Point four concluded with 'COMMENT: The well documented belief by the army that the entire Ixil Indian population is pro-EGP has created a situation in which the army can be expected to give no quarter to combatants and non-combatants alike.'[31] In the words of former legal counsel to the CEH, Jan Perlin, 'The historic attribution of particular characteristics to the "indigenous masses", an integral part of the racist construct [of Guatemala], determined the choice of military tactics against geographically defined portions of this group when it was determined that "they" constituted a threat.'[32]

Second, as explained in the previously cited October 1981 declassified US Department of State memorandum, General Lucas Garcia believed that the 'extermination' was the measure of the 'success' of his 'policy of repression'.[33] Extermination was then not simply a means, but a goal. Moreover, despite their convoluted language and censored presentation, these documents acknowledge Guatemalan army massacres of unarmed Maya and also concur with the Guatemalan army that all Ixiles are 'pro-EGP'. This concurrence between the CIA, State Department, and Guatemalan army represents the official conflation of ethnicity with political affiliation. Thus, the US Embassy and its officers in Guatemala, the US State Department and the CIA justify Guatemalan army destruction of the social, political and material culture of the Maya in general and the Ixiles in particular. Though this justification for genocide is based on the conflated idea that all Ixiles are pro-EGP, ethnicity is central to this equation. Moreover, the 1982 CIA document makes clear that the Army High Command was not only informed about the massacres, but that the 'commanding officers of the units involved have been instructed to destroy all towns and villages' and that the Army High Command was 'highly pleased with the initial results'.[34]

Thus far, I have demonstrated (1) that army massacres of Maya communities violated Genocide Convention Articles 2(a), (b) and (c); (2) that though these massacres were directed at Maya communities in the name of 'scorching communists', in fact, the Guatemalan army carried out its first genocidal campaign of massacres against the Maya because they were Maya; (3) further, that the army sought to cover this campaign against the Maya by conflating political affiliation with ethnic identity; (4) that because 'extermination' of the Maya was, in the words of General Lucas Garcia, a measure of the campaign's 'success', the genocide was both a means and an end goal; and, (5) based on declassified CIA and US State Department documents, that the Army High Command ordered, was informed about and 'highly pleased with' army massacres in February 1982.

Proving intent to commit genocide

This brings us back to the issues of intent and standard of proof, which are interrelated. First, intent is often confused with motive. In criminal law, intent means the deliberation behind the act regardless of the actual motive.[35] Intentionality defines intent.[36] Did the Guatemalan army intend to commit genocide against the Maya? Yes, because the army's commander in chief sought to exterminate the Maya with no distinction between civilians and combatants or between democratic opposition and armed insurrection.[37] Was the aim to destroy the Maya, as a group, in whole or in part? Yes, because (1) all Maya were at-risk of being 'exterminated' by virtue of their indigenous identity; (2) massacres destroyed 626 Maya villages; and, (3) all 626 villages were Maya.

By outlining the Guatemalan army's intent to commit genocide, I have also alluded to available evidence that leads us to the issue of standard of proof. Dinah Shelton suggests that '*beyond a reasonable doubt* in common law court and *conviction in time* or its equivalent in a continental system' are internationally accepted standards of proof. Moreover, citing the Inter-American Court judgment in the Velasquez-Rodriguez case, she is 'fully confident that proof can be inferred from a pattern or practice'.[38]

Ben Kiernan points out that 'Smoking Gun' internal documentation is not necessary to prove intent – though the declassified US government documents do provide this. Proof of intent can be inferred by 'a proven pattern of actions, not just from a top-down written order'.[39] 'Serial killers who are convicted by showing patterns and inferred responsibility from circumstantial evidence'[40] is one such example. Kiernan adds that 'similar actions in a pattern across a territory can be proof of command intent.'[41]

Declassified CIA and US State Department documents provide evidence of intent to commit genocide. I would also like to suggest that intent is found in the very language of the generals in command during the 'scorched earth campaign'. While Lucas Garcia spoke of 'exterminating', General Efrain Rios Montt spoke of 'taking the water away from the fish' (*quitar al agua del pez*), the water being the Maya and the fish being the guerrilla. Even here, it is clear that the general made a distinction between the guerrilla (fish) and the Maya (water). If he truly meant to 'scorch communists' and 'eliminate subversion', the fish, rather than the water, would have been his military target. If he was unable to distinguish between the Maya and the guerrillas, the metaphor would have had no meaning. Rios Montt, like Lucas Garcia before him, wanted to eliminate the Maya. The massacres were a genocidal campaign, begun under Lucas Garcia and continued under Rios Montt, which intended to destroy the Maya because they were Maya. Seven months after Rios Montt came to power, one Maya survivor said that after the massacres, 'All that was left was silence.'[42] Amnesty International issued a report condemning massacres of 'Indian' peasants resulting in more than 2,600 documented deaths, 'many of them women and children', in the first six months of the Rios Montt regime. Even with incomplete information, as early as 1982, it was clear to human rights observers that the Guatemalan 'Indians' were the target of the army's campaign of terror.[43] Again, citing Perlin, 'The truth of genocidal intent centres around the process of the construction of the "other" as the enemy.'[44]

At this point, I have demonstrated that the Guatemalan army committed genocide against the Maya with the intention to destroy the Maya in whole or in part and that genocide was both the means and the end, and furthermore, genocide was also the planned intent. Still, I want to offer further evidence of the army's strategic intent to commit genocide as well as some of the results of the genocidal campaign – both of which demonstrate that genocide was a consistent policy of the Guatemalan army through the dictatorships of Lucas Garcia and Rios Montt – each of whom had command responsibility.

Genocide as army policy from Lucas Garcia to Rios Montt

In general, the Guatemalan army has sought to elude responsibility for its genocidal campaign of massacres by claiming that massacres did not emanate from the army high command, but rather from the actions of rogue field commanders. Still, one army colonel unequivocally stated that 'a comandante could not follow his own strategy against his superiors.'[45] Former General Efraín Rios Montt became president of Guatemala when he overthrew the dictatorship of Lucas Garcia in March 1982. La Violencia was at its height during these two dictatorships. Still, Rios Montt not only claims that he had nothing to do with the massacres, but that his regime stopped the massacres begun by Lucas Garcia.

General Lucas Garcia, withdrawn from the political scene for the past decade due to advanced Alzheimer's disease, died in May 2006. Rios Montt, however, continues to play a powerful role in Guatemalan politics. He is secretary general of the FRG party, which holds a significant number of seats in the Guatemalan Congress. Rios Montt has been a member of congress and president of the congress since the peace accords and his party has held the presidency as well. Indeed, Rios Montt attempted to run for president in 1995 and continues to manoeuvre for the office. In 1995, the Guatemalan Supreme Electoral Commission banned his candidacy (and his wife's) based on the Guatemalan Constitution, which prohibits anyone who came to power through a military coup from running for president. It took the FRG and Rios Montt until 2003 to stack the courts and win his right to a presidential bid. The symbol of his FRG party is a white hand on a blue background. When I asked Maya friends in rural communities about the meaning of this symbol, I was always told, 'It is the strong/tough hand' (*la mano dura*) and 'the white hand' (*la mano blanca*). Both *la mano dura* and *la mano blanca* were names of death squads during La Violencia and death threats were often received with hand prints or drawings of hands.

Though current party politics are not my focus here, I do want to suggest that it is an ominous experience to be in a country of genocide survivors during an election with *la mano dura* plastered on every building, fence and lamppost. Outsiders, both non-Maya Guatemalans and internationals, often ask why and how the FRG could win an election in communities of massacre survivors. Though a thorough explanation requires analysis of evangelical church affiliations with Rios Montt as well as campaign practices,[46] I want to suggest that massacre survivors have no reason to believe that the power of Rios Montt to exterminate their communities has diminished, given that he has an omnipresent political party with propaganda throughout Maya communities and that his party symbol is a signifier of terror.

In this section, through an analysis of the pattern of massacres in El Quiché and Baja Verapaz during the last 12 months of Lucas Garcia's regime (March 1981–2) and the first 12 months of Rios Montt's reign (March 1982–3), I demonstrate that (1) massacres were *not* the result of rogue field commanders; (2) massacres were a systematic and strategic campaign of the army as an institution; (3) Rios Montt not only continued the campaign of massacres begun by Lucas Garcia, he actually further systematized the massacre campaign; and (4) this sustained campaign of massacres was the army's first genocidal campaign.

The Ixil and Ixcán areas are located in the northern part of El Quiché with the Ixcán jungle north of the Ixil mountain range. Between March 1981 and March 1983, the Guatemalan army carried out 77 massacres in the Ixil–Ixcán region. There are 3,102 known victims of these massacres. If we locate the number of massacres and victims by date on the calendar of the regimes, Lucas Garcia is responsible for 45 massacres with 1,678 victims from March 1981 to March 1982 and Rios Montt is responsible for 32 massacres with 1,424 victims from March 1982 to March 1983 (See Chart 21.3).[47]

If we focus only on comparing the number of massacres, we find a 15 percent drop in the number of massacres and 200 less massacre victims in the Ixil–Ixcán area during the first year of Rios Montt (See Chart 21.4). However, it would be misleading to simply conclude that the number of massacres and massacre victims decreased under Rios Montt because 1,424 Maya were killed in 32 army massacres under his regime. Moreover, rather than a decrease in genocidal activities in the area, the number of victims per massacre actually increased under Rios Montt from an average of 37 victims to 45, or an 18 percent increase in number of victims per massacre.

This increase indicates a more systematic genocidal policy which sought 'efficiency' in killing ever larger numbers of people in each massacre. Furthermore, if we limit the time of study from the last three months under Lucas Garcia and the first three months under Rios Montt, we find 775 Maya

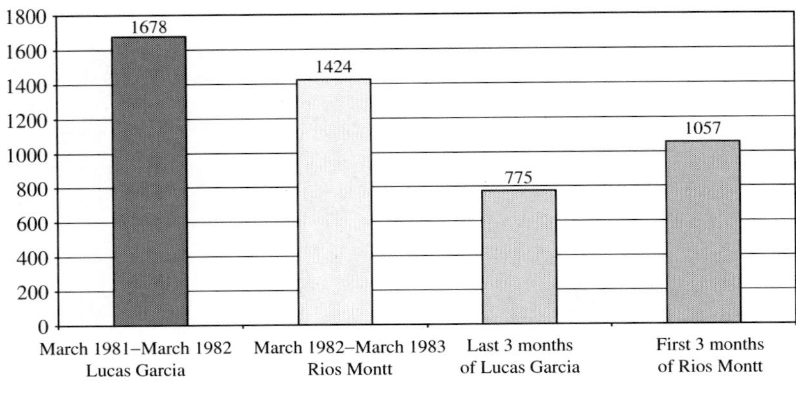

Source: CEH, 1999

Chart 21.3 Total number of massacre victims in northern El Quiche March 1981 to March 1983

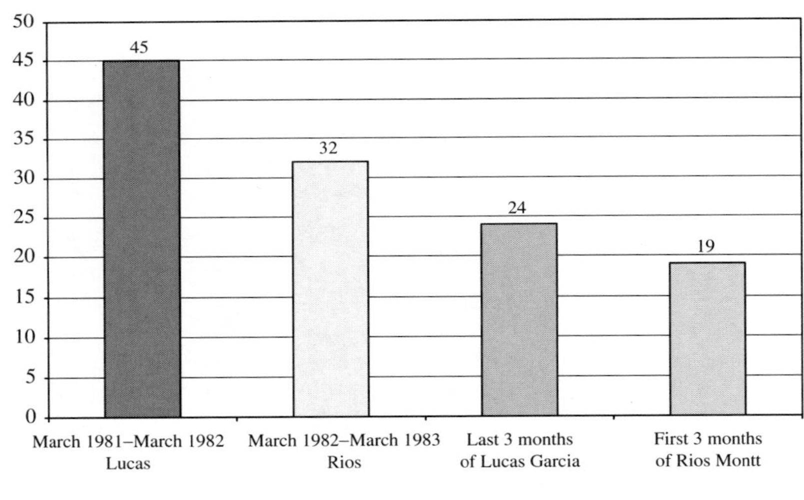

Source: CEH, 1999

Chart 21.4 Number of massacres in northern El Quiche

victims of 24 massacres under Lucas Garcia and 1,057 victims of 19 massacres under Rios Montt. Though there is a 21 percent drop in the number of known massacres, there is a 27 percent increase in the average number of victims in each massacre under Rios Montt. In the first three months of the Rios Montt regime, the average number of victims per massacre increased from 32 to 56

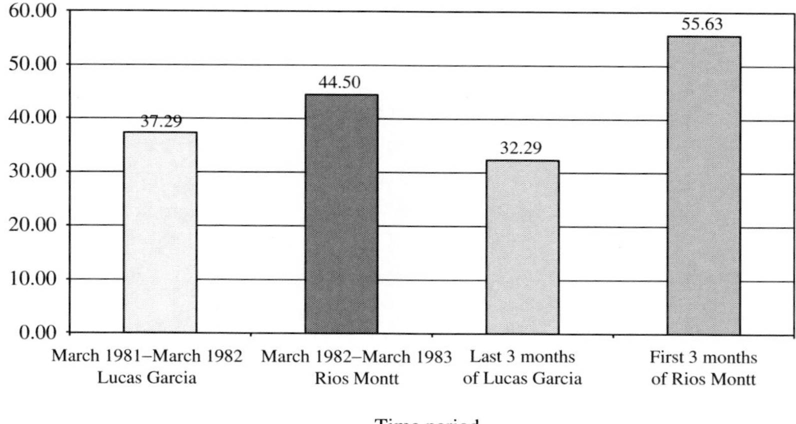

Chart 21.5 Average number of victims per massacre in northern El Quiche

(See Chart 21.5). Further, the qualitative difference between an average of 32 and 56 victims is not the size of the village; rather it is the systematic inclusion of women, children and elderly in the slaughter. Whereas it is during the last six months of the Lucas Garcia regime that the army began to include women, children and elderly as targets in some massacres, it is under Rios Montt that their inclusion became a systematic practice.

If we broaden our analysis to the entire department of El Quiché, our conclusions about the strategies and patterns of massacres in the Ixil–Ixcán areas during the regimes of Lucas Garcia and Rios Montt are systematically reaffirmed.[48] Under Lucas Garcia, from March 1981 to March 1982, 2,495 Maya were victims of 97 army massacres in the department of El Quiché. Under Rios Montt, between March 1982 and March 1983, 3,180 Maya were victims of 85 massacres in El Quiché. Here again, while there is a 13 percent drop in the number of massacres under Rios Montt, there is a 25 percent increase in the number of massacre victims during the first year of his regime (See Chart 21.6). Again, under Rios Montt, there is an increase in the efficiency of the massacres with 30 percent more victims per massacre, on average. And again, I want to emphasize that this 30 percent increase represents the systematic inclusion of women, children and elderly as massacre victims.

Fully 43 percent of all the Achi Maya killed in army massacres between January of 1980 and December of 1982, died during the first nine months of the Rios Montt regime (See Chart 21.7).[49] If we combine the massacres in the municipality of Rabinal and the departmental capital of Salama, we find the ladino-dominated Salama suffered 1 percent of massacres while the predominantly Achi-Maya Rabinal suffered 99 percent of the massacres (See Chart 21.8).

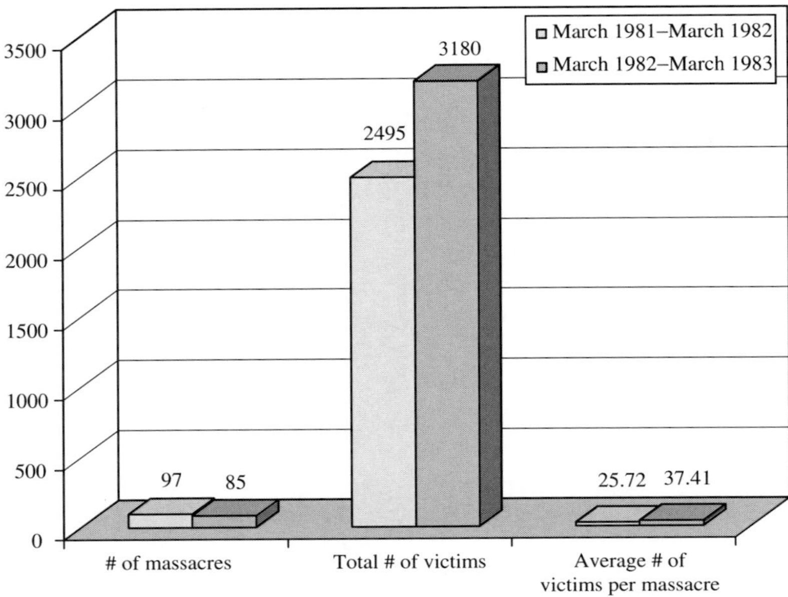

Source: CEH, 1999

Chart 21.6 EI Quiche data

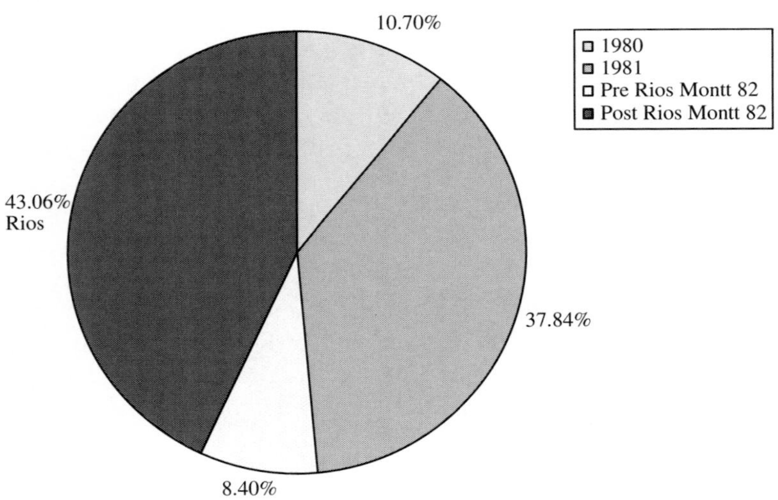

Source: CEH, 1999

Chart 21.7 Regime responsibility for percentage of massacre victims Baja Verapaz, 1980–1982

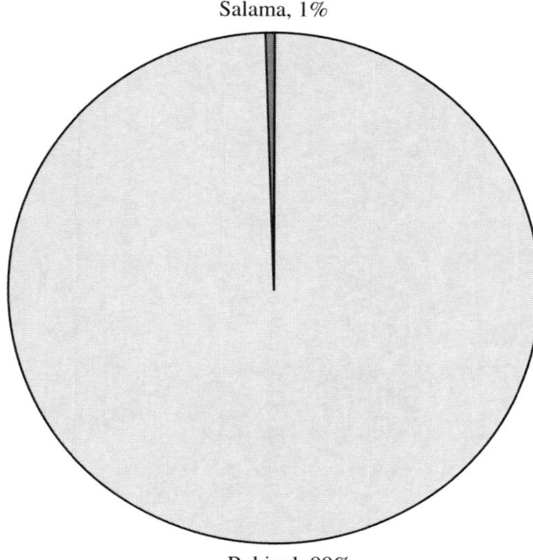

Source: CEH, 1999

Chart 21.8 Percentage of massacre victims 1980–1983 by Municipality for Salama and Rabinal, Baja Verapaz

In 1981, 422 Rabinal Achi were killed by the army in massacres under Lucas Garcia – an average of 35 massacre victims per month. Another 95 Achi died in massacres during the last three months of the Lucas Garcia regime in 1982 – an average of 32 massacre victims per month. In just the first nine months of Rios Montt's regime, 487 Rabinal Achi were killed in army massacres (See Chart 21.9). Averaging 54 massacre victims per month in Rabinal alone, there was a 64 percent increase in the number of massacre victims in Rabinal under Rios Montt.[50]

Between 1980 and 1983, 25 percent of massacres were committed by the army alone. Another 21 percent were committed by army troops with judiciales – local ladinos from Salama and Rabinal *vestido de civil con pañuelos rojos* (in civilian clothes with red bandanas). Both Rabinal Achi and ladinos refer to these men interchangeably as 'judiciales' and 'escuadrones'. Moreover, 54 percent of all Rabinal massacres were committed by the army with PAC military commissioners and/or patrollers. Under the regime of Rios Montt, military commissioners and PACs were included in every army massacre in Rabinal.[51]

Genocide is a gendered atrocity because its intention is to destroy the cultural group. This means destruction of the community's material culture as well as its reproductive capacity – thus, women and children are prime genocidal targets. One way to pinpoint the height of the genocide is to look at the ratio of male to female massacre victims. In 1981, females (including women and girls) comprised

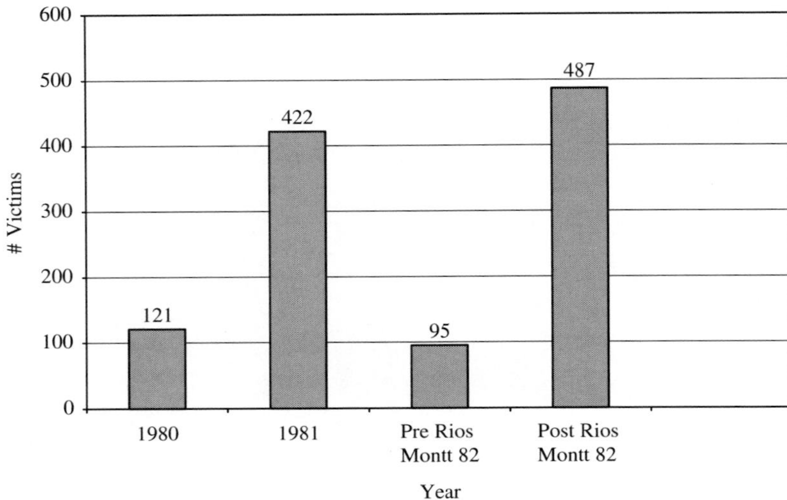

Source: CEH, 1999

Chart 21.9 Number of massacre victims – Rabinal, Baja Verpaz 1980–1982

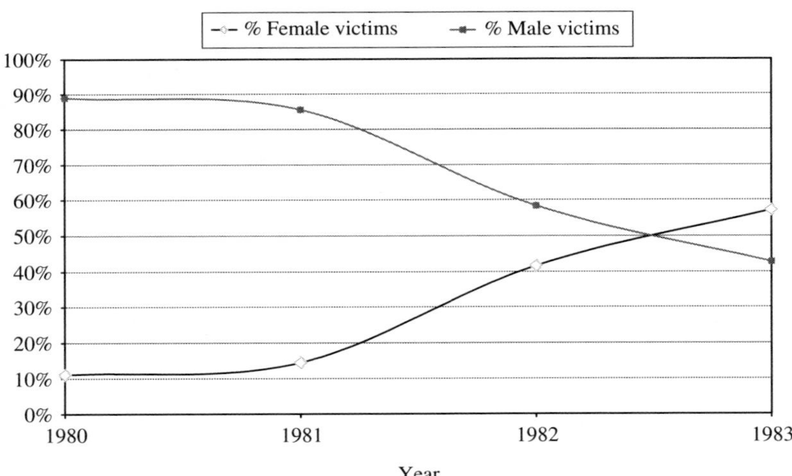

Source: CEH, 1999

Chart 21.10 Percentage of massacre victims by gender Baja Verapaz, 1980–1983

14 percent of massacre victims in Rabinal. By 1982, they made up 42 percent of massacre victims. By charting the gender composition of massacre victims over time, we see that halfway through 1982 the increase in the number of women killed in massacres rises so rapidly that the comparative percentage of men killed actually drops (See Chart 21.10).

This point of intersection represents the successful implementation of a shift in army strategy from selective massacres to genocide and is located midway through 1982 about three months after Rios Montt seized power.[52]

No doubt, the ever-increasing number of Maya massacre victims and the pattern from the Lucas Garcia regime to the rule of Rios Montt indicates an ongoing army strategy that was consistent in its target population (the Maya) and one which became increasingly efficient. Moreover, this improved efficiency was no accident and certainly not the random and coincidental outcome of rogue commanders in the field. It was the field implementation of the Guatemalan army's 'Plan de Campana Victoria 82' (Victory Campaign Plan 82) which sought to 'eliminate', 'annihilate' and 'exterminate' the 'enemy'.[53]

In her extensive study of the Guatemalan military based on interviews with high-ranking officers, Jennifer Schirmer concluded: 'The concentration of energies and forces [of Plan Victoria] resulted in the most closely coordinated, intensive massacre campaign in Guatemalan history.'[54] General Hector Gramajo, Rios Montt's Deputy Chief of Staff, told Schirmer 'proudly' that 'one of the first things we did was draw up a document for the campaign with annexes and appendices. It was a complete job with planning down to the last detail.'[55] Gramajo also told Schirmer that he was 'coordinator and supervisor of the military commanders of operations for the western zone (Alta and Baja Verapaces, El Quiché, Huerhuetenango and Chimaltenango)'; he also referred to the campaign of massacres as his 'baby'.[56] Less than one month after the Rios Montt coup, Plan Victoria was signed by the junta on 10 April 1982 and officially began 10 days later. Throughout the campaign, Gramajo and the army General Staff received hourly and daily intelligence reports about all the details of the campaign via radio transmissions.[57] A critical component of Plan Victoria was the systematic organization of civil patrols that was begun, perhaps as a pilot campaign, under Lucas Garcia but brought to fruition under Rios Montt. Fully 64 percent of army massacres during the 34-year conflict occurred between June 1981 and December 1982.[58] According to a statistical analysis of the CEH findings, 14.5 percent of Ixil Maya and 16 percent of Achi Maya were killed during La Violencia.[59]

Inclusion of PACs in Guatemalan army massacres

Given that PACs were an integral component of the 1982 Victory Campaign, I want to again look at the massacres, but this time analyzing the composition of the perpetrators. My questions here are (1) Who carried out the massacres? (2) Does this reveal a pattern? (3) If there is a pattern, what are its implications?

In the department of El Quiché during the last year of the Lucas Garcia regime, army platoons carried out 97 massacres but 16 of these massacres were different from the rest because, for the first time, army platoons carried out massacres with local PAC participation under army command.[60] Under Lucas

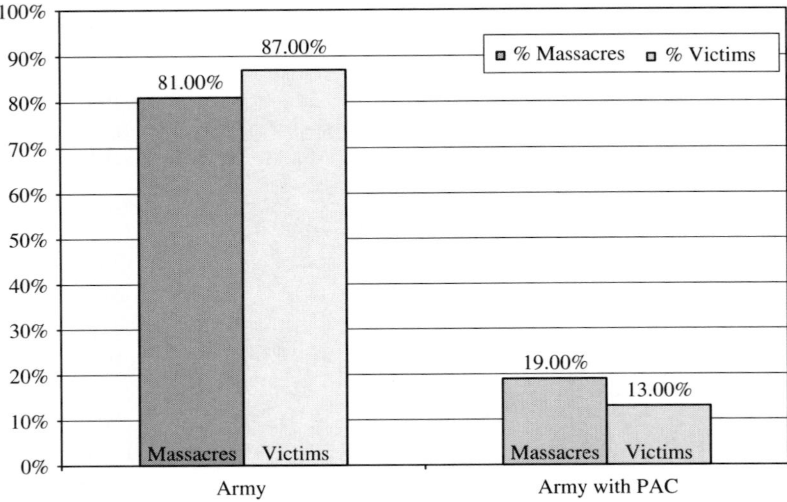

Chart 21.11 Command responsibility of army and PACS during the last 12 months of Lucas Garica Regime

Garcia, 19 percent of massacres were carried out by army platoons with PAC participation (under army command) and 81 percent of massacres were carried out by army platoons alone. Reviewing the number of victims of each massacre, one finds that 87 percent of the victims were killed in army platoon massacres and 13 percent of the victims were killed in joint army/PAC massacres (See Chart 21.11).

Each massacre was representative of a wide-scale military strategy that did not distinguish between civilians and combatants;[61] a strategy that first used terror and psychological cruelty to force communities to accede to army control. Massacres should not be seen as discrete and one-time-only incidents of state violence but rather as integral strategic operations which in their sum form the army's first genocide campaign. Nonetheless, each massacre is still significant in that it embodies the moment in which violence explodes into the lives of civilian villagers and forever changes the lives of citizens in Guatemalan society both locally and nationally. It is within the tension of this local and comparative national analysis of the massacres that we can best understand the meaning of the Guatemalan genocide.

In the Ixil Area, in the last six months of 1980, 83 Maya lost their lives in army massacres in five Ixil communities. By 1981, PACs were systematically incorporated into the army's massacre campaign. Indeed, of 79 army massacres carried out by the army in El Quiché during 1981, local PACs participated in 12 of these massacres (or 15 percent).[62] By 1982, the army had committed 131 massacres in El Quiché and local PACs participated in 41 of these massacres – doubling PAC participation in army massacres to 31 percent.[63] No doubt, this increase in PAC execution of army strategy represents both the expansion of the army's scorched earth campaign as well as the growth of army-controlled civil patrols throughout the region.

In its comprehensive investigation, the CEH found that 18 percent of human rights violations were committed by civil patrols. Further, it noted that 85 percent of those violations committed by patrollers were carried out under army order.[64] It is not insignificant that the CEH found that one out of every ten human rights violations was carried out by a military commissioner and that while these commissioners often led patrollers in acts of violence, 87 percent of the violations committed by commissioners were in collusion with the army.[65]

Less than one month after the army organized all the men of San José and San Antonio Sinaché, Zacualpa, into a PAC, army-ordered PAC violence began within the community. On 24 May 1982 (exactly two months after the coup), the arm`y called all the 800 patrollers to gather in front of the church in San Antonio Sinaché. After chastising them for failing to turn in any guerrillas in the preceding weeks, the army lieutenant sent them on a fruitless march through the mountains searching for guerrillas. When they returned empty-handed, the army and patrollers who had remained showed them the dead bodies of four PAC members and two local women. After ordering the patrollers to relinquish their palos (sticks) and machetes, the lieutenant accused Manuel Tol Canil, one of the local PAC chiefs of being a guerrilla. Two other patrollers protested that Canil was not a guerrilla and had committed no crime. The lieutenant then accused those two patrollers of also being guerrillas.[66]

The hands of the three men were bound behind their backs and they were tied to a tree in front of the church. The lieutenant ordered the patrollers to form a line in front of the tree. He picked up one of the machetes, gave it to the first man in line, and ordered him to '*Vos matalo a éste. Si vos no lo matás, te mato a vos* (You kill him this way. If you don't kill him, I will kill you).' Taking turns, the men were ordered not to hit the men with lethal blows because their deaths should be slow to extend their suffering. When the first victim died after three machete blows, the lieutenant said, 'That's too bad that he couldn't tolerate more, he died with only three blows of the machete.'[67] After all three men had been killed, the patrollers were ordered to bury them. One patroller recalled returning home after killings, 'We came home cold, we were all frightened. The elders were crying as we walked down the path. The thing is that we were all crying.'[68] Another former patroller explained the impact of this army-ordered violence in his community, 'We began to drink more *guaro* [grain alcohol] to make our hearts more tranquil to try to pass thorugh the pain these events brought to us.'[69]

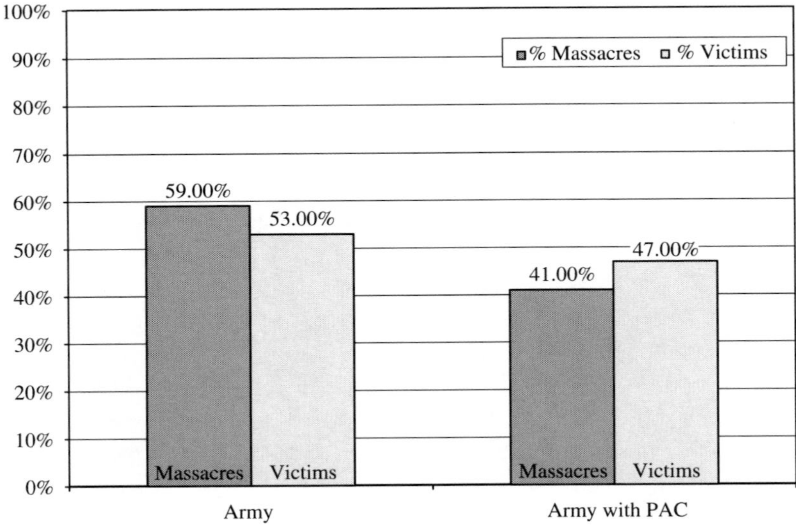

Source: CEH, 1999

Chart 21.12 Command responsibility of army and PAC under Rios Montt Regime

Plan Victoria, developed under Rios Montt, increased the centrality of the PACs to army strategy.[70] Less than one month after Rios Montt's coup, the army began an intensified and systematic forced recruitment of Maya into the PACs.[71] This further systematized the inclusion of civil patrols in the counterinsurgency begun under Lucas Garcia. Thus, it should not be surprising that army massacres with PAC participation more than doubled to account for 41 percent of army massacres under Rios Montt and that the number of victims of army/PAC massacres more than tripled to account for 47 percent of army massacre victims (See Chart 21.12).

This systematic pattern of incorporation of army-controlled civil patrols participating in army massacres at the same time that the army's official Plan Victoria campaign calls for increased organization of these PACs indicates 'beyond a shadow of a doubt' that (1) massacres were carried out by army platoons and army platoons with PAC participation; (2) the pattern of army and army/PAC massacres from Lucas Garcia to Rios Montt indicates massacres as a result of widespread army strategy and command responsibility; (3) this pattern further reveals a highly coordinated army campaign which increasingly and systematically included PACs in massacre operations under army command; (4) this pattern could only have existed as the result of a widespread army strategy with incorporation of PACs as a strategic component of the 1982 Plan Victoria; and (5) both Lucas Garcia and Rios Montt, as well as Gramajo and other army officials in the High Command, had command responsibility and were the intellectual authors of army and army/PAC massacres of the Maya during their military regimes. This sustained campaign of massacres was the army's first genocidal campaign against the Maya.

'Hunter Battalions' – the Guatemalan army's second campaign of genocide

As the Guatemalan army moved forward with Plan Victoria's first campaign of genocide committing massacres against the Maya in villages throughout the country, those who survived by fleeing into the mountains were pursued by the army. Initially, massacre survivors fled to nearby villages in the mountains seeking refuge from the army ground troops chasing them through the mountains as well as the machine gun strafing of army helicopters and the bombs being dropped from planes. These villages were soon attacked and destroyed by the army, which left only the mountain itself as refuge.

In July 1981, based on an interview with an unnamed US intelligence operative who had worked in Brazil and Colombia, Everett G. Martin reported in the *Wall Street Journal* that 'the Carter Administration's policy of turning its back on a country that violates the human rights of its citizens during the fight against guerrillas "is a coward's way out."' Martin also reported on the indoctrination of Salvadoran troops at a special training school. An unnamed Green Beret colonel explained the counterinsurgency techniques: 'There aren't any such things as special forces camps or free-fire zones in irregular warfare. We are supposed to train the local forces to play guerrilla with hunter battalions that are moving all the time. ... You make them realize their situation is hopeless and then you offer them amnesty.'[72] These same techniques were taught to Guatemalan army officials and troops at the School of the Americas.[73]

Indeed, former soldiers involved in the pursuit of civilians in flight have referred to these operations as 'hunting the deer' (*cazando el venado*). The technique was to use multiple platoons to encircle a large area. These troops would be backed up by helicopter strafing and aerial bombardment. Soldiers would begin to fire into the forested areas of the mountains on all but one side of the circle thereby forcing the civilians to flee in the direction which appeared to be safe for lack of gunfire. As civilians reached these areas, the soldiers would open fire directly onto the civilian populations. This sustained 'hunt' of the Maya and the intentional suffering and destruction it caused is the army's second campaign of genocide against the Maya.

While the army killed civilians in flight, they also forced these internal refugees to die from hunger. Empty villages were burned and their crops were destroyed by the army. Even those villagers who had dug *buzones* to hide and store corn and clothing had fared little better than those who had not. The *buzones* were most often found and destroyed or looted by the army and/or civil patrols. Civilians in flight had little more than the clothes on their back and whatever food they were able to carry lasted, at best, for only a few days. Civilians fled the army sometimes for days and sometimes for a week until they found a temporary safe haven where they would stay until the next army attack or until they drifted away in search of food and water. Wherever they landed, they were constantly pursued by hunger and thirst.

Writing of survival in Auschwitz, Primo Levi wrote: 'the physiological reserves of the organism were consumed in two or three months, and death by hunger, or by diseases induced by hunger, was the prisoner's normal destiny, avoidable only with additional food.'[74] Indeed, in the hundreds of testimonies I have taken from massacre survivors, the power of the hunger, thirst and illness of life in flight from army troops overwhelms even the event of the massacre because life in flight went on for years and during the years in flight an average of 30 percent of massacre survivors died from army attacks, hunger and illnesses associated with hunger and exposure to the elements.[75] It was the desperation of hunger that drove massacre survivors to forage for edible roots, weeds and bark in the mountains and also to search for any abandoned crops of milpa missed by the army's scorched earth campaign. Don Silverio recalls, 'It had been more than eight days without food. We were far in the mountain, but we could see the milpa. The soldiers had left. There was a youth who was very brave, he said he was going to investigate and bring back maize for all of us. We heard the explosion. Poor youth. The army had mined the milpa. In other places where we found milpa, the soldiers had shit on our sacred milpa.'[76]

'Thirst', wrote Levi, 'does not give respite. Hunger exhausts, thirst enrages.'[77] When not cold and wet from the constant rain of winter, massacre survivors in flight were hot and in search of water in the unrelenting heat of summer. Without water, there can be no life. What kind of life is there when water is so limited that one does not know from one day to the next if there will be water enough to drink? What does it mean to bring new life into the world in such dire conditions? Doña Juanita gave birth in the mountains when there was no water: 'My son was born in the mountain. He was born without clothes. He was born without food. We didn't even have any water. When my son was born, I couldn't even change because I had no other clothes and I had to stay in my own filth because there was no water. We suffered greatly in the mountain.'[78] Even when there was enough water for bathing, there was never any soap. In place of soap, people used ashes when they bathed.

Just as massacres were not the result of rogue army commanders, the hunt for Maya civilians in flight in the mountains as well as all the resulting death, privations and sufferings were the systematic enactment of the Guatemalan army's second campaign of genocide against the Maya. The goal of this campaign, which was supported by the US government, was to eliminate those Maya who survived the hundreds of army massacres.

Forced concentration of massacre survivors into army-controlled 'model villages'

The third army campaign of genocide is the forced concentration of Maya massacre survivors into army-controlled camps which the army called 'model villages'. In *Survival in Auschwitz*, Primo Levi writes of his arrival to the camp: 'we saw a large door, and above it a sign, brightly illuminated (its memory still strikes me in my dreams): Work Gives Freedom.'[79] In keeping with the Nazi fantasy of work and freedom in concentration camps, the Guatemalan Army named roads within its model villages 'Avenue of Development', 'Avenue of Security',[80] 'National Army Avenue' and 'Road of the Fallen',[81] and signposts at the entries had slogans such as: 'Guatemala is peace and development',[82] 'Welcome to Saraxoch, a totally ideologically new community', 'Anti-Subversive Village. Ideologicaly New'[83] and 'Only he who fights has the right to win. Only he who wins has the right to live.'[84]

In September of 1982, *New York Times* reporter Marlise Simons reported that Rios Montt was carrying out a 'methodical counterinsurgency program' begun when Rios Montt imposed a state of siege in July and which included military operations of 25,000 army soldiers 'aided by some 25,000 members of a newly created Civil Defense Force' Further, she wrote that the 'government's new strategy ... includes herding thousands of Indian villagers into army-controlled zones.' Simon visited displaced survivors of the army massacre of Las Pacayas village; she wrote: 'Since the massacre, the army has returned 150 villagers to Las Pacayas, where they now live in rows of military tents and improvised huts. In the presence of an army captain, the Indian men repeated the official version that the "subversives" had attacked them.' Outside the surveillance of the army, several sources confirmed the massacre was committed by the army.[85]

Model villages such as Las Pacayas were an integral part of the Army's 'Poles of Development' campaign which theoretically provided for rural development. In reality, the model villages, like the poles of development, were army-controlled resettlement work camps developed as a means of maintaining absolute control over communities of displaced Maya massacre survivors. The construction of the model villages was among the first 'food for work' projects which returning massacre survivors were forced to build. Most of these villages were built upon the burned remains of villages razed by the army. Indeed, massacre survivors often returned to their villages of origin to rebuild under army order. Because the composition of villages was determined by the army, many villages were rebuilt with Maya from different villages as well as other ethnolinguistic communities. Thus, many Maya today describe their communities as *revuelto* [scrambled]. In addition to the villages, survivors were also forced to build access roads for army vehicles.

Just as hunger had driven massacre survivors to surrender from the mountains, hunger also drove them to work for food. 'No work projects, no food. A great way of doing things', said Sergeant Corsantes, one of the commanders at the Saraxoch model village.[86] Indeed, the 1980 Santa Fe Committee's 'A New Inter-American Policy for the 80s' which served as a blueprint for the Reagan administration's Latin American policies, cynically stated 'Food is a weapon in a world at war.'[87] The Guatemalan army journal *Revista Militar* noted, 'In twenty four hours, it is possible to assemble 3,000 or more voluntary workers to undertake construction of a road, a school, irrigation projects, a whole city ...'[88]

Within the model villages, residents were called to line-up in formation and register in the morning, the afternoon, and the evening. Each day at midday, residents were also required to participate in anti-guerrilla, pro-army confessional rituals in which several local men would recount how they had been betrayed by the guerrilla and helped by the army. Residents were not allowed to leave model villages without army permission.[89]

The construction of model villages was reminiscent of the strategic hamlets developed in Vietnam by the United States and the South Vietnamese army during the Vietnam War. Model villages included at least one, and often two, military detachments of 150 soldiers who were permanently housed in army garrisons built within the village. These garrisons were most often located close to the village entrance allowing soldiers to monitor daily activities within the village. Model villages each had army/PAC patrol posts at the entrance and exit of the village. A soldier in the model village of Chisec explained, 'We have a list of names. If their names appear on the list, we take them.' Responding to a question about the fate of those taken away, the soldier said, 'They die.'[90] Thus, the grid-pattern construction plan of model village housing and its garrison layout, and land distribution was designed for army surveillance and control of the population, not for the functional development of productive agrarian communities as the army claimed in 'Poles of Development' propaganda. The model village plan destroyed the traditional village layout of scattered housing, a layout that allowed for cultivation of crops and care of livestock, replacing it with rows of tightly packed housing placed in an urban grid pattern, thus destroying agrarian production.

Genocide, terror and the sacred milpa

In his theorizing on cultures of terror, Michael Taussig wrote that the cultural elaboration of fear was integral to controlling massive populations.[91] The loss and destruction of milpa is present in every testimony not simply because it is the principle food source of the Maya, but because maize is sacred. Nobel Prize winning Guatemalan writer Miguel Angel Asturias wrote: 'The maize impoverishes the earth and makes no one rich. Neither the boss, nor the men. Sown to be eaten it is the sacred sustenance of the men who were made of maize. Sown to make money it means famine for the men who were made of maize.'[92] The Maya are the 'Men of Maize' and Maya origin stories begin with the birth of the Maya through maize.[93] Thus, Guatemalan army destruction of maize was a recurring ritual destruction of the Maya both physically and spiritually. This ritual destruction has new meaning under genocide law following the decisions of International Criminal Tribunal for the former Yugoslavia (ICTY) in its Rule 61 decision which identified three new (and more expansive) categories for consideration in the interpretation of the intent requirement for genocide: '(1) the general political doctrine of the aggressor; (2) the repetition of discriminatory and destructive acts; and (3) the perpetration of acts which violate or are perceived by the aggressor as violating the foundations of the group, whether or not they constitute the enumerated acts prohibited in the genocide definition, and so long as they are part of the same pattern of conduct.'[94]

As Perlin points out in her insightful work, the third category allows for the consideration of violations historically considered to be 'cultural genocide', violations previously excluded from legal consideration under the definition of genocide which was limited under the genocide convention to 'the construct of physical or mental destruction'.[95] Thus, in the CEH's analysis, acts of cultural destruction were considered to be 'signposts of the subjective intent of the attackers when they were committed together with the acts of physical destruction specifically proscribed in the Genocide Convention'. In the ICTY's broadened categories of intent, 'the bombing of sacred Maya lands used for religious worship ... the burning of huipiles ... the prohibition of ritual burial of the dead', and the destruction of other ritual icons 'were indicative of an intent to detroy the group, as such'. Perlin specifically notes that the 'religious and cultural significance that the Maya attribute to the cultivation of the land, and particularly of maize' was central to the CEH's conclusion that the army committed acts of genocide.[96]

For massacre survivors, the sacred milpa was prominent not only in testimonies of community loss and destruction, but also a potent symbol of community regeneration. The endurance and reinvention of ritual belief systems is an indication of their ongoing social and cultural significance. In the case of the Maya survivors, this significance is found not only in what was lost to the violence but also in what has been reconstructed in its aftermath. Just as the destruction and desecration of the milpa became a metaphor for army violation of the integrity of Maya communities, the resurrection of the milpa is a living metaphor of community rebirth.

Don Justicio, an Ixil community leader recounted the suffering and rebirth of his community through a story of the milpa:

> In the time of the violence, a moment arrived in which the sacred milpa, which gives us life, disappeared. From so much destruction of its very roots, it disappeared. Because the maize disappeared, there was a time in which the people had to live without maize. This was a time when many people died, many children died, because the sacred maize had been exterminated. But there was an elderly man who had a buzón and even though he had to displace himself many times fleeing the army, his buzón remained untouched. The sacred maize in his buzón was untouched. A moment arrived when he was able to return to his buzón to see what was there, to see if anything remained. He found a little bit of maize. And though he was hungry, he didn't eat this little bit of maize. No, he carried it back to the communities and handful by handful, he gave it to his friends, neighbours, and compañeros. Everyone had just a little bit because there wasn't very much. This was how we once again began to cultivate the sacred maize. After it was planted, we had our first harvest and once again we were able to make tortillas. After so many deaths, so much sadness, we were still able to cultivate our sacred milpa.[97]

Justice after genocide?

On 29 April 2004, the Inter-American Court issued its condemnation of the Guatemalan government for the 18 July 1982 massacre of 188 Achi-Maya in the village of Plan de Sánchez in the mountains above Rabinal, Baja Verapaz. The Inter-American Court attributed the massacre to Guatemalan Army troops. This is the first ruling by the Inter-American Court against the Guatemalan state for any of the 626 massacres carried out by the army in the early 1980s. The Court later announced the damages the Guatemalan state will be required to pay to the relatives of victims at $7.9 million.[98]

Beyond the importance of this judgment for the people of Plan de Sánchez, the Court's ruling is particularly significant because the following key points were included in the judgment: (1) there was a genocide in Guatemala; (2) this genocide was part of the framework of the internal armed conflict when the armed forces of the Guatemalan government applied their National Security Doctrine in its counterinsurgency actions; and (3) these counterinsurgency actions carried out within the Guatemalan government's National Security Doctrine took place during the regime of General Efrain Rios Montt who came to power through military coup in March of 1982.

Further, regarding the massacre in Plan de Sánchez, the Court indicated that the armed forces of the Guatemalan government had violated the following rights, each of which is consecrated in the Human Rights Convention of the Organization of American States: (1) the right to personal integrity; (2) the right to judicial protection; (3) the right to judicial guarantees of equality before the law; (4) the right to freedom of conscience; (5) the right to freedom of religion; and (6) the right to private property.[99]

The Plan de Sánchez case was considered by the Inter-American Court at the request of the Inter-American Commission which had received a petition from surviving relatives of the massacre victims. These survivors requested consideration within the Inter-American Court because of the lack of justice in the Guatemalan legal system. Since the Plan de Sánchez case was initiated in 1995, the Guatemalan Forensic Anthropology Foundation (FAFG) has carried out more than 300 exhumations of clandestine cemeteries of massacre victims in Guatemala. Each of these exhumations has included the filing of a criminal case with forensic evidence against the Guatemalan army and its agents. To date, only the Rio Negro case has been heard in a Guatemalan court and no army officials were included in the case which found three civil patrollers guilty.[100] Survivors continue to seek justice in local, national, regional and international courts.

In July 2006, the Spanish Court issued an international arrest order charging various former generals and military officials with genocide, terrorism, torture, assassination and illegal detention. Those charged include: General Efrain Rios Montt (head of state through military coup from March 1982 to August 1983); General Oscar Humberto Mejia Victores (head of state through military coup from August 1983 to January 1986); General Fernando Romeo Lucas Garcia (president of Guatemala from 1978 to March 1982); General Angel Anibal Guevara Rodriguez (Minister of Defence under Lucas Garcia); Donaldo Alvarez Ruiz (Minister of Interior under Lucas Garcia); Colonel German Chupina Barahona (Director of the National Police under Lucas Garcia); Pedro Garcia Arredondo (Chief of Command 6 of the National Police under Lucas Garcia); and General Benedicto Lucas Garcia (Army chief of staff during his brother's reign).[101] As of March 2007, none of these military officers have been extradited and each has filed numerous appeals to slow the process.[102] Moreover, they continue to make public justifications and/or deny any knowledge of human rights violations. While none of them have been jailed, the country of Guatemala is now their jail because INTERPOL agreements bind any country receiving a visitor on INTERPOL's international arrest order list as being immediately extraditable. Still, they continue to argue that self-granted amnesties give them immunity from prosecution as they live with impunity in Guatemala.

Moreover, the evidence suggests that we can and should make connections between practices and discourses of violence in the past and present. In the historigraphy of Guatemala, there is a particular lexicon that we can trace from

the 1980s (and probably earlier). In the 1980s, the military regimes: blamed the victims by calling them subversives; threatened anyone who opposed the repression; claimed amnesty for any crimes committed by the army; blamed the guerrilla for any killings or disappearances; and pleaded ignorance to the violence engulfing the country. In the 1990s, the army: blamed the massacre victims for causing the massacres; claimed the victims and survivors were subversives; threatened anyone who sought exhumations; claimed amnesty for any crimes committed; blamed the guerrilla for all violence; and pleaded ignorance for obvious army violence. After the Spanish Court issued its arrest warrant, the generals: claimed the Spanish judge was an ETA terrorist; threatened witnesses; claimed amnesty for any crimes committed; blamed the guerrillas for massacres; and pleaded ignorance. In the contemporary cases of *feminicidio* (the killing of women), extrajudicial executions and social cleansing, the justice system in general and the prosecutor's office in particular have: dismissed the victims as less than worthy by calling them gang-members; blamed gangs for all the violence; claimed social cleansing does not exist; claim witnesses will not come forward; and, continue to plead ignorance about all aspects of violence even though there are more murders per day now than there were in the late 1980s.[103] It is impunity – the violation of the law by those charged with upholding it – that connects the genocide of the past with the violence of the present. Keeping those connections clear and dissecting institutional responsibility for violence remain the tasks confronting contemporary and future scholarship on Guatemala.

Notes

1. This chapter draws on *Violencia y Genocidio en Guatemala* (Guatemala City: F&G Editores, 2003) and *Buried Secrets: Truth and Human Rights in Guatemala* (New York: Palgrave Macmillan, 2003). Special thanks to Dan Stone for his patience and for including my work on Guatemala in this volume, to Raul Figueroa Sarti for his unconditional love and support, and to Valentina for teaching me that I could write and be a mother at the same time. This chapter is dedicated to the survivors of the Guatemalan genocide. Any errors are mine.
2. All names of massacre survivors are pseudonyms.
3. URNG: Union Revolucionario Nacional Guatemalteca – Guatemalan National Revolutionary Union.
4. See Amnesty International (hereafter AI), *Guatemala: Massive Extrajudicial Executions in Rural Areas Under the Government of Efrain Rios Montt*. Special Briefing (New York: AI, 1982); AI, *Guatemala: Lack of Investigations into Past Human Rights Abuses: Clandestine Cemeteries* (London: AI, 1991); AI, *Human Rights Violations Against Indigenous Peoples of the Americas* (New York: AI, 1992); AI, *Guatemala: All the Truth, Justice for All* (New York: AI, 1998); Americas Watch (hereafter AW), *Little Hope: Human Rights in Guatemala, January 1984 to January 1985* (New York: AW, 1985); AW, *Guatemala: A Nation of Prisoners* (New York: AW, 1984); R. Carmack, *Harvest of Violence: The Maya Indians and the Guatemalan Crisis*

(Norman, OK: University of Oklahoma Press, 1988); R. Falla, *Masacres de la Selva* (Guatemala City: Editorial Universitario, 1992); Fundación de Antropología Forense de Guatemala (Guatemalan Forensic Anthropology Foundation – FAFG), *Las Masacres de Rabinal* (Guatemala City: FAFG, 1995); FAFG Exhumation Reports 1992 to 1998 on file in FAFG office; Oficina de Derechos Humanos del Arzobispado de Guatemala (ODHA), *Guatemala- Nunca Más*, Vols. 1–4; Informé Proyecto Interdiocesano de Recupaeración de la Memoria Histórica (REHMI) (Guatemala City: ODHA, 1998); S. Davis and J. Hodson, *Witness to Political Violence in Guatemala*. Impact Audit 2 (Boston, MA: Oxfam America, 1982); B. Manz, *Refugees of a Hidden War: The Aftermath of Counterinsurgency in Guatemala* (Albany, NY: State University of New York Press, 1988); C. Figueroa Ibarra, *El Recurso del Miedo – Ensayo sobre el Estado y el Terror en Guatemala* (San Jose, Costa Rica: EDUCA, 1991).

5. W. Churchill, *A Little Matter of Genocide: Holocaust and Denial in the Americas, 1492 to the Present* (San Francisco, CA: City Lights Books, 1997).
6. Falla, *Masacres de la Selva*.
7. For an excellent analysis of urban political movements, see D. Levenson-Estrada, *Trade Unionists Against Terror: Guatemala City 1954–1985* (Chapel Hill, NC: University of North Carolina Press, 1994); S. Jonas, *The Battle for Guatemala: Rebels, Death Squads and US Power* (Boulder, CO: Westview Press, 1991); J. Fried, ed. *Guatemala in Rebellion: An Unfinished History* (New York: Grove Press, 1983); and E. Galeano, *Pais Ocupado* (Mexico: Nuestro Tiempo, 1967). For a comparative analysis of Latin American movements, see A. Escobar and S. Alvarez, eds, *The Making of Social Movements in Latin* America (Boulder, CO: Westview Press, 1992). For more on urban state terror in Guatemala, see A. Peralta, *Dialectica del Terror* and Figueroa Ibarra, *El Recurso del Miedo*. See also J. Corradi, ed., *Fear at the Edge: State Terrorism in Latin America* (Boulder, CO: Westview Press, 1992). For an eloquent fictional portrayal of urban life during La Violencia, see A. Arias, *After the Bombs* (Willimantic, CT: Curbstone Press, 1990).
8. T. Barry, *Guatemala: The Politics of Counterinsurgency* (Albuquerque, NM: Inter-Hemispheric Education Center, 1986), p. 36. For excellent maps of military bases in Guatemala, see also CEH, *Memoria*, vol. II, 524–5.
9. See V. Sanford, 'The Moral Imagination of Survival: Displacement and Child Soldiers in Colombia and Guatemala', in *Troublemakers of Peacemakers? Youth and Post-Accord Peacebuilding*, ed., S. McEvoy (Notre Dame, IN: University of Notre Dame Press, 2006).
10. J. Schirmer, *The Guatemalan Military Project: A Violence Called Democracy* (Philadelphia, PA: University of Pennsylvania Press, 1998), p. 47.
11. Commission for Historical Clarification (CEH), *Guatemala: Memoria del Silencio*, 12 vols. (Guatemala City: CEH, 1999), Vol. 7, p. 53.
12. CEH, Vol. 7, p. 10. While the CEH provided comprehensive documentation of Guatemalan army human rights violations throughout the country, international and national human rights groups had been reporting these violations for years. See, for example, AW, *Closing Space: Human Rights in Guatemala* (New York: AW, 1988) and *Clandestine Detention in Guatemala* (New York: AW, 1993); AI, 'Guatemala: A Government Program of Political Murder', *New York Review of Books*, 19 March 1981, 38–40; AI, *Guatemala: The Human Rights Record* (London: AI, 1987); Davis and Hodson, *Witness to Political Violence in Guatemala*; R. Falla, ed., *Voices of the Survivors: The Massacre at Finca San Francisco* (Cambridge: Cultural Survival and Anthropology Resource Center Report No. 10, 1983). See also A. Arias 'Changing

Indian Identity: Guatemala's Violent Transition to Modernity', in *Guatemalan Indians and the State*, ed., C. Smith (Austin, TX: University of Texas Press, 1990), pp. 230–57; M. Diskin, *Trouble in Our Backyard: Central America and the United States in the 1980s* (New York: Pantheon Books, 1983).

13. Specifically violated were Articles 3, 5, 6, 9, 12, 17.2 and 20.1 of the UDHR; Articles 6, 7 and 9 of the ICPR; and, Articles 1 and 2 of the Convention against Torture.
14. Convention Against Torture, Article 2.1.
15. Guatemala became a signatory to the UDHR in 1948, the same year it was adopted by the UN. The Genocide Convention was adopted by the UN in 1948 and has been in effect since 1951. Guatemala approved signing the Genocide Convention in Decree 704 on 11 November 1949 and became an official signatory on 1 June 1950. The ICPR was adopted by the UN in 1966 and has been in effect since 1976; adopted by the UN in 1984, the Convention against Torture has been in effect since that same year. While Guatemala did not sign the ICPR until 1992 and the Convention against Torture until 1990, each of these conventions has been adopted and come into force with a majority of state signatories. When a majority of states agree to an international convention or protocol, it can be argued that this majority commitment represents a new standard of international customary law to which all states can be held accountable.
16. Specifically violated were Articles 3, 5, 6, 9, 12, 17.2 and 20.1 of the Universal Declaration of Human Rights (UDHR); Articles 6, 7 and 9 of the International Covenant of Civil and Political Rights (ICPR); and, Articles 1 and 2 of the Convention against Torture.
17. This shift from crimes against humanity to genocide is not unique to Guatemala. Indeed, the Nazi death camps were preceded by the brutal wave of selective killings by the *Einsatzgruppen* (mobile killing units) from 1941 to late 1942, which took the lives of approximately 1.5 million Jews as well as communists, partisans and Polish intellectuals, among others. See R. Rhodes, *Masters of Death: The SS-Einsatzgruppen and the Invention of the Holocaust* (New York: Knopf, 2002). For an excellent analysis of genocide in Bosnia and Rwanda, see E. Neuffer, *The Key to My Neighbor's House: Seeking Justice in Bosnia and Rwanda* (New York: Picador, 2001). On Rwanda, see also M. Mamdani, *When Victims Become Killers: Colonialism, Nativism, and the Genocide in Rwanda* (Princeton, NJ: Princeton University Press, 2001) and P. Gourevitch *'We Wish to Inform You that Tomorrow We Will Be Killed With Our Families': Stories from Rwanda* (New York: Farrar, Straus & Giroux, 1999).
18. G. Andreopoulos, 'Introduction: The Calculus of Genocide', in *Genocide: Conceptual and Historic Dimensions*, ed., G. Andreopoulos (Philadelphia, PA: University of Pennsylvania Press, 1994), pp. 14–15.
19. G. Black, *Garrison Guatemala* (London: Zed Books, 1984), p. 11.
20. US Department of State, 'Secret Memorandum. Reference: Guatemala 6366,' 5 October 1981, 1–2 Declassified January 1998.
21. Unclassified US Department of State. Confidential Action Memorandum To The Secretary of State; Subject: US Guatemala Relations: Arms Sales. No month or day specified but text indicates it was written before 4 December 1982 and after 2 November 1982, p. 1.
22. Unclassified US Dept. of State, 1982, p. 2.
23. Ibid., p. 3.
24. For known impact of La Violencia before CEH report, see n.4 above.
25. Article II of the convention. For complete Convention, see I. Brownlie, ed., *Basic Documents on Human Rights* (Oxford: Clarendon Press, 1992), pp. 31–4.

26. CEH, Vol. 5, p. 42.
27. For more on 'intentionality', see H. Fein, 'Genocide, Terror, Life Integrity, and War Crimes: The Case for Discrimination', *Genocide*, ed., Andreopoulos, pp. 95–107; A. L. Hinton, ed., *The Dark Side of Modernity: Toward an Anthropology of Genocide* (Berkeley, CA: University of California Press, 2002); D. Shelton, *Remedies in International Human Rights Law* (Oxford: Oxford University Press, 1999); P. Ronayne, *Never Again? The United States and the Prevention and Punishment of Genocide since the Holocaust* (Lanham, MD: Rowman and Littlefield Publishers, 2001); J. G. Heidenrich, *How to Prevent Genocide: A Guide for Policymakers, Scholars, and the Concerned Citizen* (Westport, CT: Praeger, 2001); A. Alvarez, *Governments, Citizens and Genocide: A Comparative and Interdisciplinary Approach* (Bloomington, IN: Indiana University Press, 2001); B. Kiernan, ed., *Genocide and Democracy in Cambodia: The Khmer Rouge, the United Nations and the International Community* (New Haven, CT: Yale University Southeast Asia Studies,1993).
28. CEH, Vol. 2, p. 315.
29. J. Perlin, 'The Guatemalan Historical Clarification Commission Finds Genocide', *ILSA Journal of International and Comparative Law*, 6 (2000), 396. See also B. Duhaime, 'Le Crime de Génocide et le Guatemala: Une Analyse Juridique', *Recherches Amérindiennes au Québec*, 29, 3 (1999): 101–6.
30. Central Intelligence Agency, 'Document Secret G5-41', 5 February 1982, p. 2. Declassified January 1998.
31. Ibid., pp. 2–3.
32. Perlin, 'The Guatemalan Commission Finds Genocide', 398.
33. Department of State, 'Secret Memorandum. Reference: Guatemala 6366. 5 October 1981', pp. 1–2. Declassified January 1998.
34. CIA, 'Document Secret', pp. 2–3.
35. See B. Kiernan, Genocide_Studies@Topica.ca, 8 March 2002.
36. Kiernan (Genocide Studies) points out that intention is determined by acts carried out deliberately rather than simply the motive behind them. Likewise, Shelton (email correspondence with author) argues that if genocide is the method to obtain land, the goal of obtaining the land does not preclude the intentionality of genocide.
37. Schirmer, *The Guatemalan Military Project*, p. 45.
38. D. Shelton, email communication with author, 12 March 2002. For more on the Velasquez–Rodriguez case, see Shelton, *Remedies in International Human Rights Law*, p. 221.
39. Kiernan, Genocide_Studies@Topica.ca.
40. Shelton, email communication with author, 12 March 2002.
41. Kiernan, Genocide_Studies@Topica.ca.
42. A. Riding, 'Guatemalans Tell of Murder of 300', *New York Times*, 5 October 1982, 7.
43. Ibid.
44. Perlin, 'The Guatemalan Historical Clarification Commission Finds Genocide', 399.
45. Schirmer, *The Guatemalan Military Project*, p. 47.
46. In the summer of 1995, I witnessed FRG campaign tactics firsthand in the K'iche' communities of San Andrés Sajcabajá. A group of party officials came to town with some 'engineers', who were ostensibly taking census information in order to bring electricity to these villages. As the 'engineers' wrote down the information and took measurements for the power lines, they explained that only houses with a blue flag (like the blue background of FRG) would receive electricity and that to obtain a blue flag, adults in the household needed to present their *cédulas* (national

identification cards) and sign a document. The document turned out to be FRG party registration. Given that the majority of local community members signed the document with their thumbprint, only those who were literate were able to see that they were not signing up for electricity, but rather for the FRG party.

47. Analysis on massacres in El Quiché in this section is based on massacre data presented in CEH, Vol. 10.
48. Ibid.
49. Analysis on massacres in Baja Verapaz in this section is based on massacre data presented in CEH, Vol. 8.
50. Analysis on massacres in Baja Verapaz in this section is based on massacre data presented in CEH, Vol. 8.
51. Analysis on massacres in Baja Verapaz in this section is based on massacre data presented in CEH, Vol. 8.
52. Analysis on massacres in Baja Verapaz in this section is based on massacre data presented in CEH, Vol. 8.
53. For more on Plan Victoria, see Schirmer, *The Guatemalan Military Project*; Barry, *Guatemala: The Politics of Counterinsurgency*; Guatemalan Church in Exile, *Guatemala: Security, Development and Democracy* (n.p.: Guatemalan Church in Exile, 1989); H. Gramajo, *De la guerra. ... A la guerra* (Guatemala City: Fondo de Cultura Editorial, S.A., 1995).
54. Schirmer, *The Guatemalan Military Project*, p. 44.
55. Ibid.
56. Ibid., p. 45.
57. Ibid., pp. 46–7.
58. Perlin, 'The Guatemalan Commission Finds Genocide', 407.
59. Ibid., 411.
60. CEH, Vol. 10, pp. 1012–213; Vol. 11, pp. 1384–8.
61. Schirmer writes (*The Guatemalan Military Project*, p. 45): 'No distinction is made between combatant and noncombatant ...'
62. CEH, Vol. 7, p. 10.
63. CEH, Vol. 10.
64. CEH, Vol. 2, pp. 226–7.
65. Ibid., p. 181.
66. CEH, Vol. 7, p. 164.
67. Ibid., p. 165.
68. Ibid., p. 166.
69. Ibid., p. 164.
70. For excellent analysis on the history and systematic incorporation of PACs into military strategy, see CEH, Vol. 2, pp. 158–234; ODHA, *Nunca Más*, Vol. 2, pp. 113–58.
71. Ejercito de Guatemala, *Las patrullas de autodefensa civil: La respuesta popular al proceso de integración socio-economico-politico en la Guatemala actual* (Guatemala City: Editorial del Ejercito, 1984), p. 16.
72. E. G. Martin, 'The Right Way to Fight Anti-Guerrilla Warfare', *Wall Street Journal*, 30 July 1981, 5.
73. Department of Defense, School of the Americas Academic Records 1947–1991, School of the Americas Yearly Lists of Guatemalan military officers trained at SOA released under Freedom of Information Act. The US Marines receive this same training. See Department of Defense, United States Marine Corps (MCI) 15 July 1997,

Operations Against Guerrilla Units, 1–23: 'Your objective is to KILL GUERRILLAS, NOT to hold terrain' [emphasis in original].

74. P. Levi, *The Drowned and the Saved* (New York: Vintage, 1988), p. 41.
75. This 30 percent draws on testimonies from massacres survivors in Ixil, K'iche', Achi, Keq'chi', and Kaqchiquel communities.
76. Nebaj testimony 6a C 3N6, 15 March 1997, p. 2.
77. Levi, *The Drowned and the Saved,* p. 79.
78. Nebaj testimony C 18 BN12, 14 March 1997, p. 1 of 1, b.
79. Levi, *Survival in Auschwitz,* p. 22.
80. 'Development as Counterinsurgency', *Central America Report,* 29 (July/August 1986): 1.
81. Guatemalan Church in Exile (GCE), 'Las Coordinadores Interinstitucionales', *Guatemalan Church in Exile,* 5, 2 (1985): 21.
82. Ibid.
83. A. Michaels, 'Poverty and Despair Prevail in Guatemala's "Model Villages"', *The Guardian,* 16 September 1987, 11.
84. Barry, *Politics of Counterinsurgency,* p. 23.
85. M. Simons, 'Massacres Spreading Terror in the Villages of the Maya', *New York Times,* 15 September 1982, 4. This article by Simons and articles by other journalists previously cited indicate there was international knowledge of the massacres and the incarceration of survivors by the Guatemalan army as the events unfolded – despite President Reagan's support of the regime. Indeed, a coalition of Native American organizations, Oxfam, and Cultural Survival, among others, ran a full-page advertisement in the *New York Times* denouncing the massacres. See 'Help Stop the War Against the Mayan Indians of Guatemala', *New York Times,* 3 January 1984, 9.
86. *Central America Report,* 29 (July/August 1986), 12.
87. *Guatemalan Church in Exile,* 4, 5 (September/October 1984), 6.
88. *Central America Report,* 29 (July/August 1986), 12.
89. *San Francisco Chronicle,* 23 January 1985, F5. In numerous testimonies in the Ixil Area as well as other Maya communities throughout the country, survivors consistently gave testimony to the need for permission from the army for any movement between or outside of villages and towns. Moreover, these authorizations quickly became a source of income through illegal taxing by military commissioners.
90. *Guatemala Human Rights Commission* (October 1987): 11.
91. Taussig, 'Culture of Terror', 469.
92. M. A. Asturias, *Hombres de Maíz* (Buenos Aires: Editorial Losada, SA, 1957), p. 12.
93. See 'Popol Vuh', trans., D. Tedlock, in *Popol Vuh - The Definitive Edition of the Mayan Book of the Dawn of Life and the Glories of Gods and Kings* (New York: Simon and Schuster, 1985); P. Mcanany, *Living with the Ancestors: Kinship and Kingship in Ancient Maya Society* (Austin, TX: University of Texas, 1995); and Asturias, *Hombres de Maíz.*
94. Perlin, 'The Guatemalan Commission Finds Genocide', 402.
95. Ibid.
96. Ibid., 402–3.
97. Nebaj testimony 3N8, 11 March 1997, p. 1 of 1.
98. www.corteidh.or.cr/seriecpdf/seriec_116_esp.pdf.
99. www.corteidh.or.cr/seriecpdf/seriec_105_esp.pdf.
100. For more on the Rio Negro Trial, see Sanford, *Buried Secrets.*

101. *El Periodico* (Guatemala), 8 July 2006, 1.
102. General Fernando Romeo Lucas Garcia appears to have died in Venezuela shortly before the arrest order was issued. The Spanish Court included his name in the Arrest Warrant because no death certificate was provided to them to demonstrate his death.
103. See P. Alston, Civil and Political Rights, Including the Questions of Disappearances and Summary Executions. Report of the Special Rapporteur on extrajudicial, summary or arbitrary executions, Philip Alston. Mission to Guatemala, 21–25 August 2006 (19 February 2007), p. 5.

22
Genocides of Indigenous Peoples

Robert K. Hitchcock and Thomas E. Koperski

Introduction

Indigenous peoples have been characterized as 'victims of progress',[1] 'invisible indigenes',[2] 'resource rebels',[3] and 'First Nations who are organizing to survive'.[4] Most, if not all peoples, who consider themselves to be indigenous or aboriginal have histories that include complex kinds of contacts with other peoples, some of which were negative. All too often, indigenous peoples have had to cope with efforts by other groups, governments, settlers, or transnational corporations to take away their lands and resources, sometimes by force or through the application of questionable means. As David Maybury-Lewis[5] notes, 'Indigenous peoples are those who are subordinated and marginalized by those who rule over them.' Patrick Brantlinger points out that the advent of Europeans in Australia, New Zealand, southern Africa, Latin America, and North America 'meant steep population declines in indigenous populations'. He goes on to say, 'One of the main causes for these declines is not mysterious: violence, warfare, genocide.'[6]

In many instances, indigenous peoples live in remote places that contain a variety of kinds of valuable resources that they wish to retain in the face of colonization. There were cases where indigenous peoples actively resisted incursions by other peoples as well as assimilation and cultural modification efforts by outside agencies. Their cultural distinctiveness and desire to maintain their lands and identities, combined with their relative lack of power as compared to state systems, resulted in indigenous peoples being prime targets of genocide. According to one non-government organization working on the issue of indigenous peoples' rights, the International Work Group for Indigenous Affairs (IWGIA), based in Denmark, 'an estimate of the number of indigenous people who die through violent means each year is 30,000.'[7]

The concept of 'indigenous peoples' is controversial, and various definitions have been offered by international organizations such as the United Nations and the World Bank, by governments, by non-government organizations, by scholars, and by members of groups who see themselves as indigenous.[8] There is no consensus on the meaning of the terms 'indigenous', 'indigenism', or 'indigeneity'.[9] A substantial number of governments do not recognize peoples within their borders as indigenous. In the case of Asia, for example, only one country, the Philippines, has officially adopted the term indigenous peoples, has a law aimed specifically at protecting the rights of indigenous peoples, and has a National Commission on Indigenous Peoples (NCIP). India has some 461 ethnic groups that are recognized as 'Scheduled Tribes'.[10] In Africa, countries such as Botswana argue that all citizens of the country are indigenous.[11]

Indigenous peoples tend to have a sense of cultural identity that members attempt to maintain, one that is generally distinct from that of the majority of the peoples in the countries where they reside. In many cases, indigenous peoples see themselves as descendants of the original inhabitants of a territory. Indigenous peoples are those that are 'aboriginal', 'native peoples', or 'first nations'. In many cases, indigenous peoples are ethnic minorities, and with very few exceptions they do not have control over the governmental machinery of the nation-states where they live. Self-identification as indigenous is an important criterion. Indigenous peoples often see themselves as marginalized, and in many countries, indigenous peoples did not have the right to vote or to take part in public policy formulation until relatively recently. Many members of indigenous groups believe that they lack a voice in civil affairs.[12]

Indigenous peoples in some cases are still on the land where their ancestors resided for generations. As the World Bank's Indigenous Peoples' Policy notes, indigenous peoples have 'collective attachment' to geographically distinct habitats or 'ancestral territories'; in other words, they have physical presence in and social, spiritual, and economic ties to lands and resources.[13] A number of indigenous peoples around the world have communal land tenure systems involving common property resource management and broad-based access. Land is held in the name of the group, not of individuals, and people do not have the right to buy or sell group land. It should be noted, however, that many indigenous peoples have been removed from their ancestral lands and the rights to those lands have been granted to the state (for example, in the form of national parks), to private companies, or to non-indigenous individuals. Most indigenous groups in the world today have suffered displacement from some or all of their ancestral lands. A substantial number of indigenous peoples reside in trans-boundary areas and thus are seen by states as being problematic as they are sometimes thought to have multiple allegiances.

There is a great deal of heterogeneity among peoples who define themselves – or who are defined by others – as indigenous. In some cases, indigenous peoples have customs and traditions that differ greatly from those of other groups.

They may speak indigenous languages, and take part in rituals and cultural activities that are distinctive. Some indigenous peoples have economies that are based in part on hunting and gathering, herding, or agriculture. At the same time, virtually all indigenous groups today are involved in the global economy to some extent, using money and earning incomes from the formal or informal economy (for example, selling crafts or natural resources such as honey, timber, or semi-precious stones). The rights to land and resources are key goals of the world's indigenous peoples, and they are enshrined in the only international human rights instrument that is binding on states, the International Labor Organization's Convention No. 169 Concerning Indigenous and Tribal Peoples in Independent Countries.[14]

Today, there are an estimated 350,000,000–600,000,000 indigenous peoples living in over half of the world's countries. It is notoriously difficult to get accurate statistics on small peoples, especially if they reside in remote places or ones where there is conflict. Many governments do not collect data on the ethnic backgrounds of the peoples in their territories. There is a dearth of reliable statistical information on indigenous peoples, in part, because of methodological difficulties in censuses, variation in the criteria used for identifying indigenous groups, and because of political pressures either to inflate or underestimate the numbers of people in question. Table 22.1 presents an estimate of current numbers and distributions of indigenous peoples. It should be stressed that these data are tentative, and that careful censuses of indigenous peoples and the use of agreed-upon criteria for indigenousness would provide a more accurate picture of the numbers and distributions of indigenous peoples world-wide. Being indigenous today sometimes confers some rights and benefits; in some parts of Latin America, such as Brazil and Peru, for example, indigenous peoples can gain title over land through land titling programmes. In the United States and Canada, members of American Indian groups and First Nations can get government health benefits. In some states in the U.S., American Indian tribes have the right to operate casinos, some of which generate substantial income for their tribal councils or their members.[15] A trend in some countries such as the U.S. is that people are identifying themselves as indigenous more now than was the case in the past.

Some members of indigenous groups want to employ a strict definition of indigenousness because they wish to limit the numbers of people who can claim indigenous identity. Governments sometimes refuse to recognize groups within their borders as indigenous because they do not want those groups to be able to appeal to international agencies such as the United Nations for assistance. Governments also have significant concerns over the possibility that indigenous groups might seek self-determination, and, in fact, genocides of indigenous peoples are often directed at groups who are challenging the state for greater recognition of their rights or seeking autonomy.[16]

Table 22.1 Estimated numbers of the world's indigenous peoples for 2005

Region	**Number of groups**	**Overall population**
North America (4 Countries)	250	328,667,927
Indians (Canada) (613 bands)		1,000,000
Indians (United States) (515 Tribes)		2,851,000
Inuit (Canada)		47,000
Central America (8 Countries)	370	147,338,108
Miskito (Nicaragua)		170,000
Zapotec (Mexico)		545,000
South America (14 Countries)	561	371,274,004
Ache (Paraguay)		1,800
Arhuaco (Colombia)		9,000
Mapuche (Argentina, Chile)		1,710,000
Yanomamo (Brazil, Venezuela)		24,700
Yora (Peru)		850
Russia	105	143,420,309
Khanty (3 Tribes)		21,500
Saami		1,775
Tribes of Siberia (30 Tribes)		199,900
Udege		1,920
Eastern Asia (7 Countries)	82	1,538,099,417
Ainu (Japan)		25,000
Bouyei (China)		3,157,700
Thao (Taiwan)		400
Melanesia (5 Countries)	1000	7,398,902
Papuans (312 Tribes)		2,209,000
South-East Asia (10 countries)	1400	571,337,070
Orang Asli (Malaysia)		130,000
Hill Tribes (Thailand)		570,000
Penan (Borneo)		12,000
South-Central Asia (14 Countries)	820	1,594,572,436
Adivasis (India)		89,500,000
Tribals (Bangladesh)		1,050,000
Australia and New Zealand	210	24,127,726
Aboriginals (Australia)		440,000
Maori (New Zealand)		550,000
Africa (57 Countries)	2000	887,223,445
Batwa (Pygmies) (8 Countries)		400,000
Bushmen (San) (6 Countries)		107,100
Hadza (Tanzania)		1,350
Maasai (Kenya, Tanzania)		1,359,000
Tuareg (6 Countries)		3,500,000
Grand Total	6798	6.5 billion 650,000,000

Note: Estimates generated by using population growth-rates and data complied from the following sources: United Nations Statistical Division, United Nations Unrepresented Nations and Peoples Organization, CIA Factbook 2005, GeoHive.com, International Mission Board, PeoplesGroups.org, Ethnologue.com, Survival International, Greenpeace, and World Bank.

The targeting of indigenous groups for genocide is a contentious issue, as will be discussed in this chapter. Some analysts see the entire 500-year history of the expansion of European states into the Americas, Africa, and Asia, and more recently the Arctic and the Pacific, as a genocidal enterprise.[17] There are debates over who, if anyone, is responsible for the destruction of indigenous groups. There are also discussions and disagreements over whether or not nation-states such as the United States or Brazil intentionally destroyed indigenous peoples on the basis of who they were. As Ronald Niezen points out, 'Indigenous peoples, like some ethnic groups, derive much of their identity from histories of state-sponsored genocide, forced settlement, relocation, political marginalization, and various formal attempts at cultural destruction.'[18] Genocides of indigenous peoples sometimes occurred because the people being targeted by the state were identified as secessionists or 'terrorists'. The Herero of South West Africa, now Namibia, were targeted by the German military for their having revolted against the colonial government in 1904 in the first genocide of the twentieth century.[19]

While historians, anthropologists, and human rights advocates have discussed genocides of indigenous peoples for well over a century, it was not until the 1980s and 1990s that comparative analyses of genocides of indigenous peoples became commonplace. Part of the reason for the expansion of interest in genocides of indigenous peoples was the massive increase in conflicts involving states and indigenous peoples, characterized by Bernard Neitschmann as 'the Third World War'.[20] Conflicts between governments and indigenous peoples were seen in many different parts of the world, including Central America (e.g. in Guatemala, Mexico, and Nicaragua), Bangladesh, Burma, Colombia, India, Indonesia, Laos, Malaysia, Peru, the Philippines, and Vietnam.[21] A second reason for the expanded interest in the human rights of indigenous peoples was the 500th anniversary (in 1992) of the arrival of Christopher Columbus in what came to be called the Americas. A third reason was the rise of indigenous activism in the 1960s and 1970s in the United States, Canada, Latin America, Asia, and the Pacific. Globalization has also played a significant role in these processes, with the expansion of governments, international agencies, and private companies into remote places and the efforts to intensify resource exploitation and utilize local labour.

In May 1992, a declaration was issued by representatives of indigenous peoples from around the world who attended the World Conference of Indigenous Peoples on Territory, Environment, and Development held in Brazil prior to the Earth Summit (the World Conference on Sustainable Development of the United Nations) in June 1992. The Kari-Oka Declaration and the Indigenous Peoples Earth Charter stated specifically, 'We continue to maintain our rights as peoples despite centuries of deprivation, assimilation, and genocide.' The Earth Charter noted 'There exist many examples of genocides against indigenous peoples.' It went on to conclude that the United Nations Genocide Convention must be changed to include a discussion of the genocide of indigenous peoples.[22] Questions were also raised about the impacts of transnational corporations on indigenous peoples.[23]

There have been debates and disagreements among analysts, governments, indigenous peoples' support groups, and indigenous peoples themselves as to whether specific sets of events constitute genocide. Some of these debates have revolved around issues of 'intent'. Others have focused on the question of whether actions taken by governments, groups, or militaries were aimed purposely at exterminating a people of the basis of who they were. A number of researchers have labelled actions taken against indigenous peoples as genocide if they included destruction of a people's culture, or, as some analysts have termed it, cultural genocide or ethnocide.[24]

This chapter focuses on the historiography and discussions of genocides of indigenous peoples primarily from the late 1960s to the present. The genocides that are addressed, however, extend over a much longer period, roughly the past 500 years. There are several reasons why there was a significant increase in attention paid to genocides and massive human rights violations in the 1960s and 1970s. It was in the late 1960s that the indigenous peoples' rights movement began to take shape. Several of the major indigenous peoples' human rights organizations were founded, including the IWGIA (1968), Survival International (1969), and Cultural Survival (1972).[25] There was a proliferation of organizations formed by indigenous peoples, such as the American Indian Movement (AIM), founded by Indian activists in 1968.[26] Liberation movements in the Third World picked up stream in southeast Asia, Africa, Latin America, and the Pacific.

There were high profile actions by indigenous peoples, such as the take-over of the island of Alcatraz in San Francisco Bay on 20 November 1969.[27] Articles were published on genocides of indigenous peoples in the late 1960s, notably one by Norman Lewis in the London *Sunday Times Magazine* that came out on 23 February 1969.[28] And it was in the late 1960s and 1970s that scholars and activists began paying greater attention to the struggles between Fourth World peoples and First, Second, and Third World states, some of it because of what they saw as illegal actions of states against indigenous peoples and both passive and active resistance to top-down development and exploitation by transnational forces.[29] In the field of anthropology, questions were raised in 1970 about the role of social scientists in the counterinsurgency efforts of the U.S. Department of Defense in southeast Asia, notably with respect to the Hill Tribes of Thailand, indigenous peoples who were drawn into struggle between pro-communist and anti-communist forces.[30] Indigenous peoples were also drawn into the anti-apartheid struggle in southern Africa, with San (Bushmen) being incorporated into the South African Defense Force (SADF) in the conflicts in Angola and Namibia.[31] As in so many instances where indigenous peoples were drawn into wars, San peoples suffered, and there were charges of genocide being perpetrated against the San.[32]

The historiography of genocide of indigenous peoples

A critical review of the literature on indigenous peoples reveals that most writers use a fairly broad definition of the concept of genocide. While some analysts use the definition of genocide as presented in Article 2 of the *United Nations Convention on the Prevention and Punishment of the Crime of Genocide,* others extend the concept to include such actions as intentional prevention of ethnic groups from practicing their traditional customs, forced resettlement, denial of access to development assistance, and destruction of the habitats or resources used by indigenous groups. In some cases, victim groups label actions as genocidal so as to bring about greater awareness of gross human rights violations on the part of the international community and, in so doing, prompt a response.

On 8 October 1948, the United Nations General Assembly adopted the *Convention on the Prevention and Punishment of Genocide.* Under Article 2 of the Genocide Convention, genocide means any of the following acts committed with intent to destroy, in whole or in part, a national, ethnical, racial, or religious group as such:

(a) Killing members of the group
(b) Causing serious bodily or mental harm to members of the group
(c) Deliberately inflicting on the group conditions of life calculated to bring about its physical destruction in whole or in part
(d) Imposing measures intended to prevent births within the group
(e) Forcibly transferring children of the group to another group.

It should be noted that the definition of genocide in the Convention was the product of a political compromise. It should also be pointed out that the Genocide Convention makes genocide a crime under international law. Acts punishable under the Genocide Convention include (a) genocide, (b) conspiring to commit genocide, (c) direct and public incitement to commit genocide, (d) attempt to commit genocide, and (e) complicity in genocide.

The use of the term 'genocide,' it is hoped by those who employ it, will bring about the condemnation of the perpetrator(s) and lead ultimately to the cessation of the actions that are harming indigenous groups and individuals. There is also a desire to see perpetrators of genocidal actions brought to justice. Primary concerns of scholars and activists dealing with indigenous peoples' genocides are (1) to understand factors involved in genocides, (2) to help develop sound conventions and warning systems to prevent genocide, and (3) to work out ways to cope with genocides and their consequences.[33]

An important criticism of the United Nations Genocide Convention revolves around the fact that it applies only to those collectivities specified in Article II, specifically, 'a national, ethnical, racial, or religious group as such.' Many indigenous peoples fall under the category of 'ethnical' collectivities, but at the same time indigenous peoples have organizations that are avowedly political in nature and have been dealt with harshly as a result. They would like to see the definition of genocide in the convention broadened to include political collectivities and classes.

Helen Fein offers a social scientific definition of genocide that is broader than that contained in the United Nations Genocide Convention: 'Genocide is sustained purposeful action by a perpetrator to physically destroy a collectivity directly or indirectly, through interdiction of the biological and sociological reproduction of group members, sustained regardless of the surrender or lack of threat offered by the victim.'[34] Indigenous peoples would like to see a definition of genocide along these lines as it is more inclusive that the current legal definition in the U.N. Genocide Convention.

Genocides involving indigenous peoples occur in a number of contexts, some of which are associated with open and hostile conflicts between groups (i.e. warfare). There are cases of genocide that have occurred in the absence of international conflict, however, as seen, for example, in the victimization of Batwa (Pygmies) during the Rwanda genocide of April–July 2004, when an estimated 30 per cent of the 30,000 Batwa in Rwanda were killed, the largest proportion of the three major ethnic groups in the country. Indigenous peoples issued calls at the United Nations and other forums for investigations of genocides of indigenous peoples. The prosecution of individuals for genocide should not, in the opinions of a number of indigenous peoples' organizations, be limited to war crimes but should include crimes against humanity, purposeful destruction of the habitats in which people live, rape, and sterilization.[35]

Groups that have been subjected to genocidal treatment often end up being victimized in a wide variety of ways: they may be enslaved; they may be deprived of their resources and property; and they may be relocated involuntarily to other places. Indigenous groups have noted that they have sometimes been exposed purposely to diseases that led to significant population losses.[36] The introduction and spread of diseases among indigenous peoples was seen as a kind of 'biological warfare' perpetrated by militaries, settlers, and the state. Some spokespersons for indigenous peoples in Africa have suggested that HIV/AIDS is an example of biological or 'germ warfare' aimed at indigenous and other Africans.[37]

Cultural genocide takes place under conditions of state imposition of educational and national language programmes, modernization, development, and nation building.[38] In many parts of the world indigenous peoples have been coerced or cajoled into giving up their languages and cultural traditions. States as diverse as Australia, Botswana, Canada, China, India, Russia, Turkey, and the

United States have required people living within their boundaries to learn national languages. In Australia, Canada, and the United States, indigenous children were removed from their families and sent to boarding schools and other state institutions where they had to learn national languages.[39] The removal of children from the families of indigenous peoples has been identified as either a genocidal action or one involving forced assimilation.[40] The widespread efforts to promote national educational curricula and the teaching of majority (as opposed to minority) languages have had significant impacts on language survival, with organizations like the United Nations Educational, Scientific, and Cultural Organization (UNESCO) predicting that half or more of the world's languages, many of them spoken by indigenous peoples, will be extinct by the end of the twenty-first century.

Eight countries, all of them containing sizable numbers of people who identify themselves as indigenous, account for more than half of all contemporary languages spoken on the planet: Papua New Guinea (832), Indonesia (731), Nigeria (515), India (398), Mexico (295), Cameroon (286), Australia (268), and Brazil (234).[41] The loss of language is part of a much larger process of the loss of cultural and intellectual property, something of great concern to indigenous peoples worldwide.[42] It is important to note, however, that there is a worldwide trend toward the teaching of mother-tongue languages, which is part of a larger process of ethnogenesis or identity enhancement.[43] In New Zealand, Maori is now an official language and is taught in over 350 schools. Efforts are on-going to promote mother-tongue language education among Native Americans, Latin American Indians, southern African San, Alaskan Indians and Inuit, Native Hawaiians, and other indigenous peoples. Some of this work is being done by faith-based groups (e.g. the Summer Institute of Linguistics) and some by anthropologists, educators, missionaries, and linguists, a number of whom are members of the Society for the Study of Indigenous Languages of the Americas or the Permanent International Committee of Linguists. As will be shown in the following discussion, issues involving both physical and cultural extinction are being addressed increasingly by social scientists, human rights workers, development personnel, members of faith-based organizations, and, importantly, indigenous peoples themselves.

A brief history of genocides of various indigenous peoples

Oral histories and stories of indigenous peoples throughout the world contain tales of massacres, murders, disappearances, enslavement, forced relocation, rapes, and taking of children away from their families. The expansion of European colonial societies in Latin America, North America, Africa, Asia, Australia, the Pacific, and the Arctic saw conflicts and mistreatment of indigenous and minority peoples, sizable numbers of whom died out as colonization and human and natural resource exploitation proceeded.[44] The contexts in which genocides of indigenous peoples varied. Indigenous groups suffered atrocities, massive human rights violations, and genocides in every part of the world (see Table 22.2). Indigenous peoples were attacked by militaries and paramilitary forces; they suffered at the hands of both right-wing and left-wing regimes, and they saw the resources upon which they depended destroyed purposely as well as unintentionally. Indigenous peoples as diverse as the San of southern Africa, the Adivasis of India, and the Maya of Central America were exposed to violence and trauma. In spite of the efforts to prevent genocide and to punish perpetrators, genocides have continued into the twenty-first century,

Table 22.2 Twentieth- and twenty-first-century cases of genocide of indigenous peoples

Group name	**Country**	**Date(s)**
Africa		
Barabaig	Tanzania	1990–2
Bubi	Equatorial Guinea	1969–79
Dinka, Nuer	Sudan	1983–2002
Efe Pygmies	Congo (DRC)	1994–present
Fur, Zagawa, Masalit	Sudan	2003–present
Herero	Namibia	1904–7
Hutu	Burundi	1972, 1988
Isaak	Somalia	1988–9
Karimojong	Uganda	1979–86
Lese	Congo (DRC)	1994–present
Mbuti Pygmies	Congo(DRC)	1994–present
Nuba	Sudan	1991–2002
San	Angola	1975–2002
Tuareg	Mali, Niger	1988–95
Tyua San	Zimbabwe	1982–3
Asia		
Agta	Philippines	1988
Amungme	Irian Jaya	1997
Armenians	Turkey	1915–18
Atta	Philippines	1987
Auyu	Irian Jaya	1989
Cham	Kampuchea	1975–9
Dani	New Guinea	1988
Higaonan	Philippines	1988
H'mong	Laos	1979–86
Jawara	India (Andamans)	1987–2001
Karen	Burma (Myanmar)	1992–present
Kurds	Iraq	1987–2003
Nasioi	Bougainville	1990–1
Penan	Malaysia	1986–9
Timorese	East Timor	1975–2002
Adivasis (Tribals)	Bangladesh	1977–1997

(*Continued*)

Table 22.2 (*Continued*)

Group name	Country	Date(s)
Central America		
Indians	El Salvador	1980–92
Maya Indians	Guatemala	1964–96
Maya Indians	Mexico	1994–9
Miskito	Nicaragua	1981–6
Latin America		
Ache	Paraguay	1952–76
Arara	Brazil	1992
Cuiva	Colombia	1967–71
Mapuche	Chile	1986
Nambiquara	Brazil	1986–7
Nunak	Colombia	1991
Paez	Colombia	1991
Pai Tavytere	Paraguay	1990–1
Ticuna	Brazil	1988
Waorani	Ecuador	1986–92
Yanomami	Brazil	1988–9, 1993
North America		
Indians	Canada	16th–19th centuries
Indians	United States	15th–19th centuries

as seen in the cases of the Batwa (Pygmies) of the Democratic Republic of the Congo. As Refugees International noted on its website in 2003, 'The Batwa have been accused of exchanging information, becoming spies, or joining an opposing side, and so often became victims of violence.'[45] There were reports by Human Rights Watch of Pygmies being cannibalized by soldiers in the Congo, which noted that 'Perpetrators have found that fear of cannibalism terrorizes victims more effectively... than does the simple fear of death.'[46] Indians in the Rio Parto area of Brazil, who live on the border of Mato Grosso and Amazonas states, were reported in June 2005 to be hunted down by heavily armed loggers who were shooting them on sight.[47] National indigenous people's organizations such as FUNAI (the National Foundation for the Indian) in Brazil and international indigenous people's advocacy organizations such as Survival International publicized the plight of the Rio Pardo Indians, and efforts were made to protect the Indians by securing land rights over indigenous territory of some 160,000 hectares. The problem facing the Indians and those who work with them, however, is ensuring that the protected status of the area is observed and loggers, miners, and settlers do not move in and take over, exterminating the residents of the region in the process.

In Brazil, Shelton Davis[48] estimated that more than 80 Indian tribes that came in contact with national society were destroyed between the beginning of the twentieth century and 1957, and the indigenous population of the Amazon dropped from approximately a million people to less than 200,000. As the indigenous peoples' support organization Survival International has noted in numerous *Urgent Action Bulletins*, Indians in Argentina, Bolivia, Brazil, Colombia, Chile, Ecuador, Paraguay, Peru, Uruguay, and Venezuela, among other countries in Latin America, have been exposed to massive human rights violations. In part because of the victimization they have experienced, groups such as the Guarani-Kaiowa in Brazil have had to cope with substantial numbers of suicides of people as young as nine years of age.[49]

It is interesting to examine the historiography of the genocides of indigenous peoples of Latin America and elsewhere. In *Thy Will Be Done: The Conquest of the Amazon: Nelson Rockefeller and the Age of Oil*, Gerard Colby and Charlotte Dennett describe in detail some of the atrocities committed against Indians in the Amazon Basin and point to people and organizations that they believe to be the perpetrators, including settlers, miners, governments, multinational corporations, missionaries, and the Central Intelligence Agency of the United States.[50] The book generated considerable interest and controversy, with faith-based groups in particular responding that the charges of missionary involvement in genocide, ethnocide, and counterinsurgency were false.[51]

In the past, the genocides and massive human rights violations perpetrated against indigenous peoples did not go unnoticed by members of colonial societies, some of whom sought actively to protect and promote the rights of indigenous peoples.[52] The Aborigines Protection Society (APS), formed in 1839, drew attention to the mistreatment of indigenous peoples in places as diverse as South Africa, Australia, and India.[53] There were different perspectives on the situations facing indigenous peoples. On the one hand, there were those individuals, characterized as 'realists', who saw cultural change, assimilation, and disintegration of indigenous societies as inevitable, and other individuals, often characterized as 'idealists', who saw that physical and cultural survival of indigenous peoples was not only possible but desirable.[54]

Part of the debate between the realists and the idealists revolved around the notion of indigenous peoples' 'preservation' and 'protection'. It was argued by the realists that the destruction of indigenous peoples and their incorporation into dominant national society was inevitable. To try and hold back this 'inevitable process' was seen as tantamount to promoting a kind of 'human zoo' approach in which indigenous societies are preserved for 'scientific curiosity, frozen in time'. On the other hand, the idealists felt that colonial policies of the British government were misguided and that indigenous peoples needed to be protected from the violence which was all too common in the culture contact situations occurring as colonialism proceeded.[55]

Many indigenous peoples, for their part, wanted not only protection but also the right of self-determination. They wanted to be able to live their own lives, free of imposition of non-indigenous concepts such as 'civilization' and Christianity. At the same time, there were those indigenous groups who accepted Christianity and were willing to modify some of their cultural practices, adopting, for example, Western styles of clothing and sending their children to school. Many indigenous groups engaged in non-indigenous work activities such as crop-growing, livestock herding, and commercial hunting (e.g. for meat or furs) for Europeans who had entered their areas. There were also what John Bodley terms 'civilization's unwilling conscripts' who were pressed into service as road builders, miners, and servants.[56] There were those indigenous groups who resisted what they saw as coercive policies of western societies, withdrawing into more remote areas or, alternatively, fighting back, as seen, for example, in the case of the Apaches of the southwestern United States and northern Mexico under Geronimo.[57] There has been a tendency on the part of states and some analysts to argue that indigenous peoples were, in effect, 'self-extinguishing,' that their 'savage customs' were the reason for their demise. In other words, states and agencies that have perpetrated genocide have blamed the victims and have attempted to avoid responsibility for their actions.[58]

One of the difficulties faced by activists, anthropologists, and others investigating genocidal acts is that most of the existing accounts are not from indigenous groups but rather come from the government, the military, or other agencies who have come in contact with these groups. Fortunately, indigenous peoples themselves are recording their experiences and telling their stories more often now than was the case in the past. This is sometimes done in autobiographical form, as can be seen in the example of Victor Montejo, a Guatemalan Quiche Maya Indian and anthropologist who described an attack on a village, Tzalala, where he was serving as a teacher in September 1978.[59] Guatemala, like some other countries in Central and South America, Africa, Asia, and the Pacific where indigenous people exist, saw oppression, genocidal massacres, and massive human rights violations over a 36-year period (1960–1996) in the twentieth century. The civil war and violence in Guatemala saw killings and disappearances of some 200,000 people, many of them members of indigenous groups.[60]

The situations of indigenous peoples in Guatemala are not without controversy, as can be seen in the first-person claims of genocidal actions by the state and the military against indigenous communities. In 1982, Rigoberta Menchu, a Quiche Maya activist produced a book with a co-author about her life, her indigenous activism, peasant resistance, and the loss of relatives at the hands of the Guatemalan military. Rigoberta Menchu subsequently received the Nobel Prize in 1992 for her support of indigenous rights. In 1999, the accuracy of Rigoberta Menchu's accounts was questioned by David Stoll, an anthropologist with extensive experience in Guatemala.[61] Stoll was careful not to criticize Rigoberta Menchu unfairly. He noted that her book was 'one of the most powerful narratives to come out of Latin America in recent times' and that it had a powerful impact on readers and had become a symbol of resistance against oppression.[62] He pointed out how important the book was in helping bring attention to the long struggle in Guatemala and how it led to pressure being brought to bear on the government and the military to negotiate for peace. Human rights imagery, he noted, played a powerful role in bringing resolution to the conflict in Guatemala.[63]

Stoll put the conflict in Guatemala in context in his book. He pointed out that while Rigoberta Menchu's book characterized the actions of the guerillas on the land as liberation fights, many peasants on the ground saw both the guerillas and government soldiers as threats to their well-being. Stoll saw a 'considerable gap between the voice of revolutionary commitment incarnated by Rigoberta and the peasant voices that [he] was listening to.'[64] Stoll struggled with the problem of taking issue with Rigoberta's powerful testimony at a crucial time in Guatemalan history – the run-up to a peace agreement – and with the idea of contradicting a native person's testimony because, as he put it, 'that would violate the right of a native person to tell her story in her own way.'[65] As an anthropologist, he was concerned with the reliability of oral testimony; at the same time, he realized full well that what came to be known in Latin America as *testimonios* reflected personal perspectives. He was of the opinion that *testimonios* were also regarded as testimony about specific events, and that reliability and accuracy were important issues.[66]

Stoll's book in some ways is an amplification and re-evaluation of some of the issues that Rigoberta Menchu raised in her work: the importance of land to the peasants of the country, the land use and development conflicts many Guatemalans were facing, the problems of 'ethnic subordination' and the struggles between indigenous and ladinos against the state and wealthy elites. He described the rise of the resistance movement and the factionalization that occurred in the social movements in Guatemala. He does not exonerate the guerillas for the human rights violations that they perpetrated, just as he does not exonerate the government and the military for their widespread violations of human rights in Guatemala. He makes the important points that one must look at both the victimizers and the victims carefully and that one should not withhold blame for those who committed atrocities. As Stoll says, 'Outsiders in search of clarity can easily overestimate the coherence and underestimate the ambiguity experienced by people trapped in a civil war.'[67] There were indeed cases, he admits, of villagers joining the insurgency as guerillas. At the same time, he points out, there were also cases where villagers opted to avoid taking part in the insurgency and who were as afraid of the guerillas as they were of the military. The degree to which the villagers were united in their opposition to the state was open to question, according to Stoll. At least some of them preferred to simply get on with their lives, growing their crops and raising their children.

There were cases, Stoll notes, where the government appointed local informers and *judiciales* (judicial police who functioned as marshals and detectives). These individuals then engaged in tracking down those who they defined as subversives and killing them extra-judicially. Although these individuals were essentially deputized by the state, which bears some responsibility for their actions, in Stoll's view, these individuals bear more of the blame for what they did.[68] Some of the peasants of Guatemala were victimized by both sides in the long civil war. Stoll concludes that 'failing to subject Rigoberta's account to critical judgment had definite costs.' He goes on to say:

> The most serious was to allow her internationally amplified voice to drown out the voices of peasants she was presumed to represent, who did not view the guerillas as a contribution to their needs, who instead viewed them as another tribulation, and who wanted the war to end far sooner than it did.[69]

The stories that Stoll heard were mainly narratives of victimization. As he noted, 'Refusing to judge whose story was more reliable would ... mean giving equal credibility to an army collaborator and the widow of the man he killed.[70] Stoll's work represents an important correction of Rigoberta's story, which, he notes, was used 'prop up at the international level a guerilla movement that had lost its credibility at home.'[71] Guerilla warfare is not an inevitable response from the poor, and human rights, peace, and justice can come about through non-violent means when indigenous peoples and others interact with the state. Stoll's account is in many ways 'the story of all poor Guatemalans' living in the midst of a civil war which had horrific consequences for tens of thousands of people, many of them indigenous peasants.

It should be stressed that Stoll's book generated major debates and controversy in the popular and academic literature.[72] Politically conservative writers seized on it as a justification for discrediting the indigenous and liberation movements in Guatemala. Liberal and left-wing writers attacked Stoll for what they saw as a deliberate effort to undermine Rigoberta Menchu and the peoples and ideals that she and her people represented. Stoll's scholarship and perspectives were attacked; it was noted, for example, that some of his interviews of individuals were conducted in the presence of other people, notably soldiers, something that could potentially bias seriously the points raised in the discussions.[73] Stoll disputes these charges, as do some of his colleagues, who argue that none of the interviews of villagers was conducted in the presence of armed soldiers. An important point arising from the debates about the work of

David Stoll is that relating to the importance of conducting interviews in private, the ways in which questions are framed, and the crucial significance of having a detailed understanding of the socio-cultural contexts in which statements are made when discussions are being held regarding complex human rights issues. Another conclusion is that, when writing about genocides and massive human rights violations, one must consider very carefully the social and political contexts and consequences of what one says.

Questions were also raised about the descriptions by anthropologists and journalists of the treatment of Ache Indians (sometimes called the Guayaki) in eastern Paraguay.[74] The Ache, who numbered some 900–1,000 people in the early 1970s, were described as having been killed off, having had their children taken away from them, chased down in 'manhunts', and treated inhumanely by the Paraguayan government and by settlers. The Paraguayan military established an Ache reservation where people were confined by force. There were charges of the deliberate withholding of food and medicine from the Ache. Entire groups of Ache were alleged to have disappeared as a result of deliberate murder, kidnappings, or the carrying out of both 'private and official hunts'. Reports on the situations faced by the Ache were published by the IWGIA in the 1970s and were followed by a series of books, reports, and media stories. The Catholic Church took a strong stance on indigenous peoples' rights, partially in response to the information on the treatment of the Ache. The government of Paraguay rejected the charges of genocide at meetings at the United Nations and in statements to the press.

Anthropologists and missionaries weighed in to the debates about what had transpired among the Ache, including ones working with or for some of the indigenous peoples' human rights organizations such as Survival International, Cultural Survival, and the IWGIA.[75] A bitter debate arose over the ways in which indigenous peoples advocacy groups portrayed the treatment of the Ache in the early 1990s.[76] Survival International reacted to an article in a New York newspaper by journalist Alexander Cockburn that said that the organization had exaggerated the facts concerning the treatment of the Ache. The charge of genocide was rejected by representatives of another indigenous peoples' advocacy group, Cultural Survival.[77] Survival International had sought to publicize the reports on the treatment of the Ache in the 1970s. The organization sponsored visits to Paraguay by observers, including Richard Arens, an international lawyer familiar with the Ache case. Survival also published a report on the Ache genocide issue.[78] When Cultural Survival's report denying that genocide was occurring in Paraguay was published, Survival International wrote to Cultural Survival, expressing their concern. Cultural Survival subsequently published an amended version of its report. Meetings between representatives of the two organizations addressed a number of issues, including the nature of the reporting, with Cultural Survival maintaining that their report was 'academic' as opposed to the more 'journalistic' reports produced by Survival International and the IWGIA.[79] A second issue discussed revolved around what was meant by the term 'genocide'. A third issue related to the nature of the evidence, including the degree to which first person testimony was utilized, when and how it was obtained, and who was responsible for the interviews and information.

Much of the debate about whether or not the Ache were subjected to genocidal treatment relates to the issue of government intent. As David Maybury-Lewis and James Howe put it in their report, 'The charge that the Paraguayan government has had an official policy of genocide against the Indians seems to us unlikely as well as unproven.'[80] The defense on the part of the government under Alfredo Stroesner was that they never had a systematic policy to exterminate the Ache or other Indian groups; instead, the Paraguayan government claimed, the approach to dealing with Indians was one of attempting to help them. The establishment of settlements was seen as one way of providing assistance to Indian peoples, though many Indians would disagree with that position given the conditions under which they lived in those settlements. The American media, in particular, was criticized for failing to pay greater attention to the 'tragedy of the Ache'.[81]

The Ache, it was argued by those who believed that genocide was being perpetrated, had to cope with a two-pronged policy, one of physical extermination, on the one hand, and enslavement and forced enculturation, on the other.[82] The International League for the Rights of Man submitted a statement to the Secretary General of the United Nations that charged the government of Paraguay with genocide, slavery, and torture. The Director of the Paraguay Indian Affairs Department was cited as being one of those individuals involved in the exploitation of young Ache women as slaves.[83] The Inter-American Commission on Human Rights of the Organization of American States also considered the Ache case. Other organizations that looked into the Ache case included the Anti-Slavery Society (now Anti-Slavery International, AAI), the U.S. Catholic Conference, the Conference of Catholic Bishops, the National Council of Churches, the Anti-Defamation League, the International Association of Democratic Lawyers, and the United Nations Sub-Commission on Prevention of Discrimination and Protection of Minorities.

In spite of the publicity, no sanctions were imposed on the Paraguayan government by the United Nations or by the United States, Paraguay's major donor. There were, however, some positive results from the publicity surrounding Ache genocide and ethnocide, including an expansion of the activities of non-government organizations working with Paraguayan Indian communities and pressure being brought to bear on the government by faith-based organizations and human rights groups to allow for greater native autonomy in Paraguay. The Paraguayan Minister of Defense, General Marcial

Samaneigo, attempted to browbeat representatives from religious organizations, government institutions, and non-government organizations into making a public degree that the accusations by Mark Munzel had been false. Debate continues about the Ache case, with some analysts suggesting, based on interviews and detailed field and archival work, that the original reports by Mark Munzel were overstated or, even worse, outright lies.[84]

Anthropologists Kim Hill and Magdalena Hurtado, who worked intensively with the Ache, question the application of the term genocide to the Ache case on the basis of their field data on Ache demography.[85] They point out that the most common cause of death was one where a person was killed by another individual. This was as true in pre-contact warfare as it was after contact. The colonists, they noted, did not want to exterminate the Ache but rather preferred to take their land and use the Ache as labourers on that land. According to Hill and Hurtado, one of the reasons that people opted to go to the reservations was to avoid warfare and conflict. Their data suggest that the Ache population was not in danger of extinction but rather it was growing rapidly at the time of the alleged genocide. Hill and Hurtado also question the accuracy of Munzel's figures on deaths and captures of children, saying the Munzel's number is almost twice the size of the entire Northern Ache population in 1968.[86]

Nevertheless, anthropologists, educators, native leaders, and members of religious organizations continue to feel that the treatment of the Ache was ethnocidal if not genocidal, and that the debate over the Ache case was positive in terms of bringing greater pressure to bear on the Paraguayan government to change their policies and resulted in increased international awareness of the severity of some of the issues faced by indigenous peoples.

Genocide and ethnocide in Australia

A third set of cases involving alleged physical and cultural genocide against indigenous peoples is that in Tasmania and the Australian mainland.[87] As Jared Diamond notes, one way in which Europeans dealt with Aboriginals was to shoot them.[88] Within a century of European colonization of Australia and Tasmania, substantial numbers of Aboriginal Australians and Tasmanians had died, some of them because of direct conflict with Europeans, and many more because of disease or starvation. Some of the classic descriptions of physical genocide perpetrated against indigenous peoples come from treatments of what happened to Tasmanian Aboriginals in the early 1800s.[89]

It should be noted that there is considerable debate about the issue of Tasmanian genocide. Issues raised in this debate range from the historical accuracy of the reports on genocide to the questions of 'intent' and 'consciousness' when it came to the actions of settlers.[90] Violet acts against Tasmanian Aboriginals began almost immediately after settlers arrived on Tasmania in

1803–4. According to Plomley,[91] British policies resulted in the destruction of some 4,000–7,000 Aboriginal Tasmanians, most of them between 1803 and 1847. Famine conditions set in early on in the Derwent River settlement in Tasmania, resulting in the settlers hunting kangaroos, emu, and other resources on which Aboriginals also depended. As settlers moved out further and further from the settlements in search of game, they came into increasing contact with Aboriginals who were also depending on those same resources. Clashes occurred, and both Aboriginals and settlers died. By 1824, the settler population had increased to some 12,000 people, and livestock numbers, especially sheep, had expanded considerably. According to Ryan [92] the sheep population increased more than twelve-fold, from 54,600 in 1816 to 791,120 in 1828. Land was allocated to settlers for grazing purposes. Efforts were made by the colonial government to engage in what in effect was an enclosure movement, dispossessing the Aboriginals and granting the land to settlers. These processes set the stage for the so-called 'Black War' (1825–30) which resulted in the killings of hundreds of Tasmanian Aboriginals as well as a number of whites. Aboriginals were labelled 'black crows' or 'black vermin' by the British settlers on Tasmania in an effort to dehumanize them. From an estimated 3,000–4,000 people in nine different sociopolitical groups, each with 6 to 15 bands (co-residential groups of people who were tied together by kinship, marriage, friendship, and reciprocity) at the time of contact, the numbers of Aboriginals declined to 'a few hundred' by the middle of the nineteenth century, in part, as a result of violence perpetrated against them.[93]

In 1825, an effort was made to establish a native reserve on Tasmania, but it failed due to economic difficulties and a concern on the part of the government with potential threats to the well-being of 'the colony' by 'bushrangers' (people, many of them settlers, who had become, in effect, outlaws).[94] Two strategies were proposed by the government authorities: either 'hunt the Aboriginals down' or relocate them elsewhere (for example, to the outer islands in Bass Strait). There were also those who maintained that Aboriginals should be given land rights and allowed to pursue their own lifestyles.[95] In November 1828, martial law was declared by the British authorities.[96] Bounties were offered to settlers for the capture of Aboriginal adults and children. The exploitation, rape, mistreatment, and killing of Aboriginal women by settler males contributed significantly to the rising tensions between settlers and Aboriginals on Tasmania.[97] The tensions ultimately led to what can be described as a guerilla war between Aboriginals and settlers, a process that, in many ways, helps set the stage for frontier genocides.[98]

It is important to note that the Aboriginals were not passive victims of extermination efforts; rather, they fought back and exacted serious losses among the settler population. Their resistance only served to fuel the desire for ruthless measures to be taken against them by the settlers. In 1830, the Tasmanian government came up with the idea of a 'final solution' to the 'Aboriginal problem'. The lieutenant governor of Tasmania, George Arthur, proposed a kind of 'game drive' in which armed settlers would be arrayed along a line some 50 m apart and would push forward, killing or capturing Aboriginals. Some 2,000 soldiers, settlers, convicts, and police constables took part in what came to be called 'the Black Line', the largest group of individuals brought together to fight Aboriginals in the history of the colonization of Australian and Tasmania. As it worked out, the forces on the Black Line encountered serious obstacles; some of the soldiers were killed in friendly fire incidents. Two Aboriginals were killed and two were captured, one of whom later escaped.

The Black Line represented the end of major hostilities between Aboriginals and settlers. Government policy changed after that, with a greater emphasis on 'civilizing' the Aboriginals, those who were left after the Black War and the decimations of disease, environmental degradation, and starvation. There were advocates who spoke out on behalf of the Tasmanian Aboriginals, notably George Robinson, who played a role as a conciliator but who contributed to Aboriginal decline through assimilation and relocation efforts.[99] The Committee for Aboriginal Affairs in Tasmania had recommended the resettlement of the remaining Aboriginals on Flinders Island, a relatively large island a significant distant away from the coast of Tasmania. Some of the children of the Aboriginals were taken from their families and taken to a boarding school in Hobart, the capital.

As Mark Crocker[100] notes, 'The Tasmanians had everything [on Flinders Island] except decent water, adequate provisions, sanitary quarters, good health, and the will to live.' Flinders Island, like so many settlement schemes for indigenous peoples around the world, became, in effect, a death trap. Mortality rates from disease and malnutrition among the Aboriginals were substantial, and some people who visited the settlement said that they thought that the policy being pursued on Flinders was aimed deliberately at extermination.[101] Eventually, 47 Aboriginals (15 adult males, 22 adult females, and 10 children) were able to petition successfully for their return to the mainland, and they were settled in a small locality at Oyster Cove, not far from Hobart. The last full-blooded Aboriginal, Truganini, died in 1876, ending what some Europeans saw as 'the Aboriginal problem', thus enabling them to reject any future Aboriginal claims for land and human rights.

But even in death, indigenous peoples' remains are all too often subjected to desecration. The Royal Society of Tasmania applied in 1878 for permission to disinter Truganini's remains so that they could keep them in their collections. While there was an agreement that her remains would not be placed on display, the Royal Society did, in fact, display her skeleton in the Tasmanian Museum and Art Gallery until 1947.[102] Indigenous peoples like the Tasmanian Aboriginals have sought to have museums, universities, and other institutions return the remains of their members along with cultural property for reburial, something that was done with the remains of Truganini after a drawn-out effort by Tasmanian Aboriginals and their supporters to have Truganini's remains repatriated. In 1976, after many efforts by the state to resist turning over the remains to Aboriginals, Truganini's remains were cremated and her ashes scattered by an Aboriginal elder over the D'Entrecasteaux Channel in keeping with Truganini's original wishes, a century after her death. Thus, it was not until the last quarter of the twentieth century that Tasmanian Aboriginals were recognized as having a common cultural identity and having rights like those of other Australians.[103]

As is the case with many of the other reported genocides of indigenous peoples, there is vigorous debate about the 'received wisdom' concerning the genocide of Tasmanian indigenous peoples.[104] The Tasmanian governments and the federal Australian government reject the charge of genocide, as do many politicians. Much of this debate revolves around the definition of genocide and the issue of 'intentionality'. A common response to the charge of genocide of indigenous peoples (or other victims of genocides and massive human rights violations) is that the deaths and destruction occurred inadvertently and were not a result of deliberate policy. Another response to the charge of genocide is that the situations of indigenous Tasmanians worsened because of 'benign neglect', not overt policy aimed at extermination. Denial of genocide has been a feature of some of the debates about what occurred in Tasmania. The failure of the 'Black Line' to capture or kill even a small percentage of the Tasmanian aboriginals was cited as evidence of a lack of a genocidal policy. The fact that there were efforts to help aboriginal Tasmanians was seen as proof that genocide was not the avowed aim of the Australian state or of individuals in Tasmania. Finally, there is also a sense of inevitability in governmental views of what happened to the indigenous peoples of Tasmania: that they were, like many other indigenous groups, 'vanishing peoples'.[105]

The debate over 'uniqueness' of specific genocides

Perhaps the most contentious debate over indigenous peoples' genocides erupted in the 1990s with the publication of two books, David Stannard's *American Holocaust: Columbus and the Conquest of the New World* and Ward Churchill's *A Little Matter of Genocide: Holocaust and Denial in the Americas: 1492 to the Present.*[106] Stannard and Churchill argued that Native Americans had been subjected to genocidal treatment, and they provided documentation of large-scale reductions in the numbers of indigenous peoples in the Americas. They questioned what they saw as a tendency in the literature on the Holocaust to characterize the Holocaust as unique. This debate, which became extremely polemical, even saw charges that people writing about the Holocaust were denying the existence of other genocides including those of Native Americans.[107]

The gist of the debate about the 'uniqueness' of the Holocaust focuses in part on the issue of whether the Holocaust was indeed different or whether it should be viewed as but one of a large number of examples of mass murder in human history.[108] The efforts to historicize the Holocaust and other genocides have seen comparisons made among various genocides. At the same time, there are those analysts who argue that such comparisons are inappropriate and that the Holocaust is unique on a number of grounds, including the planned and systematic extermination of six million Jews by a highly organized state apparatus.[109] There was also a trend in the literature in the 1990s that characterized the persecution of other groups besides Jews as examples of 'hidden' or 'forgotten' holocausts.[110] Clearly, the Holocaust had become politicized, and there were efforts to counter what some researchers saw as an attempt at 'normalization' of the Holocaust or 'demystification'.[111]

Steven Katz, in his book, *The Holocaust in Historical Context,* pointed out that the Holocaust was unique, in part, because of the deliberate intent of Hitler and the Nazis to physically eradicate every Jewish man, woman, and child.[112] He went on to redefine the term genocide, saying, 'the concept of genocide applies *only* when there is an actualized intent, however successfully carried out, to physically destroy an *entire* group (as a group is defined by the perpetrators).'[113] In his view, no other cases of mass killing warranted the term 'genocide'. Katz's position was attacked by several authors in the volume *Is the Holocaust Unique?*[114] One of the contributors, David Stannard, said that those scholars who sought to emphasize the uniqueness of the Holocaust were in essence denying all other genocides and thus were falling into the trap of diminishing the sufferings of other peoples. One impact of this tendency, he suggested, was that it provided 'a screen against which opportunistic governments today attempt to conceal their own past and ongoing genocidal actions.'[115] Stannard went on to say that public ignorance of the 'genocidal and racist horrors against indigenous peoples' that have been perpetrated by nations in the Western Hemisphere, including the United States is 'consciously aided and abetted and legitimized by the actions of Jewish uniqueness advocates'.[116]

A concern expressed by Stannard in his volume *American Holocaust* was that some victims of mass killings were seen as 'more worthy' than others.[117] Native Americans, who in Stannard's view, were killed in substantially larger numbers in North America (some 50–100 million people, he estimated) than in the Holocaust.[118] He rejected the notion that many Native American deaths were from 'natural causes' like disease, saying that Indians died directly or indirectly at the hands of Europeans and Euro-Americans.[119] Stannard describes the United States' destruction of its indigenous peoples as 'the most massive interrelated sequence of genocides in history of the world'.[120] He claims that the efforts to eradicate Native Americans were more successful than was the case for the Nazis in the Holocaust, with 90–95 per cent of the indigenous population of North America being wiped out, compared to what he calculated to be 66 per cent of European Jews.[121] In Stannard's view, the scholars who advocated the uniqueness of the Holocaust were in effect denying the existence of other genocides and were thus contributing indirectly to greater possibilities of genocides to be perpetrated in the future.

As Gavriel Rosenfeld notes, the attacks on the uniqueness concept by Stannard, Churchill, and others (e.g. Norman Finkelstein and Ruth Birn[122]) generated considerable controversy and debate among genocide scholars both in print and on the worldwide web.[123] The quality of the scholarship of Stannard and Churchill were attacked, as were their motivations and political positions. A critical issue that arises concerning the Holocaust and the destruction of Native Americans relates again to that of *intent*. While certainly there were many cases where government officials, military officers, and settlers expressed a desire for American Indians to be physically destroyed, many of the deaths that occurred were a result of the impacts of various diseases, albeit ones contracted originally through contact with Europeans and Euro-Americans. There were certainly cases of genocidal massacres, a particularly horrific example of which was the purposeful destruction by 700 U.S. volunteer soldiers of over 150 Arapaho and Cheyenne, many of them women, children, and elderly persons, at Sand Creek, Colorado on 29 November 1864.[124] Like other cases of genocidal massacres, the killings at Sand Creek were preceded by calls in Colorado for the extermination of Indians and seizing of their property.[125] Spokespersons for the Northern Arapaho Tribe, the Northern Cheyenne, as well as the Southern Cheyenne Tribe and the Arapaho Tribe of Oklahoma, have called for greater attention to be paid to the events at Sand Creek and for commemoration of the place where so many Arapaho and Cheyenne died. They, along with representatives of many Native American groups, have called for the United States to issue a formal apology to Native Americans for the treatment that they received, an apology which has yet to be made.[126]

The contexts of indigenous peoples' genocides

Indigenous peoples have been the victims of genocidal acts on the part of states and other entities (for example, transnational corporations), in part, because of some of the ways in which they have been represented in the media and in conversation by members of the state or of dominant societies. Members of indigenous communities, or indigenous peoples as collectivities, have been variously described as 'brutes', 'savages', 'vermin', 'primitives', or 'nuisances'. These negative stereotypes have been employed, in part, as justifications for actions by states and other entities such as settler organizations ranging from dispossession to extrajudicial killings and from exploitation of labour under unfair conditions to the torture and mistreatment of members of indigenous groups. Negative stereotyping of indigenous peoples is seen especially in situations where there are conflicts over resources or resistance efforts by indigenous groups in places as far apart as the Philippines, Brazil, Bangladesh, Burma, Indonesia, Guatemala, and Zimbabwe.[127]

Indigenous peoples possess a number of characteristics that are important to their identity, on the one hand, but that expose them to some degree of risk, on the other. Indigenous peoples generally possess ethnic, religious, or linguistic characteristics that are different from the dominant or numerically superior groups in the societies of which they are a part. They also tend to have a sense of cultural identity or social solidarity that many indigenous group members attempt to maintain even in the face of efforts to bring about cultural modification and change. In some cases, members of indigenous communities attempt to hide their identity so as not to suffer racial prejudice or poor treatment at the hands of others. On the other hand, there are many members of indigenous groups who proclaim their ethnic affiliation proudly and openly. Indeed, an important criterion for 'indigenousness' is the identification by people themselves of their distinct cultural identity. There are a number of cases where indigenous peoples who have resisted invasions or other actions have been defined as 'terrorists', although indigenous groups involved in the resistance see themselves as freedom fighters or as promoters of indigenous peoples self-determination.

Most, but not all, indigenous groups are ethnic minorities who tend to lack power, feel that they are marginalized from the political process, and are disenfranchised. Many, if not most, indigenous peoples prefer to reserve for themselves the right to determine who is and is not a member of their group. Their actions are sometimes viewed as exclusionary by outside agencies, which seek to usurp the rights of indigenous peoples to make decisions about group membership and affiliation. This was true, for example, of the United States, which sought to do away with the trust relationship between Indian peoples and the state in a process known as 'Termination'. The United States also sought to settle all outstanding land claims through the Indian Land Claims Commission.[128]

The government of India, like Botswana, maintains that all people in the country are indigenous. At the same time, the government of India does designate tens of millions of its citizens as 'tribals' (Adivasis, 'Scheduled Tribes'). There are also 'Scheduled Castes' designated under the Indian Constitution. These groups are provided with assistance, including places in Indian institutions of higher learning. In some cases, such as with the Nagas, the government of India is engaged in actions aimed at undermining their efforts at self-determination.[129] India has also sought to make contact with groups such as the Jarawa and the Onge on the Andaman Islands in order to settle them down, making way for timber companies, road-building operations, and tourism.[130]

The Chittagong Hill Tracts in southeastern Bangladesh, near the border with India and Burma, contain over a dozen distinct tribal peoples, known in South Asia as Adivasi and to themselves collectively as Jummas. Since the founding of the nation-state of Bangladesh in 1971, the peoples of the Chittagong Hills have had to cope with Bangladesh government efforts to pacify and control the region, carry out counter-insurgency operations, resettle people in protected villages, engage in land reform and development efforts, and encourage Bengali settlers from the plains of Bangladesh to establish homes and farms in the hills.

The peoples of the Chittagong Hill Tracts are socially, culturally, and linguistically distinct from the majority Bengali population of Bangladesh. Most of the Chittagong tribal peoples are not Muslims but rather Buddhists, Hindus, Christians, or animists, those practicing indigenous religions. The Chittagong Hill Tracts people have been the targets of religious and cultural oppression. Their traditional agricultural practices involving shifting cultivation (also known as swidden, or slash and burn, horticulture) have been criticized by the Bangladesh government, which has attempted to transform the land use and tenure system in the Chittagong Hills. The construction of a hydroelectric dam at Kaptai on the Karnafuli River in the Chittagong Hills in the early 1960s saw 100,000 people displaced and over 40 per cent of the arable land in the region inundated. The Bangladesh government has encouraged the development of commercial plantations for coffee, cocoa, and spices, mostly owned by outsiders. Timber concessions were been granted to companies and individuals, and the rate of deforestation in the Chittagong Hills expanded considerably.

Today the Chittagong Hills have some 600,000 residents, approximately 1 per cent of the total population of Bangladesh. The various indigenous groups, such as the Chakma (Saksa), Mru, Marma, and Tripura, have their own traditions, social systems, forms of leadership, and belief systems and see themselves as distinct from each other. At the same time, they identify themselves as indigenous to the areas where they reside, and they claim customary rights over the land and its resources. Bangladesh government initiatives to reform the land tenure system have met with stiff resistance. The indigenous peoples of the Chittagong Hills have formed political parties, one of which, the Jana Samhati Samiti (JSS), the People's United Party, has an armed wing, the Shanti Bahini (Peace Forces). The Shanti Bahini, which carried out attacks on government military forces, often in response to massacres and the burnings of villages, was outlawed in both Bangladesh and India.

The peoples of the Chittagong Hills have attempted to negotiate with the Bangladesh government for autonomy for the region, recognition of local peoples' land rights, the establishment of its own legislature, and land recognition of traditional tribal authorities. There has also been a strong desire among the tribal peoples of the Chittagong Hills for the cessation of settlement by outsiders in the hills. The Bangladesh government responded with increased pressure on the Chittagong Hill populations, engaging in military operations where local people were killed, their homes and farms burned, women were raped, people were forcibly relocated, and temples, churches, and traditional sacred sites destroyed. Sizable numbers of tribal peoples were displaced internally in Bangladesh, while others fled across the borders into Burma and India as refugees. International human rights groups decried what was occurring in the Chittagong Hills, and delegations were sent by organizations such as Amnesty International to investigate the situation.

The Chittagong Hill Tracts Commission is an independent body established to investigate allegations of human rights violations in southeastern Bangladesh. In November 1990, the Chittagong Hill Tracts Commission received permission to visit the region and to conduct interviews of local people, which were carried out in 1990–1. The testimonies cover a wide range of subjects, from mass murder, disappearances, and rape to destruction of property, involuntary relocation, and religious oppression.[131] Problems continue to face the dozen indigenous groups as well as many of the Bengali settlers in the Chittagong Hills today. The lack of security, on-going attacks, the failure of the government of Bangladesh to withdraw the military as per the peace agreement of 1997, dissension among various political parties and organizations, and grinding poverty characterize the Chittagong Hills in the twenty-first century.[132]

An example of a current genocide is that of Darfur in Sudan, Africa's largest country. The situation in Darfur (which means, literally, 'land of the Fur'), has been on-going since February 2003. Darfur's population was approximately 6,500,000 in 2005. Two rebel groups are operating in the Darfur region: the Sudan Liberation Army and Movement (SLA/M) and the Justice and Equality Movement. These groups drew some of the recruits from three ethnic groups in Darfur: the Fur, Zaghawa, and Massalit. These groups defined themselves as Africans (as opposed to Arabs), and many of them, like the Arab populations in Sudan, are Muslim. As John Heffernan and David Tuller note, 'While parties in the conflict refer to themselves, and each other, as "Arabs", and "Africans", the main distinguishing characteristics are not skin colour or religion – members of both groups are black and Muslim – but language, occupation, ethnicity, and culture.'[133]

There has been targeting and deliberate destruction of civilian populations by the government of Sudan and its allies (in this case, the Janjaweed militias). Gross human rights violations are being perpetrated. Rape is being used as a weapon against the civilian population. A scorched earth policy has been carried out in the region. Hundreds of villages have been destroyed. Helicopter gun ships and jet bombers have been used along with ground troops. Water sources have been poisoned, crops, and stocks of seeds destroyed, and irrigation systems disrupted. Food has been used as a weapon against the civilian population, with the government of Sudan disrupting humanitarian efforts to help local communities. People have been forced to leave their homes, and some have crossed the border into Chad as refugees while others are internally displaced in Sudan (some 2,000,000 people). The actions there fit category c of the United Nations Genocide Convention, with destruction of livelihoods and habitats of targeted populations.[134] An estimated 200,000–220,000 people have died directly at the hands of the government of Sudan and the Janjaweed, and thousands of villages have been destroyed.[135] As was the case with the Hereros in Namibia in the early part of the twentieth century, the people of Darfur are being deprived of their lives and livelihoods and are being forced into the desert where many of them face starvation.

Secretary of State Colin Powell and the U.S. House of Representatives declared the events in Darfur as constituting genocide in June 2004. United Nations Security Council Resolution 1593 referred the situation in Darfur to the International Criminal Court (ICC). Currently, there is an African Union (AU) peace-keeping force in Sudan, but it is under-funded and under-equipped. A number of international organizations are monitoring the situation in western Sudan, including the International Crisis Group, Human Rights Watch, and the United States Atrocities Documentation Team (ADT).[136] Nevertheless, the killings, ethnic cleansing, rapes, and destruction of communities go on. The government of Sudan continues to maintain that the situation in Darfur is an internal matter. No formal international sanctions have been brought to bear on the government of Sudan for its actions, although the United States, among other countries, has called for sanctions to be imposed.

In the case of West Papua (sometimes referred to as Irian Jaya), the government of Indonesia, the fourth most populous country in the world, stepped up its actions against local populations in the late 1990s.[137] There are some 312 ethnic groups who together number some 1,000,000 people in West Papua, an area the size of France. Indonesia has controlled the area since the early 1960s. Targeting of local populations has been done by the Indonesian military and militias. As of 2006, some 100,000 people had died as a result of Indonesian government actions. The situation in West Papua was exacerbated by the World-Bank funded Transmigration Programme which brought thousands of people from Java, Sumatra, and other Indonesian islands to settle in West Papua.

An armed group seeking independence from Indonesia is Organisasi Papua Merdeka (the Free Papua Movement). In late 2001 a major leader of the resistance was murdered. A Papuan Presidium Forum was established in Papua but it has had relatively little impact. Since 1999, when East Timor got independence, the Indonesian military has stepped up its pressure on West Papua. Assassinations, torture, disappearances, and destruction of villages have been carried out.[138]

The government of Indonesia has granted mineral and timber rights to transnational corporations, which also have allegedly engaged in human rights violations. These companies include Freeport McMoRan, a New Orleans-based mining company, Rio Tinto, the largest mining company on the planet, and BP (British Petroleum).[139] A paper mill that was planned for West Papua by Scott Paper was shelved in 2001 due to local and international pressures. In 2001, the Indonesian government grudgingly gave limited political autonomy and a higher share of mining revenues to West Papua. Representatives of West Papuan groups appealed what they said was genocide at the United Nations Human Rights Commission in Geneva in 2004. Thus far, however, there have been no sanctions brought to bear on Indonesia by the international community.

Human rights activists, educators, and indigenous peoples themselves have argued forcefully that cases of genocide and ethnocide should be followed up on and prosecuted to the fullest extent of the law. Indigenous peoples have called for investigations of genocides and mass human rights violations at the international, national, and local levels. Some indigenous groups have gone to court against the governments of the countries where they live, and in a number of instances, indigenous peoples sought legal judgements against transnational corporations for violations of their rights and destruction of their habitats.[140] 'Developmental genocides', as they have been called, have become increasingly common with the expansion of globalization and international trade in the latter part of the twentieth century and the new millennium. Some indigenous groups, such as the Lacandon Maya and their neighbours in Chiapas, Mexico, have resorted to high-profile tactics such as armed take-overs of property and then using the worldwide web to broadcast their views to protest what they see as unfair international trade and national development affecting their livelihoods and well-being.[141] In all of these efforts, the major foci of indigenous peoples, while diverse in many ways, has been on promoting their individual and collective human rights, including the rights to life and livelihoods. As some indigenous spokespersons have said, building on the work of Samuel Totten, 'With reference to the prediction, prevention and intervention of genocide', 'Where there is the political will, there is a way.'[142]

Conclusions

In most cases, indigenous peoples in Africa, Asia, the Americas, the Pacific, the Arctic, Australia, and New Zealand are at the bottom of the several-tiered socioeconomic systems of the countries in which they live. Sizable proportions of indigenous peoples are impoverished; they are marginalized both socially and politically; and they are all too often subjected to discriminatory treatment by governments and individuals in the states in which they reside. A major reason for this situation is that many of them were designated by colonial governments as 'wards of the state', without legal rights to participate in political decision-making or to control their own futures.

The claims of indigenous peoples around the world are relatively similar: they wish to have their human rights respected; they do not wish to be discriminated against or mistreated; they want ownership and control over their own land and natural resources; and they want the right to participate through their own institutions in the political process at the nation-state, regional, and international levels. Representatives of indigenous peoples' organizations have taken part in a number of international forums on indigenous peoples held by academic institutions and indigenous peoples' human rights and advocacy organizations and have called for recognition of their collective rights. Indigenous leaders have been elected to regional-level offices, and in one case, that of Bolivia, an indigenous leader, Evo Morales, became president of the country in 2006.

In spite of these gains, indigenous peoples continue to have to cope with the lack of compliance of nation-states, international institutions, and transnational corporations with human rights legislation and guidelines on indigenous peoples and development project implementation. The *Declaration of the Rights of Indigenous Peoples*, with its provisions on collective and individual rights and to be protected against genocide,[143] is unlikely to be accepted by many of the member states of the United Nations. While the new Human Rights Council may discuss the *Declaration of the Rights of Indigenous Peoples* and then pass it on to the General Assembly for debate, countries such as the United States, the United Kingdom, and Australia will attempt to derail it so that it cannot become an international human rights instrument. Indigenous groups and their supporters will have to continue to be vigilant about the possibility of genocides, and they will have to continue to campaign for greater recognition of the human rights and needs of indigenous peoples. Efforts will also have to be made to obtain additional information, especially first person testimonies, about genocides and the conditions that lead to genocides. Documentation of genocides is one of the ways that future genocides can be prevented.

The failure of nation-states to take strong stances against genocide and massive human rights violations is well-documented.[144] There are many reasons that have been given as to why nation-states and international agencies such as the United Nations fail to take action against genocide. In some cases, it is because they believe that it is not in their interest to intervene. In other cases, it is allegedly because they do not believe that a genocide is taking place, preferring instead to call the situation something else, such as a civil war. In still other cases, it is because the nation-state feels that it would expose their peace-keeping troops to risks that they do not feel are warranted. And there are situations where nation-states are in collusion with governments that are engaged in human rights violations of some of their own people who are labelled as 'terrorists'.

While much of the emphasis in this chapter has been on recent genocides, it should not be concluded that genocides did not occur either prior to the beginnings of recorded history. There is archaeological evidence that indicates the destruction of groups and individuals in prehistoric times, and indigenous groups today engage in warfare and retributions.[145] Some of the people in jail who face justice for genocidal actions in Rwanda in 1994, for example, are members of indigenous Batwa communities. Indigenous peoples have had to come to terms with the fact that many of their histories involve genocides and massive human rights violations. The crucial issue facing indigenous and other peoples today is how to prevent future genocides. There is also a need for coming up with early warning systems in order to predict the possibility of genocides among indigenous groups as well as other peoples.

In some ways, indigenous peoples, 'First Nations' are undergoing a kind of renaissance, with some legal and moral successes (e.g. getting more defined legal rights to land in Australia and New Zealand and in getting the remains of their ancestors and some of the cultural property repatriated to some indigenous groups).[146] Members of indigenous groups have organized themselves and have established representative bodies in virtually all of the countries where indigenous peoples reside. Indigenous peoples have sought formal apologies from governments that they believe did them great injustices, and in some instances, notably in the cases of Australia and Canada, they have had apologies made to them.[147] But apologies only solve part of the problem. What is needed now, as a Lakota spokesperson said at a September 1998 meeting at the University of Nebraska-Lincoln concerning the handling and repatriation of Indian remains and culturally significant property, is the explicit recognition of the right of indigenous peoples to exist without having to face prejudice and injustice.[148]

As Israel Charny points out, even though as humans we may care most about ourselves and those close to us, it is also a matter of self-interest to care about the genocide of others.[149] Every event of mass murder, he goes on to say, opens the door to greater possibilities of further genocidal massacres, including, potentially, our own people. Genocide is an expensive process in an economic, human, and moral sense. Humankind simply cannot be indifferent to what happens to its members. Failure to take a stand on the mistreatment of other people has significant social, political, and psychological impacts. The sense of kinship and belonging to a common humanity is crucial to long-term survival. There are those who feel as well that there is an attachment to the past, present, and future of the larger cosmos, or, as Charny says, an appreciation of the holiness of all life.[150] Certainly this is the position of many members of indigenous groups who feel strongly that they are a part of the natural world and, more broadly, the universe. There is a danger, however, in essentializing indigenous peoples, in portraying them as something other than what they are: human beings who wish to be treated with respect, dignity, and fairness.

Notes

1. See J. H. Bodley, *Victims of Progress*, 4th edn. (Mountain View, CA and London: Mayfield Publishing Company, 1999).
2. B. G. Miller, *Invisible Indigenes: The Politics of Non-Recognition* (Lincoln, NB: University of Nebraska Press, 2003).
3. A. Gedicks, *Resource Rebels: Native Challenges to Mining and Oil Corporations* (Cambridge, MA: South End Press, 2001).
4. R. Sesana, a G//ana San, spokesperson of First People of the Kalahari, a San non-government organization in Botswana.
5. D. Maybury-Lewis, 'Genocide Against Indigenous Peoples', in *Annihilating Difference: The Anthropology of Genocide*, ed. A. L. Hinton (Berkeley, CA: University of California Press, 2002), p. 43.
6. P. Brantlinger, *Dark Vanishings: Discourse on the Extinction of Primitive Races, 1800–1930* (Ithaca, NY: Cornell University Press, 2003), p. 2.
7. International Work Group for Indigenous Affairs, *IWGIA Yearbook 1987: Indigenous Peoples and Development* (Copenhagen: International Work Group for Indigenous Affairs, 1988), p. 1.
8. For discussions of definitions of the concept 'indigenous peoples', see J. R. Martinez-Cobo, *Study of the Problem of Discrimination Against Indigenous Populations: Volume V: Conclusions, Proposals, and Recommendations* (New York, United Nations, 1985), p. 48; Independent Commission on International Humanitarian Issues, *Indigenous Peoples: A global Quest for Justice* (London: Zed Books, 1987), pp. 5–13; J. Burger, *Report from the Frontier: The State of the World's Indigenous Peoples* (London: Zed Books and Cambridge, MA: Cultural Survival, Inc:, 1990), pp. 5–12; World Bank, 'Indigenous Peoples', in *The World Bank Operational Manual: Operational Policies 4.10* (Washington, D.C.: The World Bank, 2005); M. Stewart-Harawira, *The New Imperial Order: Indigenous Reponses to Globalization* (London: Zed Books, 2005); N. G. Postero, *Now We Are Citizens: Indigenous Politics in Postmulticultural Bolivia* (Stanford, CA: Stanford University Press, 2007); see especially pp. 3, 10, 11–13, 50, 84–6.
9. See D. Maybury-Lewis, *Indigenous Peoples, Ethnic Groups, and the State* (Boston, MA: Allyn and Bacon, 1997), pp. x, 7–12, 54–6; K. Coates, *A Global History of Indigenous Peoples: Struggle and Survival* (New York: Palgrave Macmillan, 2004), pp. 1–15; R. Niezen, *The Origins of Indigenism: Human Rights and the Politics of Identity* (Berkeley, CA: University of California Press, 2004), pp. 2–15, 18–23.
10. See R. Bhengra, 'Indigenous Peoples' Juridical Rights and Their Relation to the State in India', in *Vines That Won't Bind: Indigenous Peoples in Asia*, ed. C. Erni (Copenhagen: International Work Group for Indigenous Affairs, 1996), pp. 119–50; R. Bhengra, C. R. Bijoy, and S. Luithui, *The Adivasis of India* (London: Minority Rights Group International, 1998); S. Venkateswar, *Development and Ethnocide: Colonial Practices in the Andaman Islands* (Copenhagen: International Work Group for Indigenous Affairs, 2004).
11. See the Botswana government website, www.gov.bw/index.php.
12. F. Wilmer, *The Indigenous Voice in World Politics: Since Time Immemorial* (Newbury Park, CA: Sage Publications, 1993); B. R. Howard, *Indigenous Peoples and the State: The Struggle for Native Rights* (DeKalb, IL: Northern Illinois University Press, 2003).
13. World Bank, 'Indigenous Peoples', p. 2.
14. For a copy of this Convention, see S. J. Anaya, *Indigenous Peoples in International Law* (New York: Oxford University Press, 1996), pp. 193–204.

15. See E. Darian-Smith, *New Capitalists: Law, Politics, and Identity Surrounding Casino Gaming on Native American Land* (Belmont, CA: Thompson/Wadsworth, 2004).
16. See T. R. Gurr, *Minorities at Risk: A Global View of Ethnopolitical Conflicts* (Washington, D.C.: United States Institute for Peace Press, 1993); and T. R. Gurr, *Peoples Versus States: Minorities at Risk in the New Century* (Washington, D.C.: United States Institute for Peace Press, 2000), pp. 45–7.
17. For an enlightening discussion of this complex issue, see E. Barkan: 'Genocides of Indigenous Peoples: Rhetoric of Human Rights', in *The Specter of Genocide: Mass Murder in Historical Perspective*, eds, R. Gellately and B. Kiernan (Cambridge: Cambridge University Press, 2003), pp. 117–39. Some of the works he addresses include K. Sale, *The Conquest of Paradise: Christopher Columbus and the Columbian Legacy* (New York: Alfred A. Knopf, 1991); D. E. Stannard, *American Holocaust: The Conquest of the New World* (New York: Oxford University Press, 1992); and G. E. Tinker, *Missionary Conquest: The Gospel and Native American Genocide* (Minneapolis, MN: Fortress Press, 1993).
18. Niezen, *The Origins of Indigenism*, p. 5.
19. See H. Drechsler, *Let Us Die Fighting: The Struggle of the Herero and the Nama Against German Imperialism* (London: Zed Press, 1980); J. Bridgman, *The Revolt of the Hereros* (Berkeley, CA: University of California Press, 1981); K. Poewe, *The Namibian Herero: A History of Their Psychosocial Disintegration and Survival* (Lewiston, NY: The Edward Mellen Press, 1985); A. Palmer, *Colonial Genocide* (Adelaide: Crawford House Publishers, 2000); I. V. Hull, 'Military Culture and the Production of "Final Solutions" in the Colonies: The Example of Wilhelminian Germany', in *The Specter of Genocide*, eds, Gellately and Kiernan, pp. 141–62; and Jürgen Zimmerer's chapter in this volume.
20. B. Neitschmann, 'The Third World War', *Cultural Survival Quarterly*, 11, 3 (1987), 1–16.
21. See, for example, reports by Amnesty International, Anti-Slavery International, Human Rights Watch, the International Work Group for Indigenous Affairs, Survival International, and the Minority Rights Group. Examples include Center for World Indigenous Studies, *International Tribunal on Genocide in Central America* (Kenmore, WA: Center for World Indigenous Studies, 1986; www.cwis.org/fwdp/americas/itcaplan,txt); Amnesty International, *Human Rights Violations Against Indigenous Peoples of the Americas* (New York: Amnesty International, 1992); Minority Rights Group International, *World Directly of Minorities* (London: Minority Rights Group International, 1997); Anti-Slavery International and International Work Group for Indigenous Affairs, *Enslaved Peoples in the 1990s: Indigenous Peoples, Debt Bondage, and Human Rights* (London: Anti-Slavery International and Copenhagen: International Work Group for Indigenous Affairs, 1997). An excellent discussion of conflict involving indigenous and other peoples and state systems that was kept secret for many years was that in Laos in the period between 1942 and 1975, with residual effects continuing to the present; see J. Hamilton-Merritt, *Tragic Mountains: The Hmong, the Americans, and the Secret Wars for Laos, 1942–1992* (Bloomington, IN: Indiana University Press, 1992).
22. Kari-Oka Declaration and the Indigenous Peoples Earth Charter, World Conference of Indigenous Peoples on Territory, Environment and Development, 25–30 May 1992.
23. For a discussion of the impacts of multinational corporations on indigenous peoples, see A. Gedicks, *The New Resource Wars: Native and Environmental Struggles against Multinational Corporations* (Boston, MA: South End Press, 2001).

24. L. Kuper, *Genocide: Its Political Use in the Twentieth Century* (New Haven, CT: Yale University Press, 1981), pp. 31, 41; A. Palmer, 'Ethnocide', in *Genocide in Our Time*, eds, M. N. Dobkowski and I. Wallimann (Ann Arbor, MI: Pierian Press, 1992), p. 1; R. K. Hitchcock and T. Twedt, 'Physical and Cultural Genocide of Various Indigenous Peoples', in *Century of Genocide: Eyewitness Accounts and Critical Views*, eds, S. Totten, W. S. Parsons, and I. Charny (New York: Garland Publishing, 1997), p. 373; D. Maybury-Lewis, *Indigenous Peoples, Ethnic Groups, and the State*, pp. 1–7.
25. Bodley, *Victims of Progress*, pp. 170–96.
26. R. Weyler, *Blood of the Land: The U.S. Government and the Corporate War against the American Indian Movement*, 2nd edn (Philadelphia, PA: New Society Publishers, 1992).
27. T. Johnson, J. Nagel, and D. Champagne, eds, *American Indian Activism: Alcatraz to the Longest Walk* (Urbana, IL: University of Illinois Press, 1997).
28. N. Lewis, 'Genocide – From Fire and Sword to Arsenic and Bullets: Civilization Has Sent Six Million Indians to Extinction', *Sunday Times Magazine* (London) (23 February 1969). For additional discussion of these matters with relation to Central America, see Center for World Indigenous Studies, *International Tribunal on Genocide in Central America* (Kenmore, WA: Center for World Indigenous Studies, 1986).
29. For a discussion of the reactions of anthropologists to counterinsurgency operations carried out by the U.S. government in Thailand in the 1960s, see E. Wakin, *Anthropology Goes to War: Professional Ethics and Counterinsurgency in Thailand* (Madison, WI: Center for Southeast Asian Studies, University of Wisconsin-Madison, 1992).
30. See Wakin, *Anthropology Goes to War*.
31. See G. B. Kolata, '!Kung Bushmen Join South African Army', *Science*, 211 (1981), 562-4.
32. S. Souindola, 'Angola: Genocide of the Bosquimanos', *IWGIA Newsletter*, 31–2 (1981), 66–8.
33. See, for example, I. L. Horowitz, *Taking Lives: Genocide and State Power* (New Brunswick, NJ: Transaction Publishers, 1980); I. W. Charny, *How Can We Commit the Unthinkable? Genocide, the Human Cancer* (Boulder, CO: Westview Press, 1982); L. Kuper, *The Prevention of Genocide* (New Haven, CT: Yale University Press, 1985); E. Staub, *The Roots of Evil: The Origins of Genocide and Other Group Violence* (Cambridge: Cambridge University Press, 1989); A. Neier, *War Crimes: Brutality, Genocide, Terror, and the Struggle for Justice* (New York: Times Books, 1998); I. W. Charny, ed., *Encyclopedia of Genocide, Volumes I and II* (Santa Barbara, CA: ABC-Clio, 1999).
34. H. Fein, 'Genocide: A Sociological Perspective', *Current Sociology*, 38, 1 (1990), 24.
35. As noted in some of the discussions at the meetings of the Working Group on Indigenous Populations and the Permanent Forum on Indigenous Issues of the United Nations.
36. See, for example, L. A. Stiffarm with P. Lane Jr., 'The Demography of Native North America: A Question of American Indian Survival', in *The State of Native America: Genocide, Colonization, and Resistance*, ed. M. A. Jaimes (Boston, MA: South End Press, 1992), pp. 30–4.
37. Such statements were made in interviews of indigenous peoples' organizations spokespersons at meetings of Khoi and San peoples in southern Africa in 1997 and 2003 and at international meetings on indigenous peoples in Africa. People concerned with the well-being of the San have also asked whether what is happening

to the San in the Central Kalahari Game Reserve of Botswana, who, along with another group, the Bakgalagadi, were relocated out of the game reserve by the government of Botswana in 1997 and 2002. See, for example, M. Levine, 'Can Botswana Be Charged with Genocide?' *Mmegi Wa Dikgang*, 4–10 October 2002; P Kenyon, 'Row over Bushmen "Genocide,"' http://news.bbc.co.yk/go/pr/fr/-/2/hi/programmes/crossing_continents/4404816.stm 2005/11006. The BBC Radio 4's Crossing Continents program was broadcast on Thursday, 10 November 2004.

38. For further information on cultural genocide, see the chapter in this volume by Robert van Krieken.
39. See, for example, D. Adams, *Education for Extinction: American Indians and the Boarding School Experience, 1875–1928* (Lawrence, KS: University of Kansas Press, 1995); A. D. Moses, ed., *Genocide and Settler Society: Frontier Violence and Stolen Indigenous Children in Australian History* (New York: Berghahn Books, 2004).
40. See Human Rights and Equal Opportunity Commission, *Bringing Them Home: Report of the National Inquiry into the Separation of Aboriginal and Torres Strait Island Children* (Sydney: Human Rights and Equal Opportunity Commission, 1997); V. Haskins and M. D. Jacobs, 'Stolen Generations and Vanishing Indians: The Removals of Indigenous Children as a Weapon of War in the United States and Australia', In ed. J. Merten, *Children and War: A Historical Anthology* (New York: New York University Press, 2002), pp. 227–41; M. D. Jacobs, 'Maternal Colonialism: White Women and Indigenous Child Removal in the American West and Australia 1880–1940', *Western Historical Quarterly* 36, 1 (2005) 453–76; K. Ellinghaus, 'Indigenous Assimilation and Absorption in the United States and Australia,' *Pacific Historical Review* 75, 4 (2006) 563–85.
41. See P. Sampas, 'Last Words', *WorldWatch* (May–June 2001), 34–40; see also M. Krauss, 'The World's Languages in Crisis', and K. Hale, 'On Endangered Languages and the Safeguarding of Diversity', *Language*, 68, 1 (1992), 1–3, 6; D. Nettle and S. Romaine, *Vanishing Voices: The Extinction of the World's Languages* (Oxford: Oxford University Press, 2000); T. Skutnabb-Kangas, *Linguistic Genocide in Education – or Worldwide Diversity and Human Rights?* (Mahwah, NJ: Lawrence Erlbaum Associates, 2000).
42. See I. E. Daes, *A Study on the Protection of the Cultural and Intellectual Property (Heritage) of Indigenous Peoples* (New York: United Nations, 1996); D. A. Posey and G. Dutfield, *Beyond Intellectual Property: Toward Traditional Rights for Indigenous Peoples and Local Communities* (Ottawa: International Development Research Center, 1996); M. A. Bengwayan, *Intellectual and Cultural Property Rights of Indigenous and Tribal Peoples in Asia* (London: Minority Rights Group International, 2003).
43. See Bodley, *Victims of Progress*, pp. 145–69; Independent Commission on International Humanitarian Issues, *Indigenous Peoples: A Global Quest for Justice* (London: Zed Press, 1987).
44. See, for example, R. Thornton, *American Indian Holocaust and Survival: A Population History since 1492* (Norman, OK: University of Oklahoma Press, 1987); F. Chalk and K. Jonassohn, *The History and Sociology of Genocide: Analyses and Case Studies* (New Haven, CT: Yale University Press, 1990); Hitchcock and Twedt, 'Physical and Cultural Genocide'; C. Tatz, *With Intent to Destroy: Reflecting on Genocide* (London: Verso, 2003), pp. 67–106; W. Churchill, *A Little Matter of Genocide: Holocaust and Denial in the Americas, 1492 to the Present* (San Francisco, CA: City Lights Books, 1997); E. Barkan, *The Guilt of Nations: Restitution and Negotiating Historical Injustices* (New York: W. W. Norton and Company, 2000); Barkan, 'Genocides of Indigenous

Peoples', pp. 133–9; E.-I. A. Daes, 'Indigenous Peoples', in *Encyclopedia of Genocide and Crimes against Humanity*, ed. D. L. Shelton (Detroit, MI and New York: Thomson-Gale, 2005), pp. 508–16; M. Lavene, *Genocide in the Age of the Nation State, Volume 2: The Rise of the West and the Coming of Genocide* (London: I. B. Tauris, 2005).

45. Refugees International, 'Forgotten Peoples: The Batwa "Pygmy" of the Great Lakes Region of Africa', www.refugeessinternational.org/content/article/detail/892, 12 August 2003.
46. See D. Bergner, 'The Most Unconventional Weapon', *The New York Times Magazine* (28 October 2003), 48–53; www.hrw.org.
47. Survival International, 'Rio Pardo. Brazil: Uncontacted Tribe Faces Genocide', *Urgent Action Bulletin*, June 2005 (London: Survival International, 2005).
48. S. Davis, *Victims of the Miracle: Development and the Indians of Brazil* (Cambridge: Cambridge University Press, 1977), p. 5.
49. See G. Grumberg, 'Why are the Guarani Kaiowa Killing Themselves?', *IWGIA Newsletter*, 91, 2 (1991), 21–4; and the *Urgent Action Bulletins* of Survival International produced in the 1980s through to the present (London: Survival International, www.survival.org).
50. G. Colby with C. Dennett, *Thy Will Be Done: The Conquest of the Amazon: Nelson Rockefeller and the Age of Oil* (New York: HarperPerennial, 1976).
51. W. C. Townsend, Summer Institute of Linguistics, response to Colby, *Thy Will Be Done*, p. 4; T. L. Headland and K. L. Pike, 'SIL and Genocide: Well-Oiled Connections?', *Anthropology Newsletter*, 38, 2 (1997), 4–5; M. Edelman, 'Nelson Rockefeller and Latin America', *Anthropology Newsletter*, 38, 2 (1997), 36–7; Thomas Headland, Summer Institute of Linguistics, personal communications, 2003, 2005.
52. Very good discussions of the efforts of individuals and organizations to assist indigenous peoples can be found in Bodley, *Victims of Progress*, pp. 170–201; Brantlinger, *Dark Vanishings*.
53. For a discussion of the Aborigines Protection Society and other institutions concerned about the welfare of indigenous peoples in the nineteenth century, see Brantlinger, *Dark Vanishings*, pp. 68–9, 71–2, 86–93.
54. Bodley, *Victims of Progress*, pp. 170–6.
55. Ibid., pp. 170, 172–6.
56. Ibid., pp. 22–3.
57. Crocker, *Rivers of Blood, Rivers of Gold*, pp. 187–266.
58. Brantlinger, *Dark Vanishings*, pp. 2, 43.
59. V. Montejo, *Testimony: Death of a Guatemalan Village* (Willimantic, CT: Curbstone Press, 1987).
60. For a discussion of the Guatemala case, see Victoria Sanford in this volume. See also R. Falla, 'We Charge Genocide', *In Guatemala: Tyranny on Trial: Testimony of the Permanent People's Tribunal* (San Francisco, CA: Synthesis Publications, 1984), pp. 112–19; R. Falla, *Massacres in the Jungle: Ixcan, Guatemala, 1975–1982* (Boulder, CO: Westview Press, 1994); B. Manz, *Refugees of a Hidden War: The Aftermath of Counterinsurgency in Guatemala* (Albany, NY: State University of New York Press, 1988); R. Carmack, *Harvest of Violence: The Mayan Indians and the Guatemalan Crisis* (Norman, OK: University of Oklahoma Press, 1988); C. S. Smith, ed., *Guatemalan Indians and the State, 1540 to 1988* (Austin, TX: University of Texas Press, 1990); D. Stoll, *Between Two Armies in the Ixil Towns of Guatemala* (New York: Columbia University Press, 1993); K. B. Warren, *Indigenous Movements and Their Critics: Pan-Maya Activism in Guatemala* (Princeton, NJ: Princeton

University Press, 1998); J. Colajmoco, 'The Chixoy Dam: The Aya Achi Genocide: The Story of Forced Resettlement', in *Dams, Indigenous Peoples, and Ethnic Minorities*, ed., M. Colchester (Copenhagen: International Work Group for Indigenous Affairs, 1999); V. Sanford, *Buried Secrets: Truth and Human Rights in Guatemala* (New York: Palgrave Macmillan, 2003).

61. Cf. R. Menchu, I, *Rigoberta Menchu, an Indian Woman of Guatemala*, ed., E. Burgos-Debray, trans. by A. Wright (London: Verso, 1984); and D. Stoll, *Rigoberta Menchu and the Story of All Poor Guatemalans* (Boulder, CO: Westview Press, 1999).
62. Stoll, *Rigoberta Menchu*, pp. 4–5.
63. Ibid., pp. 7–8.
64. Ibid., p. 10.
65. Ibid., p. 11.
66. For an excellent discussion of the importance of first person testimony in genocide and human rights cases, see S. Totten, *First-Person Accounts of Genocidal Acts Committed in the Twentieth Century: An Annotated Bibliography* (Westport, CT: Greenwood Press, 1991), pp. xxv–xliii; S. Totten and W.S. Parsons, 'Introduction', in *Century of Genocide*, eds, Totten et al., pp. 6–9.
67. Stoll, *Rigoberta Menchu*, p. 125.
68. Ibid., p. 141.
69. Ibid., p. 217.
70. Ibid., p. 218.
71. Ibid., p. 278.
72. See A. Arias, ed., *The Rigoberta Menchu Controversy* (Minneapolis, MN: University of Minnesota Press, 2001); H. Cohen, 'The Unmaking of Rigoberta Menchu', in *Genocide, Collective Violence, and Popular Memory: The Politics of Remembrance in the Twentieth Century*, eds, D. E. Lorey and W. H Beezley, eds, (Wilmington, DE: Scholarly Resources Books, 2002), pp. 53–64.
73. Artuo Arias, as quoted in Cohen, 'The Unmaking of Rigoberta Menchu', pp. 58–9.
74. See M. Munzel, *The Ache Indians: Genocide in Paraguay* (Copenhagen: International Work Group for Indigenous Affairs, 1973); R. Arens, ed., *Genocide in Paraguay* (Philadelphia, PA: Temple University Press, 1976).
75. M. Munzel, *The Ache: Genocide Continues in Paraguay* (Copenhagen: International Work Group for Indigenous Affairs, 1974); M. Chase Sardi, 'The Present Situation of the Indians in Paraguay', in *The Situation of the Indian in South America: Contributions to the Study of Inter-Ethnic Conflict in the Non-Andean Regions of South America*, ed. W. Dostal (Geneva: World Council of Churches, 1972). K. Hill and A. Hurtado, *Ache Life History: The Ecology and Demography of a Foraging People* (New York: Aldine de Gruyter, 1995).
76. See Survival International, *The Denial of Genocide* (London: Survival International, 1993).
77. D. Maybury-Lewis and J. Howe, *The Indian Peoples of Paraguay: Their Plight and Their Prospects*. Cultural Survival Special Reports No. 2. (Cambridge, MA: Cultural Survival Inc. 1980).
78. R. J. Smith and B. Melia, *Genocide of the Ache-Guayaki?* (London: Survival International, 1978).
79. Survival International, *The Denial of Genocide*, p. 3.
80. Maybury-Lewis and Howe, *The Indian Peoples of Paraguay*, p. 40.
81. R. Arens, 'Introduction', in *Genocide in Paraguay*, ed. Arens, pp. 5–6.
82. See Munzel, *The Ache* and Arens, ed., *Genocide in Paraguay*.
83. Arens, 'Introduction', p. 12.

84. See the excellent discussions of these issues in R. H. Horst, 'Political Advocacy and Religious Allegiance; Catholic Missions and Indigenous Resistance in Paraguay, 1982–1992', paper presented at the 2000 meetings of the Latin American Studies Association, Miami, Florida. One of the interviews by Horst was of Miguel Chase Sardi (16 August 1995) who addressed directly the question of the veracity of Mark Munzel, see Horst, p. 7.
85. Hill and Hurtado, *Ache Life History*, pp. 168–9.
86. Ibid, p. 169.
87. See J. Bonwick, The Last of the Tasmanians, or The Black War of Van Diemen's Land (London: Sampson Low, 1870); C. Turnbull, *Black War: The Extermination of the Tasmanian Aborigines* (Melbourne: Cheshire-Lansdowne, 1948); T. Barta, 'Relations of Genocide: Land and Lives in the Colonization of Australia', in *Genocide and the Modern Age: Etiology and Case Studies of Mass Death*, eds, I. Wallimann and M. N. Dobkowski, pp. 237–51; J. P. Synott, 'Genocide and Cover-up Practices of the British Colonial System against Australian Aborigines, 1788–1992', *Internet on the Holocaust and Genocide*, 44–6 (1993), 15–16; J. J. Cove, *What the Bones Say: Tasmanian Aborigines, Science, and Domination* (Ottawa: Carleton University Press, 1995); Crocker, *Rivers of Blood, Rivers of Gold*, especially pp. 115–94; C. Tatz, *Genocide in Australia* (Canberra: Australian Institute of Aboriginal and Torres Strait Islander Studies, 1999); A. Palmer, *Colonial Genocide* (Adelaide: Crawford House, 2000); H. Reynolds, *An Indelible Stain? The Question of Genocide in Australia's History* (Melbourne: Viking Australia, 2001); A. D. Moses, ed., *Genocide and Settler Society: Frontier Violence and Stolen Indigenous Children in Australian History* (New York: Berghahn Books, 2004).
88. J. Diamond, *Guns, Germs, and Steel: The Fates of Human Societies*. (New York: W.W. Norton, 1997), p. 320.
89. See H. Reynolds, *The Other Side of the Frontier: Aboriginal Resistance to the European Invasion of Australia* (Victoria: Penguin Australia, 1982); H. Reynolds, *Why Weren't We Told A Personal Search for the Truth About Our History*? (Victoria: Penguin Australia, 1999); A. D. Moses, 'An Antipodean Genocide? The Origins of the Genocidal Moment in the Colonization of Australia', *Journal of Genocide Research*, 2, 1 (2000), 89–106; C. Tatz, 'Confronting Australian Genocide', *Aboriginal History* 25 (2001), 1–14; B. Kiernan, 'Australia's Aboriginal Genocide', *Yale Journal of Human Rights*, 1, 1 (2001), 49–56; A. R. Sousa, '"They Will be Hunted Down Like Wild Beasts and Destroyed!" A Comparative Study of Genocide in California and Tasmania', *Journal of Genocide Research*, 6, 2 (2004), 193–209; A. Curthoys, 'Raphael Lemkin's "Tasmania": An Introduction', *Patterns of Prejudice*, 39, 2 (2005), 168–75.
90. See K. Windschuttle, *The Fabrication of Aboriginal History, Volume One: Van Diemen's Land 1803–1847* (Paddington: Macleay Press, 2002). H. Dailey, 'Fabricating Aboriginal History,' http:Sunday.ninemsn.com.au/Sunday/cover_stories/article-1286.asp; R. Manne, *Whitewash: On Keith Windschuttle's Fabrication of Aboriginal History* (Melbourne: Black, 2003); P. Brantlinger, '"Black Armband" versus "White Blindfold" History in Australia', *Victorian Studies*, 46, 4 (2004), pp. 655–74.
91. N. J. B. Pomley, *The Aboriginal/Settler Clash in Van Diemen's Land, 1803–1831* (Hobart: University of Tasmania, 1992), pp. 10, 20.
92. L. Ryan, *The Aboriginal Tasmanians*, 2nd edn (St. Leonards: Allen & Unwin, 1996), p. 83.
93. The estimated numbers of Aboriginal Tasmanians varied; cf. Plomley, *The Aboriginal/Settler Clash in Van Diemen's Land: 1803–1831* and L. Ryan, *The Aboriginal Tasmanians*.

94. Cove, *What the Bones Say*, p. 25.
95. Diamond, *Guns, Germs, and Steel*, p. 27.
96. As B. Madley put it, 'When in November 1828 Arthur declared martial law, he implicitly institutionalized ethnic cleansing, if not genocide', p. 174, in 'Patterns of Frontier Genocide 1803–1819: The Aboriginal Tasmanians, the Yuki of California, and the Herero of Namibia,' *Journal of Genocide Research*, 6, 2 (2004), 167–92.
97. N. J. B. Plomley, *An Immigrant of 1824* (Hobart: Tasmanian Historical Research Association, 1973), p. 2.
98. Madley, 'Patterns of Frontier Genocide', 173–4.
99. N. J. B. Plomley, ed., *Weep in Silence: A History of the Flinders Island Aboriginal Settlement with the Flinders Island Journal of George Augustus Robinson* (Hobart: Blubber Head Press, 1987); N. J. B. Plomley, *Friendly Mission: The Tasmanian Journals and Papers of George Augustus Robinson: 1829–1834* (Kingsgrove: Halstead Press, 1966).
100. Ibid., p. 165.
101. Ibid., p. 166.
102. Cove, *What the Bones Say*, pp. 51–2.
103. Ibid., p. 153.
104. A. Curthoys, 'Genocide in Tasmania: The History of an Idea', in *Empire, Colony, Genocide*, ed. A. D. Moses (New York: Berghahn, 2008), for example, questions the conventional wisdom about Tasmanian genocide; see also Tony Barta's chapter in this volume.
105. Brantlinger, *Dark Vanishings*, pp. 4, 11, 15–16, 41–3, 124–30.
106. Stannard, *American Holocaust*.
107. For excellent discussions of this highly contentious debate, see G. D. Rosenfeld, 'The Politics of Uniqueness: Reflections on the Recent Polemical Term in Holocaust and Genocide Scholarship', *Holocaust and Genocide Studies*, 13, 1 (1999), 28–61; B. Rensink, 'Native American History, the Holocaust, and Comparative Genocide: Historiography, Debate, and Critical Analysis' (M.A. Thesis, Department of History, University of Nebraska-Lincoln, 2006).
108. For an example, see V. Dadrian, 'The Convergent Aspects of the Armenian and Jewish Cases of Genocide: A Reintepretation of the Concept of the Holocaust', *Holocaust and Genocide Studies*, 3, 2 (1998), 151–69.
109. See, for example, S. T. Katz, *The Holocaust in Historical Context, Volume I: The Holocaust and Mass Death Before the Modern Age* (New York: Oxford University Press, 1992); D. Lipstadt, *Denying the Holocaust: The Growing Assault on Truth and Memory* (New York: Free Press, 1993); D. J. Goldhagen, *Hitler's Willing Executioners: Ordinary Germans and the Holocaust* (New York: Alfred A. Knopf, 1996).
110. See, for example, G. Grau, *Hidden Holocaust? Gay and Lesbian Persecution in Germany, 1933–1945* (Chicago, IL: Fitzroy Dearborn, 1995); I. Chang, *The Rape of Nanking: The Forgotten Holocaust* (New York: Basic Books, 1997).
111. See, for example, Y. Bauer, *The Holocaust in Historical Perspective* (Seattle, WA: University of Washington Press, 1978), especially pp. 30–49.
112. Katz, *The Holocaust in Historical Context*, p. 10.
113. Ibid., pp. 128–9.
114. A. Rosenbaum, ed., *Is the Holocaust Unique: Perspectives on Comparative Genocide* (Boulder, CO: Westview Press, 1996). See especially the article by D. Stannard, 'Uniqueness as Denial: The Politics of Genocide Scholarship', pp. 163–208.
115. Stannard, 'Uniqueness as Denial', p. 167.
116. Ibid., p. 198.

117. Stannard, *American Holocaust*, p. 256.
118. Stannard, 'Uniqueness as Denial', p. 181; Stannard, in *American Holocaust*, p. 146, notes that 'The worst human holocaust the world had ever witnessed, roaring across two continents non-stop for four centuries and consuming the lives of countless tens of millions of people finally had leveled off. There was, at last, almost no one left to kill.'
119. Stannard, *American Holocaust*.
120. D. Stannard, 'Preface', in W. Churchill, *A Little Matter of Genocide*, p. xvi.
121. Stannard, 'Uniqueness as Denial', p. 181.
122. N. Finkelstein and R. B. Birn, *A Nation on Trial: The Goldhagen Thesis and Historical Truth* (New York: Metropolitan, 1998).
123. Rosenfeld, 'The Politics of Uniqueness', pp. 42–9.
124. S. Hoig, *The Sand Creek Massacre* (Norman, OK: University of Oklahoma Press, 1961); D. Green and D. Scott, *Finding Sand Creek* (Norman, OK: University of Oklahoma Press, 2004); S. Hoig, 'Sand Creek Massacre', in *Encyclopedia of Genocide and Crimes Against Humanity*, ed. Shelton, pp. 942–3.
125. The governor of Colorado in August 1864, had published a proclamation calling upon citizens to kill all Indians and seize their property, 'effectively extending an invitation for wholesale bloodshed and thievery.' See Green and Scott, *Finding Sand Creek*, p. 14.
126. For a discussion of the importance of apologies and admissions of wrongdoing, see Barkan, *The Guilt of Nations*.
127. See the reports of Amnesty International, Human Rights Watch, African Rights, Asia Watch, Minority Rights Group, Survival International, Cultural Survival, and the International Work Group for Indigenous Affairs. For a specific example of the way in which one indigenous group, the Karen, who number 6 million in Burma and 400,000 in Thailand, has been treated by the Burmese government and military, see the Jubilee Campaign, 'Genocide Against the Karen People in Burma', www.jubileecampaign.co.uk/world/bnrs.htm (1998); B. Rogers, *A Land Without Evil: Stopping the Genocide of Burma's Karen* (Oxford: Monarch Books, 2004).
128. See I. Sutton, ed., *Irredeemable America: The Indians' Estate and Land Claims* (Albuquerque, NM: University of New Mexico Press, 1985); J. Nagel, *American Indian Ethnic Renewal: Red Power and the Resurgence of Identity and Culture* (Oxford: Oxford University Press, 1996).
129. International Work Group for Indigenous Affairs, *The Naga Nation and Its Struggle Against Genocide* (Copenhagen: International Work Group for Indigenous Affairs, 1986).
130. S. Venkateswar, *Development and Ethnocide: Colonial Practices in the Andaman Islands*; see also some of the *Urgent Action Bulletins* of Survival International.
131. International Work Group for Indigenous Affairs, *Genocide in the Chittagong Hill Tracts, Bangladesh ... They Are Now Burning Village After Village* (Copenhagen: International Work Group for Indigenous Affairs, 1984); W. Mey, ed., *Genocide in the Chittagong Hill Tracts*. IWGIA Document No. 51 (Copenhagen: International Work Group for Indigenous Affairs, 1984); A. H. Chowdhury 'Self-Determination, the Chittagong, and Bangladesh', in *Human Rights and Environment: International Views*, ed. D. P. Forsythe (New York: St. Martin's Press, 1989), pp. 292–301; Chittagong Hill Tracts Commission, *'Life is not Ours': Land and Human Rights in the Chittagong Hill Tracts, Bangladesh: The Report of the Chittagong Hill Tracts Commission 1991*. (Copenhagen: International Work Group for Indigenous Affairs, 1991); Chittagong Hill Tracts Commission, *'Life is Not Ours': Land and Human Rights in the*

Chittagong Hill Tracts, Bangladesh. An Update of the May 1991 Report (Copenhagen: International Work Group for Indigenous Affairs, 1991); Chittagong Hill Tracts Commission (2000), *'Life is Not Ours': Land and Human Rights in the Chittagong Hill Tracts, Bangladesh: Update 4* (Copenhagen: International Work Group for Indigenous Affairs, 2000); R. C. Roy, *Land Rights of the Indigenous Peoples of the Chittagong Hill Tracts, Bangladesh* (Copenhagen: International Work Group for Indigenous Affairs, 2000); R. Jahan, 'Genocide in Bangladesh', in *Century of Genocide*, eds, Totten, Parsons and Charny, pp. 295–319.

132. I. Hume and S. Drong, 'Bangaldesh', In ed. S. Stidsen, *The Indigenous World 2006* (Copenhagen: International Work Group for Indigenous Affairs, 2006), 364–73. See also the website of Vanishing Rites, http://www.vanishingrites.com.
133. J. Heffernan and D. Tuller, 'Ending the Genocide in Darfur', *San Francisco Chronicle* (12 February 2006).
134. For a discussion of the concept of genocide in Darfur, see S. Straus, 'Darfur and the Genocide Debate', *Foreign Affairs*, 84, 1 (2005), 123–33.
135. Physicians for Human Rights, *Assault on Survival* (Boston, MA: Physicians for Human Rights, 2005). Estimates of the deaths vary considerably, in part, because of the difficulty of conducting surveys in a war-torn region and because of the assumptions made by organizations and individuals attempting to come up with numbers of people who were killed or died, J. Hagan and A. Palloni, 'Death in Darfur', *Science* 313 (2006) 1578–9. See also U.S. Department of State, *Sudan: Death Toll in Darfur* (Fact Sheet, Bureau of Intelligence and Research, Washington, D.C., March 2005).
136. For information on the Darfur situation, see the website of the United Nations Office of the High Commissioner for Human Rights (www.unhcr.org/english/docs/darfurreport.doc) and Justice Africa (www.justiceafrica.org). See also U.S. Department of State, *Documenting Atrocities in Darfur*. State Department Publication 111882, 9 September 2004 (Washington, D.C.: Department of State, 2004); J. Apsel, ed., *Darfur: Genocide before Our Eyes*. (New York: Institute for the Study of Genocide, 2005); G. Prunier, *Darfur: The Ambiguous Genocide* (Ithaca, NY: Cornell University Press, 1995); J. Flint and A. De Waal, *Darfur: A Short History of a Long War* (London: Zed Books, 2005).
137. See A. Schwarz, *A Nation in Waiting: Indonesia's Search for Stability* (London: Allen and Unwin, 1999); M. Kooistra, *Indonesia: Regional Conflicts and State Terror* (London: Minority Rights Group International, 2001).
138. C. Erni, 'West Papua', In ed. S. Stidsen, *The Indigenous World 2006* (Copenhagen: International Work Group for Indigenous Affairs, 2006) 265–72; C. Erni, personal communication, 2006.
139. D. Hyndman, *Ancestral Rain Forests and the Mountain of Gold: Indigenous Peoples and Mining in New Guinea* (Boulder, CO: Westview Press, 1994).
140. Cases brought against transnational corporations include ones in civil court in the United States; these include cases brought by the Huaorani Indians of Ecuador against Texaco (now Chevron-Texaco) for its actions (and inactions) in the Oriente region of Ecuador; one brought against Unocal, the California-based oil company (now part of British Petroleum) and Total, the French Oil company by Karen and other peoples for their actions involving the use of slave labour in the construction of a pipeline in Myanmar (Burma), and, by the Ogoni of Rivers State, Nigeria, against Royal Dutch Shell for its abysmal environmental and human rights record in the Niger Delta. See F. Wilmer, *The Indigenous Voice in World Politics*, pp. 128–31; R. K. Hitchcock, 'Indigenous Peoples, Multinational Corporations, and Human Rights',

Indigenous Affairs, 2 (1997), 6–11; Gedicks, *Resource Rebels*; S. Totten, W. S. Parsons, and R. K. Hitchcock, 'Confronting Genocide and Ethnocide of Indigenous Peoples: An Interdisciplinary Approach to Definition, Intervention, Prevention, and Advocacy', in *Annihilating Difference*, ed. Hinton, pp. 71–4; L. Girion, '1789 Law Acquires Human Rights Role', *Los Angeles Times* (16 June 2003), A1, A12.

141. N. P. Higgins, *Understanding the Chiapas Rebellion: Modernist Visions and the Invisible Indian* (Austin, TX: University of Texas Press, 1994).
142. Such a statement was made by a G//ana San leader in Botswana at a conference on Khoi and San Development held at the University of Botswana in September 2003; see also S. Totten, 'The Intervention and Prevention of Genocide: Where There *Is* the Political Will, There is a Way', in *Century of Genocide*, eds, Totten, Parsons, and Charny, pp. 469–90.
143. For a draft of the United Nations Declaration on the Rights of Indigenous Peoples, see S. J. Anaya, *Indigenous Peoples in International Law* (Oxford: Oxford University Press, 1996), pp. 190–3.
144. See S. Power, *"A Problem from Hell": America and the Age of Genocide* (New York: Basic Books, 2002) and discussions on the failure of the international community to intervene in the April–July 1994 genocide in Rwanda, such as G. Prunier, *The Rwanda Crisis: History of a Genocide* (New York: Columbia University Press, 1995); A. Des Forges, *Leave None to Tell the Story: Genocide in Rwanda* (New York: Human Rights Watch, 1999). A similar reluctance to intervene in the situation in Bosnia by the international community saw the mass killings of some 7,000 Bosnian Muslim men and boys in the so-called United Nations' safe haven of Srebrenica in July 1995; see L. Silber and A. Little, *Yugoslavia: Death of a Nation* (London: Penguin, 1997), pp. 345–53.
145. See P. Willey, *Prehistoric Warfare in the Great Plains* (Oxford: Oxford University Press, 1990); S. Krech III, 'Genocide in Tribal Society', *Nature* 371 (1994), 14–15; L. H. Keeley, *War Before Civilization: The Myth of the Peaceful Savage* (Oxford: Oxford University Press, 1996).
146. See Barkan, *The Guilt of Nations*, pp. 159–282.
147. Ibid. pp. 237–8, 245–8.
148. Documentation of this meeting was done by community members and representatives of 17 Great Plains tribes in Lincoln, Nebraska on 1–2 September 1998.
149. I. Charny, 'Preface: Which Genocide Matters More? Learning to Care about Humanity', in *Century of Genocide*, eds, Totten, Parsons, and Charny, pp. xii–xiii.
150. Ibid., p. xv.

Index